INVESTMENT MATH MADE EASY

Martin J. Miles

Prentice-Hall, Inc.
Englewood Cliffs, New Jersey

Prentice-Hall International, Inc., *London*
Prentice-Hall of Australia, Pty. Ltd., *Sydney*
Prentice-Hall Canada, Inc., *Toronto*
Prentice-Hall of India Private Ltd., *New Delhi*
Prentice-Hall of Japan, Inc., *Tokyo*
Prentice-Hall of Southeast Asia Pte. Ltd., *Singapore*
Whitehall Books, Ltd., Wellington, *New Zealand*
Editora Prentice-Hall do Brasil Ltda., *Rio de Janeiro*
Prentice-Hall Hispanoamericana, S.A., *Mexico*

Library of Congress Cataloging-in-Publication Data

Miles, Martin J., 1933-
Investment math made easy.

Includes index.
1. Investments—Mathematics. 2. Business mathematics.
I. Title.
HG4521.M4566 1986 332.6'01'51 85-30057

ISBN 0-13-503244-X
ISBN 0-13-503236-9 [PBK]

Printed in the United States of America

To my parents,
Mrs. Mary L. and the late Dr. Martin B. Miles,
and my children,
Barbara and Martin

Acknowledgments

I would like to express my indebtedness to Dr. Edwin L. Crow, mathematical statistician with the National Center for Atmospheric Research; Mr. William C. Adams, Senior Vice-President with Dean Witter; Mr. Gary Stipula, a stockbroker with Merrill Lynch; Mr. Thomas Hagerty, formerly with the Internal Revenue Service; and Mr. Daniel J. Miles. Their review and suggestions were very helpful.

I am equally indebted to Ms. Patricia Sanchez and Kathy Mayeda for the preparation of this difficult manuscript, and to Mr. E. Dean Eicher and Alison Aragon for the illustrations.

M.J.M.

About the Author

Martin J. Miles is a mathematician and real estate consultant who specializes in optimizing real estate investment decisions. He holds a real estate license in Colorado where he has been a long-term, active real estate investor.

Mr. Miles received both his Bachelor's and Master's degrees in mathematics from the University of Colorado. He has lectured in the United States, Canada, and Europe, and has written more than a score of mathematical books, articles, and theorems. Miles is also the author of *Encyclopedia of Real Estate Formulas and Tables* (Prentice-Hall, Inc., 1978) and *Real Estate Investor's Complete Handbook* (Prentice-Hall, Inc., 1982).

What This Book Will Do for You

How can you predict whether the price of your stock will go up or down? Should you put your hard-earned dollars in an ordinary life insurance policy, or would you be better off with term insurance plus an annuity? What kind of return can you expect from your investment in that oil painting or antique? How can you size up an investment in municipal bonds?

Investment Math Made Easy gives you fast answers to these questions — and more — by putting at your fingertips *easy-to-use formulas and tables for almost every investment situation.* With the help of this handy guide, you'll need only a pocket calculator or paper and pencil to size up your prospective investments, make sound investment decisions, and calculate your dollar return.

Here's why you won't make an investment move without this handy guide at your side:

- It gives you simple math formulas and tables for evaluating any investment — complete with examples.
- It covers the entire investment spectrum — from stocks, bonds, and government securities to real estate, life insurance, commodities, and collectibles.
- It shows you formulas that top analysts use to determine the financial condition of major corporations . . . the value of their stock . . . and the value of new stock offerings.
- It contains sample market quotations from the Wall Street Journal and shows how to interpret them.
- It explains the tax consequences of investments, where appropriate — so that you'll know at a glance how taxes will affect your profits.
- It is carefully organized to present each investment calculation in a simple, consistent manner. The advantage is obvious; you can easily compare one investment to another.

With its many formulas, tables, and examples covering the entire investment spectrum, *Investment Math Made Easy* is sure to be an invaluable aid to your investment program.

HOW TO GET THE MOST FROM THIS BOOK

With just two exceptions, all formulas in this book can be solved with the four basic arithmetic operations (addition, subtraction, multiplication, and division). Here are the two exceptions:

- Exponents

  EXAMPLE: Determine the value of $1.83^{2.4}$.

  SOLUTION: Using an electronic calculator having a "y^x" button,

  - enter 1.83
  - press the "y^x" button,
  - enter 2.4.

  The value is 4.26.

- Annuities

  The three annuities in this book are:

  1. The amount of $1 drawing interest, compounded at regular periods.
  2. The present value of $1 received at regular periods.
  3. The future value of $1 deposited at regular periods.

  EXAMPLE: What is the amount of $1 that is drawing interest at r=9% compounded q=4 times/year over m=12 months?

  SOLUTION: Generally, this annuity is labeled c(r,m,q). For the values in this example, it is labeled c(9,12,4). The value is listed in Table I on page 234. It is found in the column labeled c(9,m,4) at row m=12. That is,

  $$c(9,12,4) = 1.30605.$$

Table of Contents

List of Figures

List of Tables

PART I

Formulas for Evaluating Corporations and Their Securities

A business can operate as a sole proprietorship, general partnership, or limited partnership, etc. However, the favored form for large businesses is the corporation.

A corporation operates under a charter granted by the state. It is a legal entity that can own property, enter contracts, sue, be sued, borrow, employ persons, conduct affairs as a natural person, and if desired, enjoy perpetual life. In a sense, a corporation is a partnership of individuals who have contributed money to it, and in exchange, receive an ownership interest in it. Ownership is represented by stock (sometimes called capital stock). A corporation issues stock to raise capital; it can issue both common stock and preferred stock, but it cannot issue more shares than are authorized by the state. Since stock is transferable, it can be traded in markets.

Chapter 1 discusses techniques to evaluate corporations (the fundamental approach to value), and Chapter 2 discusses techniques to evaluate the market price of corporate securities (the technical approach to value).

Common stock represents a residual ownership; that is, it has a claim to corporate assets after all superior claims are satisfied. Investors buy stock to obtain part of the earnings through dividends and to obtain a capital gain resulting from a stock price that subsequently increases due to either large dividends or the prospect of them. Most corporations issue only common stock. Common stock is discussed generally throughout the first two chapters and specifically on page 35.

Preferred stock has a claim to corporate earnings and assets prior to that of common stock. However, since preferred stock usually is nonvoting stock, control of the corporation rests with common stockholders. Preferred stock is discussed on page 47.

The amount of stock the corporation issues is usually less than that authorized. Since non-issued stock is not owned, it neither votes nor draws dividends. The corporation can purchase some of its issued stock. If it does, this stock is called Treasury stock; it also neither votes nor draws dividends. However, the corporation can sell it at any price.

Stockholders have a preemptive right to purchase any additional stock which the company may issue (to maintain their interest in the corporation). This right applies to a new issue and to the old issue if the interest and control have been established. However, it does not apply to Treasury stock and stock issued to pay fair value for property.

If more stock is issued, each stockholder may be given a number of rights (equal to the number of shares he owns). The rights entitle each to purchase shares of the new issue at a stipulated price and within a stipulated short period of time. Rights are discussed on page 59.

If more stock is issued, the corporation may also issue stock purchase warrants. The warrant is purchased at a certain price, and it grants the warrant holder the right to purchase a stated number of shares of stock within a specified time, and sometimes, at a specified price. Warrants can usually be thought of as long-term rights. They are discussed on page 61.

A corporation can also issue bonds. However, whereas stock represents ownership in the corporation, bonds represent long-term indebtedness of the corporation. The bondholder receives periodic (usually semiannual) payments of interest, and the redemption value (usually the face value) will be paid at maturity. Corporate bonds are discussed on page 67.

Corporations can also raise capital by selling commercial paper. These short-term notes are discussed on page 79.

CHAPTER 1
The Fundamental Approach to Value

Why do individuals buy stock in a corporation? Because ownership in a corporation brings the prospect of future benefits. Since stockholders receive the assets of the corporation only upon its dissolution, the future benefits are usually the periodic payments of dividends from that portion of corporate earnings that the directors consider to be excess and the capital gain from the possible increased value of each share. If it were not for the prospect of receiving dividends, the stock would have little value and would be almost impossible to sell.

How is stock value determined? It is determined in the same way the value of other investments is determined: the value is the present value of all future benefits.* The value of the primary future benefits (i.e., dividends) is not known and must be estimated.** If, after you own the stock, it appears to be a more attractive investment (probably because others believe dividends will increase more than they had previously imagined), a secondary future benefit could be price appreciation. Moreover, since future benefits are not valued as highly as equal but current benefits, they must be discounted. Not only is determining the rate of discount (i.e., the rate of return) a personal decision, but it can vary as other investments become more or less attractive. Of course, current interest rates are extremely important in determining the discount. In summary, current value depends upon:

- Dividends to be received over the holding period;
- The price of the stock at the end of the holding period; and
- The discount the investor places on future benefits.

---

*Note the distinction between value and market price. Industries and corporations move in and out of favor with investors, so these two quantities are rarely equal. Profitable investments can be made by purchasing the stock of quality companies in industries currently out of favor (e.g., a company whose stock price is less than net asset value and less than 7 times earnings, even though annual earnings are increasing by 15%). See Financial Statements, page 17.

**Future dividends can be forecast by the Fundamental Approach: by examining the economy, the industry, management, supply and demand, financial statements, etc.

These values can be used in the two formulas below to estimate the present value of a share of stock; this value should be compared with the current market price. The first formula is general; it is the usual present value formula in which dividends are discounted as they are received (usually quarterly), and the market price of the stock is discounted over the holding period. To use this formula, you must estimate:

- Each periodic dividend;
- The price of the stock at the end of the holding period; and
- Your rate of return on similar investments.

The second formula (divided into two) is a less general form of the present value formula, but it uses quantities that can be more readily estimated (from earnings). To use this formula, you must estimate:

- The constant annual rate of change of earnings and dividends;
- The current periodic dividend (assumed to remain a constant fraction of earnings, called the payout ratio);
- The price-to-earnings ratio at the end of the holding period;* and
- Your rate of return on similar investments.

FORMULAS:

$$v = \begin{cases} \sum_{i=1}^{m} \frac{d_i}{c(r,i,q)} + \frac{p}{c(r,m,q)} & \text{(Variable dividends)**} \\ \left.\begin{array}{ll} F + G & \text{if } r \geq r' \\ F' + G' & \text{if } r < r' \end{array}\right\} & \text{(Constant rate of change of earnings and dividends)} \end{cases}$$

where

v = present value of a share of stock

then

d_i = periodic dividend after the ith period

d' = current periodic dividend (a fraction of e')

---

*This ratio should largely depend upon the annual rate of change of earnings.

**The "Σ" symbol means to sum the expression to the right m times where i changes from 1 through m. That is,

$$\frac{d_1}{c(r,1,q)} + \frac{d_2}{c(r,2,q)} + \ldots + \frac{d_m}{c(r,m,q)}.$$

e' = current periodic earnings

F = $d' \cdot a(x,m,q)$

F' = $d' \cdot s(z,m,q)$

G = $hqe'/c(x,m,q)$

G' = $hqe' \cdot c(z,m,q)$

h = price-to-earnings ratio after m periods

m = number of dividend periods in holding period

p = market price of stock after m periods. (Note: $p = hqe' \cdot c(r',m,q)$ if earnings change at the constant rate of r'.)

q = number of dividend (or earning) periods per year

r = investor's rate of return on similar investments

r' = annual rate of change of earnings and dividends

$x = \dfrac{r-r'}{1+r'/q}$ = an annual rate if $r \geq r'$

$z = \dfrac{r'-r}{1+r/q}$ = an annual rate if $r \leq r'$

$a(x,m,q)$ = present value of 1. (Evaluate from Table I or the formula in the introduction to Table I and a calculator.)

$c(r,i,q)$,
$c(r,m,q)$,
$c(z,m,q)$, and
$c(x,m,q)$ = amount of 1 at compound interest. (Evaluate from Table I or the formula in the introduction to Table I and a calculator.)

$s(z,m,q)$ = amount of 1. (Evaluate from Table I or the formula in the introduction to Table I and a calculator.)

EXAMPLE: (Constant rate of change of earnings and dividends): Suppose a company currently earns \$0.30 per share each quarter. It is expected that earnings will increase at an annual rate of 40%. Similar companies with similar earnings prospects sell at 50 times annual earnings. It is expected that the company will pay one-third of its earnings as dividends. Your rate of return on investments of similar risk is 15%. How much should you pay for these shares if you intend to hold them for two years?

SOLUTION: In this example,

$$e' = \$0.30,\ q = 4,\ r' = 0.40,\ h = 50,\ d' = (1/3)e' = \$0.10,$$
$$r = 0.15,\ \text{and } m = 8.$$

From this information (and since $r<r'$),

$$z = \frac{0.40-0.15}{1+0.15/4} = 0.2410.$$

From the formulas in the footnote and a calculator,

$$c(z,m,q) = c(24.10,8,4) = 1.5969,^{*}$$

and

$$s(z,m,q) = s(24.10,8,4) = 9.9064.$$

Now,

$$F' = \$0.010 \times 9.9064 = \$0.99, \text{ and}$$
$$G' = 50 \times 4 \times \$0.30 \times 1.5969 = \$95.81.$$

Now, the present value (the price you should pay) for each share is

$$v = \$0.99 + \$95.81 = \$96.80.$$

Note that the projected price of each share after 8 periods is

$$p = 50 \times 4 \times \$0.30 \times c(40,8,4) = \$60 \times 2.1436 = \$128.62.$$

Corporations are involved in every conceivable type of business. The common stock price of those involved in the same type of business tends to behave in the same way and at the same time. Moreover, certain measures of value tend to apply to the same type of business. This is especially true for those businesses that are regulated by governments (i.e., utilities, banks, insurance, and investment companies). They are regulated because a certain degree of public trust is necessary. Certainly the largest and most difficult type of business to characterize is the industrials. The following is a brief discussion of different types of businesses: industrials, banks, public utilities, insurance, and investment companies. Then, financial statements that apply to most companies are discussed.

---

*c(24.10,8,4) is determined from a calculator as $(1+0.2410/4)^8 = (1.06025)^8 = 1.5969$. It is obtained by entering 1.06025, pressing the "y^x" button, and entering 8.

INDUSTRIALS

Industrial companies are engaged in a very broad range of activities: manufacturing, merchandising, resource extraction, services, etc. Consequently, they are best described as all companies except transportations, banks, public utilities, insurance, and investment companies. It is sensible to declare these companies as non-industrial because most are regulated by governments, and consequently, they must operate in an unnatural and constrained way. On the other hand, industrials are relatively free of government control, and because their activities are so varied, the price behavior of their stocks varies considerably.

Investors using the fundamental approach should consider the following questions:

- Does the company belong to a growth industry?
- Do alternate products or services exist?
- Does it have product diversification (for stability and safety)?
- Is the company competitive within the industry (e.g., does it have a good reputation, goodwill, patents, brand names, sufficient outlets, wise management)?
- Is there sufficient demand for its products and services?
- Does the company have a high operating ratio or operating profit margin ratio?* These ratios can be affected by:
    - The difference between the product price and the cost of its raw materials.
    - Salaries for labor and the cost of operating policies imposed by labor, including strikes. Labor costs are more variable than are other costs.
    - Competition. Competition is greater if:
        - There is a large number of companies in the industry.
        - Brand names, firm names, patents, and distribution are not important.
        - The industry is not a growth industry.
        - Competitive pricing is traditional.
- Do the following government regulations affect the company?:
    - Antitrust enforcement
    - Tariffs

---

*Defined on page 24.

- Import quotas
- Export financing policies
- Excess profit tax
- Price and wage controls
- Raw material allocation

Pages 25 through 27 contain many "figures of merit" by which investors using the fundamental approach can evaluate industrial companies.

BANKS

Commercial banks are private companies that are regulated (for safety, not profit) by state and federal agencies. Their earnings come primarily from the use of their customers' deposits, and their stock (almost entirely common stock) is usually traded in the over-the-counter market. Since their earnings and dividends are relatively stable, their stock is favored by conservative investors, fire insurance companies, trust funds, and endowments.

Regulation

Government regulation of commercial banks attempts to ensure safety of deposits, not limit earnings as it does with public utilities. Generally, regulation:

- limits competition,
- limits the interest rate on time deposits,
- limits cash reserve,
- limits the quality of municipal and corporate bond investments,
- limits the quality and quantity of real estate loans,
- forbids stock investment,
- requires assets to be reviewed, and
- requires deposit insurance.

Assets

A commercial bank's total assets are divided into liquid assets and assets at risk. They are distributed roughly as follows:

- Liquid Assets
  - Cash (20%)
  - Secondary Reserves (10–20%): short-term, low interest U.S. Government securities

- Assets at Risk
  - Loans (35–55%): personal, real estate, and commercial loans
  - Bonds (10–30%): U.S., municipal, and corporate bonds as secondary reserves

The liquidity of assets is very important. A bank whose assets are relatively liquid is in a position to time its investing and thereby increase its earnings. Liquidity is often measured by this ratio:

$$\text{Liquidity} = \frac{(\text{Cash}) + (\text{Value of Bonds Maturing Within 5 Years})^*}{(\text{Total Assets})}$$

Leverage

Banks have their own resources (called capital funds) as well as those of their depositers. If a bank invests heavily in U.S. securities, the percent of capital funds-to-total resources should be near 5%; but if it invests heavily in loans, it should be nearer 10%. The following risk ratio should be about 0.15:

$$\text{Risk Ratio} = \frac{(\text{Capital Funds})}{(\text{Assets at Risk})}$$

If the bank's directors view this ratio to be too low, they may vote to reduce the dividend or issue more stock.

Earnings

A bank's earnings come from four sources:

- Loans (65%): Interest on loans
- Bonds** } (15%): Interest and capital gain.
- Real estate }
- Services (20%): Fees from trust departments, safety deposit boxes, collections, etc.

Income from loans and services is relatively stable. To stabilize other income, banks are permitted to maintain a reserve account. This account is primarily intended to cover loan losses. During prosperity, it could be viewed as a "hidden" capital item. However, some banks use the reserve account for the profits and losses from the sale of real estate and

*This ratio is similar to the working capital-to-total assets ratio used to measure liquidity of industrials (page 21).

**Only a small percentage of the bonds are corporate bonds.

bonds. Since bond prices change (inversely) with interest rates, banks time their sales and purchases around these rates. Hence, without the reserve account, these erratic earnings could offset the relatively stable earnings from loans and services.

A bank's earnings are usually measured by the indicated earnings and the net operating earnings. Before defining indicated earnings, it is first necessary to define the capital account:

Capital Account = (Capital Notes and Debentures)* + (Capital Stock) + (Surplus) + (Undivided Profits).

The indicated earnings is then defined as the dividends paid plus the change in the capital account (from one accounting period to another):

Indicated Earnings = (Dividends Paid) + (Change in Capital Account).

This is a particularly good measure of earnings if the capital account includes the profits and losses from loans, real estate, and securities.

Net operating earnings is another measure of a bank's earnings. It is defined as:

Net Operating Earnings = (Recurring Earnings) − (Recurring Expenses).

Recurring earnings are interest and fees. Recurring expenses are salaries, interest paid, taxes, supplies, etc., however, regularly occurring expenses in the reserve account are not included. The net operating earnings after taxes** is a measure of earnings favored by most analysts and is the quantity used to compute earnings/share and the price-to-earnings ratio.

An annual return on equity (i.e., earnings per invested capital) of 15% is considered good. See earnings-to-net-worth ratio, page 27.

Efficiency

A commercial bank's earnings depend primarily on its ability to gain and hold deposits. This ability depends upon management, competition from other banks and lenders,*** growth, and prosperity of

*A debenture is a bond that is backed only by the credit of the issuer. It is not secured by property as is a mortgage.

**Banks pay federal income tax at 20% of taxable income instead of 46% as do other corporations.

***Commercial banks receive competition in lending from insurance companies, finance companies, and savings and loan associations.

the region. The efficiency of a bank can be measured by the operating ratio:

$$\text{Operating Ratio} = \frac{(\text{Total Operating Expenses})}{(\text{Gross Revenue})}.$$

This ratio is smaller for larger banks (e.g., 0.5 to 0.7) since they tend to have larger accounts.

It seems that banks that are willing to take larger risks in lending also have larger profits (the losses are more than offset by the gains). Other factors in selecting a bank investment are their dividend policy (established banks tend to pay higher dividends because newer ones need to build their reserves), leverage, and size.

PUBLIC UTILITIES

Public utilities include electricity, telephone, gas, water, telegraph, and local transit. Companies that provide these services usually obtain their funds (i.e., are capitalized) by issuing investment grade bonds (representing debt), good quality preferred stock, and common stock. These companies prefer that their bondholders and stockholders are local in order to help create favorable public sentiment. They are heavily regulated by governments, primarily to control their rates. For this reason, the price of their common stock tends to behave in the same manner.

Regulation

Although it is often said that regulation covers *what* is done, not *how* it is done, this statement is becoming less true. Most public utilities operate under a long-term agreement (known as a franchise) that usually creates a monopoly in the service area. Potential investors in these companies should be aware of:

- the franchise agreement;
- the relationship between the company and the public; and
- the relationship between the company and the regulating authority (which often results from the previously stated relationship).*

---

*The Salomon Bros. Investment Company provides a rating of state authorities' attitude toward the local public utility.

The primary responsibility of the regulatory authority is the setting of rates. The rates depend upon assets and earnings; however, different governmental authorities define assets and earnings in different ways.

The assets upon which the return is determined is called the rate base valuation. This value has been defined as:

- The prudently invested historic cost of construction. This is the value of the assets when placed in service less the accumulated depreciation;
- The reproduction cost. Due to possible inflation since the assets were placed in service, this value can be substantially larger than the above value. Again, accumulated depreciation is subtracted; or
- The sum of the value of bonds, preferred stock, and common stock.

The capitalization rate uses this sum. It is defined as follows:

$$\frac{\text{(Interest Paid On Bonds)} + \text{(Dividends Paid On Preferred Stock)} + \text{(Earnings Necessary to Keep Common Stock Price at Book Value)}^{*}}{\text{(Value Of Bonds)} + \text{(Value of Preferred Stock)} + \text{(Value of Common Stock)}}$$

Regulating agencies often prefer debt (value of bonds) to be no higher than 60% of the capitalization and common stock value to be no less than 25%; preferred stock value occupies the remaining percent. Even though regulatory agencies require standard accounting practices, the value of the assets may not be obvious from studying the balance sheet: Some are not listed, some are listed when they are used in another service, the cost and depreciation are reported in different ways, some accounting procedures allow the cost of new construction and equipment to be moved from the income statement (where it reduces earnings) to the balance sheet, etc.

As far as earnings are concerned:

- The company is entitled by law to obtain "reasonable" earnings;
- The company's earnings should be sufficient to "maintain its credit standing and attract capital";
- The company should be permitted "a fair return on a fair

---

*If the common stock price exceeds book value, the company can attempt to lower the price by selling more stock or converting some bonds to common stock.

valuation of the property used and useful in the public service," etc.

Characteristics of Stock

Dependable earnings allow public utilities to pay regular, dependable dividends; dividends amount to about 75% of earnings.* Common stockholders also are frequently offered rights (to purchase more shares of common stock). (See page 59.) It is not unusual for them to be given the right to buy 6% to 7% more shares of common stock every two years at net asset value (book value), even though the stock is selling 20% higher than this (i.e., this right increases the dividend yield by 0.55% without diluting the book value).

Most utility stocks are listed on the major stock exchanges. The price of their good quality bonds and preferred stocks usually fluctuate only in response to interest rates (inversely). On the other hand, the price of lesser grade preferred and common stock fluctuate as does the price of industrial stocks (but in unison and without long-term adjustments). Utility common stocks also have higher price-to-earnings ratios than do those of industrials.

PROPERTY AND CASUALTY INSURANCE COMPANIES

Property insurance companies sell policies for fire damage and extended coverage for damage from wind, explosion, water, etc. Casualty insurance companies sell policies for casualty, workman's compensation, general liability, automobile liability, accident, health, etc. Some companies sell both property and casualty policies, and others, called reinsurance companies, share the risk (and premiums) on some large policies written by other companies.

Property and casualty insurance companies can be stock companies (that issue mostly common stock that is traded over-the-counter), but many are mutual companies (owned by their policyholders).

Property and casualty insurance stocks appeal to conservative investors, trust funds, and endowments because they usually have reasonable asset growth, safety, and steady dividend income. Their prices tend to vary as do industrial stocks of similar quality, but their dividend yields are somewhat lower.

---

*See the payout ratio on page 25.

Regulation of Investments

Property and casualty insurance companies are state regulated in the interest of policyholders (as are banks in the interest of depositors). Regulation is not aggressive, but it typically requires the company to:

- invest all funds that are not needed for cash and payables;
- invest policyholders' and creditors' money in bonds only; and
- invest stockholders' equity in bonds, preferred stock, or common stock (of banks, public utilities, high quality industrials, etc.).

Within these guidelines, the companies try to invest for steady income rather than for capital gain. That is, the primary intent of the investments is to cover unexpected losses, and the secondary intent is steady growth of assets. As a percentage of total assets, these investments tend to be:

Common Stock	33–43%
Bonds (Non-Taxable)	25–35%
Bonds (Taxable)	10–20%
Cash and Receivables	10–20%
Preferred Stock	1–3%

Underwriting

Policies are usually written for 1–3 years. The amount of insurance in force is often related to the amount of insurable assets and the owners' ability to pay premiums. For example, during the Great Depression (1929–1933), the amount of property and casualty insurance declined 40% and 32%, respectively, from the usual amount. Some companies have been notably successful in writing low-risk policies; however, this is often expected of them, and the price of their stock already reflects this success.

Often the annual net premiums earned by the companies amount to 45% of their assets, 100%–105% of all expenses and losses, and 30% of earnings. The companies invest premiums as they are received (creating a sinking fund), so the investment usually earns interest and dividends before they must be paid to satisfy a loss. Analysts frequently use the following four measures of profit from underwriting:

$$\text{Loss Ratio} = \frac{\text{(Losses Incurred During Fiscal Year)}}{\text{(Total Premiums Paid Before and During Fiscal Year)}}$$

$$\approx 0.60 \text{ to } 0.65;$$

$$\text{Expense Ratio} = \frac{\text{(Selling Expenses)* + (Operating Expenses)}}{\text{(New Premiums Collected)}}$$

$$\approx 0.35 \text{ to } 0.40;$$

*About 75% of all expenses.

$$\text{Loss and Expense Ratio} = (\text{Loss Ratio}) + (\text{Expense Ratio}) \approx 0.95 \text{ to } 1.05; \text{ and}$$

$$\text{Underwriting Profit Margin} = 1 - (\text{Loss and Expense Ratio}) \approx -0.05 \text{ to } +0.05.$$

Financial Statements

Measures of performance for property and casualty companies can be difficult to interpret because some companies insure both property and casualty, and many companies are holding companies for other companies.*

The basic item in underwriting income is the net premiums earned:

$$\text{Net Premiums Earned (NPE)} = (\text{Net Premiums Written}) - (\text{Change in Prepaid Premiums}).$$

This item is used in more detailed measures of profit and income.

The following measure of performance is recognized by regulatory and tax authorities:

$$\text{Statutory Underwriting Profit (or Loss) (SUP)} = \text{NPE} - (\text{Losses}) - (\text{Operating Expenses}).$$

Even though this measure is offically recognized, it is often misleading because the losses are recognized, not when the losses are incurred, but as premiums are received (over the term of the new policies). Because the statutory underwriting profit is often distorted, the following adjusted measure of performance has gained favor:

$$\text{Adjusted Underwriting Profit (AUP)} = \text{SUP} + 0.40 \times (\text{Change in Prepaid Fire Premiums}) + 0.35 \times (\text{Change in Prepaid Casualty Premiums}).$$

The total income (before tax) includes the statutory underwriting profit as well as the income from investments:

$$\text{Total Income (Before Tax) (TI)} = \text{SUP} + (\text{Investment Income}).^{**}$$

Another measure important to investors is the net asset value (also

---

*Holding companies control other companies through ownership of a majority of their stock.

**Investment income is rental income, dividend income, interest income, and profit from the sale of securities.

called book value). It measures the maximum amount that the company should invest and the assets remaining even if premiums decline drastically:

$$\text{Net Asset Value (NAV)} = (\text{Value of Capital Stock}) + (\text{Surplus}) + (0.35 \times \text{Prepaid Premiums}).$$

LIFE INSURANCE COMPANIES

Life insurance companies sell individual life insurance, group life insurance, annuities, and some health and accident insurance. See Part VI on page 131. About two-thirds of life insurance companies are mutual companies (i.e., owned by their policyholders), and the remainder are stock companies; their common stock is usually traded over-the-counter.

Premiums are currently based on mortality tables that were developed from data collected in 1954. Life expectancy has increased significantly since then; hence, insureds pay premiums for a significantly longer period of time than predicted by these tables, and the benefits need not be paid as soon. The result has been higher earnings.

Measures of performance for life insurance companies suffer from the same distortion as do those of property and casualty companies: the cost of acquiring new policies is accounted immediately, but the premiums are accounted when received. Premium adjustments often add 15%-30% to net income and 20%-35% to net worth.

Life insurance companies have high price-to-earnings ratios and low dividend yields (to maintain net worth at 5%-8% of total assets). They do differ, however, in management's ability to:

- minimize expenses,
- obtain insureds with low mortality,
- invest successfully,
- package policies attractively, and
- sell efficiently.

Since state law requires that most of their assets be invested in mortgages and bonds, common stock investments do not affect life insurance companies' income as much as they affect the income of property and casualty companies.

INVESTMENT COMPANIES

Investment companies pool the money received from the sale of their shares; then they buy securities that fit their investment goal. An open-end company sells and redeems its shares at their net asset value.* A closed-end company is listed on the stock exchange, and its shares can be bought or sold at the market price for a commission. Shares of all companies can be purchased either indirectly from a sales representative for a commission of about 7.5% (called a load fund), or directly from the company for no commission (called a no-load fund). The commission on a load fund is deducted from the investment funds. Recently, a number of load funds have switched to no-load, but with a redemption fee for early withdrawal.

There is a great variety of investment companies, and one can be found for most any investment objective: growth, income, speculation, taxes, safety, bonds, options, futures, money markets, etc.

Investing through an investment company provides diversification, management, and switching privileges (if the company manages more than one type of fund). Also, regularly reinvesting dividends is equivalent to dollar cost averaging (page 37).

An investment company investor need only hold his shares for more than 31 days for a gain to qualify as a long-term capital gain—even though the company must hold its invested shares for 12 months to qualify. An investor can use this short holding period to counter other short-term gain. For example, suppose he has a short-term gain from another investment that he wants to offset by an equal short-term loss. He can purchase shares in an investment company, knowing those shares will drop in value due to payment of a previously announced capital gain dividend. If he sells the shares after 31 days, he has a short-term loss on the shares and a long-term gain on the dividend.**

FINANCIAL STATEMENTS

Financial statements are usually reported annually by public corporations to stockholders. Interpretation of the financial data in these statements is central to the fundamental approach to corporate investment. However, financial statements must be read and interpreted carefully because:

- Accounting practices differ among corporations and industries;
- They are not timely since some information can be as old as a year; and
- They are invariably incomplete.

---

*Net asset value = (market price of securities) + (short-term investments) + (cash).

**This maneuver doesn't work for state income tax in the following states which consider the dividends to be ordinary income: Alabama, Arkansas, California, Delaware, Illinois, Mississippi, N. Carolina, Pennsylvania, and Wisconsin.

The most important financial statements are the balance sheet and the income statement. Data from these two statements are valuable in their own right, but especially valuable when combined to form measures or "figures of merit" for either the corporation's financial condition or the value of its securities. The most important measures are ratios because their value doesn't depend on the size of the company. They too must be used carefully; in addition to the above three problems, care must be taken when comparing data from different companies (especially companies in different industries). Many of these problems can be avoided, however, by using measures for the same company, but for different times; significant trends can be spotted this way.

Some measures, such as earnings/share and net assets/share, depend upon the number of shares of common stock outstanding. This number can be increased if the company raises funds by selling common stock, debentures or preferred stock (that is convertible to common stock), or options and warrants (permitting purchase of common stock at a given price). Some dilution is not serious if the funds are used judiciously to increase earnings. At any rate, the Securities and Exchange Commission requires earnings to be reported as if all debentures and preferred stock were converted and all options and warrants were exercised.

Balance Sheet

The balance sheet is used to obtain a financial picture of the corporation on the reporting date.* It reports the assets, liabilities, and stockholders' equity (also called net worth). The value of these items "balance" because stockholders' equity is *defined* to equal the difference between assets and liabilities (both of which are fixed); that is,

$$\text{Stockholders' Equity} = (\text{Assets}) - (\text{Liabilities}),$$

or

$$\text{Assets} = (\text{Liabilities}) + (\text{Stockholders' Equity}).$$

Assets include current assets (i.e., items convertible to cash within a year), property and equipment (i.e., land and property that can be depreciated or amortized), and other assets (which usually do not include intangible assets). Often assets are divided into current assets and fixed assets. The method of valuing each asset should be known; a corporation may determine value by the cost, market value, appraised value, etc.

---

*It is called a consolidated balance sheet if the reporting company owns or controls other corporations.

Liabilities include current liabilities (i.e., debts payable within a year) and other liabilities (i.e., debts payable later).

Stockholders' equity includes all funds invested by stockholders as well as reinvested earnings.

The sample Balance Sheet (Table 1) contains frequently listed items. They are labeled B_1 through B_{28} for convenient reference in the measure of value formulas, and a hypothetical value of each item is included for illustration.

Table 1. SAMPLE BALANCE SHEET

	Label	Item	Value (Millions)
Assets		CURRENT ASSETS (Assets receivable within a year)	
	B_1	Cash	$ 13.0
	B_2	Time Deposits	4.2
	B_3	Marketable Securities (Corporate & government)	10.3
	B_4	Receivables Due Within Year (Notes and accounts that are collectible)	23.9
	B_5	Inventory (Valued at the lower of cost or market value)	51.7
	B_6	TOTAL CURRENT ASSETS	103.1
		PROPERTY AND EQUIPMENT	
	B_7	Buildings, Fixtures & Equipment (Valued at cost)	194.7
	B_8	Accumulated Depreciation	52.5
	B_9	Land (Valued at cost)	2.1
	B_{10}	TOTAL PROPERTY AND EQUIPMENT*	144.3
		OTHER ASSETS (Valued at cost and excluding intangible assets)	
	B_{11}	Receivables Due After One Year (Notes and accounts that are collectible)	8.2
	B_{12}	Insurance Surrender Value	0.4
	B_{13}	Other	1.1
	B_{14}	TOTAL OTHER ASSETS	9.7
	B_{15}	TOTAL ASSETS	257.1

*$B_{10} = B_7 - B_8 + B_9$

Table 1. SAMPLE BALANCE SHEET (Continued)

	Label	Item	Value (Millions)
Liabilities		CURRENT LIABILITIES (Payable within a year)	
	B_{16}	Notes and Accounts Payable	$ 10.5
	B_{17}	Expenses Accrued (Unpaid wages, commissions, interest, etc.)	6.9
	B_{18}	Long-Term Debt (Currently maturing)	1.8
	B_{19}	Income Tax (Federal and other)	7.2
	B_{20}	Dividends Payable (Declared on preferred and common)	11.9
	B_{21}	TOTAL CURRENT LIABILITIES	38.3
		OTHER LIABILITIES (Payable after a year)	
	B_{22}	Long-Term Debt (Maturing after a year)[1]	43.9
	B_{23}	TOTAL LIABILITIES	82.2
Stockholders' Equity (Net Worth)	B_{24}	Preferred Stock (Value of authorized stock at par)[2]	13.2
	B_{25}	Common Stock (Value of outstanding stock at par)[3]	40.5
	B_{26}	Additional Paid-in Capital (Value from sale of stock that exceeds par)	21.7
	B_{27}	Retained Earnings (Amount reinvested in corporation)	99.5
	B_{28}	TOTAL STOCKHOLDERS' EQUITY	174.9
		TOTAL LIABILITIES AND TOTAL STOCKHOLDERS' EQUITY	257.1

[1]**7% sinking debentures due in 5 years**

[2]**$100 par, 132,000 shares authorized and outstanding**

[3]**$20 par, 3,000,000 authorized and 2,025,000 outstanding**

Measures of Value From the Balance Sheet

The first four formulas measure liquidity, the next measure worth, and the last evaluates the current market price of the stock.

Current Ratio. This is the best known ratio from the balance sheet. It is a measure of liquidity, and for most corporations, should be at least 2. A ratio of 5 or higher could mean the corporation has invested too heavily in marketable securities.

$$\text{Current Ratio} = \frac{\text{Total Current Assets}}{\text{Total Current Liabilities}}$$

$$= \frac{B_6}{B_{21}} = \frac{\$103.1}{\$38.3} = 2.69.$$

Acid Test Ratio. This is the same as the current ratio, but inventories are excluded from current assets. Often there is doubt about the value and the liquidity of inventories, so this ratio very strictly measures the corporation's ability to meet current obligations.*

$$\text{Acid Test Ratio} = \frac{(\text{Total Current Assets}) - (\text{Inventories})}{\text{Total Current Liabilities}}$$

$$= \frac{B_6 - B_5}{B_{21}} = \frac{\$103.1 - \$51.7}{\$38.3} = 1.34.$$

Working Capital-to-Total-Assets Ratio. Working capital is the excess of current assets over current liabilities. This ratio is a liquidity measure since it measures the fraction of total assets available for current operations. It is seasonal for some industries.

$$\text{Working Capital-to-Total-Assets Ratio} = \frac{\text{Working Capital}}{\text{Total Assets}}$$

$$= \frac{B_6 - B_{21}}{B_{15}} = \frac{\$103.1 - \$38.3}{\$257.1} = 0.252.$$

Working Capital-to-Inventory Ratio. Working capital is the excess of current assets over current liabilities.

$$\text{Working Capital-to-Inventory Ratio} = \frac{\text{Working Capital}}{\text{Inventory}}$$

$$= \frac{B_6 - B_{21}}{B_5} = \frac{\$103.1 - \$38.3}{\$51.7} = 1.25.$$

---

*The value of inventories to the company depends upon whether the price of raw materials has subsequently changed. Some companies hedge against price changes by investing in futures markets.

*Net Worth-to-Fixed-Assets Ratio.** Net worth is the total stockholders' equity, and fixed assets are all assets that are not current assets. This ratio is another measure of liquidity; the higher its value, the more liquid is the corporation.

$$\text{Net Worth-to-Fixed-Assets Ratio} = \frac{\text{Net Worth}}{\text{Fixed Assets}}$$

$$= \frac{B_{28}}{B_{15} - B_6} = \frac{\$174.9}{\$257.1 - \$103.1} = 1.14.$$

Net Worth-to-Total-Debt Ratio. The total debt is the sum of all long-term debts (maturing this year and later). This ratio should not be used for public utilities. A ratio that exceeds three is quite favorable.

$$\text{Net Worth-to-Total-Debt Ratio} = \frac{\text{Net Worth}}{\text{Total Debt}}$$

$$= \frac{B_{28}}{B_{18} + B_{22}} = \frac{\$174.9}{\$1.8 + \$43.9} = 3.83.$$

Price-to-Net-Asset-Value Ratio. Net asset value (also called book value) is the total assets less creditor's claims and preferred stock value; the net asset value is usually divided by the number, n, of common shares outstanding (stated in millions, as are items in the balance sheet) so that it is the net asset value per share. This is the only balance sheet ratio that evaluates the current market price, p, per share of common stock. It is a more stable figure than the price-to-earnings ratio (See the Income Statement on page 23). Notice, however, that the price is current and the net asset value is as old as one year. Usually only very profitable companies have shares selling at more than twice net asset value. A ratio less than one probably indicates that the market price is very reasonable.**

$$\text{Price-to-Net-Asset-Value Ratio} = \frac{\text{Price}}{\text{Net Asset Value}}$$

*This ratio and the following one form another ratio, the debt-to-fixed-assets ratio, that measures the extent to which fixed assets are encumbered. A low value of this ratio is preferred.

**Noted analyst Benjamin Graham replaced total assets (B_{15}) with current assets (B_6) and considered purchasing shares only if the ratio was less than 1; with this replacement, the ratio in this example would be 5.71.

$$= \frac{p}{\left[\dfrac{B_{15} - (B_{18} + B_{22} + B_{24})}{n}\right]} = \frac{\$124\text{-}5/8}{\left[\dfrac{\$257.1 - (\$1.8 + \$43.9 + \$13.2)}{2.025}\right]}$$

$$= \frac{\$124.625}{\$97.88} = 1.27.$$

Income Statement

The income statement shows profits and losses. Items from this statement are used to obtain a dynamic picture of the corporation by comparing the values from year to year.

The sample Income Statement (Table 2) contains frequently listed items. They are labeled I_1 through I_{10} for convenient use in the measure of value formulas, and hypothetical values are included for illustration.

Table 2. SAMPLE INCOME STATEMENT

	Label	Item	Value (Millions)
Income	I_1	Net Sales[1]	$243.2
Costs and Expenses	I_2	Cost of Goods Sold	160.4
	I_3	Expenses (General and administrative)[2]	29.8
	I_4	Depreciation and Amortization	5.5
	I_5	TOTAL OPERATING COSTS AND EXPENSES[3]	195.7
	I_6	Interest Charges	2.7
	I_7	Income Tax (Federal and other)	23.9
	I_8	TOTAL COSTS AND EXPENSES	222.3
Dividends	I_9	Dividends Paid on Preferred Stock	0.6
	I_{10}	Dividends Paid on Common Stock	11.3

[1]This item is often called revenues for companies such as utilities and insurance.

[2]Includes rent, maintenance, repairs, employee retirement, taxes (for property, social security, state, federal), etc.

[3]Banks and insurance companies will include gains and losses from securities transactions here.

Measures of Value From the Income Statement

Operating Ratio. This is the ratio of total operating costs and expenses-to-net sales. This important ratio varies with the type of business and is used widely in service industries. It is an index of efficiency because it is the outlay required to produce sales; a high ratio is undesirable.

$$\text{Operating Ratio} = \frac{\text{Total Operating Costs and Expenses}}{\text{Net Sales}}$$

$$= \frac{I_5}{I_1} = \frac{\$195.7}{\$243.2} = 0.80.$$

Operating Profit Margin Ratio. The operating profit is the net sales less the total operating costs and expenses. The operating profit margin can be defined as either the ratio of operating profit-to-net-sales ratio or the complement of the operating ratio (above).

$$\text{Operating Profit Margin Ratio} = \frac{\text{Operating Profit}}{\text{Net Sales}} = \frac{I_1 - I_5}{I_1}$$

$$= 1 - \text{Operating Ratio} = 1 - \frac{I_5}{I_1} = 1 - 0.80 = 0.20.$$

Interest Coverage Ratio. This is the ratio of operating profit-to-interest charges. For most businesses an interest coverage ratio of 3 is considered to be adequate. Businesses with unstable earnings should have a ratio of 4 to 5.

$$\text{Interest Coverage Ratio} = \frac{\text{Operating Profit}}{\text{Interest Charges}}$$

$$= \frac{I_1 - I_5}{I_6} = \frac{\$243.2 - \$195.7}{\$2.7} = 17.6.$$

Earnings-to-Net-Sales Ratio. Earnings (i.e., net profit) is the net sales less the total costs and expenses and dividends paid on preferred stock.

$$\text{Earnings-to-Net-Sales Ratio} = \frac{\text{Earnings}}{\text{Net Sales}}$$

$$= \frac{I_1 - I_8 - I_9}{I_1} = 1 - \frac{I_8 + I_9}{I_1} = 1 - \frac{\$222.3 + \$0.6}{\$243.2}$$

$$= 1 - 0.92 = 0.08.$$

Payout Ratio. This ratio reflects management's dividend policy. For fast, average, and slow growing companies, this ratio is about 0.3, 0.5, and 0.7, respectively. It is relatively stable for public utilities and transportation companies.

$$\text{Payout Ratio} = \frac{\text{Cash Dividend on Common Stock}}{\text{Earnings}}$$

$$= \frac{I_{10}}{I_1 - I_8 - I_9} = \frac{\$11.3}{\$243.2 - \$222.3 - \$0.6} = 0.557.$$

Price-to-Earnings Ratio. This conventional measure can have a very wide range of values. It should only be used for corporations whose earnings are stable and not cyclical. The current market price per share is p, and the number of outstanding common shares (stated in millions, as are items in the income statement) is n. A ratio less than 10 probably indicates that the market price is reasonable:*

$$\text{Price-to-Earnings Ratio} = \frac{\text{Price}}{\text{Earnings/Share}}$$

$$= \frac{p}{\left[\frac{I_1 - I_8 - I_9}{n}\right]} = \frac{\$124\text{-}5/8}{\left[\frac{\$243.2 - \$222.3 - \$0.6}{2.025}\right]} = \frac{\$124.625}{\$10.025}$$

$$= 12.43.$$

Cash Flow. Cash flow is the cash available for dividends for each share of outstanding common stock; it is not a ratio of items from the income statement. It is the earnings/share, except that non-cash items such as depreciation are not deducted:

$$\text{Cash Flow} = \frac{I_1 - I_8 - I_9 + I_4}{n} = \frac{\$243.2 - \$222.3 - \$0.6 + \$5.5}{2.025}$$

$$= \$12.74/\text{share}.$$

Measures of Value Using Ratios of Items From the Income Statement to the Balance Sheet

These measures are the ratio of net sales or earnings from the income statement to investment items from the balance sheet. Therefore, they are rates of return on investment (i.e., interest rates).

*As seen on page 41, the price-to-earnings ratio is used to estimate the market price of the surviving company after an acquisition.

Net Sales-to-Inventory Ratio. This ratio approximates inventory turnover. It doesn't necessarily equal inventory turnover because inventory is valued at the lower of cost or market value and net sales are valued at market value. A high ratio indicates merchandising ability.

$$\text{Net Sales-to-Inventory Ratio} = \frac{\text{Net Sales}}{\text{Inventory}}$$

$$= \frac{I_1}{B_5} = \frac{\$243.2}{\$51.7} = 4.70.$$

Net Sales-to-Receivables Ratio. This ratio measures the success in collecting debt. It is especially important to firms whose business is lending. A low value indicates a large fraction of bad debts. However, since many firms sell their receivables to banks and finance companies, this ratio could be difficult to interpret.

$$\text{Net Sales-to-Receivable Ratio} = \frac{\text{Net Sales}}{\text{Receivables}}$$

$$= \frac{I_1}{B_4} = \frac{\$243.2}{\$23.9} = 10.18.$$

*Net Sales-to-Fixed-Assets Ratio.** Fixed assets are all assets that are not current assets. This ratio measures the productivity of fixed assets. A high value indicates successful investment in plant and other non-current assets.

$$\text{Net Sales-to-Fixed-Assets Ratio} = \frac{\text{Net Sales}}{\text{Fixed Assets}}$$

$$= \frac{I_1}{B_{15} - B_6} = \frac{\$243.2}{\$257.1 - \$103.1} = 1.58.$$

Net Sales-to-Net-Worth Ratio. This ratio measures the productivity of invested capital.

$$\text{Net Sales-to-Net-Worth Ratio} = \frac{\text{Net Sales}}{\text{Net Worth}}$$

$$= \frac{I_1}{B_{28}} = \frac{\$243.2}{\$174.9} = 1.39.$$

*This ratio and the following one can form another ratio, the capitalization-to-fixed-asset ratio, that measures how well fixed assets are financed by permanent capital (i.e., stock).

Net Sales-to-Capitalization Ratio. This ratio measures the productivity of invested capital plus debt.

$$\text{Net Sales-to-Capitalization Ratio} = \frac{\text{Net Sales}}{\text{Capitalization}}$$

$$= \frac{I_1}{B_{18}+B_{22}+B_{28}} = \frac{\$243.2}{\$1.8+\$43.9+\$174.9} = 1.10.$$

Earnings-to-Net-Worth Ratio. This ratio measures the profitability of invested capital. It is the return on equity.

$$\text{Earnings-to-Net-Worth Ratio} = \frac{\text{Earnings}}{\text{Net Worth}}$$

$$= \frac{I_1-I_8-I_9}{B_{28}} = \frac{\$243.2-\$222.3-\$0.6}{\$174.9} = 0.12.$$

Return on Investment. This is a measure of the profitability of assets.

$$\text{Return on Investment} = \frac{\text{Net Income (After Taxes)}}{\text{Total Assets}}$$

$$= \frac{I_1-I_8-I_9}{B_{15}} = \frac{\$243.2-\$222.3-\$0.6}{\$257.1} = 0.079.$$

Earned Growth Rate. This is the annual rate at which the company's book value is increasing due to retained earnings (i.e., earnings not paid as common stock dividends).

$$\text{Earned Growth Rate} = \frac{\text{(Earnings)} - \text{(Dividends)}}{\text{(Net Asset Value)}}$$

$$= \frac{(I_1-I_8-I_9)-I_{10}}{B_{15}-(B_{18}+B_{22}+B_{24})} = \frac{(\$243.2-\$222.3-\$0.6)-\$11.3}{\$257.1-(\$1.8+\$43.9+\$13.2)}$$

$$= \frac{\$20.3-\$11.3}{\$257.1-\$58.9} = \frac{\$9}{\$198.2} = 0.045.$$

CHAPTER 2
Why Many Investors Use the Technical Approach to Value

Investors using the technical approach to value rely upon their own interpretation of the supply of, and demand for, stock. They hope to predict prices by studying past prices, trading volume, and the two together. They often don't even want to know about the nature of the company's business, because they think that this information is irrelevant (to supply and demand) and is likely to bias their judgment. Their opinion is that the fundamental approach is only useful for a long-term investment: most financial data are stale and the market has had time to adjust the price.

Even though technicians can put too much faith in their interpretation of stock market data, some of their methods can significantly improve the timing of stock purchases and sales.

RUMOR, NEWS, AND CONTRARY OPINION

Not all investors obtain corporate information simultaneously. There are some investors who are much closer to a company than others (i.e., directors, officers, employees, analysts, friends or relatives, employees of other corporations, attorneys, and printers) and who will learn about corporate information first. For our purposes, we shall refer to corporate information as news or rumor, depending upon whether it is officially announced or not.

Often, when insiders hear a significant rumor about a company, they will trade in the stock. In the case of a favorable rumor, the insiders will buy the stock—causing the price either to rise or to be unexpectedly firm. When the favorable information is actually announced, the stock's price usually will either rise less than expected or decline. This is because the insiders will have either failed to buy (because they already have done so) or they will sell if the price has subsequently increased.

Most investors are not aware of the rumor period of information dissemination and are bewildered by the price behavior just described;

they simply view the market as irrational. On the other hand, those investors who are aware of this period hold the theory which is commonly called contrary analysis (they are called contrarians). They believe that if "everyone" agrees that a stock is a good buy, it can't be: if "everyone" believes this, they probably have already acted on it, and there will be no new buyers to drive the price higher. Hence, the saying "buy on (favorable) rumor, sell on (favorable) news."

Of course, the nature of some corporation information allows it to become available to all (indiscriminately);* in this case there is no rumor, just news. In such instances, the price will behave as most investors expect; it will rise and fall in proportion to the quality of the news. In this case, investors view the market as rational.

Of course, not all rumors are true, and some that are true fail to become fact; this is especially true of acquisition rumors. Acquisition rumors usually cause prices to rise even though the acquisition may not be beneficial (see page 41). It is even sometimes wise to sell after news about an acquisition because enthusiasm and price can wane.

VOLUME

Volume is the word that is commonly used for the number of shares traded in a given period of time. Most technicians place great emphasis on volume as a tool for predicting prices. At the very least, volume indicates the amount of interest in a stock. However, volume alone indicates nothing about future prices; it must be observed with the concurrent price of the stock.

Volume and price tend to be correlated after corporate information has been announced.** In this phase, volume seems to indicate little about future prices. This situation exists most of the time.

If volume and price are not correlated, information has probably not been announced (the rumor phase). The following are easily the more interesting situations:

- If the price increases when volume does not, the supply of stock is less than the demand for it. Perhaps insiders have accumulated stock for a good reason and are reluctant to sell.
- If the price decreases when volume does not, the supply of stock is greater than the demand for it; unfavorable information is known (either by rumor or news). If it is known only to insiders, the price decline

*Even when information is announced, not all investors become aware simultaneously.

**Two quantities, such as volume and price, are correlated if they tend to move together; the magnitude of the moves is irrelevant to correlation.

could be just beginning; and if it is known by all as news, the price decline could be ending (i.e., a "selling climax").

Certainly large volume changes can occur without information (e.g., when mutual funds adjust their portfolios); for this reason, technical analysis should not be followed rigidly.

PRICE

Technicians often believe that "a picture is worth a thousand words." Therefore, they religiously study graphs of stock prices as they vary in time. The price is plotted on the vertical axis and time is plotted on the horizontal axis.* Usually these graphs are bar charts.

To create a bar chart, the technician selects a period of time such as a day or week. Then a vertical line that covers the range of prices during that period is drawn on the chart. Next, a short horizontal tick is drawn on the vertical line at the closing price for that period. The range of prices in the bar tends to be proportional to the price.

For example, the weekly range of stock prices might be approximately 10% of its price. That is, if the price is $10, it would have a weekly range of $1; if the price is $100, it would have a weekly range of $10. If the technician graphs these prices on a linear scale (i.e., a scale with equal vertical distances representing equal dollar *amounts*), the $100 stock will appear to be 10 times as volatile as is the $10 stock. If he graphs them on a logarithmic scale (i.e., a scale in which equal vertical distances represent equal *percentages***), the $100 stock and the $10 stock will appear as equally volatile.

It is important that stock prices be graphed on a logarithmic scale because:

- Otherwise the price behavior of a stock will appear distorted if the price changes from, say, $10 to $100.
- The price behavior of different stocks can be compared, regardless of price.

The trading volume during each period is usually represented by a

---

*Point and figure charts are an exception. They do not change with time, but only when prices change.

**A price changing exponentially will appear as a straight line on a logarithmic scale (because exponents and logarithms are inverse functions of each other). For example, money at compound interest appears to be a straight line whose slope is proportional to the interest rate. Also, stocks that are very low priced appear a little "jerky" because the minimum unit of change is large for the price (e.g., 1/8 is 6% of the value of a $2 stock, but 0.2% of a $60 stock).

vertical line on a linear scale at the bottom of the graph below the bar during that period.

Figure 1 are examples of logarithmic and linear charts. The weekly prices of a stock are shown on a logarithmic scale (left) and a linear scale (right).* The volume is plotted at the bottom of the logarithmic scale.

Figure 1

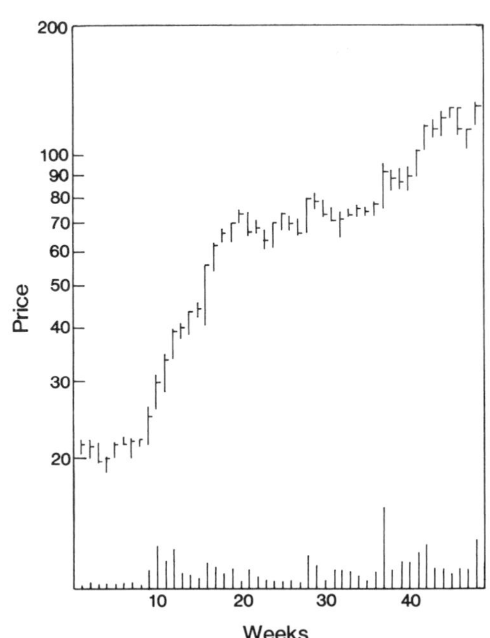

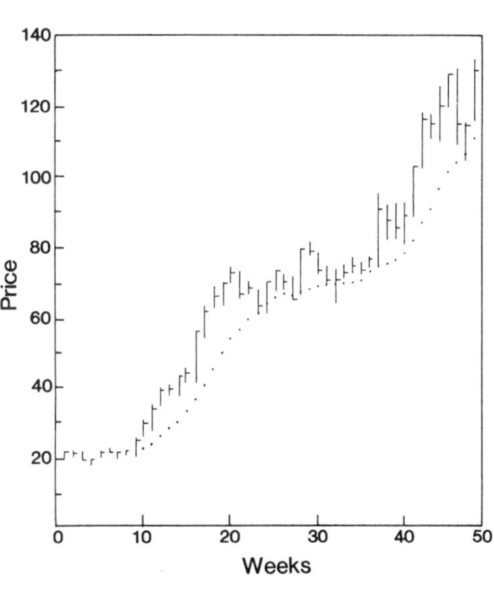

Charts can be used to predict prices, because investors usually remember the price at which they bought or sold. For example, if they bought at a given price and the price subsequently falls and then returns, they may wish to sell at that price (feeling fortunate that it returned). If many investors feel this way there will be a large supply of stock at that price, and the stock is said to have a "supply level" there. This large supply of stock will tend to cause the price to fall again.

A resistance (or support) level would occur if the price rose and then returned; the previous buyers might feel fortunate to be able to buy more shares there at that price. Moreover, even if investors do not behave in this way, enough investors believe that they will, and the myth becomes fact.

*Actually, these are called semi-logarithmic charts because the horizontal (time) scale is linear. A cycle is the price range over an order of magnitude, e.g., from 1 to 10, 10 to 100, 100 to 1000, etc.

Because reading charts is somewhat of an art, it is inevitable that some superstition will evolve too.

The Dow Theory is the oldest and most popular theory of predicting stock market price behavior. It is used to predict the trend of industrial stocks (as a group rather than individually). The theory utilizes the average price of 30 industrial stocks and the transportation stocks. It supposes that there is a primary long-term business cycle (lasting years) upon which is superimposed other minor business cycles (lasting weeks and months).

The theory says, generally, that a long-term trend in the industrials ends only when *both* the industrials and transportations change direction. Specifically,

(1) A bull market is possible if a low is higher than a previous low (in both averages);

(2) A bull market is confirmed if (1) is followed by a high that exceeds a previous high;

(3) A bear market is possible if a high is less than a previous high (in both averages);

(4) A bear market is confirmed if (3) is followed by a low that is less than a previous low.

If the Dow Theory didn't require similar price behavior in both averages (in steps 1 and 3) it would say little.

Note that these highs and lows are not carefully defined: some analysts use daily values, others use closing values. Many analysts scoff at the Dow Theory, because the market has changed considerably since its formulation. For example, the industrial average had 12 stocks then and 30 now. Also, the theory used the railroad average then and uses the transportation average now.

MOVING AVERAGE

A moving average is an average of stock prices for, say, the last 200 market days. It is recomputed each day by including the price for the current day and omitting the earliest price from the previous day's computation. The price is usually the closing price, but it needn't be.

Technicians plot the moving average on the same chart with the stock. They believe that when the moving average crosses the stock's current price, a price reversal is beginning. Since the moving average is composed of past prices, it lags the current market price. Of course, the number of days in the average determines how much it lags and how readily it responds to change. Since the moving average on any two consecutive days contains the same prices except for two (the first and last), it forms a relatively smooth curve.

Figure 2 shows a 10-week moving average of closing prices for the common stock. Since this stock has generally been rising, the moving average tends to lie below the stock prices. The following formula determines the average on the kth day for a moving average of j days.

Figure 2

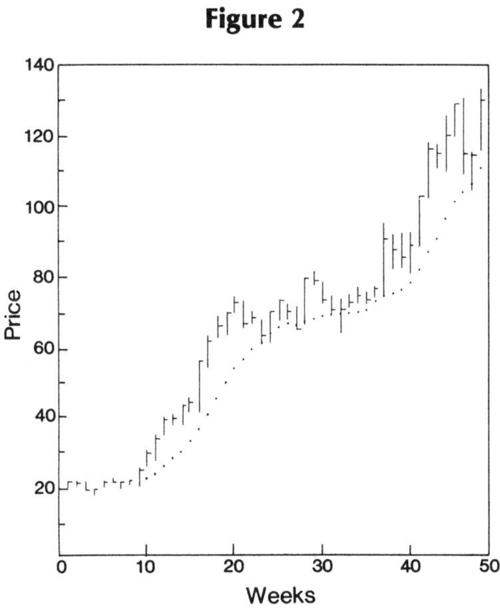

FORMULA:

$$\bar{p}_k = \frac{p_{k+1-j} + \ldots + p_k}{j} = \frac{1}{j} \sum_{i=1}^{j} p_{k+i-j}$$

where

$\bar{p}_k$ = moving average price on the kth day ($k \geq j$)

then

j = number of days in the moving average

p_k = closing market price on the kth day

p_{k+1-j} = closing market price on day $k + 1 - j$.

EXAMPLE: On six consecutive market days, the common shares of Gulf Oil closed at:

31, 32-1/2, 32-1/4, 31-3/4, 33, and 33-3/4.

Determine the five-day moving average on the fifth and sixth days.

SOLUTION: In this example,

$$\begin{aligned} j &= 5,\ p_1 = 31,\ p_2 = 32\text{-}1/2,\ p_3 = 32\text{-}1/4, \\ p_4 &= 31\text{-}3/4,\ p_5 = 33, \text{ and } p_6 = 33\text{-}3/4. \end{aligned}$$

In the first case $k = 5$. Therefore, $k+1-j = 5+1-5 = 1$. From the formula, the moving average price on the fifth day is,

$$\begin{aligned} \overline{p}_5 &= \frac{p_1 + \ldots + p_5}{5} \\ &= \frac{31 + 32\text{-}1/2 + 32\text{-}1/4 + 31\text{-}3/4 + 33}{5} \\ &= \frac{160.5}{5} = 32.1. \end{aligned}$$

In the second case $k = 6$. Therefore, $k+1-j = 6+1-5 = 2$. From the formula, the moving average price on the sixth day is,

$$\begin{aligned} \overline{p}_6 &= \frac{p_2 + \ldots + p_6}{5} \\ &= \frac{32\text{-}1/2 + 32\text{-}1/4 + 31\text{-}3/4 + 33 + 33\text{-}3/4}{5} \\ &= \frac{163.25}{5} = 32.65. \end{aligned}$$

CHAPTER 3
Yield and Value Made Easy

COMMON STOCK

Common stock is the residual ownership of a corporation; that is, it has a claim to corporate assets after all superior claims (such as claims of bond and preferred stockholders) are satisfied.* It also has the basic voting control in the corporation.

All corporations issue common stock, and most issue *only* common stock. Each share represents a unit of ownership of the corporation. The owner of the shares has no liability, and the risk is limited to the amount of the investment.

Even though preferred stock has priority over common stock to receive a dividend from earnings, the amount is limited. Common stock is more popular than preferred stock because the amount of dividend is not contractually limited (i.e., common stock can participate in the growth of the company). This potential and uncertainty as to dividends cause large changes in the supply of, and demand for, stock. Therefore, common stock has wide price movement and a concomitantly large potential for capital gain or loss.

Stock dividends are taxed as ordinary income (the first $100 is exempt each year), and capital gain after six months is taxed as capital gain. Buying commissions add to the basis, and selling commissions subtract from the sale price.

Common stock has been discussed in Chapters 1 and 2, so little needs to be added here. However, the following will discuss the yield on a share of common stock, the yield on a common stock investment, dividends, dollar cost averaging, and the expected price of a share of common stock after a merger.

Yield

When computing the yield, it is important to distinguish between the current yield on the stock and the yield on the investment. The current

*In this way, the common stockholder is similar to the owner of real estate. (See Figure 23.)

yield is simply the yield (not including commissions) if you held the stock for a year and if both the price and the annual dividend remain unchanged.

FORMULAS:

$$y_c = \frac{d}{p_1}$$

$$Y = \frac{A-B}{C}$$

$$y = (1+Y)^{1/t}-1$$

where

y_c = current annual yield on the stock

Y = total yield on the investment (over its term)

y = annual yield on the investment

then

A = $p_2 + td$

B = $p_1 + c_1 + c_2$

C = $mp_1 + c_1$

c_1, c_2 = commission per share when the stock is bought and sold, respectively

d = annual cash dividend

m = margin, expressed as a decimal ($m=1$ if margin is not used). If the use of margin incurs interest charges, add the per share charge to c_2

p_1, p_2 = price when the stock is bought and sold, respectively

t = time investment is held, in years

EXAMPLE: Mark Meredith bought 100 shares of IBM common stock at $40 without using margin. The commission was $60. He held the stock for three years during which time he received quarterly dividends of $0.86/share. He sold the stock at $68 and paid a $76 commission. What was (a) the current annual yield on the stock when he bought it, and (b) his annual yield?

SOLUTION: In this example,

$p_1 = \$40,\ m = 1,\ c_1 = \$60/100 = \$0.60,\ t = 3,$

$d = \$0.86 \times 4 = \$3.44,\ p_2 = \$68,$ and $c_2 = \$76/100 = \$0.76.$

(a) The current annual yield on the stock is,

$$y_c = \frac{\$3.44}{\$40} = 0.086 = 8.6\%.$$

(b) In this case,

$$C = 1 \times \$40 + \$0.60 = \$40.60,$$

$$B = \$40 + \$0.60 + \$0.76 = \$41.36, \text{ and}$$

$$A = \$68 + 3 \times \$3.44 = \$78.32.$$

Now the total yield on the investment is,

$$Y = \frac{\$78.32-\$41.36}{\$40.60} = \frac{\$36.96}{\$40.60} = 0.9103 = 91.03\%,$$

and the annual yield on the investment is

$$y = (1+0.9103)^{1/3}-1 = 1.9103^{.3333}-1 = 1.2408-1 = 0.2408 = 24.08\%.*$$

Dollar-Cost Averaging

Dollar-cost averaging is a method of buying shares which assures that your average price per share is less than or equal to the average of the prices at the times of purchase.

This lower average price is achieved by periodically investing the same number of *dollars* at each time of purchase. In this way, more shares are purchased when the price is low, and fewer shares are purchased when the price is high. On the other hand, if the same number of *shares* is purchased each time, the average price of the purchased shares equals the average of the prices at the time of purchase.

Even if dollar-cost averaging didn't result in a lower average purchase price, it can be argued that purchasing shares only at given

---

*If an electronic calculator is used to determine the annual yield, enter 1.9103, press the "y^x" button, and enter .3333.

periods of time defeats the propensity to buy on rallies (and to sell on declines).

FORMULAS:

$$p_s = \frac{p_1 + \ldots + p_m}{m}$$

$$p_d = \frac{k_1 p_1 + \ldots + k_m p_m}{k_1 + \ldots + k_m}$$

where

p_s = average price of shares when an equal number of shares is purchased periodically

p_d = average price of shares when an equal number of dollars is invested periodically (dollar-cost averaging)

then

$k_1,\ldots,k_m$ = number of shares purchased in each period

m = number of periods

$p_1,\ldots,p_m$ = price of shares in each period.

EXAMPLE (Comparison): Suppose that after three equal periods, shares of IBM Corporation were selling at \$70, \$40, and \$100. The amount of \$2,800 is invested each period. Which of the following two plans results in a lower average price: (a) an equal number of shares is purchased, and (b) an equal number of dollars is invested (i.e., dollar-cost averaging)?

SOLUTION: In this example,

$m = 3$, $p_1 = \$70$, $p_2 = \$40$, and $p_3 = \$100$.

(a) The average price of the shares is,

$$p_s = \frac{\$70 + \$40 + \$100}{3} = \frac{\$210}{3} = \$70.$$

(b) In this case,

$$k_1 = \frac{\$2800}{\$70} = 40,\ k_2 = \frac{\$2800}{\$40} = 70,\ \text{and } k_3 = \frac{\$2800}{\$100}$$
$$= 28.$$

Now, the average price of the shares is,

$$p_d = \frac{40 \times \$70 + 70 \times \$40 + 28 \times \$100}{40 + 70 + 28}$$

$$= \frac{\$2800 + \$2800 + \$2800}{138}$$

$$= \frac{\$8400}{138} = \$60.87.$$

In this example, dollar-cost averaging resulted in an average price that is $9/share less than that which resulted from the other method.

Dividends

Common stock represents the residual ownership of a corporation that is entitled to earnings and assets after other limited claims. Directors of the corporation vote upon the amount of earnings, if any, to be paid to stockholders as dividends. The dividends are paid as either cash dividends or stock dividends. The dividends can be regarded as a return *on* the investment, similar to interest. The current dividend yield (interest rate) can be determined by dividing the current annual dividend by the current price of each share.

Cash Dividends: Cash dividends are paid periodically (usually quarterly) by companies that are well-established. The directors' policy for cash dividends can be measured as a ratio of the dividend-to-cash flow or as a ratio of the dividend-to-earnings. The ratio of dividends-to-earnings is called the payout ratio. This ratio depends upon many factors, but is often 0.40–0.50 for stable industrials, 0.50–0.60 for transportations, and 0.60–0.70 for utilities.

Cash dividends are taxed as ordinary income in the year they are received.

FORMULA:

$$\boxed{y_c = \frac{d}{p}}$$

where

y_c = current annual yield on the stock

then

d = annual cash dividend from each share

p = current price of each share.

EXAMPLE: When IBM was paying an annual cash dividend of \$3.80, its stock was selling at \$113. What was the current annual yield at that time?

SOLUTION: In this example,

$$d = \$3.80, \text{ and } p = \$113.$$

The current annual yield was,

$$y_c = \frac{\$3.80}{\$113} = 0.0336 = 3.36\%.$$

Stock Dividends: Stock dividends are often issued by companies that are young, growing, and short of cash. They are usually stated as a percentage of stock owned. For example, a 5% stock dividend provides 5 more shares for every 100 shares owned. Stock dividends typically amount to 2%-10% of common stock owned. On the other hand, a stock dividend of 25% or more is usually called a stock split. Both stock dividends and stock splits increase the number of shares outstanding, but because they don't increase assets, they correspondingly decrease the book value/share.

A stock dividend lowers the investor's basis, and is thus exempt from income tax until the stock is sold. When it is sold, it is subject to tax as a capital gain. Moreover, the holding period is considered to be the holding period of the shares on which the dividend was paid. These two features (delayed tax and long holding period) add to the attractiveness of stock dividends with respect to cash dividends.

FORMULAS:

$$y_c = d$$

$$b = \frac{p}{1 + d}$$

where

y_c = current annual yield on the stock

b = basis resulting from stock dividend

then

d = annual stock dividend, expressed as the ratio of the number of new shares per 100 shares

p = purchase price of each share.

EXAMPLE: When NVF Company was issuing a 5% stock dividend every other quarter, the common stock was selling at \$3.75. Determine (a) the current annual yield on the stock dividend, and (b) the basis after two dividends.

SOLUTION: In this example,

$$d = 0.05 \times 2 = 0.10, \text{ and } p = \$3.75.$$

Now, (a) The current annual yield on the stock dividend is,

$$y_c = d = 0.10 = 10\%,$$

and (b) The basis after two dividends is,

$$b = \frac{\$3.75}{1+0.10} = \frac{\$3.75}{1.10} = \$3.41.$$

Market Price of the Surviving Company's Stock After an Acquisition

There are many reasons that a company might wish to acquire another.* To accomplish this, a company may offer cash or stock for the stock of the company to be acquired. If an acquisition does occur, a very important consideration to the investor would be the market price of the shares of the combined company.

The following formulas determine the anticipated market price of the combined company, assuming it will inherit the price/earning ratio that the market has assigned to the acquiring company (Company A), which it often does.

FORMULAS:

$$p = \begin{cases} \dfrac{p_a}{e_a} \cdot \dfrac{e_a n_a + e_b n_b}{n_a} & \text{(Acquired from Cash)} \\[2ex] \dfrac{p_a}{e_a} \cdot \left[\dfrac{e_a n_a + e_b n_b}{n_a + n_b \left(1 - \dfrac{p_b}{p_a}\right)} \right]^{**} & \text{(Acquired from Stock)} \end{cases}$$

---

*Low priced and highly profitable companies are prime candidates.

**Of course, acquisition of Company B by Company A by stock can occur only if the market considers Company A to be worth more than Company B. That is, $p_a n_a > p_b n_b$.

where

p = anticipated market price of shares of combined company

then

e_a, e_b = annual earnings of companies A and B, respectively

n_a, n_b = number of outstanding shares of companies A and B, respectively

p_a, p_b = price of shares of companies A and B, respectively, before acquisition attempt is rumored (or known).

EXAMPLE (Cash): Suppose the shares of Company A have been selling at $32. It has had earnings of $2/share on 2,000,000 shares outstanding. It wishes to acquire Company B from its earnings. Company B has earnings of $1.2/share on 1,000,000 shares outstanding. What will be the price of the combined company if the price/earning ratio of Company A is preserved?

SOLUTION: In this example,

$$p_a = \$32,\ e_a = \$2,\ n_a = 2{,}000{,}000,\ e_b = \$1.2, \text{ and}$$
$$n_b = 1{,}000{,}000.$$

Now, the price of the shares of the combined companies is expected to be:

$$\begin{aligned} p &= \frac{\$32}{\$2} \cdot \left(\frac{\$2 \times 2{,}000{,}000 + \$1.2 \times 1{,}000{,}000}{2{,}000{,}000}\right) \\ &= 16 \cdot \left(\frac{\$4{,}000{,}000 + \$1{,}200{,}000}{2{,}000{,}000}\right) \\ &= 16 \cdot \left(\frac{\$5{,}200{,}000}{2{,}000{,}000}\right) \\ &= 16 \times \$2.6 \\ &= \$41.60. \end{aligned}$$

This is the price if the price-to-earnings ratio of Company A is preserved. The price of its shares increase from $32 to $41.60.

EXAMPLE (Stock): Suppose the shares of Company A had been selling at $32. It has had earnings of $2/share on 2,000,000 shares outstanding. It wishes to acquire Company B with a stock offer. The shares of Company B have been selling at \$16. It too had earnings of \$2/share on 2,000,000 shares outstanding. Company A offers one share of its stock for two shares of stock in Company B. If this offer is accepted by Company B, what will be the price of the combined stock if the price/earning ratio of Company A prevails?

SOLUTION: In this example,

$$p_a = \$32,\ e_a = \$2,\ n_a = 2{,}000{,}000,\ p_b = \$16,$$

$$e_b = \$2, \text{ and } n_b = 2{,}000{,}000.$$

Now, the price of the shares of the combined companies is expected to be:

$$\begin{aligned} p &= \frac{\$32}{\$2} \cdot \left(\frac{\$2 \times 2{,}000{,}000 + \$2 \times 2{,}000{,}000}{2{,}000{,}000 + 2{,}000{,}000(1 - \frac{\$16}{\$32})} \right) \\ &= 16 \cdot \left(\frac{\$4{,}000{,}000 + \$4{,}000{,}000}{2{,}000{,}000 + 2{,}000{,}000 \times (1/2)} \right) \\ &= 16 \cdot \left(\frac{\$8{,}000{,}000}{3{,}000{,}000} \right) \\ &= 16 \times \$2.667 \\ &= \$42.67. \end{aligned}$$

That is, if the price-to-earnings ratio of Company A prevails, its shares increase in price from \$32 to \$42.67.

Beta

Beta is the name given to a measure of the variability of the price of a single stock relative to the variability of the average price of a group of stocks (such as Standard and Poor's 500 Price Index).*

It is determined in the following way:

- On, say, n occasions, note the price of the subject stock and the average price of the group.
- Plot these n points in two dimensions: Plot the price of the subject stock on the vertical axis and the price of the average on the horizontal axis. The result is a "scattering" of n points.

---

*The quantities needn't be price; they could be yield, price/earnings ratios, etc.

- Determine the slope of the line that "best" fits these points (called the regression line).*

Now, Beta (denoted by β) is the name usually given to the slope of this line. (A line making a 45° angle with the horizontal has a slope of 1.) For example, if $\beta=1.25$, the variability of the subject stock is 25% greater than that of the average.**

FORMULA:

$$\boxed{\beta = \frac{A}{B}}$$

where

β = the relative variability (i.e., slope of the regression line)

then

$$A = \sum_{i=1}^{n} (p_i - \overline{p})(p_{ai} - \overline{p}_a)$$

$$B = \sum_{i=1}^{n} (p_{ai} - \overline{p}_a)^2$$

n = number of observations

p_i = the price of the subject stock on the ith observation

$$\overline{p} = \frac{1}{n}\sum_{i=1}^{n} p_i = \text{the average price of the subject stock}$$

---

*The best fitting straight line is the one that renders a minimum the sum of the squares of the vertical distance between the points and the line. Beta should not be used with fewer than 11 points, nor when correlation does not exist (i.e., when there is no systematic relationship).

**Some authors say that Beta measures risk. It doesn't. Risk is defined in terms of probability: Risk = (Amount at Risk)×(Probability of Loss). This formula shows that risk is proportional to the *mean* (i.e., probability of loss), whereas Beta measures the relative *variability* of two investments.

p_{ai} = the price of the average stock on the ith observation

$$\bar{p}_a = \frac{1}{n}\sum_{i=1}^{n} p_{ai} = \text{the average price of the average stock.}$$

EXAMPLE: On six observations, IBM common stock was selling at,

68, 69, 63, 58, 53, and 55.

At the same time, the New York Composite Index for industrials (an average) was,

77, 72, 78, 70, 72, and 63.*

Determine Beta for IBM relative to the Index for these observations. These points and the regression line are shown in Figure 3.

Figure 3

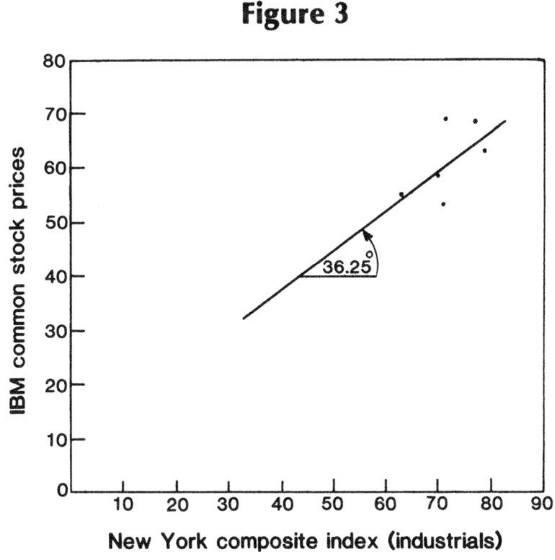

SOLUTION: In this example,

$n = 6.$

---

*These few observations are inadequate and are used only for illustration.

The prices are,

$$p_1 = 68,\ p_2 = 69,\ p_3 = 63,\ p_4 = 58,\ p_5 = 53,\ p_6 = 55,$$

$$p_{a1} = 77,\ p_{a2} = 72,\ p_{a3} = 78,\ p_{a4} = 70,\ p_{a5} = 72, \text{ and } p_{a6} = 63.$$

The average prices for IBM and the composite average are,

$$\overline{p} = \frac{1}{6}\sum_{i=1}^{6} p_i = (1/6)(68+69+63+58+53+55)$$

$$= (1/6)\times 366 = 61, \text{ and}$$

$$\overline{p_a} = \frac{1}{6}\sum_{i=1}^{6} p_{ai} = (1/6)(77+72+78+70+72+63)$$

$$= (1/6)\times 432 = 72.$$

The numerator in the Beta formula is,

$$A = \sum_{i=1}^{6} (p_i - \overline{p})(p_{ai} - \overline{p_a})$$

$$= (68-61)(77-72) + (69-61)(72-72) + (63-61)(78-72)$$

$$+ (58-61)(70-72) + (53-61)(72-72) + (55-61)(63-72)$$

$$= 7\times 5 + 8\times 0 + 2\times 6 + (-3)\times(-2) + (-8)\times 0$$
$$+ (-6)\times(-9)$$

$$= 35 + 0 + 12 + 6 - 0 + 54$$

$$= 107.$$

The denominator in the Beta formula is,

$$B = \sum_{i=1}^{6} (p_{ai} - \overline{p_a})^2$$

$$= (77-72)^2 + (72-72)^2 + (78-72)^2$$

$$+ (70-72)^2 + (72-72)^2 + (63-72)^2$$

$$= 5^2 + 0^2 + 6^2 + (-2)^2 + 0^2 + (-9)^2$$

$$= 25 + 0 + 36 + 4 + 0 + 81$$

$$= 146.$$

Now, Beta is,

$$\beta = \frac{A}{B} = \frac{107}{146} = 0.733.$$

This slope corresponds to an angle of 36.25°.* For this period of time, the price of IBM has varied less than has the Index.

PREFERRED STOCK

Preferred stock has a claim to corporate earnings and assets prior to that of common stock; however, there is no guarantee. Since preferred stockholders are owners of the company, their claim to earnings and assets is behind that of creditors, such as bondholders. A corporation issues preferred stock in order to raise capital to acquire another company, for expansion, improvements, etc. Some corporations issue more than one class of preferred stock, each with a different priority.

Preferred stock can have several features:

Voting: The stockholders can usually vote only when dividends are late or the company is in financial trouble.

Callable: The corporation has the right to buy the callable shares at a specified price (usually a few points above par and after five years). It may choose to exercise this option if the yield exceeds the yield on currently issued preferred stock or if it has surplus cash. Even if the shares are not callable, merger or recapitalization can cause them to be replaced by those that are callable.

Cumulative: Both current and late dividends are to be paid ahead of common stock dividends. Without this feature, late dividends are lost forever to the preferred stockholder. Even with this feature, late dividends belong to the current stockholder.

Participation: The stockholders can obtain extra dividends or special disbursements such as rights. This feature is not usual, but it causes preferred stock to increase in price because the stockholder can participate in the prosperity of the company.

*That is, the angle above the horizontal (in degrees) is obtained from $\tan^{-1} \beta$.

Convertible: This feature provides the right to exchange preferred shares for a specified number of shares of common or other stock. The number of shares often decreases with time. This feature allows holders to share in the higher value of common stock that usually accompanies economic success; hence, preferred stock with this feature will vary more in price than without it. This feature also induces investors to accept a lower dividend rate. As an alternative to convertibility, the corporation may attach warrants to the preferred stock so that the holder may purchase common stock and retain the preferred stock.

If the corporation liquidates involuntarily, preferred stockholders usually receive either par value or a stated value plus the accumulated dividend. If liquidation is voluntary, they usually receive an additional premium.

Eighty-five percent of preferred stock dividend income from an American corporation that is paid to another American corporation is exempt from taxation. Hence, there is more propensity for corporations to invest in preferred stock than there is for individuals.

The investor in preferred stock has much less opportunity for capital gain than in common stock. The reason for this is not that he has more secure dividend income; it is because the dividend is fixed unless there is a participation or convertible feature. Also, common stock prices vary more than preferred stock prices for the following chain of reasons:

- Corporate earnings are relatively unstable.
- Dividends are paid from earnings.
- Preferred stockholders are paid dividends before common stockholders (therefore, common stock dividends are less stable than preferred stock dividends).
- Common stock prices vary with expected dividends (among other factors, of course).

The current annual yield on preferred stock will compare with similar investments such as corporate bonds with a BAA rating; and since the dividend is fixed, the price cannot change greatly. (See the formula on page 36).

Preferred stock is traded in the same market or exchange as is common stock. Most newspapers list the price of the preferred stock with the common, and include both the dividend (expressed either in dollars or as a percent of par value) and the current annual yield.

The following formulas can be used to determine the current annual yield on a preferred stock and the yield on a preferred stock investment.

Since investors in preferred stock value the safety of dividends, the formulas on page 51 should be used to measure safety. The dividend coverage is considered by most analysts to be the most reliable measure of safety, particularly when comparing preferred stocks within the same industry.

FORMULAS:

$$y_c = \begin{cases} \dfrac{d}{p_1} & \text{(Current annual before-tax yield on preferred stock)} \\ \dfrac{d}{p_1} \bullet (1-0.15r_t) & \text{(Current annual after-tax yield on preferred stock for corporations)} \\ \dfrac{d}{p_1} \bullet (1-r_t) & \text{(Current annual after-tax yield on preferred stock for individuals)} \end{cases}$$

$$y_m = \frac{d+D}{E}$$

$$Y = \frac{A-B}{C}$$

$$y = (1+Y)^{1/t}-1$$

where

y_c = current annual yield on the preferred stock

y_m = approximate annual yield on the callable preferred stock

Y = total yield on the investment

y = annual yield on the investment

then

$A = p_2+td$

$B = p_1+c_1+c_2$

$C = mp_1+c_1$

c_1, c_2 = commission per share to buy and sell the stock, respectively

$$D = \frac{p_2 - p_1}{n}$$

d = annual dividend per share

$$E = \frac{p_2 + p_1}{2}$$

m = margin expressed as a decimal. If none used, m=1

n = number of years after purchased and until callable

p_1 = current market price or purchase price

p_2 = sale price or called price

r_t = corporate or individual income tax rate, expressed as a decimal

t = time investment held, in years.

EXAMPLE 1 (Tax): Dr. M.J. Connors is a professional corporation. As such, 85% of preferred stock dividends is excluded from federal income tax. He owns 1,000 shares of GTE preferred. It is rated BBB+ by Standard and Poor's, and pays a quarterly dividend of $0.62/share. The stock is currently selling at 19-1/2. Assume Dr. Connors' tax rate is 46% (both as an individual and as a corporation), and compare the current annual yields after tax for each case.

SOLUTION: In this example,

$$d = 4 \times \$0.62 = \$2.48,\ p_1 = \$19.50, \text{ and } r_t = 0.46.$$

Now, the current yield after tax as a corporation is,

$$y_c = \frac{\$2.48}{\$19.50} \times (1 - 0.15 \times 0.46)$$

$$= \frac{\$2.48}{\$19.50} \times 0.931 = 0.118 = 11.8\%,$$

and the current yield after tax as an individual is,

$$y_c = \frac{\$2.48}{\$19.50} \times (1 - 0.46)$$

$$= \frac{\$2.48}{\$19.50} \times 0.54 = 0.069 = 6.9\%.$$

EXAMPLE 2 (Callable): Consolidated Edison of New York preferred pays a quarterly dividend of $1.25 and will be called at 100 in five years. It is currently selling at 54-1/2. What is (a) the current annual yield, and (b) the "yield-to-call" (i.e., yield until called)?

SOLUTION: In this example,

$$d = \$1.25 \times 4 = \$5.00,\ p_2 = \$100.00,\ n = 5 \text{ years, and } p_1 = \$54.50.$$

Now,

(a) The current annual yield is,

$$y_c = \frac{\$5.00}{\$54.50} = 0.092 = 9.2\%, \text{ and}$$

(b) In this case,

$$D = \frac{\$100.00 - \$54.50}{5} = \$9.10, \text{ and}$$

$$E = \frac{\$100.00 + \$54.50}{2} = \$77.25.$$

The "yield-to-call" is,

$$y_m = \frac{\$5.00 + \$9.10}{\$77.25} = 0.183 = 18.3\%.$$

FORMULAS:

Measures of Preferred Dividend Safety*

	Dividend Coverage	Earnings/ Share	Assets/ Share	Yield/ Share
First Priority Preferred	$\frac{(I_1 - I_8) + I_6}{I_{9,1} + I_6}$	$\frac{(I_1 - I_8)}{n_1}$	$\frac{B_{15}}{n_1}$	$\frac{d_1}{p_1}$
Second Priority Preferred	$\frac{(I_1 - I_8) + I_6}{I_{9,1} + I_{9,2} + I_6}$	$\frac{(I_1 - I_8) - I_{9,1}}{n_2}$	$\frac{B_{15} - I_{9,1}}{n_2}$	$\frac{d_2}{p_2}$

then

I_1, I_6, I_8 = net sales, interest charges, and total costs and expenses, respectively

*Most of these quantities are defined in the Balance Sheet (page 19) and Income Statement (page 23).

$I_{9,1}, I_{9,2}$ = Item I_9 (dividends paid on preferred stock), but separated into dividends for first and second priority preferred, respectively

B_{15} = total assets

n_1, n_2 = number of outstanding shares of first and second priority preferred, respectively

d_1, d_2 = annual dividend per share on first and second priority preferred, respectively

p_1, p_2 = current market price of first and second priority preferred, respectively.

EXAMPLE 3 (Dividend Coverage): Suppose the company whose income statement is shown on page 23 had issued two preferred stocks, and of the total \$600,000 preferred stock dividend, \$400,000 was paid on the first preferred and \$200,000 was paid on the second preferred. Determine the dividend coverage for each issue. Express all values per millions of dollars.

SOLUTION: In this example,

$$I_1 = \$243.2,\ I_8 = \$222.3,\ I_6 = \$2.7,$$

$$I_{9,1} = \$0.4, \text{ and } I_{9,2} = \$0.2.$$

Now the dividend coverage for the first preferred stock is,

$$\frac{(\$243.2 - \$222.3) + \$2.7}{\$0.4 + \$2.7} = \frac{\$20.9 + \$2.7}{\$0.4 + \$2.7} = \frac{\$23.6}{\$3.1} = 7.61,$$

and the dividend coverage for the second preferred stock is,

$$\frac{(\$243.2 - \$222.3) + \$2.7}{\$0.4 + \$0.2 + \$2.7} = \frac{\$20.9 + \$2.7}{\$0.6 + \$2.7} = \frac{\$23.6}{\$3.3} = 7.15.$$

The second preferred dividend is nearly as secure as the first.

OPTIONS

Options are contracts giving the right to buy or sell a specified number of shares of common stock (usually 100) at a specified price and within a specified period of time.* The price is called the striking price,

*The expiration date is the Saturday following the third Friday of the quoted month.

and terms range from one month to one year. Options are calls (giving the right to buy) or puts (giving the right to sell). Options can be purchased or sold (also said to be written).

The cost to buy an option (called a premium) depends upon the duration of the contract, the difference between the current price of the common stock and the contract (striking) price, the volatility of the common stock and market conditions. The premium can range from 2% to 25% of the price of the common stock.* Options are traded in markets such as the Chicago Board Options Exchange.

Figure 4 shows the Wall Street Journal quotations for options for Dupont common stock.** There are 18 possible calls and 18 possible puts: six different strike prices and three months. In this case, on September 30, 8 options were not offered (denoted by s), and 12 options were not traded (denoted by r). The common stock closed at 52, and the five October call options had (strike price)+(option price)=51-5/8, 51-3/4, 52-1/4, 52-11/16, and 55-3/8.***

Call Options

A call option gives the investor the right to buy a specified number of shares of common stock (usually 100) at a specified price and within a specified period of time. The call option is used much more than the put option. However, fewer than one-half of purchased call options are exercised. Three types of investors use call options:

- Call options are bought by those who believe the value of the common stock will increase. They will exercise their option and buy the common stock at the striking price, having spent only about 15% of the purchase price. They receive the difference between the current market price and the striking price (less commissions).
- Call options are bought by those who have sold short the common stock and want to reduce their risk from a rising stock value.****
- Call options are sold (written) by those who believe the value will not increase much (if at all) during the contract period. They needn't own the stock. If they do own the stock, they are referred to as covered, otherwise they are referred to as uncovered.

---

*Some data show that the average premium for a call option (when the price of the common equals the striking price) can be estimated by $u=(p/25)\bullet k^{0.58}$ where u, p, and k are the premium/share, the price/share of the stock, and the months remaining until the expiration date, respectively.

**Reprinted by permission of the Wall Street Journal © Dow Jones & Company, Inc., 1983.

***In this case, the October options are to expire in 22 days.

****Common stock is said to be sold short by an investor if he does not own the stock. The investor borrows it and then sells it in the hope of buying it at a lower price in the future.

Figure 4

Listed Options Quotations

Closing prices of all options. Sales unit usually is 100 shares. Security description includes exercise price. Stock close is New York or American exchange final price.

Option & NY Close	Strike Price	Calls–Last Oct	Calls–Last Jan	Calls–Last Apr	Puts–Last Oct	Puts–Last Jan	Puts–Last Apr
56½	... 55	2¼	5¼	r	9-16	2⅜	r
56½	... 60	9-16	2¾	4½	r	4¾	r
Burrgh	..40	13⅝	r	s	r	r	s
53¾	... 45	8⅞	r	r	r	r	r
53¾	... 50	3⅞	5¼	r	5-16	1¾	r
53¾	... 55	9-16	2⅞	4¼	2¼	r	r
53¾	... 60	1-16	1¼	2⅜	r	r	r
C Tel	20	4⅜	4⅝	r	r	r	r
24½	... 25	7-16	r	1¾	r	1⅜	r
Cooper	.. 30	4¾	r	r	r	¾	r
34½	... 35	¾	2⅛	r	1¼	2⅝	r
CrZel	25	4½	r	5½	r	r	r
29⅝	... 30	½	r	2¼	1¼	r	r
DartK	.. 65	r	5¼	r	r	1⅛	r
68¼	... 70	½	2⅜	r	r	r	r
68¼	... 75	⅛	r	1¾	r	r	r
Dig Eq	..90	r	16⅞	r	⅛	1 11-16	2⅝
102¾	.. 95	8¾	12½	r	½	3	4⅜
102¾	. 100	4¾	10¼	r	1 9-16	4⅞	6⅛
102¾	. 110	⅞	5⅜	r	7½	10	11
102¾	. 120	⅛	3⅛	6	r	r	r
102¾	. 130	r	1	3¼	r	r	r
102¾	. 140	r	½	s	r	r	s
Disney	.. 55	7¼	r	r	1-16	1	1¾
62	 60	2¾	5	8¼	11-16	2 9-16	r
62	. 65	7-16	3	5¼	3⅞	4¾	6
62	 70	1-16	1⅝	3⅝	8	r	r
62	 75	1-16	¾	s	12⅝	r	s
62	 80	r	½	s	17⅝	r	s
du Pnt	.. 35	16⅝	s	s	r	s	s
52	 40	11¾	r	s	r	r	s
52	 45	7¼	7¾	r	r	½	r
52	 50	2 11-16	4⅛	5¾	9-16	1 15-16	r
52	 55	⅜	2	3⅛	3⅜	4½	r
52	 60	s	⅝	r	s	r	r
FstCh	. 29¾	r	r	s	5-16	r	s
Goodyr	..30	¾	2⅛	r	7-16	r	r
30⅜	... 35	1-16	⅝	1	r	r	r
Gould	... 30	2½	3⅝	5⅜	5-16	1 5-16	2
32	[illegible]	[illegible]	[illegible]	2 7-16	3⅛	[illegible]	4¼
32	[illegible]	[illegible]	[illegible]	[illegible]	[illegible]	[illegible]	[illegible]

Put Options

A put option is a contract giving the holder the right to sell stock (usually 100 shares) at a specified price during a specified period of time. Put options are bought and sold as are calls, but the price is expected to move in the opposite direction.

Straddle Strategy

A straddle is a strategy containing both a put option and a call option on the same common stock, for the same period of time, and at the same striking price. However, the two can be exercised separately, if at all. The premium is higher than for each option separately.

A straddle would be used by an investor who forecasts a price move either both ways (so he could exercise both options) or either way (so he could exercise at least one option). Conversely, a straddle would be written by an investor who anticipates very little price move.

Spread Strategy

A spread is a strategy containing both a put option and a call option on the same common stock, for the same period of time, but at different striking prices: the price for the call option is higher than that for the common stock and the price for the put option is lower. Because of this price spread, the risk for the writer is less than that for the writer of the straddle; the reward (i.e., the premium) is also less.

Strip and Strap Strategies

These strategies contain three options on the same common stock, over the same period of time, and at the same price: the strip has two put options and one call option, and the strap has two call options and one put option.

Table 3 lists possible actions, depending upon your anticipation of the price of the common stock and your position in it, if any.

The following three tables, starting on page 57, contain formulas for the total yield from investments in calls, puts, and straddles, respectively. They include those quantities resulting from the option investments only, not from the option and common stock ownership (e.g., dividends).

Table 3. OPTION STRATEGIES

	Anticipate Price Increase	Anticipate Price Decrease	Anticipate Large Price Change*	Anticipate Small Price Change*	Anticipate No Change
Own Stock	Buy Call or Write Put	Buy Put or Write Call	Buy Straddle	Write Straddle	Write Call
Have Sold Short	Buy Call or Write Put	Buy Put or Write Call	Buy Straddle	Write Straddle	Write Put
Have No Position	Buy Call or Write Put	Buy Put or Write Call	Buy Straddle	Write Straddle	Write Straddle

***Either up, down, or both.**

FORMULAS:

$$Y = \frac{A-B}{C}$$

$$y = (1+Y)^{1/t}-1$$

where

Y = total yield on the option investment

y = annual yield on the option investment

then

A, B, and C: (Found in one of the tables for calls, puts, and straddles on page 57)

c_c, c_p = commission per share on the call and put option, respectively

c_{ce}, c_{pe} = commission per share on the common stock at exercise price for the call and put option, respectively

c_{cs}, c_{ps} = commission per share on the common stock at striking price for the call and put option, respectively

p_{ce}, p_{pe} = exercise price of the call and put option, respectively

p_{cs}, p_{ps} = striking price of the call and put option, respectively

t = time option held, in years

u = premium per share to buy the option.

EXAMPLE 1 (Purchase a Call): In May, IBM common stock was selling at 62-3/4, and a call to purchase 100 shares of the stock in January at 60 cost \$7-1/2. One option contract was purchased for an \$18 commission. Five months later (October) it is selling at 72-1/2. It is purchased at 60 for a \$54 commission and sold at 72-1/2 for a \$68 commission. What is the yield on this call option?

SOLUTION: In this example,

p_{cs} = \$60, $u = \$7.50$, $c_c = \$18/100 = \$0.18$, $t = 5/12$,

p_{ce} = \$72.50, $c_{cs} = \$54/100 = \$0.54$, and

c_{ce} = \$68/100 = \$0.68.

CALLS

	Call Option Purchased	Call Option Written
Call Exercised	$A = p_{ce}$ $B = u+c_c+p_{cs}+c_{cs}+c_{ce}$ $C = u+c_c$	$A = p_{cs}+u$ $B = p_{ce}+c_c$ (Stock Owned) $C = c_c$ $A = p_{cs}+u$ $B = p_{ce}+c_{ce}+c_c$ (Stock Not Owned) $C = c_c$
Call Not Exercised	$A = \$0$ $B = u+c_c$ $C = B$	$A = u$ $B = c_c$ $C = c_c$

PUTS

	Put Option Purchased	Put Option Written
Put Exercised	$A = p_{ps}$ $B = u+c_p+p_{pe}+c_{pe}+c_{ps}$ $C = u+c_p$	$A = p_{pe}+u$ $B = p_{ps}+c_p$ (Stock Owned) $C = c_p$ $A = p_{pe}+u$ $B = p_{ps}+c_p+c_{pe}$ (Stock Not Owned) $C = c_p$
Put Not Exercised	$A = \$0$ $B = u+c_p$ $C = B$	$A = u$ $B = c_p$ $C = c_p$

STRADDLES

	Straddle Purchased	Straddle Written
Call Exercised & Put Exercised	$A = p_{ce}$ $B = u+c_c+c_p+p_{pe}+c_{pe}+c_{ps}+c_{ce}+c_{cs}$ $C = u+c_c+c_p$*	$A = p_{pe}+u$ $B = p_{ce}+c_c+c_p+c_{ce}+c_{pe}$** $C = c_c+c_p$
Call Exercised & Put Not Exercised	$A = p_{ce}$ $B = p_{cs}+u+c_c+c_p+c_{cs}+c_{ce}$ $C = u+c_c+c_p$	$A = p_{cs}+u$ $B = p_{ce}+c_c+c_p+c_{ce}$** $C = c_c+c_p$

***The sum, c_c+c_p, is the commission for the straddle.**

****If stock is not owned, include the commission, c_{ce} or c_{pe}, to purchase it at the market price when the options are exercised.**

STRADDLES cont'd

	Straddle Purchased	Straddle Written
Call Exercised & Put Exercised	$A = p_{ps}$ $B = p_{pe}+u+c_c+c_p+c_{pe}+c_{ps}$ $C = u+c_c+c_p$	$A = p_{pe}+u$ $B = p_{ps}+c_c+c_p+c_{pe}$** $C = c_c+c_p$
Call Not Exercised & Put Not Exercised	$A = \$0$ $B = u+c_c+c_p$ $C = B$	$A = u$ $B = c_c+c_p$ $C = B$

****If stock is not owned, include the commission, c_{ce} or c_{pe}, to purchase it at the market price when the options are exercised.**

Now,

$$A = \$72.50,$$

$$B = \$7.50 + \$0.18 + \$60.00 + \$0.54 + \$0.68 = \$68.90, \text{ and}$$

$$C = \$7.50 + \$0.18 = \$7.68.$$

The total yield is,

$$Y = \frac{\$72.50-\$68.90}{\$7.68} = \frac{\$3.6}{\$7.68} = 0.4688 = 46.88\%.$$

The annual yield is,

$$y = (1+0.4688)^{1/t}-1 = (1.4688)^{12/5} - 1$$
$$= 2.5160-1 = 1.5160 = 151.60\%.$$

EXAMPLE 2 (Write a Call): In January, IBM was selling at 58-1/2. The owner of 135 shares felt pessimistic about the long-term outlook for the market and decided to write a call option (for 100 shares) for 12 months, with a striking price of 60 and a premium of $10. The commission to sell the option was $20. In October, after 10 months, the option was exercised at 72-1/2. The owner delivered the shares (no selling or selling commissions necessary). What is his total and annual yield?

SOLUTION: In this example,

$$p_{cs} = \$60,\ u = \$10,\ c_c = \$20/100 = \$0.20,\ t = 10/12, \text{ and}$$

$$p_{ce} = \$72.50.$$

Now,

$$A = \$60.00 + \$10.00 = \$70.00,$$

$$B = \$72.50 + \$0.20 = \$72.70, \text{ and}$$

$$C = \$0.20.$$

The total yield is,

$$Y = \frac{\$70.00 - \$72.70}{\$0.20} = \frac{-\$2.70}{\$0.20} = -13.50 = -1350\%.$$

Since the total yield is less than -1 (i.e., less than -100%), the annual yield cannot be computed by the formula.

RIGHTS

When a corporation issues more stock, current shareholders have the right to purchase the shares (because a shareholder has a right to maintain his proportionate ownership in the corporation). This privilege is evidenced by a certificate called a warrant. Shareholders can exercise the rights (by purchasing more shares), sell the rights, or simply let them expire after the subscription period (which lasts about one month).* The right usually allows the new shares to be purchased at a price less than the current market price (e.g., 5%–10% less).

The market price of rights can fall during the subscription period because, as rights are exercised, the supply of stock increases; if demand does not increase as much, the price of the stock (and of the rights) will fall.

The theoretical value of a right depends upon whether the evaluation date is before or after the date that non-shareholders can exercise the right (called the ex-right date).

If the market price of the common stock is the same before and after the ex-right date (i.e., $p_b = p_a$), the theoretical value of the right is higher after the ex-right date, by the factor $(n+1)/n$ where n is the number of owned shares required to purchase one new share.

Owners of the common stock can open a special subscription account with their broker for 90 days after the rights are issued. This account permits purchase of the stock for 25% margin without interest.

---

*When subscription periods are extensive, the rights are usually called warrants.

FORMULAS:

$$v_b = \frac{p_b - p_s}{n+1} \quad \text{(before ex-right date)}$$

$$v_a = \frac{p_a - p_s}{n} \quad \text{(after ex-right date)}$$

$$Y = \frac{A-B}{C}$$

$$y = (1+Y)^{1/t} - 1$$

where

v_b, v_a = theoretical value of the right before and after the ex-right date, respectively

Y = total yield from exercising the rights

y = annual yield from exercising the rights

then

A = p_b

B = p_s+2c

C = mp_s+2c

c = commission per share on the common stock acquired from rights

m = margin of the special subscription account, expressed as a decimal. If none used, $m=1$.

n = number of old shares required to purchase one new share

p_b, p_a = market price of the common stock before and after the ex-right date, respectively

p_s = subscription price of the new common stock

t = time investment held, in years.

EXAMPLE: Southwestern Public Service issued rights that allowed common stockholders to buy 1 share of new common stock at $10.95 for each 10 shares held. Since you own 800 shares of common stock, you acquire 80 rights. Five days before the rights expired (the ex-right date), the common stock was selling at 11-3/4. (a) What is the theoretical value of each right? (b) What is your total yield if you deposit the rights in a special subscription account, exercise your 80 rights to buy 80 shares of common stock with 25% margin, and immediately sell at 11-3/4 for a $28 commission?

SOLUTION: In this example,

$$p_s = \$10.95,\ n = 10,\ p_b = \$11.75,\ m = 0.25, \text{ and}$$

$$c = \$28/80 = \$0.35.$$

Now,

(a) The theoretical value of each right is,

$$v_b = \frac{\$11.75-\$10.95}{10+1} = \frac{\$0.80}{11} = \$0.073.$$

(b) To determine the total yield, compute

$$A = \$11.75,$$

$$B = \$10.95 + 2\times\$0.35 = \$11.65, \text{ and}$$

$$C = 0.25\times\$10.95 + 2\times\$0.35 = \$3.44.$$

The total yield from exercising the rights through the special subscription account is,

$$Y = \frac{\$11.75-\$11.65}{3.44} = \frac{\$0.10}{\$3.44} = 0.029 = 2.9\%.$$

Since the stock is immediately sold, the annual yield is infinite.

WARRANTS

A warrant is an option which gives its owner the right to purchase a stated number of shares of stock (usually common stock) at a stated price and usually within a stated period of time (e.g., 5, 10, 20 years, and even in perpetuity).* When the warrants are issued, the price at which they can be exercised (i.e., the striking price) is greater than the current price of the stock. They are long-term rights and are issued by the corporation to raise money for operations or to retire debt. Sometimes they are attached to

*Technically, however, a warrant is a piece of paper which is evidence of ownership of something less than a stock or bond (such as a right of a fractional share of stock). They pay no dividend, have no voting rights, are not registered, and are usually issued in bearer form.

preferred stock and bond certificates (in place of the convertible feature) to make these securities more attractive to investors.

Warrants are usually purchased by investors who want leverage in the common stock that they believe will increase in price. They are also purchased by investors who want to limit their potential loss after they have sold short the common stock. Warrants are traded on the major stock exchanges and over the counter.

The value of warrants depends upon the exercise price of the warrant and the price of the common stock. The following formulas can be used to determine the yields on both the warrant and the common stock, and the theoretical yields when the common stock is priced higher than the exercise price.

FORMULAS:

Market Values	Theoretical Values (When $p_{c2}>p_s$)*
$Y_w = \frac{A_w - B_w}{C_w}$	$v_{wi} = n(p_{ci} - p_s)$ where $i=1,2$
$Y_c = \frac{A_c - B_c}{C_c}$	$Y_w = \frac{p_{c2} - p_{c1}}{p_{c1} - p_s}$**
$y_w = (1+Y_w)^{1/t} - 1$	$Y_c = \frac{p_{c2} - p_{c1}}{p_{c1}}$
$y_c = (1+Y_c)^{1/t} - 1$	$\hat{Y} = \frac{1}{1-\hat{p}}$

where

Y_w, Y_c = total yield on the warrant and common stock, respectively

y_w, y_c = annual yield on warrant and common stock, respectively

$\hat{Y} = Y_w/Y_c$ = ratio of the theoretical total yields (theoretical leverage), excluding dividends and commissions

*The formulas for theoretical values ignore dividends on the common stock and commissions.

**If the market price of the warrant equals the theoretical value, $p_{w1}=v_{w1}$, and $p_{w2}=v_{w2}$. Then

$$Y_w = \frac{p_{w2} - p_{w1}}{p_{w1}} = \frac{n(p_{c2} - p_s) - n(p_{c1} - p_s)}{n(p_{c1} - p_s)} = \frac{p_{c2} - p_{c1}}{p_{c1} - p_s}.$$

then

A_c	=	$P_{c2}+td$
A_w	=	p_{w2}
B_c	=	$p_{c1}+c_{c1}+c_{c2}$
B_w	=	$p_{w1}+p_{w2}+c_{w2}$
C_c	=	$m_c p_{c1}+c_{c1}$
C_w	=	$m_w p_w+c_{w1}$
c_{c1},c_{c2}	=	commission per share to buy and sell the common stock, respectively
c_{w1},c_{w2}	=	commission per warrant to buy and sell the warrant, respectively
d	=	annual dividend per share paid on common stock
m_c	=	margin to buy the common stock, expressed as a decimal. If not used, let $m_c=1$
m_w	=	margin to buy the warrant, expressed as a decimal. If not used, let $m_w=1$
n	=	number of shares of the common stock covered in the warrant
p_{c1},p_{c2}	=	price of the common stock when purchased and sold, respectively
p_s	=	striking price of the common stock
p_{w1},p_{w2}	=	price of the warrant when acquired and disposed, respectively
p	=	p_s/p_{c1} (when $p_s<p_{c1}$)
t	=	time investment held, in years
v_{w1},v_{w2}	=	theoretical value of the warrant (when exercisable) at an earlier and later time, respectively.

Consider the warrant investment under the following two conditions of the price of the common stock:

1. Price of the Common Stock Is Less Than the Striking Price (i.e., $p_{c2}<p_s$). The warrant cannot be exercised profitably, so its value depends

entirely upon the hope that the price of the common stock will exceed the striking price (particularly since warrants pay no dividends). The price of the warrant depends upon the price of the common stock and will be correlated with it (i.e., they are correlated if they tend to move in the same direction at the same time, but not necessarily by the same amount). If the warrant gives the right to buy one share of common stock, the price of the warrant will be less than that of the common stock and will tend to vary more (relative to its price), particularly when the price of the common stock is falling.

EXAMPLE 1 ($p_{c2}<p_s$): Chrysler Corporation warrants give the right to buy one share of common stock at 13. Consider two cases in which the price of the common stock was less than the striking price:

A. (Price of Common Stock Falling.) When the common stock was selling at 7, the warrant was selling at 3-3/8. Later, because the common stock was selling at 3-1/4, the warrant was selling at 1-1/4. What yield would have been achieved on common stock and warrant investments during this time without using margin and without considering commissions or dividends (which weren't paid on the common stock during this period)?

B. (Price of Common Stock Rising.) When the common stock was selling at 3-1/4, the warrant was selling at 1-1/4. Later, because the common stock was selling at 6-1/4, the warrant was selling at 2-3/8. What yield would have been achieved on common stock and warrant investments during this time, without using margin and without considering commissions or dividends (which weren't paid on the common stock during this time)?

SOLUTION A: In this example,

$$p_{c1} = \$7.00,\ p_{w1} = \$3.375,\ p_{c2} = \$3.25,\ p_{w2} = \$1.25.$$

Now,

$$A_c = \$3.25,\ B_c = \$7.00,\ C_c = \$7.00,\ A_w = \$1.250,$$

$$B_w = \$3.375, \text{ and } C_w = \$3.375.$$

The total yield on the common stock would have been

$$Y_c = \frac{\$3.25-\$7.00}{\$7.00} = \frac{-\$3.75}{\$7.00} = -\ 0.536 = -53.6\%,$$

and the total yield on the warrant would have been

$$Y_w = \frac{\$1.250-\$3.375}{\$1.250} = \frac{-\$2.125}{\$1.250} = -1.70 = -170\%.$$

In this case, the warrant is a worse investment than the common stock.

SOLUTION B: In this example,

$$p_{c1} = \$3.25,\ p_{w1} = \$1.25,\ p_{c2} = \$6.25, \text{ and } p_{w2} = \$2.375.$$

Now,

$$A_c = \$6.25,\ B_c = \$3.25,\ C_c = \$3.25,\ A_w = \$2.375,$$

$$B_w = \$1.25, \text{ and } C_w = \$1.25.$$

The total yield on the common stock would have been

$$Y_c = \frac{\$6.25-\$3.25}{\$3.25} = \frac{\$3.00}{\$3.25} = 0.923 = 92.3\%,$$

and the total yield on the warrant would have been

$$Y_w = \frac{\$2.375-\$1.250}{\$1.25} = \frac{\$1.125}{\$1.25} = 0.900 = 90.0\%.$$

In this case, the warrants and the common stock are almost equally good investments.

2. Price of the Common Stock Is Greater Than the Striking Price (i.e., $p_{c2}>p_s$). In this case, the warrant can be exercised profitably. Its theoretical value is given by v_{w1} and v_{w2} (corresponding to two arbitrarily different prices of the common stock). In practice, the price of the warrant will vary about the theoretical value, depending upon the concurrent market prices of the common stock and the warrant.

Figure 5 shows the weekly closing prices of the Mattel, Inc. common stock less the weekly closing prices of the warrant as they varied about the exercise (striking) price for 19 consecutive weeks.

When the price of the common stock exceeds the striking price, the warrant should be selling at a price that provides leverage relative to the common stock (i.e., its yield is greater). Figure 6 is a graph of the theoretical leverage, $\hat{Y}=Y_w/Y_c$, as the ratio, $\hat{p}=p_s/p_{c1}$, varies between zero and one. The more p_{c1} exceeds p_s, the less the leverage. For example, when the common stock is selling at twice the striking price, the yield on the warrant is twice the yield on the common stock.

EXAMPLE 2 ($p_{c2}>p_s$): Mattel, Inc. warrants provided the right to buy one share of common stock at 4. When the common stock was selling at 13, the warrant was selling at 9. Later when the common stock was selling at 19-1/2, the warrant was selling at 14-1/2. Without using margin and without considering commissions or dividends, what would have been (a) the total yield on the common stock, (b) the total yield on the warrant, (c) the theoretical value of the warrant (on the later date), and (d) the leverage (on the later date)?

SOLUTION: In this example,

$n = 1, p_s = \$4.00, p_{c1} = \$13.00, p_{w1} = \$9.00,$

$p_{c2} = \$19.50, p_{w2} = \$14.50, \text{ and } p = \$4.00/\$13.00 = 0.307.$

(a) The total yield on the common stock would have been

$$Y_c = \frac{\$19.50-\$13.00}{\$13.00} = \frac{\$6.50}{\$13.00} = 0.50 = 50\%.$$

(b) The total yield on the warrant would have been

$$Y_w = \frac{\$19.50-\$13.00}{\$13.00-\$4.00} = \frac{\$6.50}{\$9.00} = 0.722 = 72.2\%.$$

(c) The theoretical value of the warrant is

$v_{w2} = 1\times(\$19.50-\$4.00) = \$15.50.$
(The market price of the warrant was $14.50.)

(d) The theoretical leverage (of the warrant relative to the common stock) is

$$\hat{Y} = \frac{1}{1-0.307} = \frac{1}{0.693} = 1.44.$$

That is, the yield on the warrant investment is 1.44 times as high as the yield on the common stock investment.

Figure 5

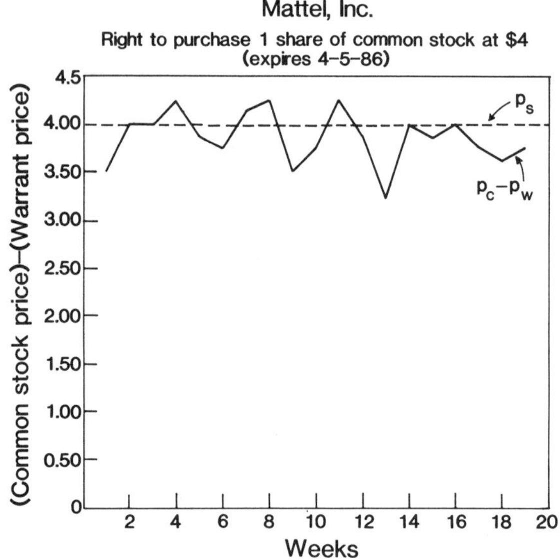

Figure 6

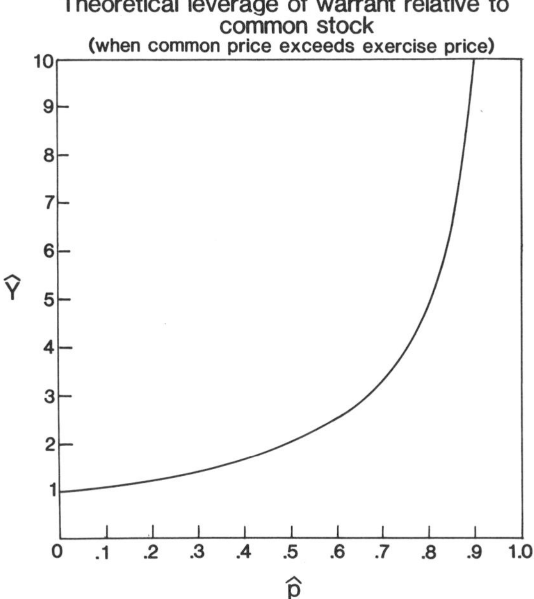

CORPORATE BONDS

Corporate bonds are promissory notes issued by corporations to raise money. They usually have a face value of $1,000. The number of bonds in each issue can be very large, and each bond contains the same features (as specified in a written contract called an indenture).

Interest is usually paid semiannually at a fixed rate. Maturities range from a few years to many years (such as 50), and the corporation promises to pay the owner the face value at maturity. During its term, the bond usually can be traded in a secondary market. Most bonds are traded in the over-the-counter market. Only odd lots of bonds are traded in the New York and American stock exchanges. The price of the traded bonds tends to vary inversely with the interest rates paid on currently issued bonds that are similar. Figure 7 is a schematic diagram showing how a bond price would tend to respond to changing interest rates over its term.

The following discusses frequently occurring features of corporate bonds, the yield on corporate bond investments, and the special situations arising from the conversion feature.

Features

Security. Bonds can be either secured or not secured by assets. Those that are not secured (by a lien or pledge) are called debentures, and due to

Figure 7

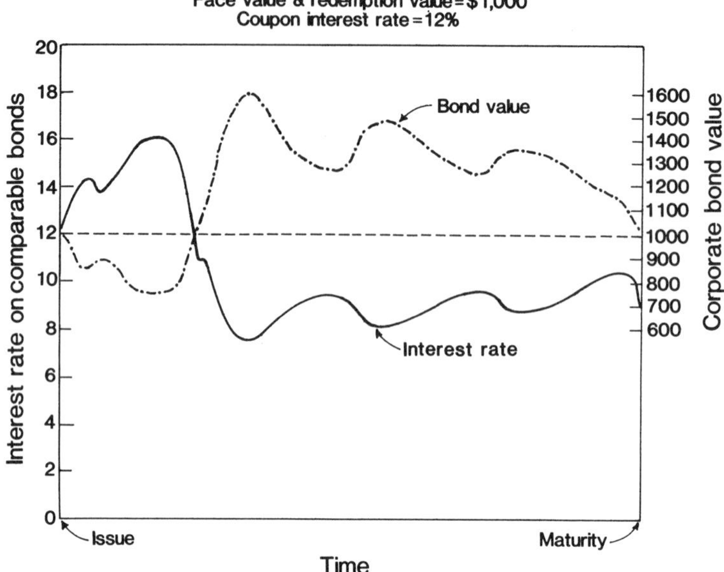

their greater risk, tend to incorporate features that yield more than do secured bonds. If the corporation defaults on the bond contract, its property may be:

- Placed in the possession of a trustee in bankruptcy while its finances are reorganized. That is, new securities may be issued according to the corporation's ability to pay and according to priority: secured creditors, unsecured creditors,* preferred stockholders, and finally, common stockholders; or
- Liquidated. Secured bondholders have first claim on specified assets and a prorata claim on unspecified assets.

Maturity. Terms of bonds usually range from 10 to 50 years. Most bonds have fixed maturities; however, some permit extensions, and others mature in installments over the life of the issue (called serial bonds).

Callable. A bond is said to be callable if it can be paid by the company prior to maturity. Most bonds are callable, but at 3%–10% above face value. This premium is of little value to the owner:

- If interest rates rise, the bond price will fall, and the company will not call the bonds.

---

*Bondholders are creditors. Unlike stockholders, they are not owners of the corporation.

- If interest rates fall, the bond price will rise, the company may call the bonds, and the investor will not be able to duplicate the bond rate in a similar investment.

Conversion. Bonds with the conversion feature may be exchanged for a stated number of shares of common stock.* The number of shares often diminishes with time. Investors convert readily when the total stock price exceeds the bond price, particularly if the stock pays a dividend. Of course, the stock price is not high enough for profitable conversion when the bond is issued. Instead of the conversion privilege, some bonds either have attached warrants that can be used to purchase stock at a certain price and time (while retaining the bond), or grant extra participation in the earnings of the company by increasing the interest rate. Conversion will dilute the value of common stock unless the company uses the bond proceeds to increase the earnings equally.

Debt and Dividend Limitation. Some bond contracts limit the amount of long-term debt the company can incur and the amount of dividend it can pay.

Modification of Indenture. Some bond contracts permit the contract to be modified if the holders of 2/3 or 3/4 of the bonds consent. Modifications usually involve freeing property from the mortgage, issuing more bonds, increasing the debt and dividend limit, etc. Primary bond features such as the interest rate, term, and amount of principal payment are usually not modifiable.

Guarantee. Sometimes the interest payments (or both interest payments and principal) are guaranteed by a third party, such as a lessee whose net rent payments exceed the bond obligation.

The quality of corporate bonds depends upon the features contained in the indenture, the corporation's ability to adhere to the contract, liquidity of the bonds, and liquidity of the corporate assets. Quality among bonds ranges widely, and the highest quality corporate bonds have yields only one-quarter percent above Treasury Bonds of similar maturity. More speculative bonds are held by individuals who prefer a capital gain made possible by the greater price movement. Investment services such as Moody's and Standard and Poor's grade corporate bonds according to quality (see Municipal Bonds, page 105).

Since the amount of interest paid on a bond is fixed by contract, the relative value of the interest portion of the investment is affected by the change in the consumer price index. On the other hand, the relative value of the principal (price of the bond) is affected by the change in interest

*Bonds without this feature are called straight bonds.

rates (as depicted in Figure 7). Of course, the corporation's ability to pay affects both interest and principal.

Like common stock, bond prices are quoted in multiples of 1/8, and "on the basis of 100." For example:

- A $1,000 bond selling at $900 is quoted as 90, and
- A $500 bond selling at $450 is quoted as 90.

The quoted price of the bond does not include interest that has accrued since the last interest payment. The purchase price of the bond depends upon whether or not the company is currently in default on interest payments:

- If there has been a default on an interest payment, it is assumed that interest will not be paid, and the accrued interest is not added to the purchase price. These bonds are said to be "traded flat," and an "f" is usually listed next to the maturity date in financial publications.
- If there has not been a default on an interest payment, accrued interest is prorated from the last interest payment date to the day before you pay for the bond and added to the purchase price; 30-day months are used for proration.

Figure 8 shows the Wall Street Journal quotations of some corporate bonds. Notice that the current yield is not quoted on the Bally corporate bond since it is convertible to common stock.

EXAMPLE 1 (Interest and Price): A $1,000 bond pays 8% interest on February 1 and August 1 (i.e., $40 for each six months). On April 23, you instruct your broker to buy it, and on April 26 he pays for it. How much of the annual $80 interest will be added to the purchase price?

SOLUTION:

- Two full months have elapsed since February 1 (2×30 days $= 60$ days)
- Twenty-five full days have elapsed in April before payment
- Since all months are assumed to have 30 days, a year is assumed to have 360 days.

Now, the accrued interest to be added to the purchase price is

$$\$80 \times \left(\frac{60+25}{360}\right) = \$80 \times \left(\frac{85}{360}\right) = \$80 \times 0.2361 = \$18.89.$$

Yield on a Bond

The first four formulas determine the yield on a *bond,* and the last two determine the yield on the *bond investment.* The yields on the bond

Figure 8

New York Exchange Bonds

Bonds	Cur Yld	Vol	High	Low	Close	Net Chg.
CORPORATION BONDS						
...Gn 11s...		142	126½	125		1
AmMot 6s88	cv	11	102	100	100	
ASug 5.3s93	8.7	2	61	61	61	
ATT 3¼s84	3.4	35	94½	94 3-16	94½	+ 7-16
ATT 4⅜s85	4.7	40	92½	92¼	92¼	
ATT 4⅜s85r	4.7	21	92¼	92⅛	92¼	
ATT 2⅝s86	3.1	50	84⅜	84⅜	84⅜	+ ⅛
ATT 2⅞s87	3.6	2	80	80	80	
ATT 3⅞s90	5.6	81	69¾	69¼	69½	- ¼
ATT 8¾00	11.	134	77½	77⅛	77½	+ ⅛
ATT 7s01	11.	104	64⅞	64⅝	64¾	
ATT 7⅛s03	11.	21	64⅝	64⅜	64⅜	
ATT 8.80s05	12.	200	76⅝	76	76⅜	+ ⅝
ATT 8⅝s07	12.	7	74⅝	74¼	74⅝	+ ⅜
ATT 10⅜90	11.	66	94⅞	94⅞	94⅞	+ ½
ATT 13¼91	13.	235	105½	105	105¼	
Ancp 13⅞02	cv	42	98	97¼	97⅞	- ⅛
Anhr 9.9s86	10.	5	96⅜	96⅜	96⅜	⅞
Anxtr 8¼03	cv	16	107	107	107	+ 1
Arco 8s84	8.1	4	99⅜	99⅜	99⅜	⅛
ArizP 7.45s02	12.	24	63	62⅛	63	
Armr 5s84	5.0	23	99½	99½	99½	
Atchn 4s95r	7.8	1	51¼	51¼	51¼	
ARich 11⅜10	12.	42	94	92⅝	92⅝	⅝
ARch d7s91	9.2	66	75⅞	75⅞	75⅞	¼
AvcoC 5½93	cv	43	75½	75	75	½
AvcoC 7½93	11.	6	66⅛	66⅛	66⅛	+ ¼
AvcoF 11s90	11.	2	96⅛	96⅛	96⅛	
BldwU 10s09	26.	181	38¾	37⅜	38	¾
Baily 6s98	cv	5	91	91	91	+ 1
Bally 10s06	cv	152	97	96¼	96¼	- ¼
B O 4½10A	cv	5	170⅝	170⅝	170⅝	
Bal... ¼07	12...		...⅛	69⅛	69⅛	

are the nominal annual yield, the current annual yield, the approximate yield to maturity (or to call date), and the exact yield to maturity (or to call date).

The nominal yield is the coupon interest rate. This yield results when the bond is purchased at face value and will be redeemed at that price. The current annual yield is the coupon rate, adjusted for the current purchase price. This yield is used to evaluate speculative bonds in which the principal is at risk. The yield to maturity (or to call date) can be approximated by the bond salesman's method (i.e., y_m) or determined precisely by iteration. The bond salesman's method is fairly accurate when the face value, purchase price, and redemption price are all fairly close (within about 10%) and the maturity is not greater than, say, 10 years. The yield from the exact method must be determined by trial and error; that is, values of y_r are repeatedly selected to render the two sides of the equation as nearly equal as desired. The yield to maturity might provide an initial value for y_r.

The last two formulas are used to determine the total and annual yield on a *bond investment.*

FORMULAS:

$$y_n = r_b$$

$$y_c = r_b \bullet \frac{v_{bf}}{p_{bl}}$$

$$y_m = \frac{r_b v_{bf} + D}{E}$$

$$p_{bl} = [F \cdot a(y_r,k,q) + G/c(y_r,k,q)](1+y_r t')^{*}$$

(Exact yield on bond to maturity or call date)

$$Y = \frac{A-B}{C}$$

$$y = (1+Y)^{1/t} - 1$$

where

y_n = nominal annual yield (coupon rate) on the bond

y_c = current annual yield on the bond

y_m = approximate annual yield to maturity (or call date) on the bond

y_r = annual rate of return on the bond

Y = total yield on the bond investment

y = annual yield on the bond investment

then

$A = p_{b2} + jv_{bf}(r_b/q)$

$B = p_{bl} + c_{bl} + c_{b2}$

$C = mp_{bl} + c_{bl}$

c_{bl}, c_{b2} = commission per bond to buy and sell the bond, respectively

---

*When the face value, redemption value, and purchase price are equal and the bond is purchased on a coupon date, the yield from both the approximate and exact methods equals the nominal yield, $y_n = y_c = y_m = y_r = r_b$.

D	=	$\frac{v_{br}-p_{b1}}{k}$
E	=	$\frac{v_{br}+p_{b1}}{2}$
F	=	$v_{bf}(r_b/q)$
G	=	v_{br}
j	=	number of full interest periods bond held
k	=	number of full or partial interest periods until maturity (or to call date)
m	=	margin to buy bond, expressed as a decimal. If not used, let m=l
p_{b1},p_{b2}	=	purchase price and sale price of the bond, respectively
q	=	number of interest periods per year
r_b	=	annual interest rate on bond (coupon rate), expressed as a decimal
t	=	time investment held, in years
t′	=	time since the last bond interest period, expressed as a fraction of a 360-day year (full months are assumed to have 30 days)
v_{bf}	=	face value of the bond
v_{br}	=	redemption value of the bond (usually the face value)
$a(y_r,k,q)$	=	present value of an annuity of 1. (Table I)
$c(y_r,k,q)$	=	amount of l at compound interest. (Table I)

EXAMPLE 2 (Yield): Xerox Corporation issued convertible bonds with a coupon interest rate of 6%, payable semiannually, and redeemable at face value ($1,000) in 1995. The bond is currently selling at $720 and has exactly 20 interest periods remaining. Determine the yield on the bond by each of the first four methods.

SOLUTION: In this example,

r_b = 0.06, q = 2, v_{bf} = $1,000, v_{br} = $1,000,

p_{bl} = $720, k = 20, and t′ = 0.

Now,

- The nominal yield is

$$y_n = 0.06 = 6\%.$$

- The current yield is

$$y_c = 0.06 \times \frac{\$1{,}000}{\$720} = 0.083 = 8.3\%.$$

- To determine the approximate yield to maturity by the bond salesman's method, first determine

$$D = \frac{\$1{,}000-\$720}{20} = \$14, \text{ and}$$

$$E = \frac{\$1{,}000+\$720}{2} = \$860.$$

Then,

$$y_m = \frac{0.06\times\$1{,}000+\$14}{\$860} = \frac{\$60+\$14}{\$860} = \frac{\$74}{\$860} = 0.086 = 8.6\%.$$

- The exact yield to maturity requires trial and error selection of yields in order to render the two sides of the equation as nearly equal as desired. In this case,

$$F = \$1{,}000(0.06/2) = \$30, \text{ and } G = \$1{,}000.$$

From the formula

$$\$720 = \left[\$30 \bullet a(y_r,20,2) + \$1{,}000/c(y_r,20,2)\right] \bullet (1+y_r\times 0).$$

It is efficient to select y_r near the yield determined by the bond salesman's method. Select $y_r = 8.00\%$. From Table I or an electronic calculator,

$$a(8,20,2) = 13.5903, \text{ and } c(8,20,2) = 2.1911.$$

Now, the right side of the equation is as follows:

$$= \$30\times 13.5903 + \$1{,}000/2.1911$$

$$= \$407.71 + \$456.39$$

$$= \$864.10.$$

Subsequent trials show that

y_r = 9.00% renders the right side equal to $804.87,

y_r = 10.00% renders the right side equal to $750.76,

y_r = 10.50% renders the right side equal to $725.45, and

y_r = 10.75% renders the right side equal to $713.21.

The last two prices straddle the price of the left side (i.e., $720); linear interpolation (Appendix B) reveals the yield by the exact method to be y_r=10.61% (rendering the right side equal to $720.03).

Conversion Feature

The conversion feature creates a hybrid security. If the common stock is priced too low for profitable conversion, the price of the bond tends to respond to the prevailing interest rates (as do bonds without this feature); as seen in the following formulas, the theoretical value would be v_{bi} (i for interest). If the common stock is priced high enough for profitable conversion to common stock, the price of the bond will tend to respond to the price of the common stock;* the theoretical value would be v_{bc} (c for conversion).

Two sets of formulas are of interest with the conversion feature. The following set deals strictly with conversion, and the set on page 78 deals with the use of this feature to hedge against falling bond prices by selling short the common stock.

FORMULAS (for Conversion):

$$p_c = \frac{p_b}{n}$$

$$v_{bc} = np_c$$

$$v_{bi} = \frac{r_b v_{bf}}{r}$$

$$r = \frac{r_b v_{bf}}{np_c}$$

$$d = \frac{r_b v_{bf}}{n}$$

*A commission is not charged upon conversion.

where

p_c = purchase price of the common stock

v_{bf}, v_{bc}, v_{bi} = face value, conversion value, and interest value of the bond, respectively

r = current annual interest rate on similar bonds

d = annual common stock dividend

then

n = number of shares of common stock for which the bond can be converted

p_b = purchase price of the bond

r_b = annual interest rate on the bond (coupon rate)

EXAMPLE 3 (Conversion): Xerox Corporation issued convertible bonds with a \$1,000 face value, paying 6%, and due in 1995. They carry an A rating, and each bond can be converted to 10.87 shares of common stock. The bonds are currently being traded at 72 (on the basis of 100). The common stock is quoted at 42-3/8 and pays an annual dividend of \$3/share. (a) What common stock price would be equivalent to the \$720 bond; (b) What current annual interest rate on similar bonds would cause the bond to tend to be equivalent to the 42-3/8 stock; and (c) What annual common stock dividend would equal the annual bond interest?

SOLUTION: In this example,

$$v_{bf} = \$1{,}000,\ r_b = 0.06,\ n = 10.87,\ p_b = \$720, \text{ and } p_c = \$42.375.$$

Now

(a) The common stock price that is equivalent to the \$720 bond is

$$p_c = \frac{p_b}{n} = \frac{\$720}{10.87} = \$66.24,$$

(b) The current annual interest rate on similar bonds that would cause the bond to be equivalent to the 42-3/8 stock price is

$$r = \frac{r_b v_{bf}}{np_c} = \frac{0.06\times\$1{,}000}{10.87\times\$42.375} = \frac{\$60}{\$460.62}$$

$$= 0.1303 = 13.03\%, \text{ and}$$

(c) The annual common stock dividend that would equal the bond interest is

$$d = \frac{r_b v_{bf}}{n} = \frac{0.06 \times \$1{,}000}{10.87} = \frac{\$60}{10.87} = \$5.52.$$

Figure 9 shows the current annual interest rates (on similar corporate bonds) and common stock prices at which equitable conversion could occur for the bond in this example. It is a graph of the formula for r as p_c changes.

Figure 9

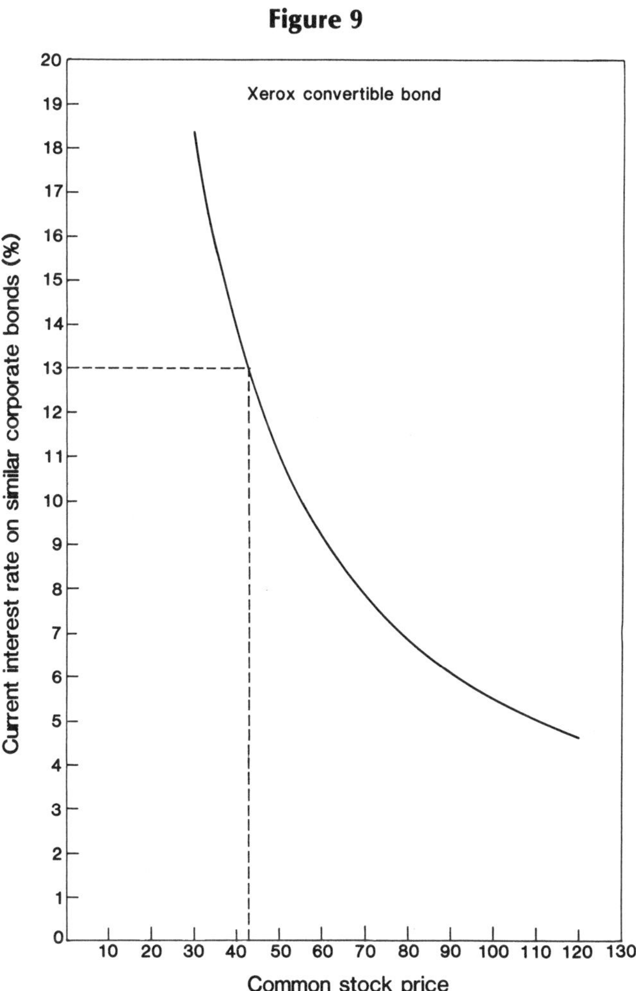

Selling Short to Hedge a Convertible Bond Investment

Sometimes the convertible bond investment is hedged by selling short the common stock. The following formulas determine the yield resulting from the hedge.

FORMULAS (for Hedging):

$$Y = \frac{A-B}{C}$$

$$y = (1+Y)^{1/t}-1$$

where

Y = total yield on the investment

y = annual yield on the investment

then

A = $p_{b2}n_b+r_b v_{bf} n_b t+p_{c1}n_c$

B = $p_{b1}n_b+p_{c2}n_c+c_{c1}+c_{c2}+c_{b1}+c_{b2}$

C = $mp_{b1}n_b+c_{b1}+c_{c1}$

c_{b1},c_{b2} = commission to buy and sell the bond, respectively

c_{c1},c_{c2} = commission to short sell and buy the common stock, respectively

m = margin for the bond, expressed as a decimal. If not used, $m=1$

n_b,n_c = number of bonds and shares of common stock, respectively

p_{b1},p_{b2} = purchase price and later price of the bond, respectively

p_{c1},p_{c2} = short sale price and later price of the common stock, respectively

r = current annual interest rate on similar bonds (illustrated in Figure 9)

r_b = annual interest rate on the bond (coupon rate)

t = time investment held, in years

v_{bf} = face value of the bond

EXAMPLE 4 (Hedging): Xerox Corporation issued convertible bonds with a $1,000 face value, paying 6%, and due in 1995. Each bond can be converted into 10.87 shares of common stock. The bonds are currently being traded at 72 (on the basis of 100), and the common stock is selling at 42-3/8. Suppose you purchase 10 bonds (without margin) for a commission of \$50, but you are worried about rising interest rates. To protect against the resulting falling bond price, you sell short 100 shares of Xerox common stock for a commission of \$70. Determine the total yield if, after one year, the interest rate on similar bonds increases by 20%, and the common stock falls to 34. At this time you purchase the common stock for a commission of \$65, but retain the bond.

SOLUTION: In this example,

$$v_{bf} = \$1{,}000,\ r_b = 0.06,\ p_{b1} = \$720,$$

$$p_{c1} = \$42.375,\ n_b = 10,\ m = 1,\ c_{b1} = \$50,\ n_c = 100,$$

$$c_{c1} = \$70,\ t = 1,\ p_{b2} = p_{b1}/1.20 = \$720/1.20 = \$600,$$

$$p_{c2} = \$34,\ c_{c2} = \$65, \text{ and } c_{b2} = \$0.$$

Now

$$\begin{aligned} A &= \$600\times10 + \$0.06\times\$1{,}000\times1 + \$42.375\times100 \\ &= \$6{,}000 + \$60 + \$4{,}237.50 \\ &= \$10{,}297.50, \end{aligned}$$

$$\begin{aligned} B &= \$720\times10 + \$34\times100 + \$70 + \$65 + \$50 + \$0 \\ &= \$10{,}785, \text{ and} \end{aligned}$$

$$C = \$720\times10 + \$50 + \$70 = \$7{,}320.$$

The total yield is

$$Y = \frac{\$10{,}297.50-\$10{,}785}{\$7{,}320} = \frac{-\$487.50}{\$7{,}320} = -0.0666 = -6.66\%.$$

Figure 10 shows the total yield from this example over time for the nine combinations, resulting from three interest rate scenarios ($r=r_{b/2}$, r_b, and $2r_b$) and three common stock price scenarios ($p_{c2}=p_{c1/2}$, p_{c1}, and $2p_{c1}$). Notice that the three curves near the bottom of the figure have a discontinuous slope (i.e., a "dog leg") where the bond can be equitably converted to common stock.

COMMERCIAL PAPER

Commercial paper is a term that refers to short-term unsecured promissory notes issued by corporations to provide short-term working capital. This method of raising capital is usually less costly for them than obtaining a bank loan. Commercial paper is usually issued at a discount

Figure 10

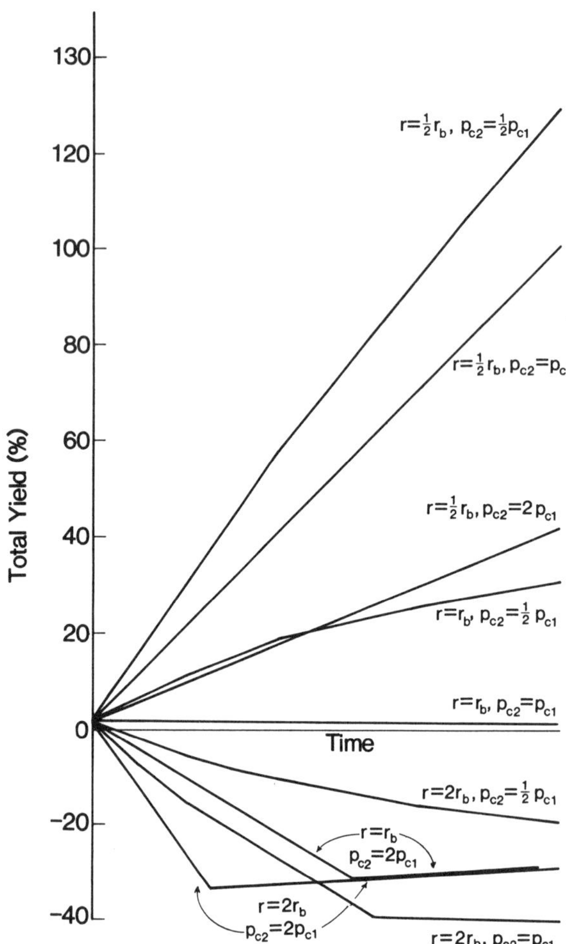

from face value and bears no interest. However, it can be issued at face value (in which case it would bear interest). The yield on commercial paper is usually about one-half percent lower than the bank prime rate and higher than the rate on Treasury bills. Default in commercial paper is very rare.

The minimum investment amount is usually $100,000 (sometimes $25,000 if the maturity exceeds 30 days); for this reason most investors are institutions.

Most commercial paper matures in 30 days or less, and very rarely does the term exceed 270 days.* Even though most paper is held to

*The Securities and Exchange Commission does not require an issue to be registered if the maturity is 270 days or less, and if the proceeds are used for current transactions.

maturity, it can be traded in a secondary market unless the issuer retains a prepayment privilege. Even though more than one thousand firms issue paper, the secondary market is relatively inactive because the characteristics of commercial paper vary so widely (causing uncertainty), and their maturities are so short.

Firms such as Moody's, Standard and Poor's, and Fitch rate commercial paper according to risk. For example, Standard and Poor's rates paper from A through D and subdivides the A rating into A-1, A-2, and A-3.

Goldman Sachs, Merrill Lynch, and others deal regularly in commercial paper. They often determine the discount from face value and charge the issuer 0.125% for the placement.

The following formulas can be used to determine the yield from an investment in commercial paper, the equivalent bond yield, and the purchase price in terms of dollars and discount.

FORMULAS:

$$Y = \frac{A-B}{C}$$

$$y = (1+Y)^{\frac{365}{t}} - 1$$

$$y_b = \frac{365d}{360-dt} \ *$$

$$p_1 = \frac{p_2}{(1+y_b \frac{t}{365})}$$

$$d \doteq \frac{p_2-p_1}{p_2} \bullet \frac{360}{t} = \frac{360y_b}{365+y_bt}$$

where

Y = total yield on the investment

y = annual yield on the investment

y_b = equivalent bond yield, expressed as a decimal (the yield quoted in market transactions)

p_1 = purchase price in dollars (the ask if bought in a secondary market)

*To compare commercial paper with certificates of deposit and other interest-bearing instruments, substitute 365 with 360. This yield is then called the money market yield.

d = ask price in terms of discount, expressed as a decimal (the ask quoted in market transactions)

then

$A = p_2$

$B = p_1 + c$

$C = B$

c = commission if a new issue is bought through a bank or a broker

p_2 = selling price in dollars (the bid if sold prematurely in a secondary market, or face value if held until maturity)

t = days until maturity (Table II)

EXAMPLE: The Haskins Furniture Companies issued commercial paper in denominations of $100,000 at an 8% discount to mature in 90 days. Determine the equivalent bond interest yield.

SOLUTION: In this example,

$d = 0.08$, and $t = 90$.

Now, the equivalent bond interest yield is

$$y_b = \frac{365 \times 0.08}{360 - 0.08 \times 90} = \frac{29.20}{360 - 7.2} = \frac{29.20}{352.8} = 0.0828 = 8.28\%.$$

PART II
How to Evaluate Federal Government Securities

CHAPTER 4
Treasury Bills

Treasury bills are marketable short-term securities issued by the federal government to finance the national debt. They mature in 91 days, 182 days, or 364 days. They are purchased below face value in denominations as small as $1,000. Treasury bills can be held until maturity or sold prematurely. Since they bear no interest, the investor profits from the difference between the purchase price and the face value (if held to maturity) or between the purchase price and the sale price (if sold prematurely).*

The purchase price of newly issued bills is determined by a weekly auction (on Mondays). Bids are forwarded to Federal Reserve Banks by banks and brokers. The Treasury allots bills first to the highest bidders and later to lower bidders, until it no longer needs money.

Treasury bills can be purchased without cost from the Treasury, a Federal Reserve Bank, or a branch.** They can be purchased for a commission from other banks or a stock broker. No certificate is issued, and ownership is held in book entry form.

Treasury bills that are purchased in the secondary market are bought at the ask price and sold at the bid (or redeemed at face value if held to maturity).

---

*Bankers' acceptances and commercial paper are also discount securities, and the formulas for them are the same as those for Treasury bills.

**Obtain a form from them; mail the completed form with a certified check payable to the Federal Reserve Bank in your district.

The Wall Street Journal lists the current quotes under the heading "Treasury Issues" (see Figure 11). For each issue, it lists the maturity date, the bid and ask price (in terms of the yield), and the yield (the bond equivalent yield). The yield is stated in terms of the bond yield, because Treasury bills are the only Treasury security that does not bear interest. The Treasury calculates the discount as if the year has 360 days. However, bond interest is calculated on the basis of a 365-day year.

Figure 11

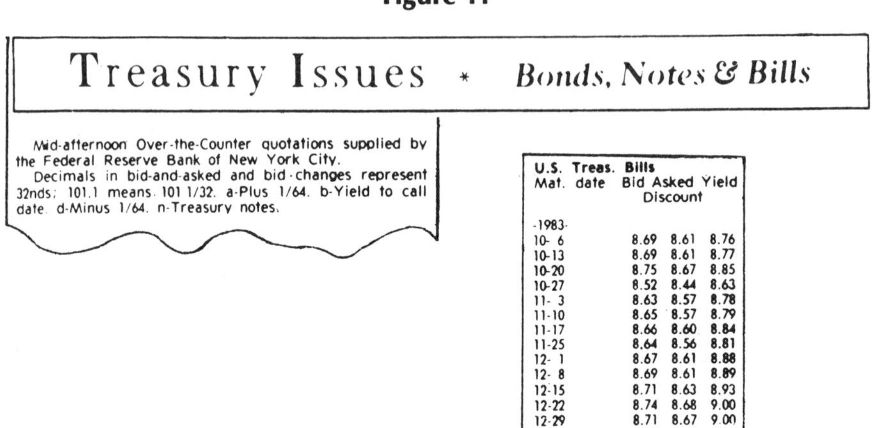

Treasury Issues * *Bonds, Notes & Bills*

Mid-afternoon Over-the-Counter quotations supplied by the Federal Reserve Bank of New York City.
Decimals in bid-and-asked and bid-changes represent 32nds; 101.1 means 101 1/32. a-Plus 1/64. b-Yield to call date. d-Minus 1/64. n-Treasury notes.

U.S. Treas. Bills

Mat. date	Bid	Asked	Yield
	Discount		
-1983-			
10- 6	8.69	8.61	8.76
10-13	8.69	8.61	8.77
10-20	8.75	8.67	8.85
10-27	8.52	8.44	8.63
11- 3	8.63	8.57	8.78
11-10	8.65	8.57	8.79
11-17	8.66	8.60	8.84
11-25	8.64	8.56	8.81
12- 1	8.67	8.61	8.88
12- 8	8.69	8.61	8.89
12-15	8.71	8.63	8.93
12-22	8.74	8.68	9.00
12-29	8.71	8.67	9.00

Since Treasury bills are guaranteed by the federal government, there is no risk (for bills purchased from the Treasury). Consequently, the yield is lower than on any other security. They require no security and are very liquid. The gain or loss from an investment in Treasury bills is taxed as ordinary income in the year it is disposed.

The following formulas can be used to determine the yield from an investment in Treasury bills, the equivalent bond yield, and the purchase price in terms of dollars and discount.*

FORMULAS:

$$Y = \frac{A-B}{C}$$

$$y = (1+Y)^{\frac{365}{t}} - 1$$

*Treasury bills can also be traded in financial futures markets. These markets and the yield curve are discussed on page 117.

$$y_b = \frac{365d}{360-dt}\ *$$

$$p_1 = \frac{p_2}{1+y_b \frac{t}{365}}$$

$$d = \frac{p_2-p_1}{p_2} \bullet \frac{360}{t} = \frac{360y_b}{365+y_b t}$$

where

Y = total yield on the investment

y = annual yield on the investment

y_b = equivalent bond yield, expressed as a decimal (the yield that is quoted in market transactions)

p_1 = purchase price of the bill (the ask if bought in the secondary market)

d = ask price of the bill in terms of discount (as quoted in market transactions)

then

A = p_2

B = p_1+c

C = B

c = commission if a new issue is bought through a bank or broker; e.g., $15–$25 per transaction

p_2 = selling price of the bill (the bid if sold prematurely in a secondary market, or face value if held until maturity)

t = days until maturity (Table II).

---

*To compare Treasury bills with certificates of deposit and other interest-bearing instruments, substitute 365 with 360. This yield is then called the money market yield on a bill.

EXAMPLE: On October 3, Cindy Johnson wants to buy a Treasury bill that matures on the 29th of December. The price is quoted in terms of discount from face value: Bid, 8.71; Ask, 8.67; and Yield, 9.00. Suppose the bill is purchased from a member bank of the Federal Reserve System (so that there is no commission). On the basis of 100, (a) what is the purchase price, and (b) what is the annual yield on the investment?

SOLUTION: There are 87 days until maturity, so $t=87$. Since the basis is 100, $p_2=\$100$, and the yield is $y_b=0.0900$. Hence,

(a) the purchase price (ask) is

$$p_1 = \frac{\$100}{1+0.0900\times\frac{87}{365}} = \frac{\$100}{1+0.0900\times0.23836}$$

$$= \frac{\$100}{1+0.021452} = \frac{\$100}{1.021452} = \$97.90.$$

(b) In this case,

$A = \$100$, $B = \$97.90$, and $C = B$.

The total yield on the investment is

$$Y = \frac{\$100-\$97.90}{\$97.90} = \frac{\$\ 2.10}{\$97.90}$$

$$= 0.021452 = 2.15\%.$$

The annual yield on the investment is

$$y = (1+Y)^{\frac{365}{87}} - 1$$

$$= (1+0.021452)^{4.19540} - 1$$

$$= (1.021452)^{4.19540} - 1$$

$$= 1.0931 - 1 = 0.0931 = 9.31\%.$$

CHAPTER 5
Treasury Bonds and Notes

Treasury bonds and notes are issued by the Treasury in order to pay the federal debt. The two instruments differ in their maturities: Notes mature in one to ten years, and bonds mature in ten years or more. Unlike Treasury bills, bonds and notes are issued at (or near) face value ($1,000) and bear a fixed rate of interest that is paid semiannually. They are auctioned by the Federal Reserve to those bidding the lowest yield (i.e., the lowest interest rate), and are redeemed at maturity for face value.

Existing bonds and notes are traded in secondary markets and can be bought (at the ask) and sold (at the bid) through brokers. Their price is quoted on the basis of 100, and rises and falls as interest rates on similar new issues are lower or higher, respectively.

The interest rate is often called the coupon rate. Since the bearer of a bond and note is usually not known, the bearer must send a coupon to the issuer's paying agent in order to receive the semiannual interest payment. The price of these securities gradually rises as the interest date nears and then falls by the amount of interest when it is paid.

Since Treasury bonds and notes are issued by the federal government they are risk-free (if purchased at face value), are extremely liquid, and can be used for collateral. Because of these desirable features, they can bear a low-interest rate.

Treasury bonds and notes that are traded in secondary markets are listed in financial publications such as the Wall Street Journal. As an example, Figure 12 lists the coupon (interest) rate, the maturity date, the bid price, the ask price, the bid price change, and the current yield. Prices are quoted on the basis of 100, but the numbers that follow the decimal are not fractions of 10 or 100; they are fractions of 32. That is, 102.21 is 102-21/32 (i.e., 102.65625).

Interest is taxed as ordinary income in the year it is received. If bonds or notes are purchased at face value and held until maturity, there is neither capital gain nor loss. Otherwise, there probably will be. A capital gain can be reported as such, or amortized and deducted from ordinary income.

The first four formulas can be used to determine the yield of the

Treasury bond or note (i.e., y_n, y_c, y_m, and y_r), and the next two formulas determine the yield from the Treasury bond or note investment.*

Figure 12

Treasury Issues * *Bonds, Notes & Bills*

Mid-afternoon Over-the-Counter quotations supplied by the Federal Reserve Bank of New York City.

Decimals in bid-and-asked and bid-changes represent 32nds; 101.1 means 101 1/32. a-Plus 1/64. b-Yield to call date. d-Minus 1/64. n-Treasury notes.

Rate	Mat. Date	Bid	Asked	Bid Chg.	Yld.
	1989 Oc[illegible]		[illegible].14	+ .6	[illegible]
10¾s,	1989 Nov n	97.19	97.27	+ .12	11.25
10½s,	1990 Jan n	96.8	96.16	+ .10	11.30
3½s,	1990 Feb	90.28	91.28	+ .20	5.01
10½s,	1990 Apr n	96.4	96.12	+ .9	11.30
8¼s,	1990 May	87.4	87.20	+ .5	10.93
10¾s,	1990 Jul n	97.5	97.9	+ .9	11.34
10¾s,	1990 Aug n	97	97.8	+ .8	11.34
11½s,	1990 Oct n	100.17	100.25	+ .9	11.33
13s,	1990 Nov n	106.30	107.6	+ .7	11.49
14½s,	1991 May n	114.5	114.13	+ .11	11.60
14⅞s,	1991 Aug n	116.6	116.14	+ .9	11.63
14¼s,	1991 Nov n	113.10	113.18	+ .10	11.62
14⅝s,	1992 Feb n	115.18	115.26	+ .8	11.62
13¾s,	1992 May n	111.4	111.12	+ .10	11.62
4¼s,	1987-92 Aug	91.4	92.4	+ .4	5.38
7¼s,	1992 Aug	78.1	78.9	+ .11	11.19
10½s,	1992 Nov n	95.1	96.1	+ .11	11.21
4s,	1988-93 Feb	91.18	92.2	+ .6	5.07
6¾s,	1993 Feb	74.22	76.6	+ .8	11.08
7⅞s,	1993 Feb	80.19	81.3	+ .12	11.18
10⅞s,	1993 Feb n	96.30	97.2	+ .8	11.40
10⅛s,	1993 May n	93.4	93.12	+ .10	11.27
7½s,	1988-93 Aug	78	78.16	+ .14	11.14
8⅝s,	1993 Aug	84.9	84.17	+ .11	11.26
11⅞s,	1993 Aug n	102.21	102.29	+ .12	11.37
8⅝s,	1993 Nov	84.2	84.10	+ .11	11.27
9s,	1994 Feb	85.26	86.2	+ .6	11.32
4⅛s,	1989-94 May	91.25	92.25	+ .13	5.01
8¾s,	1994 Aug	84.3	84.11	+ .10	11.29
10⅛s,	1994 Nov	92.10	92.18	+ .10	11.31
3s,	1995 Feb	91.9	92.9	– .1	3.84
10½s,	1995 Feb	94.2	94.10	+ .11	11.41
10⅜s,	1995 May	93.4	93.12	+ .8	11.42
12⅝s,	1995 May	106.30	107.6	+ .10	11.48
11½s,	1995 Nov	100.6	100.14	+ .14	11.43
7s,	1993-98 May	70.7	70.23	+ .12	11.09
3½s,	1998 Nov	92.5	93.5	+ .1	4.11
8½s,	1994-99 May	79.2	79.10	+ .5	11.36
7⅞s,	1995-00 Feb	74.7	74.15	+ .3	11.34
8⅜s,	1995-00 Aug	77.14	77.22	+ .6	11.38
11¾s,	2001 Feb	100.25	101	+ .9	11.61
13⅛s,	2001 May	110.27	111.3	+ .8	11.63
8s,	1996-01 Aug	74.20	74.28	+ .8	11.31
13⅜s,	2001 Aug	112.22	112.30	+ .7	11.63
15¾s,	2001 Nov	130.18	131.2	+ .9	11.61
14¼s,	2002 Feb	119.23	119.31	+ .14	11.60
11⅝s,	2002 Nov	99.25	100.1	+ .11	11.62
10¾s,	2003 Feb	93.17	93.25	+ .11	11.57
10¾s,	2003 May	93.5	93.13		11.61
11⅛s,	2003 Aug	96.10	96.18	+ .8	11.57
11⅞s,	2003 Nov	101.25	102.9	+ .9	11.57
8¼s,	2000-05 May	76.2	76.10	+ .14	11.17
7⅝s,	2002-07 Feb	70.20	70.28	+ .8	11.15
7⅞s,	2002-07 Nov	72.10	72.18	+ .6	11.18
8⅜s,	2003-08 Aug	75.31	76.7	+ .5	11.23
8¾s,	2003-08 Nov	78.18	78.26	+ .6	11.31
9⅛s,	20[illegible] May	81.17	81.[illegible]	[illegible]	[illegible]1.32

*Treasury bonds and notes can also be traded in the financial futures markets. These markets and the yield curve are discussed on page 117.

FORMULAS:

$$y_n = r$$

$$y_c = r_b \cdot \frac{v_{bf}}{p_{b1}}$$

$$y_m = \frac{r_b v_{bf} + D}{E}$$

$$p_{b1} = v_{bf} \cdot [F \cdot a(y_r,k,2) + G/c(y_r,k,2)] \cdot (1+y_r t')$$

$$Y = \frac{A-B}{C}$$

$$y = (1+Y)^{1/t} - 1$$

where

y_n = annual nominal yield on the bond or note

y_c = annual current yield on the bond or note

y_m = approximate annual yield to maturity on the bond or note

y_r = exact annual yield to maturity (rate of return) on the bond or note

Y = total yield on the investment

y = annual yield on the investment

then

$A = p_{b2} + j v_{bf} \cdot (r_b/2)$

$B = p_{b1}$

$C = B$

$D = \dfrac{v_{bf} - p_{b1}}{k}$

$E = \dfrac{v_{bf} - p_{b1}}{2}$

$F = r_b/2$

$G = 1$

j = number of full interest periods investment held

k = number of semiannual interest periods until maturity

p_{b1} = purchase (ask) price of the bond or note

p_{b2} = selling price of the bond or note (bid or face value if held until maturity)

r_b = coupon interest rate on the bond or note, expressed as a decimal

t = time the investment held, in years

t' = time since the last bond interest period, expressed as a fraction of a 360-day year. Full months are assumed to have 30 days (Table II)

v_{bf} = face value of the bond or note

$a(y_r,k,2)$ = present value of an annuity of 1 (Table I)

$c(y_r,k,2)$ = amount of 1 at compound interest (Table I)

EXAMPLE: Suppose you buy ten Treasury notes that bear interest of 15-3/8% to be paid semiannually and mature in five years. The note is quoted at 114.2 bid and 115 ask (on the basis of 100). You hold them for six interest periods, and because similar issues currently bear a lower interest rate, they are selling at 118.60 bid and 118.30 ask. (a) What is your total yield over the three years, (b) what is your annual yield, and (c) what is the exact yield to maturity that causes your notes to sell at 118.30 ask?

SOLUTION: In this example,

r_b = 0.15375, $k = 10$, $p_{b1} = \$1,150.00$, $v_{bf} = \$1,000.00$,

j = 6, and $p_{b2} = \$1,180.60$.

Now,
(a) In this case,

$$A = \$1,180.60 + 6 \times \$1,000.00 \times (0.15375/2) = \$1,641.85,$$

$$B = \$1,150.00, \text{ and}$$

$$C = \$1,150.00.$$

The total yield on the investment is

$$Y = \frac{\$1{,}641.85-\$1{,}150.00}{\$1{,}150.00} = \frac{\$491.85}{\$1{,}150.00}$$

$$= 0.4277 = 42.77\%.$$

(b) Since the notes have been held three years, $t=3$. Now, the annual yield on the investment is

$$y = (1+0.4277)^{1/3} - 1 = (1.4277)^{0.3333} - 1$$

$$= 1.1260 - 1 = 0.1260 = 12.60\%.$$

(c) To determine the current interest rate on similar notes, we must use the formula for p_{bl} and determine y_r. Due to the nature of the two annuity functions, it is not possible to rearrange the formula and solve it for y_r. However, by trial and error we can approximate y_r (i.e., by determining p_{bl} for different values of y_r until p_{bl} is sufficiently close to \$118.06). It is efficient to begin by selecting y_r to be near the rate determined by the bond salesman's method (i.e., y_m). It was found that when $y_r=12\%$, $p_{bl}=\$112.43$, and when $y_r=10\%$, $p_{bl}=\$120.75$. Linear interpolation (Appendix B) shows that $p_{bl}=\$118.06$ when the annual yield to maturity is $y_r=10.65\%$.

CHAPTER 6
Savings Bonds

Savings bonds are issued by the Treasury to help pay the federal debt. They are risk free and can be redeemed upon request after six months. However, they cannot be transferred, sold, or used as collateral.

Savings bonds are issued in registration form in the name of individuals (single or co-ownership), organizations, or fiduciaries. They can be purchased and redeemed at most financial institutions at no charge. Two types of savings bonds are currently being issued by the Treasury, Series EE and Series HH. They both have ten-year maturities, but differ in many ways.

Series EE Bonds

These bonds are issued in face amounts from $50 to $10,000. However, they are purchased at 50% of face value. After six months they can be redeemed to provide a minimum annual yield from 4.04% to 7.51%. However, if held at least five years, they will provide an annual yield that is the maximum of:

- 7.5%, or
- 85% of the average yield on Treasury bonds and notes whose maturities are approximately five years.

This yield is compounded semiannually. Table 4 lists redemption values and yields based on the 7.5% annual yield. No more than $30,000 (face amount) can be purchased in the same name in any calendar year.

Interest on EE bonds is considered to be the difference between the redemption value and the amount paid. It is exempt from state income tax, but subject to estate, inheritance, gift, and other excise tax (whether federal or state). It is also subject to federal income tax, and can be reported on either a cash basis (in the year received upon redemption) or an accrual basis (in the year the interest occurred).

Series HH Bonds

Due to the low volume of sales, HH bonds can no longer be purchased, but they can be acquired through exchange of Series E and EE

Table 4. SERIES EE BONDS

Years & Months After Issue	Issue Price								Annual Yield		
	$25.00	$37.50	$ 50.00	$100.00	$250.00	$500.00	$2500.00	$5000.00	From Issue Date to Start of Period (Percent)	During Each Period (Percent)	From Start of Period to Maturity (Percent)
		Redemption Value During Each Period									
0-0 to 0-2	$25.00	$37.50	$ 50.00	$100.00	$250.00	$500.00	$2500.00	$ 5000.00	----	4.85	7.50
0-2 to 0-3	25.18	37.77	50.36	100.72	251.80	503.60	2518.00	5036.00	4.35	3.84	7.56
0-3 to 0-4	25.26	37.89	50.52	101.04	252.60	505.20	2526.00	5052.00	4.18	3.83	7.59
0-4 to 0-5	25.34	38.01	50.68	101.36	253.40	506.80	2534.00	5068.00	4.09	3.82	7.62
0-5 to 0-6	25.42	38.13	50.84	101.66	254.20	508.40	2542.00	5084.00	4.04	4.77	7.66
0-6 to 0-7	25.52	38.28	51.04	102.08	255.20	510.40	2552.00	5104.00	4.16	5.71	7.68
0-7 to 0-8	25.64	38.46	51.28	102.56	256.40	512.80	2564.00	5128.00	4.38	6.64	7.70
0-8 to 0-9	25.78	38.67	51.56	103.12	257.80	515.60	2578.00	5156.00	4.66	7.56	7.71
0-9 to 0-10	25.94	38.91	51.88	103.76	259.40	518.80	2594.00	5188.00	4.98	6.56	7.71
0-10 to 0-11	26.08	39.12	52.16	104.32	260.80	521.60	2608.00	5216.00	5.14	7.48	7.72
0-11 to 1-0	26.24	39.36	52.48	104.96	262.40	524.80	2624.00	5248.00	5.35	7.43	7.72
1-0 to 1-1	26.40	39.60	52.80	105.60	264.00	528.80	2640.00	5280.00	5.52	6.45	7.72
1-1 to 1-2	26.54	39.81	53.08	106.16	265.40	530.80	2654.00	5308.00	5.59	6.41	7.74
1-2 to 1-3	26.68	40.02	53.36	106.72	266.80	533.60	2668.00	5336.00	5.65	5.46	7.75
1-3 to 1-4	26.80	40.20	53.60	107.20	268.00	536.00	2680.00	5360.00	5.64	6.35	7.77
1-4 to 1-5	26.94	40.41	53.88	107.76	269.40	538.80	2694.00	5388.00	5.68	6.32	7.78
1-5 to 1-6	27.08	40.62	54.16	108.32	270.80	541.60	2708.00	5416.00	5.72	6.28	7.80
1-6 to 2-0	27.22	40.83	54.44	108.88	272.20	544.40	2722.00	5444.00	5.75	6.76	7.81
2-0 to 2-6	28.14	42.21	56.28	112.56	281.40	562.80	2814.00	5628.00	6.00	7.25	7.88
2-6 to 3-0	29.16	43.74	58.32	116.64	291.60	583.20	2916.00	5832.00	6.25	7.82	7.92
3-0 to 3-6	30.30	45.45	60.60	121.20	303.00	606.00	3030.00	6060.00	6.51	8.18	7.93
3-6 to 4-0	31.54	47.31	63.08	126.16	315.40	630.80	3154.00	6308.00	6.75	8.88	7.91
4-0 to 4-6	32.94	49.41	65.88	131.76	329.40	658.80	3294.00	6588.00	7.02	9.23	7.83
4-6 to 5-0	34.46	51.69	68.92	137.84	344.60	689.20	3446.00	6892.00	7.26	9.75	7.70
5-0 to 5-6	36.14	54.21	72.28	144.56	361.40	722.80	3614.00	7228.00	7.51	7.53	7.50
5-6 to 6-0	37.50	56.25	75.00	150.00	375.00	750.00	3750.00	7500.00	7.51	7.47	7.50
6-0 to 6-6	38.90	58.35	77.80	155.60	389.00	778.00	3890.00	7780.00	7.51	7.51	7.50
6-6 to 7-0	40.36	60.54	80.72	161.44	403.60	807.20	4036.00	8072.00	7.51	7.43	7.50
7-0 to 7-6	41.86	62.79	83.72	167.44	418.60	837.20	4186.00	8372.00	7.50	7.55	7.51
7-6 to 8-0	43.44	65.16	86.88	173.76	434.40	868.80	4344.00	8688.00	7.50	7.46	7.50
8-0 to 8-6	45.06	67.59	90.12	180.24	450.60	901.20	4506.00	9012.00	7.50	7.55	7.51
8-6 to 9-0	46.76	70.14	93.52	187.04	467.60	935.20	4676.00	9352.00	7.50	7.44	7.50
9-0 to 9-6	48.50	72.75	97.00	194.00	486.00	970.00	4850.00	9700.00	7.50	7.51	7.53
9-6 to 10-0	50.32	75.48	100.64	201.28	503.20	1006.40	5032.00	10064.00	7.50	7.55	7.55
10-0	52.22	78.33	104.44	208.88	522.20	1044.40	5222.00	10444.00	7.50	----	----

bonds and savings notes. They are issued at face value in amounts from $500 to $10,000. To maintain parity with the Series EE bonds, they pay interest of 7.5% compounded semiannually; interest is paid by check. Table 5 lists the amount of interest and the yields for each period of time. No more than $20,000 can be exchanged in the same name in any calendar year.

Investors are interested in exchanging Series EE bonds for Series HH bonds because tax on the interest they earned is deferred until the Series HH bonds are redeemed. At that time, they are subject to the same tax as are the Series EE bonds (and using the cash basis).

EXAMPLE: Suppose you purchase three Series EE bonds for $250 each (face value of $500 each). You choose to report the interest on the cash basis and hold them until maturity. At this time each bond is worth $522.20. To defer tax on the interest ($272.50/bond), you choose to exchange the bonds for Series HH bonds. You have the option of either receiving three bonds and $22.20 × 3 = $66.60 (to be taxed now) or adding $433.40 and receiving four bonds. The semiannual interest checks on the Series HH bonds are subject to tax in the year they are received, but the $272.20 interest on each Series EE bond is not subject to tax until the Series HH bonds are redeemed.

Table 5. SERIES HH BONDS

Period of Time Bond Is Held After Issue Date	Issue Price				Annual Yield		
	$500	$1,000	$5,000	$10,000	From Issue to Each Interest Payment Date	For Half-Year Period Preceding Interest Payment Date	From Each Interest Payment Date to Maturity
	Amount of Semi-Annual Interest for each Denomination						
					Percent	Percent	Percent
.5 years	$18.75	$37.50	$187.50	$375.00	7.50	7.50	7.50
1.0 years	18.75	37.50	187.50	375.00	7.50	7.50	7.50
1.5 years	18.75	37.50	187.50	375.00	7.50	7.50	7.50
2.0 years	18.75	37.50	187.50	375.00	7.50	7.50	7.50
2.5 years	18.75	37.50	187.50	375.00	7.50	7.50	7.50
3.0 years	18.75	37.50	187.50	375.00	7.50	7.50	7.50
3.5 years	18.75	37.50	187.50	375.00	7.50	7.50	7.50
4.0 years	18.75	37.50	187.50	375.00	7.50	7.50	7.50
4.5 years	18.75	37.50	187.50	375.00	7.50	7.50	7.50
5.0 years	18.75	37.50	187.50	375.00	7.50	7.50	7.50
5.5 years	18.75	37.50	187.50	375.00	7.50	7.50	7.50
6.0 years	18.75	37.50	187.50	375.00	7.50	7.50	7.50
6.5 years	18.75	37.50	187.50	375.00	7.50	7.50	7.50
7.0 years	18.75	37.50	187.50	375.00	7.50	7.50	7.50
7.5 years	18.75	37.50	187.50	375.00	7.50	7.50	7.50
8.0 years	18.75	37.50	187.50	375.00	7.50	7.50	7.50
8.5 years	18.75	37.50	187.50	375.00	7.50	7.50	7.50
9.0 years	18.75	37.50	187.50	375.00	7.50	7.50	7.50
9.5 years	18.75	37.50	187.50	375.00	7.50	7.50	7.50
10.0 years	18.75	37.50	187.50	375.00	7.50	7.50	----

CHAPTER 7
Government National Mortgage Association Certificates

The Government National Mortgage Association (GNMA) is a wholly owned government corporation that was created to help financial institutions such as savings and loan associations, banks, and mortgage brokers raise money for real estate loans. It does this by buying their existing mortgages. These purchased mortgages are easily sold to investors indirectly by the GNMA when it issues certificates that are mortgage-backed and guaranteed.*

That is, the purchaser is guaranteed to receive full and timely monthly payments. Like mortgage payments, each payment consists of some return of principal and the interest on the remaining principal. The principal portion is not taxed since it is merely being returned, but the interest portion is taxed as ordinary income. These certificates are usually issued in minimum denominations of $25,000, but some brokerage firms sell minimum denominations of $10,000.

The term of these certificates is usually about 12 years, but it is not listed in financial quotations. Prepayment is permitted. Liquidity is no problem since many brokerage firms maintain a secondary market in the certificates. The price increases and decreases as current interest rates decrease and increase, respectively. Figure 13 shows an example of GNMA certificate quotations as listed in the Wall Street Journal.

GNMA certificates can be compared to corporate bonds; however, the payments are monthly instead of semiannually, and the principal is returned gradually over the term instead of at the term.**

The formula to determine the yield is the same as that for a mortgage or a bond (with 12 payment periods per year instead of 2); the yield is determined by trial and error. GNMA certificates are bought at the ask and sold at the bid, so there are no explicit commissions.***

---

*The mortgage payments are "passed through" to the holder of the certificate.

**If the principal is reinvested as received (creating a sinking fund), the yield can exceed that on corporate bonds.

***GNMA certificates are also traded in the financial futures markets. These markets and the yield curve are discussed on page 152.

Figure 13

Government, Agency and Miscellaneous Securities

Mid-afternoon Over-the-Counter quotations; sources on request.
Decimals in bid-and-asked and bid changes represent 32nds; 101.1 means 101 1/32. a-Plus 1/64. b-Yield to call date. d-Minus 1/64. n-Treasury notes.

GNMA Issues

Rate	Mat	Bid	Asked	Yld
8.00		76.22	76.30	11.75
9.00		81.3	81.11	12.04
9.50		84.2	84.10	12.04
10.00		86.2	86.10	12.22
11.00		91.2	91.10	12.40
11.50		93.15	93.23	12.50
12.50		98.19	98.27	12.65
13.00		101.1	101.9	12.74
13.50		103.9	103.17	12.86
14.00		105.4	105.12	13.05
15.00		107.13	107.21	13.62
16.00		107.17	107.25	14.54

FORMULA:

$$p_c = 100 \cdot [F \cdot a(y_r,k,12) + G/c(y_r,k,12)]$$

where

y_r = annual yield on the certificate investment if held until maturity

then

F = $r_c/12$

G = 1

k = number of remaining months of the mortgage

p_c = bid price of the certificate (on the basis of 100)

r_c = annual interest rate on the certificate, expressed as a decimal

$a(y_r,k,12)$ = present value of 1 (Table I)

$c(y_r,k,12)$ = amount of 1 at compound interest (Table I)

EXAMPLE: A 9% GNMA certificate is selling at 68.2 (the bid on the basis of 100) and has 12 years remaining. Determine the yield on the certificate investment if it is held until maturity.

SOLUTION: In this example,

$$r_c = 0.09,\ p_c = 68.2,\ \text{and } k = 12 \times 12 = 144.$$

The functions $a(y_r,144,12)$ and $c(y_r,144,12)$ must be evaluated using trial values of y_r until the two sides of the equation are as near in value as desired. For example, from Table I or an electronic calculator,

$$a(14.5,144,12) = 68.08052,\ \text{and } c(14.5,144,12) = 5.63824.$$

In this case

$$F = 0.09/12 = 0.0075,\ \text{and } G = 1.$$

Then, from the formula

$$\begin{aligned} 68.2 &= 100(0.0075 \times 68.08052 + 1/5.63824) \\ &= 100(0.51060 + 0.17736) \\ &= 100 \times 0.68796 \\ &= 68.796. \end{aligned}$$

Also, for $y_r = 15\%$,

$$a(15,144,12) = 66.62772,\ \text{and } c(15,144,12) = 5.98253.$$

Then

$$\begin{aligned} 68.2 &= 100(0.0075 \times 66.62772 + 1/5.98253) \\ &= 100(0.49971 + 0.16715) \\ &= 100 \times 0.66686 \\ &= 66.686. \end{aligned}$$

Since $66.686 < 68.2 < 68.796$, the yield is between 14.5% and 15%. Linear interpolation (see Appendix B) provides this good approximation:

$$\begin{aligned} y_r &= \left(\frac{68.796-68.2}{68.796-66.686}\right) \times 0.15 + \left(\frac{68.2-66.686}{68.796-66.686}\right) \times 0.145 \\ &= \frac{0.596}{2.110} \times 0.15 + \frac{1.514}{2.110} \times 0.145 \end{aligned}$$

$$= 0.04237 + 0.10404$$

$$= 0.14641 = 14.641\%$$

This is essentially the yield on the certificate investment if held until maturity, because it renders the right side of the formula equal to 68.19.

PART III

How to Measure the Value of a Mortgage Investment

New and existing mortgages are often traded. Their value depends upon the difference between economic and contract interest rates, the remaining term, the risk, etc. The formulas in this section will show you how to determine the yield, the purchase price, and the discount.

If there is no prepayment, the mortgage yield, y_r, can be determined from the first formula if either the purchase price or the discount from the loan balance is known. If there is prepayment, the yield can be determined from the formula for the purchase price. In either case, the yield cannot be determined explicitly. However, it can be determined by the method shown in the following example. Also, Figure 14 can be used to estimate the yield or the purchase price for mortgages with monthly payments and no prepayment.

The purchase price that will provide the desired yield, y_r, can be determined from the second formula. Notice that this formula can be used either when there is prepayment or when there is not. (If not, set k=0, in which case a(r,k,q)=0.)

After the purchase price that provides the required yield has been determined, the discount, r′, can be determined from the third formula.

The amount of each payment that is considered capital gain is determined by the ratio of the purchase price-to-remaining balance. The remainder of the payment is ordinary income.

All of these formulas are for amortized loans. However, they can be used for non-amortized loans (loans where the payments consist of interest only) simply by replacing both a(r,m,q) and a(r,k,q) with q/r.*

*That is, a non-amortized loan can be characterized mathematically as an amortized loan whose term is infinite. Hence, from the formula in the introduction to Table I, we see that letting $m \to \infty$ and $k \to \infty$ reduces a(r,m,q) and a(r,k,q) equal to q/r.

Figure 14

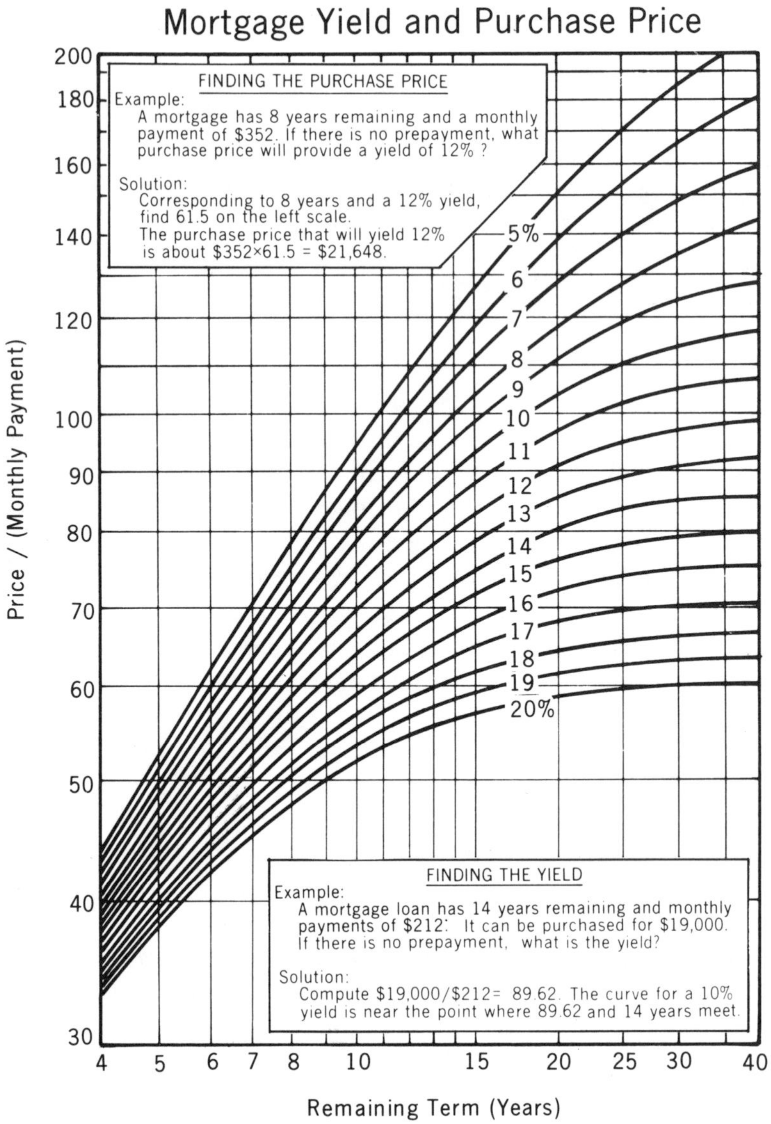

FORMULAS:

$$a(y_r,k,q) = \frac{p_m}{p} = \frac{p_m}{B} \cdot a(r,m,q) = (1-r') \cdot a(r,k,q) \quad \text{(yield)}$$

$$p_m = B \cdot \frac{s(y_r,j-i,q)+a(r,k,q)}{c(y_r,j-i,q)+a(r,m,q)} \quad \text{(purchase price)}$$

$$r' = 1 - \frac{p_m}{B} \qquad \text{(discount)}$$

$$p_c = p \cdot \frac{p_m}{B}$$

$$p_i = p - p_c$$

where

y_r = annual yield on the mortgage

p_m = purchase price that results in the required yield

r' = discount on the mortgage balance, expressed as a decimal

p_c, p_i = amount of each payment that is recognized as capital gain and ordinary income, respectively

then

B = original amount of mortgage

i = number of payment periods from inception until purchase of the mortgage

j = number of payment periods from inception until the balloon payment

k = number of payment periods remaining after the balloon payment

m = nq = total number of payment periods (note: $m=j+k$)

n = number of years (term of the mortgage)

p = amount of each periodic payment

q = number of payment periods per year

r = annual mortgage interest rate

$a(y_r,k,q)$, etc. = present value of an annuity of 1 (Table I)

$c(y_r,j-i,q)$ = amount of 1 at compound interest (Table I)

$s(y_r,j-i,q)$ = amount of an annuity of 1 (Table I)

EXAMPLE 1 (Yield): An amortized loan has 84 remaining monthly payments of \$324.43. If it can be purchased for \$17,840.00, what is the yield?

SOLUTION: In this example,

$$k = 84,\ q = 12,\ p = \$324.43, \text{ and } p_m = \$17,840.00.$$

From the first formula,

$$a(y_r,84,12) = \frac{\$17,840.00}{\$324.43} = 54.9887.$$

From Table I, locate the section with monthly payments (i.e., q=12) and the row corresponding to 84 periods (i.e., m=84). Scan this row, and find two consecutive values of $a(y_r,84,12)$ that bracket 54.9887. The yield is between these two interest rates. Interpolation (Appendix B) would show that the yield is y_r=12.99%.

EXAMPLE 2 (Purchase Price): A five-year amortized loan of \$16,000 at 8% interest with monthly payments is purchased after 11 payments. What must the purchase price be if there is to be a yield of 10% when (a) there is no prepayment, and (b) there is a balloon payment 48 payments after the mortgage is executed?

SOLUTION: In this example,

$$n = 5 \text{ years},\ B = \$16,000,\ r = 8\%,\ q = 12,\ m = nq = 60,\ i = 11, \text{ and}$$

$$y_r = 10\%.$$

(a) Since there is no prepayment, j=m=60, and k=0. Now, from the second formula,

$$p_m = \$16,000 \times \frac{s(10,60-11,12) + a(8,0,12)}{c(10,60-11,12) \cdot a(8,60,12)}$$

$$= \$16,000 \times \frac{s(10,49,12) + 0}{c(10,49,12) \cdot a(8,60,12)}.^*$$

From Table I

$$s(10,49,12) = 60.2118459,$$

$$c(10,49,12) = 1.5017654, \text{ and}$$

$$a(8,60,12) = 49.3184333.$$

*When k = 0, a(r,k,q) = 0.

Now

$$p_m = \$16{,}000 \times \left(\frac{60.2118459 + 0}{1.5017654 \times 49.3184333} \right)$$

$$= \$13{,}007.40.$$

(b) In this case, a balloon payment is due after 48 months. That is, j=48 and k=12. Now

$$p_m = \$16{,}000 \times \frac{s(10,48 - 11,12) + a(8,12,12)}{c(10,48 - 11,12) \cdot a(8,60,12)}$$

$$p_m = \$16{,}000 \times \frac{s(10,37,12) + a(8,12,12)}{c(10,37,12) \cdot a(8,60,12)} .$$

From Table I

$$s(10,37,12) = 43.1300029,$$

$$c(10,37,12) = 1.3594167,$$

$$a(8,12,12) = 11.4957818, \text{ and}$$

$$a(8,60,12) = 49.3184333.$$

Now

$$p_m = \$16{,}000 \times \left(\frac{43.1300029 + 11.4957818}{1.3594167 \times 49.3184333} \right)$$

$$= \$16{,}000 \times \frac{54.6257847}{67.044302}$$

$$= \$13{,}036.34.$$

PART IV
How to Invest in Municipal Bonds

Bonds are interest-bearing certificates of indebtedness. Municipal bonds are issued by states, municipalities (i.e., counties, cities, and states), districts (i.e., school, road, and assessment districts), departments, and authorities.*

The outstanding feature of municipal bonds is their tax-free interest. The interest received is not subject to federal income tax and is usually not subject to state tax if the bonds were issued in that state. Because of this feature, municipal bonds are usually purchased by individuals in high-income tax brackets, private funds, corporations, and banks.

Figure 15 relates the non-taxed municipal bond yield to an equivalent yield required from a taxed investment at 1984 rates. For example, a 10% yield on a municipal bond requires a 16.1% yield on a taxed investment if the investor is an unmarried person whose taxable income is $100,000.

*Municipal notes are also issued to cover debt of one month to one year. They bear interest and are issued in denominations of $5,000 to $5,000,000. They are tax free in the same way as are municipal bonds.

Figure 15

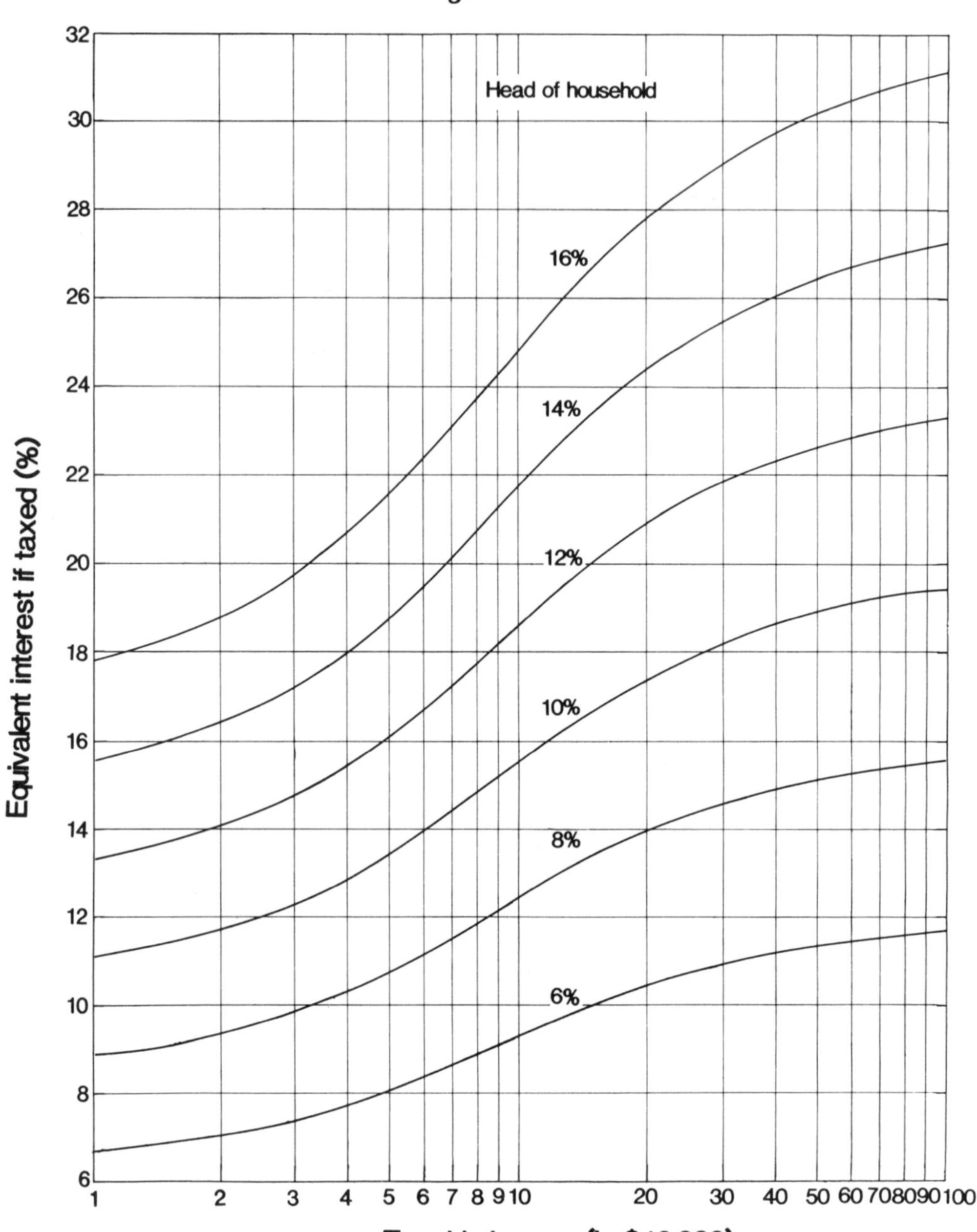
Head of household
16%
14%
12%
10%
8%
6%
Equivalent interest if taxed (%)
6
8
10
12
14
16
18
20
22
24
26
28
30
32
1
2
3
4
5
6
7
8
9
10
20
30
40
50
60
70
80
90
100
Taxable income (in $10,000)

Figure 15 (*Continued*)

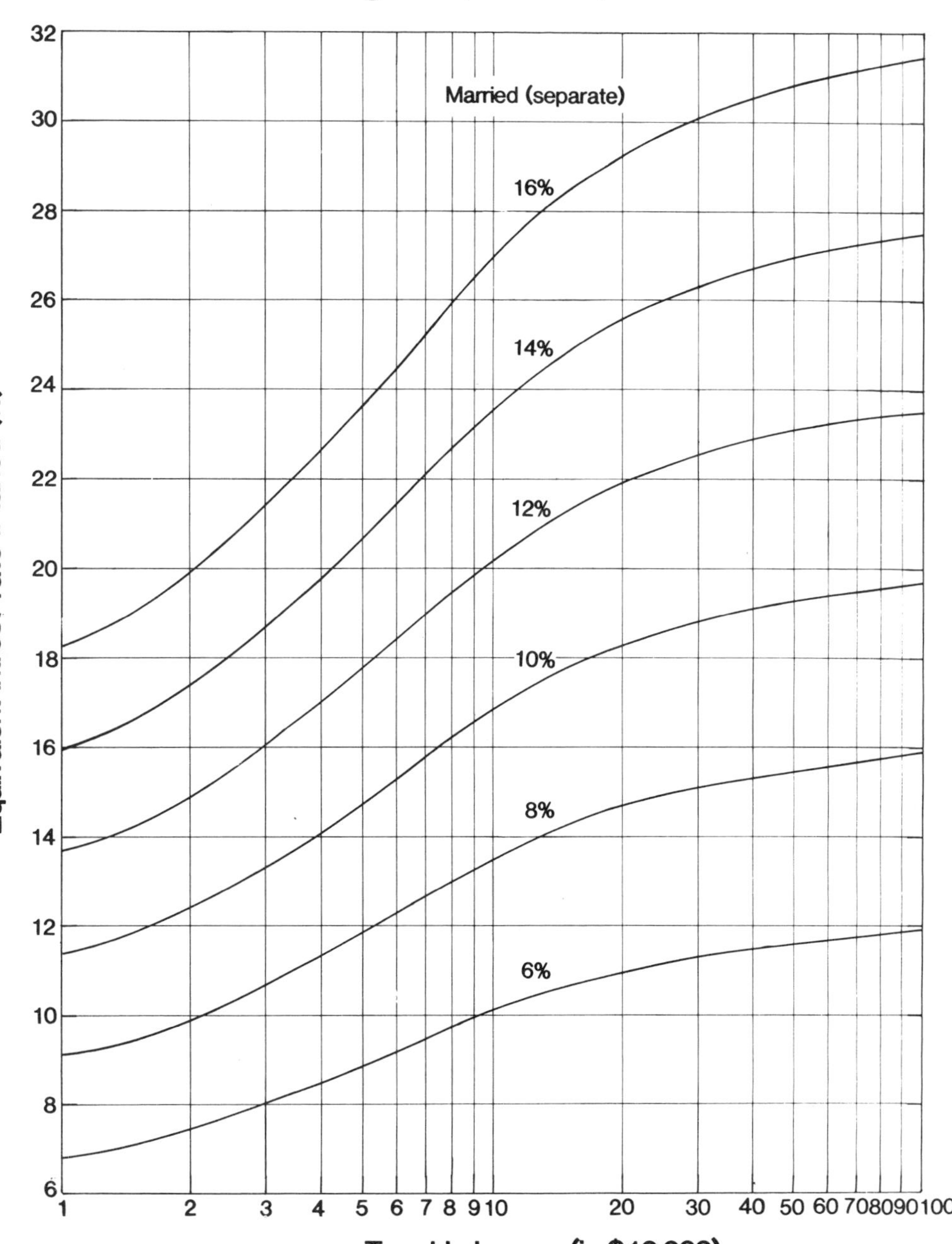

Figure 15 (*Continued*)

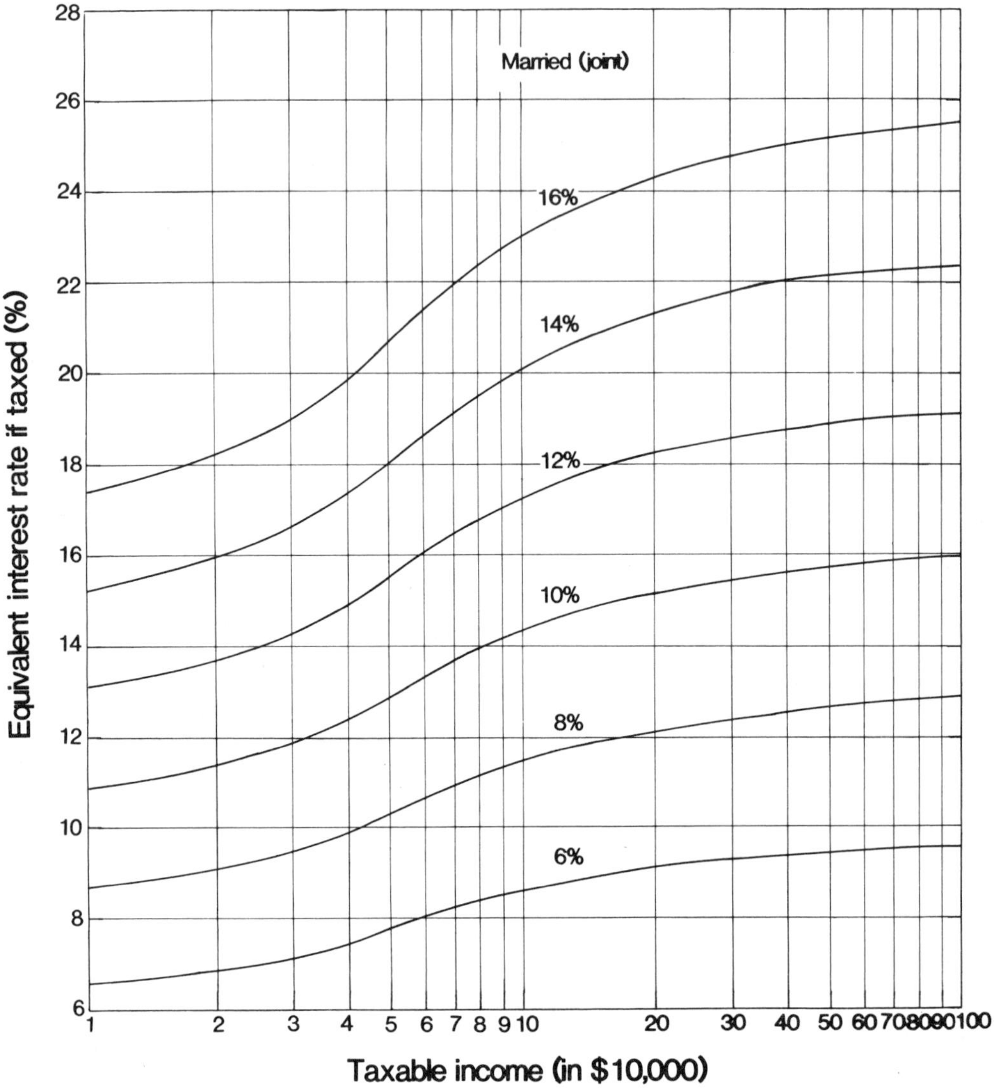

Figure 15 (*Continued*)

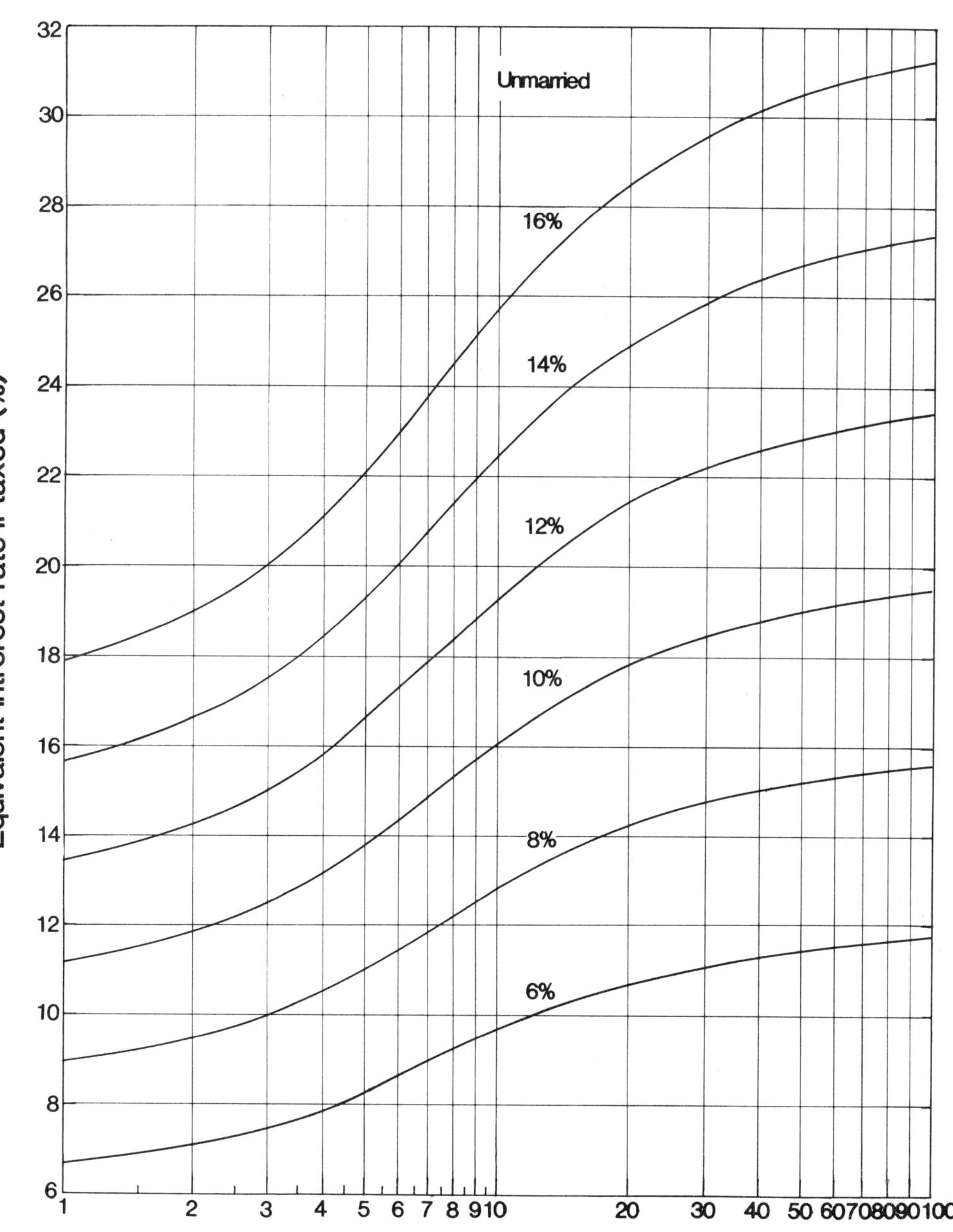

Figure 15 (*Continued*)

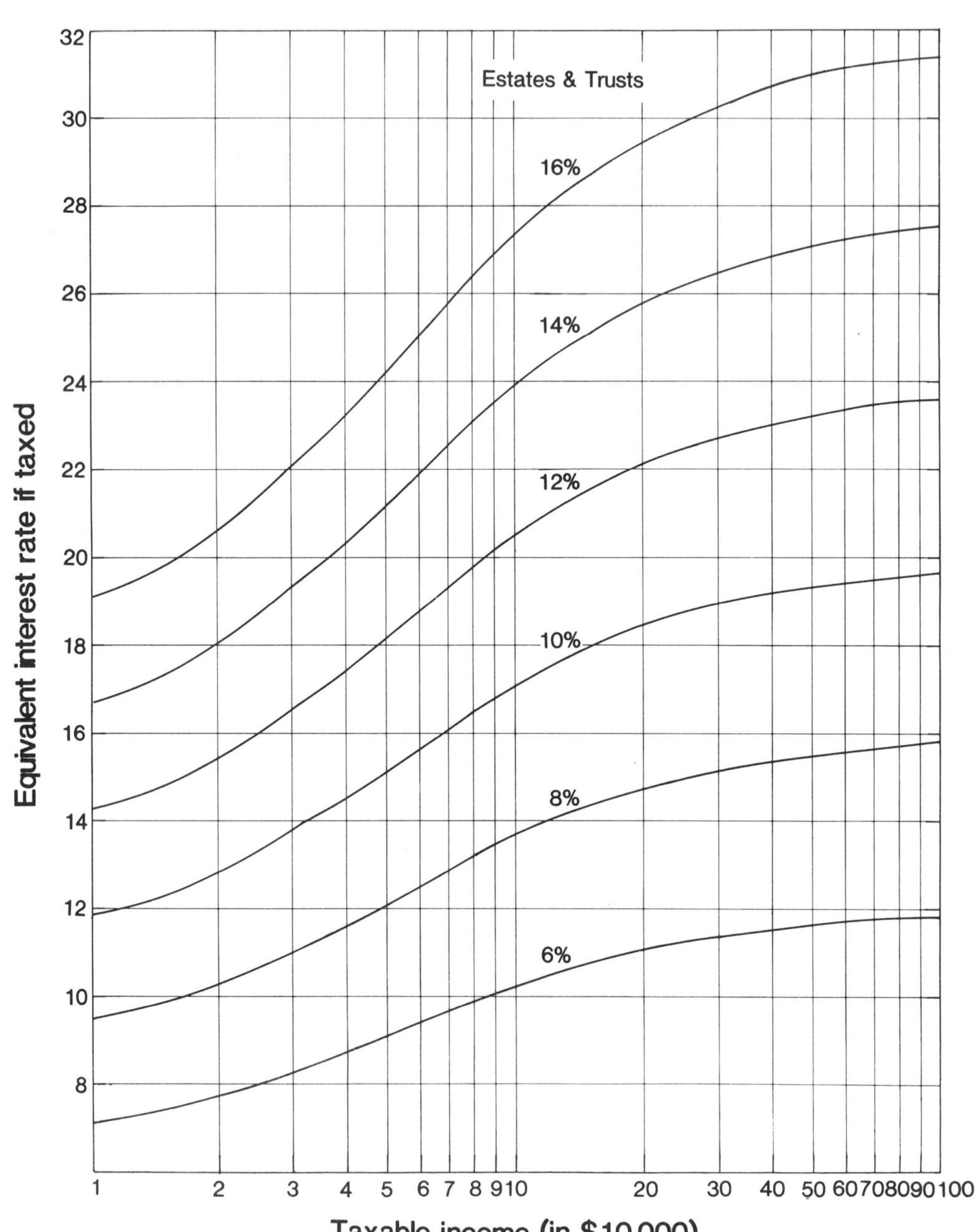

The safety of municipal bonds depends upon the debtor's ability to pay the principal and interest. Some investment services such as Moody's and Standard & Poor's grade municipal bonds into nine categories according to safety as shown in Table 6:

Table 6. MUNICIPAL BONDS RATINGS

Grade Description	Moody's	Standard & Poor's
Best Quality	Aaa	AAA
High Quality	Aa	AA
Upper-Medium	A	A
Medium*	Baa	BBB
Speculative	Ba	BB
Low	B	B
Poor-Default	Caa	CCC
Highly Speculative-Default	Ca	CC
Lowest Quality	C	C

***Lowest acceptable grade as an investment by commercial banks.**

The ways in which the debtor raises the money to pay the debt affects the safety of the investment. The three common ways are from:

- any tax the debtor chooses (for a full faith and credit bond or a general obligation bond)
- a specific tax (for a special tax bond)
- a specific earnings (for a revenue bond)*

Some municipal bonds mature on a single date (called straight bonds), while most mature in installments over the life of the bond (called serial bonds, which are often issued to pay for depreciable assets such as schools or roads).

Like other bonds, municipal bonds pay interest semiannually. The coupon (or contract) interest rate is paid on the face value.

Issued bonds can be purchased at face value from the securities firms that participate in underwriting the issue. On the other hand, existing bonds can be bought and sold through securities firms that maintain a (secondary) market in them. They are bought and sold in multiples of five.

---

*Some revenue bonds are paid by a corporation that has an agreement with the government. These are called industrial revenue bonds.

Figure 16 shows quotations as listed in the Wall Street Journal for revenue bonds. It lists two prices: The lower bid price and the higher ask price as if the face value were 100.* The difference between these prices is dictated by the market (activity, risk, etc.) and is often 2%–4% of the bid price, but it can be much larger. The column farthest to the right lists the change in the bid price since the close of the last market day. No explicit commission is charged on either the purchase or the sale: The investor purchases the bonds at the ask price; if he holds them until maturity, he receives the face value; if he sells them prematurely, he receives the current bid price. There is not an active market in many bonds, so liquidity should be considered.

Figure 16

Tax-Exempt Bonds

Here are current prices of several active tax-exempt revenue bonds issued by toll roads and other public authorities.

Agency	Coupon	Mat	Bid	Asked	Chg.
Alabama G.O.	8⅜s	'01	93	95	....
Bat Park City Auth NY	6⅜s	'14	65½	67½	....
Chelan Cnty PU Dist	5s	'13	63	65	....
Clark Cnty Arpt Rev	10½s	'07	99	101	....
Columbia St Pwr Exch	3⅞s	'03	69	71	....
Dela River Port Auth	6½s	'11	70½	72½	....
Douglas Cnty PU Dist	4s	'18	44	46	....
Ga Mun El Auth Pwr Rev	8s	'15	82	86	....
Intermountain Pwr	7½s	'18	73	77	....
Intermountain Pwr	10½s	'18	99	101	....
Intermountain Pwr	14s	'21	119½	123½	.
Jacksonville Elec Rev	9¼s	'13	92½	95½	..
Loop	6½s	'08	66½	69½	....
MAC	7½s	'92	89	93	.
MAC	7½s	'95	86½	90½	....
MAC-n	8s	'86	99½	103½	....
MAC	8s	'91	97	101	....
MAC	9.7s	'08	98	102	..
MAC	9¾s	'92	101½	105½	...
MAC	10¼s	'93	110	114	....
Mass Port Auth Rev	6s	'11	68	71	
Massachusetts G.O.	6½s	'00	74	77	...
Mass Wholesale	6⅜s	'15	54	57	....
Mass Wholesale	13⅜s	'17	106	109	....
Metro Transit Auth	9¼s	'15	93½	96½	....
Michigan Public Pwr	10⅝s	'18	102	104	..
Nebraska Pub Pwr Dist	7.1s	'17	72	76	....
NJ Turnpike Auth	4¾s	'06	62½	64½	....
NJ Turnpike Auth	5.7s	'13	69	71	....
NJ Turnpike Auth	6s	'14	73	75	....
NY Mtge Agency Rev	9¾s	'13	101½	10[illegible]	....
NY [illegible] Es[illegible]	[illegible]	'10	64	[illegible]	

The demand for municipal bonds changes with:

- The current yield available from other securities, particularly high-grade taxable bonds,
- The supply of money that is subject to high tax rates, and
- The supply of tax-exempt bonds.

---

*Commonly referred to as "on the basis of 100."

Although the interest received from a municipal bond investment is exempt from federal income tax, the capital gain or loss is treated as capital gain. Hence, the quoted yield may include some profits that will be subject to tax.

The first four formulas can be used to determine the yield on the bond (i.e., y_n, y_c, y_m, and y_r), and the next two formulas determine the yield on the municipal bond investment.

FORMULAS:

$$y_n = r_b$$

$$y_c = r_b \bullet \frac{v_{bf}}{p_{b1}}$$

$$y_m = \frac{r_b v_{bf} + D}{E}$$

$$p_{b1} = [F \bullet a(y_r,k,q) + G/c(y_r,k,q)] \bullet (1+y_r t') \text{ (Exact yield to maturity)}$$

$$Y = \frac{A-B}{C}$$

$$y = (1+Y)^{1/t} - 1$$

where

y_n = annual nominal yield on the bond

y_c = annual current yield on the bond

y_m = approximate annual yield to maturity on the bond

y_r = exact annual yield to maturity on the bond

Y = total yield on the bond investment

y = annual yield on the bond investment

then

$A = p_{b2} + j v_{bf}(r_b/q)$

$B = p_{b1}$

$C = B$

$$D = \frac{v_{bf} - p_{b1}}{k}$$

$$E = \frac{v_{bf} + p_{b1}}{2}$$

$F = v_{bf}(r_b/q)$

$G = v_{br}$

j = number of full interest periods bond held

k = number of full or partial interest periods until maturity

p_{b1} = ask when purchased (p_{b1}=100, if purchased when issued)

p_{b2} = bid when sold (p_{b2}=100, if held to maturity)

q = number of interest periods per year

r_b = annual interest rate on the bond, expressed as a decimal

t = time investment held, in years

t' = time since last bond interest period, expressed as a factor of a 360-day year (full months are assumed to have 30 days)

v_{bf} = face value of the bond

v_{br} = redemption value of the bond

$a(y_r,k,q)$ = present value of an annuity of 1 (Table I)

$c(y_r,k,q)$ = amount of 1 at compound interest (Table I)

EXAMPLE 1 (Effective Interest Rate): The contract interest rate on the Intermountain Power municipal bond is 10-1/2%. Suppose your taxable income is $30,000, and you are married and filing jointly. From Figure 15 estimate the interest rate comparable to that of an otherwise equivalent investment whose interest income is taxed.

SOLUTION: Find your taxable income along the bottom of Figure 15. Move up until you come to the curve labelled 10-1/2% (i.e., 1/4 of the vertical distance between 10% and 12%). Then, follow left and read 12.5% on the left margin. This is the approximate interest rate you would have to achieve on an otherwise equivalent investment whose interest income is taxed.

EXAMPLE 2 (Yield): The Michigan Public Power Bond is a revenue municipal bond that bears interest at 10-5/8% to be paid semiannually. It matures in the year 2018. The bid and ask prices (on the basis of 100) are 97 and 98-1/2, respectively. Suppose they are purchased, held for 30 months, and sold when the bid and ask prices are 101 and 103, respectively. What is the total yield and the annual yield?

SOLUTION: In this example,

$$r_b = 0.10625,\ q = 2,\ v_{bf} = \$100,\ p_{b1} = \$98.50,\ j = 5, \text{ and}$$

$$p_{b2} = \$101.00.$$

Now

$$A = \$101.00 + 5\times\$100\times(0.10625/2) = \$127.5625,$$

$$B = \$98.50, \text{ and}$$

$$C = \$98.50.$$

The total yield on the investment is

$$Y = \frac{\$127.5625-\$98.50}{\$98.50}$$

$$= \frac{\$29.0625}{\$98.50}$$

$$= 0.2951 = 29.51\%.$$

The annual yield on the investment is

$$y = (1+0.2951)^{1/2.5} - 1 = (1.2951)^{0.4} - 1$$

$$= 1.1090 - 1 = 0.1090 = 10.90\%.$$

PART V

Futures Contracts and the Yield Curve

Traditionally, the word "futures" refers to commodity futures. However, in 1972 trading began in financial futures. This is the trading in contracts of financial instruments such as Treasury bills, Treasury bonds, Treasury notes, commercial paper, mortgage certificates, and foreign currency.

First, let us discuss futures trading in terms of the traditional futures—the commodity futures. Then we will discuss financial futures.

CHAPTER 8
Understanding Commodity Futures

There are two types of commodity markets: the spot market where the commodities are (physically) traded and the futures market where contracts are (financially) traded for commodities to be delivered in the future. However, not all commodities are acceptable for futures trading. The commodity must be storable and in adequate supply, must be available in standard units and in definable grades, and must have many producers and buyers. Commodity futures generally fall into five classes: grains and oil seeds, livestock and meat, food and fiber, metals and petroleum, and wood. Each commodity has its own unit of quantity (e.g., pounds, bushels, etc.). The minimum number of units that can be traded in a single transaction (e.g., 50,000 lbs., 5,000 bu, etc.) is the size of a contract.

Commodity futures exist because these commodities take time to produce, and the market price may change over the production period. This means that those who have invested in a phase of the production are taking a risk that the price will not change over that phase, particularly those investing in the early phases. Most of these investors are interested in profiting from their phase of production only, not from the variations of the marketplace. Since (through their contribution) they have an investment in the commodity (i.e., they are said to be "long" in the commodity), they will counter their investment by selling contracts equal to it (i.e., by going "short").

The buyer of these contracts is speculating that the price will be higher when the product is deliverable. The producer profits by adding value to the product, not by gambling on the market price of the product when it is deliverable. This maneuver to reduce or avoid risk is called "hedging." The buyer of his contracts (who is now said to be "long" in the commodity) is speculating; whether he gains or loses, he has served a purpose.

For example, the "producers" of grain are the farmers, millers, grain merchants, storers, bakers, etc. The owner of a grain storage elevator may buy wheat from farmers in July (when it is harvested). A banker may lend him 90% of the purchase price. The owner intends to store the wheat until December (his contribution). To protect himself from a lower market price in December, he will sell contracts at the current price of wheat plus the cost of storage for this time period.

These contracts can be purchased for 5%–15% of the contract price and are traded in exchanges (such as the Chicago Board of Trade Exchange) as "December wheat." The price of the contracts will vary daily, depending upon the anticipated price of wheat in December. As the December delivery date approaches, the commodity future is traded near a price called the cash or spot price. Nearly all speculators will sell the contracts before their term so as not to take delivery of the commodity.*

The commodity futures market differs from the stock market in several important ways:

- Futures contracts expire within 17 months or less, whereas stocks are traded in perpetuity.
- Futures contracts pay no dividends, whereas all stocks either do or there is hope that they will.
- Both purchases and short sales of futures contracts are treated equally and made with equally low margin, 1%–15% of the contract price. Purchases and short sales of stocks are not treated equally.

Although commodity futures prices vary no more than stock prices, the low margin available for commodities simulates greater price volatility and forces most speculators either to liquidate their interest or to contribute more equity in order to maintain the required margin. (A margin call is issued when the current margin is 25% less than the minimum required for that contract.) Because of the low margin, brokers' commissions are an unusually significant portion of the investment: they are generally 0.1% to 1.3% of the contract price, about 10% of the investment.

The number of outstanding contracts is called the open interest. The volume is the number of contracts traded during a certain period of time.

Theoretically the price of a contract for a later month should exceed the price of a contract for an earlier month due to costs for storage, insurance, interest, etc. However, this is not always true due to the anticipated differences in either supply, demand, or both. Speculators often seize on this anomaly by buying contracts for the month whose

---

*However, maybe 2% of the speculators will take delivery (and incur costs for delivery and storage) because selling would result in a short-term capital gain. They hold the commodity until their gain qualifies as a long-term gain, and then sell to the spot market.

price is thought to be too low, and/or selling an equal number of contracts in the month whose price is thought to be too high. These combined contracts are called spreads. Spreads sometimes constitute one-third of the open interest.

Fundamental Approach to Commodity Futures Speculation

Users of the fundamental approach attempt to analyze the supply of and demand for the commodity (not the contracts). The fundamental approach has more meaning in the commodity futures market than in the stock market, because there is less "insider" knowledge and more external effects, such as:

- weather
- seasons
- international currency
- labor
- politics
- price supports
- government reports on stocks and production
- market newsletters
- warehouse receipts
- elevator prices
- export commitments
- trade between countries

The U.S. Department of Agriculture is very influential in commodity futures because it:

- issues reports on crops, news, and research,
- supervises the exchanges,
- buys and sells commodities in huge quantities,
- sets support prices (to encourage or discourage production), and
- restricts marketing.

Technical Approach to Commodity Futures Speculation

Users of the technical approach analyze the prices of a commodity and the supply of and demand for the open interest (i.e., number of contracts outstanding on the commodity). They pay little attention to the supply of and demand for the commodity.

These investors employ a great variety of mathematical tools, mostly statistical, to forecast prices:

- Moving Averages—They might use many different periods of time (i.e., number of trading days), different intra-day prices, bands about the moving average, smoothing techniques, etc. (See page 32.)
- Regression Curves—If there is a suspected systematic relationship between two or more quantities, they can be observed and measured on many occasions. If a systematic relationship does exist among them, a line (or plane in the case of more than two quantities) can be determined that "best" fits the data. Then the formula of the line (or plane) provides a way to forecast prices based upon the other values. (See page 43.)
- Bar Charts—These charts of commodity prices are studied for the same patterns as are charts of stock prices. They are discussed on page 30.
- Point and Figure Charts.
- Contrary Opinion. (See page 28.)

There is great similarity in technical analysis as applied to commodity futures and stocks. However, in commodity futures there is less interest in trading volume. Commodities with unusually small volume can have large price changes, and are often avoided for this reason alone.

Figure 17 shows sample quotations of commodity futures as listed in the Wall Street Journal. Table 7 summarizes the exchanges and contract size for most commodities. The following formulas can be used to determine the yield from a commodity investment.

FORMULAS:

$$Y = \frac{A-B}{C}$$

$$y = (1+Y)^{1/t} - 1$$

where

Y = total yield on the investment

y = annual yield on the investment

Continued on page 124

Figure 17

Futures Prices

Open Interest Reflects Previous Trading Day.

	Open	High	Low	Settle	Change	Lifetime High	Lifetime Low	Open Interest
–GRAINS AND OILSEEDS–								
CORN (CBT) 5,000 bu.; cents per bu.								
Dec	352	355	305¾	354¾	+ 3¼	376½	253	108,920
Mar	356	358	354	357½	+ 4	386¼	278½	65,453
May	355	359	354½	358½	+ 4¾	390	285	19,490
July	353½	358	352½	357½	+ 6	388	288¼	26,952
Sept	327	330	326½	330	+ 3¾	356½	320	2,589
Dec	307½	309½	304½	308	+ ½	330	296	11,108
Est vol 37,800; vol Thur 78,426; open int 224,512, –1,122.								
CORN (MCE) 1,000 bu.; cents per bu.								
Dec	352	355½	350⅞	354¾	+ 3¼	381	253¼	8,269
Mar	356	358½	354½	357½	+ 4	386¼	278½	2,661
May	354	359½	354	358½	+ 4¾	390	285½	1,510
July	353	358	353	357½	+ 6	388⅛	288½	2,251
Sept	329	329	327½	330	+ 3¾	355	321	146
Dec	308	309½	305	308	+ ½	330	296⅞	1,695
Est vol 3,000; vol Thur 2,222; open int 16,532, –131.								
OATS (CBT) 5,000 bu.; cents per bu.								
Dec	189	190¾	188	190½	+ 2¼	207½	161¾	6,317
Mar	198¾	200½	198	200	+ 2¼	219	172	1,352
May	205	207	204½	206	+ 2	226	177	402
July	210	213¼	210	211¼	+ 2¾	229	189½	328
Sept	214½	214½	212½	213¾	+ 2¾	219	208	35
Est vol 3,500; vol Thur 2,148; open int 8,434, –381.								
SOYBEANS (CBT) 5,000 bu.; cents per bu.								
Nov	861	871	845	866	+ 12	986½	568½	68,729
Jan	872	885	858	881	+ 17	982	594	28,624
Mar	880	892	867	890½	+ 17½	993½	616	18,650
May	878	890	867	890	+ 19½	996	630	7,404
July	868	882	858½	881	+ 18½	992½	639½	11,627
Aug	844	850	835	850	+ 11	956¾	640	2,929
Sept	769	775	763	774½	+ 9½	860	710	2,324
Nov	698	702	689	701½	+ 10½	772¼	671	7,737
Est vol 67,200; vol Thur 85,459; open int 148,024, +87.								
SOYBEANS (MCE) 1,000 bu.; cents per bu.								
Nov	858	872	845	866	+ 12	968½	568	6,318
Jan.	870	885	858	881	+ 17	982	596	1,462
Mar	882	893	866⅞	890½	+ 17½	993½	620½	1,862
May	881	889	868	890	+ 19½	996	636	833
July	867	880	859	881	+ 18½	992½	645	641
Aug	844	847	838	850	+ 11	955	646	185
Sept	771	775	770	774½	+ 9½	853	710	84
Nov	696	704	690⅛	701½	+ 10½	772¼	663	297
Est vol 3,000; vol Thur 9,954; open int 11,682, +492								
SOYBEAN MEAL (CBT) 100 tons; $ per ton.								
Oct	228.00	236.00	226.50	235.50	+ 5.80	264.50	163.00	5,740
Dec	234.00	240.00	231.00	239.50	+ 4.80	268.50	166.50	30,821
Jan.	235.00	240.50	232.00	239.50	+ 4.20	268.50	174.50	10,026
Mar	237.00	241.00	234.00	239.80	+ 2.10	268.50	179.50	6,461
May	237.00	241.00	234.00	240.00	+ 2.50	267.50	185.00	3,045
July	237.00	241.50	235.00	241.50	+ 3.50	267.50	188.00	2,827
Aug	228.00	235.00	227.00	232.50	+ 5.00	251.00	192.[illegible]	1,619
Sept	[illegible]	222.00	[illegible]	[illegible]	+ 3.50	243.[illegible]	[illegible]	[illegible]779

Table 7. EXCHANGES AND CONTRACT SIZES FOR MOST COMMODITIES

Commodity	Exchange*	Contract Size
Grains and Oil Seeds		
Corn	CBT, MCE	5,000 bu
Oats	CBT	5,000 bu
Soybeans	CBT, MCE	5,000 bu
Soybean Meal	CBT	100 tons
Soybean Oil	CBT, MPLS	60,000 lbs.
Wheat	CBT, KC, MCE	5,000 bu
Barley	WPG	20 metric tons
Flaxseed	WPG	20 metric tons
Rapeseed	WPG	20 metric tons
Rye	WPG	20 metric tons
Livestock and Meat		
Cattle (Feeder)	CME	44,000 lbs.
Cattle (Live)	CME	40,000 lbs.
Hogs	CME	30,000 lbs.
Pork Bellies	CME	38,000 lbs.
Food and Fiber		
Cocoa	CSCE	10 metric tons
Coffee	CSCE	37,500 lbs.
Cotton	CTN	50,000 lbs.
Orange Juice	CTN	15,000 lbs.
Sugar (World)	CSCE	112,000 lbs.
Sugar (Domestic)	CSCE	112,000 lbs.
Metals and Petroleum		
Copper	CMX	25,000 lbs.
Gold	CMX, IMM	100 troy ounces
Platinum	NYM	50 troy ounces
Palladium	NYM	100 troy ounces
Silver	CMX, CBT	5,000 troy ounces
NY Gasoline	NYM	42,000 gal.
Heating Oil	NYM	42,000 gal.
Crude Oil	NYM	42,000 gal.
Wood		
Lumber	CME	130,000 board feet

***CBT—Chicago Board of Trade; CME—Chicago Mercantile Exchange; CMX—Commodity Exchange, New York; CSCE—Coffee, Sugar & Cocoa Exchange, New York; CTN—New York Cotton Exchange; IMM—International Monetary Market at CMF, Chicago; KC—Kansas City Board of Trade; MPLS—Minneapolis Grain Exchange; NYFE—New York Futures Exchange, unit of New York Stock Exchange; NYM—New York Mercantile Exchange; WPG—Winnipeg Commodity Exchange.**

then

$A = p_{c2}$

$B = p_{c1}+c_1+c_2$

$C = mp_{c1}+c_1$

c_1,c_2 = initial and final commission, respectively

m = initial margin, expressed as a decimal

p_{c1},p_{c2} = initial and final price of the investment, respectively

t = holding period, in years

EXAMPLE (Speculator's Yield): In April, a November contract for soybeans (5,000 bu) was purchased at \$6.90/bu (quoted as 690). The cost was (\$6.90/bu)×(5,000 bu)=\$34,500. The margin was 4.4%, and the commission was \$25. After four months, the contract was sold for \$7.10/bu for a \$25 commission. Determine the total and annual yield.

SOLUTION: In this example,

$p_{c1} = \$34{,}500,\ m = 0.044,\ c_1 = \$25,\ t = 4/12 = 1/3,$

$p_{c2} = (\$7.1/\text{bu})\times(5{,}000\ \text{bu}) = \$35{,}550,\ \text{and}\ c_2 = \$25.$

Now

$A = \$35{,}550,$

$B = \$34{,}500 + \$25 + \$25 = \$34{,}550,\ \text{and}$

$C = 0.044\times\$34{,}500 + \$25 = \$1{,}543.$

The total yield is

$$Y = \frac{\$35{,}550-\$34{,}550}{\$1{,}543} = \frac{\$1{,}000}{\$1{,}543} = 0.648 = 64.8\%.$$

The annual yield is

$$y = (1+0.648)^3 - 1 = (1.648)^3 - 1 = 4.48 - 1 = 3.48$$
$$= 348\%.$$

CHAPTER 9
Financial Futures—The New Investment

Financial futures include financial instruments such as Treasury bills, notes and bonds, bank certificates of deposit, Government National Mortgage Association (GNMA) certificates, Eurodollars, and major foreign currencies. Financial futures also include major stock market indices. Figure 18 shows sample quotations of financial futures and financial futures options as listed in the Wall Street Journal. Table 8 lists the financial instruments, currencies, and indices. For each entry, it lists the exchange in which they traded, the contract size, and the minimum margin for each trader, speculators and hedgers.

FEATURES

Financial futures trading began in 1972, and the principles that apply to commodity futures also apply to financial futures. The price of debt instruments and foreign currencies change primarily with interest rates, and stock indices change from many factors (including interest rates).

The traders, again, are hedgers and speculators. Speculators trade in financial futures for profit, but hedgers trade to protect an existing position. Typically, hedgers are holders of fixed income securities, lenders, builders with construction loans, mortgage banks, savings and loan associations, and corporations of all kinds that want to be protected against the higher costs of borrowing. The yield formulas for commodity futures (page 121) also apply to financial futures.

EXAMPLE (Speculator's Yield): Suppose you expect interest rates to decrease over the next few months. You buy 10 futures contracts of 5-year Treasury notes at 8-1/2%. They are selling at 95 so each contract is $95,000 (see Table 8), and the margin is 1.5%. Three months later, interest rates have declined, and the notes are selling at 99.4 (i.e., 99-4/32). If both the buying and selling commissions are $480, what is the total yield?

Figure 18

Futures Prices

Open Interest Reflects Previous Trading Day.

- FINANCIAL -

BRITISH POUND (IMM) – 25,000 pounds; $ per pound

	Open	High	Low	Settle	Change	Lifetime High	Lifetime Low	Open Interest
Dec	1.4950	1.5010	1.4925	1.4945	– .0005	1.6425	1.4460	17,277
Mar	1.4960	1.5015	1.4950	1.4955	– .0010	1.6010	1.4470	1,790
June	....	....	....	1.4965	– .0015	1.5400	1.4860	201
Sept	....	....	....	1.4975	– .0020	1.5240	1.5050	3

Est vol 4,347; vol Thur 8,161; open Int 19,271, +1,213.

CANADIAN DOLLAR (IMM) – 100,000 dlrs.; $ per Can $

	Open	High	Low	Settle	Change	Lifetime High	Lifetime Low	Open Interest
Dec	.8120	.8126	.8120	.8124	+ .0006	.8171	.8005	4,204
Mar	.8127	.8130	.8126	.8127	+ .0005	.8169	.8040	973
June	.8129	.8130	.8129	.8130	+ .0006	.8168	.8100	192
Sept		....	....	.8132	+ .0005	.8147	8128	2

Est vol '942; vol Thur 736; open Int 5,371, – 197.

JAPANESE YEN (IMM) 12.5 million yen; $ per yen (.00)

	Open	High	Low	Settle	Change	Lifetime High	Lifetime Low	Open Interest
Dec	.4260	.4281	.4260	.4271	+ .0021	.4416	.4082	35,336
Mar	.4293	.4309	.4293	.4302	+ .0022	.4329	.4125	1,540
June	.4335	.4335	.4343	.4335	+ .0023	.4335	.4180	100

Est vol 14,371; vol Thur 13.634; open Int 36 976, - 806

SWISS FRANC (IMM) – 125,000 francs-$ per franc

	Open	High	Low	Settle	Change	Lifetime High	Lifetime Low	Open Interest
Dec	.4757	.4782	.4754	.4774	+ .0025	.5450	.4634	28,512
Mar	.4815	.4842	.4815	.4832	+ .0026	.5170	.4695	1,282
June		....	....	.4870	+ .0012	.5045	.4752	74
Sept		....	....	.4935	+ .0020	.4945	.4844	8

Est vol 20,053; vol Thur 14,253; open Int 29,876, – 340.

W. GERMAN MARK (IMM) - 125,000 marks; $ per mark

	Open	High	Low	Settle	Change	Lifetime High	Lifetime Low	Open Interest
Dec	.3821	.3839	.3820	.3835	+ .0014	.4400	.3710	25,781
Mar	.3858	.3872	.3858	.3871	+ .0015	.4100	.3758	1,933
June		....	....	.3904	+ .0007	.3960	.3813	74
Sept		....	....	.3943	+ .0015	3946	.3885	14

Est vol 9,887; vol Thur 9,315; open Int 27,802, + 1,504.

EURODOLLAR (IMM) – $1 million; pts of 100%

	Open	High	Low	Settle	Chg	Yield Settle	Yield Chg	Open Interest
Dec	90.03	90.11	90.01	90.09	+ .09	9.91	– .09	16,319
Mar	89.66	89.74	89.65	89.72	+ .09	10.28	– .09	12,033
June	89.38	89.46	89.38	89.46	+ .11	10.54	– .11	4,940
Sept	89.13	89.19	89.13	89.19	+ .07	10.81	– .07	745
Dec	88.86	88.92	88.86	88.92	+ .04	11.08	.04	65
Mar	....	....	....	88.72	+ .04	11.28	.04	26

Est vol 2,783; vol Thur 3,164; open Int 34,128, + 794.

GNMA 8% (CBT) - $100,000 prncpl; pts. 32nds. of 100%

	Open	High	Low	Settle	Chg	Yield Settle	Yield Chg	Open Interest
Dec	68-31	69-05	68-27	68-27	– 1	13.408	+ .008	26,300
Mar.	68-02	68-08	67-29	67-29	– 2	13.625	+ .015	10,568
June	67-16	67-16	67-06	67-06	– 2	13.794	+ .015	4,163
Sept	....	....	....	66-21	– 2	13.921	+ .015	1,321
Dec	66-14	66-14	66-07	66-07	– 2	14.027	+ .016	1,389
Mar	....	....	....	65-27	– 2	14.118	+ .015	187
June	....	....	....	65-17	– 2	14.195	+ .016	282
Sept	65-11	65-11	65-09	65-09	– 2	14.257	+ .016	131
Dec				65-03	– 2	14.30[illegible]		2[illegible]

Futures Options

Chicago Board of Trade

TREASURY BONDS – $100,000; points and 64ths of 100%

Strike Price	Calls – Last Dec	Calls – Last Mar	Calls – Last Jun	Puts – Last Dec	Puts – Last Mar	Puts – Last Jun
66	6-47	....	....	0-02	0-30	....
68	4-49	4-55	5-00	0-07	0-54	....
70	3-08	3-37	3-58	0-25	1-27	....
72	1-48	2-28	2-60	0-61	2-16	....
74	0-53	1-41	2-09	2-00	3-25	....
76	0-19	1-01	....	3-38	4-46	....
78	0-07	0-42	....	4-46	....	....
80	0-03	0-21	....	....	....	....
82	0-01	....	....	....	....	....

Est. total vol. 7,500
Calls: Thurs. vol. 3,904; open int. 41,354
Puts: Thurs. vol. 2,465; open int. 17,287

Comex, New York

GOLD – 100 troy ounces; dollars per troy ounce.

Strike Price	Calls – Last Dec	Calls – Last Feb	Calls – Last Apr	Puts – Last Dec	Puts – Last Feb	Puts – Last Apr
380	29.00	....	....	2.80	5.00	5.50
400	14.50	23.00	29.50	6.50	8.50	11.50
420	5.30	12.50	19.00	16.50	18.00	19.00
440	1.70	7.00	11.50	33.00	30.50	30.50
460	.60	3.70	7.00	52.00	46.50	45.00
480	.20	2.40	3.80	72.00	....	61.00
500	.10	....	2.60	92.00	....	80.00
530	.10	....	1.50	....	....	....
560	.10	....	....	....	....	....
590	.10	....	....	....	....	....
620	.10	....	....	....	....	....

Est. total vol. 4,500
Calls: Thurs vol. 1,706; open int. 15,457
Puts: Thurs vol. 676; open int. 6,535

Chicago Mercantile Exchange

S&P 500 STOCK INDEX – Price = $500 times premium.

Strike Price	Calls – Settle Dec	Calls – Settle Mar	Calls – Settle Jun	Puts – Settle Dec	Puts – Settle Mar
135	....	....	....	....	....
140	....	....	....	....	....
145	....	....	....	.05	....
150	....	....	....	.20	....
155	13.80	....	....	.50	1.70
160	9.45	12.85	....	1.20	....
165	5.65	9.60	....	2.40	....
170	3.00	6.40	....	4.80	6.25
175	1.50	4.40	....	8.20	....
180	.75	3.10	....	12.40	....
185	.35	....	4.00	....	....

Estimated total vol. 771
Calls: Thurs vol. 138; open int. 5,256
Puts: Thurs vol. 48; open int. 1,225

N.Y. Futures Exchange

NYSE Composite Index – Price = $500 times premium.

Strike Price	Calls – Settle Dec.	Calls – Settle Mar.	Calls – Settle Jun.	Puts – Settle Dec.	Puts – Settle Mar.	Puts – Settle Jun.
90	7.65	....	....	.35	1.25	....
92	6.00	7.80	....	.70	1.75	....
94	4.45	6.50	....	1.15	2.45	....
96	3.10	5.30	7.05	1.80	3.25	4.25
98	2.20	4.10	6.05	2.90	4.15	5.25
100	1.45	3.30	5.15	4.15	5.25	6.35
102	.85	2.60	4.35	5.55	6.55	7.55
104	.55	2.00	3.65	7.25	7.95	8.85
106	.25	1.60	....	....	....	....

Estimated total vol. 952
Calls: Thurs. vol. 524; open int. 4,601
Puts: Thurs. vol. 42; open int. 3,726

Table 8. EXCHANGES, CONTRACT SIZE, AND MINIMUM MARGIN FOR MOST FINANCIAL FUTURES

	Exchange*	Contract Size	Minimum Margin/Contract	
			Speculators	Hedgers
Debt Instruments				
Treasury Bills	I.M.M.	$1,000,000	$1,500	$1,500
Treasury Notes	C.B.T.	100,000	1,500	1,500
Treasury Bonds	C.B.T.	100,000	2,000	1,500
Bank and Eurodollar CDs	I.M.M.	1,000,000	1,500	1,500
GNMA Certificates	C.B.T.	100,000	2,000	1,500
Foreign Currencies				
British	I.M.M.	25,000 pounds	1,500	1,500
Canadian	I.M.M.	100,000 U.S. dollars	900	900
Japanese	I.M.M.	2,500,000 yen	1,500	1,500
Swiss	I.M.M.	125,000 francs	2,000	2,000
German	I.M.M.	125,000 marks	1,500	1,500
Stock Indices				
NYSE	N.Y.F.E.	Index × $500	3,500	1,500
S&P 500	C.M.E.	Index × $500	6,000	3,000
Value Line	K.C.B.T.	Index × $500	6,500	2,500

***International Monetary Market (I.M.M.); Chicago Board of Trade (C.B.T.); New York Futures Exchange (N.Y.F.E.); Chicago Mercantile Exchange (C.M.E.); and Kansas City Board of Trade (K.C.B.T.). Eurodollar is a deposit of a dollar-denominated outside of the U.S. (but begun in Europe).**

SOLUTION: In this example,

p_{c1} = \$95,000, $m = 0.015$, p_{c2} = \$99,125, and $c_1 = c_2$ = \$480.

Now

A = \$99,125

B = \$95,000 + \$480 + \$480 = \$95,960, and

C = 0.015×\$95,000 + \$480 = \$1,905.

The total yield is

$$Y = \frac{\$99{,}125 - \$95{,}960}{\$1{,}905} = \frac{\$3{,}165}{\$1{,}905} = 1.6614 = 166.14\%.$$

THE YIELD CURVE

The profitability of investments in financial instruments depends upon future interest rates. This is true for the spot (cash) markets as well as for the futures markets. Forecasting interest rates is very difficult; many investors believe investing in interest-bearing issues can be aided by studying the yields on several similar investments with different maturities.* Generally, investments with longer maturities provide higher yields because of the greater risk inherent in their extensive term. Yield curves drawn as a function of maturity date exhibiting this pattern (i.e., a continually decreasing positive slope) are considered to be normal. Figure 19 shows a normal yield curve and an abnormal one.

Figure 19

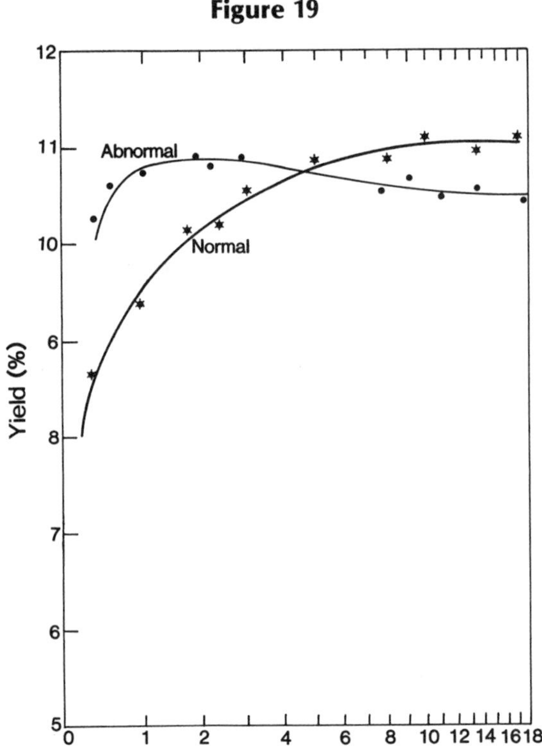

*These yields are bond equivalent yields.

Some data defining the curve will fail to lie on the smooth curve because

- An abnormally high yield might result from a large issue;
- An abnormally low yield might result from an issue that matures near a tax date (i.e., bought heavily for sale near that date); or
- Some special characteristics of some issues, such as those required to pay federal estate tax when owed by a decedent. These "flower bonds" are accepted at par and are in great demand.

The normal yield curve exists when investors have no strong feeling about a change in interest rates. That is, a curve that deviates from the normal does so usually because of investors' unusual expectations. The abnormal curve in Figure 19 would exist because investors believe interest rates will rise and they seek the relatively high rates for a long period of time; this demand causes the price to rise and the yield to fall. However, an investor using the yield curve might believe that the abnormal situation will probably return to the normal. Hence, he will buy issues with short maturities as he believes their yield will fall because the price will rise.

PART VI
Is Life Insurance An Investment?

A life insurance policy is a contract in which the insuring company promises to pay certain sums of money (called benefits) upon death or other contingency of human life. In turn, the policyholder promises to pay to the company periodic sums of money (called premiums). The policyholder need not be the insured.

Life insurance is not a typical investment and, in some cases, not an investment at all. However, the annual premiums and benefits can be so substantial that they can influence an investment plan. At the least, life insurance is a hedge against the ultimate loss.

The following chapters discuss the types of policies that can be purchased, how premiums are determined, a reasonable insurance-investment plan, and the yield on policies.

CHAPTER 10
What Type of Policy Is Best for You?

Life insurance policies can allow the holder to participate in the profits of the company (called participation policies) or not (called nonparticipation policies). They can also provide pure protection in the event of death, or provide some protection together with a "savings account."

All states require life insurance companies to maintain a certain reserve of capital. To comply, the company estimates its income from premiums and interest and its expenses from benefits paid and operating expenses. However, to provide a cushion for the unexpected, it sells policies that allow participation in the profits of the company. Those who purchase these policies provide the cushion by paying unusually large premiums.* Then some of the premium not needed to meet the reserve requirement is returned (but usually only after the policy is 1 to 3 years old) and *called* a dividend. These "dividends" can be taken in the form of:

- cash paid to the policyholder,
- a premium-reducing sum that is retained by the company,
- an interest-bearing sum that is retained by the company, or
- a face-value increasing sum that is retained by the company.

The dividends are not taxable (since they are merely a return of excess premium), and they are paid at different rates, depending upon the companies' anticipated needs and desires. Most companies begin with smaller dividends that are increased over the term of the policy, but some do the opposite. Dividend requirements that differ among companies render participation policies more difficult to evaluate than are nonparticipating policies.

---

*About 50% higher (than for nonparticipating policies) for younger policyholders and 25% higher for older policyholders.

Consider the following three types of policies that provide pure protection and three types that mix protection with a savings account.

POLICIES WITH PURE PROTECTION

Policies with pure protection are called term policies, and the benefits are paid only if the insured dies during the term of the policy.

One-Year Renewable Term Insurance

One-year renewable term insurance is renewable each year and, because the probability of dying increases each year, the premiums also increase each year. This policy can be renewed until age 100 (age 75 in some states), and then it can be converted to another type of policy. It can be purchased for group life insurance, and appeals to those whose future financial obligations are uncertain.

Level Term Insurance

Level term insurance is modeled after property insurance. Both the annual premiums and the face value remain constant over the term. Terms are usually 5, 10, 15, 20, 25, and 30 years, or until age 65.

A variation of this type of policy can be obtained by paying an additional premium in the first year in exchange for lower annual premiums. Insurance companies incur large costs from lapsed policies, and this variation tends to discourage lapsing. The following transpires when the policy is not allowed to lapse:

- If the policyholder is alive at its term, at least twice the additional premium is returned.
- If the policyholder is not alive at its term, the additional premium is given to the beneficiary; some companies also add the accumulated interest.

Decreasing Term Insurance

The premium in decreasing term insurance is constant, but the benefits decrease with time. This policy appeals to those whose obligations also decrease with time, e.g., a father whose children are grown. Another example of a decreasing obligation is the decreasing balance of a mortgage loan; in fact, the face value generally decreases at this rate (making it similar to mortgage insurance). One-year renewable term insurance (above) can be used as decreasing term insurance if the face value decreases with each renewal. Family income plans are essentially decreasing term policies.

POLICIES WITH SOME PROTECTION AND SOME SAVINGS

These policies provide some protection and they provide cash (surrender) value as well. The cash value increases with time and protection decreases with time. The sum of the two is never less than the face value. That is, if cash value exceeds the face value, the excess is retained by the company.

The policyholder can always either borrow an amount as large as the cash value or take the cash; however, cash is not available until the policy is 1 to 3 years old. If the policyholder borrows cash and then the insured dies, the beneficiary receives the face value less the loan balance.* On the other hand, the policyholder must surrender the policy if he takes the cash (for this reason, cash value is often called surrender value).** The cash value is not taxable until it exceeds the difference between the sum of the premiums and the sum of the dividends. Most policies permit the company as long as six months to either grant a loan or permit withdrawal of cash.

Three types of policies that mix protection with cash value are: ordinary life, limited payment life, and endowment life insurance. (All cash value policies can be considered to be endowment policies.)

Ordinary Life Insurance

Ordinary life insurance (also called whole or straight life insurance) requires constant annual premiums over the life of the insured. The face value remains constant, but after a period of time, the pure protection is gradually replaced by cash value. Its term extends to the insured's 100th birthday. This policy has been the most popular; however, its long term, coupled with the fear of inflation, has diminished its appeal. (For instance, the risk inherent to long-term investments causes long-term financial instruments to bear higher interest rates than do short-term instruments.)

Most ordinary life insurance policies can be converted to an annuity policy (e.g., at age 65). In this case, monthly payments are made either only to the policyholder until his death, or to the policyholder until his death and then to his heirs for a fixed number of years.*** Once it is converted to an annuity policy, it is no longer a life insurance policy; in fact, it rewards living: Life insurance protects against early death, and an annuity policy protects against late death.

---

*As an alternative, he may borrow from other lenders and use the cash value as collateral.

**There are alternatives to surrender: the policy can be kept at a reduced face value or converted to a term policy.

***At the rate of about 0.7% per month of face value.

Limited Payment Life Insurance

Limited payment life insurance is identical to ordinary life insurance with one exception: the premium is paid either over the remaining life of the insured or over a predetermined number of years (whichever occurs first). Generally, premiums are paid for 20 years, 30 years, or until age 65.

Naturally, these premiums are higher than for ordinary life insurance premiums. Even though it is comforting to anticipate the early termination of paying premiums, there are some disadvantages to this type of policy:

- High premiums occur when most policyholders can least afford them (e.g., the coexistence of young, dependent children coupled with lower beginning salaries).
- The future value of the premiums is higher than those of ordinary life insurance; i.e., higher premiums paid sooner earn more interest for the company, not the policyholder.
- If inflation occurs over the remaining life of the insured, the fixed benefits will have diminished value relative to the higher premiums which were paid earlier.

Endowment Life Insurance

Endowment life insurance has a fixed face value. The constant premiums are paid by the policyholder either over the term or until the death of the insured, whichever occurs first.*

If the insured dies before the term, the face value is paid to the beneficiary and is not taxed. Otherwise, the face value is paid to the policyholder. This amount can be paid in a single payment at the term or in a series of monthly payments for as long as the insured lives (or even to the beneficiary after the policyholder dies, if desired).

The premiums on an endowment policy are very high compared to other types of life insurance. For example, a 20-year endowment policy for $50,000 purchased at age 35 can have annual premiums of $2,200.

It should be mentioned that features of the policies discussed here can be combined (to confound potential policyholders further). Some say that combination policies include what the policyholder needs and what the insurance salesman wants.

---

*It is possible to have larger premiums paid over a period shorter than the term. Such an arrangement is similar to that of limited payment life insurance.

CHAPTER 11
How Premiums Are Determined

When investigating premiums, you must begin with the mortality table. Periodically, deaths among a random large number of American males and females are observed separately. The number that die before each age (from 0 through 100) is noted. From this information, the methods of mathematical statistics are employed to determine the expected remaining life for each age and sex. This information is listed for males in Table 9 and illustrated in Figure 20.* For example, a 30-year-old male has an expected remaining life of 41.25 years. Since the rate of death increases with age, so too must the rate of the cost of insurance, the premium.

The premium is known in the industry as the gross premium. The gross premium is the net premium plus an amount called loading.

THE NET PREMIUM

The net premium is determined mathematically, using the mortality table and the concept of the present value of an annuity. The company makes the following three assumptions

- The mortality of insureds will be that as given in the table.
- Premiums are invested when received at the annual rate of interest, r.
- The present value of the premiums and interest received equals the present value of the benefits (i.e., the company is assumed to have no expenses, profits, losses, etc.). The present value calculations use the interest rate, r. (See Appendix C.)

Since premiums are received over many years, the interest rate, r, cannot be a current rate; rather, it is a nominal conservative rate that is "certain" to be obtained over those years. In fact, the achieved rate should

*This table, called the Commissioners' Standard Table, was last tabulated in 1958 from data collected between 1950 and 1954. To adapt this information to females, add 3 to the expected remaining life after age 12. Since people live longer now, policyholders pay more premiums, and the company can invest the benefits for a longer period of time.

Table 9. COMMISSIONERS' 1958 STANDARD ORDINARY MORTALITY TABLE FOR MALES

Age	Expectation of Life	Age	Expectation of Life
0	68.30	50	23.63
1	67.78	51	22.82
2	66.90	52	22.03
3	66.00	53	21.25
4	65.10	54	20.47
5	64.19	55	19.71
6	63.27	56	18.97
7	62.35	57	18.23
8	61.43	58	17.51
9	60.51	59	16.81
10	59.58	60	16.12
11	58.65	61	15.44
12	57.72	62	14.78
13	56.80	63	14.14
14	55.87	64	13.51
15	54.95	65	12.90
16	54.03	66	12.31
17	53.11	67	11.73
18	52.19	68	11.17
19	51.28	69	10.64
20	50.37	70	10.12
21	49.46	71	9.63
22	48.55	72	9.15
23	47.64	73	8.69
24	46.73	74	8.24
25	45.82	75	7.81
26	44.90	76	7.39
27	43.99	77	6.98
28	43.08	78	6.59
29	42.16	79	6.21
30	41.25	80	5.85
31	40.34	81	5.51
32	39.43	82	5.19
33	38.51	83	4.89
34	37.60	84	4.60
35	36.69	85	4.32
36	35.78	86	4.06
37	34.88	87	3.80
38	33.97	88	3.55
39	33.07	89	3.31
40	32.18	90	3.06
41	31.29	91	2.82
42	30.41	92	2.58
43	29.54	93	2.33
44	28.67	94	2.07
45	27.81	95	1.80
46	26.95	96	1.51
47	26.11	97	1.18
48	25.27	98	.83
49	24.45	99	.50

Figure 20

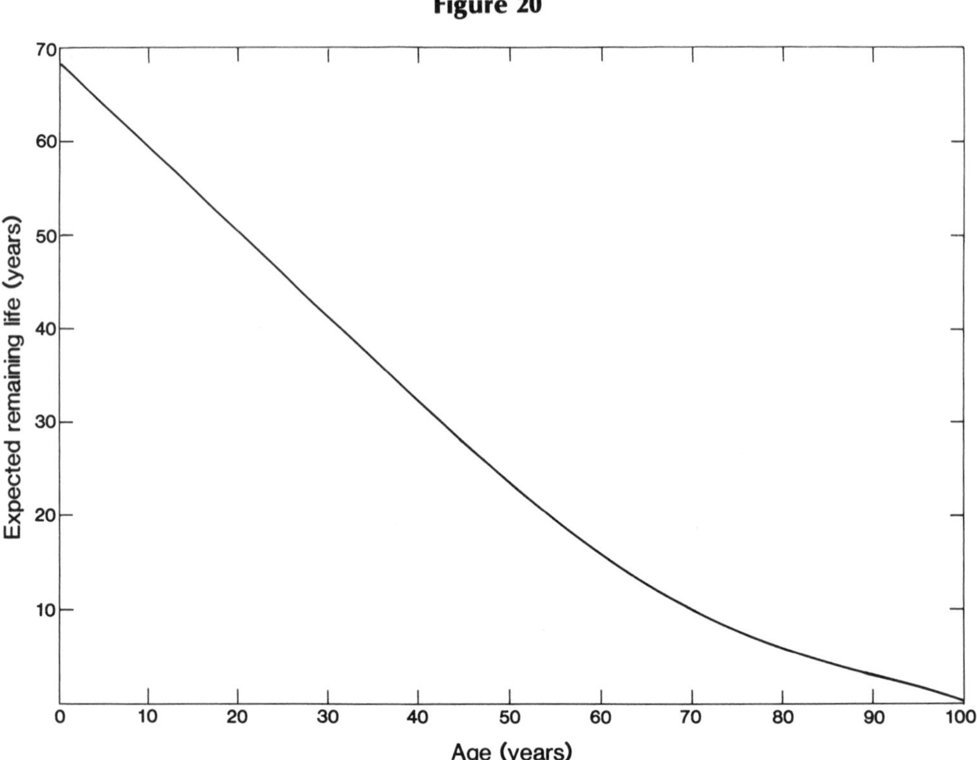

be comfortably higher. The nominal rate of 4.5% is widely used. Interest is received from loans to policyholders from their savings account, investments in bonds, etc.

The net premiums for all life insurance policies are actuarially equal. This means that if your premiums were net premiums, your investments also were to draw interest at the rate r, and you were to live the expected remaining number of years, you could not financially favor one policy over another.

The following formulas can be used to determine the annual net premium for four common types of policies.

FORMULAS:

$$
u = \begin{cases}
\dfrac{1}{1.045} - \dfrac{L_{j+1}}{L_j} & \text{Ordinary Life} \\[2ex]
\dfrac{\dfrac{L_j}{1.045} - L_{j+1}}{L_j - L_{j+n}} & \text{Limited Payment Life} \\[2ex]
\dfrac{1}{1.045} - \dfrac{L_{j+1} - L_{j+n+1}}{L_j - L_{j+n}} & \text{Level Term Life*} \\[2ex]
\dfrac{1}{1.045} - \dfrac{L_{j+1} - L_{j+n}}{L_j - L_{j+n}} & \text{Endowment Life}
\end{cases}
$$

where

u = annual net premium for a policy whose face value is 1.

then

j = age (in years) of male insured when policy is purchased; for females subtract 3 years after age 12.

L_i = a function listed in Table 10. It is computed using the interest rate 4.5% and i years where i represents j, j+1, j+n, or j+n+1 in the formulas.**

n = number of years over which the annual premiums are to be paid (same as the term except for limited payment life).

EXAMPLE (Ordinary Life): As a 35-year-old male, you purchase a $100,000 ordinary life insurance policy. What is your annual net premium?

---

*This is the formula for one year renewable term insurance if n=1.

**This rate varies among companies and states. The function L in the formulas is the same as the function N in actuarial tables, except that L has been normalized so that L_{99}=1.00.

Table 10. VALUES OF A FUNCTION USED TO COMPUTE ANNUAL NET INSURANCE PREMIUMS

i	L_i	i	L_i	i	L_i	i	L_i
0	2605175.79	50	168435.37	25	754959.37	75	12371.72
1	2483468.64	51	156628.90	26	716182.16	76	10520.17
2	2367827.05	52	145424.85	27	679146.41	77	8878.36
3	2257360.00	53	134800.94	28	643774.96	78	7431.64
4	2151810.59	54	124735.77	29	609994.05	79	6165.87
5	2050953.83	55	115208.93	30	577733.43	80	5067.32
6	1954575.30	56	106200.81	31	546926.24	81	4122.46
7	1862471.55	57	97692.67	32	517508.46	82	3317.73
8	1774448.57	58	89666.61	33	489419.14	83	2639.55
9	1690322.19	59	82105.51	34	462599.88	84	2074.41
10	1609917.49	60	74993.02	35	436995.05	85	1608.99
11	1533068.30	61	68313.34	36	412551.63	86	1230.41
12	1459617.38	62	62051.31	37	389219.51	87	926.52
13	1389415.88	63	56192.21	38	366951.07	88	685.97
14	1322322.05	64	50721.71	39	345701.22	89	498.39
15	1258202.18	65	45625.88	40	325427.65	90	354.48
16	1196928.75	66	40891.10	41	306090.15	91	246.02
17	1138379.49	67	36504.06	42	287650.69	92	165.91
18	1082437.77	68	32451.79	43	270073.03	93	108.09
19	1028991.75	69	28721.52	44	253322.44	94	67.48
20	977933.67	70	25300.67	45	237365.79	95	39.86
21	929159.28	71	22176.43	46	222171.39	96	21.80
22	882568.77	72	19335.59	47	207709.08	97	10.58
23	838066.13	73	16764.28	48	193950.24	98	4.15
24	795559.08	74	14448.02	49	180867.62	99	1.00

SOLUTION: In this example, j=35. From Table 10, L_{35}=436995.05, and L_{36}=412551.63. Now, the annual net premium for the amount 1 is

$$\begin{aligned} u &= \frac{1}{1.045} - \frac{412551.63}{436995.05} \\ &= 0.95693780 - 0.94406477 \\ &= 0.0128730. \end{aligned}$$

The annual net premium for a \$100,000 policy is

$$\$100{,}000 \times 0.0128730 = \$1{,}287.30.$$

LOADING

Loading is the other component of the (gross) premium. It is simply a term for the charge for a variety of the company's expenses and profits. Most expenses are normal operating expenses, but the following are policy-dependent:

- Cost of lapsed policies;
- Cost to administer the policy (higher for participating and cash value policies);
- Costs dependent upon the age of the insured; and
- Commissions paid to salesmen; they are much higher for ordinary life than for term policies.

The amount of loading varies, not only among types of policies but among companies as well.* However, it is said by the industry that loading is equitable among policyholders. At any rate, the variation in loading makes it difficult to compare policies, particularly for those with participation and cash value.

*Organizations that sell life insurance policies to their members have low operating expenses and usually less loading.

CHAPTER 12
How to Discover a Reasonable Insurance-Investment Plan

There is no substitute for the protection provided by insurance: Its ability to furnish certain and immediate protection is unique. Other investments can provide protection through appreciation, but this appreciation is not certain, usually is achieved only after a period of time, and often is not liquid.

However, there are many substitutes for the savings component of non-term policies. The yield from these policies is very low. Even though the cash value is almost certain to be available and is usually not taxable, these two features are not unique to life insurance. High-quality municipal bonds have these features and bear higher interest rates. Even though income from other investments might be taxable, the yield is sufficiently high to counter this feature.

Since it is imprudent to be unprotected, it makes no sense to compare other investments with the protection component of insurance. However, it makes very good sense to compare other investments with the savings component. A reasonable plan is to buy term insurance (for protection only) instead of buying a cash value type of policy, and invest the portion of the premium that you have saved.

EXAMPLE: Suppose a 35-year-old male requires $100,000 protection over 30 years. He can purchase a $100,000 ordinary life policy until age 99 with annual premiums of $2,000. The face value is constant, and it is represented by the horizontal line in Figure 21.* On the other hand, he can purchase a $100,000 level term policy for 30 years with annual premiums of $1,000. Then he can invest the difference of the two premiums (i.e., $1,000) annually at interest (in this case 6%, and compounded annually). This total value (protection plus investment) is shown in Figure 21 over 30 years, i.e., from age 35 to 65. At 30 years the level term policy matures (i.e., the protection vanishes), and the

*Some values in this example come from quantities that are compounded. Therefore, they are best represented on a semi-logarithmic scale.

Figure 21

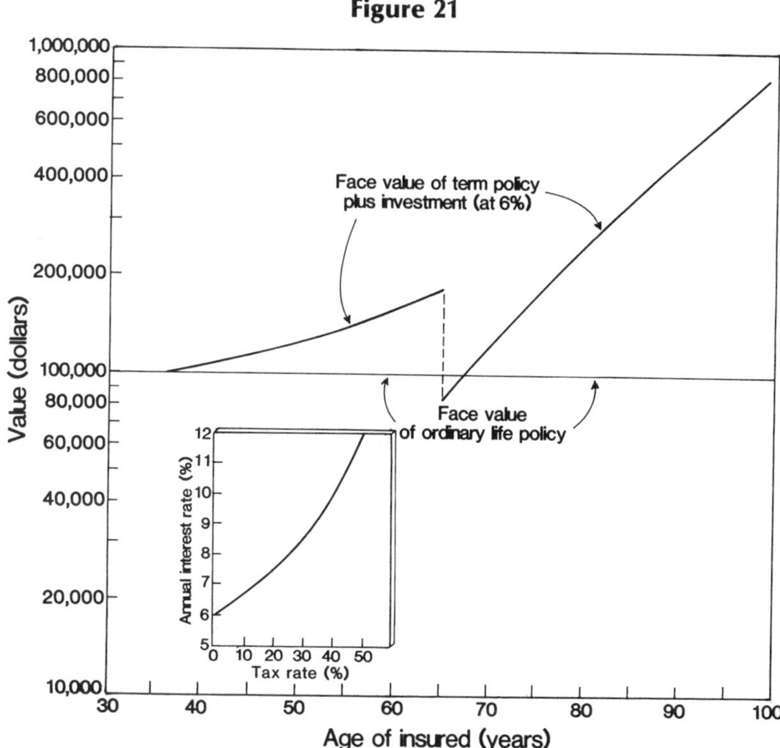

investment has a value of $83,801. From this time, he pays no premium, so he invests the $2,000 (still at 6% interest) annually until age 99. At age 99 the investment is worth $828,517, and the ordinary life policy is worth $100,000 (all cash value).

However, the comparison should not favor the protection plus investment alternative so overwhelmingly: the $100,000 cash value is tax-free, and interest on the investment would have been taxed annually as ordinary income. The small insert graph in Figure 21 shows how to account for tax in the example. That is, the figure is correct if each year you paid tax at 0% and earned 6% interest, paid tax at 20% and earned 7.5% interest, paid tax at 40% and earned 8.58% interest, etc.

The following formula can be used to compare the two strategies for any tax rate that is constant over the term of the investment.

FORMULAS:

$$v_o = v_{fo} \qquad 0 \le i < 99$$

$$v_t = \begin{cases} F + G & 0 \le i < n \\ (F'+G')/(a(r',q,q) & n \le i < 99 \end{cases}$$

where

v_o, v_t = value of ordinary life and term policy (plus investment), respectively

then

$F = (u_o - u_t) \cdot s(r', iq, q)/a(r', q, q)$

$F' = (u_o - u_t) \cdot s(r', nq, q) \cdot c[r', (i-n)q, q]$

$G = v_{ft}$

$G' = u_o \cdot s[r', (i-n)q, q]/a(r', q, q)$

i = number of years after insured

j = age of insured when insured, in years

n = term of policy, in years

q = number of interest periods per year for investment

r = annual interest rate on investment

$$r' = \begin{cases} r \text{ if tax is not considered} \\ r(1-r_t) \text{ if tax is considered} \end{cases}$$

t = income tax rate, expressed as a decimal

u_o, u_t = annual (gross) premium on ordinary life and term policy, respectively

v_{fo}, v_{ft} = face value of ordinary life and term policy, respectively

$a(r', q, q)$ = present value of an annuity of $1 (Table I)

$c[r', (i-n)q, q]$ = amount of $1 at compound interest (Table I)

$s[r', (i-n)q, q]$, $s[r', iq, q]$, and $s(r', nq, q)$ = amount of an annuity of $1 (Table I)

EXAMPLE: Using the above example, determine the value of these two investments after 10 years and 50 years, if (a) you purchase the ordinary life policy and pay annual premiums until your death or until you reach 99 years, and (b) you purchase the level term insurance policy and pay annual premiums, and annually invest the difference in the premiums (between ordinary life and term) at 8% compounded quarterly until your death or until you reach 99 years. You pay income tax at the rate of 25% each year.

SOLUTION: In this example,

$j = 35$, $v_{fo} = v_{ft} = \$100{,}000$, $n = 30$, $u_o = \$2{,}000$,

$u_t = \$1{,}000$, $i = 10$ and 50, $r = 8\%$, $r_t = 0.25$,

$r' = r(1-r_t) = 6\%$, and $q = 4$.

(a) The value of the ordinary life policy is constant: $v_o = \$100{,}000$.
(b) The value of the level term policy plus investment varies:

(i) When i = 10,

$F = (\$2{,}000-\$1{,}000) \cdot s(6,10\times4,4)/a(6,4,4)$, and
$G = \$100{,}000$.

From Table I, s(6,40,4)=54.26789, and a(6,4,4)=3.85438.
Now

$F = \$1{,}000\times54.26789/3.85438 = \$14{,}079.54$.

The value of the term policy and investment after 10 years is

$$v_t = \$14{,}079.54 + \$100{,}000 = \$114{,}079.54.$$

(ii) When i = 50,

$F' = (\$2{,}000-\$1{,}000) \cdot s(6,30\times4,4) \cdot c[6,(50-30)\times4,4]$, and

$G' = \$2{,}000 \cdot s[6,(50-30)\times4,4]$.

From Table I, s(6,120,4)=331.28819, c(16,80,4)=3.29066, s(6,80,4) = 152.71085, and a(6,4,4) = 3.85438.

Now

$F' = \$1{,}000\times331.28819\times3.29066 = \$1{,}090{,}156.80$, and

$G' = \$2{,}000\times152.71085 = \$305{,}421.70$.

The value of the term policy and investment after 50 years is

$$
\begin{aligned}
v_t &= (\$1{,}090{,}156.80+\$305{,}421.70)/3.85438 \\
&= \$1{,}395{,}578.50/3.85438 \\
&= \$362{,}076.00
\end{aligned}
$$

Hence, the $100,000 ordinary life policy is exceeded in value by the combination term policy and investment plan after 10 years (i.e., $114,590.49) and greatly exceeded after 50 years (i.e., $362,076.00).

CHAPTER 13
How to Determine the Yield on Your Policy

The yield from most investments is rather easy to imagine: It is the net amount gained for the amount required to obtain the investment. However, the yield from an insurance investment is not so easy to imagine:

- If the beneficiary is not the policyholder, the yield to the beneficiary is infinite, and the yield to the policyholder (in the case of term insurance) is zero. Even though these observations are technically true, the policyholder wouldn't purchase the policy if he didn't consider the interests of the beneficiary to be his interests also.
- The yield to the beneficiary occurs only upon the ultimate loss (death) and the yield is increased by early death of the insured (who is usually the policyholder).

Yield formulas can either account for the present value of money or not. If you would not invest otherwise, for any reason (because you believe that you must be insured), the present value is ignored and the factor b_k is simply, k (the number of premiums). If, instead you elect to invest the money spent as premiums, use the alternate formula for b_k (that treats the amount of the premium as an annual deposit in a sinking fund). The same statements apply to b_n.

FORMULAS:

Ordinary Life

$$Y = \frac{1}{ub_k} - 1$$

Limited Payment Life

$$Y = \begin{cases} \dfrac{1}{ub_k} & k \le n \\ \dfrac{1}{ub_n c(r,k-n,q)^*} - 1 & n < k \end{cases}$$

*If you choose $b_n = n$, then set $c(r,k-n,q) = 1$.

Level Term Life

$$Y = \begin{cases} \dfrac{1}{ub_k} - 1 & k \le n \\ -1 & n < k \end{cases}$$

Endowment Life

$$Y = \begin{cases} \dfrac{1}{ub_k} - 1 & k \le n \\ \dfrac{1}{ub_n} - 1 & n < k \end{cases}$$

where

Y = total yield on the investment

then

$$b_k = \begin{cases} s(r,kq,q)/a(r,q,q) & \text{if present value considered} \\ k & \text{if present value not considered} \end{cases}$$

$$b_n = \begin{cases} s(r,nq,q)/a(r,q,q) & \text{if present value considered} \\ n & \text{if present value not considered} \end{cases}$$

k = number of years insured lives after purchasing the policy

n = number of years over which annual premiums are to be paid (same as the term except for limited payment life)

q = number of investment periods per year

r = policyholder's usual rate of return on similar investments

u = annual (gross) premium on a life insurance policy whose face value is 1

y = $(1+Y)^{1/k}-1$ = annual yield on the investment

a(r,q,q) = present value of an annuity of 1 (Table I)

c(r,k−n,q) = amount of 1 at compound interest (Table I)

s(r,kq,q), s(r,nq,q) = amount of an annuity of 1 (Table I)

EXAMPLE: A 35-year-old male buys a 20-year limited payment life policy for $100,000. The annual premiums are $3,000. Determine the total yield if he dies 30 years later. Assume (a) the premiums would not have been invested otherwise, and (b) the premiums would have been invested in Treasury bonds that pay 8% interest semiannually.

SOLUTION: In this example,

$$n = 20,\ u = \$3{,}000/\$100{,}000 = 0.03, \text{ and } k = 30.$$

(a) In this case, $b_{30}=30$, and since $n<k$, $c(r,k-n,q)=1$. The total yield if the premiums had not been invested otherwise is

$$Y = \frac{1}{0.03 \times 30} - 1 = 0.111 = 11.1\%.$$

(b) In this case, $r = 8\%$, and $q = 2$.
Now,

$$b_n = s(r,nq,q)/a(r,q,q) = s(8,40,2)/a(8,2,2),$$

and

$$c(r,k-n,q) = c(8,10,2).$$

From Table I

$$b_{30} = 95.02552/1.886095 = 50.38215,$$

and

$$c(8,10,2) = 1.48024.$$

Finally, the total yield if the premiums had been invested in Treasury bonds is

$$Y = \frac{1}{0.03 \times 50.38215 \times 1.48024} - 1 = 0.447 - 1$$

$$= -0.553 = -55.3\%.$$

That is, if the premiums would have been invested in Treasury bonds, as they should have been; their return renders the negative yield from the policy.

PART VII
How to Measure the True Value of Collectibles

A collectible property is one that has rare quality or quantity. Collectors will purchase them for their quality; investors will purchase them for their quantity (and perhaps quality). Collectibles could include vacant land as well as the usual coins, stamps, paintings by well-known artists, antiques, cars, oriental rugs, etc.

People who invest in collectibles expect to profit when the demand for them exceeds the supply. Certainly, in many cases, it is difficult for supply to increase, i.e., the supply of coins, stamps, and cars cannot increase after their year of manufacture; the supply of antiques, oriental rugs, and paintings cannot really increase if they are valued for their period and artisan. However, with collectible property, even though each parcel of land is unique, the supply can increase when similar parcels become available—through demolition or altered use.

The demand for collectibles often depends on fashion and use, and is not so easily predicted. Collectible properties are not in great demand by investors when interest rates are high because they pay no interest.

Collectibles have several common features:

- They do not pay interest or dividends;
- They cost rent (for storage), insurance, or are taxed;
- Most are purchased at a considerable markup (an implicit commission), and sales tax is often charged; hence, they should be held for a long time;
- There is often a great lack of liquidity;
- Their price tends to keep up with inflation, particularly when interest rates are low or the economy is strong; and

- Any profit that results is from capital gain. The income tax on long-term capital gain is only 40% of that on ordinary income (that would result from interest and dividends).

An investor in collectibles should have a good estimate of his capital gain over the intended holding period. Then the following two methods can be employed to determine the annual yield and the present value of the collectible:

- Figure 22 converts the capital gain into an annual yield for holding periods up to 10 years. For example, a 400% increase over 7 years results from a 21.90% annual yield. The following formulas can be used to obtain these results for values not shown in the figure.
- Also, since the only profit from collectibles comes at the end of the holding period (which may be extensive), its present value, p_1, should be estimated. This value depends upon your estimate of its value at the end of the holding period and *your* usual rate of return on similar investments.

Figure 22

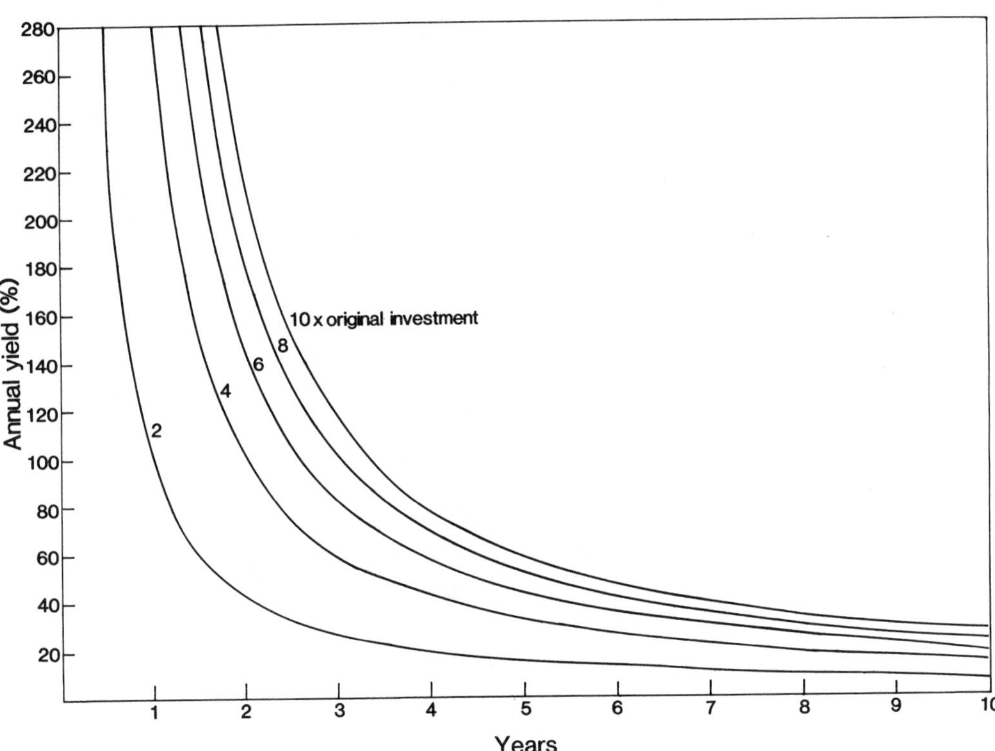

FORMULAS:

$$Y = \frac{p_2 - p_1 - c}{p_1}$$

$$y = (1+Y)^{1/t} - 1$$

$$p_1 = p_2 / c(y_r, t, 1)^*$$

where

Y = total yield on the investment

y = annual yield on the investment

p_1 = present value or purchase price, including sales tax

then

c = holding costs

p_2 = net sale price

t = holding period, in years

y_r = annual rate of return on similar investments

$c(y_r,t,1)$ = amount of 1 at compound interest (Table I)

EXAMPLE (Annual Yield): Jim Knowles bought some 1903 Liberty Head dollars 10 years ago for $1,000. He keeps them in a bank's safety deposit box for which he pays $2/month. If he could now sell them for 2-1/2 times his original investment, what would his annual yield be?

SOLUTION: In this example,

p_1 = \$1,000, t = 10 years, $c = 120 \times \$2 = \$240$, and

$p_2 = \$1{,}000 \times 2.5 = \$2{,}500$.

Now, the total yield is

$$Y = \frac{\$2{,}500 - \$1{,}000 - \$240}{\$1{,}000} = \frac{\$1{,}260}{\$1{,}000} = 126\%.$$

*For simplicity, the formula ignores holding costs.

The annual yield is

$$y = (1+1.26)^{1/10} - 1 = 2.26^{0.10} - 1 = 1.0850 - 1$$
$$= 0.0850 = 8.5\%.$$

EXAMPLE (Present Value): Suppose you expect a parcel of vacant land to be worth $300,000 in 7 years. Your annual rate of return on similar investments is about 15%. Ignoring holding costs, what is the present value of the parcel (to you)?

SOLUTION: In this example,

$$p_2 = \$300{,}000,\ t = 7, \text{ and } y_r = 15\%.$$

From Table I

$$c(15,7,1) = 2.66002.$$

Now, the present value of the parcel is

$$p_1 = \frac{\$300{,}000}{2.66002} = \$112{,}781.$$

This is the maximum price you should pay for the land if your prediction is true.

PART VIII
How to Understand a Real Estate Investment

A real estate investment can take many forms: vacant land, residential rental buildings, office buildings, warehouses, shopping centers, commercial buildings, etc. However, with the exception of vacant land, they can all be viewed in much the same way. They usually involve leverage, mortgage loans, rental income, operating expenses, depreciation, and similar income tax computations.

WHY REAL ESTATE INVESTMENTS ARE GENERALLY PROFITABLE

Due to inflation, leverage, and the tax advantages of real estate ownership, great profits have been obtained even by relatively unsophisticated investors.

Improved real estate exists because of the contributions of land, labor, capital, entrepreneurs, and the many different building materials available. Therefore, in the absence of periodic supply and demand fluctuations of local real estate markets, it is only natural to expect its value to follow prevailing prices.

In addition, because real estate is usually a leveraged investment (similar to margin in the futures markets), inflation can provide unusually large profits. For example, suppose a rental house is purchased for $60,000 using a $15,000 down payment and a $45,000 mortgage loan. If the value of the house increases by 10% to $66,000, the $15,000 investment has a value of $15,000 + $6,000 = $21,000, a 40% increase. (Actually, it is greater because the loan principal has also been reduced somewhat.)

Furthermore, income tax laws greatly favor real estate over other investments. They permit deducting loan interest, operating expenses, and depreciation of the improved portion (as well as personal property) at a rate that greatly exceeds accrued depreciation. Then, if the property is sold by the installment method, the capital gain is taxed at a rate even lower than the 40% of ordinary income that is available to other investments qualifying for a long-term gain; in this case, it is not unusual to pay tax on capital gain at the rate of only 13% of the ordinary income rate.

However, it is often difficult to estimate the profits and yield from a real estate investment because of its many components, most of which require some degree of computation. (For one method of doing this, see the ten-step procedure diagram and the corresponding forms on which the values can be listed in Chapter 5.) The example on page 211 shows how a rather typical real estate investment produces an annual yield of 27% before tax and 24% after tax!

THE COMPONENTS OF A REAL ESTATE INVESTMENT

Scheduled gross income is the maximum income a property can generate. Effective gross income is the income received. Therefore, the effective gross income is the scheduled gross income less vacancies and collection losses.

Vacancies and collection losses tend to increase when there is a surplus of comparable properties, when scheduled rent exceeds the economic rent, or when the tenant fails to pay.

Effective gross income is often used as a measure of property value. The gross income multiplier is the ratio of the property value-to-annual-effective gross income. For instance, a property offered for $480,000 with an annual effective gross income of $80,000 is said to be "offered at six times gross." When comparing similar properties, the gross income multiplier is probably a good measure of value.

Net operating income is effective gross income less operating expenses (e.g., property taxes, utilities, maintenance, etc). The net income multiplier is the ratio of property value-to-annual-net operating income.* Among similar properties, the net operating income can vary widely due to management decisions concerning maintenance expenses or due to irregularly occurring large expenses such as roof and furnace repair. Older properties, for example, often have extensive maintenance costs.

Cash flow is net operating income less debt service. When property values are anticipated to increase, property is often bought even though

*The property capitalization rate (page 162) is the reciprocal of this ratio.

the cash flow is zero or negative; the buyer anticipates his reward in the form of future cash flow and capital gain. On the other hand, when property values are expected to remain stable or even fall, buyers must be lured by financing arranged to provide favorable cash flow, a small down payment, etc.

Cash flow is used to determine the rate of return for the owner (the equity investor). If cash flow is computed before income tax, it is called cash throw-off, and if it is computed after income tax, it is called net spendable income.

Figure 23 depicts these demands on scheduled gross income. In it, you'll see that scheduled gross income first goes to "other" (appearing in the form of vacancies and collection losses). The resulting effective gross income first serves land and labor (operating expenses). Then the resulting net operating income serves capital (debt service). Finally, the remainder serves entrepreneurship (cash flow). Notice the similarity between the entrepreneur in real estate and the common stock investor: both are the last to be served from earnings.

Figure 23

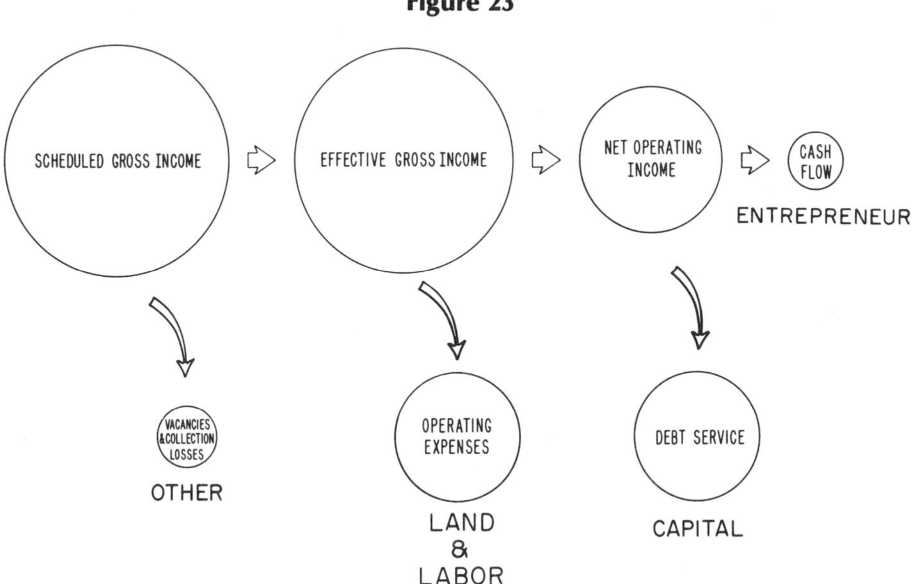

CHAPTER 14
How Real Estate Is Appraised

Real estate value can be estimated by the most cursory of investigations (such as by using the gross multiple) or by an extensive program of data collection and statistical analysis. Whether the investor consults a professional appraiser or estimates value himself, it is important to know the methods employed by the professional: the cost, income, and market approaches.*

The cost approach uses the current reproduction cost of an improvement and subtracts its estimated accrued depreciation. The estimated value of the land is then added to this value to estimate the property value.

The income approach uses the annual net operating income of the property and the estimated current capitalization rate of similar properties. Then, depending on the judgment of the appraiser, one of several possible formulas is used to estimate property values.

The market approach, the most fundamental of the three, uses sampling of recent comparable sales to estimate the property value.

It is interesting to note that the cost approach relies on the present (reproduction cost) and the past (accrued depreciation); the income approach relies on the present (income and capitalization rate) and the future (income and reversion); and the market approach relies on the present (comparable sales).

Table 11 lists the approaches to value that are generally appropriate for properties with certain characteristics.

An appraiser will use as many of the three approaches as are applicable to the subject property. Then, he will use his judgment to assign weights to each approach to obtain a single estimate of fair market

---

*Real estate appraisal is similar to determining stock value from the fundamental approach.

Table 11. APPROACHES TO VALUE THAT ARE APPROPRIATE FOR SOME PROPERTIES

		Approaches to value that are appropriate		
		Cost	Income	Market*
Property Characteristics	Newer improvement without income potential	X		X
	Newer improvement with income potential	X	X	X
	Older improvement without income potential			X
	Older improvement with income potential		X	X
	No improvement without income potential			X
	No improvement with income potential		X	X

***The market method can't be used when there are no recent comparable sales.**

value.* Although this process is called reconciliation or correlation, it is simply a weighted average of the three approaches to value.

EXAMPLE: Suppose a property has been appraised at $50,000, $52,000, and $49,000 by the cost, income, and market approaches, respectively. Also suppose that, because of the peculiarities of the subject property, the appraiser feels the respective approaches should be weighted by 60%, 10%, and 30%.** Then, if v_p is the final estimate of property value, we have:

$$\begin{aligned} v_p &= 0.60 \times \$50{,}000 + 0.10 \times \$52{,}000 + 0.30 \times \$49{,}000 \\ &= \$30{,}000 + \$5{,}200 + \$14{,}700 \\ &= \$49{,}900. \end{aligned}$$

The following discusses the important aspects of the cost, income, and market approaches.

---

*Fair market value, as defined by the courts, is "the price that a property will bring in a competitive market under all conditions requisite to a fair sale which would result from negotiations between a buyer and a seller, each acting prudently, with knowledge and without undue pressure." Value can be distorted by legal aspects of property, by need for a quick sale, etc.

The importance of judgment in all aspects of appraisal can't be overemphasized; appraising is not an exact science, and there are many conceivable ways in which a property can fail to fit guidelines.

**Of course, each weight must be non-negative, and the three must sum to 1.

COST APPROACH

The cost approach to value estimates the reproduction cost of the improvement, subtracts the estimated accrued depreciation, and then adds the estimated value of the land (as if vacant):

$$\begin{aligned} \text{property value} &= \text{(reproduction cost of improvement)} \\ &\quad - \text{(accrued depreciation of improvement)} \\ &\quad + \text{(value of land).} \end{aligned}$$

This approach to value is used most often to appraise newer properties (because accrued depreciation is difficult to estimate in older properties), and properties for which the other two approaches to value cannot be used. For instance, the income approach cannot be used for properties without income potential, and the market approach cannot be used for properties that are rarely sold (e.g., institutional properties such as churches, schools, libraries, etc.). The cost approach is also used whenever the value of the improvement must be separated from the value of the land such as required for ad valorem taxations, accounting, feasibility studies, etc.

Since the cost approach to value utilizes three distinct components (reproduction cost, accrued depreciation, and land value), it is useful to examine them separately.

Reproduction Cost

The reproduction cost is the cost to substitute the improvement with a new replica.* Theoretically, the reproduction cost is the upper limit on the value of an improvement, because no intelligent buyer would pay more than the cost to reproduce the improvement.

Three methods can be used to estimate the direct costs of reproduction. They are presented in order of decreasing detail (and increasing utility):

Quantity Survey Method. This method to estimate reproduction cost considers every unit (component) used in construction (e.g., the number of nails, the amount of each type of pipe, the cubic yards of concrete, etc.), its price, and the labor cost to complete each unit of the improvement. It is quite accurate, but very time consuming. The current

---

*Replacement cost, on the other hand, is the cost to substitute the improvement with a new one of like utility. This concept is used when the reproduction cost cannot be used (i.e., when materials and building techniques are no longer available to construct a replica).

cost of building components can be obtained from builders, building suppliers, and some building cost services.

Unit-in-Place Method. This method is a modified quantity survey method. The components and labor are still included, but in an aggregate way. That is, the reproduction cost of a roof is estimated after it is completed and in place. This method, while not so time consuming as the quantity survey method, is still considered to be rather impractical.

Comparison Method. This method uses the area or volume of the subject improvement. Then a standard improvement, similar to the subject property, is found in cost estimating manuals. The standard improvement is a certain size (area or volume), and the cost per unit size of the subject property increases or decreases as it is smaller or larger, respectively, than the standard. That is, costs are proportionately higher for smaller improvements than for larger ones. No improvement will be exactly like the standard; there will be characteristics, such as quality, equipment, and design that differ from the standard, and the appraiser must make appropriate adjustments.

Accrued Depreciation

Accrued depreciation is the loss of value that an improvement has suffered from all sources since its inception. Real estate appraisers generally agree that accrued depreciation or diminished utility can come from three sources:

Physical Deterioration. Depreciation is accrued due to the damages of use and time. This form of depreciation begins the instant an improvement is constructed, and continues until replacement or demolition.

Functional Obsolescence. Depreciation is accrued from the loss of appeal and utility. Value is lost in a rather unpredictable manner.

Economic Obsolescence. Depreciation is accrued from either unfavorable zoning or unfavorable supply and demand. Diminished utility results from causes external to the property and can be considered as "locational obsolescence." It is thought to be incurable since the property owner cannot solve the problem.

Land Value

The value of the land (as if vacant) is determined by the market approach. That is, the value is based on recent sales of comparable sites.

INCOME APPROACH

Industrial, residential rental, and commercial properties can be appraised by several formulas that depend on the actual or potential net operating income and the capitalization rate.

The selection of the most appropriate formula for appraisal depends on assumptions about the future income, the estimated holding period, the relative certainty of values of the physical components (i.e., land and building), the judgment of the appraiser, etc.

The selection of the proper capitalization rate also depends on some of the above factors; the resultant property value is very sensitive to the capitalization rate. The capitalization rate and the appraisal formulas are discussed separately below.

Capitalization Rate

Capitalization is the process of converting income into a capital value (the original investment). The rate at which income is converted into a capital value is called the capitalization rate. Conceptually, the capitalization rate for these or any investment is the sum of two rates: the interest rate (the rate of return *on* invested capital) and the recapture rate (the rate of return *of* invested capital).

A real estate investment is usually composed of two separate investments, a mortgage loan and the investor's equity. Not only does the property have a capitalization rate, but each investment component also has a capitalization rate.

If the invested capital is a mortgage loan, the lender's investment is the loan amount. Each payment of an amortized loan consists of an amount of interest and an amount of principal. The interest is the return *on* his investment, and the principal is the return *of* his investment. The mortgage capitalization rate is the sum of these two rates. It is also expressible as the ratio of annual payment-to-loan amount; this ratio is called the annual mortgage constant.

If the invested capital is the original equity (down payment) in an income property, the return on the investment consists of some or all of the cash flow. Any cash flow in excess of the return on capital can be regarded as a return of capital. The equity capitalization rate is the sum of these rates, and is also expressible as the ratio of annual cash flow-to-down payment.

The property value is the sum of the mortgage amount and the investor's equity. Hence, the property interest rate can be thought of as the weighted average of the mortgage interest rate and the equity interest rate. The property recapture rate can be thought of as the weighted average of the mortgage recapture rate and the equity recapture rate. The property capitalization rate is the sum of the property interest rate and the property recapture rate. It is also expressible as the ratio of annual net operating income-to-property value or as the reciprocal of the net income multiplier (i.e., if property is valued at "8 times net," its capitalization rate is 12.5%.

FORMULAS:

Rates	Investment: Mortgage	Investment: Equity	Investment: Property
Interest	$r_m =$ (specified by contract)	$r_e = \dfrac{r_p - t\,r_m}{1 - t}$ (if $t < 1$)	$r_p = \begin{cases} t\,r_m + (1 - t)r_e & \text{(band of investment rate)} \\ r_1 + r_2 + r_3 + r_4 & \text{(component rate)} \end{cases}$
Recapture	$r'_m = \dfrac{q}{s(r_m,m,q)}$	$r'_e = \dfrac{r'_p - t\,r'_m}{1 - t}$ (if $t < 1$)	$r'_p = \begin{cases} t\,r'_m + (1 - t)r'_e & \text{(band of investment rate)} \\ \dfrac{1}{s(r,k,1)} & * \end{cases}$
Capitalization	$z_m = \begin{cases} r_m + r'_m \\ \dfrac{x_m}{v_m} & \text{(reciprocal of net income multiplier)} \\ \dfrac{q}{a(r_m,m,q)} \end{cases}$	$z_e = \begin{cases} r_e + r'_e \\ \dfrac{x_e}{v_e} & \text{(comparison rate)} \\ \dfrac{z_p - tz_m}{1 - t} & \text{(if } t < 1) \end{cases}$	$z_p = \begin{cases} r_p + r'_p \\ \dfrac{x_p}{v_p} & \text{(comparison rate)} \\ tz_m + (1 - t)z_e & \text{(band of investment rate)} \\ tz_m + (1 - t)z_e + \dfrac{\left[1 - h - t\dfrac{s(r_m,j,q)}{s(r_m,m,q)}\right]}{s(z_e,n,1)} & \text{(Ellwood rate)} \end{cases}$

*It is conventional to assume that deposits in a sinking fund are made annually. However, they are probably made q times a year (e.g., $q = 12$). In this case, $r'_p = q/s(r,kq,q)$. If $r = 0$, recapture is according to the straight-line method; if $r = r_i$, recapture is according to the Hoskold method; if $r = r_p$, recapture is according to the Inwood method.

where

r_m, r_e, r_p = interest rate for mortgage, equity, and property, respectively

r'_m, r'_e, r'_p = recapture rate for mortgage, equity, and property, respectively

z_m, z_e, z_p = capitalization rate for mortgage, equity, and property, respectively

then

h = forecast-to-present property value ratio

j = nq = number of mortgage interest periods until the end of income projection period

k = number of remaining years of economic life of improvement

m = total number of mortgage interest periods

n = number of years in income projection period (for the Ellwood rate. See the explanation of Ellwood rate, below.)

q = number of mortgage interest periods per year

r_1 = safe rate (such as that paid on government bonds)

r_2 = risk rate (for possible declining income)

r_3 = non-liquidity rate

r_4 = management rate (for burden of clerical duties associated with ownership)

t = v_m/v_p = loan-to-value ratio

v_m, v_e, v_p = present value of mortgage, equity, and property, respectively)

x_m, x_e, x_p = annual mortgage payment, cash flow, and net operating income, respectively

$a(r_m, m, q)$ = present value of an annuity of 1 (Table I)

$s(r_m, m, q)$ etc. = amount of an annuity of 1 (Table I)

The three important capitalization rates are the comparison rate, the band of investment rate, and the Ellwood rate.

Comparison Rate. The property capitalization rate,

$$z_p = \frac{x_p}{v_p},$$

is the ratio of annual net operating income-to-present value of the property. This ratio is the reciprocal of the commonly used net income multiplier.

Band of Investment Rate. The financial components of the property (mortgage and equity) each have their own capitalization rate. The band of investment rate is the weighted average of these rates.

EXAMPLE: Consider a property for which the mortgage capitalization rate (annual mortgage constant) is 9.26%, and the equity capitalization rate is 12%. If the loan-to-value ratio is 75%, what is the property capitalization rate by the band of investment method?

SOLUTION: In this example, $z_m = 0.0926$, $z_e = 0.12$, and $t = 0.75$. Then the property capitalization rate is

$$\begin{aligned} z_p &= 0.75 \times .0926 + 0.25 \times 0.12 \\ &= 0.0695 + 0.03 = 0.0995 \\ &= 9.95\% \end{aligned}$$

Ellwood Rate. The Ellwood rate is the band of investment rate plus an additional term. This term depends on the mortgage amortization and the changed property value that occurs during the estimated holding period. The bracketed portion of the additional term is the fraction of property value that must be replaced. This fraction is the change in investor's equity (through loan amortization and changed property value) during the holding period, divided by the original property value. Replacement is accomplished by depositing an amount annually in a sinking fund at interest equal to the investor's equity capitalization rate, z_e.

Appraisal Formulas

Two types of formulas are used to estimate value by the income approach: direct capitalization and the formulas of the residual techniques. It would be a mistake, however, to think of the two types as distinct since direct capitalization is also one of the terms in each of the residual techniques.

Direct Capitalization. Direct capitalization is simply the ratio of annual net operating income to the capitalization rate. In this way, income is converted to a capital value. Generally, direct capitalization is used for properties for which one of the residual techniques is not applicable.

FORMULA:

$$\boxed{v_p = \frac{x_p}{z_p}}$$

where

v_p = present value of property

then

x_p = annual net operating income

z_p = property capitalization rate

EXAMPLE: Suppose a commercial property has an annual net operating income of $100,000, and five appraisers independently estimate the property capitalization rate to be 0.105, 0.092, 0.100, 0.098, and 0.110. Determine the property value by direct capitalization.

SOLUTION: The average capitalization rate is $z_p = 0.101 = 10.1\%$. Since the annual net operating income is $x_p = \$100{,}000$, the property value by the direct capitalization method is

$$v_p = \frac{\$100{,}000}{0.101} = \$990{,}099$$

Residual Techniques. Residual techniques are often used when the value of one of the physical components (land or building) is well known and the other is not. In such cases, the value of the better-known component is determined by the cost or market approach; then the income attributable to the lesser-known component is considered residual. There are three residual techniques: building, land, and property.

The *building residual technique* assumes that the value of the land is reasonably well known, but the value of the building is not. The value of the land is determined by the market approach. The annual net operating income attributable to the land is subtracted from the annual net operating income from the property. The value of the building is determined by capitalizing the residual amount (due to the building) at the property capitalization rate. The value of the property is the sum of the value of the land and the building.

The *land residual technique* assumes that the value of the building is reasonably well known, but the value of the land is not. The value of the building is determined by the cost approach. The annual net operating income attributable to the building is subtracted from the annual net operating income from the property. The value of the land is determined by capitalizing this residual amount (due to the land) at the property interest rate. The value of the property is the sum of the value of the building and the land.

The *property residual technique* assumes that the two property components, land and building, can't be separated. All net operating income is attributed to the property as a whole and capitalized at the property capitalization rate. The land value is assumed to be known and is discounted at the property interest rate over a period that is the estimated useful life of the building, the remaining term of the lease, etc.

Table 12 lists the type(s) of residual techniques that are appropriate, given certain assumptions about the value of the land and buildings. Formulas and examples for each technique follow the table.

FORMULAS:

$$v_p = \begin{cases} \dfrac{x_p - r_p v_\ell}{z_p} + v_\ell & \text{(building residual technique)} \\[2ex] \dfrac{x_p - z_p v_b}{r_p} + v_b & \text{(land residual technique)} \\[2ex] \dfrac{x_p}{z_p} + \dfrac{v_\ell}{c(r_p,k,1)} & \text{(property residual technique)} \end{cases}$$

where

v_p = present value of the property

then

k = remaining useful life of the building or the remaining term of a long-term lease (years)

r_p = property interest rate

v_b = present value of the building

v = present value of the land

x_p = annual net operating income from the property

z_p = property capitalization rate*

$c(r_p,k,l)$ = amount of l at compound interest (Table I)

Table 12. RESIDUAL TECHNIQUE(S) APPROPRIATE TO ESTIMATE PROPERTY VALUE

			Land	
			Land Value Well Known (By Market Approach)	Land Value not Well Known
Building	Building Value Well Known (By Cost Approach)	Building does not exist*	Land residual Building residual	Land residual
		Building new and represents highest and best use	Land residual Building residual	Land residual
		Building old, but accrued depreciation known	Building residual	Property residual
		Building old, but represents highest and best use	Property residual Building residual	Property residual
	Building Value not Well Known	Building new, but doesn't represent highest and best use	Building residual	Property residual
		Building old, and accrued depreciation not well known	Building residual	Property residual
		Building old, but has stable long-term lease	Property residual Building residual	Property residual

***Determine a hypothetical value for the land by assuming it is put to its highest and best use.**

*If recapture is deposited annually in a sinking fund at the property interest rate (the Inwood method of recapture), then $z_p = 1/a(r_p,k,l)$.

EXAMPLE (Building Residual Technique): Consider an older apartment building located in a transitional neighborhood. Because the building is older, there has been considerable accrued depreciation, and its value is difficult to determine by the cost approach. However, since it is located in a transitional neighborhood, there are enough recent comparable sales of lots to estimate the land value by the market approach at $150,000. The annual net operating income from the building is $50,500. The interest rate for similar properties is 8%, and the property capitalization rate is 11%; the method of recapture is not specified here, but the rate is included implicitly as 3%. Determine the property value by the building residual technique.

SOLUTION: In this example,

$v_\ell = \$150{,}000$, $x_p = \$50{,}500$, $r_p = 0.08$, and $z_p = 0.11$.

Now, the property value by the building residual technique is

$$\begin{aligned} v_p &= \frac{x_p - r_p v_l}{z_p} + v_\ell \\ &= \frac{\$50{,}500 - 0.08 \times \$150{,}000}{0.11} + \$150{,}000 \\ &= \frac{\$50{,}500 - \$12{,}000}{0.11} + \$150{,}000 \\ &= \frac{\$38{,}500}{0.11} + \$150{,}000 \\ &= \$350{,}000 + \$150{,}000 \\ &= \$500{,}000. \end{aligned}$$

Market Approach

The market approach to value requires collecting data from recent sales of comparable properties and analyzing the data to estimate the value of the subject property. The phrase "recent sales of comparable properties" is a way of saying that the market data and the subject property should come from the same statistical population.

Time is measured by change, and change will be noticed not only in fashion, but also in prices. Fashion in real estate (measured by functional obsolescence) changes relatively slowly. If prices are changing very slowly, "recent" could include the last several years. On the other hand, if they are changing rapidly, "recent" may include only the last few months.

The concept "comparable" is a highly subjective one. In the strictest sense, no two properties are exactly alike; even if two buildings are identical, their location can't be. To determine comparability, one should list the characteristics of the subject property and order them according to their importance in determining value. Clearly, the most important characteristics of comparable properties should be nearly the same, e.g., function, location, design, etc.

Single regression analysis is used to estimate value when it seems to depend on one important measurable characteristic. For instance, if we feel that floor area is the most important characteristic in determining value in one-bedroom apartments, floor area is the single characteristic. Single regression analysis, using the sale price and the floor area obtained from several properties, can be used to estimate the value of a subject property with known floor area.

Multiple regression analysis is used when value is thought to depend on more than one characteristic. (Such is always the case, of course, but multiple regression analysis is complicated and often avoided for this reason alone.)

CHAPTER 15
Mortgage Payments Determined Easily

The payments on an amortized loan are usually constant and made at equal intervals of time. The payments consist of an amount of interest and an amount of principal. The amount of interest is the loan balance, multiplied by the periodic interest rate. The amount of principal directly reduces the loan balance. Since the balance becomes progressively smaller, the amount of interest does also. Finally, since the payments are constant, the amount of principal becomes equally larger.

Since the payments constitute an annuity to the lender, the size of the payment is determined from the formula for the present value of an annuity. The payment must be such that the present value of the annuity equals the amount loaned. Of course, the rate of return on the investment is the interest rate on the loan. The formula for the present value of an annuity with constant payments and constant interest rate is

$$B = p \cdot \sum_{i=1}^{m} \frac{1}{(1 + r/q)^i} = p \cdot a(r,m,q).$$

This formula can also be solved for the periodic payment of an amortized loan:

$$p = B/a(r,m,q).$$

The constant payment can be determined from one of the following formulas. However, if the period is monthly, the payment can be found in Table I or estimated quickly from Figure 24.

Figure 24

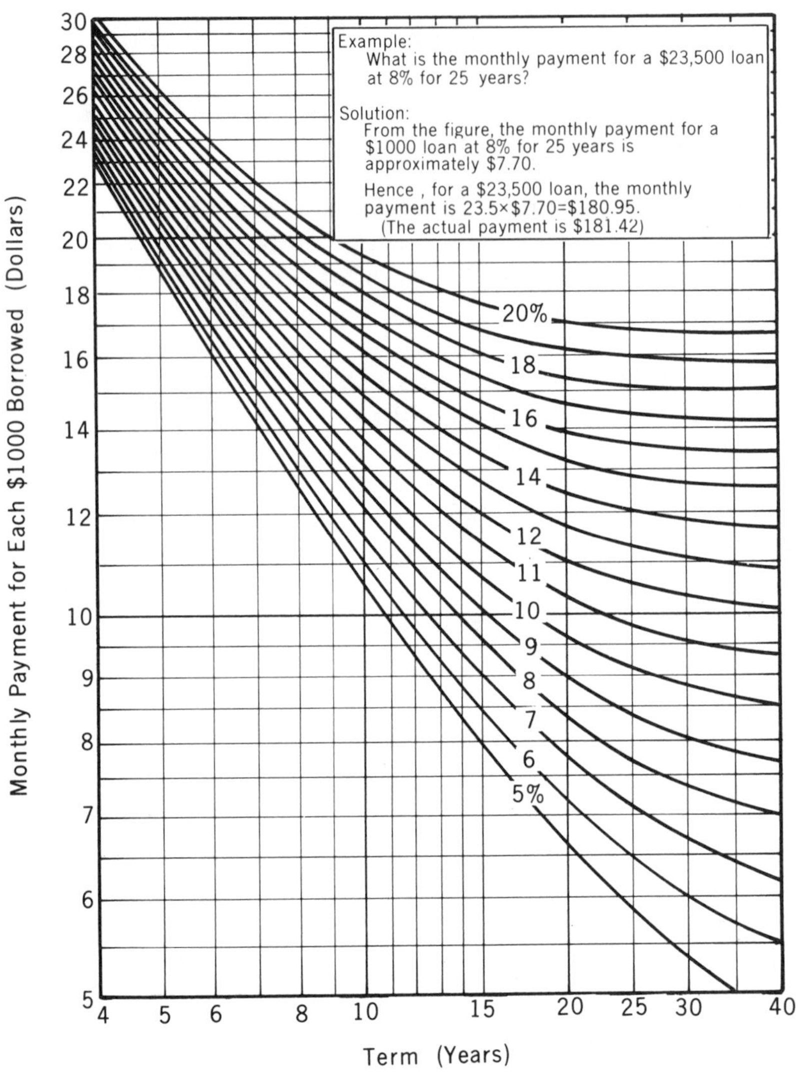

FORMULAS:

$$p = \begin{cases} B/a(r,m,q) & \text{(complete amortization)} \\ B/a(r,j,q) = B_j/s(r,j,q) & \text{(partial amortization)} \end{cases}$$

where

p = amount of periodic payment

then

B = amount of loan

B_j = loan balance after the jth period

j = number of payment periods after which the balance, B_j, remains

m = total number of payments

q = number of periods per year

r = annual interest rate

a(r,m,q),
a(r,j,q) = present value of an annuity of 1 (Table I)

s(r,j,q) = amount of an annuity of 1 (Table I)

EXAMPLE 1 (Complete Amortization): J. O. Miller obtained a $35,300 loan at 10% interest with monthly payments for 25 years. How much must each payment be in order to completely amortize the loan at its term?

SOLUTION: In this example,

$$B = \$35{,}300,\ r = 10\%,\ q = 12,\ \text{and}\ m = 25 \times 12 = 300.$$

From Table I,

$$a(r,m,q) = a(10,300,12) = 110.04723.$$

Now, from the formula, the monthly payment is

$$p = \$35{,}300/110.04723 = \$320.77.$$

EXAMPLE 2 (Partial Amortization): J. O. Miller wants to lend $16,000 at 8% with monthly payments for three years. At the end of three years, he wants to receive a single balloon payment of $5,000. (In the 36th period, he will receive the regular payment plus the balloon.) What monthly payment will accomplish this?

SOLUTION: In this example,

$$B = \$16{,}000,\ r = 8\%,\ q = 12,\ j = 36,\ \text{and}\ B_j = \$5{,}000.$$

From Table I

$$a(r,j,q) = a(8,36,12) = 31.91181, \text{ and}$$
$$s(r,j,q) = s(8,36,12) = 40.53556.$$

Now, from the formula, the monthly payment is

$$\begin{aligned} p &= \$16{,}000/31.91181 - \$5{,}000/40.53556 \\ &= \$501.38 - \$123.35 \\ &= \$378.03. \end{aligned}$$

CHAPTER 16
Interest Payments Computed for You

Interest is the consideration for the use of money. It is usually paid at a fixed rate on the loan balance.*

Each payment of a non-amortized loan consists of interest only. In this case, the principal (loan balance) remains until the term of the loan, at which time it is usually paid in a single payment. Because the loan balance is constant, the amount of interest in each payment is also constant.

Each payment of an amortized loan consists of an amount of interest (at a fixed rate on the loan balance) and an amount of principal. The amount of principal reduces the loan balance. Since the loan balance is continually decreasing, so too is the amount of interest in each payment.

Since investment interest is a tax deduction, it is necessary to determine the amount of interest paid during the tax year. The amount of interest can be determined from the following formulas. Also, Table 13 lists the amount of interest paid through each month for the first 50 months of an amortized loan of $1,000. It includes terms of 5, 10, . . ., 40 years and interest rates from 9% through 14.75%. Of course, the interest paid between any two periods can be determined by subtracting one value from the other.

FORMULAS:

$$I = Brt \qquad \text{(non-amortized loans)}$$

$$\left.\begin{aligned} I_j &= p \cdot [j+a(r,m-j,q) - a(r,m,q)] \\ I'_j &= p \cdot [12+a(r,m-j,q) - a(r,m-j+12,q)] \end{aligned}\right\} \text{(amortized loans)}$$

---

*Sometimes the rate of interest is required to change in response to changes in a standard rate, such as the prime rate.

where

I = amount of interest from the beginning

I_j = amount of interest through the jth period

I'_j = amount of interest between any 12-month period ending in the jth month

then

B = amount of principal

B_j = balance after j payments

m = nq = total number of periods

n = number of years

p = amount of each periodic payment

q = number of periods per year

r = interest rate, expressed as a decimal

t = time from the beginning, expressed as a fraction of a year

$a(r,m,q)$,
$a(r,m-j+12,q)$,
$a(r,m-j,q)$ = present value of an annuity of 1 (Table I) (Note: $a(r,0,q) = 0$)

EXAMPLE 1 (Interest between Two Periods): A five-year amortized loan at 8% interest has monthly payments of $324.43. How much interest is paid between the 23rd and 40th payments?

SOLUTION: To find the interest paid between the 23rd and 40th payments, it is necessary to first determine I_{23} and I_{40}, and then the difference, $I_{40} - I_{23}$.

In this example,

n = 5 years, $r = 8\%$, $q = 12$, $m = nq = 60$, and

p = $324.43.

From Table I,

$a(r,m,q) = a(8,60,12) = 49.318433$.

When $j = 23$,

$$a(r, m - j, q) = a(8,37,12) = 32.693847.$$

Now, from the formula, the interest paid through the 23rd payment is

$$I_{23} = \$324.43 \times (23 + 32.693847 - 49.318433)$$
$$= \$324.43 \times 6.375414$$
$$= \$2{,}068.38.$$

Proceeding in the same way, we find

$$I_{40} = \$3{,}032.60.$$

Therefore, the amount of interest paid between the 23rd and 40th payment is

$$I_{40} - I_{23} = \$3{,}032.60 - \$2{,}068.38$$
$$= \$964.22.$$

EXAMPLE 2 (Using Table 13): How much interest has been paid after the first 15 monthly payments of an $80,000 loan at 10% amortized over 25 years?

SOLUTION: From page 186, corresponding to 25-year loans, the interest paid on $1,000 is $124.5986. Therefore, 80 × $124.5986 = $9,967.89 interest has been paid on $80,000.

Table 13. 5-YEAR TERM—INTEREST RATE

J	9.00	9.25	9.50	9.75	10.00	10.25	10.50	10.75	11.00	11.25	11.50	11.75
1	7.5000	7.7083	7.9167	8.1250	8.3333	8.5417	8.7500	8.9583	9.1667	9.3750	9.5833	9.7917
2	14.9006	15.3151	15.7297	16.1444	16.5591	16.9738	17.3885	17.8033	18.2181	18.6329	19.0477	19.4626
3	22.2009	22.8196	23.4384	24.0573	24.6763	25.2953	25.9145	26.5338	27.1531	27.7726	28.3921	29.0117
4	29.4004	30.2210	31.0418	31.8628	32.6841	33.5054	34.3270	35.1488	35.9708	36.7929	37.6152	38.4377
5	36.4981	37.5185	38.5392	39.5602	40.5815	41.6032	42.6251	43.6474	44.6699	45.6928	46.7160	47.7395
6	43.4934	44.7113	45.9296	47.1484	48.3677	49.5875	50.8077	52.0284	53.2496	54.4712	55.6932	56.9157
7	50.3855	51.7986	53.2123	54.6267	56.0418	57.4575	58.8739	60.2909	61.7085	63.1268	64.5457	65.9652
8	57.1736	58.7796	60.3864	61.9941	63.6027	65.2122	66.8225	68.4337	70.0457	71.6586	73.2723	74.8868
9	63.8569	65.6534	67.4510	69.2496	71.0496	72.8506	74.6526	76.4558	78.2600	80.0653	81.8717	83.6791
10	70.4346	72.4193	74.4053	76.3927	78.3815	80.3717	82.3632	84.3561	86.3503	88.3459	90.3428	92.3410
11	76.9060	79.0763	81.2483	83.4220	85.5974	87.7745	89.9532	92.1335	94.3155	96.4990	98.6842	100.8710
12	83.2702	85.6238	87.9793	90.3369	92.5964	95.0580	97.4215	99.7869	102.1543	104.5237	106.8949	109.2681
13	89.5265	92.0607	94.5973	97.1362	99.6775	102.2211	104.7670	107.3152	109.8657	112.4185	114.9735	117.5308
14	95.6740	98.3864	101.1014	103.8192	106.5397	109.2629	111.9888	114.7174	117.4485	120.1823	122.9188	125.6578
15	101.7120	104.5998	107.4908	110.3849	113.2821	116.1824	119.0857	121.9921	124.9015	127.8140	130.7294	133.6478
16	107.6395	110.7002	113.7644	116.8322	119.9035	122.9784	126.0566	129.1384	132.2236	135.3121	138.4041	141.4995
17	113.4558	116.6866	119.9215	123.1603	126.4031	129.6499	132.9005	136.1550	139.4134	142.6756	145.9416	149.2114
18	119.1600	122.5583	125.9610	129.3682	132.7798	136.1958	139.6162	143.0408	146.4698	149.9031	153.3406	156.7823
19	124.7513	128.3143	131.8821	135.4549	139.0326	142.6151	146.2025	149.7947	153.3916	156.9933	160.5997	164.2108
20	130.2289	133.9536	137.6838	141.4194	145.1604	148.9068	152.6584	156.4154	160.1776	163.9450	167.7176	171.4955
21	135.5919	139.4756	143.3652	147.2608	151.1623	155.0696	158.9827	162.9017	166.8264	170.7569	174.6930	178.6348
22	140.8394	144.8791	148.9253	152.9780	157.0370	161.1025	165.1743	169.2525	173.3369	177.4276	181.5245	185.6276
23	145.9705	150.1633	154.3631	158.5699	162.7837	167.0044	171.2320	175.4665	179.7078	183.9558	188.2107	192.4722
24	150.9845	155.3273	159.6777	164.0357	168.4012	172.7742	177.1547	181.5425	185.9377	190.3403	194.7501	199.1672
25	155.8804	160.3702	164.8682	169.3743	173.8885	178.4108	182.9411	187.4793	192.0255	196.5796	201.1415	205.7113
26	160.6573	165.2910	169.9334	174.5846	179.2444	183.9129	188.5900	193.2756	197.9698	202.6724	207.3834	212.1028
27	165.3143	170.0887	174.8725	179.6656	184.4680	189.2795	194.1003	198.9302	203.7692	208.6173	213.4743	218.3404
28	169.8506	174.7625	179.6844	184.6163	189.5579	194.5094	199.4707	204.4418	209.4225	214.4129	219.4129	224.4224
29	174.2652	179.3114	184.3682	189.4355	194.5133	199.6015	204.7001	209.8091	214.9283	220.0578	225.1976	230.3475
30	178.5573	183.7344	188.9228	194.1223	199.3329	204.5545	209.7872	215.0308	220.2853	225.5507	230.8269	236.1139
31	182.7258	188.0306	193.3471	198.6755	204.0155	209.3673	214.7306	220.1056	225.4921	230.8901	236.2995	241.7203
32	186.7700	192.1989	197.6403	203.0940	208.5602	214.0386	219.5293	225.0322	230.5473	236.0745	241.6137	247.1650
33	190.6887	196.2384	201.8011	207.3769	212.9656	218.5673	224.1819	229.8093	235.4495	241.1025	246.7681	252.4464
34	194.4812	200.1481	205.8286	211.5229	217.2307	222.9522	228.6871	234.4356	240.1974	245.9726	251.7611	257.5629
35	198.1464	203.9269	209.7218	215.5309	221.3543	227.1919	233.0437	238.9096	244.7895	250.6834	256.5913	262.5130
36	201.6835	207.5740	213.4795	219.3999	225.3352	231.2854	237.2503	243.2300	249.2244	255.2334	261.2569	267.2950
37	205.0913	211.0882	217.1007	223.1287	229.1722	235.2313	241.3057	247.3955	253.5006	259.6209	265.7565	271.9072
38	208.3691	214.4685	220.5842	226.7161	232.8642	239.0283	245.2085	251.4046	257.6167	263.8447	270.0885	276.3480
39	211.5157	217.7140	223.9291	230.1611	236.4098	242.6752	248.9573	255.2560	261.5713	267.9030	274.2512	280.6157
40	214.5303	220.8235	227.1342	233.4624	239.8079	246.1708	252.5509	258.9482	265.3627	271.7943	278.2430	284.7087
41	217.4117	223.7961	230.1985	236.6189	243.0573	249.5137	255.9879	262.4799	268.9897	275.5172	282.0623	288.6251
42	220.1591	226.6306	233.1207	239.6294	246.1567	252.7025	259.2668	265.8495	272.4506	279.0699	285.7075	292.3633
43	222.7714	229.3260	235.8998	242.4928	249.1049	255.7361	262.3864	269.0557	275.7438	282.4509	289.1768	295.9215
44	225.2476	231.8912	238.5346	245.2077	251.9006	258.6131	265.3452	272.0969	278.8680	285.6586	292.4687	299.2980
45	227.5867	234.2952	241.0240	247.7731	254.5425	261.3321	268.1418	274.9717	281.8215	288.6914	295.5813	302.4910
46	229.7877	236.5669	243.3669	250.1877	257.0294	263.8918	270.7748	277.6785	284.6028	291.5476	298.5129	305.4987
47	231.8495	238.6951	245.5620	252.4503	259.3599	266.2908	273.2428	280.2160	287.2103	294.2256	301.2620	308.3192
48	233.7710	240.6787	247.6083	254.5597	261.5328	268.5277	275.5443	282.5826	289.6424	296.7237	303.8265	310.9508
49	235.5513	242.5167	249.5045	256.5145	263.5468	270.6013	277.6779	284.7766	291.8974	299.0402	306.2050	313.3916
50	237.1892	244.2079	251.2494	258.3136	265.4005	272.5100	279.6421	286.7967	293.9738	301.1734	308.3954	315.6397

Table 13. 5-YEAR TERM—INTEREST RATE (*Continued*)

J	12.00	12.25	12.50	12.75	13.00	13.25	13.50	13.75	14.00	14.25	14.50	14.75
1	10.0000	10.2083	10.4167	10.6250	10.8333	11.0417	11.2500	11.4583	11.6667	11.8750	12.0833	12.2917
2	19.8776	20.2925	20.7075	21.1225	21.5375	21.9526	22.3677	22.7828	23.1980	23.6132	24.0284	24.4436
3	29.6314	30.2513	30.8711	31.4911	32.1112	32.7314	33.3516	33.9719	34.5924	35.2129	35.8334	36.4541
4	39.2604	40.0833	40.9063	41.7295	42.5529	43.3765	44.2002	45.0241	45.8482	46.6725	47.4969	48.3214
5	48.7632	49.7873	50.8117	51.8363	52.8613	53.8865	54.9120	55.9379	56.9639	57.9903	59.0169	60.0438
6	58.1387	59.3620	60.5859	61.8101	63.0348	64.2600	65.4855	66.7115	67.9379	69.1647	70.3919	71.6195
7	67.3854	68.8061	70.2275	71.6495	73.0721	74.4953	75.9191	77.3434	78.7684	80.1939	81.6200	83.0466
8	76.5021	78.1183	79.7353	81.3530	82.9716	84.5910	86.2111	87.8320	89.4538	91.0762	92.6995	94.3234
9	85.4876	87.2971	89.1077	90.9193	92.7319	94.5455	96.3601	98.1757	99.9923	101.8099	103.6285	105.4480
10	94.3405	96.3413	98.3434	100.3467	102.3514	104.3573	106.3644	108.3728	110.3824	112.3933	114.4053	116.4186
11	103.0594	105.2494	107.4409	109.6340	111.8286	114.0247	116.2224	118.4216	120.6223	122.8244	125.0280	127.2331
12	111.6431	114.0201	116.3989	118.7795	121.1620	123.5463	125.9324	128.3204	130.7101	133.1016	135.4948	137.8898
13	120.0902	122.6519	125.2158	127.7818	130.3500	132.9204	135.4928	138.0674	140.6441	143.2229	145.8038	148.3867
14	128.3993	131.1435	133.8902	136.6394	139.3911	142.1453	144.9020	147.6611	150.4226	153.1866	155.9530	158.7218
15	136.5691	139.4934	142.4206	145.3507	148.2836	151.2194	154.1580	157.0995	160.0438	162.9908	165.9406	168.8931
16	144.5981	147.7002	150.8055	153.9141	157.0260	160.1411	163.2594	166.3809	169.5057	172.6335	175.7645	178.8987
17	152.4850	155.7623	159.0434	162.3281	165.6165	168.9086	172.2043	175.5036	178.8065	182.1129	185.4229	188.7364
18	160.2283	163.6784	167.1327	170.5912	174.0537	177.5203	180.9910	184.4657	187.9444	191.4270	194.9136	198.4042
19	167.8266	171.4470	175.0720	178.7016	182.3358	185.9745	189.6176	193.2653	196.9174	200.5739	204.2348	207.9000
20	175.2784	179.0665	182.8596	186.6578	190.4611	194.2693	198.0825	201.9006	205.7236	209.5515	213.3843	217.2218
21	182.5823	186.5354	190.4940	194.4582	198.4279	202.4031	206.3837	210.3697	214.3611	218.3579	222.3600	226.3674
22	189.7368	193.8521	197.9736	202.1010	206.2345	210.3740	214.5194	218.6708	222.8280	226.9910	231.1599	235.3345
23	196.7404	201.0152	205.2967	209.5847	213.8793	218.1803	222.4878	226.8018	231.1221	235.4488	239.7818	244.1211
24	203.5916	208.0231	212.4617	216.9075	221.3603	225.8202	230.2870	234.7608	239.2415	243.7291	248.2236	252.7248
25	210.2888	214.8741	219.4671	224.0677	228.6759	233.2917	237.9151	242.5459	247.1843	251.8300	256.4831	261.1435
26	216.8306	221.5667	226.3110	231.0636	235.8243	240.5932	245.3701	250.1551	254.9482	259.7492	264.5581	269.3749
27	223.2153	228.0992	232.9919	237.8934	242.8036	247.7225	252.6502	257.5864	262.5312	267.4845	272.4464	277.4166
28	229.4415	234.4700	239.5080	244.5553	249.6120	254.6780	259.7532	264.8376	269.9312	275.0339	280.1456	285.2664
29	235.5075	240.6775	245.8576	251.0477	256.2477	261.4576	266.6774	271.9069	277.1461	282.3951	287.6537	292.9219
30	241.4116	246.7200	252.0391	257.3687	262.7088	268.0594	273.4205	278.7920	284.1737	289.5658	294.9681	300.3806
31	247.1524	252.5959	258.0505	263.5164	268.9934	274.4815	279.9807	285.4908	291.0119	296.5438	302.0866	307.6402
32	252.7282	258.3033	263.8903	269.4891	275.0996	280.7219	286.3558	292.0013	297.6583	303.3269	309.0069	314.6983
33	258.1372	263.8406	269.5565	275.2848	281.0255	286.7785	292.5437	298.3212	304.1109	309.9126	315.7265	321.5523
34	263.3779	269.2061	275.0474	280.9017	286.7690	292.6493	298.5424	304.4484	310.3672	316.2987	322.2429	328.1997
35	268.4486	274.3980	280.3611	286.3379	292.3283	298.3323	304.3498	310.3807	316.4251	322.4828	328.5538	334.6381
36	273.3475	279.4145	285.4958	291.5914	297.7013	303.8254	309.9636	316.1159	322.2822	328.4625	334.6567	340.8647
37	278.0730	284.2538	290.4497	296.6604	302.8860	309.1265	315.3817	321.6516	327.9361	334.2353	340.5490	346.8771
38	282.6233	288.9142	295.2208	301.5429	307.8804	314.2335	320.6019	326.9856	333.3846	339.7988	346.2282	352.6726
39	286.9966	293.3938	299.8072	306.2368	312.6825	319.1442	325.6219	332.1156	338.6252	345.1505	351.6917	358.2485
40	291.1913	297.6908	304.2071	310.7402	317.2900	323.8565	330.4396	337.0393	343.6554	350.2880	356.9369	363.6022
41	295.2054	301.8032	308.4184	315.0511	321.7010	328.3682	335.0526	341.7542	348.4729	355.2086	361.9612	368.7308
42	299.0372	305.7293	312.4393	319.1673	325.9133	332.6771	339.4587	346.2580	353.0751	359.9097	366.7620	373.6317
43	302.6849	309.4670	316.2677	323.0869	329.9247	336.7809	343.6554	350.5483	357.4595	364.3889	371.3364	378.3020
44	306.1467	313.0146	319.9016	326.8078	333.7331	340.6773	347.6405	354.6227	361.6236	368.6434	375.6818	382.7389
45	309.4206	316.3699	323.3390	330.3278	337.3362	344.3642	351.4116	358.4786	365.5649	372.6705	379.7954	386.9396
46	312.5048	319.5312	326.5779	333.6448	340.7319	347.8391	354.9663	362.1135	369.2806	376.4676	383.6745	390.9011
47	315.3974	322.4964	329.6162	336.7567	343.9179	351.0997	358.3021	365.5249	372.7683	380.0320	387.3161	394.6204
48	318.0965	325.2635	332.4517	339.6612	346.8919	354.1437	361.4165	368.7103	376.0251	383.3608	390.7174	398.0947
49	320.6001	327.8304	335.0825	342.3562	349.6516	356.9686	364.3071	371.6671	379.0485	386.4513	393.8755	401.3208
50	322.9063	330.1952	337.5062	344.8394	352.1947	359.5721	366.9714	374.3926	381.8358	389.3007	396.7874	404.2958

Table 13. 10-YEAR TERM—INTEREST RATE

J	9.00	9.25	9.50	9.75	10.00	10.25	10.50	10.75	11.00	11.25	11.50	11.75
1	7.5000	7.7083	7.9167	8.1250	8.3333	8.5417	8.7500	8.9583	9.1667	9.3750	9.5833	9.7917
2	14.9612	15.3774	15.7936	16.2098	16.6260	17.0422	17.4585	17.8748	18.2911	18.7074	19.1238	19.5401
3	22.3834	23.0069	23.6304	24.2540	24.8776	25.5013	26.1251	26.7490	27.3729	27.9969	28.6209	29.2450
4	29.7663	30.5965	31.4268	32.2573	33.0879	33.9186	34.7495	35.5805	36.4117	37.2429	38.0743	38.9058
5	37.1095	38.1459	39.1825	40.2194	41.2565	42.2938	43.3313	44.3690	45.4070	46.4452	47.4836	48.5221
6	44.4128	45.6548	46.8972	48.1399	49.3830	50.6264	51.8701	53.1142	54.3586	55.6033	56.8483	58.0936
7	51.6759	53.1229	54.5705	56.0185	57.4671	58.9161	60.3656	61.8155	63.2659	64.7167	66.1680	67.6196
8	58.8984	60.5499	62.2021	63.8549	65.5084	67.1625	68.8173	70.4726	72.1286	73.7851	75.4423	77.0999
9	66.0801	67.9354	69.7917	71.6487	73.5066	75.3654	77.2249	79.0852	80.9463	82.8081	84.6707	86.5340
10	73.2206	75.2792	77.3389	79.3996	81.4614	83.5242	85.5880	87.6528	89.7185	91.7852	93.8528	95.9213
11	80.3197	82.5809	84.8434	87.1072	89.3723	91.6387	93.9062	96.1750	98.4449	100.7160	102.9882	105.2615
12	87.3770	89.8402	92.3049	94.7712	97.2390	99.7084	102.1791	104.6514	107.1250	109.6000	112.0764	114.5541
13	94.3923	97.0567	99.7231	102.3912	105.0612	107.7329	110.4064	113.0815	115.7584	118.4368	121.1169	123.7986
14	101.3651	104.2302	107.0975	109.9669	112.8384	115.7120	118.5876	121.4651	124.3446	127.2261	130.1094	132.9945
15	108.2952	111.3603	114.4279	117.4979	120.5703	123.6451	126.7222	129.8017	132.8833	135.9672	139.0533	142.1414
16	115.1824	118.4467	121.7138	124.9838	128.2565	131.5319	134.8100	138.0908	141.3740	144.6599	147.9481	151.2389
17	122.0261	125.4889	128.9550	132.4243	135.8966	139.3721	142.8505	146.3320	149.8163	153.3035	156.7935	160.2863
18	128.8262	132.4868	136.1511	139.8189	143.4903	147.1651	150.8433	154.5249	158.2097	161.8977	165.5889	169.2832
19	135.5823	139.4400	143.3017	147.1675	151.0371	154.9107	158.7880	162.6690	166.5537	170.4420	174.3339	178.2292
20	142.2940	146.3480	150.4065	154.4694	158.5367	162.6083	166.6841	170.7640	174.8480	178.9360	183.0279	187.1237
21	148.9611	153.2106	157.4651	161.7245	165.9887	170.2576	174.5312	178.8094	183.0920	187.3791	191.6705	195.9662
22	155.5831	160.0274	164.4771	168.9322	173.3926	177.8582	182.3289	186.8047	191.2853	195.7709	200.2612	204.7562
23	162.1599	166.7981	171.4422	176.0923	180.7481	185.4097	190.0768	194.7494	199.4275	204.1109	208.7995	213.4932
24	168.6909	173.5222	178.3600	183.2043	188.0548	192.9115	197.7744	202.6433	207.5180	212.3986	217.2848	222.1767
25	175.1759	180.1995	185.2302	190.2678	195.3122	200.3634	205.4213	210.4857	215.5564	220.6335	225.7168	230.8062
26	181.6146	186.8296	192.0522	197.2824	202.5200	207.7649	213.0170	218.2762	223.5423	228.8152	234.0948	239.3810
27	188.0065	193.4121	198.8259	204.2478	209.6778	215.1156	220.5612	226.0143	231.4750	236.9431	242.4184	247.9008
28	194.3514	199.9466	205.5507	211.1636	216.7850	222.4150	228.0532	233.6997	239.3542	245.0167	250.6870	256.3649
29	200.6488	206.4328	212.2263	218.0292	223.8414	229.6626	235.4928	241.3318	247.1794	253.0356	258.9001	264.7729
30	206.8985	212.8703	218.8524	224.8445	230.8464	236.8581	242.8794	248.9101	254.9500	260.9991	267.0572	273.1241
31	213.1000	219.2588	225.4284	231.6088	237.7997	244.0010	250.2125	256.4341	262.6656	268.9069	275.1577	281.4180
32	219.2531	225.5978	231.9541	238.3218	244.7008	251.0908	257.4918	263.9034	270.3256	276.7583	283.2011	289.6540
33	225.3572	231.8870	238.4290	244.9832	251.5493	258.1272	264.7166	271.3175	277.9296	284.5528	291.1868	297.8316
34	231.4122	238.1259	244.8527	251.5924	258.3447	265.1095	271.8867	278.6759	285.4770	292.2899	299.1144	305.9502
35	237.4175	244.3143	251.2249	258.1490	265.0867	272.0375	279.0014	285.9780	292.9674	299.9691	306.9832	314.0092
36	243.3729	250.4517	257.5450	264.6527	271.7747	278.9106	286.0602	293.2235	300.4001	307.5899	314.7926	322.0081
37	249.2780	256.5377	263.8127	271.1030	278.4083	285.7283	293.0628	300.4117	307.7747	315.1516	322.5422	329.9462
38	255.1323	262.5719	270.0277	277.4994	284.9870	292.4901	300.0086	307.5422	315.0906	322.6537	330.2312	337.8230
39	260.9356	268.5539	276.1893	283.8416	291.5105	299.1957	306.8971	314.6144	322.3473	330.0957	337.8593	345.6378
40	266.6873	274.4834	282.2973	290.1290	297.9781	305.8445	313.7278	321.6278	329.5443	337.4770	345.4257	353.3901
41	272.3872	280.3598	288.3513	296.3613	304.3896	312.4360	320.5002	328.5819	336.6809	344.7970	352.9298	361.0793
42	278.0348	286.1829	294.3507	302.5379	310.7444	318.9697	327.2137	335.4762	343.7567	352.0551	360.3712	368.7046
43	283.6298	291.9522	300.2952	308.6585	317.0420	325.4452	333.8680	342.3101	350.7711	359.2509	367.7491	376.2655
44	289.1717	297.6672	306.1843	314.7226	323.2819	331.8619	340.4624	349.0830	357.7235	366.3836	375.0630	383.7614
45	294.6602	303.3276	312.0175	320.7297	329.4637	338.2194	346.9965	355.7946	364.6134	373.4527	382.3123	391.1917
46	300.0948	308.9330	317.7946	326.6793	335.5869	344.5171	353.4696	362.4441	371.4402	380.4577	389.4962	398.5556
47	305.4752	314.4828	323.5149	332.5710	341.6511	350.7546	359.8813	369.0310	378.2033	387.3978	396.6143	405.8525
48	310.8010	319.9768	329.1780	338.4044	347.6556	356.9313	366.2311	375.5548	384.9021	394.2725	403.6659	413.0818
49	316.0717	325.4144	334.7836	344.1789	353.6000	363.0466	372.5184	382.0149	391.5360	401.0812	410.6503	420.2429
50	321.2869	330.7952	340.3311	349.8941	359.4839	369.1001	378.7426	388.4108	398.1045	407.8233	417.5669	427.3350

Table 13. 10-YEAR TERM—INTEREST RATE (*Continued*)

J	12.00	12.25	12.50	12.75	13.00	13.25	13.50	13.75	14.00	14.25	14.50	14.75
1	10.0000	10.2083	10.4167	10.6250	10.8333	11.0417	11.2500	11.4583	11.6667	11.8750	12.0833	12.2917
2	19.9565	20.3729	20.7894	21.2058	21.6223	22.0388	22.4553	22.8718	23.2883	23.7048	24.1214	24.5380
3	29.8692	30.4934	31.1176	31.7420	32.3663	32.9908	33.6153	34.2398	34.8644	35.4890	36.1137	36.7384
4	39.7374	40.5692	41.4010	42.2330	43.0651	43.8972	44.7295	45.5619	46.3944	47.2269	48.0596	48.8924
5	49.5609	50.5999	51.6390	52.6784	53.7179	54.7576	55.7975	56.8375	57.8777	58.9181	59.9586	60.9993
6	59.3392	60.5851	61.8312	63.0777	64.3244	65.5714	66.8187	68.0662	69.3139	70.5619	71.8101	73.0586
7	69.0717	70.5242	71.9771	73.4304	74.8841	76.3381	77.7925	79.2473	80.7024	82.1578	83.6136	85.0697
8	78.7582	80.4169	82.0762	83.7361	85.3964	87.0572	88.7185	90.3803	92.0426	93.7053	95.3684	97.0320
9	88.3980	90.2627	92.1281	93.9941	95.8608	97.7282	99.5961	101.4647	103.3339	105.2037	107.0740	108.9449
10	97.9907	100.0610	102.1321	104.2041	106.2769	108.3504	110.4248	112.4999	114.5758	116.6524	118.7298	120.8078
11	107.5359	109.8114	112.0879	114.3655	116.6440	118.9235	121.2040	123.4854	125.7678	128.0510	130.3351	132.6201
12	117.0331	119.5134	121.9949	124.4777	126.9617	129.4468	131.9332	134.4206	136.9091	139.3988	141.8894	144.3812
13	126.4818	129.1665	131.8527	134.5403	137.2294	139.9199	142.6117	145.3049	147.9994	150.6951	153.3921	156.0904
14	135.8815	138.7702	141.6606	144.5528	147.4466	150.3420	153.2391	156.1377	159.0378	161.9394	164.8425	167.7470
15	145.2317	148.3240	151.4183	154.5145	157.6127	160.7128	163.8147	166.9184	170.0239	173.1311	176.2400	179.3506
16	154.5319	157.8274	161.1251	164.4251	167.7272	171.0315	174.3380	177.6465	180.9570	184.2695	187.5840	190.9003
17	163.7817	167.2798	170.7805	174.2838	177.7895	181.2977	184.8083	188.3213	191.8365	195.3540	198.8737	202.3956
18	172.9805	176.6809	180.3841	184.0902	187.7991	191.5108	195.2252	198.9422	202.6618	206.3840	210.1086	213.8357
19	182.1279	186.0299	189.9352	193.8437	197.7554	201.6701	205.5879	209.5087	213.4323	217.3588	221.2881	225.2200
20	191.2232	195.3264	199.4333	203.5438	207.6578	211.7752	215.8959	220.0200	224.1473	228.2777	232.4113	236.5479
21	200.2660	204.5700	208.8779	213.1899	217.5057	221.8253	226.1486	230.4756	234.8061	239.1402	243.4777	247.8185
22	209.2558	213.7599	218.2684	222.7813	227.2985	231.8198	236.3453	240.8747	245.4082	249.9454	254.4865	259.0312
23	218.1920	222.8957	227.6043	232.3176	237.0356	241.7583	246.4854	251.2169	255.9527	260.6928	265.4371	270.1854
24	227.0741	231.9768	236.8849	241.7982	246.7165	251.6399	256.5682	261.5014	266.4392	271.3817	276.3287	281.2802
25	235.9015	241.0027	246.1097	251.2224	256.3406	261.4642	266.5932	271.7275	276.8669	282.0113	287.1607	292.3149
26	244.6737	249.9728	255.2781	260.5896	265.9071	271.2305	276.5597	281.8946	287.2350	292.5810	297.9323	303.2889
27	253.3902	258.8865	264.3896	269.8993	275.4155	280.9381	286.4670	292.0020	297.5430	303.0900	308.6428	314.2013
28	262.0504	267.7433	273.4435	279.1508	284.8651	290.5864	296.3144	302.0490	307.7901	313.5377	319.2915	325.0514
29	270.6537	276.5426	282.4392	288.3436	294.2554	300.1747	306.1013	312.0350	317.9757	323.9232	329.8775	335.8385
30	279.1996	285.2837	291.3762	297.4769	303.5857	309.7024	315.8270	321.9592	328.0989	334.2460	340.4003	346.5617
31	287.6875	293.9661	300.2538	306.5502	312.8553	319.1688	325.4908	331.8209	338.1590	344.5051	350.8589	357.2203
32	296.1168	302.5893	309.0713	315.5628	322.0635	328.5733	335.0920	341.6194	348.1554	354.6999	361.2526	367.8134
33	304.4869	311.1525	317.8283	324.5141	331.2098	337.9151	344.6299	351.3540	358.0873	364.8295	371.5806	378.3404
34	312.7972	319.6552	326.5240	333.4034	340.2933	347.1935	354.1038	361.0240	367.9539	374.8934	381.8422	388.8003
35	321.0472	328.0967	335.1578	342.2301	349.3136	356.4079	363.5129	370.6285	377.7544	384.8905	392.0365	399.1924
36	329.2361	336.4765	343.7291	350.9935	358.2698	365.5575	372.8567	380.1670	387.4882	394.8202	402.1628	409.5157
37	337.3635	344.7939	352.2371	359.6930	367.1612	374.6417	382.1342	389.6385	397.1544	404.6816	412.2201	419.7695
38	345.4288	353.0483	360.6814	368.3278	375.9873	383.6597	391.3448	399.0424	406.7522	414.4740	422.2077	429.9530
39	353.4311	361.2390	369.0611	376.8972	384.7472	392.6108	400.4877	408.3778	416.2808	424.1965	432.1247	440.0651
40	361.3701	369.3653	377.3756	385.4006	393.4402	401.4941	409.5621	417.6440	425.7394	433.8483	441.9703	450.1052
41	369.2450	377.4267	385.6242	393.8373	402.0657	410.3091	418.5674	426.8402	435.1273	443.4285	451.7435	460.0722
42	377.0551	385.4224	393.8063	402.2066	410.6229	419.0550	427.5026	435.9656	444.4435	452.9363	461.4436	469.9653
43	384.7999	393.3518	401.9212	410.5077	419.1110	427.7309	436.3671	445.0193	453.6873	462.3709	471.0697	479.7835
44	392.4786	401.2143	409.9681	418.7399	427.5293	436.3361	445.1599	454.0006	462.8578	471.7313	480.6208	489.5260
45	400.0907	409.0090	417.9464	426.9025	435.8770	444.8698	453.8804	462.9086	471.9541	481.0167	490.0961	499.1919
46	407.6354	416.7354	425.8553	434.9947	444.1535	453.3312	462.5277	471.7425	480.9755	490.2262	499.4945	508.7801
47	415.1121	424.3927	433.6941	443.0159	452.3578	461.7196	471.1009	480.5014	489.9209	499.3589	508.8153	518.2897
48	422.5201	431.9802	441.4620	450.9652	460.4893	470.0341	479.5993	489.1845	498.7895	508.4139	518.0575	527.7198
49	429.8587	439.4973	449.1585	458.8418	468.5471	478.2739	488.0220	497.7909	507.5805	517.3903	527.2200	537.0694
50	437.1272	446.9432	456.7826	466.6451	476.5304	486.4382	496.3681	506.3197	516.2928	526.2871	536.3021	546.3375

Table 13. 15-YEAR TERM—INTEREST RATE

J	9.00	9.25	9.50	9.75	10.00	10.25	10.50	10.75	11.00	11.25	11.50	11.75
1	7.5000	7.7083	7.9167	8.1250	8.3333	8.5417	8.7500	8.9583	9.1667	9.3750	9.5833	9.7917
2	14.9802	15.3968	15.8133	16.2299	16.6466	17.0632	17.4798	17.8965	18.3132	18.7299	19.1466	19.5633
3	22.4404	23.0651	23.6899	24.3147	24.9395	25.5644	26.1893	26.8143	27.4393	28.0644	28.6895	29.3146
4	29.8805	30.7132	31.5461	32.3790	33.2120	34.0451	34.8783	35.7116	36.5450	37.3784	38.2119	39.0455
5	37.3003	38.3410	39.3818	40.4228	41.4639	42.5052	43.5466	44.5882	45.6299	46.6717	47.7136	48.7557
6	44.6997	45.9482	47.1969	48.4459	49.6950	50.9444	52.1941	53.4439	54.6939	55.9441	57.1944	58.4450
7	52.0785	53.5347	54.9912	56.4480	57.9052	59.3627	60.8204	62.2785	63.7368	65.1954	66.6542	68.1133
8	59.4366	61.1004	62.7645	64.4292	66.0942	67.7597	69.4255	71.0918	72.7584	74.4253	76.0926	77.7602
9	66.7739	68.6450	70.5168	72.3891	74.2619	76.1353	78.0092	79.8836	81.7585	83.6338	85.5096	87.3857
10	74.0900	76.1685	78.2477	80.3276	82.4082	84.4894	86.5713	88.6538	90.7369	92.8206	94.9048	96.9896
11	81.3850	83.6706	85.9571	88.2445	90.5327	92.8218	95.1116	97.4022	99.6935	101.9855	104.2781	106.5714
12	88.6586	91.1512	93.6449	96.1397	98.6354	101.1322	103.6299	106.1285	108.6279	111.1282	113.6293	116.1312
13	95.9107	98.6102	101.3109	104.0129	106.7161	109.4205	112.1260	114.8325	117.5401	120.2487	122.9582	125.6686
14	103.1411	106.0473	108.9550	111.8641	114.7746	117.6865	120.5997	123.5141	126.4298	129.3466	132.2645	135.1835
15	110.3497	113.4624	116.5769	119.6930	122.8107	125.9300	129.0508	132.1731	135.2967	138.4217	141.5481	144.6756
16	117.5363	120.8554	124.1764	127.4994	130.8242	134.1508	137.4792	140.8092	144.1408	147.4740	150.8086	154.1447
17	124.7007	128.2259	131.7534	135.2831	138.8149	142.3488	145.8845	149.4222	152.9617	156.5030	160.0460	163.5908
18	131.8428	135.5740	139.3078	143.0441	146.7827	150.5236	154.2668	158.0120	161.7594	165.5087	169.2599	173.0130
19	138.9623	142.8994	146.8393	150.7820	154.7273	158.6752	162.6256	166.5784	170.5334	174.4907	178.4502	182.4117
20	146.0592	150.2019	154.3478	158.4967	162.6486	166.8033	170.9608	175.1210	179.2838	183.4490	187.6166	191.7865
21	153.1333	157.4814	161.8330	166.1880	170.5463	174.9078	179.2723	183.6398	188.0101	192.3832	196.7589	201.1371
22	160.1843	164.7376	169.2948	173.8557	178.4203	182.9883	187.5598	192.1344	196.7122	201.2931	205.8768	210.4634
23	167.2121	171.9705	176.7330	181.4997	186.2704	191.0448	195.8230	200.6048	205.3900	210.1785	214.9702	219.7650
24	174.2166	179.1797	184.1475	189.1197	194.0963	199.0770	204.0618	209.0506	214.0430	219.0392	224.0388	229.0418
25	181.1975	186.3652	191.5380	196.7156	201.8979	207.0848	212.2760	217.4716	222.6713	227.8749	233.0823	238.2935
26	188.1548	193.5268	198.9043	204.2870	209.6749	215.0678	220.4654	225.8677	231.2744	236.6854	242.1006	247.5198
27	195.0881	200.6642	206.2462	211.8340	217.4272	223.0259	228.6297	234.2385	239.8522	245.4705	251.0933	256.7205
28	201.9974	207.7773	213.5637	219.3561	225.1546	230.9589	236.7687	242.5839	248.4044	254.2299	260.0603	265.8953
29	208.8824	214.8659	220.8563	226.8534	232.8568	238.8665	244.8822	250.9037	256.9308	262.9634	269.0012	275.0440
30	215.7430	221.9299	228.1241	234.3254	240.5337	246.7486	252.9700	259.1976	265.4313	271.6708	277.9159	284.1664
31	222.5790	228.9689	235.3667	241.7721	248.1849	254.6049	261.0318	267.4654	273.9054	280.3517	286.8040	293.2622
32	229.3901	235.9829	242.5840	249.1933	255.8104	262.4352	269.0674	275.7068	282.3530	289.0060	295.6654	302.3310
33	236.1763	242.9716	249.7757	256.5886	263.4099	270.2393	277.0766	283.9216	290.7739	297.6334	304.4997	311.3727
34	242.9373	249.9348	256.9418	263.9580	270.9831	278.0170	285.0592	292.1096	299.1678	306.2336	313.3068	320.3870
35	249.6730	256.8724	264.0818	271.3011	278.5299	285.7680	293.0149	300.2705	307.5345	314.8065	322.0863	329.3736
36	256.3831	263.7841	271.1958	278.6179	286.0501	293.4921	300.9435	308.4041	315.8736	323.3517	330.8380	338.3323
37	263.0674	270.6697	278.2834	285.9080	293.5434	301.1891	308.8448	316.5102	324.1850	331.8689	339.5616	347.2628
38	269.7259	277.5291	285.3444	293.1713	301.0095	308.8587	316.7184	324.5885	332.4684	340.3580	348.2569	356.1647
39	276.3581	284.3621	292.3787	300.4076	308.4484	316.5007	324.5643	332.6387	340.7236	348.8186	356.9235	365.0378
40	282.9641	291.1684	299.3860	307.6165	315.8596	324.1149	332.3820	340.6606	348.9502	357.2505	365.5612	373.8819
41	289.5435	297.9478	306.3661	314.7980	323.2431	331.7011	340.1715	348.6539	357.1481	365.6535	374.1698	382.6967
42	296.0962	304.7001	313.3187	321.9517	330.5986	339.2589	347.9324	356.6185	365.3169	374.0271	382.7489	391.4818
43	302.6220	311.4252	320.2438	329.0775	337.9258	346.7882	355.6644	364.5539	373.4564	382.3713	391.2983	400.2370
44	309.1207	318.1227	327.1410	336.1751	345.2245	354.2887	363.3674	372.4601	381.5663	390.6856	399.8177	408.9620
45	315.5920	324.7926	334.0102	343.2443	352.4945	361.7602	371.0411	380.3366	389.6464	398.9699	408.3067	417.6564
46	322.0358	331.4345	340.8510	350.2849	359.7355	369.2024	378.6852	388.1833	397.6963	407.2238	416.7652	426.3200
47	328.4518	338.0483	347.6634	357.2966	366.9473	376.6151	386.2995	395.9999	405.7159	415.4470	425.1927	434.9526
48	334.8399	344.6338	354.4470	364.2791	374.1297	383.9980	393.8836	403.7861	413.7048	423.6393	433.5891	443.5537
49	341.1999	351.1906	361.2017	371.2324	381.2823	391.3508	401.4374	411.5416	421.6627	431.8004	441.9540	452.1231
50	347.5315	357.7187	367.9271	378.1561	388.4050	398.6734	408.9606	419.2662	429.5894	439.9299	450.2871	460.6604

Table 13. 15-YEAR TERM—INTEREST RATE (*Continued*)

J	12.00	12.25	12.50	12.75	13.00	13.25	13.50	13.75	14.00	14.25	14.50	14.75
1	10.0000	10.2083	10.4167	10.6250	10.8333	11.0417	11.2500	11.4583	11.6667	11.8750	12.0833	12.2917
2	19.9800	20.3967	20.8135	21.2302	21.6470	22.0637	22.4805	22.8973	23.3141	23.7309	24.1477	24.5645
3	29.9397	30.5649	31.1902	31.8154	32.4407	33.0660	33.6913	34.3166	34.9420	35.5674	36.1928	36.8182
4	39.8791	40.7128	41.5466	42.3804	43.2142	44.0482	44.8821	45.7161	46.5502	47.3843	48.2185	49.0527
5	49.7978	50.8401	51.8824	52.9249	53.9675	55.0101	56.0528	57.0956	58.1385	59.1814	60.2244	61.2675
6	59.6957	60.9466	62.1976	63.4488	64.7001	65.9515	67.2031	68.4548	69.7066	70.9585	72.2105	73.4626
7	69.5726	71.0321	72.4918	73.9518	75.4119	76.8723	78.3328	79.7934	81.2543	82.7153	84.1764	85.6377
8	79.4282	81.0964	82.7649	84.4337	86.1028	87.7721	89.4416	91.1113	92.7813	94.4515	96.1219	97.7924
9	89.2623	91.1393	93.0166	94.8943	96.7723	98.6507	100.5293	102.4083	104.2875	106.1670	108.0467	109.9267
10	99.0748	101.1605	103.2467	105.3334	107.4204	109.5079	111.5957	113.6839	115.7725	117.8614	119.9506	122.0401
11	108.8654	111.1599	113.4550	115.7506	118.0468	120.3434	122.6406	124.9381	127.2362	129.5346	131.8334	134.1325
12	118.6338	121.1372	123.6412	126.1459	128.6512	131.1571	133.6636	136.1706	138.6782	141.1862	143.6947	146.2036
13	128.3800	131.0922	133.8052	136.5189	139.2335	141.9487	144.6646	147.3811	150.0983	152.8161	155.5344	158.2532
14	138.1036	141.0246	143.9466	146.8695	149.7933	152.7179	155.6433	158.5694	161.4963	164.4239	167.3521	170.2809
15	147.8044	150.9343	154.0653	157.1973	160.3304	163.4645	166.5994	169.7353	172.8719	176.0094	179.1476	182.2866
16	157.4822	160.8209	164.1610	167.5022	170.8446	174.1882	177.5327	180.8783	184.2249	187.5724	190.9207	194.2699
17	167.1367	170.6844	174.2335	177.7839	181.3357	184.8888	188.4430	191.9984	195.5549	199.1125	202.6710	206.2305
18	176.7678	180.5243	184.2825	188.0422	191.8034	195.5660	199.3300	203.0953	206.8618	210.6295	214.3983	218.1682
19	186.3752	190.3405	194.3078	198.2767	202.2473	206.2196	210.1933	214.1686	218.1452	222.1231	226.1023	230.0828
20	195.9586	200.1328	204.3091	208.4873	212.6674	216.8493	221.0329	225.2181	229.4048	233.5931	237.7828	241.9738
21	205.5178	209.9009	214.2862	218.6737	223.0633	227.4548	231.8483	236.2435	240.6405	245.0392	249.4394	253.8411
22	215.0527	219.6445	224.2389	228.8356	233.4347	238.0359	242.6393	247.2446	251.8519	256.4610	261.0718	265.6843
23	224.5628	229.3635	234.1669	238.9729	243.7814	248.5924	253.4056	258.2211	263.0387	267.8583	272.6798	277.5031
24	234.0481	239.0575	244.0698	249.0851	254.1031	259.1238	264.1470	269.1727	274.2006	279.2308	284.2631	289.2973
25	243.5082	248.7262	253.9476	259.1721	264.3996	269.6300	274.8632	280.0991	285.3374	290.5782	295.8213	301.0666
26	252.9428	258.3696	263.7999	269.2336	274.6706	280.1108	285.5539	291.0000	296.4488	301.9002	307.3542	312.8105
27	262.3518	267.9872	273.6264	279.2693	284.9158	290.5657	296.2188	301.8751	307.5344	313.1966	318.8614	324.5289
28	271.7349	277.5788	283.4268	289.2789	295.1348	300.9945	306.8576	312.7242	318.5940	324.4669	330.3427	336.2214
29	281.0917	287.1441	293.2010	299.2622	305.3276	311.3969	317.4701	323.5469	329.6272	335.7109	341.7977	347.8877
30	290.4222	296.6830	302.9486	309.2189	315.4937	321.7727	328.0559	334.3430	340.6338	346.9283	353.2262	359.5274
31	299.7259	306.1950	312.6694	319.1487	325.6328	332.1215	338.6147	345.1120	351.6135	358.1187	364.6277	371.1403
32	309.0026	315.6800	322.3630	329.0513	335.7447	342.4431	349.1462	355.8538	362.5658	369.2819	376.0021	382.7259
33	318.2521	325.1377	332.0292	338.9264	345.8291	352.7371	359.6501	366.5680	373.4906	380.4176	387.3488	394.2841
34	327.4741	334.5677	341.6677	348.7738	355.8857	363.0032	370.1262	377.2543	384.3874	391.5253	398.6677	405.8144
35	336.6683	343.9699	351.2782	358.5931	365.9141	373.2412	380.5740	387.9124	395.2560	402.6048	409.9583	417.3165
36	345.8343	353.3438	360.8605	368.3840	375.9142	383.4507	390.9934	398.5419	406.0961	413.6556	421.2204	428.7900
37	354.9721	362.6893	370.4141	378.1463	385.8855	393.6314	401.3839	409.1426	416.9072	424.6776	432.4535	440.2347
38	364.0812	372.0060	379.9389	387.8796	395.8277	403.7830	411.7452	419.7140	427.6891	435.6704	443.6574	451.6500
39	373.1614	381.2937	389.4346	397.5836	405.7406	413.9051	422.0770	430.2559	438.4414	446.6335	454.8317	463.0358
40	382.2123	390.5520	398.9007	407.2581	415.6238	423.9975	432.3790	440.7679	449.1638	457.5666	465.9760	474.3915
41	391.2338	399.7807	408.3371	416.9026	425.4770	434.0598	442.6508	451.2496	459.8560	468.4695	477.0899	485.7170
42	400.2254	408.9794	417.7434	426.5170	435.2999	444.0917	452.8922	461.7008	470.5174	479.3417	488.1732	497.0117
43	409.1870	418.1479	427.1193	436.1008	445.0921	454.0929	463.1026	472.1211	481.1480	490.1828	499.2254	508.2753
44	418.1181	427.2857	436.4644	445.6537	454.8534	464.0629	473.2819	482.5101	491.7471	500.9925	510.2461	519.5074
45	427.0186	436.3927	445.7785	455.1755	464.5833	474.0015	483.4297	492.8675	502.3146	511.7705	521.2350	530.7076
46	435.8880	445.4685	455.0613	464.6657	474.2816	483.9083	493.5455	503.1929	512.8499	522.5163	532.1916	541.8756
47	444.7261	454.5128	464.3123	474.1241	483.9478	493.7829	503.6291	513.4859	523.3528	533.2296	543.1157	553.0109
48	453.5326	463.5253	473.5313	483.5503	493.5817	503.6251	513.6801	523.7461	533.8229	543.9099	554.0068	564.1131
49	462.3071	472.5056	482.7180	492.9440	503.1829	513.4344	523.6981	533.9733	544.2597	554.5569	564.8645	575.1819
50	471.0493	481.4534	491.8720	502.3047	512.7511	523.2106	533.6827	544.1670	554.6630	565.1703	575.6884	586.2168

Table 13. 20-YEAR TERM—INTEREST RATE

J	9.00	9.25	9.50	9.75	10.00	10.25	10.50	10.75	11.00	11.25	11.50	11.75
1	7.5000	7.7083	7.9167	8.1250	8.3333	8.5417	8.7500	8.9583	9.1667	9.3750	9.5833	9.7917
2	14.9888	15.4055	15.8222	16.2389	16.6557	17.0724	17.4892	17.9060	18.3227	18.7395	19.1563	19.5731
3	22.4662	23.0914	23.7166	24.3418	24.9670	25.5922	26.2175	26.8428	27.4681	28.0935	28.7188	29.3442
4	29.9323	30.7659	31.5996	32.4333	33.2671	34.1010	34.9348	35.7688	36.6027	37.4367	38.2708	39.1048
5	37.3869	38.4290	39.4712	40.5136	41.5560	42.5985	43.6411	44.6837	45.7265	46.7692	47.8121	48.8550
6	44.8299	46.0806	47.3314	48.5824	49.8335	51.0848	52.3362	53.5876	54.8392	56.0909	57.3426	58.5944
7	52.2612	53.7205	55.1800	56.6398	58.0997	59.5597	61.0200	62.4803	63.9409	65.4015	66.8623	68.3232
8	59.6808	61.3488	63.0170	64.6855	66.3542	68.0232	69.6924	71.3618	73.0313	74.7011	76.3710	78.0410
9	67.0886	68.9652	70.8422	72.7195	74.5972	76.4751	78.3533	80.2318	82.1105	83.9895	85.8686	87.7480
10	74.4844	76.5698	78.6555	80.7418	82.8284	84.9153	87.0027	89.0903	91.1783	93.2665	95.3551	97.4438
11	81.8683	84.1623	86.4570	88.7521	91.0478	93.3438	95.6404	97.9373	100.2346	102.5322	104.8302	107.1285
12	89.2400	91.7429	94.2464	96.7505	99.2552	101.7605	104.2663	106.7726	109.2793	111.7864	114.2940	116.8019
13	96.5996	99.3112	102.0236	104.7368	107.4507	110.1652	112.8803	115.5960	118.3123	121.0290	123.7462	126.4639
14	103.9468	106.3673	109.7887	112.7109	115.6340	118.5578	121.4824	124.4076	127.3334	130.2599	133.1869	136.1143
15	111.2817	114.4110	117.5414	120.6727	123.8051	126.9383	130.0723	133.2071	136.3427	139.4789	142.6158	145.7532
16	118.6041	121.9423	125.2817	128.6222	131.9638	135.3065	138.6501	141.9946	145.3399	148.6860	152.0329	155.3804
17	125.9140	129.4610	133.0094	136.5592	140.1102	143.6623	147.2155	150.7698	154.3250	157.8811	161.4380	164.9957
18	133.2112	136.9671	140.7246	144.4836	148.2440	152.0057	155.7686	159.5327	163.2978	167.0640	170.8310	174.5990
19	140.4957	144.4605	148.4271	152.3953	156.3651	160.3364	164.3091	168.2831	172.2583	176.2346	180.2119	184.1902
20	147.7673	151.9410	156.1167	160.2942	164.4736	168.6545	172.8370	177.0209	181.2062	185.3928	189.5805	193.7693
21	155.0259	159.4086	163.7934	168.1803	172.5691	176.9598	181.3522	185.7461	190.1416	194.5385	198.9366	203.3360
22	162.2715	166.8631	171.4571	176.0534	180.6518	185.2522	189.8545	194.4585	199.0643	203.6716	208.2803	212.8903
23	169.5040	174.3045	179.1077	183.9133	188.7213	193.5315	198.3438	203.1581	207.9741	212.7919	217.6112	222.4320
24	176.7233	181.7327	186.7450	191.7601	196.7777	201.7978	206.8201	211.8446	216.8710	221.8993	226.9294	231.9611
25	183.9292	189.1475	194.3690	199.5935	204.8208	210.0507	215.2832	220.5179	225.7549	230.9938	236.2347	241.4773
26	191.1217	196.5489	201.9796	207.4135	212.8505	218.2904	223.7329	229.1780	234.6255	240.0752	245.5270	250.9806
27	198.3006	203.9368	209.5767	215.2200	220.8667	226.5165	232.1693	237.8248	243.4829	249.1433	254.8061	260.4709
28	205.4659	211.3110	217.1600	223.0129	228.8693	234.7291	240.5921	246.4580	252.3268	258.1981	264.0719	269.9479
29	212.6175	218.6714	224.7297	230.7920	236.8582	242.9280	249.0012	255.0777	261.1572	267.2394	273.3243	279.4117
30	219.7552	226.0180	232.2854	238.5572	244.8332	251.1131	257.3966	263.6836	269.9739	276.2671	282.5632	288.8620
31	226.8790	233.3506	239.8272	246.3085	252.7942	259.2842	265.7781	272.2757	278.7768	285.2811	291.7885	298.2987
32	233.9888	240.6692	247.3549	254.0457	260.7412	267.4413	274.1455	280.8538	287.5658	294.2812	301.0000	307.7217
33	241.0843	247.9735	254.8684	261.7687	268.6740	275.5842	282.4988	289.4178	296.3407	303.2673	310.1975	317.1309
34	248.1656	255.2636	262.3676	269.4773	276.5925	283.7128	290.8379	297.9675	305.1015	312.2393	319.3810	326.5260
35	255.2326	262.5392	269.8523	277.1715	284.4965	291.8270	299.1625	306.5030	313.8479	321.1971	328.5502	335.9071
36	262.2850	269.8004	277.3225	284.8512	292.3860	299.9256	307.4727	315.0239	322.5799	330.1404	337.7052	345.2739
37	269.3229	277.0469	284.7781	292.5162	300.2608	308.0116	315.7662	323.5302	331.2973	339.0693	346.8457	354.6263
38	276.3461	284.2787	292.2189	300.1664	308.1209	316.0818	324.0489	332.0217	340.0000	347.9834	355.9716	363.9642
39	283.3545	291.4956	299.6448	307.8017	315.9660	324.1371	332.3147	340.4984	348.6879	356.8828	365.0827	373.2874
40	290.3479	298.6975	307.0557	315.4220	323.7960	332.1773	340.5655	348.9601	357.3608	365.7672	374.1790	382.5957
41	297.3264	305.8844	314.4515	323.0271	331.6109	340.2024	348.8011	357.4066	366.0186	374.6366	383.2602	391.8891
42	304.2897	313.0561	321.8320	330.6170	339.4105	348.2122	357.0214	365.8379	374.6611	383.4907	392.3263	401.1674
43	311.2377	320.2124	329.1972	338.1914	347.1947	356.2065	365.2263	374.2537	383.2883	392.3295	401.3770	410.4304
44	318.1704	327.3534	336.5469	345.7504	354.9633	364.1853	373.4156	382.6540	391.8999	401.1528	410.4123	419.6780
45	325.0876	334.4787	343.8809	353.2936	362.7163	372.1483	381.5893	391.0386	400.4958	409.9604	419.4320	428.9101
46	331.9891	341.5884	351.1993	360.8211	370.4534	380.0956	389.7470	399.4073	409.0759	418.7522	428.4359	438.1264
47	338.8750	348.6823	358.5018	368.3327	378.1746	388.0268	397.8889	407.7601	417.6400	427.5281	437.4239	447.3269
48	345.7450	355.7603	365.7883	375.8283	385.8797	395.9420	406.0145	416.0967	426.1880	436.2879	446.3958	456.5113
49	352.5991	362.8222	373.0587	383.3077	393.5686	403.8410	414.1240	424.4171	434.7198	445.0315	455.3516	465.6795
50	359.4371	369.8680	380.3128	390.7708	401.2412	411.7235	422.2170	432.7211	443.2352	453.7586	464.2909	474.8315

Table 13. 20-YEAR TERM—INTEREST RATE (*Continued*)

J	12.00	12.25	12.50	12.75	13.00	13.25	13.50	13.75	14.00	14.25	14.50	14.75
1	10.0000	10.2083	10.4167	10.6250	10.8333	11.0417	11.2500	11.4583	11.6667	11.8750	12.0833	12.2917
2	19.9899	20.4067	20.8235	21.2403	21.6571	22.0739	22.4907	22.9075	23.3244	23.7412	24.1580	24.5748
3	29.9696	30.5950	31.2204	31.8458	32.4712	33.0967	33.7221	34.3475	34.9730	35.5985	36.2239	36.8494
4	39.9389	40.7731	41.6072	42.4414	43.2756	44.1098	44.9440	45.7782	46.6124	47.4467	48.2810	49.1152
5	49.8979	50.9409	51.9839	53.0269	54.0700	55.1131	56.1563	57.1994	58.2426	59.2858	60.3290	61.3722
6	59.8463	61.0983	62.3503	63.6024	64.8545	66.1067	67.3589	68.6111	69.8634	71.1157	72.3680	73.6203
7	69.7841	71.2452	72.7064	74.1676	75.6289	77.0903	78.5517	80.0132	81.4747	82.9362	84.3978	85.8594
8	79.7112	81.3815	83.0520	84.7225	86.3931	88.0638	89.7346	91.4054	93.0763	94.7473	96.4183	98.0893
9	89.6275	91.5071	93.3870	95.2669	97.1470	99.0272	100.9075	102.7878	104.6683	106.5488	108.4293	110.3099
10	99.5328	101.6219	103.7113	105.8008	107.8905	109.9803	112.0702	114.1602	116.2504	118.3406	120.4308	122.5211
11	109.4270	111.7258	114.0248	116.3240	118.6234	120.9230	123.2227	125.5226	127.8225	130.1226	132.4227	134.7229
12	119.3101	121.8186	124.3274	126.8364	129.3457	131.8552	134.3648	136.8746	139.3846	141.8947	144.4048	146.9151
13	129.1819	131.9003	134.6190	137.3380	140.0572	142.7768	145.4965	148.2164	150.9365	153.6567	156.3770	159.0975
14	139.0423	141.9706	144.8994	147.8285	150.7579	153.6876	156.6175	159.5477	162.4781	165.4086	168.3393	171.2701
15	148.8912	152.0297	155.1686	158.3079	161.4476	164.5876	167.7279	170.8684	174.0092	177.1502	180.2914	183.4327
16	158.7285	162.0772	165.4263	168.7760	172.1261	175.4766	178.8274	182.1785	185.5298	188.8814	192.2332	195.5852
17	168.5540	172.1130	175.6726	179.2328	182.7934	186.3545	189.9159	193.4777	197.0398	200.6021	204.1647	207.7275
18	178.3677	182.1372	185.9073	189.6780	193.4493	197.2211	200.9933	204.7660	208.5389	212.3122	216.0857	219.8595
19	188.1694	192.1495	196.1302	200.1117	204.0938	208.0764	212.0596	216.0432	220.0272	224.0115	227.9961	231.9809
20	197.9591	202.1498	206.3413	210.5336	214.7267	218.9203	223.1145	227.3092	231.5043	235.6999	239.8957	244.0918
21	207.7365	212.1380	216.5404	220.9437	225.3478	229.7525	234.1579	238.5639	242.9703	247.3772	251.7845	256.1920
22	217.5016	222.1140	226.7274	231.3418	235.9570	240.5731	245.1898	249.8071	254.4250	259.0434	263.6622	268.2813
23	227.2542	232.0776	236.9022	241.7278	246.5543	251.3817	256.2099	261.0388	265.8683	270.6983	275.5288	280.3597
24	236.9942	242.0288	247.0646	252.1015	257.1395	262.1784	267.2182	272.2588	277.3000	282.3418	287.3841	292.4268
25	246.7216	251.9673	257.2145	262.4629	267.7124	272.9630	278.2145	283.4669	288.7200	293.9737	299.2280	304.4828
26	256.4361	261.8932	267.3517	272.8117	278.2729	283.7353	289.1987	294.6630	300.1281	305.5939	311.0603	316.5273
27	266.1376	271.8061	277.4763	283.1479	288.8210	294.4952	300.1706	305.8470	311.5242	317.2023	322.8810	328.5603
28	275.8261	281.7061	287.5879	293.4714	299.3563	305.2426	311.1301	317.0187	322.9083	328.7987	334.6898	340.5816
29	285.5013	291.5930	297.6866	303.7819	309.8789	315.9773	322.0771	328.1780	334.2800	340.3829	346.4867	352.5911
30	295.1631	301.4666	307.7720	314.0794	320.3886	326.6993	333.0114	339.3248	345.6394	351.9549	358.2714	364.5886
31	304.8115	311.3268	317.8442	324.3637	330.8851	337.4082	343.9329	350.4589	356.9862	363.5145	370.0438	376.5740
32	314.4463	321.1734	327.9030	334.6347	341.3685	348.1041	354.8414	361.5802	368.3203	375.0616	381.8039	388.5471
33	324.0672	331.0064	337.9482	344.8923	351.8386	358.7868	365.7368	372.6885	379.6415	386.5959	393.5513	400.5078
34	333.6743	340.8256	347.9796	355.1362	362.2951	369.4561	376.6190	383.7836	390.9498	398.1173	405.2861	412.4559
35	343.2674	350.6309	357.9973	365.3664	372.7380	380.1118	387.4877	394.8655	402.2449	409.6258	417.0080	424.3913
36	352.8463	360.4220	368.0009	375.5827	383.1671	390.7539	398.3429	405.9339	413.5267	421.1211	428.7168	436.3138
37	362.4108	370.1989	377.9904	385.7849	393.5823	401.3822	409.1844	416.9888	424.7951	432.6031	440.4125	448.2233
38	371.9609	379.9615	387.9656	395.9729	403.9833	411.9964	420.0121	428.0299	436.0498	444.0715	452.0948	460.1195
39	381.4964	389.7095	397.9263	406.1466	414.3702	422.5966	430.8257	439.0572	447.2908	455.5264	463.7637	472.0024
40	391.0171	399.4428	407.8725	416.3058	424.7426	433.1824	441.6251	450.0703	458.5178	466.9674	475.4188	483.8718
41	400.5229	409.1613	417.8039	426.4504	435.1005	443.7538	452.4102	461.0693	469.7308	478.3945	487.0601	495.7275
42	410.0137	418.8648	427.7204	436.5801	445.4437	454.3106	463.1808	472.0538	480.9295	489.8074	498.6875	507.5693
43	419.4893	428.5532	437.6219	446.6949	455.7720	464.8527	473.9367	483.0239	492.1137	501.2061	510.3006	519.3971
44	428.9495	438.2263	447.5082	456.7946	466.0852	475.3798	484.6779	493.9792	503.2834	512.5902	521.8994	531.2106
45	438.3942	447.8840	457.3791	466.8789	476.3833	485.8918	495.4040	504.9196	514.4383	523.9598	533.4837	543.0098
46	447.8233	457.5261	467.2344	476.9479	486.6660	496.3885	506.1149	515.8450	525.5783	535.3145	545.0533	554.7945
47	457.2365	467.1524	477.0741	487.0012	496.9332	506.8698	516.8106	526.7551	536.7031	546.6542	556.6081	566.5644
48	466.6338	476.7628	486.8980	497.0387	507.1847	517.3355	527.4907	537.6499	547.8127	557.9788	568.1478	578.3194
49	476.0149	486.3571	496.7058	507.0603	517.4204	527.7854	538.1551	548.5290	558.9068	569.2880	579.6722	590.0592
50	485.3797	495.9352	506.4974	517.0658	527.6400	538.2194	548.8037	559.3925	569.9852	580.5816	591.1813	601.7838

Table 13. 25-YEAR TERM—INTEREST RATE

J	9.00	9.25	9.50	9.75	10.00	10.25	10.50	10.75	11.00	11.25	11.50	11.75
1	7.5000	7.7083	7.9167	8.1250	8.3333	8.5417	8.7500	8.9583	9.1667	9.3750	9.5833	9.7917
2	14.9959	15.4127	15.8294	16.2462	16.6630	17.0798	17.4965	17.9133	18.3301	18.7468	19.1636	19.5804
3	22.4877	23.1130	23.7383	24.3636	24.9889	25.6142	26.2395	26.8649	27.4902	28.1155	28.7408	29.3661
4	29.9753	30.8092	31.6432	32.4771	33.3111	34.1451	34.9790	35.8130	36.6469	37.4809	38.3148	39.1488
5	37.4587	38.5014	39.5441	40.5868	41.6295	42.6722	43.7149	44.7576	45.8003	46.8431	47.8857	48.9284
6	44.9379	46.1894	47.4410	48.6925	49.9441	51.1957	52.4472	53.6988	54.9504	56.2019	57.4535	58.7050
7	52.4129	53.8733	55.3338	56.7943	58.2548	59.7154	61.1759	62.6364	64.0970	65.5575	67.0180	68.4785
8	59.8836	61.5530	63.2226	64.8921	66.5617	68.2313	69.9009	71.5705	73.2401	74.9097	76.5792	78.2488
9	67.3499	69.2285	71.1072	72.9859	74.8647	76.7434	78.6222	80.5010	82.3798	84.2585	86.1372	88.0159
10	74.8119	76.8998	78.9877	81.0757	83.1637	85.2518	87.3398	89.4279	91.5159	93.6039	95.6919	97.7799
11	82.2695	84.5667	86.8640	89.1613	91.4588	93.7562	96.0536	98.3511	100.6485	102.9459	105.2433	107.5406
12	89.7227	92.2294	94.7361	97.2429	99.7498	102.2567	104.7637	107.2706	109.7775	112.2844	114.7913	117.2980
13	97.1715	99.8877	102.6039	105.3203	108.0368	110.7533	113.4699	116.1864	118.9030	121.6194	124.3358	127.0522
14	104.6158	107.5416	110.4675	113.3936	116.3198	119.2460	122.1722	125.0985	128.0247	130.9509	133.8770	136.8030
15	112.0555	115.1911	118.3268	121.4626	124.5986	127.7346	130.8707	134.0067	137.1428	140.2788	143.4147	146.5505
16	119.4908	122.8361	126.1817	129.5274	132.8733	136.2192	139.5652	142.9112	146.2572	149.6030	152.9489	156.2945
17	126.9214	130.4767	134.0322	137.5879	141.1438	144.6998	148.2558	151.8118	155.3678	158.9237	162.4795	166.0352
18	134.3474	138.1127	141.8783	145.6441	149.4101	153.1762	156.9423	160.7085	164.4746	168.2406	172.0066	175.7724
19	141.7688	145.7442	149.7199	153.6960	157.6722	161.6485	165.6249	169.6013	173.5776	177.5539	181.5301	185.5061
20	149.1855	153.3711	157.5571	161.7434	165.9299	170.1166	174.3033	178.4901	182.6768	186.8634	191.0499	195.2362
21	156.5974	160.9934	165.3898	169.7865	174.1834	178.5805	182.9777	187.3749	191.7721	196.1691	200.5661	204.9628
22	164.0046	168.6110	173.2178	177.8250	182.4325	187.0402	191.6479	196.2557	200.8634	205.4711	210.0785	214.6858
23	171.4070	176.2239	181.0413	185.8591	190.6772	195.4955	200.3140	205.1324	209.9508	214.7691	219.5873	224.4052
24	178.8046	183.8321	188.8602	193.8887	198.9175	203.9466	208.9758	214.0050	219.0342	224.0633	229.0922	234.1209
25	186.1973	191.4355	196.6744	201.9137	207.1534	212.3933	217.6334	222.8735	228.1136	233.3536	238.5933	243.8328
26	193.5851	199.0342	204.4838	209.9341	215.3847	220.8356	226.2867	231.7378	237.1889	242.6398	248.0906	253.5411
27	200.9680	206.6279	212.2886	217.9498	223.6115	229.2735	234.9356	240.5979	246.2601	251.9221	257.5840	263.2456
28	208.3459	214.2168	220.0885	225.9609	231.8337	237.7069	243.5803	249.4537	255.3271	261.2004	267.0735	272.9462
29	215.7188	221.8008	227.8837	233.9673	240.0513	246.1358	252.2205	258.3053	264.3900	270.4746	276.5590	282.6430
30	223.0866	229.3798	235.6740	241.9689	248.2643	254.5602	260.8563	267.1525	273.4486	279.7447	286.0405	292.3359
31	230.4494	236.9539	243.4594	249.9657	256.4726	262.9799	269.4876	275.9953	282.5030	289.0106	295.5179	302.0249
32	237.8070	244.5229	251.2398	257.9576	264.6761	271.3951	278.1143	284.8337	291.5531	298.2724	304.9913	311.7099
33	245.1595	252.0868	259.0153	265.9447	272.8749	279.8056	286.7366	293.6677	300.5989	307.5299	314.4606	321.3909
34	252.5067	259.6456	266.7858	273.9269	281.0689	288.2114	295.3542	302.4972	309.6403	316.7831	323.9257	331.0679
35	259.8487	267.1993	274.5512	281.9042	289.2580	296.6124	303.9672	311.3222	318.6772	326.0321	333.3866	340.7408
36	267.1855	274.7478	282.3115	289.8764	297.4422	305.0087	312.5755	320.1426	327.7097	335.2767	342.8433	350.4095
37	274.5169	282.2910	290.0667	297.8436	305.6215	313.4001	321.1791	328.9584	336.7377	344.5169	352.2957	360.0741
38	281.8429	289.8290	297.8168	305.8058	313.7959	321.7867	329.7780	337.7696	345.7612	353.7527	361.7438	369.7345
39	289.1636	297.3617	305.5616	313.7628	321.9652	330.1683	338.3720	346.5760	354.7801	362.9840	371.1876	379.3906
40	296.4788	304.8890	313.3011	321.7147	330.1295	338.5451	346.9612	355.3778	363.7943	372.2108	380.6269	389.0425
41	303.7885	312.4110	321.0354	329.6614	338.2886	346.9168	355.5456	364.1747	372.8039	381.4330	390.0618	398.6900
42	311.0927	319.9275	328.7643	337.6028	346.4427	355.2835	364.1250	372.9668	381.8088	390.6507	399.4922	408.3332
43	318.3913	327.4385	336.4879	345.5390	354.5915	363.6451	372.6994	381.7541	390.8090	399.8637	408.9181	417.9719
44	325.6843	334.9440	344.2060	353.4698	362.7351	372.0016	381.2688	390.5365	399.8043	409.0720	418.3394	427.6062
45	332.9717	342.4440	351.9186	361.3953	370.8735	380.3529	389.8332	399.3139	408.7948	418.2756	427.7561	437.2359
46	340.2534	349.9363	359.6258	369.3153	379.0066	388.6990	398.3924	408.0863	417.7804	427.4744	437.1681	446.8611
47	347.5294	357.4270	367.3274	377.2299	387.1343	397.0399	406.9465	416.8537	426.7611	436.6684	446.5754	456.4818
48	354.7995	364.9100	375.0234	385.1390	395.2566	405.3755	415.4954	425.6160	435.7368	445.8576	455.9780	466.0978
49	362.0639	372.3873	382.7137	393.0426	403.3734	413.7057	424.0391	434.3732	444.7075	455.0418	465.3758	475.7091
50	369.3224	379.8588	390.3984	400.9405	411.4848	422.0306	432.5775	443.1252	453.6732	464.2211	474.7687	485.3157

Table 13. 25-YEAR TERM—INTEREST RATE (*Continued*)

J	12.00	12.25	12.50	12.75	13.00	13.25	13.50	13.75	14.00	14.25	14.50	14.75
1	10.0000	10.2083	10.4167	10.6250	10.8333	11.0417	11.2500	11.4583	11.6667	11.8750	12.0833	12.2917
2	19.9971	20.4139	20.8307	21.2474	21.6642	22.0809	22.4977	22.9145	23.3312	23.7480	24.1647	24.5815
3	29.9914	30.6167	31.2420	31.8673	32.4925	33.1178	33.7431	34.3683	34.9936	35.6189	36.2441	36.8693
4	39.9827	40.8166	41.6506	42.4845	43.3184	44.1522	44.9861	45.8200	46.6538	47.4877	48.3215	49.1553
5	49.9711	51.0138	52.0564	53.0990	54.1416	55.1842	56.2268	57.2693	58.3118	59.3543	60.3968	61.4393
6	59.9565	61.2080	62.4595	63.7109	64.9623	66.2137	67.4650	68.7164	69.9676	71.2189	72.4701	73.7213
7	69.9389	71.3993	72.8597	74.3201	75.7804	77.2406	78.7009	80.1610	81.6212	83.0813	84.5413	86.0013
8	79.9183	81.5877	83.2571	84.9265	86.5958	88.2650	89.9342	91.6034	93.2725	94.9415	96.6104	98.2793
9	89.8946	91.7731	93.6517	95.5301	97.4085	99.2869	101.1651	103.0433	104.9214	106.7995	108.6774	110.5553
10	99.8677	101.9556	104.0433	106.1310	108.2186	110.3061	112.3935	114.4808	116.5681	118.6552	120.7422	122.8292
11	109.8378	112.1350	114.4320	116.7290	119.0259	121.3227	123.6193	125.9159	128.2123	130.5087	132.8048	135.1009
12	119.8047	122.3113	124.8178	127.3242	129.8305	132.3366	134.8426	137.3485	139.8542	142.3598	144.8653	147.3706
13	129.7684	132.4846	135.2006	137.9165	140.6322	143.3478	146.0633	148.7786	151.4937	154.2087	156.9235	159.6381
14	139.7289	142.6547	145.5803	148.5058	151.4312	154.3563	157.2813	160.2061	163.1307	166.0552	168.9794	171.9034
15	149.6861	152.8217	155.9571	159.0923	162.2273	165.3621	168.4967	171.6311	174.7653	177.8993	181.0330	184.1665
16	159.6401	162.9855	166.3307	169.6757	173.0205	176.3651	179.7094	183.0535	186.3974	189.7410	193.0843	196.4274
17	169.5907	173.1461	176.7012	180.2561	183.8108	187.3652	190.9194	194.4733	198.0269	201.5802	205.1333	208.6860
18	179.5380	183.3034	187.0686	190.8335	194.5982	198.3626	202.1267	205.8904	209.6539	213.4170	217.1799	220.9423
19	189.4819	193.4574	197.4328	201.4078	205.3826	209.3570	213.3311	217.3049	221.2783	225.2514	229.2240	233.1963
20	199.4223	203.6082	207.7937	211.9790	216.1640	220.3485	224.5328	228.7166	232.9001	237.0831	241.2658	245.4480
21	209.3593	213.7555	218.1515	222.5471	226.9423	231.3371	235.7316	240.1256	244.5192	248.9124	253.3051	257.6973
22	219.2928	223.8995	228.5059	233.1119	237.7176	242.3228	246.9275	251.5318	256.1357	260.7390	265.3419	269.9442
23	229.2228	234.0401	238.8571	243.6736	248.4897	253.3054	258.1206	262.9353	267.7494	272.5630	277.3761	282.1887
24	239.1492	244.1772	249.2048	254.2320	259.2588	264.2850	269.3107	274.3358	279.3604	284.3844	289.4078	294.4307
25	249.0720	254.3109	259.5493	264.7872	270.0246	275.2615	280.4978	285.7335	290.9687	296.2031	301.4370	306.6702
26	258.9912	264.4410	269.8902	275.3390	280.7873	286.2349	291.6819	297.1283	302.5741	308.0191	313.4635	318.9071
27	268.9067	274.5675	280.2278	285.8875	291.5467	297.2052	302.8630	308.5202	314.1767	319.8324	325.4874	331.1416
28	278.8186	284.6904	290.5618	296.4326	302.3028	308.1723	314.0411	319.9091	325.7764	331.6429	337.5086	343.3734
29	288.7266	294.8098	300.8923	306.9743	313.0556	319.1362	325.2160	331.2950	337.3732	343.4505	349.5270	355.6026
30	298.6309	304.9254	311.2193	317.5125	323.8050	330.0968	336.3877	342.6778	348.9671	355.2554	361.5428	367.8292
31	308.5314	315.0373	321.5426	328.0473	334.5511	341.0542	347.5563	354.0576	360.5580	367.0573	373.5557	380.0531
32	318.4280	325.1455	331.8624	338.5785	345.2938	352.0082	358.7217	365.4343	372.1458	378.8564	385.5659	392.2743
33	328.3207	335.2499	342.1784	349.1061	356.0330	362.9589	369.8839	376.8078	383.7307	390.6525	397.5732	404.4927
34	338.2095	345.3505	352.4907	359.6301	366.7686	373.9062	381.0427	388.1781	395.3125	402.4456	409.5776	416.7084
35	348.0943	355.4472	362.7993	370.1505	377.5008	384.8501	392.1982	399.5453	406.8911	414.2357	421.5791	428.9212
36	357.9751	365.5400	373.1041	380.6672	388.2294	395.7905	403.3504	410.9091	418.4666	426.0228	433.5777	441.1312
37	367.8519	375.6289	383.4050	391.1802	398.9544	406.7274	414.4992	422.2697	430.0389	437.8068	445.5733	453.3383
38	377.7245	385.7138	393.7021	401.6895	409.6757	417.6607	425.6445	433.6270	441.6080	449.5877	457.5658	465.5425
39	387.5930	395.7946	403.9953	412.1949	420.3933	428.5905	436.7864	444.9808	453.1739	461.3654	469.5553	477.7437
40	397.4574	405.8714	414.2845	422.6965	431.1072	439.5167	447.9247	456.3313	464.7364	473.1399	481.5417	489.9419
41	407.3175	415.9441	424.5697	433.1942	441.8174	450.4392	459.0595	467.6784	476.2956	484.9111	493.5250	502.1371
42	417.1734	426.0127	434.8509	443.6879	452.5237	461.3580	470.1907	479.0219	487.8514	496.6791	505.5051	514.3293
43	427.0249	436.0770	445.1280	454.1778	463.2261	472.2730	481.3183	490.3619	499.4038	508.4438	517.4820	526.5183
44	436.8721	446.1371	455.4010	464.6636	473.9247	483.1843	492.4422	501.6984	510.9527	520.2052	529.4557	538.7042
45	446.7150	456.1930	465.6698	475.1453	484.6193	494.0917	503.5624	513.0312	522.4982	531.9631	541.4260	550.8869
46	456.5534	466.2445	475.9345	485.6230	495.3100	504.9953	514.6788	524.3604	534.0401	543.7176	553.3931	563.0663
47	466.3873	476.2917	486.1948	496.0965	505.9966	515.8950	525.7914	535.6859	545.5784	555.4687	565.3568	575.2426
48	476.2167	486.3345	496.4509	506.5659	516.6792	526.7907	536.9002	547.0077	557.1131	567.2162	577.3170	587.4155
49	486.0415	496.3728	506.7027	517.0310	527.3576	537.6824	548.0051	558.3257	568.6441	578.9602	589.2738	599.5851
50	495.8617	506.4066	516.9500	527.4919	538.0319	548.5701	559.1061	569.6399	580.1715	590.7006	601.2272	611.7512

Table 13. 30-YEAR TERM—INTEREST RATE

J	9.00	9.25	9.50	9.75	10.00	10.25	10.50	10.75	11.00	11.25	11.50	11.75
1	7.5000	7.7083	7.9167	8.1250	8.3333	8.5417	8.7500	8.9583	9.1667	9.3750	9.5833	9.7917
2	14.9975	15.4142	15.8310	16.2477	16.6645	17.0812	17.4980	17.9147	18.3315	18.7482	19.1650	19.5817
3	22.4923	23.1176	23.7429	24.3681	24.9934	25.6187	26.2439	26.8692	27.4944	28.1196	28.7449	29.3701
4	29.9846	30.8185	31.6524	32.4862	33.3201	34.1539	34.9878	35.8216	36.6554	37.4892	38.3230	39.1568
5	37.4743	38.5169	39.5594	40.6020	41.6445	42.6871	43.7296	44.7721	45.8146	46.8570	47.8995	48.9419
6	44.9614	46.2127	47.4641	48.7154	49.9667	51.2180	52.4693	53.7205	54.9718	56.2230	57.4741	58.7253
7	52.4458	53.9060	55.3662	56.8264	58.2866	59.7467	61.2069	62.6670	64.1270	65.5870	67.0470	68.5069
8	59.9275	61.5967	63.2659	64.9350	66.6042	68.2733	69.9423	71.6113	73.2803	74.9492	76.6180	78.2868
9	67.4066	69.2848	71.1631	73.0413	74.9194	76.7975	78.6756	80.5536	82.4316	84.3095	86.1873	88.0650
10	74.8829	76.9703	79.0577	81.1450	83.2323	85.3196	87.4068	89.4939	91.5809	93.6678	95.7547	97.8415
11	82.3566	84.6532	86.9498	89.2464	91.5429	93.8393	96.1357	98.4320	100.7282	103.0243	105.3202	107.6161
12	89.8275	92.3334	94.8393	97.3452	99.8510	102.3568	104.8624	107.3680	109.8734	112.3787	114.8839	117.3890
13	97.2956	100.0109	102.7263	105.4416	108.1568	110.8719	113.5869	116.3018	119.0166	121.7312	124.4457	127.1600
14	104.7609	107.6858	110.6106	113.5354	116.4601	119.3847	122.3092	125.2335	128.1577	131.0817	134.0056	136.9292
15	112.2234	115.3579	118.4923	121.6267	124.7610	127.8952	131.0292	134.1630	137.2967	140.4302	143.5635	146.6966
16	119.6831	123.0273	126.3714	129.7155	133.0594	136.4032	139.7469	143.0904	146.4336	149.7767	153.1195	156.4621
17	127.1399	130.6939	134.2478	137.8016	141.3553	144.9089	148.4623	152.0155	155.5684	159.1211	162.6735	166.2257
18	134.5939	138.3577	142.1215	145.8852	149.6488	153.4122	157.1754	160.9383	164.7010	168.4634	172.2256	175.9874
19	142.0449	146.0188	149.9925	153.9662	157.9397	161.9130	165.8861	169.8589	173.8315	177.8037	181.7756	185.7472
20	149.4931	153.6770	157.8608	162.0445	166.2280	170.4114	174.5944	178.7772	182.9597	187.1419	191.3236	195.5050
21	156.9383	161.3323	165.7263	170.1201	174.5138	178.9072	183.3004	187.6933	192.0858	196.4779	200.8696	205.2609
22	164.3805	168.9848	173.5890	178.1931	182.7970	187.4006	192.0040	196.6070	201.2096	205.8118	210.4135	215.0148
23	171.8198	176.6344	181.4490	186.2634	191.0776	195.8915	200.7051	205.5183	210.3311	215.1435	219.9554	224.7668
24	179.2561	184.2811	189.3061	194.3309	199.3555	204.3798	209.4038	214.4273	219.4504	224.4730	229.4951	234.5167
25	186.6893	191.9249	197.1604	202.3957	207.6308	212.8656	218.1000	223.3339	228.5674	233.8003	239.0327	244.2645
26	194.1195	199.5657	205.0118	210.4577	215.9034	221.3487	226.7937	232.2381	237.6821	243.1254	248.5682	254.0103
27	201.5466	207.2035	212.8603	218.5169	224.1733	229.8293	235.4849	241.1399	246.7944	252.4483	258.1015	263.7540
28	208.9706	214.8383	220.7059	226.5733	232.4405	238.3072	244.1735	250.0392	255.9044	261.7689	267.6326	273.4957
29	216.3915	222.4701	228.5486	234.6269	240.7049	246.7825	252.8596	258.9361	265.0120	271.0871	277.1616	283.2352
30	223.8093	230.0988	236.3883	242.6776	248.9666	255.2551	261.5431	267.8305	274.1172	280.4031	286.6883	292.9726
31	231.2238	237.7245	244.2251	250.7254	257.2255	263.7250	270.2240	276.7223	283.2200	289.7168	296.2127	302.7078
32	238.6352	245.3471	252.0588	258.7703	265.4815	272.1922	278.9023	285.6117	292.3203	299.0280	305.7349	312.4408
33	246.0434	252.9665	259.8895	266.8123	273.7347	280.6566	287.5779	294.4984	301.4181	308.3370	315.2548	322.1716
34	253.4484	260.5828	267.7172	274.8513	281.9851	289.1183	296.2508	303.3826	310.5135	317.6435	324.7724	331.9002
35	260.8500	268.1959	275.5418	282.8874	290.2326	297.5772	304.9211	312.2642	319.6064	326.9475	334.2876	341.6266
36	268.2484	275.8059	283.3633	290.9204	298.4771	306.0332	313.5886	321.1431	328.6967	336.2492	343.8005	351.3507
37	275.6435	283.4126	291.1816	298.9504	306.7187	314.4865	322.2534	330.0194	337.7844	345.5483	353.3111	361.0725
38	283.0353	291.0161	298.9969	306.9774	314.9574	322.9368	330.9154	338.8930	346.8696	354.8450	362.8192	370.7920
39	290.4237	298.6163	306.8089	315.0012	323.1931	331.3843	339.5746	347.7640	355.9522	364.1392	372.3249	380.5091
40	297.8086	306.2132	314.6178	323.0220	331.4258	339.8288	348.2310	356.6322	365.0321	373.4308	381.8281	390.2239
41	305.1902	313.8068	322.4234	331.0397	339.6554	348.2704	356.8846	365.4976	374.1094	382.7199	391.3289	399.9363
42	312.5684	321.3971	330.2257	339.0541	347.8820	356.7091	365.5352	374.3603	383.1840	392.0064	400.8272	409.6464
43	319.9431	328.9840	338.0248	347.0654	356.1055	365.1448	374.1830	383.2201	392.2559	401.2902	410.3229	419.3539
44	327.3143	336.5674	345.8206	355.0735	364.3259	373.5774	382.8279	392.0772	401.3251	410.5714	419.8161	429.0591
45	334.6819	344.1475	353.6131	363.0784	372.5431	382.0070	391.4698	400.9314	410.3915	419.8500	429.3068	438.7617
46	342.0461	351.7241	361.4022	371.0800	380.7572	390.4336	400.1088	409.7827	419.4551	429.1259	438.7949	448.4619
47	349.4067	359.2973	369.1879	379.0783	388.9681	398.8570	408.7448	418.6311	428.5160	438.3991	448.2803	458.1595
48	356.7636	366.8669	376.9703	387.0733	397.1758	407.2773	417.3777	427.4766	437.5740	447.6695	457.7631	467.8546
49	364.1170	374.4330	384.7492	395.0650	405.3802	415.6945	426.0076	436.3192	446.6291	456.9372	467.2432	477.5471
50	371.4667	381.9956	392.5246	403.0533	413.5814	424.1085	434.6344	445.1588	455.6814	466.2021	476.7207	487.2370

Table 13. 30-YEAR TERM—INTEREST RATE (*Continued*)

J	12.00	12.25	12.50	12.75	13.00	13.25	13.50	13.75	14.00	14.25	14.50	14.75
1	10.0000	10.2083	10.4167	10.6250	10.8333	11.0417	11.2500	11.4583	11.6667	11.8750	12.0833	12.2917
2	19.9984	20.4152	20.8319	21.2487	21.6654	22.0821	22.4988	22.9156	23.3323	23.7490	24.1657	24.5824
3	29.9953	30.6205	31.2457	31.8709	32.4961	33.1213	33.7465	34.3717	34.9968	35.6220	36.2471	36.8723
4	39.9906	40.8244	41.6581	42.4918	43.3256	44.1593	44.9930	45.8266	46.6603	47.4940	48.3276	49.1612
5	49.9843	51.0267	52.0690	53.1114	54.1537	55.1960	56.2382	57.2805	58.3227	59.3649	60.4071	61.4492
6	59.9764	61.2274	62.4785	63.7295	64.9804	66.2314	67.4823	68.7332	69.9840	71.2348	72.4856	73.7363
7	69.9668	71.4266	72.8864	74.3462	75.8059	77.2655	78.7251	80.1847	81.6442	83.1036	84.5630	86.0224
8	79.9556	81.6243	83.2929	84.9614	86.6299	88.2983	89.9667	91.6350	93.3032	94.9714	96.6395	98.3076
9	89.9427	91.8203	93.6978	95.5752	97.4526	99.3298	101.2070	103.0841	104.9611	106.8381	108.7149	110.5917
10	99.9281	102.0147	104.1012	106.1875	108.2738	110.3600	112.4460	114.5320	116.6179	118.7036	120.7893	122.8749
11	109.9119	112.2075	114.5030	116.7984	119.0937	121.3888	123.6838	125.9787	128.2735	130.5681	132.8626	135.1571
12	119.8939	122.3986	124.9033	127.4077	129.9121	132.4162	134.9203	137.4241	139.9279	142.4315	144.9349	147.4382
13	129.8742	132.5881	135.3019	138.0156	140.7290	143.4423	146.1554	148.8683	151.5811	154.2937	157.0061	159.7183
14	139.8527	142.7759	145.6990	148.6219	151.5445	154.4670	157.3892	160.3113	163.2331	166.1547	169.0762	171.9974
15	149.8294	152.9621	156.0945	159.2266	162.3586	165.4902	168.6217	171.7529	174.8839	178.0146	181.1452	184.2755
16	159.8044	163.1465	166.4883	169.8298	173.1711	176.5121	179.8528	183.1933	186.5334	189.8734	193.2130	196.5524
17	169.7776	173.3292	176.8804	180.4314	183.9821	187.5325	191.0825	194.6323	198.1817	201.7309	205.2798	208.8283
18	179.7489	183.5101	187.2709	191.0314	194.7916	198.5514	202.3109	206.0700	209.8288	213.5872	217.3453	221.1031
19	189.7184	193.6893	197.6597	201.6298	205.5995	209.5689	213.5378	217.5064	221.4745	225.4423	229.4098	233.3768
20	199.6860	203.8666	208.0468	212.2266	216.4059	220.5848	224.7633	228.9414	233.1190	237.2962	241.4730	245.6494
21	209.6518	214.0422	218.4322	222.8217	227.2107	231.5993	235.9874	240.3750	244.7621	249.1488	253.5350	257.9208
22	219.6157	224.2160	228.8158	233.4152	238.0140	242.6122	247.2100	251.8072	256.4040	261.0002	265.5959	270.1911
23	229.5776	234.3879	239.1977	244.0069	248.8156	253.6236	258.4311	263.2381	268.0445	272.8503	277.6555	282.4603
24	239.5376	244.5580	249.5778	254.5970	259.6155	264.6335	269.6508	274.6675	279.6836	284.6991	289.7139	294.7282
25	249.4957	254.7262	259.9561	265.1853	270.4139	275.6418	280.8690	286.0955	291.3213	296.5465	301.7711	306.9950
26	259.4518	264.8925	270.3326	275.7719	281.2105	286.6484	292.0856	297.5220	302.9577	308.3927	313.8270	319.2605
27	269.4059	275.0569	280.7072	286.3568	292.0055	297.6535	303.3007	308.9471	314.5927	320.2375	325.8816	331.5249
28	279.3579	285.2194	291.0800	296.9399	302.7988	308.6569	314.5142	320.3706	326.2262	332.0810	337.9349	343.7880
29	289.3080	295.3799	301.4510	307.5211	313.5904	319.6587	325.7262	331.7927	337.8583	343.9230	349.9869	356.0498
30	299.2560	305.5384	311.8200	318.1006	324.3802	330.6589	336.9365	343.2132	349.4890	355.7637	362.0376	368.3104
31	309.2019	315.6950	322.1871	328.6782	335.1683	341.6573	348.1453	354.6322	361.1182	367.6030	374.0869	380.5698
32	319.1457	325.8495	332.5523	339.2540	345.9546	352.6541	359.3524	366.0497	372.7458	379.4409	386.1349	392.8278
33	329.0874	336.0020	342.9156	349.8279	356.7391	363.6491	370.5579	377.4656	384.3720	391.2773	398.1815	405.0845
34	339.0269	346.1525	353.2768	360.3999	367.5218	374.6424	381.7618	388.8799	395.9967	403.1123	410.2267	417.3399
35	348.9643	356.3009	363.6361	370.9700	378.3026	385.6339	392.9639	400.2925	407.6198	414.9458	422.2705	429.5939
36	358.8996	366.4471	373.9934	381.5382	389.0817	396.6237	404.1643	411.7036	419.2414	426.7778	434.3129	441.8466
37	368.8326	376.5913	384.3486	392.1044	399.8588	407.6117	415.3631	423.1130	430.8614	438.6083	446.3538	454.0979
38	378.7634	386.7333	394.7018	402.6687	410.6340	418.5978	426.5600	434.5207	442.4798	450.4373	458.3933	466.3478
39	388.6919	396.8732	405.0528	413.2309	421.4073	429.5821	437.7553	445.9267	454.0966	462.2647	470.4313	478.5963
40	398.6182	407.0108	415.4018	423.7911	432.1787	440.5646	448.9487	457.3311	465.7117	474.0906	482.4678	490.8433
41	408.5422	417.1463	425.7487	434.3493	442.9482	451.5452	460.1403	468.7337	477.3252	485.9149	494.5028	503.0889
42	418.4638	427.2796	436.0935	444.9055	453.7156	462.5239	471.3302	480.1345	488.9370	497.7376	506.5363	515.3331
43	428.3832	437.4105	446.4360	455.4595	464.4811	473.5006	482.5181	491.5336	500.5471	509.5587	518.5682	527.5758
44	438.3001	447.5393	456.7764	466.0115	475.2445	484.4754	493.7043	502.9310	512.1556	521.3781	530.5985	539.8169
45	448.2147	457.6657	467.1146	476.5613	486.0059	495.4483	504.8885	514.3265	523.7623	533.1959	542.6273	552.0566
46	458.1269	467.7898	477.4505	487.1090	496.7652	506.4192	516.0708	525.7202	535.3672	545.0120	554.6544	564.2947
47	468.0366	477.9115	487.7842	497.6545	507.5225	517.3881	527.2512	537.1120	546.9704	556.8264	566.6800	576.5312
48	477.9439	488.0309	498.1156	508.1978	518.2776	528.3549	538.4297	548.5020	558.5718	568.6390	578.7038	588.7662
49	487.8487	498.1479	508.4447	518.7389	529.0306	539.3197	549.6062	559.8901	570.1713	580.4500	590.7261	600.9996
50	497.7510	508.2625	518.7715	529.2778	539.7815	550.2824	560.7807	571.2762	581.7691	592.2592	602.7466	613.2314

Table 13. 40-YEAR TERM—INTEREST RATE

J	9.00	9.25	9.50	9.75	10.00	10.25	10.50	10.75	11.00	11.25	11.50	11.75
1	7.5000	7.7083	7.9167	8.1250	8.3333	8.5417	8.7500	8.9583	9.1667	9.3750	9.5833	9.7917
2	14.9006	15.3151	15.7297	16.1444	16.5591	16.9738	17.3885	17.8033	18.2181	18.6329	19.0477	19.4626
3	22.2009	22.8196	23.4384	24.0573	24.6763	25.2953	25.9145	26.5338	27.1531	27.7726	28.3921	29.0117
4	29.4004	30.2210	31.0418	31.8628	32.6841	33.5054	34.3270	35.1488	35.9708	36.7929	37.6152	38.4377
5	36.4981	37.5185	38.5392	39.5602	40.5815	41.6032	42.6251	43.6474	44.6699	45.6928	46.7160	47.7395
6	43.4934	44.7113	45.9296	47.1464	48.3677	49.5875	50.8077	52.0284	53.2496	54.4712	55.6932	56.9157
7	50.3855	51.7986	53.2123	54.6267	56.0418	57.4575	58.8739	60.2909	61.7085	63.1268	64.5457	65.9552
8	57.1736	58.7796	60.3864	61.9941	63.6027	65.2122	66.8225	68.4337	70.0457	71.6586	73.2723	74.8868
9	63.8569	65.6534	67.4510	69.2498	71.0496	72.8506	74.6526	76.4558	78.2600	80.0653	81.8717	83.6791
10	70.4346	72.4193	74.4053	76.3927	78.3815	80.3717	82.3632	84.3561	86.3503	88.3459	90.3428	92.3410
11	76.9060	79.0763	81.2483	83.4220	85.5974	87.7745	89.9532	92.1335	94.3155	96.4990	98.6842	100.8710
12	83.2702	85.6238	87.9793	90.3369	92.6964	95.0580	97.4215	99.7869	102.1543	104.5237	106.8949	109.2681
13	89.5265	92.0607	94.5973	97.1362	99.6775	102.2211	104.7670	107.3152	109.8657	112.4185	114.9735	117.5308
14	95.6740	98.3864	101.1014	103.8192	106.5397	109.2629	111.9888	114.7174	117.4485	120.1823	122.9188	125.6578
15	101.7120	104.5998	107.4908	110.3849	113.2821	116.1824	119.0857	121.9921	124.9015	127.8140	130.7294	133.6478
16	107.6395	110.7002	113.7644	116.8322	119.9035	122.9784	126.0566	129.1384	132.2236	135.3121	138.4041	141.4995
17	113.4558	116.6866	119.9215	123.1603	126.4031	129.6499	132.9005	136.1550	139.4134	142.6756	145.9416	149.2114
18	119.1600	122.5583	125.9610	129.3682	132.7798	136.1958	139.6162	143.0408	146.4698	149.9031	153.3406	156.7823
19	124.7513	128.3143	131.8821	135.4549	139.0326	142.6151	146.2025	149.7947	153.3916	156.9933	160.5997	164.2108
20	130.2289	133.9536	137.6838	141.4194	145.1604	148.9068	152.6584	156.4154	160.1776	163.9450	167.7176	171.4955
21	135.5919	139.4756	143.3652	147.2608	151.1623	155.0696	158.9827	162.9017	166.8264	170.7569	174.6930	178.6348
22	140.8394	144.8791	148.9253	152.9780	157.0370	161.1025	165.1743	169.2525	173.3369	177.4276	181.5245	185.6276
23	145.9705	150.1633	154.3631	158.5699	162.7837	167.0044	171.2320	175.4665	179.7078	183.9558	188.2107	192.4722
24	150.9845	155.3273	159.6777	164.0357	168.4012	172.7742	177.1547	181.5425	185.9377	190.3403	194.7501	199.1672
25	155.8804	160.3702	164.8682	169.3743	173.8885	178.4108	182.9411	187.4793	192.0255	196.5796	201.1415	205.7113
26	160.6573	165.2910	169.9334	174.5846	179.2444	183.9129	188.5900	193.2756	197.9698	202.6724	207.3834	212.1028
27	165.3143	170.0887	174.8725	179.6656	184.4680	189.2795	194.1003	198.9302	203.7692	208.6173	213.4743	218.3404
28	169.8506	174.7625	179.6844	184.6163	189.5579	194.5094	199.4707	204.4418	209.4225	214.4129	219.4129	224.4224
29	174.2652	179.3114	184.3682	189.4355	194.5133	199.6015	204.7001	209.8091	214.9283	220.0578	225.1976	230.3475
30	178.5573	183.7344	188.9228	194.1223	199.3329	204.5545	209.7872	215.0308	220.2853	225.5507	230.8269	236.1139
31	182.7258	188.0306	193.3471	198.6755	204.0155	209.3673	214.7306	220.1056	225.4921	230.8901	236.2995	241.7203
32	186.7700	192.1989	197.6403	203.0940	208.5602	214.0386	219.5293	225.0322	230.5473	236.0745	241.6137	247.1650
33	190.6887	196.2384	201.8011	207.3769	212.9656	218.5673	224.1819	229.8093	235.4495	241.1025	246.7681	252.4464
34	194.4812	200.1481	205.8286	211.5229	217.2307	222.9522	228.6871	234.4356	240.1974	245.9726	251.7611	257.5629
35	198.1464	203.9269	209.7218	215.5309	221.3543	227.1919	233.0437	238.9096	244.7895	250.6834	256.5913	262.5130
36	201.6835	207.5740	213.4795	219.3999	225.3352	231.2854	237.2503	243.2300	249.2244	255.2334	261.2569	267.2950
37	205.0913	211.0882	217.1007	223.1287	229.1722	235.2313	241.3057	247.3955	253.5006	259.6209	265.7565	271.9072
38	208.3691	214.4685	220.5842	226.7161	232.8642	239.0283	245.2085	251.4046	257.6167	263.8447	270.0885	276.3480
39	211.5157	217.7140	223.9291	230.1611	236.4098	242.6752	248.9573	255.2560	261.5713	267.9030	274.2512	280.6157
40	214.5303	220.8235	227.1342	233.4624	239.8079	246.1708	252.5509	258.9482	265.3627	271.7943	278.2430	284.7087
41	217.4117	223.7961	230.1985	236.6189	243.0573	249.5137	255.9879	262.4799	268.9897	275.5172	282.0623	288.6251
42	220.1591	226.6306	233.1207	239.6294	246.1567	252.7025	259.2668	265.8495	272.4506	279.0699	285.7075	292.3633
43	222.7714	229.3260	235.8998	242.4928	249.1049	255.7361	262.3864	269.0557	275.7438	282.4509	289.1768	295.9215
44	225.2476	231.8812	238.5346	245.2077	251.9006	258.6131	265.3452	272.0969	278.8680	285.6586	292.4687	299.2980
45	227.5867	234.2952	241.0240	247.7731	254.5425	261.3321	268.1418	274.9717	281.8215	288.6914	295.5813	302.4910
46	229.7877	236.5668	243.3669	250.1877	257.0294	263.8918	270.7748	277.6785	284.6028	291.5476	298.5129	305.4987
47	231.8495	238.6951	245.5620	252.4503	259.3599	266.2908	273.2428	280.2160	287.2103	294.2256	301.2620	308.3192
48	233.7710	240.6787	247.6083	254.5597	261.5328	268.5277	275.5443	282.5826	289.6424	296.7237	303.8265	310.9508
49	235.5513	242.5167	249.5045	256.5145	263.5468	270.6013	277.6779	284.7766	291.8974	299.0402	306.2050	313.3916
50	237.1892	244.2079	251.2494	258.3136	265.4005	272.5100	279.6421	286.7967	293.9738	301.1734	308.3954	315.6397

Table 13. 40-YEAR TERM—INTEREST RATE (*Continued*)

J	12.00	12.25	12.50	12.75	13.00	13.25	13.50	13.75	14.00	14.25	14.50	14.75
1	10.0000	10.2083	10.4167	10.6250	10.8333	11.0417	11.2500	11.4583	11.6667	11.8750	12.0833	12.2917
2	19.8776	20.2925	20.7075	21.1225	21.5375	21.9526	22.3677	22.7828	23.1980	23.6132	24.0284	24.4436
3	29.6314	30.2513	30.8711	31.4911	32.1112	32.7314	33.3516	33.9719	34.5924	35.2129	35.8334	36.4541
4	39.2604	40.0833	40.9063	41.7295	42.5529	43.3765	44.2002	45.0241	45.8482	46.6725	47.4969	48.3214
5	48.7632	49.7873	50.8117	51.8363	52.8613	53.8865	54.9120	55.9379	56.9639	57.9903	59.0169	60.0438
6	58.1387	59.3620	60.5859	61.8101	63.0348	64.2600	65.4855	66.7115	67.9379	69.1647	70.3919	71.6195
7	67.3854	68.8061	70.2275	71.6495	73.0721	74.4953	75.9191	77.3434	78.7684	80.1939	81.6200	83.0466
8	76.5021	78.1183	79.7353	81.3530	82.9716	84.5910	86.2111	87.8320	89.4538	91.0762	92.6995	94.3234
9	85.4876	87.2971	89.1077	90.9193	92.7319	94.5455	96.3601	98.1757	99.9923	101.8099	103.6285	105.4480
10	94.3405	96.3413	98.3434	100.3467	102.3514	104.3573	106.3644	108.3728	110.3824	112.3933	114.4053	116.4186
11	103.0594	105.2494	107.4409	109.6340	111.8286	114.0247	116.2224	118.4216	120.6223	122.8244	125.0280	127.2331
12	111.6431	114.0201	116.3989	118.7795	121.1620	123.5463	125.9324	128.3204	130.7101	133.1016	135.4948	137.6898
13	120.0902	122.6519	125.2158	127.7818	130.3500	132.9204	135.4928	138.0674	140.6441	143.2229	145.8038	148.3867
14	128.3993	131.1435	133.8902	136.6394	139.3911	142.1453	144.9020	147.6611	150.4226	153.1866	155.9530	158.7218
15	136.5691	139.4934	142.4206	145.3507	148.2836	151.2194	154.1580	157.0995	160.0438	162.9908	165.9406	168.8931
16	144.5981	147.7002	150.8055	153.9141	157.0260	160.1411	163.2594	166.3809	169.5057	172.6335	175.7645	178.8987
17	152.4850	155.7623	159.0434	162.3281	165.6165	168.9086	172.2043	175.5036	178.8065	182.1129	185.4229	188.7364
18	160.2283	163.6784	167.1327	170.5912	174.0537	177.5203	180.9910	184.4657	187.9444	191.4270	194.9136	198.4042
19	167.8266	171.4470	175.0720	178.7016	182.3358	185.9745	189.6176	193.2653	196.9174	200.5739	204.2348	207.9000
20	175.2784	179.0665	182.8596	186.6578	190.4611	194.2693	198.0825	201.9006	205.7236	209.5515	213.3843	217.2218
21	182.5823	186.5354	190.4940	194.4582	198.4279	202.4031	206.3837	210.3697	214.3611	218.3579	222.3600	226.3674
22	189.7368	193.8521	197.9736	202.1010	206.2345	210.3740	214.5194	218.6708	222.8280	226.9910	231.1599	235.3345
23	196.7404	201.0152	205.2967	209.5847	213.8793	218.1803	222.4878	226.8018	231.1221	235.4488	239.7818	244.1211
24	203.5916	208.0231	212.4617	216.9075	221.3603	225.8202	230.2870	234.7608	239.2415	243.7291	248.2236	252.7248
25	210.2888	214.8741	219.4671	224.0677	228.6759	233.2917	237.9151	242.5459	247.1843	251.8300	256.4831	261.1435
26	216.8306	221.5667	226.3110	231.0636	235.8243	240.5932	245.3701	250.1551	254.9482	259.7492	264.5581	269.3749
27	223.2153	228.0992	232.9919	237.8934	242.8036	247.7225	252.6502	257.5864	262.5312	267.4845	272.4464	277.4166
28	229.4415	234.4700	239.5080	244.5553	249.6120	254.6780	259.7532	264.8376	269.9312	275.0339	280.1456	285.2664
29	235.5075	240.6775	245.8576	251.0477	256.2477	261.4576	266.6774	271.9069	277.1461	282.3951	287.6537	292.9219
30	241.4116	246.7200	252.0391	257.3687	262.7088	268.0594	273.4205	278.7920	284.1737	289.5658	294.9681	300.3806
31	247.1524	252.5959	258.0505	263.5164	268.9934	274.4815	279.9807	285.4908	291.0119	296.5438	302.0866	307.6402
32	252.7282	258.3033	263.8903	269.4891	275.0996	280.7219	286.3558	292.0013	297.6583	303.3269	309.0069	314.6983
33	258.1372	263.8406	269.5565	275.2848	281.0255	286.7785	292.5437	298.3212	304.1109	309.9126	315.7265	321.5523
34	263.3779	269.2061	275.0474	280.9017	286.7690	292.6493	298.5424	304.4484	310.3672	316.2987	322.2429	328.1997
35	268.4486	274.3980	280.3611	286.3379	292.3283	298.3323	304.3498	310.3807	316.4251	322.4828	328.5538	334.6381
36	273.3475	279.4145	285.4958	291.5914	297.7013	303.8254	309.9636	316.1159	322.2822	328.4625	334.6567	340.8647
37	278.0730	284.2538	290.4497	296.6604	302.8860	309.1265	315.3817	321.6516	327.9361	334.2353	340.5490	346.8771
38	282.6233	288.9142	295.2208	301.5429	307.8804	314.2335	320.6019	326.9856	333.3846	339.7988	346.2282	352.6726
39	286.9966	293.3938	299.8072	306.2368	312.6825	319.1442	325.6219	332.1156	338.6252	345.1505	351.6917	358.2485
40	291.1913	297.6908	304.2071	310.7402	317.2900	323.8565	330.4396	337.0393	343.6554	350.2880	356.9369	363.6022
41	295.2054	301.8032	308.4184	315.0511	321.7010	328.3682	335.0526	341.7542	348.4729	355.2086	361.9612	368.7308
42	299.0372	305.7293	312.4393	319.1673	325.9133	332.6771	339.4587	346.2580	353.0751	359.9097	366.7620	373.6317
43	302.6849	309.4670	316.2677	323.0869	329.9247	336.7809	343.6554	350.5483	357.4595	364.3889	371.3364	378.3020
44	306.1467	313.0146	319.9016	326.8078	333.7331	340.6773	347.6405	354.6227	361.6236	368.6434	375.6818	382.7389
45	309.4206	316.3699	323.3390	330.3278	337.3362	344.3642	351.4116	358.4786	365.5649	372.6705	379.7954	386.9396
46	312.5048	319.5312	326.5779	333.6448	340.7319	347.8391	354.9663	362.1135	369.2806	376.4676	383.6745	390.9011
47	315.3974	322.4964	329.6162	336.7567	343.9179	351.0997	358.3021	365.5249	372.7683	380.0320	387.3161	394.6204
48	318.0965	325.2635	332.4517	339.6612	346.8919	354.1437	361.4165	368.7103	376.0251	383.3608	390.7174	398.0947
49	320.6001	327.8304	335.0825	342.3562	349.6516	356.9686	364.3071	371.6671	379.0485	386.4513	393.8755	401.3208
50	322.9063	330.1952	337.5062	344.8394	352.1947	359.5721	366.9714	374.3926	381.8358	389.3007	396.7874	404.2958

CHAPTER 17
Understanding Depreciation

Tangible personal property and improved real property will depreciate with time, fashion, and use. To account for this presumed loss of value, the Treasury permits an annual deduction from ordinary income.

The rules for the depreciation allowance for real property have changed greatly since 1981. Prior to 1981, the rate of the depreciation allowance depended upon whether the property was new or used, commercial or residential rental, etc. The rate was determined by one of three formulas: straight line, sum-of-the-years' digits, and declining balance (using one of three rates).

The Economic Recovery Act of 1981 introduced the Accelerated Cost Recovery System (ACRS). It specifies that property placed into service after 1980 (and before 3/16/84) could be depreciated over 15 years according to a table (Table 14.a) or over 15, 35, or 45 years using the straight-line formula. If the property was placed into service during the second half of the month, it is considered to be placed into service in the following month.

The Tax Reform Act of 1984 continues the ACRS, but specifies that property placed into service after 3/15/84 could be depreciated over 18 years according to a table (Table 14.b) or over 18, 35, or 45 years using the straight-line formula. According to this act, depreciation begins the month the property is placed into service (regardless of the time of the month).

Table 14.a. PROPERTY PLACED INTO SERVICE AFTER 1980 AND BEFORE 3/16/84

Annual and Cumulative Fraction of the Unadjusted Basis That May Be Recovered*

All Real Property (Except Low-Income Housing)

Year of Use	Month of the Year the Property Is Placed into Service																							
	1		2		3		4		5		6		7		8		9		10		11		12	
	a_n	A_n	a_n	A_n	a_n	A_n	a_n	A_n	a_n	A_n	a_n	A_n	a_n	A_n	a_n	A_n	a_n	A_n	a_n	A_n	a_n	A_n	a_n	A_n
1	.12	.12	.11	.11	.10	.10	.09	.09	.08	.08	.07	.07	.06	.06	.05	.05	.04	.04	.03	.03	.02	.02	.01	.01
2	.10	.22	.10	.21	.11	.21	.11	.20	.11	.19	.11	.18	.11	.17	.11	.16	.11	.15	.11	.14	.11	.13	.12	.13
3	.09	.31	.09	.30	.09	.30	.09	.29	.10	.29	.10	.28	.10	.27	.10	.26	.10	.25	.10	.24	.10	.23	.10	.23
4	.08	.39	.08	.38	.08	.38	.08	.37	.08	.37	.08	.36	.09	.36	.09	.35	.09	.34	.09	.33	.09	.32	.09	.32
5	.07	.46	.07	.45	.07	.45	.07	.44	.07	.44	.07	.43	.08	.44	.08	.43	.08	.42	.08	.41	.08	.40	.08	.40
6	.06	.52	.06	.51	.06	.51	.06	.50	.07	.51	.07	.50	.07	.51	.07	.50	.07	.49	.07	.48	.07	.47	.07	.47
7	.06	.58	.06	.57	.06	.57	.06	.56	.06	.57	.06	.56	.06	.57	.06	.56	.06	.55	.06	.54	.06	.53	.06	.53
8	.06	.64	.06	.63	.06	.63	.06	.62	.06	.63	.06	.62	.05	.62	.06	.62	.06	.61	.06	.60	.06	.59	.06	.59
9	.06	.70	.06	.69	.06	.69	.06	.68	.05	.68	.06	.68	.05	.67	.05	.67	.05	.66	.06	.66	.06	.65	.06	.65
10	.05	.75	.06	.75	.05	.74	.06	.74	.05	.73	.05	.73	.05	.72	.05	.72	.05	.71	.05	.71	.06	.71	.05	.70
11	.05	.80	.05	.80	.05	.79	.05	.79	.05	.78	.05	.78	.05	.77	.05	.77	.05	.76	.05	.76	.05	.76	.05	.75
12	.05	.85	.05	.85	.05	.84	.05	.84	.05	.83	.05	.83	.05	.82	.05	.82	.05	.81	.05	.81	.05	.81	.05	.80
13	.05	.90	.05	.90	.05	.89	.05	.89	.05	.88	.05	.88	.05	.87	.05	.87	.05	.86	.05	.86	.05	.86	.05	.85
14	.05	.95	.05	.95	.05	.94	.05	.94	.05	.93	.05	.93	.05	.92	.05	.92	.05	.91	.05	.91	.05	.91	.05	.90
15	.05	1.00	.05	1.00	.05	.99	.05	.99	.05	.98	.05	.98	.05	.97	.05	.97	.05	.96	.05	.96	.05	.96	.05	.95
16	—	—	—	—	.01	1.00	.01	1.00	.02	1.00	.02	1.00	.03	1.00	.03	1.00	.04	1.00	.04	1.00	.04	1.00	.05	1.00

***These tables do not apply for taxable years of less than 12 months.**

Table 14.b. PROPERTY PLACED INTO SERVICE AFTER 6/22/84*

Annual and Cumulative Fraction of the Unadjusted Basis That May Be Recovered†

All Real Property (Except Low-Income Housing)

Year of Use	Month of the Year the Property Is Placed into Service: 1		2		3		4		5		6		7		8		9		10		11		12	
	a_n	A_n	a_n	A_n	a_n	A_n	a_n	A_n	a_n	A_n	a_n	A_n	a_n	A_n	a_n	A_n	a_n	A_n	a_n	A_n	a_n	A_n	a_n	A_n
1	.09	.09	.09	.09	.08	.08	.07	.07	.06	.06	.05	.05	.04	.04	.04	.04	.03	.03	.02	.02	.01	.01	.004	.004
2	.09	.18	.09	.18	.09	.17	.09	.16	.09	.15	.09	.14	.09	.13	.09	.13	.09	.12	.10	.12	.10	.11	.100	.104
3	.08	.26	.08	.26	.08	.25	.08	.24	.08	.23	.08	.22	.08	.21	.08	.21	.09	.21	.09	.21	.09	.20	.090	.194
4	.07	.33	.07	.33	.07	.32	.07	.31	.07	.30	.08	.30	.08	.29	.08	.29	.08	.29	.08	.29	.08	.28	.080	.274
5	.07	.40	.07	.40	.07	.39	.07	.38	.07	.37	.07	.37	.07	.36	.07	.36	.07	.36	.07	.36	.07	.35	.070	.344
6	.06	.46	.06	.46	.06	.45	.06	.44	.06	.43	.06	.43	.06	.42	.06	.42	.06	.42	.06	.42	.06	.41	.060	.404
7	.05	.51	.05	.51	.05	.50	.05	.49	.06	.49	.06	.49	.06	.48	.06	.48	.06	.48	.06	.48	.06	.47	.060	.464
8	.05	.56	.05	.56	.05	.55	.05	.54	.05	.54	.05	.54	.05	.53	.05	.53	.05	.53	.05	.53	.05	.52	.050	.514
9	.05	.61	.05	.61	.05	.60	.05	.59	.05	.59	.05	.59	.05	.58	.05	.58	.05	.58	.05	.58	.05	.57	.050	.564
10	.05	.66	.05	.66	.05	.65	.05	.64	.05	.64	.05	.64	.05	.63	.05	.63	.05	.63	.05	.63	.05	.62	.050	.614
11	.05	.71	.05	.71	.05	.70	.05	.69	.05	.69	.05	.69	.05	.68	.05	.68	.05	.68	.05	.68	.05	.67	.050	.664
12	.05	.76	.05	.76	.05	.75	.05	.74	.05	.74	.05	.74	.05	.73	.05	.73	.05	.73	.05	.73	.05	.72	.050	.714
13	.04	.80	.04	.80	.04	.79	.05	.79	.04	.78	.04	.78	.05	.78	.04	.77	.04	.77	.04	.77	.05	.77	.050	.764
14	.04	.84	.04	.84	.04	.83	.04	.83	.04	.82	.04	.82	.04	.82	.04	.81	.04	.81	.04	.81	.04	.81	.040	.804
15	.04	.88	.04	.88	.04	.87	.04	.87	.04	.86	.04	.86	.04	.86	.04	.85	.04	.85	.04	.85	.04	.85	.040	.844
16	.04	.92	.04	.92	.04	.91	.04	.91	.04	.90	.04	.90	.04	.90	.04	.89	.04	.89	.04	.89	.04	.89	.040	.884
17	.04	.96	.04	.96	.04	.95	.04	.95	.04	.94	.04	.94	.04	.94	.04	.93	.04	.93	.04	.93	.04	.93	.040	.924
18	.04	1.00	.03	.99	.04	.99	.04	.99	.04	.98	.04	.98	.04	.98	.04	.97	.04	.97	.04	.97	.04	.97	.040	.964
19	—	—	.01	1.00	.01	1.00	.01	1.00	.02	1.00	.02	1.00	.02	1.00	.03	1.00	.03	1.00	.03	1.00	.03	1.00	.036	1.000

*These tables do not apply for taxable years of less than 12 months.

†The table for property placed into service after 3/15/84 and before 6/23/84 is not included.

THE ANNUAL FRACTION OF RECOVERY

Table 14 lists the fraction of the unadjusted basis of the property that can be deducted annually. The taxpayer can elect to use the straight-line method instead of the table.

FORMULAS:

$$\left.\begin{aligned} a_n &= \frac{1}{k} \\ A_n &= \frac{n}{k} \end{aligned}\right\} \text{straight-line method}$$

where

a_n = rate of cost recovery in the nth year (all rates are equal for the straight-line method)

A_n = cumulative cost recovery through the nth year

then

k = recovery period in years

n = number of years since the property was placed into service.

Figure 25 shows the rate of recovery (a_n in Table 14.a) for the two methods, and Figure 26 shows the cumulative recovery (A_n in Table 14.a) for the two methods.

The recovery deduction in the year of disposition is proportional to the number of months the property was held. To compute the annual recovery deduction from the table, multiply the appropriate fraction by the unadjusted basis of the improvement.

EXAMPLE: Sandra Giles bought a small apartment complex on September 17, 1983. The unadjusted basis of the building is $300,000. How much can she recover in the first two calendar years if she (1) uses the ACRS or (2) elects to use the straight-line method over 15 years?

SOLUTION:

(1) Using the ACRS with a 15-year recovery period, the fraction of the unadjusted basis that can be recovered is listed in column 9 (since

September is the ninth month) of Table 14.a. Corresponding to the first two years, $a_1 = 0.04$ and $a_2 = 0.11$. Therefore, Ms. Giles can recover

$$0.04 \times \$300{,}000 = \$12{,}000$$

in the first year and

$$0.11 \times \$300{,}000 = \$33{,}000$$

in the second year.

(2) Using the straight-line method, $k = 15$, and $a_1 = a_2 = .0666667$. Since Ms. Giles bought the property in the second half of September, she can recover the unadjusted basis for only the last three months of the year. Therefore, she can recover

$$0.0666667 \times \frac{3}{12} \times \$300{,}000 = \$5{,}000$$

in the first year and

$$0.0666667 \times \$300{,}000 = \$20{,}000$$

in the second year.

Figure 25

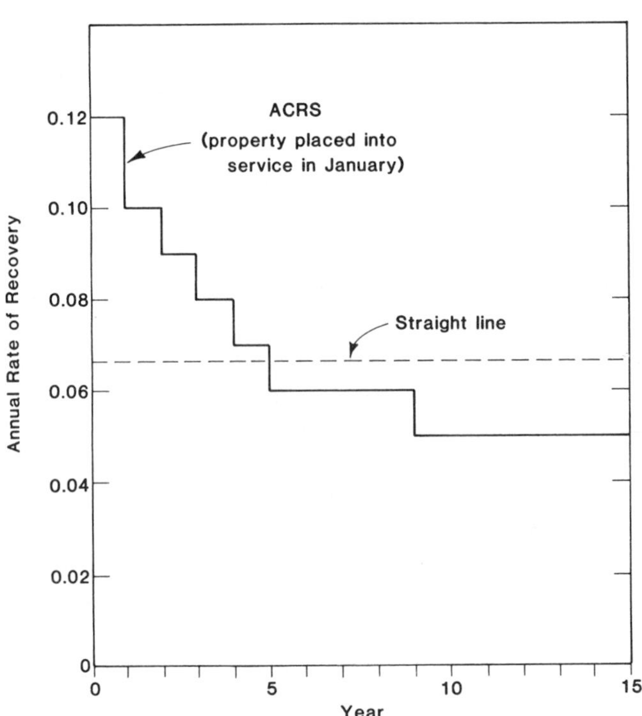

Figure 26

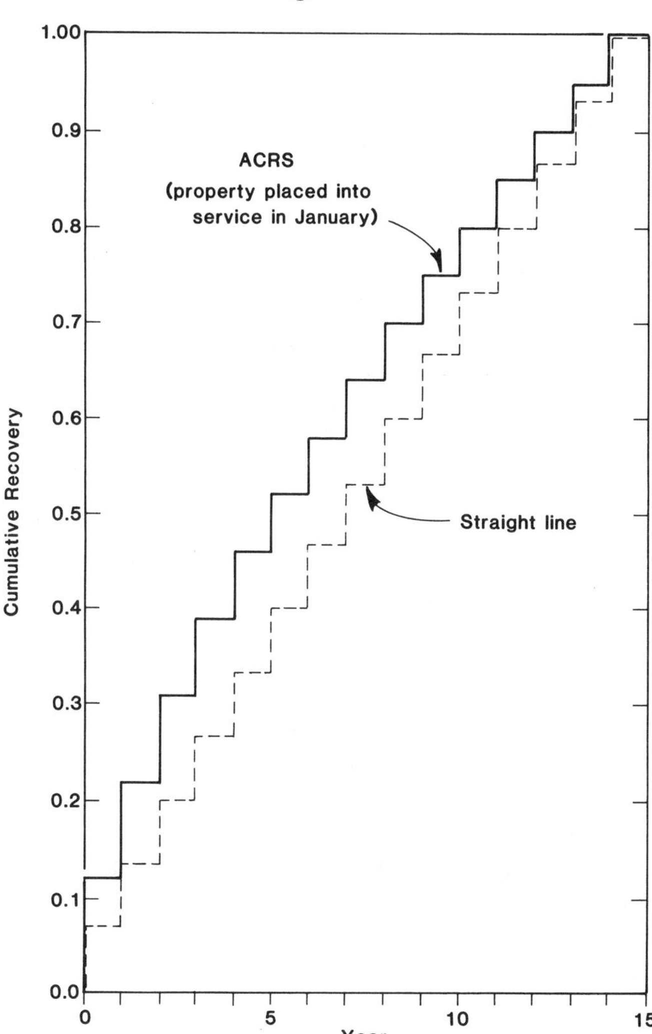
1.00
0.9
0.8
0.7
0.6
0.5
0.4
0.3
0.2
0.1
0.0
Cumulative Recovery
ACRS
(property placed into
service in January)
Straight line
0
5
10
15
Year

DEPRECIATION RECAPTURE

The taxpayer must consider two factors when choosing the accelerated method of cost recovery: the disadvantage of depreciation recapture in the year of disposition and the advantage of the annual tax savings.

Depreciation recapture is that part of the capital gain that is treated as ordinary income in the year of disposition. As shown in Table 15, the amount of depreciation recapture depends upon the type of property and the method of cost recovery.

Table 15. DEPRECIATION RECAPTURE FOR DIFFERENT TYPES OF PROPERTY AND RECOVERY METHODS

		Type of Property	
		Residential	**Non-Residential**
Recovery Method	ACRS	Amount of recovery that exceeds recovery from the straight-line method	Total amount of recovery
	Straight-Line	None	None

The taxpayer has the advantage of using more money each year if he uses the accelerated method. Figure 25 shows that the deductions from the ACRS exceed those from the straight-line method for the first five or six years.

EXAMPLE: What is the value of the excess deduction for each $100,000 of depreciable residential property that is disposed after five years by an investor who normally receives 15% annually from his investments?

SOLUTION: If the property is acquired in January, the excess deduction for each of the first five years is

$5,333, $3,333, $2,333, $1,333, and $333.

The total excess deduction is $12,665. The tax on these amounts is saved and it can be invested. Finally, upon disposition of the property, the tax on $12,665 is paid as ordinary income. The net advantage of using the accelerated depreciation is the use of the money over the holding period.

CHAPTER 18

Capital Gain and the Unrealized Benefit of the Installment Sale

A regular sale is one in which all payments are made to the seller in the year of the sale, usually at the closing (of the sale contract).

According to the Treasury, a sale is an installment sale if at least one payment is made to the seller after the year of the sale. The seller can, but needn't, also receive payments in the year of the sale. The installment sale applies to the sale of real property and to the casual sale of personal property. This method of reporting capital gain allows the seller to pay tax in the year the capital gain is received.

An installment sale is automatically reported as one, unless the seller elects to report it otherwise. He might so elect to do this if he anticipates being in a higher tax bracket when he receives installments or if he chooses income averaging.

The Treasury forbids the use of the installment sale to certain buyers under certain conditions. That is, it cannot be used in sales to the following entities if they resell the property within two years: a parent, spouse, child, grandchild, controlled corporation, trust or estate.*

The tax advantage of the installment sale over the regular sale can be substantial. For example, suppose a property is sold for $750,000. If the seller has a basis of $500,000 and selling costs of $40,000, his capital gain is $210,000. With this in mind, consider the recognized capital gain from the two methods of sale:

- *Regular sale.* The buyer obtains third-party financing, so that the seller receives all of his gain upon sale. His recognized capital gain is $210,000.

*The two-year rule does not apply in some cases when tax avoidance was not the reason for sale (e.g., death foreclosure, etc.). Notice that the two-year rule does not apply to a sale to a brother or sister.

- *Installment sale.* There is no third-party financing, so the seller takes a wraparound mortgage and receives his gain in installments. His total recognized capital gain is 0.28 × \$210,000 = \$58,800.

In the sale of this property, the installment sale method results in recognized capital gain tax that is only 28% of that resulting from the regular method. This percentage is computed in the following example in this section.

The formula shows how the recognized capital gain is determined in an installment sale.

FORMULAS:

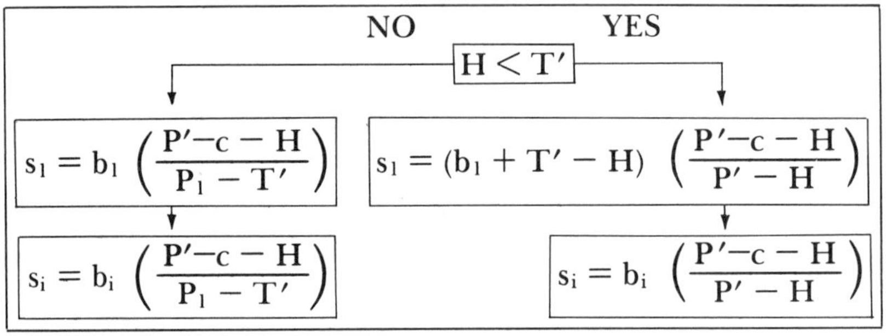

Test: $H < T'$

NO	YES
$s_1 = b_1 \left(\dfrac{P'-c-H}{P_1 - T'}\right)$	$s_1 = (b_1 + T' - H) \left(\dfrac{P'-c-H}{P' - H}\right)$
$s_i = b_i \left(\dfrac{P'-c-H}{P_1 - T'}\right)$	$s_i = b_i \left(\dfrac{P'-c-H}{P' - H}\right)$

where

s_1 = recognized capital gain in the year of the sale

s_i = recognized capital gain deferred to the ith year (i=2,3, . . .)

then

b_1 = amount received from the buyer in the year of the sale

b_i = amount received from the buyer in the ith year (i=2,3, . . .)*

c = selling costs

---

*Must include liabilities of the seller that are paid by the buyer (e.g., liens, taxes, etc.), principal payments to the seller on a purchase money mortgage, demand notes, bonds, readily marketable securities, etc. The amount received from the buyer does *not* include interest paid to the seller.

H = basis of property

P' = sale price of the property*

$P'-c$ = amount realized from sale of the property (i.e., sale price less selling costs)

T' = amount of buyer's indebtedness that is payable to a third party. (If only a purchase money mortgage is taken, $T'=\$0$).

EXAMPLE: Stan Nicholas sold an apartment building for $750,000. His basis is $500,000, and his selling costs are $40,000. The buyer gives $150,000 as a down payment, and Mr. Nicholas takes a $600,000 wraparound mortgage. Hence, there is no third-party financing. Mr. Nicholas also receives principal payments of $10,000 in each of the first two years. What is his recognized capital gain in each of the first two years?

SOLUTION: In this example,

$P' = \$750{,}000,\ H = \$500{,}000,$
$P'-c = \$750{,}000 - \$40{,}000 = \$710{,}000,$
$T' = \$0,\ b_1 = \$150{,}000 + \$10{,}000 = \$160{,}000,$ and $b_2 = \$10{,}000.$

From the flow diagram (following No), the recognized capital gain in the first year is

$$
\begin{aligned}
s_1 &= \$160{,}000 \left(\frac{\$710{,}000 - \$500{,}000}{\$750{,}000 - \$0}\right) \\
&= \$160{,}000 \left(\frac{\$210{,}000}{\$750{,}000}\right) \\
&= \$160{,}000 \times 0.28 \\
&= \$44{,}800.
\end{aligned}
$$

The recognized capital gain in the second year is

$$
\begin{aligned}
s_2 &= \$10{,}000 \times 0.28 \\
&= \$2{,}800.
\end{aligned}
$$

*The contract price is defined as the larger of $P'-H$ and $P'-T'$.

CHAPTER 19
Computing the Yield

Computing the yield for a real estate investment is more difficult than for other investments. This is so because the value of many components must be determined. Moreover, income tax is so important to a real estate investment that its effect should also be included in the yield calculations. However, it is very important to be able to estimate the yield. Even though the many components must be determined, no real estate investment should be undertaken without doing it.

This chapter contains a relatively simple ten-step procedure diagram to lead you to the yield. The diagram can be used to compute the yield in three ways: without the effect of income tax, including the effect of income tax while selling the regular way, and including tax while using the installment sale. (See Figure 27 on page 204.) Values determined at each step can be listed on the forms that correspond to one of these yield calculations (see Tables 16, 17, and 18 on pages 206 through 208.)* The boxes in the procedure diagram and the boxes in the forms are numbered to correspond to the following ten steps:

Step 1

P. This is the price for which the property is acquired. Property is usually acquired by purchase, although it needn't be. It may also be acquired by conversion, exchange, gift, a life estate, repossession, surviving a spouse, or surviving a joint tenancy. In any case, P is essentially the basis of the property when it is acquired.

A. This is the down payment and any other amount you contribute to acquire the property.

B, r, and **m.** These are the loan amount, the interest rate, and the term (in months) of the loan, respectively. These quantities are necessary to determine the total amount of interest paid each year (to be discussed in Step 2).** Use this procedure separately for all loans on the property.

---

*A computer program that determines the yield by these procedures is available on a disc. For information write: Convex Corporation, 4720 Cheyenne, Boulder, CO 80303.

**It is assumed that loan payments are monthly.

j. This is the number of months you intend to hold this investment. The holding period ends when you dispose of the property, except in the case of an installment sale. Then it ends with the last installment of principal.

P′. This is the value received when the property is disposed of (or later in the case of an installment sale). Although property is usually disposed of by sale, it needn't be. It can be disposed of by casualty, exchange, involuntary conversion, and repossession.

c. This is the selling cost, usually the sale commission. The seller pays the commission, never the buyer.

Step 2

g_i. This is the total income received each year. It is the scheduled gross income less vacancy and collection losses.

e_i. This is the sum of the operating expenses each year. It includes utilities, taxes (other than income tax), maintenance, insurance, services, supplies, etc.

i_i. This is the interest you pay on loans for the property each year. It can be determined readily from Table 13 on pages 178 through 191. For any period (in months), simply subtract the entry for the beginning month from the entry for the ending month. Then multiply that amount by the number of thousands of dollars that constitute the loan amount. See the example on page 176.

f_i. This quantity is not the cash flow, although very nearly. It would be the cash flow if the principal part of the loan payments were subtracted from it.*

Step 3

d_i. This is the depreciation claimed each year. The value of improved property does, in fact, change with time because of use, fashion, and/or utility. The Treasury considers this change to be a loss of value (which is usually a reasonable assumption). Until 1981, investors computed the depreciation according to one of three or four formulas, including the straight-line method. Now the investor can use either the straight-line method or values listed in Table 14 (the ACRS). In any case, the annual depreciation deduction is a fraction of the basis of the improvement when placed into service. (See page 192.)

$\overline{d_i}$. This is the straight-line depreciation each year the property is owned.

---

*The fraction of the total of the monthly payments that is principal after j months is $\frac{s(r,j,q)}{j \cdot a(r,m,q)}$. See page 226 for definitions.

Figure 27

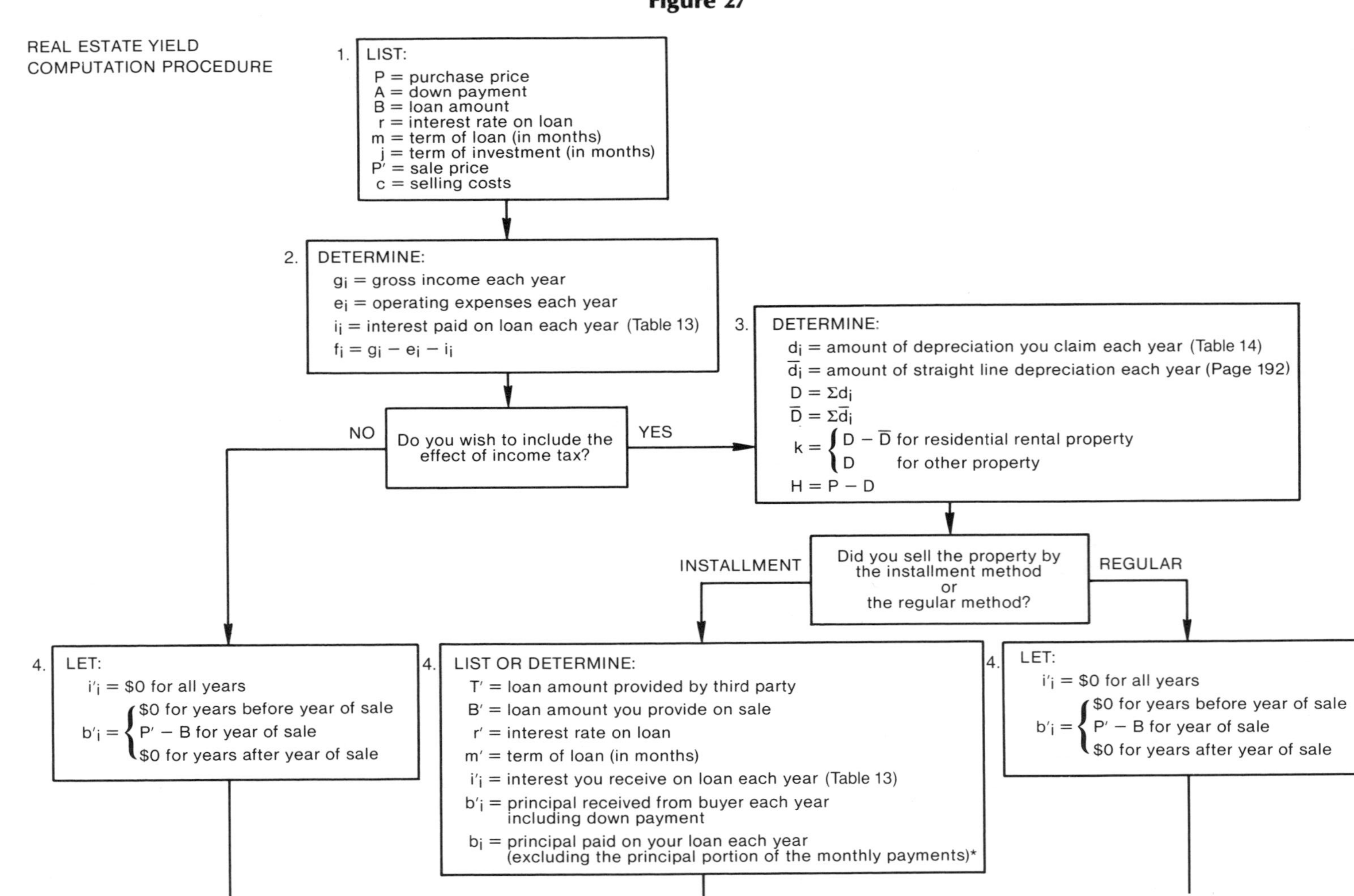

REAL ESTATE YIELD
COMPUTATION PROCEDURE
1. LIST:
P = purchase price
A = down payment
B = loan amount
r = interest rate on loan
m = term of loan (in months)
j = term of investment (in months)
P′ = sale price
c = selling costs
2. DETERMINE:
g_i = gross income each year
e_i = operating expenses each year
i_i = interest paid on loan each year (Table 13)
$f_i = g_i - e_i - i_i$
Do you wish to include the effect of income tax?
NO
YES
3. DETERMINE:
d_i = amount of depreciation you claim each year (Table 14)
$\overline{d}_i$ = amount of straight line depreciation each year (Page 192)
$D = \Sigma d_i$
$\overline{D} = \Sigma \overline{d}_i$
$k = \begin{cases} D - \overline{D} & \text{for residential rental property} \\ D & \text{for other property} \end{cases}$
$H = P - D$
Did you sell the property by the installment method or the regular method?
INSTALLMENT
REGULAR
4. LET:
i'_i = \$0 for all years
$b'_i = \begin{cases} \$0 \text{ for years before year of sale} \\ P' - B \text{ for year of sale} \\ \$0 \text{ for years after year of sale} \end{cases}$
4. LIST OR DETERMINE:
T′ = loan amount provided by third party
B′ = loan amount you provide on sale
r′ = interest rate on loan
m′ = term of loan (in months)
i'_i = interest you receive on loan each year (Table 13)
b'_i = principal received from buyer each year including down payment
b_i = principal paid on your loan each year (excluding the principal portion of the monthly payments)*
4. LET:
i'_i = \$0 for all years
$b'_i = \begin{cases} \$0 \text{ for years before year of sale} \\ P' - B \text{ for year of sale} \\ \$0 \text{ for years after year of sale} \end{cases}$

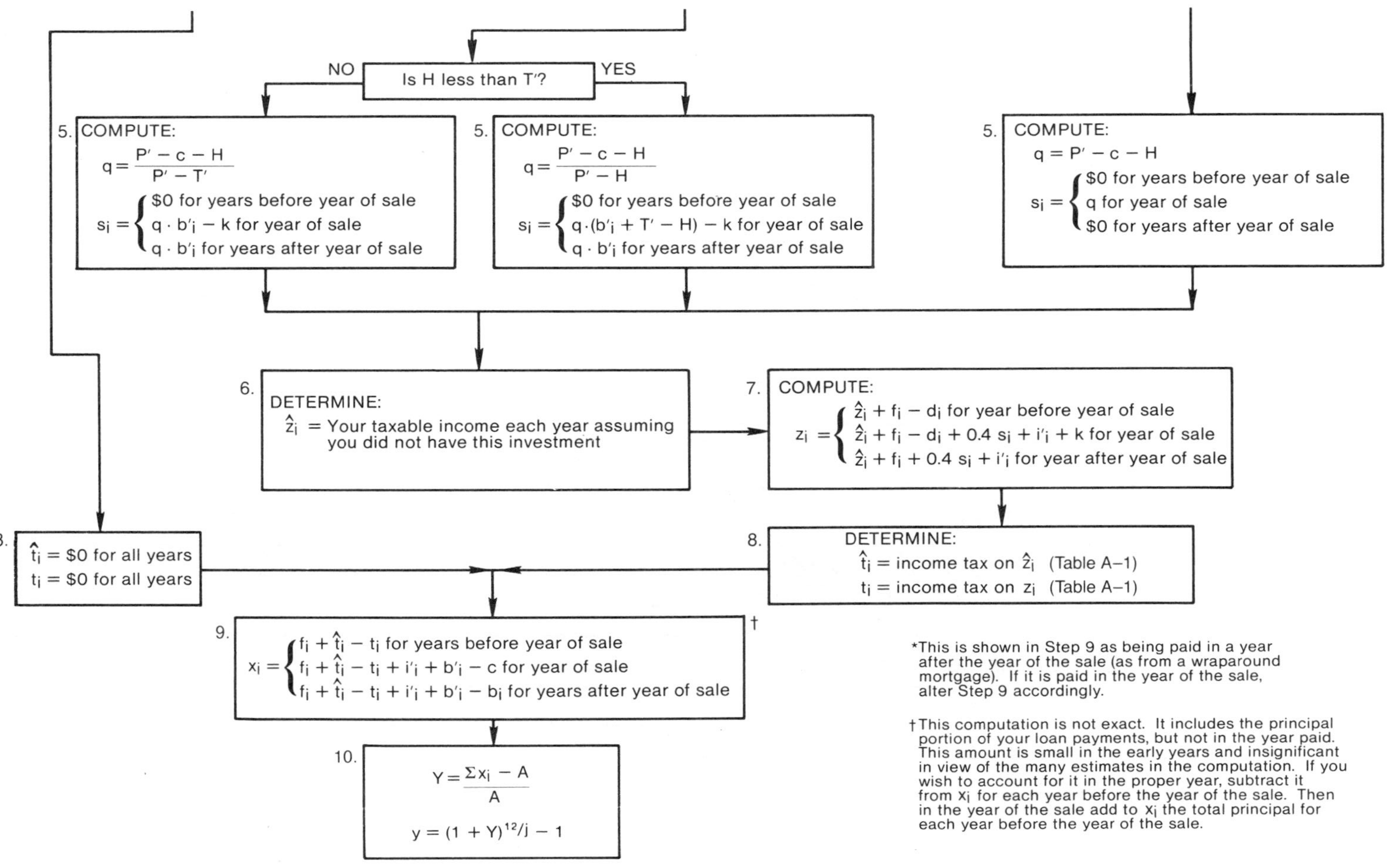

*This is shown in Step 9 as being paid in a year after the year of the sale (as from a wraparound mortgage). If it is paid in the year of the sale, alter Step 9 accordingly.

†This computation is not exact. It includes the principal portion of your loan payments, but not in the year paid. This amount is small in the early years and insignificant in view of the many estimates in the computation. If you wish to account for it in the proper year, subtract it from x_i for each year before the year of the sale. Then in the year of the sale add to x_i the total principal for each year before the year of the sale.

Table 16. REGULAR SALE—TAX NOT INCLUDED

1							
P	A	B	r	m	j	P′	c

	2				3
i	g_i	e_i	i_i	f_i	
1					
2					
3					
4					
5					

	4			5
i		i'_i	b'_i	
1				
2				
3				
4				
5				

	6	7	8		9	10
I			$\hat{t}_i$	t_i	x_i	Yields
1			\$0	\$0		Y=
2			0	0		y=
3			0	0		
4			0	0		
5			0	0		

Table 17. REGULAR SALE—TAX INCLUDED

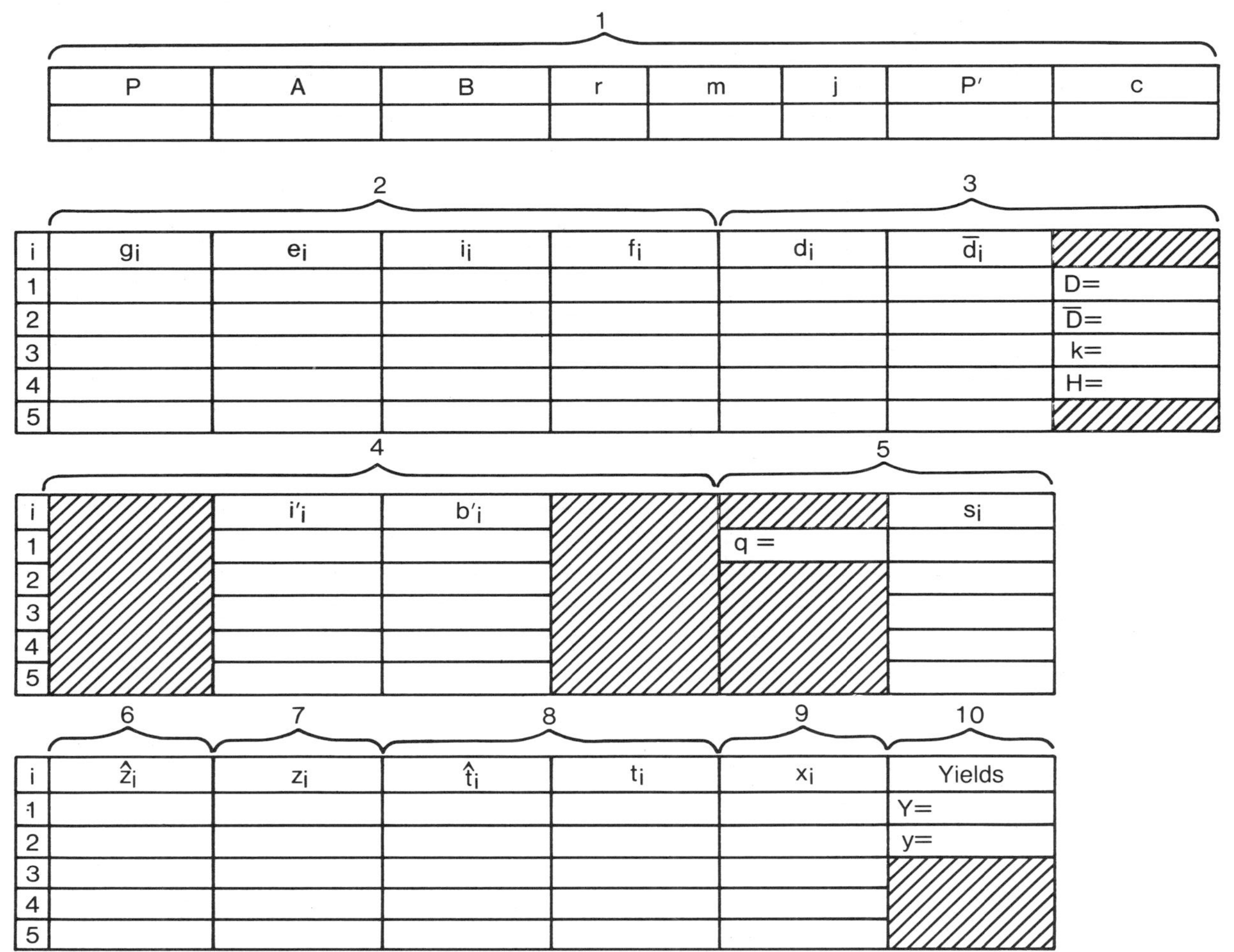

1							
P	A	B	r	m	j	P'	c

	2				3		
i	g_i	e_i	i_i	f_i	d_i	$\bar{d}_i$	
1							$D=$
2							$\bar{D}=$
3							$k=$
4							$H=$
5							

	4				5	
i		i'_i	b'_i			s_i
1					$q=$	
2						
3						
4						
5						

	6	7	8		9	10
i	$\hat{z}_i$	z_i	$\hat{t}_i$	t_i	x_i	Yields
1						$Y=$
2						$y=$
3						
4						
5						

Table 18. INSTALLMENT SALE—TAX INCLUDED

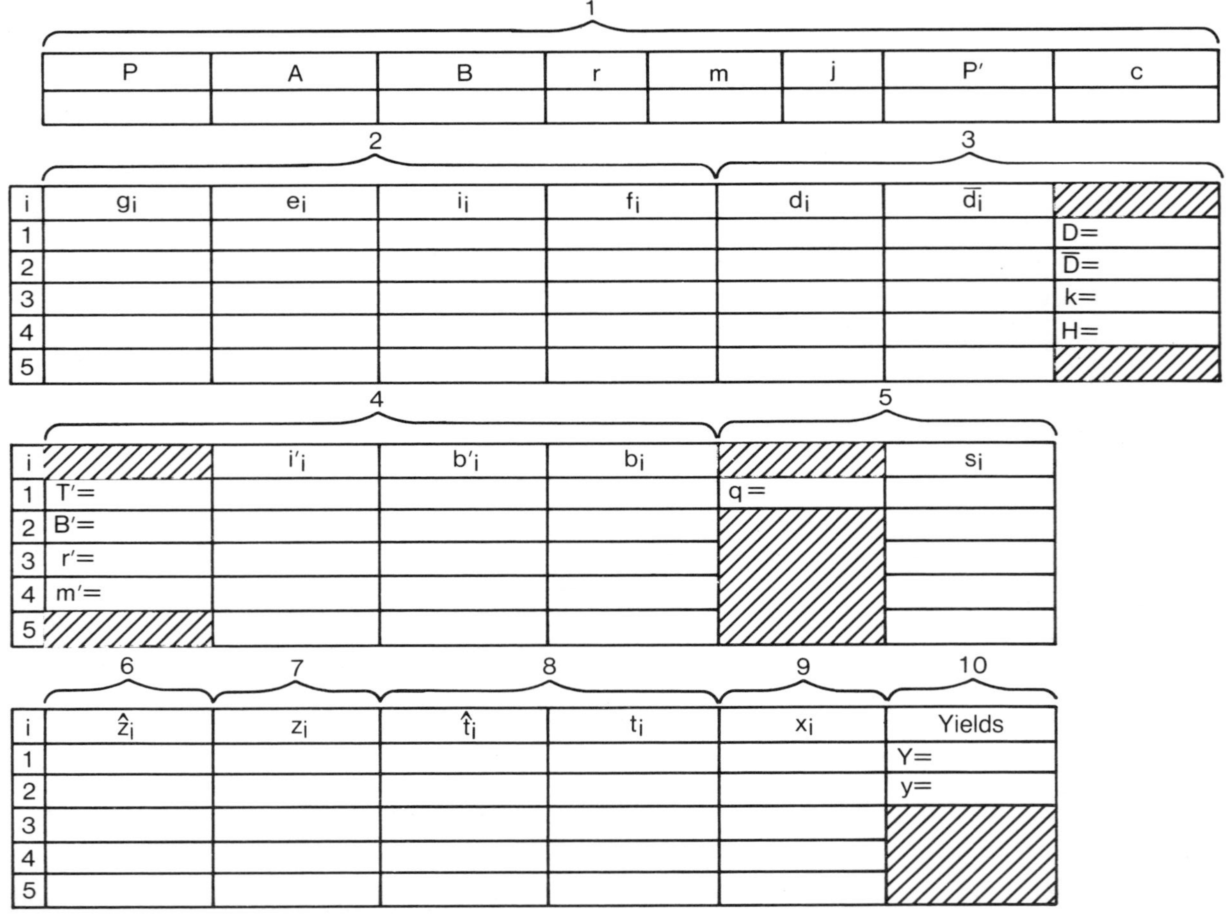

1							
P	A	B	r	m	j	P′	c

i	g_i (2)	e_i (2)	i_i (2)	f_i (2)	d_i (3)	$\overline{d_i}$ (3)	(3)
1							$D=$
2							$\overline{D}=$
3							$k=$
4							$H=$
5							

i	(4)	i'_i (4)	b'_i (4)	b_i (4)	(5)	s_i (5)
1	$T'=$				$q=$	
2	$B'=$					
3	$r'=$					
4	$m'=$					
5						

i	$\hat{z}_i$ (6)	z_i (7)	$\hat{t}_i$ (8)	t_i (8)	x_i (9)	Yields (10)
1						$Y=$
2						$y=$
3						
4						
5						

D, $\overline{D}$. This is the sum of the accrued depreciation and the straight-line depreciation, respectively, over the period of time the property is held. If the straight-line method was used, $D = \overline{D}$.

k. This is the amount of depreciation recapture. It is zero if the straight-line method is used. This amount is added to your ordinary income in the year of sale (or other disposition). Notice that if the property is not residential rental property (e.g., commercial), the depreciation recapture is the total amount of depreciation claimed. However, if the property is residential rental property (such as a rental house or apartment building) it is only the amount that exceeds straight-line depreciation. If you use the accelerated method of depreciation, your annual ordinary income has been reduced more than it would have been using the straight-line method. However, upon sale (or other disposition) the capital gain is more because the adjusted basis is lower.

H. This is the adjusted basis of the property. Usually the basis is only adjusted by the claimed depreciation, i.e., $H = P - D$.

Step 4

T′. This is the amount of third party financing obtained by the buyer when you sell by the installment method.

B′, r′, and **m′.** This is the amount, interest rate, and term (in months) of a loan, respectively, that you give the buyer when you sell by the installment method.

i_i'. This is the amount of interest paid to you each year on the loan. It is zero unless and until you sell by the installment method.

b_i'. In the case of a regular sale, this quantity is zero except in the year of the sale. Then it is the difference between the sale price and your original loan amount. In the case of the installment sale, it is the total principal paid by the buyer (including down payment).

b_i. This is the principal paid on your loan each year (not including the principal portion of each monthly payment) when you sell by the installment method. It is shown in Step 9 as being paid in a year after the year of the sale (as if it were paid from the principal of a wraparound mortgage). If it is paid in the year of the sale, subtract it that year instead.

Step 5

q. In the case of property sold by the regular method, this is the amount of capital gain to be taxed. In the case of property sold by the installment method, it is a ratio called the gross profit ratio; notice that it is always less than or equal to 1.

s_i. This is the amount to be taxed at the capital gain rate (i.e., 40% of the ordinary income rate) each year. Since the gross profit ratio never exceeds 1, the capital gain tax paid on property sold by the installment method is always less than that sold by the regular way (frequently it is only one third as much).

Step 6

$\hat{z}_i$. This is your estimate of your taxable income each year, assuming you do not hold this investment.

Step 7

z_i. This is your taxable income each year, assuming you do hold this investment.*

Step 8

$\hat{t}_i$,t_i. This is the amount of tax on $\hat{z}_i$ and z_i, respectively, each year. It is determined from the tax tables on page 222.

Step 9

x_i. This is your net profit (or loss) each year due to this investment.

Step 10

Y,y. These are the total and annual yields on this investment, respectively. Notice that, in the case of an installment sale, the annual yield is computed over a longer period of time than in the case of a regular sale; hence, it will tend to be smaller (as it should be).

*This must also be an estimate since $\hat{z}_i$ is an estimate.

CHAPTER 20
An Example of a Yield Calculation

The following example is intended to show how to compute the yield on most any real estate investment. It includes the simplest case of a regular sale with no tax consequence, a regular sale with tax consequences, and an installment sale with tax consequences.* This rather typical example shows the benefit of a real estate investment relative to other investments under the current tax laws.

The solution to the example is obtained by following the steps of the procedure diagram and listing the values on the corresponding form.

EXAMPLE: Suppose you purchased a rental house in April of 1983 for $80,000. Your down payment was $20,000, and you obtained a $60,000 mortgage loan at 10% interest that is amortized by constant monthly payments over 30 years.

You held the property for 30 months (i.e., 8 months this year, 12 months next year, and 10 months the following year). The gross income and operating expenses (not including interest on your mortgage) are listed for these three years in the following table:

Year, i	Gross Income, g_i	Operating Expenses, e_i
1	$6,400	$1,387
2	$9,000	$2,344
3	$8,930	$1,972

You sell the property for $100,000 and incur $7,000 selling costs (mostly commission).

(a) If you wish to compute the yield without the effect of income tax, stop here, and go to part (a) of the solution. Otherwise, neglecting this investment, your taxable income is $25,000 the year you purchased the property and it increases by $1,000 each year thereafter; you and your

*There is no reason to use the installment sale without tax consequences.

spouse file a joint income tax return. While you owned the property, you claimed depreciation by the ACRS method. You consider the building portion of the property to be worth $60,000 when purchased.

(b) If you sold the property the regular way (i.e., receive all of the gain in the year of the sale), and wish to compute the yield including income tax, stop here, and go to part (b) of the solution. Otherwise, you sell the property by the installment method. The buyer pays you a $30,000 down payment, and you take a wraparound mortgage for $70,000 at 11% (interest only). You require the loan balance to be paid after 18 months (e.g., a balloon payment). At this time, you pay the balance of your $60,000 mortgage loan.

(c) Compute the yield including income tax. Go to part (c) of the solution.

SOLUTION:

(a) Follow the procedure diagram and list the values from each step on Table 16.

Step 1

$P = \$80{,}000$, $A = \$20{,}000$, $B = \$60{,}000$, $r = 10\%$, $m = 12 \times 30 = 360$ months, $j = 30$ months, $P' = \$100{,}000$, and $c = \$7{,}000$.

Step 2

- $g_1 = \$6{,}400$, $g_2 = \$9{,}000$, and $g_3 = \$8{,}930$.
- $e_1 = \$1{,}387$, $e_2 = \$2{,}344$, and $e_3 = \$1{,}972$.
- Find the amount of interest for each $1,000 in Table 13.

  $i_1 = 60(\$66.6042 - \$0) = \$3{,}996$,

  $i_2 = 60(\$166.2280 - \$66.6042) = \$5{,}977$, and

  $i_3 = 60\ (\$248.9666 - \$166.2280) = \$4{,}964$.
- $f_1 = g_1 - e_1 - i_1 = \$6{,}400 - \$1{,}387 - \$3{,}996 = \$1{,}017$,

  $f_2 = g_2 - e_2 - i_2 = \$9{,}000 - \$2{,}344 - \$5{,}977 = \$679$, and

  $f_3 = g_3 - e_3 - i_3 = \$8{,}930 - \$1{,}972 - \$4{,}964 = \$1{,}994$.

[Step 3 is not needed in this case.]

Step 4

- $i'_i = \$0$ for all years.
- $b'_1 = \$0$,

  $b'_2 = \$0$, and

  $b'_3 = P' - B = \$100{,}000 - \$60{,}000 = \$40{,}000$.*

[Steps 5 through 7 are not needed in this case.]

*The principal part of the mortgage payments is not shown explicitly. However, it is accounted for implicitly since it is neither shown as reducing annual cash flow nor as reducing the loan balance.

Step 8

- $\hat{t}_i = \$0$ for all years.
- $t_i = \$0$ for all years.

Step 9

- $x_1 = f_1 + \hat{t}_1 - t_1$
  $= \$1,017 + \$0 - \$0 = \$1,017,$
  $x_2 = f_2 + \hat{t}_2 - t_2$
  $= \$679 + \$0 - \$0 = \$679,$ and
  $x_3 = f_3 + \hat{t}_3 - t_3 + b'_3 + i'_3 - c$
  $= \$1,994 + \$0 - \$0 + \$40,000 + \$0 - \$7,000 = \$34,994.$

Step 10

Now,

- The total yield is

$$Y = \frac{\sum_{i=1}^{3} x_i - A}{A}$$

$$= \frac{(\$1,017 + \$679 + \$34,994) - \$20,000}{\$20,000}$$

$$= \frac{\$36,690 - \$20,000}{\$20,000} = \frac{\$16,690}{\$20,000} = 0.8345 = 83.45\%.$$

- The annual yield is

$$y = (1+Y)^{12/j} - 1 = (1+0.8345)^{12/30} - 1 = (1.8345)^{0.4} - 1$$
$$= 1.2747 - 1 = 0.2747 = 27.47\%.$$

This completes the yield calculations when tax is not considered.

(b) Follow the procedure diagram, and list the value from each step on Table 17.

Step 1

$P = \$80,000$, $A = \$20,000$, $B = \$60,000$, $r = 10\%$, $m = 12 \times 30 = 360$ months, $j = 30$ months, $P' = \$100,000$, and $c = \$7,000$.

Step 2

- $g_1 = \$6,400$, $g_2 = \$9,000$, and $g_3 = \$8,930$.
- $e_1 = \$1,387$, $e_2 = \$2,344$, and $e_3 = \$1,972$.
- Find the amount of interest for each \$1,000 in Table 13.
  $i_1 = 60(\$66.6042 - \$0) = \$3,996,$
  $i_2 = 60(\$166.2280 - \$66.6042) = \$5,977,$ and
  $i_3 = 60(\$248.9666 - \$166.2280) = \$4,964.$

- $f_1 = g_1 - e_1 - i_1 = \$6{,}400 - \$1{,}387 - \$3{,}996 = \$1{,}017$,
  $f_2 = g_2 - e_2 - i_2 = \$9{,}000 - \$2{,}344 - \$5{,}977 = \$679$, and
  $f_3 = g_3 - e_3 - i_3 = \$8{,}930 - \$1{,}972 - \$4{,}964 = \$1{,}994$.

Step 3

The building is considered to be worth $60,000.

- Depreciation is claimed according to the ACRS (Table 14).
  $d_1 = \$60{,}000 \times 0.09 = \$5{,}400$ (since the property is placed into service in April).
  $d_2 = \$60{,}000 \times 0.11 = \$6{,}600$, and
  $d_3 = \$60{,}000 \times 0.09 \times \frac{10}{12} = \$4{,}500$ (since you held the property only 10 months in the third year).

- The straight-line depreciation during the same time is determined from the formula on page 195.

$$\overline{d_1} = \$60{,}000 \times \frac{8}{12} \times \frac{1}{15} = \$2{,}667,$$

$$\overline{d_2} = \$60{,}000 \times \frac{12}{12} \times \frac{1}{15} = \$4{,}000, \text{ and}$$

$$\overline{d_3} = \$60{,}000 \times \frac{10}{12} \times \frac{1}{15} = \$3{,}333.$$

- Compute the sum of the ACRS depreciation:
  $D = \$5{,}400 + \$6{,}600 + \$4{,}500 = \$16{,}500$.
- Compute the sum of the straight-line depreciation:
  $\overline{D} = \$2{,}667 + \$4{,}000 + \$3{,}333 = \$10{,}000$.
- Compute the difference (called depreciation recapture):
  $k = D - \overline{D} = \$16{,}500 - \$10{,}000 = \$6{,}500$.
- Compute the adjusted bases of the property:
  $H = P - D = \$80{,}000 - \$16{,}500 = \$63{,}500$.

Step 4

Let

- $i'_1 = \$0$ for all years.
- $b'_1 = \$0$,
  $b'_2 = \$0$, and
  $b'_3 = P' - B = \$100{,}000 - \$60{,}000 = \$40{,}000$.

Step 5

Compute

- $q = P' - c - H = \$100{,}000 - \$7{,}000 - \$63{,}500$
  $= \$29{,}500$.

- $s_3 = q = \$29{,}500.$

Step 6

From information in the example,

- $\hat{z}_i = \$25{,}000$, $\hat{z}_2 = \$26{,}000$, and $\hat{z}_3 = \$27{,}000$.

Step 7

- $$\begin{aligned} z_1 &= \hat{z}_1 + f_1 - d_1 \\ &= \$25{,}000 + \$1{,}017 - \$5{,}400 = \$20{,}617, \\ z_2 &= \hat{z}_2 + f_2 - d_2 \\ &= \$26{,}000 + \$679 - \$6{,}600 = \$20{,}079, \text{ and} \\ z_3 &= \hat{z}_3 + f_3 - d_3 + 0.4 \times s_3 + i'_3 + k \\ &= \$27{,}000 + \$1{,}994 - \$4{,}500 + 0.4 \times \$29{,}500 + \$0 \\ &\quad + \$6{,}500 = \$42{,}794. \end{aligned}$$

Step 8

From Income Tax Tables such as those in Appendix A,

- The income tax, not considering this investment, is $\hat{t}_1 = \$3{,}565$, $\hat{t}_2 = \$3{,}815$, and $\hat{t}_3 = \$4{,}065$.
- The income tax, considering this investment, is $t_1 = \$2{,}589$, $t_2 = \$2{,}475$, and $t_3 = \$8{,}780$.

Step 9

- $$\begin{aligned} x_1 &= f_1 + \hat{t}_1 - t_1 \\ &= \$1{,}017 + \$3{,}565 - \$2{,}589 = \$1{,}993, \\ x_2 &= f_2 + \hat{t}_2 - t_2 \\ &= \$679 + \$3{,}815 - \$2{,}475 = \$2{,}019, \text{ and} \\ x_3 &= f_3 + \hat{t}_3 - t_3 + b'_3 + i'_3 - c \\ &= \$1{,}994 + \$4{,}065 - \$8{,}780 + \$40{,}000 + \$0 - \$7{,}000 \\ &= \$30{,}279. \end{aligned}$$

Step 10

Now

- The total yield from this investment is

$$Y = \frac{\sum_{i=1}^{3} x_i - A}{A} = \frac{(\$1{,}993 + \$2{,}019 + \$30{,}279) - \$20{,}000}{\$20{,}000}$$

$$= \frac{\$34{,}291 - \$20{,}000}{\$20{,}000} = \frac{\$14{,}291}{\$20{,}000} = 0.7146 = 71.46\%.$$

- The annual yield is

$$y = (1 + Y)^{12/j} - 1 = (1 + 0.7146)^{12/30} - 1 = (1.7146)^{0.4} - 1 = 1.2407 - 1 = 0.2407 = 24.07\%.$$

This completes the yield calculations for a regular sale when tax is considered.

(c) Follow the procedure diagram and list the values from each step on Table 18:

Step 1

$P = \$80,000$, $A = \$20,000$, $B = \$60,000$, $r = 10\%$, $m = 12 \times 30 = 360$ months, $j = 48$ months, $P' = \$100,000$, and $c = \$7,000$.

Step 2

- $g_1 = \$6,400$, $g_2 = \$9,000$, $g_3 = \$8,930$, $g_4 = \$0$, and $g_5 = \$0$.
- $e_1 = \$1,387$, $e_2 = \$2,344$, $e_3 = \$1,972$, $e_4 = \$0$, and $e_5 = \$0$.
- Find the amount of interest for each \$1,000 in Table 13.
  $i_1 = 60\ (\$66.6042 - \$0) = \$3,996$,
  $i_2 = 60\ (\$166.2280 - \$66.6042) = \$5,977$,
  $i_3 = 60\ (\$265.4815 - \$166.2280) = \$5,955$,
  $i_4 = 60\ (\$364.3259 - \$265.4815) = \$5,931$, and
  $i_5 = 60\ (\$397.1758 - \$364.3259) = \$1,971$.
- $f_1 = g_1 - e_1 - i_1 = \$6,400 - \$1,387 - \$3,996 = \$1,017$,
  $f_2 = g_2 - e_2 - i_2 = \$9,000 - \$2,344 - \$5,977 = \$679$,
  $f_3 = g_3 - e_3 - i_3 = \$8,930 - \$1,972 - \$5,955 = \$1,003$,
  $f_4 = g_4 - e_4 - i_4 = \$0 - \$0 - \$5,931 = -\$5,931$, and
  $f_5 = g_5 - e_5 - i_5 = \$0 - \$0 - \$1,971 = -\$1,971$.

Step 3

The building is considered to be worth \$60,000.

- Depreciation is claimed according to the ACRS (Table 14).
  $d_1 = \$60,000 \times 0.09 = \$5,400$ (since the property is placed into service in April).
  $d_2 = \$60,000 \times 0.11 = \$6,600$, and
  $d_3 = \$60,000 \times 0.09 \times \frac{10}{12} = \$4,500$ (since you held the property only 10 months in the third year).
- The straight-line depreciation during the same time is determined from the formula on page 195.

$$\overline{d_1} = \$60,000 \times \frac{8}{12} \times \frac{1}{15} = \$2,667,$$

$$\overline{d_2} = \$60,000 \times \frac{12}{12} \times \frac{1}{15} = \$4,000, \text{ and}$$

$$\overline{d_3} = \$60,000 \times \frac{10}{12} \times \frac{1}{15} = \$3,333.$$

- Compute the sum of the ACRS depreciation:
  $D = \$5,400 + \$6,600 + \$4,500 = \$16,500$.
- Compute the sum of the straight-line depreciation:
  $\overline{D} = \$2,667 + \$4,000 + \$3,333 = \$10,000$.
- Compute the difference (called depreciation recapture):
  $k = D - \overline{D} = \$16,500 - \$10,000 = \$6,500$.
- Compute the adjusted basis of the property:
  $H = P - D = \$80,000 - \$16,500 = \$63,500$.

Step 4

From the information in the example,

- $T' = \$0$.
- $B' = \$70,000$, $r' = 11\%$, and $m' = 18$ months.
- interest is simple interest on the loan balance, so, for each year, the interest depends only upon the number of months:

$$i'_3 = \frac{2}{12} \times 0.11 \times \$70,000 = \$1,283,$$

$$i'_4 = \frac{12}{12} \times 0.11 \times \$70,000 = \$7,700, \text{ and}$$

$$i'_5 = \frac{4}{12} \times 0.11 \times \$70,000 = \$2,567.$$

- $b'_3 = \$30,000$, $b'_4 = \$0$, and $b'_5 = \$70,000$.
- Since your loan must be paid from the buyer's balloon payment in the fifth (last) year,
  $b_5 = \$60,000$, and $b_i = \$0$ for all other years.

Since $H = \$63,500$, and $T' = \$0$, use the formulas in block number 5 on the left.

Step 5

- $$q = \frac{\$100,000 - \$7,000 - \$63,500}{\$100,000 - \$0} = \frac{\$29,500}{\$100,000} = 0.295$$
- $s_3 = 0.295 \times \$30,000 - \$6,500 = \$2,350$,
  $s_4 = 0.295 \times \$0 = \$0$, and
  $s_5 = 0.295 \times \$70,000 = \$20,650$.

Step 6

From information in the example,

- $\hat{z}_1 = \$25,000$, $\hat{z}_2 = \$26,000$, $\hat{z}_3 = \$27,000$,
  $\hat{z}_4 = \$28,000$, and $\hat{z}_5 = \$29,000$.

Step 7

- $z_1 = \hat{z}_1 + f_1 - d_1$
  $= \$25{,}000 + \$1{,}017 - \$5{,}400 = \$20{,}617,$
  $z_2 = \hat{z}_2 + f_2 - d_2$
  $= \$26{,}000 + \$679 - \$6{,}600 = \$20{,}079,$
  $z_3 = \hat{z}_3 + f_3 - d_3 + 0.4 \times s_3 + i'_3 + k$
  $= \$27{,}000 + \$1{,}003 - \$4{,}500 + 0.4 \times \$2{,}350$
  $+ \$1{,}283 + \$6{,}500 = \$32{,}226$
  $z_4 = \hat{z}_4 + f_4 + 0.4 \times s_4 + i'_4$
  $= \$28{,}000 - \$5{,}955 + 0.4 \times \$0 + \$7{,}700$
  $= \$29{,}745$, and
  $z_5 = \hat{z}_5 + f_5 + 0.4 \times s_5 + i'_5$
  $= \$29{,}000 - \$1{,}971 + 0.4 \times \$20{,}650 + \$2{,}567$
  $= \$37{,}856.$

Step 8

From Income Tax Tables such as those in Appendix A,

- The income tax, not considering this investment, is $\hat{t}_1 = \$3{,}565$, $\hat{t}_2 = \$3{,}815$, $\hat{t}_3 = \$4{,}065$, $\hat{t}_4 = \$4{,}565$, and $\hat{t}_5 = \$4{,}565$.
- The income tax, considering this investment, is $t_1 = \$2{,}589$, $t_2 = \$2{,}475$, $t_3 = \$5{,}441$, $t_4 = \$4{,}751$, and $t_5 = \$7{,}150$.

Step 9

- $x_1 = f_1 + \hat{t}_1 - t_1$
  $= \$1{,}017 + \$3{,}565 - \$2{,}589 = \$1{,}993,$
  $x_2 = f_2 + \hat{t}_2 - t_2$
  $= \$679 + \$3{,}815 - \$2{,}475 = \$2{,}019,$
  $x_3 = f_3 + \hat{t}_3 - t_3 + b'_3 + i'_3 - c$
  $= \$1{,}003 + \$4{,}065 - \$5{,}441 + \$30{,}000 + \$1{,}283$
  $- \$7{,}000 = \$23{,}910,$
  $x_4 = f_4 + \hat{t}_4 - t_4 + b'_4 + i'_4 - b_4$
  $= -\$5{,}931 + \$4{,}315 - \$4{,}751 + \$0 + \$7{,}700 - \$0$
  $= \$1{,}333$, and
  $x_5 = f_5 + \hat{t}_5 - t_5 + b'_5 + b'_5 + i'_5 - b_5$
  $= -\$1{,}971 + \$4{,}565 - \$7{,}150 + \$70{,}000 + \$2{,}567$
  $- \$60{,}000 = \$8{,}011.$

Step 10

Now,

- The total yield on the investment is

$$Y = \frac{\sum_{i=1}^{5} x_i - A}{A}$$

$$= \frac{(\$1{,}993 + \$2{,}019 + \$23{,}910 + \$1{,}333 + \$8{,}011) - \$20{,}000}{\$20{,}000}$$

$$= \frac{\$37{,}266 - \$20{,}000}{\$20{,}000} = \frac{\$17{,}266}{\$20{,}000} = 0.8633 = 86.33\%.$$

- The annual yield is

$$y = (1 + Y)^{12/j} - 1 = (1 + 0.8633)^{12/48} - 1$$

$$= (1.8621)^{0.25} - 1$$

$$= 1.1683 - 1 = 16.83\%*$$

*Using the present value technique (Appendix C), the annual yield (rate of return) is 21.5%.

APPENDIX A
Income Tax Rates

Individuals computing tax according to the regular method and whose tax table income and exemptions do not exceed certain limits use one of the tax tables A, B, C, or D (not listed here). In this case tax is paid on an amount called *tax table income.*

Those individuals who exceed these limits or who compute their tax by other than the regular method* use one of the tables in this section. Figure A-1 depicts these tables. In this case, tax is paid on an amount called *taxable income.* The taxpayer is free to use the method that results in the least tax.

FORMULA:

$$\boxed{t = T(z)}$$

where

t = amount of tax using the regular method

z = taxable income or tax table income

$T(z)$ = amount of tax due on the amount z.(See the tax schedules on pages 222–223.)

T_t = income tax rate

EXAMPLE: Evan Dutton is a bachelor whose taxable income is $29,000. (a) How much income tax must he pay using the regular method, and (b) what percent of his taxable income is this?

SOLUTION: Since Mr. Dutton is single and not the head of a household, he must use the schedule for single taxpayers. (a) From this table, he must pay

$$\$5{,}705 + 0.40 \times \$200 = \$5{,}785$$

*For example, the alternative tax method, income averaging, or foreign income exclusion.

That is,

$$t = T(z) = T(\$29{,}000) = \$6{,}772.$$

(b) The percent of tax is

$$r_t = \frac{T(z)}{z} = \frac{\$6{,}772}{\$29{,}000} = 0.233 = 23.3\%$$

Figure A-1. PERCENTAGE OF TAXABLE INCOME THAT IS TAXED

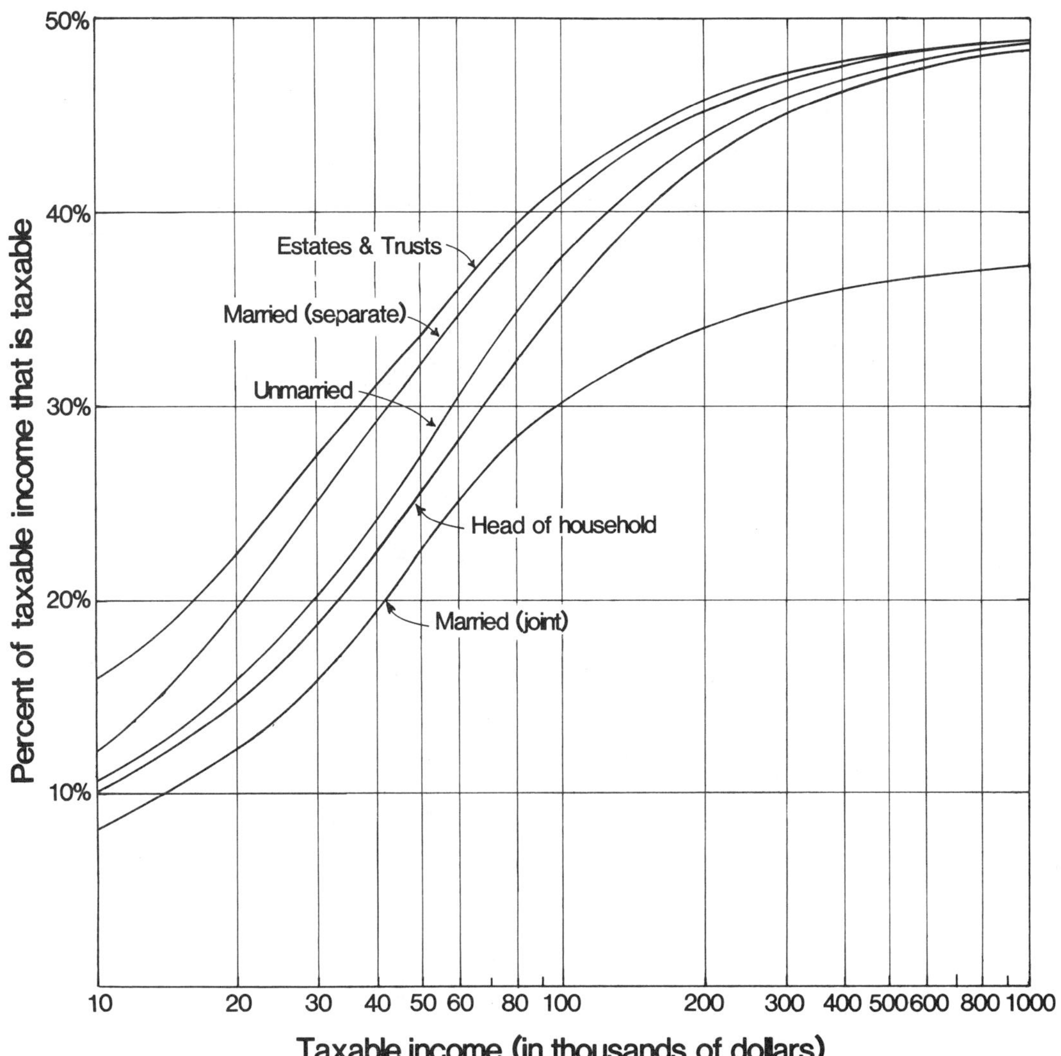

Table A-1. 1985 FEDERAL INCOME TAX RATES

SCHEDULE X—Single Taxpayers

If line 5 of Form 1040 is: Over—	but not over—	The tax is:	of the amount over—
$0	$2,390	—0—	
2,390	3,540	— 11%	$2,390
3,540	4,580	$126.50 + 12%	3,540
4,580	6,760	251.30 + 14%	4,580
6,760	8,850	556.50 + 15%	6,760
8,850	11,240	870.00 + 16%	8,850
11,240	13,430	1,252.40 + 18%	11,240
13,430	15,610	1,646.60 + 20%	13,430
15,610	18,940	2,082.60 + 23%	15,610
18,940	24,460	2,848.50 + 26%	18,940
24,460	29,970	4,283.70 + 30%	24,460
29,970	35,490	5,936.70 + 34%	29,970
35,490	43,190	7,813.50 + 38%	35,490
43,190	57,550	10,739.50 + 42%	43,190
57,550	85,130	16,770.70 + 48%	57,550
85,130	—	30,009.10 + 50%	85,130

SCHEDULE Z—Heads of Household

If line 5 of Form 1040 is: Over—	but not over—	The tax is:	of the amount over—
$0	$2,390	—0—	
2,390	4,580	— 11%	$2,390
4,580	6,760	$240.90 + 12%	4,580
6,760	9,050	502.50 + 14%	6,760
9,050	12,280	823.10 + 17%	9,050
12,280	15,610	1,372.20 + 18%	12,280
15,610	18,940	1,971.60 + 20%	15,610
18,940	24,460	2,637.60 + 24%	18,940
24,460	29,970	2,962.40 + 28%	24,460
29,970	35,490	5,505.20 + 32%	29,970
35,490	46,520	7,271.60 + 35%	35,490
46,520	63,070	11,132.10 + 42%	46,520
63,070	85,130	18,083.10 + 45%	63,070
85,130	112,720	28,010.10 + 48%	85,130
112,720	—	41,253.30 + 50%	112,720

SCHEDULE Y—Married Taxpayers and Qualifying Widows and Widowers

Married Filing Joint Returns and Qualifying Widows and Widowers				Married Filing Separate Returns			
If line 5 of Form 1040 is:		The tax is:		If line 5 of Form 1040 is:		The tax is:	
Over—	but not over—		of the amount over—	Over—	but not over—		of the amount over—
$0	$3,540	—0—		$0	$1,770	—0—	
3,540	5,720	— 11%	$3,540	1,770	2,860	— 11%	1,770
5,720	7,910	$239.80 + 12%	5,720	2,860	3,955	$119.90 + 12%	2,860
7,910	12,390	502.60 + 14%	7,910	3,955	6,195	251.30 + 14%	3,955
12,390	16,650	1,129.80 + 16%	12,390	6,195	8,325	564.90 + 16%	6,195
16,650	21,020	1,811.40 + 18%	16,650	8,325	10,510	905.70 + 18%	8,325
21,020	25,600	2,598.00 + 22%	21,020	10,510	12,800	1,299.00 + 22%	10,510
25,600	31,120	3,605.60 + 25%	25,600	12,800	15,560	1,802.80 + 25%	12,800
31,120	36,630	4,985.60 + 28%	31,120	15,560	18,315	2,492.80 + 28%	15,560
36,630	47,670	6,528.40 + 33%	36,630	18,315	23,835	3,264.20 + 33%	18,315
47,670	62,450	10,171.60 + 38%	47,670	23,835	31,225	5,085.80 + 38%	23,835
62,450	89,090	15,788.00 + 42%	62,450	31,225	44,545	7,894.00 + 42%	31,225
89,090	113,860	26,976.80 + 45%	89,090	44,545	56,930	13,488.40 + 45%	44,545
113,860	169,020	38,123.30 + 49%	113,860	56,930	84,510	19,061.65 + 49%	56,930
169,020	—	65,151.70 + 50%	169,020	84,510	—	32,575.85 + 50%	84,510

APPENDIX B
Interpolation

Often it is necessary to know a value that is not listed in a table. If the formula from which the table is derived is known, the unknown value can theoretically be determined. However, often either the formula is not known or it is quite complicated. In either event, the unknown value can be estimated by using the two nearest tabulated values. If the unknown value lies beyond the table, it can sometimes be estimated by *extrapolation.* On the other hand, if the unknown value lies between two listed values, it can be estimated by *interpolation.*

By interpolating we assume that the formula is a straight line.* This assumption is of course usually not true, but it generally provides a good estimate of the true value.

As an example, Figure B.1 shows a portion of a curve, some of whose values might be listed in a table. Consider the listed values y_1 and y_2 corresponding to x_1 and x_2. Also consider a straight line through the points $P_1 = (x_1, y_1)$ and $P_2 = (x_2, y_2)$. The straight line, although not identical to the curve, can be used to approximate values on the curve between x_1 and x_2.

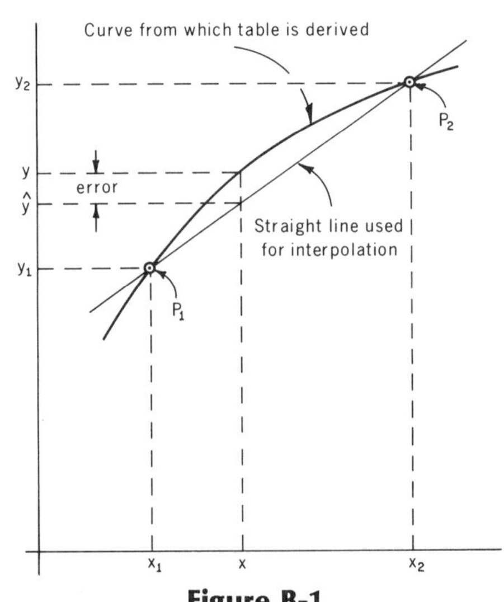

Figure B-1

For instance, the value on the curve corresponding to x is y and the value on the straight line corresponding to x is $\hat{y}$. Therefore, $\hat{y}$ is the estimate of y obtained by using linear interpolation.

The following formula determines the estimate of y.

*The word interpolation usually refers to linear interpolation although it needn't be so restrictive.

FORMULA:

$$\hat{y} = \left(\frac{x_2 - x}{x_2 - x_1}\right) \cdot y_1 + \left(\frac{x - x_1}{x_2 - x_1}\right) \cdot y_2$$

where

$\hat{y}$ = estimate of y using linear interpolation

y = nonlisted value, to be estimated by $\hat{y}$

x_1, x_2 = first and second listed parameter values that straddle x

then

x = nonlisted parameter value (between x_1 and x_2)

y_1, y_2 = first and second listed value corresponding to x_1 and x_2, respectively

EXAMPLE: Find the present value of an annuity of 1 corresponding to q = 1, r = 10%, and m = 20.25 (see Table I).

SOLUTION: Since m=20.25 is the non-listed parameter value (i.e., x = 20.25)., we will interpolate. Let

$$x_1 = 20, \text{ and } x_2 = 21$$

be the nearest listed values that straddle x.

The present values of an annuity of 1 corresponding to x_1 and x_2 (obtained from Table I) are

y_1 = a(10,20,1) = 8.51356, and y_2 = a(10,21,1) = 8.64869.

Now, using the formula, the estimate of y is

$$\begin{aligned}\hat{y} &= \left(\frac{21 - 20.25}{21 - 20}\right) \times 8.51356 + \left(\frac{20.25 - 20}{21 - 20}\right) \times 8.64869 \\ &= .75 \times 8.51356 + .25 \times 8.64869 \\ &= 6.38517 + 2.16217 \\ &= 8.54734\end{aligned}$$

(Note: The actual value using the formula in Appendix C is y = 8.54856. These two values differ by only 0.01427%.)

APPENDIX C
Annuities

INTRODUCTION

An annuity is a series of payments to be received over a period of time.

It is natural to think of an annuity as a series of equal payments received regularly from a pension fund, trust fund, etc. However, the concept is much more general than that and is applicable to many aspects of investments. The mortgage lender receives an annuity in the traditional sense because he receives equal monthly payments. However, cash flow and dividends received by the investor constitutes an annuity, usually with variable payments. Even capital gain is an annuity consisting of a single payment to be received in the future. In fact, the methods used to evaluate an annuity can (and should) be used to evaluate any payment to be received in the future.

Three methods are commonly used to evaluate an annuity. The most elementary method is simply to sum the payments. But since the payments are made over a period of time, and time has value,* most investors prefer to evaluate an annuity in ways that account for time, such as by the present value of an annuity and the amount (future value) of an annuity.

For example, suppose payments of the amounts $x_1, x_2, \ldots, x_n$ are received annually over n years. The following describes the three methods to evaluate an annuity.

A. *The Sum of an Annuity.* The sum of the annuity is simply the sum of the payments (as if time has no value):

$$\sum_{i=1}^{n} x_1 = x_1 + x_2 + \ldots + x_n.^{**}$$

---

*Time has no inherent value, but can have it if used beneficially. Of course, all investors believe they will use it beneficially. Hence, the saying, "Time has value."

**The mathematical notation $\sum_{i=1}^{n}$ means: sum all the values, x_i, for $i = 1$ through $i = n$.

B. *The Present Value of an Annuity.* If you normally invest money at the annual rate of interest, r, the first payment is not worth x_1 to you, but only $x_1/(1+r)$ because you had to wait a year to receive it. In other words, its present value is $x_1/(1 + r)$. In the same way, the present value of the second payment is $x_2/(1 + r)$,* the present value of the third payment is $x_3/(1+r)^3$, etc. Now the present value, A, of the annuity is the sum of the present values of all n payments:

$$A = \sum_{i=1}^{n} \frac{x_i}{(1+r)^i} = \frac{x_1}{(1+r)^1} + \frac{x_2}{(1+r)^2} + \ldots + \frac{x_n}{(1+r)^n}.$$

C. *The Amount of an Annuity.* The concept of the amount of an annuity is derived from the assumption that each payment can be invested at the rate of interest, r, from the time it is received until the annuity terminates.

That is, the first payment is invested at the rate r for the remaining $n - 1$ years of the annuity (i.e., interest is compounded for $n - 1$ years). Hence, its amount is $x_1(1 + r)^{n-1}$. The second payment is invested for $n - 2$ years, and its amount is $x_2(1 + r)^{n-2}$. Finally, the last payment cannot be invested at all, so its amount is simply x_n. Then the amount, S, of the annuity is the sum of the amounts of all n payments:

$$S = \sum_{i=1}^{n} x_i(1+r)^{n-i} = x_1(1+r)^{n-1} + x_2(1+r)^{n-2} + \ldots + x_n(1+r)^{n-n}.$$

Figure C-1 shows the relationship among the sum, the present value, and the amount of an annuity for equal payments and for two interest rates (1% and 5%). Notice that the sum is a straight line because equal payments are being received at equal intervals of time. The amount of the annuity is greater than the sum because the payments are being invested with interest as they are received. Conversely, the present value is less than the sum because you must wait to receive payments that you otherwise could have invested. Of course, all three formulas are equal if time has no value; i.e., $r = 0$.

Annuities are separated into three types, depending upon when they begin. An annuity is called an ordinary annuity if it begins now, and payments are made at the end of each period. An annuity is called an annuity due if it begins now, and payments are made at the beginning of each period (as in rent). An annuity is called a deferred annuity if it begins at some future date (then it can be called a deferred ordinary annuity or a

*Recall that $(1 + r)^{n-n} = (1 + r)^0 = 1$.

deferred annuity due, depending upon when the payments are considered to have been made within the period).

Figure C-1

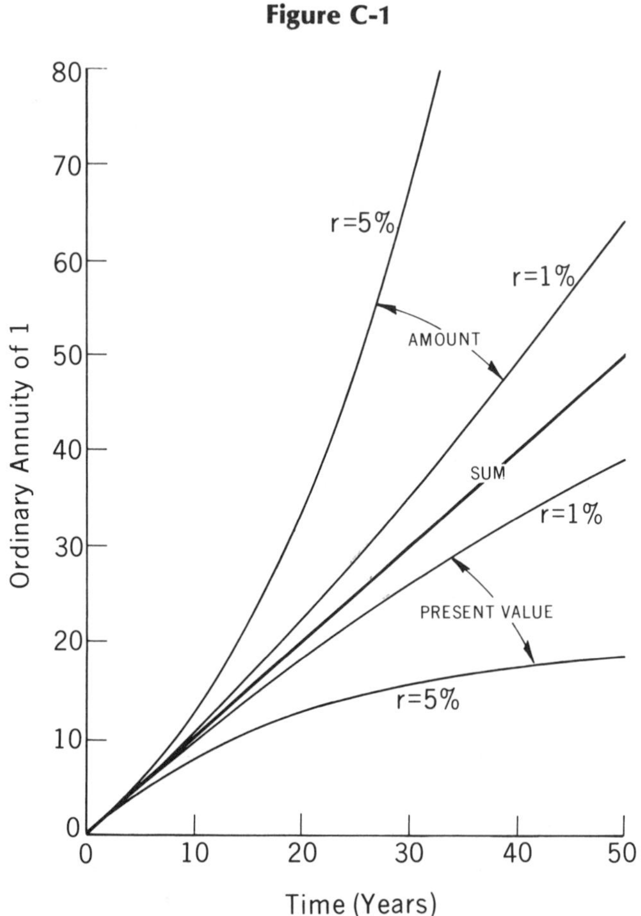

AMOUNT OF AN ANNUITY

The amount of an annuity is the amount accumulated at its term if each payment is promptly invested when it is received.

Whereas the present value of an annuity expresses the penalty for having to wait for payments, the amount of an annuity expresses the benefit for having invested them from the time they are received. For example, payments can be periodically deposited in an interest-bearing account (called a sinking fund).

FORMULAS:

INCOME			
Constant	Ordinary Annuity	$x \cdot \sum_{i=1}^{m} (1 + r/q)^{m-i} = x \cdot s(r,m,q)$
	Annuity Due	$x \cdot \sum_{i=1}^{m} (1 + r/q)^{m+1-i} = x \cdot s(r,m,q) \cdot c(r,1,q)$
Variable	Ordinary Annuity	$\sum_{i=1}^{m} x_1(1 + r/q)^{m-i} = \sum_{i=1}^{m} x_1 \cdot c(r,m-i,q)$
	Annuity Due	$\sum_{i=1}^{m} x_1(1 + r/q)^{m+1-i} = \sum_{i=1}^{m} x_1 \cdot c(r,m+1-i,q)$

EXAMPLE: Mark Meredith owes \$5,000 in four years. Suppose he deposits a fixed sum at the end of each month in an account that draws interest at 8% compounded monthly. How large must each deposit be so that the amount will be \$5,000 in four years?

SOLUTION: The deposits constitute an ordinary annuity with constant income and a constant interest rate. The formula for the amount of an ordinary annuity is

$$S = x \cdot s(r,m,q).$$

Since we must determine x, the monthly deposit, the formula must be solved for x:

$$x = S/s(r,m,q).$$

In this example, S = \$5,000, n = 4, q = 12, m = nq = 48, and r = 8%.

From Table I,

$$s(r,m,q) = s(8,48,12) = 56.34992.$$

The monthly deposits must be

$$\begin{aligned} x &= \$5,000/56.34992 \\ &= \$88.73. \end{aligned}$$

PRESENT VALUE OF AN ANNUITY

The present value of an annuity measures the penalty for having to wait to receive the payments. Since the payments are received over a period of time, and time has value,* the value of each payment is less than its face value. How much less? This depends on the rate of return (interest rate) you could achieve if you had the payment to invest. Figure C-2 shows the present value of an ordinary annuity for various interest rates. It can be used for a quick estimate of the present value of 1.

Figure C-2

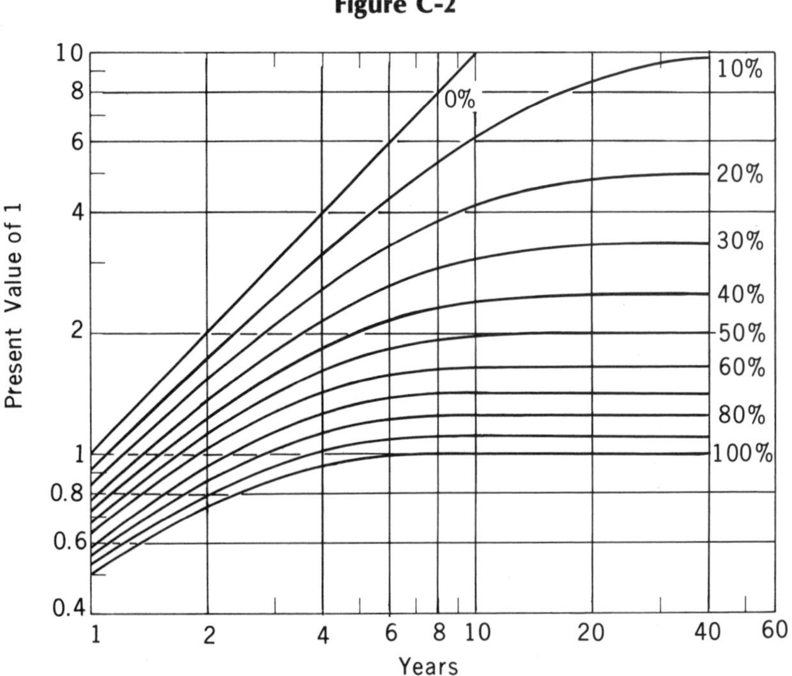

*Time has no inherent value but can have it if used beneficially. Of course all investors believe they will use it beneficially. Hence, the saying, "Time has value."

FORMULA:

INCOME	Constant	Ordinary Annuity	$x \cdot \sum_{i=1}^{m} \frac{1}{(1 + r/q)^{i}} = x \cdot a(r,m,q)$
		Annuity Due	$x \cdot \sum_{i=1}^{m} \frac{1}{(1 + r/q)^{i-1}} = x \cdot a(r,m,q) \cdot c(r,1,q)$
		Deferred Ordinary Annuity	$x \cdot \sum_{i=1}^{m} \frac{1}{(1 + r/q)^{i+v}} = x \cdot a(r,m,q)/c(r,v,q)$
	Variable	Ordinary Annuity	$\sum_{i=1}^{m} \frac{x_1}{(1 + r/q)^{1}} = \sum_{i=1}^{m} \frac{x_1}{c(r,i,q)}$
		Annuity Due	$\sum_{i=1}^{m} \frac{x_1}{(1 + r/q)^{1-i}} = \sum_{i=1}^{m} \frac{x_1}{c(r,i - 1,q)}$
		Deferred Ordinary Annuity	$\sum_{i=1}^{m} \frac{x_1}{(1 + r/q)^{1+v}} = \sum_{i=1}^{m} \frac{x_1}{c(r,i + v,q)}$

where

A = present value of an annuity

then

m = nq = total number of periods

n = number of years of annuity

q = number of periods per year

r = constant annual interest rate

v = number of periods the annuity is deferred

x = constant periodic payment

x_i = payment in the ith period

a(r,m,q) = present value of an annuity of 1 (Table I)

c(r,l,q),c(r,v,q), etc. = amount of 1 at compound interest* (Table I)

EXAMPLE (Constant Income): Suppose you expect to receive a $5,000 cash flow at the beginning of each month for 10 years. If you normally expect a 10% return on your investments, what is the present value of this annuity due?

SOLUTION: In this example,

$$x = \$5{,}000,\ q = 12,\ n = 10,\ m = nq = 120, \text{ and } r = 10\%.$$

Now,

$A = x \cdot a(r,m,q) \cdot c(r,l,q).$

From Table I,

$a(r,m,q) = a(10,120,12) = 75.6711633$, and

$c(r,l,q) = c(10,1,12) = 1.0083333.$

Now, the present value of this annuity due is

$$A = \$5{,}000 \times 75.6711633 \times 1.0083333 = \$381{,}508.77.$$

*Note that when compounding occurs continually, the amount of 1 is defined by e^{rn}: $\lim_{q \to \infty} (1+r/q)^{nq} = e^{rn}$.

TABLE I
Annuities

This table lists values of the three functions needed to solve interest problems covering a year or more. The functions are:

The amount of 1 at compound interest,

$$c(r,m,q) = (1 + r/q)^m,$$

the present value of an annuity of 1,

$$a(r,m,q) = \frac{(1 + r/q)^m - 1}{(r/q)(1 + r/q)^m},$$

and the amount of an annuity of 1,

$$s(r,m,q) = \frac{(1 + r/q)^m - 1}{(r/q)}.$$

where

r = annual interest rate, expressed as a decimal

q = number of interest periods per year

m = nq = total number of interest periods, and n is the number of years

(Annuities are discussed in Appendix C.)

Table I. ANNUITIES

M	C(5,M, 1)	A(5,M, 1)	S(5,M, 1)	M	C(6,M, 1)	A(6,M, 1)	S(6,M, 1)	M	C(7,M, 1)	A(7,M, 1)	S(7,M, 1)
1	1.05000	.95238	1.00000	1	1.06000	.94340	1.00000	1	1.07000	.93458	1.00000
2	1.10250	1.85941	2.05000	2	1.12360	1.83339	2.06000	2	1.14490	1.80802	2.07000
3	1.15763	2.72325	3.15250	3	1.19102	2.67301	3.18360	3	1.22504	2.62432	3.21490
4	1.21551	3.54595	4.31012	4	1.26248	3.46511	4.37462	4	1.31080	3.38721	4.43994
5	1.27628	4.32948	5.52563	5	1.33823	4.21236	5.63709	5	1.40255	4.10020	5.75074
6	1.34010	5.07569	6.80191	6	1.41852	4.91732	6.97532	6	1.50073	4.76654	7.15329
7	1.40710	5.78637	8.14201	7	1.50363	5.58238	8.39384	7	1.60578	5.38929	8.65402
8	1.47746	6.46321	9.54911	8	1.59385	6.20979	9.89747	8	1.71819	5.97130	10.25980
9	1.55133	7.10782	11.02656	9	1.68948	6.80169	11.49132	9	1.83846	6.51523	11.97799
10	1.62889	7.72173	12.57789	10	1.79085	7.36009	13.18079	10	1.96715	7.02358	13.81645
11	1.71034	8.30641	14.20679	11	1.89830	7.88687	14.97154	11	2.10485	7.49867	15.78360
12	1.79586	8.86325	15.91713	12	2.01220	8.38384	16.86994	12	2.25219	7.94269	17.88845
13	1.88565	9.39357	17.71298	13	2.13293	8.85268	18.88214	13	2.40985	8.35765	20.14064
14	1.97993	9.89864	19.59863	14	2.26090	9.29498	21.01507	14	2.57853	8.74547	22.55049
15	2.07893	10.37966	21.57856	15	2.39656	9.71225	23.27597	15	2.75903	9.10791	25.12902
16	2.18287	10.83777	23.65749	16	2.54035	10.10590	25.67253	16	2.95216	9.44665	27.88805
17	2.29202	11.27407	25.84037	17	2.69277	10.47726	28.21288	17	3.15882	9.76322	30.84022
18	2.40662	11.68959	28.13238	18	2.85434	10.82760	30.90565	18	3.37993	10.05909	33.99903
19	2.52695	12.08532	30.53900	19	3.02560	11.15812	33.75999	19	3.61653	10.33560	37.37896
20	2.65330	12.46221	33.06595	20	3.20714	11.46992	36.78559	20	3.86968	10.59401	40.99549
21	2.78596	12.82115	35.71925	21	3.39956	11.76408	39.99273	21	4.14056	10.83553	44.86518
22	2.92526	13.16300	38.50521	22	3.60354	12.04158	43.39229	22	4.43040	11.06124	49.00574
23	3.07152	13.48857	41.43048	23	3.81975	12.30338	46.99583	23	4.74053	11.27219	53.43614
24	3.22510	13.79864	44.50200	24	4.04893	12.55036	50.81558	24	5.07237	11.46933	58.17667
25	3.38635	14.09394	47.72710	25	4.29187	12.78336	54.86451	25	5.42743	11.65358	63.24904
26	3.55567	14.37519	51.11345	26	4.54938	13.00317	59.15638	26	5.80735	11.82578	68.67647
27	3.73346	14.64303	54.66913	27	4.82235	13.21053	63.70577	27	6.21387	11.98671	74.48382
28	3.92013	14.89813	58.40258	28	5.11169	13.40616	68.52811	28	6.64884	12.13711	80.69769
29	4.11614	15.14107	62.32271	29	5.41839	13.59072	73.63980	29	7.11426	12.27767	87.34653
30	4.32194	15.37245	66.43885	30	5.74349	13.76483	79.05819	30	7.61226	12.40904	94.46079
31	4.53804	15.59281	70.76079	31	6.08810	13.92909	84.80168	31	8.14511	12.53181	102.07304
32	4.76494	15.80268	75.29883	32	6.45339	14.08404	90.88978	32	8.71527	12.64656	110.21815
33	5.00319	16.00255	80.06377	33	6.84059	14.23023	97.34316	33	9.32534	12.75379	118.93343
34	5.25335	16.19290	85.06696	34	7.25103	14.36814	104.18375	34	9.97811	12.85401	128.25876
35	5.51602	16.37419	90.32031	35	7.68609	14.49825	111.43478	35	10.67658	12.94767	138.23688
36	5.79182	16.54685	95.83632	36	8.14725	14.62099	119.12087	36	11.42394	13.03521	148.91346
37	6.08141	16.71129	101.62814	37	8.63609	14.73678	127.26812	37	12.22362	13.11702	160.33740
38	6.38548	16.86789	107.70955	38	9.15425	14.84602	135.90421	38	13.07927	13.19347	172.56102
39	6.70475	17.01704	114.09502	39	9.70351	14.94907	145.05846	39	13.99482	13.26493	185.64029
40	7.03999	17.15909	120.79977	40	10.28572	15.04630	154.76197	40	14.97446	13.33171	199.63511
41	7.39199	17.29437	127.83976	41	10.90286	15.13802	165.04768	41	16.02267	13.39412	214.60957
42	7.76159	17.42321	135.23175	42	11.55703	15.22454	175.95054	42	17.14426	13.45245	230.63224
43	8.14967	17.54591	142.99334	43	12.25045	15.30617	187.50758	43	18.34435	13.50696	247.77650
44	8.55715	17.66277	151.14301	44	12.98548	15.38318	199.75803	44	19.62846	13.55791	266.12085
45	8.98501	17.77407	159.70016	45	13.76461	15.45583	212.74351	45	21.00245	13.60552	285.74931
46	9.43426	17.88007	168.68516	46	14.59049	15.52437	226.50812	46	22.47262	13.65002	306.75176
47	9.90597	17.98102	178.11942	47	15.46592	15.58903	241.09861	47	24.04571	13.69161	329.22439
48	10.40127	18.07716	188.02539	48	16.39387	15.65003	256.56453	48	25.72891	13.73047	353.27009
49	10.92133	18.16872	198.42666	49	17.37750	15.70757	272.95840	49	27.52993	13.76680	378.99900
50	11.46740	18.25593	209.34800	50	18.42015	15.76186	290.33590	50	29.45703	13.80075	406.52893

M	C(8,M, 1)	A(8,M, 1)	S(8,M, 1)
1	1.08000	.92593	1.00000
2	1.16640	1.78326	2.08000
3	1.25971	2.57710	3.24640
4	1.36049	3.31213	4.50611
5	1.46933	3.99271	5.86660
6	1.58687	4.62288	7.33593
7	1.71382	5.20637	8.92280
8	1.85093	5.74664	10.63663
9	1.99900	6.24689	12.48756
10	2.15892	6.71008	14.48656
11	2.33164	7.13896	16.64549
12	2.51817	7.53608	18.97713
13	2.71962	7.90378	21.49530
14	2.93719	8.24424	24.21492
15	3.17217	8.55948	27.15211
16	3.42594	8.85137	30.32428
17	3.70002	9.12164	33.75023
18	3.99602	9.37189	37.45024
19	4.31570	9.60360	41.44626
20	4.66096	9.81815	45.76196
21	5.03383	10.01680	50.42292
22	5.43654	10.20074	55.45676
23	5.87146	10.37106	60.89330
24	6.34118	10.52876	66.76476
25	6.84848	10.67478	73.10594
26	7.39635	10.80998	79.95442
27	7.98806	10.93516	87.35077
28	8.62711	11.05108	95.33883
29	9.31727	11.15841	103.96594
30	10.06266	11.25778	113.28321
31	10.86767	11.34980	123.34587
32	11.73708	11.43500	134.21354
33	12.67605	11.51389	145.95062
34	13.69013	11.58693	158.62667
35	14.78534	11.65457	172.31680
36	15.96817	11.71719	187.10215
37	17.24563	11.77518	203.07032
38	18.62528	11.82887	220.31595
39	20.11530	11.87858	238.94122
40	21.72452	11.92461	259.05652
41	23.46248	11.96723	280.78104
42	25.33948	12.00670	304.24352
43	27.36664	12.04324	329.58301
44	29.55597	12.07707	356.94965
45	31.92045	12.10840	386.50562
46	34.47409	12.13741	418.42607
47	37.23201	12.16427	452.90015
48	40.21057	12.18914	490.13216
49	43.42742	12.21216	530.34274
50	46.90161	12.23348	573.77016

M	C(9,M, 1)	A(9,M, 1)	S(9,M, 1)
1	1.09000	.91743	1.00000
2	1.18810	1.75911	2.09000
3	1.29503	2.53129	3.27810
4	1.41158	3.23972	4.57313
5	1.53862	3.88965	5.98471
6	1.67710	4.48592	7.52333
7	1.82804	5.03295	9.20043
8	1.99256	5.53482	11.02847
9	2.17189	5.99525	13.02104
10	2.36736	6.41766	15.19293
11	2.58043	6.80519	17.56029
12	2.81266	7.16073	20.14072
13	3.06580	7.48690	22.95338
14	3.34173	7.78615	26.01919
15	3.64248	8.06069	29.36092
16	3.97031	8.31256	33.00340
17	4.32763	8.54363	36.97370
18	4.71712	8.75563	41.30134
19	5.14166	8.95011	46.01846
20	5.60441	9.12855	51.16012
21	6.10881	9.29224	56.76453
22	6.65860	9.44243	62.87334
23	7.25787	9.58021	69.53194
24	7.91108	9.70661	76.78981
25	8.62308	9.82258	84.70090
26	9.39916	9.92897	93.32398
27	10.24508	10.02658	102.72313
28	11.16714	10.11613	112.96822
29	12.17218	10.19828	124.13536
30	13.26768	10.27365	136.30754
31	14.46177	10.34280	149.57522
32	15.76333	10.40624	164.03699
33	17.18203	10.46444	179.80032
34	18.72841	10.51784	196.98234
35	20.41397	10.56682	215.71075
36	22.25123	10.61176	236.12472
37	24.25384	10.65299	258.37595
38	26.43668	10.69082	282.62978
39	28.81598	10.72552	309.06646
40	31.40942	10.75736	337.88245
41	34.23627	10.78657	369.29187
42	37.31753	10.81337	403.52813
43	40.67611	10.83795	440.84566
44	44.33696	10.86051	481.52177
45	48.32729	10.88120	525.85873
46	52.67674	10.90018	574.18602
47	57.41765	10.91760	626.86276
48	62.58524	10.93358	684.28041
49	68.21791	10.94823	746.86565
50	74.35752	10.96168	815.08355

M	C(10,M, 1)	A(10,M, 1)	S(10,M, 1)
1	1.10000	.90909	1.00000
2	1.21000	1.73554	2.10000
3	1.33100	2.48685	3.31000
4	1.46410	3.16987	4.64100
5	1.61051	3.79079	6.10510
6	1.77156	4.35526	7.71561
7	1.94872	4.86842	9.48717
8	2.14359	5.33493	11.43589
9	2.35795	5.75902	13.57948
10	2.59374	6.14457	15.93742
11	2.85312	6.49506	18.53117
12	3.13843	6.81369	21.38428
13	3.45227	7.10336	24.52271
14	3.79750	7.36669	27.97498
15	4.17725	7.60608	31.77248
16	4.59497	7.82371	35.94973
17	5.05447	8.02155	40.54470
18	5.55992	8.20141	45.59917
19	6.11591	8.36492	51.15909
20	6.72750	8.51356	57.27500
21	7.40025	8.64869	64.00250
22	8.14027	8.77154	71.40275
23	8.95430	8.88322	79.54302
24	9.84973	8.98474	88.49733
25	10.83471	9.07704	98.34706
26	11.91818	9.16095	109.18177
27	13.10999	9.23722	121.09994
28	14.42099	9.30657	134.20994
29	15.86309	9.36961	148.63093
30	17.44940	9.42691	164.49402
31	19.19434	9.47901	181.94342
32	21.11378	9.52638	201.13777
33	23.22515	9.56943	222.25154
34	25.54767	9.60857	245.47670
35	28.10244	9.64416	271.02437
36	30.91268	9.67651	299.12681
37	34.00395	9.70592	330.03949
38	37.40434	9.73265	364.04343
39	41.14478	9.75696	401.44778
40	45.25926	9.77905	442.59256
41	49.78518	9.79914	487.85181
42	54.76370	9.81740	537.63699
43	60.24007	9.83400	592.40069
44	66.26408	9.84909	652.64076
45	72.89048	9.86281	718.90484
46	80.17953	9.87528	791.79532
47	88.19749	9.88662	871.97485
48	97.01723	9.89693	960.17234
49	106.71896	9.90630	1057.18957
50	117.39085	9.91481	1163.90853

Table I. ANNUITIES (*Continued*)

M	C(11,M, 1)	A(11,M, 1)	S(11,M, 1)
1	1.11000	.90090	1.00000
2	1.23210	1.71252	2.11000
3	1.36763	2.44371	3.34210
4	1.51807	3.10245	4.70973
5	1.68506	3.69590	6.22780
6	1.87041	4.23054	7.91286
7	2.07616	4.71220	9.78327
8	2.30454	5.14612	11.85943
9	2.55804	5.53705	14.16397
10	2.83942	5.88923	16.72201
11	3.15176	6.20652	19.56143
12	3.49845	6.49236	22.71319
13	3.88328	6.74987	26.21164
14	4.31044	6.98187	30.09492
15	4.78459	7.19087	34.40536
16	5.31089	7.37916	39.18995
17	5.89509	7.54879	44.50084
18	6.54355	7.70162	50.39594
19	7.26334	7.83929	56.93949
20	8.06231	7.96333	64.20283
21	8.94917	8.07507	72.26514
22	9.93357	8.17574	81.21431
23	11.02627	8.26643	91.14788
24	12.23916	8.34814	102.17415
25	13.58546	8.42174	114.41331
26	15.07986	8.48806	127.99877
27	16.73865	8.54780	143.07864
28	18.57990	8.60162	159.81729
29	20.62369	8.65011	178.39719
30	22.89230	8.69379	199.02088
31	25.41045	8.73315	221.91317
32	28.20560	8.76860	247.32362
33	31.30821	8.80054	275.52922
34	34.75212	8.82932	306.83744
35	38.57485	8.85524	341.58955
36	42.81808	8.87859	380.16441
37	47.52807	8.89963	422.98249
38	52.75616	8.91859	470.51056
39	58.55934	8.93567	523.26673
40	65.00087	8.95105	581.82607
41	72.15096	8.96491	646.82693
42	80.08757	8.97740	718.97790
43	88.89720	8.98865	799.06547
44	98.67589	8.99878	887.96267
45	109.53024	9.00791	986.63856
46	121.57857	9.01614	1096.16880
47	134.95221	9.02355	1217.74737
48	149.79695	9.03022	1352.69958
49	166.27462	9.03624	1502.49653
50	184.56483	9.04165	1668.77115

M	C(12,M, 1)	A(12,M, 1)	S(12,M, 1)
1	1.12000	.89286	1.00000
2	1.25440	1.69005	2.12000
3	1.40493	2.40183	3.37440
4	1.57352	3.03735	4.77933
5	1.76234	3.60478	6.35285
6	1.97382	4.11141	8.11519
7	2.21068	4.56376	10.08901
8	2.47596	4.96764	12.29969
9	2.77308	5.32825	14.77566
10	3.10585	5.65022	17.54874
11	3.47855	5.93770	20.65458
12	3.89598	6.19437	24.13313
13	4.36349	6.42355	28.02911
14	4.88711	6.62817	32.39260
15	5.47357	6.81086	37.27971
16	6.13039	6.97399	42.75328
17	6.86604	7.11963	48.88367
18	7.68997	7.24967	55.74971
19	8.61276	7.36578	63.43968
20	9.64629	7.46944	72.05244
21	10.80385	7.56200	81.69874
22	12.10031	7.64465	92.50258
23	13.55235	7.71843	104.60289
24	15.17863	7.78432	118.15524
25	17.00006	7.84314	133.33387
26	19.04007	7.89566	150.33393
27	21.32488	7.94255	169.37401
28	23.88387	7.98442	190.69889
29	26.74993	8.02181	214.58275
30	29.95992	8.05518	241.33268
31	33.55511	8.08499	271.29261
32	37.58173	8.11159	304.84772
33	42.09153	8.13535	342.42945
34	47.14252	8.15656	384.52098
35	52.79962	8.17550	431.66350
36	59.13557	8.19241	484.46312
37	66.23184	8.20751	543.59869
38	74.17966	8.22099	609.83053
39	83.08122	8.23303	684.01020
40	93.05097	8.24378	767.09142
41	104.21709	8.25337	860.14239
42	116.72314	8.26194	964.35948
43	130.72991	8.26959	1081.08262
44	146.41750	8.27642	1211.81253
45	163.98760	8.28252	1358.23003
46	183.66612	8.28796	1522.21764
47	205.70605	8.29282	1705.88375
48	230.39078	8.29716	1911.58980
49	258.03767	8.30104	2141.98058
50	289.00219	8.30450	2400.01825

M	C(13,M, 1)	A(13,M, 1)	S(13,M, 1)
1	1.13000	.88496	1.00000
2	1.27690	1.66810	2.13000
3	1.44290	2.36115	3.40690
4	1.63047	2.97447	4.84980
5	1.84244	3.51723	6.48027
6	2.08195	3.99755	8.32271
7	2.35261	4.42261	10.40466
8	2.65844	4.79877	12.75726
9	3.00404	5.13166	15.41571
10	3.39457	5.42624	18.41975
11	3.83586	5.68694	21.81432
12	4.33452	5.91765	25.65018
13	4.89801	6.12181	29.98470
14	5.53475	6.30249	34.88271
15	6.25427	6.46238	40.41746
16	7.06733	6.60388	46.67173
17	7.98608	6.72909	53.73906
18	9.02427	6.83991	61.72514
19	10.19742	6.93797	70.74941
20	11.52309	7.02475	80.94683
21	13.02109	7.10155	92.46992
22	14.71383	7.16951	105.49101
23	16.62663	7.22966	120.20484
24	18.78809	7.28288	136.83147
25	21.23054	7.32998	155.61956
26	23.99051	7.37167	176.85010
27	27.10928	7.40856	200.84061
28	30.63349	7.44120	227.94989
29	34.61584	7.47009	258.58338
30	39.11590	7.49565	293.19922
31	44.20096	7.51828	332.31511
32	49.94709	7.53830	376.51608
33	56.44021	7.55602	426.46317
34	63.77744	7.57170	482.90338
35	72.06851	7.58557	546.68082
36	81.43741	7.59785	618.74933
37	92.02428	7.60872	700.18674
38	103.98743	7.61833	792.21101
39	117.50580	7.62684	896.19845
40	132.78155	7.63438	1013.70424
41	150.04315	7.64104	1146.48579
42	169.54876	7.64694	1296.52895
43	191.59010	7.65216	1466.07771
44	216.49682	7.65678	1657.66781
45	244.64140	7.66086	1874.16463
46	276.44478	7.66448	2118.80603
47	312.38261	7.66768	2395.25082
48	352.99234	7.67052	2707.63342
49	398.88135	7.67302	3060.62577
50	450.73593	7.67524	3459.50712

M	C(14,M, 1)	A(14,M, 1)	S(14,M, 1)	M	C(15,M, 1)	A(15,M, 1)	S(15,M, 1)	M	C(16,M, 1)	A(16,M, 1)	S(16,M, 1)
1	1.14000	.87719	1.00000	1	1.15000	.86957	1.00000	1	1.16000	.86207	1.00000
2	1.29960	1.64666	2.14000	2	1.32250	1.62571	2.15000	2	1.34560	1.60523	2.16000
3	1.48154	2.32163	3.43960	3	1.52088	2.28323	3.47250	3	1.56090	2.24589	3.50560
4	1.68896	2.91371	4.92114	4	1.74901	2.85498	4.99338	4	1.81064	2.79818	5.06650
5	1.92541	3.43308	6.61010	5	2.01136	3.35216	6.74238	5	2.10034	3.27429	6.87714
6	2.19497	3.88867	8.53552	6	2.31306	3.78448	8.75374	6	2.43640	3.68474	8.97748
7	2.50227	4.28830	10.73049	7	2.66002	4.16042	11.06680	7	2.82622	4.03857	11.41387
8	2.85259	4.63886	13.23276	8	3.05902	4.48732	13.72682	8	3.27841	4.34359	14.24009
9	3.25195	4.94637	16.08535	9	3.51788	4.77158	16.78584	9	3.80296	4.60654	17.51851
10	3.70722	5.21612	19.33730	10	4.04556	5.01877	20.30372	10	4.41144	4.83323	21.32147
11	4.22623	5.45273	23.04452	11	4.65239	5.23371	24.34928	11	5.11726	5.02864	25.73290
12	4.81790	5.66029	27.27075	12	5.35025	5.42062	29.00167	12	5.93603	5.19711	30.85017
13	5.49241	5.84236	32.08865	13	6.15279	5.58315	34.35192	13	6.88579	5.34233	36.78620
14	6.26135	6.00207	37.58107	14	7.07571	5.72448	40.50471	14	7.98752	5.46753	43.67199
15	7.13794	6.14217	43.84241	15	8.13706	5.84737	47.58041	15	9.26552	5.57546	51.65951
16	8.13725	6.26506	50.98035	16	9.35762	5.95423	55.71747	16	10.74800	5.66850	60.92503
17	9.27646	6.37286	59.11760	17	10.76126	6.04716	65.07509	17	12.46768	5.74870	71.67303
18	10.57517	6.46742	68.39407	18	12.37545	6.12797	75.83636	18	14.46251	5.81785	84.14072
19	12.05569	6.55037	78.96923	19	14.23177	6.19823	88.21181	19	16.77652	5.87746	98.60323
20	13.74349	6.62313	91.02493	20	16.36654	6.25933	102.44358	20	19.46076	5.92884	115.37975
21	15.66758	6.68696	104.76842	21	18.82152	6.31246	118.81012	21	22.57448	5.97314	134.84051
22	17.86104	6.74294	120.43600	22	21.64475	6.35866	137.63164	22	26.18640	6.01133	157.41499
23	20.36158	6.79206	138.29704	23	24.89146	6.39884	159.27638	23	30.37622	6.04425	183.60138
24	23.21221	6.83514	158.65862	24	28.62518	6.43377	184.16784	24	35.23642	6.07263	213.97761
25	26.46192	6.87293	181.87083	25	32.91895	6.46415	212.79302	25	40.87424	6.09709	249.21402
26	30.16658	6.90608	208.33274	26	37.85680	6.49056	245.71197	26	47.41412	6.11818	290.08827
27	34.38991	6.93515	238.49933	27	43.53531	6.51353	283.56877	27	55.00038	6.13636	337.50239
28	39.20449	6.96066	272.88923	28	50.06561	6.53351	327.10408	28	63.80044	6.15204	392.50277
29	44.69312	6.98304	312.09373	29	57.57545	6.55088	377.16969	29	74.00851	6.16555	456.30322
30	50.95016	7.00266	356.78685	30	66.21177	6.56598	434.74515	30	85.84988	6.17720	530.31173
31	58.08318	7.01988	407.73701	31	76.14354	6.57911	500.95692	31	99.58586	6.18724	616.16161
32	66.21483	7.03498	465.82019	32	87.56507	6.59053	577.10046	32	115.51959	6.19590	715.74746
33	75.48490	7.04823	532.03501	33	100.69983	6.60046	664.66552	33	134.00273	6.20336	831.26706
34	86.05279	7.05985	607.51991	34	115.80480	6.60910	765.36535	34	155.44317	6.20979	965.26979
35	98.10018	7.07005	693.57270	35	133.17552	6.61661	881.17015	35	180.31407	6.21534	1120.71295
36	111.83420	7.07899	791.67288	36	153.15185	6.62314	1014.34568	36	209.16432	6.22012	1301.02703
37	127.49099	7.08683	903.50708	37	176.12463	6.62881	1167.49753	37	242.63062	6.22424	1510.19135
38	145.33973	7.09371	1030.99808	38	202.54332	6.63375	1343.62216	38	281.45151	6.22779	1752.82197
39	165.68729	7.09975	1176.33781	39	232.92482	6.63805	1546.16549	39	326.48376	6.23086	2034.27348
40	188.88351	7.10504	1342.02510	40	267.86355	6.64178	1779.09031	40	378.72116	6.23350	2360.75724
41	215.32721	7.10969	1530.90861	41	308.04308	6.64502	2046.95385	41	439.31654	6.23577	2739.47840
42	245.47301	7.11376	1746.23582	42	354.24954	6.64785	2354.99693	42	509.60719	6.23774	3178.79494
43	279.83924	7.11733	1991.70883	43	407.38697	6.65030	2709.24647	43	591.14434	6.23943	3688.40213
44	319.01673	7.12047	2271.54807	44	468.49502	6.65244	3116.63344	44	685.72744	6.24089	4279.54648
45	363.67907	7.12322	2590.56480	45	538.76927	6.65429	3585.12846	45	795.44383	6.24214	4965.27391
46	414.59414	7.12563	2954.24387	46	619.58466	6.65591	4123.89773	46	922.71484	6.24323	5760.71774
47	472.63732	7.12774	3368.83801	47	712.52236	6.65731	4743.48239	47	1070.34921	6.24416	6683.43257
48	538.80655	7.12960	3841.47534	48	819.40071	6.65853	5456.00475	48	1241.60509	6.24497	7753.78179
49	614.23946	7.13123	4380.28188	49	942.31082	6.65959	6275.40546	49	1440.26190	6.24566	8995.38687
50	700.23299	7.13266	4994.52135	50	1083.65744	6.66051	7217.71628	50	1670.70380	6.24626	10435.64877

Table I. ANNUITIES (*Continued*)

M	C(5,M, 2)	A(5,M, 2)	S(5,M, 2)
1	1.02500	.97561	1.00000
2	1.05063	1.92742	2.02500
3	1.07689	2.85602	3.07562
4	1.10381	3.76197	4.15252
5	1.13141	4.64583	5.25633
6	1.15969	5.50813	6.38774
7	1.18869	6.34939	7.54743
8	1.21840	7.17014	8.73612
9	1.24886	7.97087	9.95452
10	1.28008	8.75206	11.20338
11	1.31209	9.51421	12.48347
12	1.34489	10.25776	13.79555
13	1.37851	10.98318	15.14044
14	1.41297	11.69091	16.51895
15	1.44830	12.38138	17.93193
16	1.48451	13.05500	19.38022
17	1.52162	13.71220	20.86473
18	1.55966	14.35336	22.38635
19	1.59865	14.97889	23.94601
20	1.63862	15.58916	25.54466
21	1.67958	16.18455	27.18327
22	1.72157	16.76541	28.86286
23	1.76461	17.33211	30.58443
24	1.80873	17.88499	32.34904
25	1.85394	18.42438	34.15776
26	1.90029	18.95061	36.01171
27	1.94780	19.46401	37.91200
28	1.99650	19.96489	39.85980
29	2.04641	20.45355	41.85630
30	2.09757	20.93029	43.90270
31	2.15001	21.39541	46.00027
32	2.20376	21.84918	48.15028
33	2.25885	22.29188	50.35403
34	2.31532	22.72379	52.61289
35	2.37321	23.14516	54.92821
36	2.43254	23.55625	57.30141
37	2.49335	23.95732	59.73395
38	2.55568	24.34860	62.22730
39	2.61957	24.73034	64.78298
40	2.68506	25.10278	67.40255
41	2.75219	25.46612	70.08762
42	2.82100	25.82061	72.83981
43	2.89152	26.16645	75.66080
44	2.96381	26.50385	78.55232
45	3.03790	26.83302	81.51613
46	3.11385	27.15417	84.55403
47	3.19170	27.46748	87.66789
48	3.27149	27.77315	90.85958
49	3.35328	28.07137	94.13107
50	3.43711	28.36231	97.48435
51	3.52304	28.64616	100.92146
52	3.61111	28.92308	104.44449
53	3.70139	29.19325	108.05561
54	3.79392	29.45683	111.75700
55	3.88877	29.71398	115.55092
56	3.98599	29.96486	119.43969
57	4.08564	30.20962	123.42569
58	[illegible]	[illegible]	[illegible]

M	C(6,M, 2)	A(6,M, 2)	S(6,M, 2)
1	1.03000	.97087	1.00000
2	1.06090	1.91347	2.03000
3	1.09273	2.82861	3.09090
4	1.12551	3.71710	4.18363
5	1.15927	4.57971	5.30914
6	1.19405	5.41719	6.46841
7	1.22987	6.23028	7.66246
8	1.26677	7.01969	8.89234
9	1.30477	7.78611	10.15911
10	1.34392	8.53020	11.46388
11	1.38423	9.25262	12.80780
12	1.42576	9.95400	14.19203
13	1.46853	10.63496	15.61779
14	1.51259	11.29607	17.08632
15	1.55797	11.93794	18.59891
16	1.60471	12.56110	20.15688
17	1.65285	13.16612	21.76159
18	1.70243	13.75351	23.41444
19	1.75351	14.32380	25.11687
20	1.80611	14.87747	26.87037
21	1.86029	15.41502	28.67649
22	1.91610	15.93692	30.53678
23	1.97359	16.44361	32.45288
24	2.03279	16.93554	34.42647
25	2.09378	17.41315	36.45926
26	2.15659	17.87684	38.55304
27	2.22129	18.32703	40.70963
28	2.28793	18.76411	42.93092
29	2.35657	19.18845	45.21885
30	2.42726	19.60044	47.57542
31	2.50008	20.00043	50.00268
32	2.57508	20.38877	52.50276
33	2.65234	20.76579	55.07784
34	2.73191	21.13184	57.73018
35	2.81386	21.48722	60.46208
36	2.89828	21.83225	63.27594
37	2.98523	22.16724	66.17422
38	3.07478	22.49246	69.15945
39	3.16703	22.80822	72.23423
40	3.26204	23.11477	75.40126
41	3.35990	23.41240	78.66330
42	3.46070	23.70136	82.02320
43	3.56452	23.98190	85.48389
44	3.67145	24.25427	89.04841
45	3.78160	24.51871	92.71986
46	3.89504	24.77545	96.50146
47	4.01190	25.02471	100.39650
48	4.13225	25.26671	104.40840
49	4.25622	25.50166	108.54065
50	4.38391	25.72976	112.79687
51	4.51542	25.95123	117.18077
52	4.65089	26.16624	121.69620
53	4.79041	26.37499	126.34708
54	4.93412	26.57766	131.13749
55	5.08215	26.77443	136.07162
56	5.23461	26.96546	141.15377
57	5.39165	27.15094	146.38838
58	[illegible]	[illegible]	[illegible]

M	C(7,M, 2)	A(7,M, 2)	S(7,M, 2)
1	1.03500	.96618	1.00000
2	1.07123	1.89969	2.03500
3	1.10872	2.80164	3.10622
4	1.14752	3.67308	4.21494
5	1.18769	4.51505	5.36247
6	1.22926	5.32855	6.55015
7	1.27228	6.11454	7.77941
8	1.31681	6.87396	9.05169
9	1.36290	7.60769	10.36850
10	1.41060	8.31661	11.73139
11	1.45997	9.00155	13.14199
12	1.51107	9.66333	14.60196
13	1.56396	10.30274	16.11303
14	1.61869	10.92052	17.67699
15	1.67535	11.51741	19.29568
16	1.73399	12.09412	20.97103
17	1.79468	12.65132	22.70502
18	1.85749	13.18968	24.49969
19	1.92250	13.70984	26.35718
20	1.98979	14.21240	28.27968
21	2.05943	14.69797	30.26947
22	2.13151	15.16712	32.32890
23	2.20611	15.62041	34.46041
24	2.28333	16.05837	36.66653
25	2.36324	16.48151	38.94986
26	2.44596	16.89035	41.31310
27	2.53157	17.28536	43.75906
28	2.62017	17.66702	46.29063
29	2.71188	18.03577	48.91080
30	2.80679	18.39205	51.62268
31	2.90503	18.73628	54.42947
32	3.00671	19.06887	57.33450
33	3.11194	19.39021	60.34121
34	3.22086	19.70068	63.45315
35	3.33359	20.00066	66.67401
36	3.45027	20.29049	70.00760
37	3.57103	20.57053	73.45787
38	3.69601	20.84109	77.02889
39	3.82537	21.10250	80.72491
40	3.95926	21.35507	84.55028
41	4.09783	21.59910	88.50954
42	4.24126	21.83488	92.60737
43	4.38970	22.06269	96.84863
44	4.54334	22.28279	101.23833
45	4.70236	22.49545	105.78167
46	4.86694	22.70092	110.48403
47	5.03728	22.89944	115.35097
48	5.21359	23.09124	120.38826
49	5.39606	23.27656	125.60185
50	5.58493	23.45562	130.99791
51	5.78040	23.62862	136.58284
52	5.98271	23.79576	142.36324
53	6.19211	23.95726	148.34595
54	6.40883	24.11330	154.53806
55	6.63314	24.26405	160.94689
56	6.86530	24.40971	167.58003
57	7.10559	24.55045	174.44533
58	7.35428	24.68642	181.55092

59	4.29248	30.68137	131.69911	59	5.72000	27.50583	157.33343	59	7.61168	24.81780	188.90520
60	4.39979	30.90866	135.99159	60	5.89160	27.67556	163.05344	60	7.87809	24.94473	196.51688
61	4.50978	31.13040	140.39138	61	6.06835	27.84035	168.94504	61	8.15382	25.06738	204.39497
62	4.62253	31.34673	144.90116	62	6.25040	28.00034	175.01339	62	8.43921	25.18587	212.54880
63	4.73809	31.55778	149.52369	63	6.43791	28.15567	181.26379	63	8.73458	25.30036	220.98801
64	4.85654	31.76369	154.26179	64	6.63105	28.30648	187.70171	64	9.04029	25.41097	229.72259
65	4.97796	31.96458	159.11833	65	6.82998	28.45289	194.33276	65	9.35670	25.51785	238.76288
66	5.10241	32.16056	164.09629	66	7.03488	28.59504	201.16274	66	9.68419	25.62111	248.11958
67	5.22997	32.35177	169.19870	67	7.24593	28.73305	208.19762	67	10.02313	25.72088	257.80376
68	5.36072	32.53831	174.42866	68	7.46331	28.86704	215.44355	68	10.37394	25.81727	267.82689
69	5.49473	32.72030	179.78938	69	7.68721	28.99712	222.90686	69	10.73703	25.91041	278.20084
70	5.63210	32.89786	185.28411	70	7.91782	29.12342	230.59406	70	11.11283	26.00040	288.93786
71	5.77291	33.07108	190.91622	71	8.15536	29.24604	238.51189	71	11.50177	26.08734	300.05069
72	5.91723	33.24008	196.68912	72	8.40002	29.36509	246.66724	72	11.90434	26.17134	311.55246
73	6.06516	33.40495	202.60635	73	8.65202	29.48067	255.06726	73	12.32099	26.25251	323.45680
74	6.21679	33.56581	208.67151	74	8.91158	29.59288	263.71928	74	12.75222	26.33092	335.77779
75	6.37221	33.72274	214.88830	75	9.17893	29.70183	272.63086	75	13.19855	26.40669	348.53001
76	6.53151	33.87584	221.26050	76	9.45429	29.80760	281.80978	76	13.66050	26.47989	361.72856
77	6.69480	34.02521	227.79202	77	9.73792	29.91029	291.26407	77	14.13862	26.55062	375.38906
78	6.86217	34.17094	234.48682	78	10.03006	30.00999	301.00200	78	14.63347	26.61896	389.52768
79	7.03372	34.31311	241.34899	79	10.33096	30.10679	311.03206	79	15.14564	26.68498	404.16115
80	7.20957	34.45182	248.38271	80	10.64089	30.20076	321.36302	80	15.67574	26.74878	419.30679
81	7.38981	34.58714	255.59228	81	10.96012	30.29200	332.00391	81	16.22439	26.81041	434.98252
82	7.57455	34.71916	262.98209	82	11.28892	30.38059	342.96403	82	16.79224	26.86996	451.20691
83	7.76392	34.84796	270.55664	83	11.62759	30.46659	354.25295	83	17.37997	26.92750	467.99915
84	7.95801	34.97362	278.32056	84	11.97642	30.55009	365.88054	84	17.98827	26.98309	485.37913
85	8.15696	35.09621	286.27857	85	12.33571	30.63115	377.85695	85	18.61786	27.03680	503.36739
86	8.36089	35.21582	294.43553	86	12.70578	30.70986	390.19266	86	19.26948	27.08870	521.98525
87	8.56991	35.33251	302.79642	87	13.08695	30.78627	402.89844	87	19.94392	27.13884	541.25474
88	8.78416	35.44635	311.36633	88	13.47956	30.86045	415.98539	88	20.64195	27.18728	561.19865
89	9.00376	35.55741	320.15049	89	13.88395	30.93248	429.45496	89	21.36442	27.23409	581.84061
90	9.22886	35.66577	329.15425	90	14.30047	31.00241	443.34890	90	22.11218	27.27932	603.20503
91	9.45958	35.77148	338.38311	91	14.72948	31.07030	457.64937	91	22.88610	27.32301	625.31720
92	9.69607	35.87462	347.84269	92	15.17137	31.13621	472.37885	92	23.68712	27.36523	648.20331
93	9.93847	35.97524	357.53875	93	15.62651	31.20021	487.55022	93	24.51616	27.40602	671.89042
94	10.18693	36.07340	367.47722	94	16.09530	31.26234	503.17672	94	25.37423	27.44543	696.40659
95	10.44160	36.16917	377.66415	95	16.57816	31.32266	519.27203	95	26.26233	27.48350	721.78082
96	10.70264	36.26261	388.10576	96	17.07551	31.38122	535.85019	96	27.18151	27.52029	748.04314
97	10.97021	36.35376	398.80840	97	17.58777	31.43808	552.92569	97	28.13286	27.55584	775.22465
98	11.24447	36.44269	409.77861	98	18.11540	31.49328	570.51346	98	29.11751	27.59018	803.35752
99	11.52558	36.52946	421.02308	99	18.65887	31.54687	588.62887	99	30.13663	27.62337	832.47503
100	11.81372	36.61411	432.54865	100	19.21863	31.59891	607.28773	100	31.19141	27.65543	862.61166

Table I. ANNUITIES (*Continued*)

M	C(8,M, 2)	A(8,M, 2)	S(8,M, 2)	M	C(9,M, 2)	A(9,M, 2)	S(9,M, 2)	M	C(10,M, 2)	A(10,M, 2)	S(10,M, 2)
1	1.04000	.96154	1.00000	1	1.04500	.95694	1.00000	1	1.05000	.95238	1.00000
2	1.08160	1.88609	2.04000	2	1.09203	1.87267	2.04500	2	1.10250	1.85941	2.05000
3	1.12486	2.77509	3.12160	3	1.14117	2.74896	3.13702	3	1.15763	2.72325	3.15250
4	1.16986	3.62990	4.24646	4	1.19252	3.58753	4.27819	4	1.21551	3.54595	4.31012
5	1.21665	4.45182	5.41632	5	1.24618	4.38998	5.47071	5	1.27628	4.32948	5.52563
6	1.26532	5.24214	6.63298	6	1.30226	5.15787	6.71689	6	1.34010	5.07569	6.80191
7	1.31593	6.00205	7.89829	7	1.36086	5.89270	8.01915	7	1.40710	5.78637	8.14201
8	1.36857	6.73274	9.21423	8	1.42210	6.59589	9.38001	8	1.47746	6.46321	9.54911
9	1.42331	7.43533	10.58280	9	1.48610	7.26879	10.80211	9	1.55133	7.10782	11.02656
10	1.48024	8.11090	12.00611	10	1.55297	7.91272	12.28821	10	1.62889	7.72173	12.57789
11	1.53945	8.76048	13.48635	11	1.62285	8.52892	13.84118	11	1.71034	8.30641	14.20679
12	1.60103	9.38507	15.02581	12	1.69588	9.11858	15.46403	12	1.79586	8.86325	15.91713
13	1.66507	9.98565	16.62684	13	1.77220	9.68285	17.15991	13	1.88565	9.39357	17.71298
14	1.73168	10.56312	18.29191	14	1.85194	10.22283	18.93211	14	1.97993	9.89864	19.59863
15	1.80094	11.11839	20.02359	15	1.93528	10.73955	20.78405	15	2.07893	10.37966	21.57856
16	1.87298	11.65230	21.82453	16	2.02237	11.23402	22.71934	16	2.18287	10.83777	23.65749
17	1.94790	12.16567	23.69751	17	2.11338	11.70719	24.74171	17	2.29202	11.27407	25.84037
18	2.02582	12.65930	25.64541	18	2.20848	12.15999	26.85508	18	2.40662	11.68959	28.13238
19	2.10685	13.13394	27.67123	19	2.30786	12.59329	29.06356	19	2.52695	12.08532	30.53900
20	2.19112	13.59033	29.77808	20	2.41171	13.00794	31.37142	20	2.65330	12.46221	33.06595
21	2.27877	14.02916	31.96920	21	2.52024	13.40472	33.78314	21	2.78596	12.82115	35.71925
22	2.36992	14.45112	34.24797	22	2.63365	13.78442	36.30338	22	2.92526	13.16300	38.50521
23	2.46472	14.85684	36.61789	23	2.75217	14.14777	38.93703	23	3.07152	13.48857	41.43048
24	2.56330	15.24696	39.08260	24	2.87601	14.49548	41.68920	24	3.22510	13.79864	44.50200
25	2.66584	15.62208	41.64591	25	3.00543	14.82821	44.56521	25	3.38635	14.09394	47.72710
26	2.77247	15.98277	44.31174	26	3.14068	15.14661	47.57064	26	3.55567	14.37519	51.11345
27	2.88337	16.32959	47.08421	27	3.28201	15.45130	50.71132	27	3.73346	14.64303	54.66913
28	2.99870	16.66306	49.96758	28	3.42970	15.74287	53.99333	28	3.92013	14.89813	58.40258
29	3.11865	16.98371	52.96629	29	3.58404	16.02189	57.42303	29	4.11614	15.14107	62.32271
30	3.24340	17.29203	56.08494	30	3.74532	16.28889	61.00707	30	4.32194	15.37245	66.43885
31	3.37313	17.58849	59.32834	31	3.91386	16.54439	64.75239	31	4.53804	15.59281	70.76079
32	3.50806	17.87355	62.70147	32	4.08998	16.78889	68.66625	32	4.76494	15.80268	75.29883
33	3.64838	18.14765	66.20953	33	4.27403	17.02286	72.75623	33	5.00319	16.00255	80.06377
34	3.79432	18.41120	69.85791	34	4.46636	17.24676	77.03026	34	5.25335	16.19290	85.06696
35	3.94609	18.66461	73.65222	35	4.66735	17.46101	81.49662	35	5.51602	16.37419	90.32031
36	4.10393	18.90828	77.59831	36	4.87738	17.66604	86.16397	36	5.79182	16.54685	95.83632
37	4.26809	19.14258	81.70225	37	5.09686	17.86224	91.04134	37	6.08141	16.71129	101.62814
38	4.43881	19.36786	85.97034	38	5.32622	18.04999	96.13820	38	6.38548	16.86789	107.70955
39	4.61637	19.58448	90.40915	39	5.56590	18.22966	101.46442	39	6.70475	17.01704	114.09502
40	4.80102	19.79277	95.02552	40	5.81636	18.40158	107.03032	40	7.03999	17.15909	120.79977
41	4.99306	19.99305	99.82654	41	6.07810	18.56611	112.84669	41	7.39199	17.29437	127.83976
42	5.19278	20.18563	104.81960	42	6.35162	18.72355	118.92479	42	7.76159	17.42321	135.23175
43	5.40050	20.37079	110.01238	43	6.63744	18.87421	125.27640	43	8.14967	17.54591	142.99334
44	5.61652	20.54884	115.41288	44	6.93612	19.01838	131.91384	44	8.55715	17.66277	151.14301
45	5.84118	20.72004	121.02939	45	7.24825	19.15635	138.84997	45	8.98501	17.77407	159.70016
46	6.07482	20.88465	126.87057	46	7.57442	19.28837	146.09821	46	9.43426	17.88007	168.68516
47	6.31782	21.04294	132.94539	47	7.91527	19.41471	153.67263	47	9.90597	17.98102	178.11942
48	6.57053	21.19513	139.26321	48	8.27146	19.53561	161.58790	48	10.40127	18.07716	188.02539
49	6.83335	21.34147	145.83373	49	8.64367	19.65130	169.85936	49	10.92133	18.16872	198.42666
50	7.10668	21.48218	152.66708	50	9.03264	19.76201	178.50303	50	11.46740	18.25593	209.34800
51	7.39095	21.61749	159.77377	51	9.43910	19.86795	187.53566	51	12.04077	18.33898	220.81540
52	7.68659	21.74758	167.16472	52	9.86386	19.96933	196.97477	52	12.64281	18.41807	232.85617
53	7.99405	21.87267	174.85131	53	10.30774	20.06634	206.83863	53	13.27495	18.49340	245.49897
54	8.31381	21.99296	182.84536	54	10.77159	20.15918	217.14537	54	13.93870	18.56515	258.77392
55	8.64637	22.10861	191.15917	55	11.25631	20.24802	227.91796	55	14.63563	18.63347	272.71262
56	8.99222	22.21982	199.80554	56	11.76284	20.33303	239.17427	56	15.36741	18.69854	287.34825
57	9.35191	22.32675	208.79776	57	12.29217	20.41439	250.93711	57	16.13578	18.76052	302.71566

59	10.11503	22.52843	227.87566	59	13.42336	20.56673	276.07460	59	17.78970	18.87575	335.79402
60	10.51963	22.62349	237.99069	60	14.02741	20.63802	289.49795	60	18.67919	18.92929	353.58372
61	10.94041	22.71489	248.51031	61	14.65864	20.70624	303.52536	61	19.61315	18.98028	372.26290
62	11.37803	22.80278	259.45073	62	15.31828	20.77152	318.18400	62	20.59380	19.02883	391.87605
63	11.83315	22.88729	270.82875	63	16.00760	20.83399	333.50228	63	21.62349	19.07508	412.46985
64	12.30648	22.96855	282.66190	64	16.72794	20.89377	349.50989	64	22.70467	19.11912	434.09334
65	12.79874	23.04668	294.96838	65	17.48070	20.95098	366.23783	65	23.83990	19.16107	456.79801
66	13.31068	23.12181	307.76712	66	18.26733	21.00572	383.71853	66	25.03190	19.20102	480.63791
67	13.84311	23.19405	321.07780	67	19.08936	21.05811	401.98587	67	26.28349	19.23907	505.66981
68	14.39684	23.26351	334.92091	68	19.94839	21.10824	421.07523	68	27.59766	19.27530	531.95330
69	14.97271	23.33030	349.31775	69	20.84606	21.15621	441.02362	69	28.97755	19.30981	559.55096
70	15.57162	23.39451	364.29046	70	21.78414	21.20211	461.86968	70	30.42643	19.34268	588.52851
71	16.19448	23.45626	379.86208	71	22.76442	21.24604	483.65382	71	31.94775	19.37398	618.95494
72	16.84226	23.51564	396.05656	72	23.78882	21.28808	506.41824	72	33.54513	19.40379	650.90268
73	17.51595	23.57273	412.89882	73	24.85932	21.32830	530.20706	73	35.22239	19.43218	684.44782
74	18.21659	23.62762	430.41478	74	25.97799	21.36680	555.06638	74	36.98351	19.45922	719.67021
75	18.94525	23.68041	448.63137	75	27.14700	21.40363	581.04436	75	38.83269	19.48497	756.65372
76	19.70306	23.73116	467.57662	76	28.36861	21.43888	608.19136	76	40.77432	19.50950	795.48640
77	20.49119	23.77996	487.27969	77	29.64520	21.47262	636.55997	77	42.81304	19.53285	836.26072
78	21.31083	23.82689	507.77087	78	30.97923	21.50490	666.20517	78	44.95369	19.55510	879.07376
79	22.16327	23.87201	529.08171	79	32.37330	21.53579	697.18440	79	47.20137	19.57628	924.02745
80	23.04980	23.91539	551.24498	80	33.83010	21.56534	729.55770	80	49.56144	19.59646	971.22882
81	23.97179	23.95711	574.29478	81	35.35245	21.59363	763.38779	81	52.03951	19.61568	1020.79026
82	24.93066	23.99722	598.26657	82	36.94331	21.62070	798.74025	82	54.64149	19.63398	1072.82978
83	25.92789	24.03579	623.19723	83	38.60576	21.64660	835.68356	83	57.37356	19.65141	1127.47126
84	26.96500	24.07287	649.12512	84	40.34302	21.67139	874.28932	84	60.24224	19.66801	1184.84483
85	28.04360	24.10853	676.09012	85	42.15846	21.69511	914.63234	85	63.25435	19.68382	1245.08707
86	29.16535	24.14282	704.13373	86	44.05559	21.71781	956.79079	86	66.41707	19.69887	1308.34142
87	30.33196	24.17579	733.29908	87	46.03809	21.73953	1000.84638	87	69.73792	19.71321	1374.75849
88	31.54524	24.20749	763.63104	88	48.10980	21.76032	1046.88446	88	73.22482	19.72687	1444.49642
89	32.80705	24.23797	795.17628	89	50.27474	21.78021	1094.99426	89	76.88606	19.73987	1517.72124
90	34.11933	24.26728	827.98333	90	52.53711	21.79924	1145.26901	90	80.73037	19.75226	1594.60730
91	35.48411	24.29546	862.10267	91	54.90128	21.81746	1197.80611	91	84.76688	19.76406	1675.33767
92	36.90347	24.32256	897.58677	92	57.37183	21.83489	1252.70739	92	89.00523	19.77529	1760.10455
93	38.37961	24.34861	934.49024	93	59.95356	21.85156	1310.07922	93	93.45549	19.78599	1849.10978
94	39.91479	24.37367	972.86985	94	62.65148	21.86753	1370.03278	94	98.12826	19.79619	1942.56527
95	41.51139	24.39776	1012.78465	95	65.47079	21.88280	1432.68426	95	103.03468	19.80589	2040.69353
96	43.17184	24.42092	1054.29603	96	68.41698	21.89742	1498.15505	96	108.18641	19.81513	2143.72821
97	44.89872	24.44319	1097.46788	97	71.49574	21.91140	1566.57203	97	113.59573	19.82394	2251.91462
98	46.69466	24.46461	1142.36659	98	74.71305	21.92479	1638.06777	98	119.27552	19.83232	2365.51035
99	48.56245	24.48520	1189.06125	99	78.07514	21.93760	1712.78082	99	125.23929	19.84031	2484.78586
100	50.50495	24.50500	1237.62370	100	81.58852	21.94985	1790.85596	100	131.50126	19.84791	2610.02516

Table I. ANNUITIES (*Continued*)

M	C(11,M, 2)	A(11,M, 2)	S(11,M, 2)
1	1.05500	.94787	1.00000
2	1.11303	1.84632	2.05500
3	1.17424	2.69793	3.16803
4	1.23882	3.50515	4.34227
5	1.30696	4.27028	5.58109
6	1.37884	4.99553	6.88805
7	1.45468	5.68297	8.26689
8	1.53469	6.33457	9.72157
9	1.61909	6.95220	11.25626
10	1.70814	7.53763	12.87535
11	1.80209	8.09254	14.58350
12	1.90121	8.61852	16.38559
13	2.00577	9.11708	18.28680
14	2.11609	9.58965	20.29257
15	2.23248	10.03758	22.40866
16	2.35526	10.46216	24.64114
17	2.48480	10.86461	26.99640
18	2.62147	11.24607	29.48120
19	2.76565	11.60765	32.10267
20	2.91776	11.95038	34.86832
21	3.07823	12.27524	37.78608
22	3.24754	12.58317	40.86431
23	3.42615	12.87504	44.11185
24	3.61459	13.15170	47.53800
25	3.81339	13.41393	51.15259
26	4.02313	13.66250	54.96598
27	4.24440	13.89810	58.98911
28	4.47784	14.12142	63.23351
29	4.72412	14.33310	67.71135
30	4.98395	14.53375	72.43548
31	5.25807	14.72393	77.41943
32	5.54726	14.90420	82.67750
33	5.85236	15.07507	88.22476
34	6.17424	15.23703	94.07712
35	6.51383	15.39055	100.25136
36	6.87209	15.53607	106.76519
37	7.25005	15.67400	113.63727
38	7.64880	15.80474	120.88732
39	8.06949	15.92866	128.53613
40	8.51331	16.04612	136.60561
41	8.98154	16.15746	145.11892
42	9.47553	16.26300	154.10046
43	9.99668	16.36303	163.57599
44	10.54650	16.45785	173.57267
45	11.12655	16.54773	184.11917
46	11.73851	16.63292	195.24572
47	12.38413	16.71366	206.98423
48	13.06526	16.79020	219.36837
49	13.78385	16.86275	232.43363
50	14.54196	16.93152	246.21748
51	15.34177	16.99670	260.75944
52	16.18557	17.05848	276.10121
53	17.07577	17.11705	292.28677
54	18.01494	17.17255	309.36255
55	19.00576	17.22517	327.37749
56	20.05108	17.27504	346.38325

M	C(12,M, 2)	A(12,M, 2)	S(12,M, 2)
1	1.06000	.94340	1.00000
2	1.12360	1.83339	2.06000
3	1.19102	2.67301	3.18360
4	1.26248	3.46511	4.37462
5	1.33823	4.21236	5.63709
6	1.41852	4.91732	6.97532
7	1.50363	5.58238	8.39384
8	1.59385	6.20979	9.89747
9	1.68948	6.80169	11.49132
10	1.79085	7.36009	13.18079
11	1.89830	7.88687	14.97164
12	2.01220	8.38384	16.86994
13	2.13293	8.85268	18.88214
14	2.26090	9.29498	21.01507
15	2.39656	9.71225	23.27597
16	2.54035	10.10590	25.67253
17	2.69277	10.47726	28.21288
18	2.85434	10.82760	30.90565
19	3.02560	11.15812	33.75999
20	3.20714	11.46992	36.78559
21	3.39956	11.76408	39.99273
22	3.60354	12.04158	43.39229
23	3.81975	12.30338	46.99583
24	4.04893	12.55036	50.81558
25	4.29187	12.78336	54.86451
26	4.54938	13.00317	59.15638
27	4.82235	13.21053	63.70577
28	5.11169	13.40616	68.52811
29	5.41839	13.59072	73.63980
30	5.74349	13.76483	79.05819
31	6.08810	13.92909	84.80168
32	6.45339	14.08404	90.88978
33	6.84059	14.23023	97.34316
34	7.25103	14.36814	104.18375
35	7.68609	14.49825	111.43478
36	8.14725	14.62099	119.12087
37	8.63609	14.73678	127.26812
38	9.15425	14.84602	135.90421
39	9.70351	14.94907	145.05846
40	10.28572	15.04630	154.76197
41	10.90286	15.13802	165.04768
42	11.55703	15.22454	175.95054
43	12.25045	15.30617	187.50758
44	12.98548	15.38318	199.75803
45	13.76461	15.45583	212.74351
46	14.59049	15.52437	226.50812
47	15.46592	15.58903	241.09861
48	16.39387	15.65003	256.56453
49	17.37750	15.70757	272.95840
50	18.42015	15.76186	290.33590
51	19.52536	15.81308	308.75606
52	20.69689	15.86139	328.28142
53	21.93870	15.90697	348.97831
54	23.25502	15.94998	370.91701
55	24.65032	15.99054	394.17203
56	26.12934	16.02881	418.82235

M	C(13,M, 2)	A(13,M, 2)	S(13,M, 2)
1	1.06500	.93897	1.00000
2	1.13423	1.82063	2.06500
3	1.20795	2.64848	3.19922
4	1.28647	3.42580	4.40717
5	1.37009	4.15568	5.69364
6	1.45914	4.84101	7.06373
7	1.55399	5.48452	8.52287
8	1.65500	6.08875	10.07686
9	1.76257	6.65610	11.73185
10	1.87714	7.18883	13.49442
11	1.99915	7.68904	15.37156
12	2.12910	8.15873	17.37071
13	2.26749	8.59974	19.49981
14	2.41487	9.01384	21.76730
15	2.57184	9.40267	24.18217
16	2.73901	9.76776	26.75401
17	2.91705	10.11058	29.49302
18	3.10665	10.43247	32.41007
19	3.30859	10.73471	35.51672
20	3.52365	11.01851	38.82531
21	3.75268	11.28498	42.34895
22	3.99661	11.53520	46.10164
23	4.25639	11.77014	50.09824
24	4.53305	11.99074	54.35463
25	4.82770	12.19788	58.88768
26	5.14150	12.39237	63.71538
27	5.47570	12.57500	68.85688
28	5.83162	12.74648	74.33257
29	6.21067	12.90749	80.16419
30	6.61437	13.05868	86.37486
31	7.04430	13.20063	92.98923
32	7.50218	13.33393	100.03353
33	7.98982	13.45909	107.53571
34	8.50916	13.57661	115.52553
35	9.06225	13.68696	124.03469
36	9.65130	13.79057	133.09695
37	10.27864	13.88786	142.74825
38	10.94675	13.97921	153.02688
39	11.65829	14.06499	163.97363
40	12.41607	14.14553	175.63192
41	13.22312	14.22115	188.04799
42	14.08262	14.29216	201.27111
43	14.99799	14.35884	215.35373
44	15.97286	14.42144	230.35172
45	17.01110	14.48023	246.32459
46	18.11682	14.53543	263.33568
47	19.29441	14.58725	281.45250
48	20.54855	14.63592	300.74692
49	21.88421	14.68161	321.29547
50	23.30668	14.72452	343.17967
51	24.82161	14.76481	366.48635
52	26.43502	14.80264	391.30796
53	28.15329	14.83816	417.74298
54	29.98326	14.87151	445.89627
55	31.93217	14.90282	475.87953
56	34.00776	14.93223	507.81170

57	21.15389	17.32232	366.43433
58	22.31735	17.36712	387.58821
59	23.54481	17.40960	409.90557
60	24.83977	17.44985	433.45037
61	26.20596	17.48801	458.29014
62	27.64729	17.52418	484.49610
63	29.16789	17.55847	512.14339
64	30.77212	17.59096	541.31127
65	32.46459	17.62177	572.08339
66	34.25014	17.65096	604.54798
67	36.13390	17.67864	638.79812
68	38.12126	17.70487	674.93201
69	40.21793	17.72974	713.05327
70	42.42992	17.75330	753.27120
71	44.76356	17.77564	795.70112
72	47.22556	17.79682	840.46468
73	49.82296	17.81689	887.69024
74	52.56323	17.83591	937.51320
75	55.45420	17.85395	990.07643
76	58.50418	17.87104	1045.53063
77	61.72191	17.88724	1104.03482
78	65.11662	17.90260	1165.75673
79	68.69803	17.91716	1230.87335
80	72.47643	17.93095	1299.57139
81	76.46263	17.94403	1372.04781
82	80.66807	17.95643	1448.51044
83	85.10482	17.96818	1529.17852
84	89.78558	17.97932	1614.28334
85	94.72379	17.98987	1704.06892
86	99.93360	17.99988	1798.79271
87	105.42995	18.00936	1898.72631
88	111.22859	18.01835	2004.15626
89	117.34617	18.02688	2115.38485
90	123.80021	18.03495	2232.73102
91	130.60922	18.04261	2356.53122
92	137.79272	18.04987	2487.14044
93	145.37132	18.05675	2624.93316
94	153.36675	18.06327	2770.30449
95	161.80192	18.06945	2923.67123
96	170.70102	18.07531	3085.47315
97	180.08958	18.08086	3256.17418
98	189.99451	18.08612	3436.26376
99	200.44420	18.09111	3626.25826
100	211.46864	18.09584	3826.70247

57	27.69710	16.06492	444.95169
58	29.35893	16.09898	472.64879
59	31.12046	16.13111	502.00772
60	32.98769	16.16143	533.12818
61	34.96695	16.19003	566.11587
62	37.06497	16.21701	601.08282
63	39.28887	16.24246	638.14779
64	41.64620	16.26647	677.43666
65	44.14497	16.28912	719.08286
66	46.79367	16.31049	763.22783
67	49.60129	16.33065	810.02150
68	52.57737	16.34967	859.62279
69	55.73201	16.36762	912.20016
70	59.07593	16.38454	967.93217
71	62.62049	16.40051	1027.00810
72	66.37772	16.41558	1089.62859
73	70.36038	16.42979	1156.00630
74	74.58200	16.44320	1226.36668
75	79.05692	16.45585	1300.94868
76	83.80034	16.46778	1380.00560
77	88.82836	16.47904	1463.80594
78	94.15806	16.48966	1552.63429
79	99.80754	16.49968	1646.79235
80	105.79599	16.50913	1746.59989
81	112.14375	16.51805	1852.39588
82	118.87238	16.52646	1964.53964
83	126.00472	16.53440	2083.41202
84	133.56500	16.54188	2209.41674
85	141.57890	16.54895	2342.98174
86	150.07364	16.55561	2484.56065
87	159.07806	16.56190	2634.63428
88	168.62274	16.56783	2793.71234
89	178.74010	16.57342	2962.33508
90	189.46451	16.57870	3141.07519
91	200.83238	16.58368	3330.53970
92	212.88232	16.58838	3531.37208
93	225.65526	16.59281	3744.25441
94	239.19458	16.59699	3969.90967
95	253.54625	16.60093	4209.10425
96	268.75903	16.60465	4462.65050
97	284.88457	16.60816	4731.40953
98	301.97765	16.61147	5016.29411
99	320.09631	16.61460	5318.27175
100	339.30208	16.61755	5638.36806

57	36.21827	14.95984	541.81946
58	38.57245	14.98577	578.03773
59	41.07966	15.01011	616.61018
60	43.74984	15.03297	657.68984
61	46.59358	15.05443	701.43968
62	49.62216	15.07458	748.03326
63	52.84760	15.09350	797.65542
64	56.28270	15.11127	850.50303
65	59.94107	15.12795	906.78572
66	63.83724	15.14362	966.72679
67	67.98666	15.15833	1030.56404
68	72.40580	15.17214	1098.55070
69	77.11217	15.18511	1170.95649
70	82.12446	15.19728	1248.06867
71	87.46255	15.20872	1330.19313
72	93.14762	15.21945	1417.65568
73	99.20221	15.22953	1510.80330
74	105.65036	15.23900	1610.00552
75	112.51763	15.24788	1715.65587
76	119.83128	15.25623	1828.17351
77	127.62031	15.26407	1948.00478
78	135.91563	15.27142	2075.62510
79	144.75015	15.27833	2211.54073
80	154.15891	15.28482	2356.29087
81	164.17924	15.29091	2510.44978
82	174.85089	15.29663	2674.62902
83	186.21619	15.30200	2849.47990
84	198.32025	15.30704	3035.69610
85	211.21106	15.31178	3234.01634
86	224.93978	15.31622	3445.22741
87	239.56087	15.32040	3670.16719
88	255.13232	15.32431	3909.72805
89	271.71592	15.32800	4164.86038
90	289.37746	15.33145	4436.57630
91	308.18699	15.33470	4725.95376
92	328.21915	15.33774	5034.14076
93	349.55339	15.34060	5362.35990
94	372.27436	15.34329	5711.91330
95	396.47220	15.34581	6084.18766
96	422.24289	15.34818	6480.65986
97	449.68868	15.35040	6902.90275
98	478.91844	15.35249	7352.59143
99	510.04814	15.35445	7831.50987
100	543.20127	15.35629	8341.55802

Table I. ANNUITIES (*Continued*)

M	C(14,M, 2)	A(14,M, 2)	S(14,M, 2)	M	C(15,M, 2)	A(15,M, 2)	S(15,M, 2)	M	C(16,M, 2)	A(16,M, 2)	S(16,M, 2)
1	1.07000	.93458	1.00000	1	1.07500	.93023	1.00000	1	1.08000	.92593	1.00000
2	1.14490	1.80802	2.07000	2	1.15563	1.79557	2.07500	2	1.16640	1.78326	2.08000
3	1.22504	2.62432	3.21490	3	1.24230	2.60053	3.23062	3	1.25971	2.57710	3.24640
4	1.31080	3.38721	4.43994	4	1.33547	3.34933	4.47292	4	1.36049	3.31213	4.50611
5	1.40255	4.10020	5.75074	5	1.43563	4.04588	5.80839	5	1.46933	3.99271	5.86660
6	1.50073	4.76654	7.15329	6	1.54330	4.69385	7.24402	6	1.58687	4.62288	7.33593
7	1.60578	5.38929	8.65402	7	1.65905	5.29660	8.78732	7	1.71382	5.20637	8.92280
8	1.71819	5.97130	10.25980	8	1.78348	5.85730	10.44637	8	1.85093	5.74664	10.63663
9	1.83846	6.51523	11.97799	9	1.91724	6.37889	12.22985	9	1.99900	6.24689	12.48756
10	1.96715	7.02358	13.81645	10	2.06103	6.86408	14.14709	10	2.15892	6.71008	14.48656
11	2.10485	7.49867	15.78360	11	2.21561	7.31542	16.20812	11	2.33164	7.13896	16.64549
12	2.25219	7.94269	17.88845	12	2.38178	7.73528	18.42373	12	2.51817	7.53608	18.97713
13	2.40985	8.35765	20.14064	13	2.56041	8.12584	20.80551	13	2.71962	7.90378	21.49530
14	2.57853	8.74547	22.55049	14	2.75244	8.48915	23.36592	14	2.93719	8.24424	24.21492
15	2.75903	9.10791	25.12902	15	2.95888	8.82712	26.11836	15	3.17217	8.55948	27.15211
16	2.95216	9.44665	27.88805	16	3.18079	9.14151	29.07724	16	3.42594	8.85137	30.32428
17	3.15882	9.76322	30.84022	17	3.41935	9.43396	32.25804	17	3.70002	9.12164	33.75023
18	3.37993	10.05909	33.99903	18	3.67580	9.70601	35.67739	18	3.99602	9.37189	37.45024
19	3.61653	10.33560	37.37896	19	3.95149	9.95908	39.35319	19	4.31570	9.60360	41.44626
20	3.86968	10.59401	40.99549	20	4.24785	10.19449	43.30468	20	4.66096	9.81815	45.76196
21	4.14056	10.83553	44.86518	21	4.56644	10.41348	47.55253	21	5.03383	10.01680	50.42292
22	4.43040	11.06124	49.00574	22	4.90892	10.61719	52.11897	22	5.43654	10.20074	55.45676
23	4.74053	11.27219	53.43614	23	5.27709	10.80669	57.02790	23	5.87146	10.37106	60.89330
24	5.07237	11.46933	58.17667	24	5.67287	10.98297	62.30499	24	6.34118	10.52876	66.76476
25	5.42743	11.65358	63.24904	25	6.09834	11.14695	67.97786	25	6.84848	10.67478	73.10594
26	5.80735	11.82578	68.67647	26	6.55572	11.29948	74.07620	26	7.39635	10.80998	79.95442
27	6.21387	11.98671	74.48382	27	7.04739	11.44138	80.63192	27	7.98806	10.93516	87.35077
28	6.64884	12.13711	80.69769	28	7.57595	11.57338	87.67931	28	8.62711	11.05108	95.33883
29	7.11426	12.27767	87.34653	29	8.14414	11.69617	95.25526	29	9.31727	11.15841	103.96594
30	7.61226	12.40904	94.46079	30	8.75496	11.81039	103.39940	30	10.06266	11.25778	113.28321
31	8.14511	12.53181	102.07304	31	9.41158	11.91664	112.15436	31	10.86767	11.34980	123.34587
32	8.71527	12.64656	110.21815	32	10.11745	12.01548	121.56593	32	11.73708	11.43500	134.21354
33	9.32534	12.75379	118.93343	33	10.87625	12.10742	131.68338	33	12.67605	11.51389	145.95062
34	9.97811	12.85401	128.25876	34	11.69197	12.19295	142.55963	34	13.69013	11.58693	158.62667
35	10.67658	12.94767	138.23688	35	12.56887	12.27251	154.25161	35	14.78534	11.65457	172.31680
36	11.42394	13.03521	148.91346	36	13.51154	12.34652	166.82048	36	15.96817	11.71719	187.10215
37	12.22362	13.11702	160.33740	37	14.52490	12.41537	180.33201	37	17.24563	11.77518	203.07032
38	13.07927	13.19347	172.56102	38	15.61427	12.47941	194.85691	38	18.62528	11.82887	220.31595
39	13.99482	13.26493	185.64029	39	16.78534	12.53899	210.47118	39	20.11530	11.87858	238.94122
40	14.97446	13.33171	199.63511	40	18.04424	12.59441	227.25652	40	21.72452	11.92461	259.05652
41	16.02267	13.39412	214.60957	41	19.39756	12.64596	245.30076	41	23.46248	11.96723	280.78104
42	17.14426	13.45245	230.63224	42	20.85237	12.69392	264.69832	42	25.33948	12.00670	304.24352
43	18.34435	13.50696	247.77650	43	22.41630	12.73853	285.55069	43	27.36664	12.04324	329.58301
44	19.62846	13.55791	266.12085	44	24.09752	12.78003	307.96699	44	29.55597	12.07707	356.94965
45	21.00245	13.60552	285.74931	45	25.90484	12.81863	332.06452	45	31.92045	12.10840	386.50562
46	22.47262	13.65002	306.75176	46	27.84770	12.85454	357.96935	46	34.47409	12.13741	418.42607
47	24.04571	13.69161	329.22439	47	29.93628	12.88794	385.81706	47	37.23201	12.16427	452.90015
48	25.72891	13.73047	353.27009	48	32.18150	12.91902	415.75333	48	40.21057	12.18914	490.13216
49	27.52993	13.76680	378.99900	49	34.59511	12.94792	447.93483	49	43.42742	12.21216	530.34274
50	29.45703	13.80075	406.52893	50	37.18975	12.97481	482.52995	50	46.90161	12.23348	573.77016
51	31.51902	13.83247	435.98595	51	39.97898	12.99982	519.71969	51	50.65374	12.25323	620.67177
52	33.72535	13.86212	467.50497	52	42.97740	13.02309	559.69867	52	54.70604	12.27151	671.32551
53	36.08612	13.88984	501.23032	53	46.20071	13.04474	602.67607	53	59.08252	12.28843	726.03155
54	38.61215	13.91573	537.31644	54	49.66576	13.06487	648.87678	54	63.80913	12.30410	785.11408
55	41.31500	13.93994	575.92859	55	53.39069	13.08360	698.54253	55	68.91386	12.31861	848.92320
56	44.20705	13.96256	617.24359	56	57.39499	13.10103	751.93322	56	74.42696	12.33205	917.83706

57	47.30155	13.98370	661.45065
58	50.61265	14.00346	708.75219
59	54.15554	14.02192	759.36484
60	57.94643	14.03918	813.52038
61	62.00268	14.05531	871.46681
62	66.34286	14.07038	933.46949
63	70.98686	14.08447	999.81235
64	75.95595	14.09764	1070.79922
65	81.27286	14.10994	1146.75516
66	86.96196	14.12144	1228.02802
67	93.04930	14.13219	1314.98998
68	99.56275	14.14223	1408.03928
69	106.53214	14.15162	1507.60203
70	113.98939	14.16039	1614.13417
71	121.96865	14.16859	1728.12357
72	130.50646	14.17625	1850.09222
73	139.64191	14.18341	1980.59867
74	149.41684	14.19010	2120.24058
75	159.87602	14.19636	2269.65742
76	171.06734	14.20220	2429.53344
77	183.04205	14.20767	2600.60078
78	195.85500	14.21277	2783.64283
79	209.56485	14.21755	2979.49783
80	224.23439	14.22201	3189.06268
81	239.93079	14.22617	3413.29707
82	256.72595	14.23007	3653.22786
83	274.69677	14.23371	3909.95381
84	293.92554	14.23711	4184.65058
85	314.50033	14.24029	4478.57612
86	336.51535	14.24326	4793.07645
87	360.07143	14.24604	5129.59180
88	385.27643	14.24864	5489.66323
89	412.24578	14.25106	5874.93965
90	441.10298	14.25333	6287.18543
91	471.98019	14.25545	6728.28841
92	505.01880	14.25743	7200.26860
93	540.37012	14.25928	7705.28740
94	578.19603	14.26101	8245.65751
95	618.66975	14.26262	8823.85354
96	661.97663	14.26413	9442.52329
97	708.31499	14.26555	10104.49992
98	757.89704	14.26687	10812.81491
99	810.94984	14.26810	11570.71196
100	867.71633	14.26925	12381.66179

57	61.69962	13.11723	809.32822
58	66.32709	13.13231	871.02783
59	71.30162	13.14633	937.35492
60	76.64924	13.15938	1008.65654
61	82.39793	13.17152	1085.30578
62	88.57778	13.18281	1167.70371
63	95.22111	13.19331	1256.28149
64	102.36270	13.20308	1351.50260
65	110.03990	13.21217	1453.86530
66	118.29289	13.22062	1563.90519
67	127.16486	13.22848	1682.19808
68	136.70222	13.23580	1809.36294
69	146.95489	13.24260	1946.06516
70	157.97650	13.24893	2093.02005
71	169.82474	13.25482	2250.99655
72	182.56160	13.26030	2420.82129
73	196.25372	13.26539	2603.38289
74	210.97275	13.27013	2799.63661
75	226.79570	13.27454	3010.60935
76	243.80538	13.27864	3237.40505
77	262.09078	13.28246	3481.21043
78	281.74759	13.28601	3743.30122
79	302.87866	13.28931	4025.04881
80	325.59456	13.29238	4327.92747
81	350.01415	13.29524	4653.52203
82	376.26521	13.29790	5003.53618
83	404.48510	13.30037	5379.80139
84	434.82149	13.30267	5784.28650
85	467.43310	13.30481	6219.10798
86	502.49058	13.30680	6686.54108
87	540.17737	13.30865	7189.03166
88	580.69068	13.31037	7729.20904
89	624.24248	13.31197	8309.89972
90	671.06066	13.31346	8934.14220
91	721.39021	13.31485	9605.20286
92	775.49448	13.31614	10326.59307
93	833.65657	13.31734	11102.08755
94	896.18081	13.31846	11935.74412
95	963.39437	13.31949	12831.92493
96	1035.64895	13.32046	13795.31930
97	1113.32262	13.32136	14830.96825
98	1196.82181	13.32219	15944.29087
99	1286.58345	13.32297	17141.11268
100	1383.07721	13.32369	18427.69613

57	80.38112	12.34449	992.26402
58	86.81161	12.35601	1072.64514
59	93.75654	12.36668	1159.45676
60	101.25706	12.37655	1253.21330
61	109.35763	12.38570	1354.47036
62	118.10624	12.39416	1463.82799
63	127.55474	12.40200	1581.93423
64	137.75912	12.40926	1709.48897
65	148.77985	12.41598	1847.24808
66	160.68223	12.42221	1996.02793
67	173.53681	12.42797	2156.71016
68	187.41976	12.43330	2330.24698
69	202.41334	12.43825	2517.66673
70	218.60641	12.44282	2720.08007
71	236.09492	12.44706	2938.68648
72	254.98251	12.45098	3174.78140
73	275.38111	12.45461	3429.76391
74	297.41160	12.45797	3705.14502
75	321.20453	12.46108	4002.55662
76	346.90089	12.46397	4323.76115
77	374.65296	12.46664	4670.66205
78	404.62520	12.46911	5045.31501
79	436.99522	12.47140	5449.94021
80	471.95483	12.47351	5886.93543
81	509.71122	12.47548	6358.89026
82	550.48812	12.47729	6868.60148
83	594.52717	12.47897	7419.08960
84	642.08934	12.48053	8013.61677
85	693.45649	12.48197	8655.70611
86	748.93301	12.48331	9349.16260
87	808.84765	12.48455	10098.09561
88	873.55546	12.48569	10906.94326
89	943.43990	12.48675	11780.49872
90	1018.91509	12.48773	12723.93862
91	1100.42830	12.48864	13742.85371
92	1188.46256	12.48948	14843.28200
93	1283.53956	12.49026	16031.74456
94	1386.22273	12.49098	17315.28413
95	1497.12055	12.49165	18701.50686
96	1616.89019	12.49227	20198.62741
97	1746.24141	12.49284	21815.51760
98	1885.94072	12.49337	23561.75901
99	2036.81598	12.49386	25447.69973
100	2199.76126	12.49432	27484.51570

Table I. ANNUITIES (*Continued*)

M	C(5,M, 4)	A(5,M, 4)	S(5,M, 4)	M	C(6,M, 4)	A(6,M, 4)	S(6,M, 4)	M	C(7,M, 4)	A(7,M, 4)	S(7,M, 4)
1	1.01250	.98765	1.00000	1	1.01500	.98522	1.00000	1	1.01750	.98280	1.00000
2	1.02516	1.96312	2.01250	2	1.03023	1.95588	2.01500	2	1.03531	1.94870	2.01750
3	1.03797	2.92653	3.03766	3	1.04568	2.91220	3.04522	3	1.05342	2.89798	3.05281
4	1.05095	3.87806	4.07563	4	1.06136	3.85438	4.09090	4	1.07186	3.83094	4.10623
5	1.06408	4.81784	5.12657	5	1.07728	4.78264	5.15227	5	1.09062	4.74786	5.17809
6	1.07738	5.74601	6.19065	6	1.09344	5.69719	6.22955	6	1.10970	5.64900	6.26871
7	1.09085	6.66273	7.26804	7	1.10984	6.59821	7.32299	7	1.12912	6.53464	7.37841
8	1.10449	7.56812	8.35889	8	1.12649	7.48593	8.43284	8	1.14888	7.40505	8.50753
9	1.11829	8.46234	9.46337	9	1.14339	8.36052	9.55933	9	1.16899	8.26049	9.65641
10	1.13227	9.34553	10.58167	10	1.16054	9.22218	10.70272	10	1.18944	9.10122	10.82540
11	1.14642	10.21780	11.71394	11	1.17795	10.07112	11.86326	11	1.21026	9.92749	12.01484
12	1.16075	11.07931	12.86036	12	1.19562	10.90751	13.04121	12	1.23144	10.73955	13.22510
13	1.17526	11.93018	14.02112	13	1.21355	11.73153	14.23683	13	1.25299	11.53764	14.45654
14	1.18995	12.77055	15.19638	14	1.23176	12.54338	15.45038	14	1.27492	12.32201	15.70953
15	1.20483	13.60055	16.38633	15	1.25023	13.34323	16.68214	15	1.29723	13.09288	16.98445
16	1.21989	14.42029	17.59116	16	1.26899	14.13126	17.93237	16	1.31993	13.85050	18.28168
17	1.23514	15.22992	18.81105	17	1.28802	14.90765	19.20136	17	1.34303	14.59508	19.60161
18	1.25058	16.02955	20.04619	18	1.30734	15.67256	20.48938	18	1.36653	15.32686	20.94463
19	1.26621	16.81931	21.29677	19	1.32695	16.42617	21.79672	19	1.39045	16.04606	22.31117
20	1.28204	17.59932	22.56298	20	1.34686	17.16864	23.12367	20	1.41478	16.75288	23.70161
21	1.29806	18.36969	23.84502	21	1.36706	17.90014	24.47052	21	1.43954	17.44755	25.11639
22	1.31429	19.13056	25.14308	22	1.38756	18.62082	25.83758	22	1.46473	18.13027	26.55593
23	1.33072	19.88204	26.45737	23	1.40838	19.33086	27.22514	23	1.49036	18.80125	28.02065
24	1.34735	20.62423	27.78808	24	1.42950	20.03041	28.63352	24	1.51644	19.46069	29.51102
25	1.36419	21.35727	29.13544	25	1.45095	20.71961	30.06302	25	1.54298	20.10878	31.02746
26	1.38125	22.08125	30.49963	26	1.47271	21.39863	31.51397	26	1.56998	20.74573	32.57044
27	1.39851	22.79630	31.88087	27	1.49480	22.06762	32.98668	27	1.59746	21.37173	34.14042
28	1.41599	23.50252	33.27938	28	1.51722	22.72672	34.48148	28	1.62541	21.98695	35.73788
29	1.43369	24.20002	34.69538	29	1.53998	23.37608	35.99870	29	1.65386	22.59160	37.36329
30	1.45161	24.88891	36.12907	30	1.56308	24.01584	37.53868	30	1.68280	23.18585	39.01715
31	1.46976	25.56929	37.58068	31	1.58653	24.64615	39.10176	31	1.71225	23.76988	40.69995
32	1.48813	26.24127	39.05044	32	1.61032	25.26714	40.68829	32	1.74221	24.34386	42.41220
33	1.50673	26.90496	40.53857	33	1.63448	25.87895	42.29861	33	1.77270	24.90797	44.15441
34	1.52557	27.56046	42.04530	34	1.65900	26.48173	43.93309	34	1.80372	25.46238	45.92712
35	1.54464	28.20786	43.57087	35	1.68388	27.07559	45.59209	35	1.83529	26.00725	47.73084
36	1.56394	28.84727	45.11551	36	1.70914	27.66068	47.27597	36	1.86741	26.54275	49.56613
37	1.58349	29.47878	46.67945	37	1.73478	28.23713	48.98511	37	1.90009	27.06904	51.43354
38	1.60329	30.10250	48.26294	38	1.76080	28.80505	50.71989	38	1.93334	27.58628	53.33362
39	1.62333	30.71852	49.86623	39	1.78721	29.36458	52.48068	39	1.96717	28.09463	55.26696
40	1.64362	31.32693	51.48956	40	1.81402	29.91585	54.26789	40	2.00160	28.59423	57.23413
41	1.66416	31.92784	53.13318	41	1.84123	30.45896	56.08191	41	2.03663	29.08524	59.23573
42	1.68497	32.52132	54.79734	42	1.86885	30.99405	57.92314	42	2.07227	29.56780	61.27236
43	1.70603	33.10748	56.48231	43	1.89688	31.52123	59.79199	43	2.10853	30.04207	63.34462
44	1.72735	33.68640	58.18834	44	1.92533	32.04062	61.68887	44	2.14543	30.50817	65.45315
45	1.74895	34.25817	59.91569	45	1.95421	32.55234	63.61420	45	2.18298	30.96626	67.59858
46	1.77081	34.82288	61.66464	46	1.98353	33.05649	65.56841	46	2.22118	31.41647	69.78156
47	1.79294	35.38062	63.43545	47	2.01328	33.55319	67.55194	47	2.26005	31.85894	72.00274
48	1.81535	35.93148	65.22839	48	2.04348	34.04255	69.55522	48	2.29960	32.29380	74.26278
49	1.83805	36.47554	67.04374	49	2.07413	34.52468	71.60870	49	2.33984	32.72118	76.56238
50	1.86102	37.01288	68.88179	50	2.10524	34.99969	73.68283	50	2.38079	33.14121	78.90222
51	1.88429	37.54358	70.74281	51	2.13682	35.46767	75.78807	51	2.42245	33.55401	81.28301
52	1.90784	38.06773	72.62710	52	2.16887	35.92874	77.92489	52	2.46485	33.95972	83.70547
53	1.93169	38.58542	74.53494	53	2.20141	36.38300	80.09376	53	2.50798	34.35845	86.17031
54	1.95583	39.09671	76.46662	54	2.23443	36.83054	82.29517	54	2.55187	34.75032	88.67829
55	1.98028	39.60169	78.42246	55	2.26794	37.27147	84.52960	55	2.59653	35.13545	91.23016
56	2.00503	40.10043	80.40274	56	2.30196	37.70588	86.79754	56	2.64197	35.51395	93.82669

57	2.03010	40.59302	82.40777	57	2.33649	38.13387	89.09951	57	2.68820	35.88595	96.46866
58	2.05547	41.07952	84.43787	58	2.37154	38.55554	91.43600	58	2.73525	36.25155	99.15686
59	2.08117	41.56002	86.49334	59	2.40711	38.97097	93.80754	59	2.78311	36.61086	101.89210
60	2.10718	42.03459	88.57451	60	2.44322	39.38027	96.21465	60	2.83182	36.96399	104.67522
61	2.13352	42.50330	90.68169	61	2.47987	39.78352	98.65787	61	2.88137	37.31104	107.50703
62	2.16019	42.96622	92.81521	62	2.51707	40.18080	101.13774	62	2.93180	37.65213	110.38841
63	2.18719	43.42343	94.97540	63	2.55482	40.57222	103.65481	63	2.98310	37.98735	113.32020
64	2.21453	43.87499	97.16259	64	2.59314	40.95785	106.20963	64	3.03531	38.31681	116.30331
65	2.24221	44.32098	99.37713	65	2.63204	41.33779	108.80277	65	3.08843	38.64060	119.33861
66	2.27024	44.76146	101.61934	66	2.67152	41.71210	111.43481	66	3.14247	38.95882	122.42704
67	2.29862	45.19651	103.88958	67	2.71160	42.08089	114.10634	67	3.19747	39.27157	125.56951
68	2.32735	45.62618	106.18820	68	2.75227	42.44423	116.81793	68	3.25342	39.57893	128.76698
69	2.35644	46.05055	108.51555	69	2.79355	42.80219	119.57020	69	3.31036	39.88102	132.02040
70	2.38590	46.46968	110.87200	70	2.83546	43.15487	122.36375	70	3.36829	40.17790	135.33076
71	2.41572	46.88363	113.25790	71	2.87799	43.50234	125.19921	71	3.42723	40.46968	138.69905
72	2.44592	47.29247	115.67362	72	2.92116	43.84467	128.07720	72	3.48721	40.75645	142.12628
73	2.47649	47.69627	118.11954	73	2.96498	44.18194	130.99836	73	3.54824	41.03828	145.61349
74	2.50745	48.09508	120.59604	74	3.00945	44.51422	133.96333	74	3.61033	41.31526	149.16173
75	2.53879	48.48897	123.10349	75	3.05459	44.84160	136.97278	75	3.67351	41.58748	152.77206
76	2.57053	48.87800	125.64228	76	3.10041	45.16414	140.02737	76	3.73780	41.85501	156.44557
77	2.60266	49.26222	128.21281	77	3.14692	45.48191	143.12778	77	3.80321	42.11795	160.18336
78	2.63519	49.64170	130.81547	78	3.19412	45.79498	146.27470	78	3.86977	42.37636	163.98657
79	2.66813	50.01649	133.45066	79	3.24203	46.10343	149.46882	79	3.93749	42.63033	167.85634
80	2.70148	50.38666	136.11880	80	3.29066	46.40732	152.71085	80	4.00639	42.87993	171.79382
81	2.73525	50.75225	138.82028	81	3.34002	46.70672	156.00152	81	4.07650	43.12524	175.80022
82	2.76944	51.11334	141.55553	82	3.39012	47.00170	159.34154	82	4.14784	43.36633	179.87672
83	2.80406	51.46996	144.32498	83	3.44097	47.29231	162.73165	83	4.22043	43.60327	184.02456
84	2.83911	51.82219	147.12904	84	3.49259	47.57863	166.17264	84	4.29429	43.83614	188.24499
85	2.87460	52.17006	149.96815	85	3.54498	47.86072	169.66523	85	4.36944	44.06500	192.53928
86	2.91053	52.51364	152.84276	86	3.59815	48.13864	173.21020	86	4.44590	44.28993	196.90872
87	2.94692	52.85298	155.75329	87	3.65213	48.41246	176.80836	87	4.52371	44.51099	201.35462
88	2.98375	53.18813	158.70021	88	3.70691	48.68222	180.46048	88	4.60287	44.72824	205.87833
89	3.02105	53.51914	161.68396	89	3.76251	48.94800	184.16739	89	4.68342	44.94176	210.48120
90	3.05881	53.84606	164.70501	90	3.81895	49.20985	187.92990	90	4.76538	45.15161	215.16462
91	3.09705	54.16895	167.76382	91	3.87623	49.46784	191.74885	91	4.84877	45.35785	219.93000
92	3.13576	54.48785	170.86087	92	3.93438	49.72201	195.62508	92	4.93363	45.56054	224.77877
93	3.17496	54.80282	173.99663	93	3.99339	49.97242	199.55946	93	5.01997	45.75974	229.71240
94	3.21464	55.11389	177.17159	94	4.05329	50.21913	203.55285	94	5.10782	45.95552	234.73237
95	3.25483	55.42113	180.38623	95	4.11409	50.46220	207.60614	95	5.19720	46.14793	239.84018
96	3.29551	55.72457	183.64106	96	4.17580	50.70168	211.72023	96	5.28815	46.33703	245.03739
97	3.33671	56.02427	186.93657	97	4.23844	50.93761	215.89604	97	5.38070	46.52288	250.32554
98	3.37842	56.32026	190.27328	98	4.30202	51.17006	220.13448	98	5.47486	46.70554	255.70624
99	3.42065	56.61261	193.65170	99	4.36655	51.39907	224.43650	99	5.57067	46.88505	261.18110
100	3.46340	56.90134	197.07234	100	4.43205	51.62470	228.80304	100	5.66816	47.06147	266.75177

Table I. ANNUITIES (*Continued*)

M	C(5,M, 4)	A(5,M, 4)	S(5,M, 4)	M	C(6,M, 4)	A(6,M, 4)	S(6,M, 4)	M	C(7,M, 4)	A(7,M, 4)	S(7,M, 4)
101	3.50670	57.18651	200.53575	101	4.49853	51.84700	233.23509	101	5.76735	47.23486	272.41992
102	3.55053	57.46816	204.04244	102	4.56600	52.06601	237.73362	102	5.86828	47.40527	278.18727
103	3.59491	57.74633	207.59297	103	4.63449	52.28178	242.29962	103	5.97097	47.57275	284.05555
104	3.63985	58.02106	211.18789	104	4.70401	52.49437	246.93411	104	6.07546	47.73734	290.02652
105	3.68535	58.29241	214.82773	105	4.77457	52.70381	251.63813	105	6.18178	47.89911	296.10199
106	3.73141	58.56040	218.51308	106	4.84619	52.91016	256.41270	106	6.28997	48.05809	302.28377
107	3.77806	58.82509	222.24449	107	4.91888	53.11346	261.25889	107	6.40004	48.21434	308.57374
108	3.82528	59.08651	226.02255	108	4.99267	53.31375	266.17777	108	6.51204	48.36790	314.97378
109	3.87310	59.34470	229.84783	109	5.06756	53.51108	271.17044	109	6.62600	48.51882	321.48582
110	3.92151	59.59970	233.72093	110	5.14357	53.70550	276.23799	110	6.74196	48.66715	328.11182
111	3.97053	59.85156	237.64244	111	5.22072	53.89704	281.38156	111	6.85994	48.81292	334.85378
112	4.02016	60.10031	241.61297	112	5.29903	54.08576	286.60229	112	6.97999	48.95619	341.71372
113	4.07041	60.34598	245.63313	113	5.37852	54.27168	291.90132	113	7.10214	49.09699	348.69371
114	4.12129	60.58862	249.70355	114	5.45920	54.45486	297.27984	114	7.22643	49.23537	355.79585
115	4.17281	60.82827	253.82484	115	5.54109	54.63533	302.73904	115	7.35289	49.37137	363.02228
116	4.22497	61.06496	257.99765	116	5.62420	54.81313	308.28013	116	7.48157	49.50504	370.37517
117	4.27778	61.29872	262.22262	117	5.70856	54.98831	313.90433	117	7.61249	49.63640	377.85673
118	4.33126	61.52960	266.50041	118	5.79419	55.16089	319.61289	118	7.74571	49.76550	385.46922
119	4.38540	61.75763	270.83166	119	5.88111	55.33093	325.40709	119	7.88126	49.89239	393.21493
120	4.44021	61.98285	275.21706	120	5.96932	55.49845	331.28819	120	8.01918	50.01709	401.09620
121	4.49572	62.20528	279.65727	121	6.05886	55.66350	337.25751	121	8.15952	50.13964	409.11538
122	4.55191	62.42497	284.15299	122	6.14975	55.82611	343.31638	122	8.30231	50.26009	417.27490
123	4.60881	62.64194	288.70490	123	6.24199	55.98632	349.46612	123	8.44760	50.37847	425.57721
124	4.66642	62.85624	293.31371	124	6.33562	56.14415	355.70811	124	8.59543	50.49481	434.02481
125	4.72475	63.06789	297.98013	125	6.43066	56.29966	362.04374	125	8.74585	50.60915	442.62024
126	4.78381	63.27693	302.70488	126	6.52712	56.45287	368.47439	126	8.89891	50.72152	451.36610
127	4.84361	63.48339	307.48870	127	6.62502	56.60381	375.00151	127	9.05464	50.83196	460.26501
128	4.90415	63.68730	312.33230	128	6.72440	56.75252	381.62653	128	9.21309	50.94050	469.31964
129	4.96546	63.88869	317.23646	129	6.82526	56.89903	388.35093	129	9.37432	51.04718	478.53274
130	5.02752	64.08759	322.20191	130	6.92764	57.04338	395.17619	130	9.53837	51.15202	487.90706
131	5.09037	64.28404	327.22944	131	7.03156	57.18560	402.10384	131	9.70530	51.25506	497.44543
132	5.15400	64.47807	332.31981	132	7.13703	57.32571	409.13539	132	9.87514	51.35632	507.15073
133	5.21842	64.66970	337.47380	133	7.24409	57.46376	416.27242	133	10.04795	51.45584	517.02587
134	5.28365	64.85896	342.69223	134	7.35275	57.59976	423.51651	134	10.22379	51.55365	527.07382
135	5.34970	65.04589	347.97588	135	7.46304	57.73376	430.86926	135	10.40271	51.64978	537.29761
136	5.41657	65.23050	353.32558	136	7.57498	57.86577	438.33230	136	10.58476	51.74426	547.70032
137	5.48428	65.41284	358.74215	137	7.68861	57.99583	445.90728	137	10.76999	51.83711	558.28507
138	5.55283	65.59293	364.22642	138	7.80394	58.12397	453.59589	138	10.95846	51.92836	569.05506
139	5.62224	65.77080	369.77925	139	7.92100	58.25022	461.39983	139	11.15024	52.01805	580.01353
140	5.69252	65.94647	375.40149	140	8.03981	58.37460	469.32083	140	11.34537	52.10619	591.16376
141	5.76368	66.11997	381.09401	141	8.16041	58.49714	477.36064	141	11.54391	52.19281	602.50913
142	5.83572	66.29133	386.85769	142	8.28282	58.61787	485.52105	142	11.74593	52.27795	614.05304
143	5.90867	66.46057	392.69341	143	8.40706	58.73682	493.80386	143	11.95148	52.36162	625.79897
144	5.98253	66.62772	398.60208	144	8.53316	58.85401	502.21092	144	12.16063	52.44385	637.75045
145	6.05731	66.79281	404.58460	145	8.66116	58.96947	510.74409	145	12.37344	52.52467	649.91108
146	6.13302	66.95586	410.64191	146	8.79108	59.08322	519.40525	146	12.58998	52.60410	662.28453
147	6.20969	67.11690	416.77493	147	8.92294	59.19529	528.19633	147	12.81030	52.68216	674.87451
148	6.28731	67.27595	422.98462	148	9.05679	59.30571	537.11927	148	13.03448	52.75888	687.68481
149	6.36590	67.43304	429.27193	149	9.19264	59.41449	546.17606	149	13.26259	52.83428	700.71929
150	6.44547	67.58819	435.63783	150	9.33053	59.52166	555.36870	150	13.49468	52.90839	713.98188
151	6.52604	67.74142	442.08330	151	9.47049	59.62726	564.69923	151	13.73084	52.98121	727.47656
152	6.60762	67.89276	448.60934	152	9.61255	59.73129	574.16972	152	13.97113	53.05279	741.20740
153	6.69021	68.04223	455.21696	153	9.75673	59.83378	583.78227	153	14.21562	53.12314	755.17853
154	6.77384	68.18986	461.90717	154	9.90308	59.93476	593.53900	154	14.46440	53.19227	769.39416
155	6.85851	68.33566	468.68101	155	10.05163	60.03424	603.44208	155	14.71752	53.26022	783.85856
156	6.94424	68.47967	475.53952	156	10.20241	60.13226	613.49372	156	14.97508	53.32699	798.57608
157	7.03105	68.62189	482.48377	157	10.35544	60.22883	623.69612	157	15.23715	53.39262	813.55116
158	7.11894	68.76236	489.51481	158	10.51077	60.32397	634.05156	158	15.50380	53.45712	828.78831

161	7.38925	69.17346	511.13969	161	10.99089	60.60104	666.05923	161	16.33207	53.64404	876.11839
162	7.48161	69.30712	518.52894	162	11.15575	60.69068	677.05012	162	16.61788	53.70422	892.45046
163	7.57513	69.43913	526.01055	163	11.32309	60.77899	688.20587	163	16.90870	53.76336	909.06835
164	7.66982	69.56951	533.58568	164	11.49293	60.86600	699.52896	164	17.20460	53.82149	925.97704
165	7.76569	69.69828	541.25550	165	11.66533	60.95173	711.02190	165	17.50568	53.87861	943.18164
166	7.86276	69.82546	549.02120	166	11.84031	61.03618	722.68722	166	17.81203	53.93475	960.68732
167	7.96105	69.95107	556.88396	167	12.01791	61.11939	734.52753	167	18.12374	53.98993	978.49935
168	8.06056	70.07513	564.84501	168	12.19818	61.20137	746.54545	168	18.44090	54.04416	996.62309
169	8.16132	70.19766	572.90557	169	12.38115	61.28214	758.74363	169	18.76362	54.09745	1015.06399
170	8.26334	70.31868	581.06689	170	12.56687	61.36171	771.12478	170	19.09198	54.14983	1033.82761
171	8.36663	70.43820	589.33023	171	12.75537	61.44011	783.69165	171	19.42609	54.20131	1052.91959
172	8.47121	70.55625	597.69686	172	12.94671	61.51735	796.44703	172	19.76605	54.25190	1072.34568
173	8.57710	70.67284	606.16807	173	13.14091	61.59345	809.39373	173	20.11196	54.30162	1092.11173
174	8.68431	70.78799	614.74517	174	13.33802	61.66842	822.53464	174	20.46391	54.35049	1112.22369
175	8.79287	70.90172	623.42948	175	13.53809	61.74229	835.87266	175	20.82203	54.39851	1132.68760
176	8.90278	71.01404	632.22235	176	13.74116	61.81506	849.41075	176	21.18642	54.44571	1153.50964
177	9.01406	71.12498	641.12513	177	13.94728	61.88676	863.15191	177	21.55718	54.49210	1174.69606
178	9.12674	71.23455	650.13920	178	14.15649	61.95740	877.09919	178	21.93443	54.53769	1196.25324
179	9.24082	71.34276	659.26594	179	14.36884	62.02700	891.25568	179	22.31828	54.58250	1218.18767
180	9.35633	71.44964	668.50676	180	14.58437	62.09556	905.62451	180	22.70885	54.62653	1240.50595
181	9.47329	71.55520	677.86309	181	14.80313	62.16312	920.20888	181	23.10626	54.66981	1263.21481
182	9.59170	71.65946	687.33638	182	15.02518	62.22967	935.01201	182	23.51062	54.71234	1286.32107
183	9.71160	71.76243	696.92809	183	15.25056	62.29524	950.03719	183	23.92205	54.75415	1309.83168
184	9.83300	71.86413	706.63969	184	15.47932	62.35984	965.28775	184	24.34069	54.79523	1333.75374
185	9.95591	71.96457	716.47268	185	15.71151	62.42349	980.76707	185	24.76665	54.83561	1358.09443
186	10.08036	72.06377	726.42859	186	15.94718	62.48620	996.47857	186	25.20007	54.87529	1382.86108
187	10.20636	72.16175	736.50895	187	16.18639	62.54798	1012.42575	187	25.64107	54.91429	1408.06115
188	10.33394	72.25852	746.71531	188	16.42918	62.60885	1028.61214	188	26.08979	54.95262	1433.70222
189	10.46312	72.35409	757.04925	189	16.67562	62.66881	1045.04132	189	26.54636	54.99029	1459.79201
190	10.59390	72.44849	767.51237	190	16.92575	62.72790	1061.71694	190	27.01092	55.02731	1486.33837
191	10.72633	72.54172	778.10627	191	17.17964	62.78610	1078.64269	191	27.48361	55.06370	1513.34929
192	10.86041	72.63379	788.83260	192	17.43734	62.84345	1095.82234	192	27.96458	55.09946	1540.83290
193	10.99616	72.72473	799.69301	193	17.69890	62.89995	1113.25967	193	28.45396	55.13460	1568.79748
194	11.13361	72.81455	810.68917	194	17.96438	62.95562	1130.95857	194	28.95190	55.16914	1597.25144
195	11.27278	72.90326	821.82279	195	18.23384	63.01046	1148.92294	195	29.45856	55.20309	1626.20334
196	11.41369	72.99088	833.09557	196	18.50735	63.06449	1167.15679	196	29.97408	55.23645	1655.66189
197	11.55637	73.07741	844.50927	197	18.78496	63.11773	1185.66414	197	30.49863	55.26924	1685.63598
198	11.70082	73.16287	856.06563	198	19.06674	63.17018	1204.44910	198	31.03236	55.30146	1716.13461
199	11.84708	73.24728	867.76645	199	19.35274	63.22185	1223.51584	199	31.57542	55.33313	1747.16696
200	11.99517	73.33065	879.61353	200	19.64303	63.27276	1242.86858	200	32.12799	55.36426	1778.74239

Table I. ANNUITIES (*Continued*)

M	C(8,M, 4)	A(8,M, 4)	S(8,M, 4)	M	C(9,M, 4)	A(9,M, 4)	S(9,M, 4)	M	C(10,M, 4)	A(10,M, 4)	S(10,M, 4)
1	1.02000	.98039	1.00000	1	1.02250	.97800	1.00000	1	1.02500	.97561	1.00000
2	1.04040	1.94156	2.02000	2	1.04551	1.93447	2.02250	2	1.05063	1.92742	2.02500
3	1.06121	2.88388	3.06040	3	1.06903	2.86990	3.06801	3	1.07689	2.85602	3.07562
4	1.08243	3.80773	4.12161	4	1.09308	3.78474	4.13704	4	1.10381	3.76197	4.15252
5	1.10408	4.71346	5.20404	5	1.11768	4.67945	5.23012	5	1.13141	4.64583	5.25633
6	1.12616	5.60143	6.30812	6	1.14283	5.55448	6.34780	6	1.15969	5.50813	6.38774
7	1.14869	6.47199	7.43428	7	1.16854	6.41025	7.49062	7	1.18869	6.34939	7.54743
8	1.17166	7.32548	8.58297	8	1.19483	7.24718	8.65916	8	1.21840	7.17014	8.73612
9	1.19509	8.16224	9.75463	9	1.22171	8.06571	9.85399	9	1.24886	7.97087	9.95452
10	1.21899	8.98259	10.94972	10	1.24920	8.86622	11.07571	10	1.28008	8.75206	11.20338
11	1.24337	9.78685	12.16872	11	1.27731	9.64911	12.32491	11	1.31209	9.51421	12.48347
12	1.26824	10.57534	13.41209	12	1.30605	10.41478	13.60222	12	1.34489	10.25776	13.79555
13	1.29361	11.34837	14.68033	13	1.33544	11.16360	14.90827	13	1.37851	10.98318	15.14044
14	1.31948	12.10625	15.97394	14	1.36548	11.89594	16.24371	14	1.41297	11.69091	16.51895
15	1.34587	12.84926	17.29342	15	1.39621	12.61217	17.60919	15	1.44830	12.38138	17.93193
16	1.37279	13.57771	18.63929	16	1.42762	13.31263	19.00540	16	1.48451	13.05500	19.38022
17	1.40024	14.29187	20.01207	17	1.45974	13.99768	20.43302	17	1.52162	13.71220	20.86473
18	1.42825	14.99203	21.41231	18	1.49259	14.66766	21.89276	18	1.55966	14.35336	22.38635
19	1.45681	15.67846	22.84056	19	1.52617	15.32290	23.38535	19	1.59865	14.97889	23.94601
20	1.48595	16.35143	24.29737	20	1.56051	15.96371	24.91152	20	1.63862	15.58916	25.54466
21	1.51567	17.01121	25.78332	21	1.59562	16.59043	26.47203	21	1.67958	16.18455	27.18327
22	1.54598	17.65805	27.29898	22	1.63152	17.20335	28.06765	22	1.72157	16.76541	28.86286
23	1.57690	18.29220	28.84496	23	1.66823	17.80279	29.69917	23	1.76461	17.33211	30.58443
24	1.60844	18.91393	30.42186	24	1.70577	18.38904	31.36740	24	1.80873	17.88499	32.34904
25	1.64061	19.52346	32.03030	25	1.74415	18.96238	33.07317	25	1.85394	18.42438	34.15776
26	1.67342	20.12104	33.67091	26	1.78339	19.52311	34.81732	26	1.90029	18.95061	36.01171
27	1.70689	20.70690	35.34432	27	1.82352	20.07150	36.60071	27	1.94780	19.46401	37.91200
28	1.74102	21.28127	37.05121	28	1.86454	20.60783	38.42422	28	1.99650	19.96489	39.85980
29	1.77584	21.84438	38.79223	29	1.90650	21.13235	40.28877	29	2.04641	20.45355	41.85630
30	1.81136	22.39646	40.56808	30	1.94939	21.64533	42.19525	30	2.09757	20.93029	43.90270
31	1.84759	22.93770	42.37944	31	1.99325	22.14702	44.14466	31	2.15001	21.39541	46.00027
32	1.88454	23.46833	44.22703	32	2.03810	22.63767	46.13791	32	2.20376	21.84918	48.15028
33	1.92223	23.98856	46.11157	33	2.08396	23.11753	48.17602	33	2.25885	22.29188	50.35403
34	1.96068	24.49859	48.03380	34	2.13085	23.58683	50.25998	34	2.31532	22.72379	52.61289
35	1.99989	24.99862	49.99448	35	2.17879	24.04580	52.39083	35	2.37321	23.14516	54.92821
36	2.03989	25.48884	51.99437	36	2.22782	24.49467	54.56962	36	2.43254	23.55625	57.30141
37	2.08069	25.96945	54.03425	37	2.27794	24.93366	56.79744	37	2.49335	23.95732	59.73395
38	2.12230	26.44064	56.11494	38	2.32920	25.36299	59.07538	38	2.55568	24.34860	62.22730
39	2.16474	26.90259	58.23724	39	2.38160	25.78288	61.40457	39	2.61957	24.73034	64.78298
40	2.20804	27.35548	60.40198	40	2.43519	26.19352	63.78618	40	2.68506	25.10278	67.40255
41	2.25220	27.79949	62.61002	41	2.48998	26.59513	66.22137	41	2.75219	25.46612	70.08762
42	2.29724	28.23479	64.86222	42	2.54601	26.98790	68.71135	42	2.82100	25.82061	72.83981
43	2.34319	28.66156	67.15947	43	2.60329	27.37203	71.25735	43	2.89152	26.16645	75.66080
44	2.39005	29.07996	69.50266	44	2.66186	27.74771	73.85064	44	2.96381	26.50385	78.55232
45	2.43785	29.49016	71.89271	45	2.72176	28.11512	76.52251	45	3.03790	26.83302	81.51613
46	2.48661	29.89231	74.33056	46	2.78300	28.47444	79.24426	46	3.11385	27.15417	84.55403
47	2.53634	30.28658	76.81718	47	2.84561	28.82586	82.02726	47	3.19170	27.46748	87.66789
48	2.58707	30.67312	79.35352	48	2.90964	29.16955	84.87287	48	3.27149	27.77315	90.85958
49	2.63881	31.05208	81.94059	49	2.97511	29.50567	87.78251	49	3.35328	28.07137	94.13107
50	2.69159	31.42361	84.57940	50	3.04205	29.83440	90.75762	50	3.43711	28.36231	97.48435
51	2.74542	31.78785	87.27099	51	3.11049	30.15589	93.79966	51	3.52304	28.64616	100.92146
52	2.80033	32.14495	90.01641	52	3.18048	30.47031	96.91016	52	3.61111	28.92308	104.44449
53	2.85633	32.49505	92.81674	53	3.25204	30.77781	100.09064	53	3.70139	29.19325	108.05561
54	2.91346	32.83828	95.67307	54	3.32521	31.07854	103.34267	54	3.79392	29.45683	111.75700
55	2.97173	33.17479	98.58653	55	3.40003	31.37265	106.66788	55	3.88877	29.71398	115.55092
56	3.03117	33.50469	101.55826	56	3.47653	31.66030	110.06791	56	3.98599	29.96486	119.43969

57	3.09179	33.82813	104.58943	57	3.55475	31.94161	113.54444	57	4.08564	30.20962	123.42569
58	3.15362	34.14523	107.68122	58	3.63473	32.21673	117.09919	58	4.18778	30.44841	127.51133
59	3.21670	34.45610	110.83484	59	3.71651	32.48580	120.73392	59	4.29248	30.68137	131.69911
60	3.28103	34.76089	114.05154	60	3.80013	32.74895	124.45043	60	4.39979	30.90866	135.99159
61	3.34665	35.05969	117.33257	61	3.88564	33.00631	128.25057	61	4.50978	31.13040	140.39138
62	3.41358	35.35264	120.67922	62	3.97306	33.25801	132.13621	62	4.62253	31.34673	144.90116
63	3.48186	35.63984	124.09281	63	4.06246	33.50416	136.10927	63	4.73809	31.55778	149.52369
64	3.55149	35.92141	127.57466	64	4.15386	33.74490	140.17173	64	4.85654	31.76369	154.26179
65	3.62252	36.19747	131.12616	65	4.24733	33.98034	144.32559	65	4.97796	31.96458	159.11833
66	3.69497	36.46810	134.74868	66	4.34289	34.21061	148.57292	66	5.10241	32.16055	164.09629
67	3.76887	36.73343	138.44365	67	4.44061	34.43580	152.91581	67	5.22997	32.35177	169.19870
68	3.84425	36.99356	142.21253	68	4.54052	34.65604	157.35642	68	5.36072	32.53831	174.42866
69	3.92114	37.24859	146.05678	69	4.64268	34.87143	161.89694	69	5.49473	32.72030	179.78938
70	3.99956	37.49862	149.97791	70	4.74714	35.08208	166.53962	70	5.63210	32.89786	185.28411
71	4.07955	37.74374	153.97747	71	4.85395	35.28810	171.28676	71	5.77291	33.07108	190.91622
72	4.16114	37.98406	158.05702	72	4.96317	35.48959	176.14071	72	5.91723	33.24008	196.68912
73	4.24436	38.21967	162.21816	73	5.07484	35.68664	181.10388	73	6.06516	33.40495	202.60635
74	4.32925	38.45066	166.46252	74	5.18902	35.87935	186.17871	74	6.21679	33.56581	208.67151
75	4.41584	38.67711	170.79177	75	5.30577	36.06783	191.36774	75	6.37221	33.72274	214.88830
76	4.50415	38.89913	175.20761	76	5.42515	36.25215	196.67351	76	6.53151	33.87584	221.26050
77	4.59424	39.11680	179.71176	77	5.54722	36.43242	202.09865	77	6.69480	34.02521	227.79202
78	4.68612	39.33019	184.30600	78	5.67203	36.60873	207.64588	78	6.86217	34.17094	234.48682
79	4.77984	39.53940	188.99212	79	5.79965	36.78115	213.31792	79	7.03372	34.31311	241.34899
80	4.87544	39.74451	193.77196	80	5.93015	36.94978	219.11757	80	7.20957	34.45182	248.38271
81	4.97295	39.94560	198.64740	81	6.06357	37.11470	225.04771	81	7.38981	34.58714	255.59228
82	5.07241	40.14275	203.62034	82	6.20000	37.27599	231.11129	82	7.57455	34.71916	262.98209
83	5.17386	40.33603	208.69275	83	6.33950	37.43373	237.31129	83	7.76392	34.84796	270.55664
84	5.27733	40.52552	213.86661	84	6.48214	37.58800	243.65080	84	7.95801	34.97362	278.32056
85	5.38288	40.71129	219.14394	85	6.62799	37.73888	250.13294	85	8.15696	35.09621	286.27857
86	5.49054	40.89342	224.52682	86	6.77712	37.88643	256.76093	86	8.36089	35.21582	294.43553
87	5.60035	41.07198	230.01735	87	6.92961	38.03074	263.53805	87	8.56991	35.33251	302.79642
88	5.71235	41.24704	235.61770	88	7.08552	38.17187	270.46766	88	8.78416	35.44635	311.36633
89	5.82660	41.41867	241.33006	89	7.24495	38.30990	277.55318	89	9.00376	35.55741	320.15049
90	5.94313	41.58693	247.15666	90	7.40796	38.44489	284.79813	90	9.22886	35.66577	329.15425
91	6.06200	41.75189	253.09979	91	7.57464	38.57691	292.20608	91	9.45958	35.77148	338.38311
92	6.18324	41.91362	259.16179	92	7.74507	38.70602	299.78072	92	9.69607	35.87462	347.84269
93	6.30690	42.07218	265.34502	93	7.91933	38.83230	307.52579	93	9.93847	35.97524	357.53875
94	6.43304	42.22762	271.65192	94	8.09752	38.95579	315.44512	94	10.18693	36.07340	367.47722
95	6.56170	42.38002	278.08496	95	8.27971	39.07657	323.54263	95	10.44160	36.16917	377.66415
96	6.69293	42.52943	284.64666	96	8.46600	39.19469	331.82234	96	10.70264	36.26261	388.10576
97	6.82679	42.67592	291.33959	97	8.65649	39.31021	340.28834	97	10.97021	36.35376	398.80840
98	6.96333	42.81953	298.16638	98	8.85126	39.42319	348.94483	98	11.24447	36.44269	409.77861
99	7.10259	42.96032	305.12971	99	9.05041	39.53368	357.79609	99	11.52558	36.52946	421.02308
100	7.24465	43.09835	312.23231	100	9.25405	39.64174	366.84650	100	11.81372	36.61411	432.54865

Table I. ANNUITIES (*Continued*)

M	C(8,M, 4)	A(8,M, 4)	S(8,M, 4)
101	7.38954	43.23368	319.47695
102	7.53733	43.36635	326.86649
103	7.68808	43.49642	334.40382
104	7.84184	43.62394	342.09190
105	7.99867	43.74896	349.93374
106	8.15865	43.87153	357.93241
107	8.32182	43.99170	366.09106
108	8.48826	44.10951	374.41288
109	8.65802	44.22501	382.90114
110	8.83118	44.33824	391.55916
111	9.00781	44.44926	400.39034
112	9.18796	44.55810	409.39815
113	9.37172	44.66480	418.58611
114	9.55916	44.76941	427.95783
115	9.75034	44.87197	437.51699
116	9.94535	44.97252	447.26733
117	10.14425	45.07110	457.21268
118	10.34714	45.16775	467.35693
119	10.55408	45.26250	477.70407
120	10.76516	45.35539	488.25815
121	10.98047	45.44646	499.02331
122	11.20008	45.53574	510.00378
123	11.42408	45.62328	521.20386
124	11.65256	45.70910	532.62793
125	11.88561	45.79323	544.28049
126	12.12332	45.87572	556.16610
127	12.36579	45.95659	568.28942
128	12.61310	46.03587	580.65521
129	12.86537	46.11360	593.26832
130	13.12267	46.18980	606.13368
131	13.38513	46.26451	619.25636
132	13.65283	46.33776	632.64148
133	13.92589	46.40956	646.29431
134	14.20440	46.47996	660.22020
135	14.48849	46.54899	674.42460
136	14.77826	46.61665	688.91310
137	15.07383	46.68299	703.69136
138	15.37530	46.74803	718.76519
139	15.68281	46.81180	734.14049
140	15.99647	46.87431	749.82330
141	16.31640	46.93560	765.81976
142	16.64272	46.99568	782.13616
143	16.97558	47.05459	798.77888
144	17.31509	47.11235	815.75446
145	17.66139	47.16897	833.06955
146	18.01462	47.22448	850.73094
147	18.37491	47.27890	868.74556
148	18.74241	47.33225	887.12047
149	19.11726	47.38456	905.86288
150	19.49960	47.43585	924.98014
151	19.88959	47.48612	944.47974
152	20.28739	47.53541	964.36934
153	20.69313	47.58374	984.65672
154	21.10700	47.63112	1005.34986
155	21.52914	47.67757	1026.45685
156	21.95972	47.72310	1047.98599
157	22.39891	47.76775	1069.94571
158	22.84689	47.81152	1092.34463

M	C(9,M, 4)	A(9,M, 4)	S(9,M, 4)
101	9.46226	39.74742	376.10055
102	9.67516	39.85078	385.56281
103	9.89285	39.95186	395.23797
104	10.11544	40.05072	405.13083
105	10.34304	40.14741	415.24627
106	10.57576	40.24196	425.58931
107	10.81371	40.33444	436.15507
108	11.05702	40.42488	446.97879
109	11.30581	40.51333	458.03581
110	11.56019	40.59983	469.34162
111	11.82029	40.68443	480.90180
112	12.08625	40.76717	492.72209
113	12.35819	40.84809	504.80834
114	12.63625	40.92723	517.16653
115	12.92056	41.00462	529.80277
116	13.21128	41.08031	542.72334
117	13.50853	41.15434	555.93461
118	13.81247	41.22674	569.44314
119	14.12325	41.29755	583.25561
120	14.44102	41.36679	597.37886
121	14.76595	41.43452	611.81989
122	15.09818	41.50075	626.58583
123	15.43789	41.56552	641.68401
124	15.78524	41.62888	657.12191
125	16.14041	41.69083	672.90715
126	16.50357	41.75142	689.04755
127	16.87490	41.81068	705.55113
128	17.25459	41.86864	722.42603
129	17.64281	41.92532	739.68062
130	18.03978	41.98075	757.32343
131	18.44567	42.03497	775.36321
132	18.86070	42.08799	793.80888
133	19.28507	42.13984	812.66958
134	19.71898	42.19055	831.95464
135	20.16266	42.24015	851.67362
136	20.61632	42.28865	871.83628
137	21.08018	42.33609	892.45260
138	21.55449	42.38249	913.53278
139	22.03946	42.42786	935.08727
140	22.53535	42.47223	957.12673
141	23.04240	42.51563	979.66208
142	23.56085	42.55808	1002.70448
143	24.09097	42.59959	1026.26533
144	24.63302	42.64018	1050.35630
145	25.18726	42.67988	1074.98932
146	25.75397	42.71871	1100.17658
147	26.33344	42.75669	1125.93055
148	26.92594	42.79383	1152.25399
149	27.53177	42.83015	1179.18993
150	28.15124	42.86567	1206.72170
151	28.78464	42.90041	1234.87294
152	29.43230	42.93439	1263.65758
153	30.09452	42.96762	1293.08987
154	30.77165	43.00011	1323.18440
155	31.46401	43.03190	1353.95604
156	32.17195	43.06298	1385.42006
157	32.89582	43.09338	1417.59201
158	33.63598	43.12311	1450.48783

M	C(10,M, 4)	A(10,M, 4)	S(10,M, 4)
101	12.10906	36.69669	444.36237
102	12.41179	36.77726	456.47143
103	12.72208	36.85595	468.88322
104	13.04013	36.93255	481.60530
105	13.36614	37.00736	494.64543
106	13.70029	37.08035	508.01156
107	14.04280	37.15156	521.71185
108	14.39387	37.22104	535.75465
109	14.75371	37.28882	550.14852
110	15.12256	37.35494	564.90223
111	15.50062	37.41946	580.02478
112	15.88814	37.48240	595.52540
113	16.28534	37.54380	611.41354
114	16.69247	37.60371	627.69888
115	17.10978	37.66215	644.39135
116	17.53753	37.71918	661.50113
117	17.97597	37.77481	679.03866
118	18.42537	37.82908	697.01463
119	18.88600	37.88203	715.43999
120	19.35815	37.93369	734.32599
121	19.84210	37.98408	753.68414
122	20.33816	38.03325	773.52625
123	20.84661	38.08122	793.86440
124	21.36778	38.12802	814.71101
125	21.90197	38.17368	836.07879
126	22.44952	38.21822	857.98076
127	23.01076	38.26168	880.43028
128	23.58603	38.30408	903.44103
129	24.17568	38.34544	927.02706
130	24.78007	38.38580	951.20274
131	25.39957	38.42517	975.98280
132	26.03456	38.46358	1001.38237
133	26.68542	38.50105	1027.41693
134	27.35256	38.53761	1054.10236
135	28.03637	38.57328	1081.45492
136	28.73728	38.60808	1109.49129
137	29.45571	38.64203	1138.22857
138	30.19211	38.67515	1167.68429
139	30.94691	38.70746	1197.87639
140	31.72058	38.73899	1228.82330
141	32.51360	38.76975	1260.54389
142	33.32644	38.79975	1293.05748
143	34.15960	38.82903	1326.38392
144	35.01359	38.85759	1360.54352
145	35.88893	38.88545	1395.55711
146	36.78615	38.91263	1431.44603
147	37.70580	38.93916	1468.23218
148	38.64845	38.96503	1505.93799
149	39.61466	38.99027	1544.58644
150	40.60503	39.01490	1584.20110
151	41.62015	39.03893	1624.80613
152	42.66066	39.06237	1666.42628
153	43.72717	39.08524	1709.08694
154	44.82035	39.10755	1752.81411
155	45.94086	39.12932	1797.63446
156	47.08938	39.15055	1843.57532
157	48.26662	39.17127	1890.66471
158	49.47328	39.19148	1938.93133

161	24.24531	47.93775	1162.26526	161	35.95787	43.20843	1553.68321	161	53.27731	39.24921	2091.09259
162	24.73021	47.97818	1186.51056	162	36.76692	43.23563	1589.64108	162	54.60925	39.26752	2144.36991
163	25.22482	48.01782	1211.24077	163	37.59418	43.26223	1626.40801	163	55.97448	39.28539	2198.97915
164	25.72931	48.05669	1236.46559	164	38.44005	43.28824	1664.00219	164	57.37384	39.30282	2254.95363
165	26.24390	48.09480	1262.19490	165	39.30495	43.31368	1702.44224	165	58.80819	39.31982	2312.32747
166	26.76878	48.13215	1288.43880	166	40.18931	43.33857	1741.74719	166	60.27839	39.33641	2371.13566
167	27.30415	48.16878	1315.20757	167	41.09357	43.36290	1781.93650	167	61.78535	39.35260	2431.41405
168	27.85023	48.20468	1342.51172	168	42.01818	43.38670	1823.03007	168	63.32999	39.36839	2493.19940
169	28.40724	48.23989	1370.36196	169	42.96359	43.40998	1865.04825	169	64.91323	39.38379	2556.52939
170	28.97538	48.27440	1398.76920	170	43.93027	43.43274	1908.01183	170	66.53607	39.39882	2621.44262
171	29.55489	48.30823	1427.74458	171	44.91870	43.45500	1951.94210	171	68.19947	39.41349	2687.97869
172	30.14599	48.34140	1457.29947	172	45.92937	43.47678	1996.86080	172	69.90445	39.42779	2756.17816
173	30.74891	48.37393	1487.44546	173	46.96278	43.49807	2042.79017	173	71.65207	39.44175	2826.08261
174	31.36389	48.40581	1518.19437	174	48.01944	43.51889	2089.75294	174	73.44337	39.45536	2897.73468
175	31.99117	48.43707	1549.55826	175	49.09988	43.53926	2137.77239	175	75.27945	39.46865	2971.17804
176	32.63099	48.46771	1581.54942	176	50.20463	43.55918	2186.87226	176	77.16144	39.48161	3046.45749
177	33.28361	48.49776	1614.18041	177	51.33423	43.57866	2237.07689	177	79.09047	39.49425	3123.61893
178	33.94928	48.52721	1647.46402	178	52.48925	43.59771	2288.41112	178	81.06774	39.50659	3202.70940
179	34.62827	48.55609	1681.41330	179	53.67026	43.61634	2340.90037	179	83.09443	39.51862	3283.77714
180	35.32083	48.58440	1716.04157	180	54.87784	43.63456	2394.57063	180	85.17179	39.53036	3366.87157
181	36.02725	48.61216	1751.36240	181	56.11259	43.65239	2449.44847	181	87.30108	39.54182	3452.04336
182	36.74779	48.63937	1787.38965	182	57.37512	43.66982	2505.56106	182	89.48361	39.55299	3539.34444
183	37.48275	48.66605	1824.13744	183	58.66606	43.68686	2562.93618	183	91.72070	39.56389	3628.82805
184	38.23240	48.69221	1861.62019	184	59.98605	43.70353	2621.60225	184	94.01372	39.57453	3720.54875
185	38.99705	48.71785	1899.85259	185	61.33574	43.71984	2681.58830	185	96.36406	39.58491	3814.56247
186	39.77699	48.74299	1938.84964	186	62.71579	43.73578	2742.92403	186	98.77316	39.59503	3910.92653
187	40.57253	48.76764	1978.62664	187	64.12690	43.75137	2805.63982	187	101.24249	39.60491	4009.69970
188	41.38398	48.79180	2019.19917	188	65.56975	43.76663	2869.76672	188	103.77355	39.61455	4110.94219
189	42.21166	48.81549	2060.58315	189	67.04507	43.78154	2935.33647	189	106.36789	39.62395	4214.71574
190	43.05590	48.83872	2102.79482	190	68.55358	43.79613	3002.38154	190	109.02709	39.63312	4321.08364
191	43.91701	48.86149	2145.85071	191	70.09604	43.81039	3070.93513	191	111.75277	39.64207	4430.11073
192	44.79535	48.88381	2189.76773	192	71.67320	43.82435	3141.03117	192	114.54659	39.65080	4541.86350
193	45.69126	48.90570	2234.56308	193	73.28585	43.83799	3212.70437	193	117.41025	39.65931	4656.41008
194	46.60509	48.92716	2280.25434	194	74.93478	43.85134	3285.99022	194	120.34551	39.66762	4773.82034
195	47.53719	48.94819	2326.85943	195	76.62081	43.86439	3360.92500	195	123.35415	39.67573	4894.16585
196	48.48793	48.96882	2374.39662	196	78.34478	43.87715	3437.54581	196	126.43800	39.68364	5017.51999
197	49.45769	48.98903	2422.88455	197	80.10754	43.88963	3515.89059	197	129.59895	39.69136	5143.95799
198	50.44684	49.00886	2472.34224	198	81.90996	43.90184	3595.99813	198	132.83892	39.69888	5273.55694
199	51.45578	49.02829	2522.78909	199	83.75293	43.91378	3677.90809	199	136.15990	39.70623	5406.39586
200	52.48490	49.04734	2574.24487	200	85.63737	43.92546	3761.65102	200	139.56389	39.71339	5542.55576

Table I. ANNUITIES (*Continued*)

M	C(11,M, 4)	A(11,M, 4)	S(11,M, 4)	M	C(12,M, 4)	A(12,M, 4)	S(12,M, 4)	M	C(13,M, 4)	A(13,M, 4)	S(13,M, 4)
1	1.02750	.97324	1.00000	1	1.03000	.97087	1.00000	1	1.03250	.96852	1.00000
2	1.05576	1.92042	2.02750	2	1.06090	1.91347	2.03000	2	1.06606	1.90656	2.03250
3	1.08479	2.84226	3.08326	3	1.09273	2.82861	3.09090	3	1.10070	2.81507	3.09856
4	1.11462	3.73943	4.16805	4	1.12551	3.71710	4.18363	4	1.13648	3.69498	4.19926
5	1.14527	4.61258	5.28267	5	1.15927	4.57971	5.30914	5	1.17341	4.54720	5.33574
6	1.17677	5.46237	6.42794	6	1.19405	5.41719	6.46841	6	1.21155	5.37259	6.50915
7	1.20913	6.28941	7.60471	7	1.22987	6.23028	7.66245	7	1.25092	6.17200	7.72069
8	1.24238	7.09431	8.81384	8	1.26677	7.01969	8.89234	8	1.29158	6.94625	8.97162
9	1.27655	7.87768	10.05622	9	1.30477	7.78611	10.15911	9	1.33355	7.69612	10.26319
10	1.31165	8.64008	11.33276	10	1.34392	8.53020	11.46388	10	1.37689	8.42240	11.59675
11	1.34772	9.38207	12.64442	11	1.38423	9.25262	12.80780	11	1.42164	9.12581	12.97364
12	1.38478	10.10420	13.99214	12	1.42576	9.95400	14.19203	12	1.46785	9.80708	14.39529
13	1.42287	10.80701	15.37692	13	1.46853	10.63496	15.61779	13	1.51555	10.46690	15.86313
14	1.46199	11.49101	16.79979	14	1.51259	11.29607	17.08632	14	1.56481	11.10596	17.37868
15	1.50220	12.15670	18.26178	15	1.55797	11.93794	18.59891	15	1.61566	11.72490	18.94349
16	1.54351	12.80457	19.76398	16	1.60471	12.56110	20.15688	16	1.66817	12.32436	20.55915
17	1.58596	13.43511	21.30749	17	1.65285	13.16612	21.76159	17	1.72239	12.90495	22.22733
18	1.62957	14.04877	22.89344	18	1.70243	13.75351	23.41444	18	1.77837	13.46726	23.94972
19	1.67438	14.64600	24.52301	19	1.75351	14.32380	25.11687	19	1.83616	14.01187	25.72808
20	1.72043	15.22725	26.19740	20	1.80611	14.87747	26.87037	20	1.89584	14.53935	27.56424
21	1.76774	15.79295	27.91783	21	1.86029	15.41502	28.67649	21	1.95745	15.05021	29.46008
22	1.81635	16.34350	29.68557	22	1.91610	15.93692	30.53678	22	2.02107	15.54500	31.41753
23	1.86630	16.87932	31.50192	23	1.97359	16.44361	32.45288	23	2.08675	16.02421	33.43860
24	1.91763	17.40080	33.36822	24	2.03279	16.93554	34.42647	24	2.15457	16.48834	35.52536
25	1.97036	17.90832	35.28585	25	2.09378	17.41315	36.45926	25	2.22460	16.93786	37.67993
26	2.02455	18.40226	37.25621	26	2.15659	17.87684	38.55304	26	2.29690	17.37323	39.90453
27	2.08022	18.88297	39.28075	27	2.22129	18.32703	40.70963	27	2.37155	17.79490	42.20143
28	2.13743	19.35083	41.36098	28	2.28793	18.76411	42.93092	28	2.44862	18.20329	44.57297
29	2.19621	19.80616	43.49840	29	2.35657	19.18845	45.21885	29	2.52820	18.59883	47.02160
30	2.25660	20.24930	45.69461	30	2.42726	19.60044	47.57542	30	2.61037	18.98192	49.54980
31	2.31866	20.68059	47.95121	31	2.50008	20.00043	50.00258	31	2.69521	19.35295	52.16017
32	2.38242	21.10033	50.26987	32	2.57508	20.38877	52.50276	32	2.78280	19.71230	54.85537
33	2.44794	21.50883	52.65229	33	2.65234	20.76579	55.07784	33	2.87324	20.06034	57.63817
34	2.51526	21.90641	55.10023	34	2.73191	21.13184	57.73018	34	2.96662	20.39742	60.51141
35	2.58443	22.29334	57.61548	35	2.81386	21.48722	60.46208	35	3.06304	20.72389	63.47803
36	2.65550	22.66992	60.19991	36	2.89828	21.83225	63.27594	36	3.16258	21.04009	66.54107
37	2.72852	23.03642	62.85541	37	2.98523	22.16724	66.17422	37	3.26537	21.34633	69.70365
38	2.80356	23.39311	65.58393	38	3.07478	22.49246	69.15945	38	3.37149	21.64294	72.96902
39	2.88066	23.74025	68.38749	39	3.16703	22.80822	72.23423	39	3.48107	21.93021	76.34052
40	2.95987	24.07810	71.26814	40	3.26204	23.11477	75.40126	40	3.59420	22.20843	79.82158
41	3.04127	24.40691	74.22802	41	3.35990	23.41240	78.66330	41	3.71101	22.47790	83.41578
42	3.12491	24.72692	77.26929	42	3.46070	23.70136	82.02320	42	3.83162	22.73889	87.12680
43	3.21084	25.03837	80.39419	43	3.56452	23.98190	85.48389	43	3.95615	22.99166	90.95842
44	3.29914	25.34148	83.60504	44	3.67145	24.25427	89.04841	44	4.08472	23.23647	94.91457
45	3.38986	25.63647	86.90417	45	3.78160	24.51871	92.71986	45	4.21748	23.47358	98.99929
46	3.48309	25.92357	90.29404	46	3.89504	24.77545	96.50146	46	4.35454	23.70323	103.21677
47	3.57887	26.20299	93.77712	47	4.01190	25.02471	100.39650	47	4.49607	23.92564	107.57131
48	3.67729	26.47493	97.35600	48	4.13225	25.26671	104.40840	48	4.64219	24.14106	112.06738
49	3.77842	26.73959	101.03329	49	4.25622	25.50166	108.54065	49	4.79306	24.34969	116.70957
50	3.88232	26.99717	104.81170	50	4.38391	25.72976	112.79687	50	4.94884	24.55176	121.50263
51	3.98909	27.24785	108.69402	51	4.51542	25.95123	117.18077	51	5.10967	24.74747	126.45147
52	4.09879	27.49183	112.68311	52	4.65089	26.16624	121.69620	52	5.27574	24.93702	131.56114
53	4.21150	27.72927	116.78189	53	4.79041	26.37499	126.34708	53	5.44720	25.12060	136.83688
54	4.32732	27.96036	120.99340	54	4.93412	26.57766	131.13749	54	5.62423	25.29840	142.28407
55	4.44632	28.18527	125.32071	55	5.08215	26.77443	136.07162	55	5.80702	25.47060	147.90831
56	4.56859	28.40415	129.76703	56	5.23461	26.96546	141.15377	56	5.99575	25.63739	153.71533

57	4.69423	28.61718	134.33563	57	5.39165	27.15094	145.38838	57	6.19061	25.79892	159.71107
58	4.82332	28.82451	139.02986	58	5.55340	27.33101	151.78003	58	6.39180	25.95537	165.90168
59	4.95596	29.02629	143.85318	59	5.72000	27.50583	157.33343	59	6.59954	26.10690	172.29349
60	5.09225	29.22266	148.80914	60	5.89160	27.67556	163.05344	60	6.81402	26.25366	178.89303
61	5.23229	29.41378	153.90139	61	6.06835	27.84035	168.94504	61	7.03548	26.39579	185.70705
62	5.37618	29.59979	159.13368	62	6.25040	28.00034	175.01339	62	7.26413	26.53346	192.74253
63	5.52402	29.78082	164.50986	63	6.43791	28.15567	181.26379	63	7.50022	26.66679	200.00666
64	5.67593	29.95700	170.03388	64	6.63105	28.30648	187.70171	64	7.74397	26.79592	207.50688
65	5.83202	30.12847	175.70981	65	6.82998	28.45289	194.33276	65	7.99565	26.92099	215.25085
66	5.99240	30.29534	181.54183	66	7.03488	28.59504	201.16274	66	8.25551	27.04212	223.24650
67	6.15719	30.45776	187.53423	67	7.24593	28.73305	208.19762	67	8.52382	27.15944	231.50202
68	6.32651	30.61582	193.69142	68	7.46331	28.86704	215.44355	68	8.80084	27.27306	240.02583
69	6.50049	30.76966	200.01793	69	7.68721	28.99712	222.90686	69	9.08687	27.38311	248.82667
70	6.67926	30.91937	206.51843	70	7.91782	29.12342	230.59406	70	9.38219	27.48969	257.91354
71	6.86294	31.06508	213.19768	71	8.15536	29.24604	238.51189	71	9.68711	27.59292	267.29573
72	7.05167	31.20689	220.06062	72	8.40002	29.36509	246.66724	72	10.00194	27.69291	276.98284
73	7.24559	31.34491	227.11229	73	8.65202	29.48067	255.06726	73	10.32701	27.78974	286.98478
74	7.44484	31.47923	234.35788	74	8.91158	29.59288	263.71928	74	10.66263	27.88352	297.31179
75	7.64957	31.60996	241.80272	75	9.17893	29.70183	272.63086	75	11.00917	27.97436	307.97442
76	7.85994	31.73718	249.45229	76	9.45429	29.80760	281.80978	76	11.36697	28.06233	318.98359
77	8.07609	31.86101	257.31223	77	9.73792	29.91029	291.26407	77	11.73639	28.14754	330.35056
78	8.29818	31.98151	265.38832	78	10.03006	30.00999	301.00200	78	12.11783	28.23006	342.08695
79	8.52638	32.09880	273.68649	79	10.33096	30.10679	311.03206	79	12.51166	28.30999	354.20477
80	8.76085	32.21294	282.21287	80	10.64089	30.20076	321.36302	80	12.91828	28.38740	366.71643
81	9.00178	32.32403	290.97373	81	10.96012	30.29200	332.00391	81	13.33813	28.46237	379.63471
82	9.24933	32.43215	299.97550	82	11.28892	30.38059	342.96403	82	13.77162	28.53498	392.97284
83	9.50368	32.53737	309.22483	83	11.62759	30.46659	354.25295	83	14.21919	28.60531	406.74446
84	9.76503	32.63977	318.72851	84	11.97642	30.55009	365.88054	84	14.68132	28.67342	420.96365
85	10.03357	32.73944	328.49355	85	12.33571	30.63115	377.85695	85	15.15846	28.73939	435.64497
86	10.30950	32.83644	338.52712	86	12.70578	30.70986	390.19265	86	15.65111	28.80329	450.80343
87	10.59301	32.93084	348.83662	87	13.08695	30.78627	402.89844	87	16.15977	28.86517	466.45455
88	10.88431	33.02272	359.42962	88	13.47956	30.86045	415.98539	88	16.68497	28.92510	482.61432
89	11.18363	33.11213	370.31394	89	13.88395	30.93248	429.46496	89	17.22723	28.98315	499.29928
90	11.49118	33.19915	381.49757	90	14.30047	31.00241	443.34890	90	17.78711	29.03937	516.52651
91	11.80719	33.28385	392.98875	91	14.72948	31.07030	457.64937	91	18.36519	29.09382	534.31362
92	12.13189	33.36628	404.79595	92	15.17137	31.13621	472.37885	92	18.96206	29.14656	552.67881
93	12.46552	33.44650	416.92783	93	15.62651	31.20021	487.55022	93	19.57833	29.19763	571.64088
94	12.80832	33.52457	429.39335	94	16.09530	31.26234	503.17672	94	20.21462	29.24710	591.21920
95	13.16055	33.60056	442.20167	95	16.57816	31.32266	519.27203	95	20.87160	29.29502	611.43383
96	13.52246	33.67451	455.36221	96	17.07551	31.38122	535.85019	96	21.54993	29.34142	632.30543
97	13.89433	33.74648	468.88467	97	17.58777	31.43808	552.92569	97	22.25030	29.38636	653.85535
98	14.27642	33.81653	482.77900	98	18.11540	31.49328	570.51346	98	22.97343	29.42989	676.10565
99	14.66902	33.88470	497.05542	99	18.65887	31.54687	588.62887	99	23.72007	29.47205	699.07909
100	15.07242	33.95104	511.72445	100	19.21863	31.59891	607.28773	100	24.49097	29.51288	722.79916

Table I. ANNUITIES (*Continued*)

M	C(11,M, 4)	A(11,M, 4)	S(11,M, 4)	M	C(12,M, 4)	A(12,M, 4)	S(12,M, 4)	M	C(13,M, 4)	A(13,M, 4)	S(13,M, 4)
101	15.48691	34.01561	526.79687	101	19.79519	31.64942	626.50636	101	25.28693	29.55243	747.29013
102	15.91280	34.07846	542.28378	102	20.38905	31.69847	646.30156	102	26.10875	29.59073	772.57706
103	16.35041	34.13962	558.19659	103	21.00072	31.74609	666.69060	103	26.95729	29.62782	798.68581
104	16.80004	34.19914	574.54700	104	21.63074	31.79232	687.69132	104	27.83340	29.66375	825.64310
105	17.26204	34.25707	591.34704	105	22.27966	31.83720	709.32206	105	28.73799	29.69855	853.47650
106	17.73675	34.31345	608.60908	106	22.94805	31.88078	731.60172	106	29.67197	29.73225	882.21449
107	18.22451	34.36832	626.34583	107	23.63649	31.92308	754.54977	107	30.63631	29.76489	911.88646
108	18.72568	34.42172	644.57034	108	24.34559	31.96416	778.18627	108	31.63199	29.79651	942.52277
109	19.24064	34.47370	663.29603	109	25.07596	32.00404	802.53185	109	32.66003	29.82712	974.15476
110	19.76976	34.52428	682.53667	110	25.82823	32.04276	827.60781	110	33.72148	29.85678	1006.81479
111	20.31343	34.57351	702.30642	111	26.60308	32.08035	853.43604	111	34.81743	29.88550	1040.53627
112	20.87205	34.62142	722.61985	112	27.40117	32.11684	880.03913	112	35.94900	29.91332	1075.35370
113	21.44603	34.66805	743.49190	113	28.22321	32.15227	907.44030	113	37.11734	29.94026	1111.30270
114	22.03579	34.71343	764.93792	114	29.06991	32.18667	935.66351	114	38.32365	29.96635	1148.42003
115	22.64178	34.75759	786.97372	115	29.94200	32.22007	964.73341	115	39.56917	29.99162	1186.74368
116	23.26443	34.80058	809.61549	116	30.84026	32.25250	994.67542	116	40.85517	30.01610	1226.31285
117	23.90420	34.84241	832.87992	117	31.76547	32.28398	1025.51568	117	42.18296	30.03981	1267.16802
118	24.56156	34.88313	856.78412	118	32.71843	32.31454	1057.28115	118	43.55391	30.06277	1309.35098
119	25.23701	34.92275	881.34568	119	33.69999	32.34421	1089.99958	119	44.96941	30.08500	1352.90489
120	25.93102	34.96131	906.58269	120	34.71099	32.37302	1123.69957	120	46.43091	30.10654	1397.87430
121	26.64413	34.99885	932.51371	121	35.75232	32.40099	1158.41056	121	47.93992	30.12740	1444.30521
122	27.37684	35.03537	959.15784	122	36.82489	32.42815	1194.16288	122	49.49797	30.14760	1492.24513
123	28.12970	35.07092	986.53468	123	37.92963	32.45451	1230.98776	123	51.10665	30.16717	1541.74310
124	28.90327	35.10552	1014.66438	124	39.06752	32.48011	1268.91739	124	52.76762	30.18612	1592.84975
125	29.69811	35.13919	1043.56765	125	40.23955	32.50496	1307.98492	125	54.48256	30.20448	1645.61737
126	30.51481	35.17196	1073.26576	126	41.44673	32.52909	1348.22446	126	56.25325	30.22225	1700.09993
127	31.35397	35.20386	1103.78057	127	42.69014	32.55251	1389.67120	127	58.08148	30.23947	1756.35318
128	32.21620	35.23490	1135.13454	128	43.97084	32.57526	1432.35133	128	59.96913	30.25615	1814.43466
129	33.10215	35.26511	1167.35074	129	45.28997	32.59734	1476.33217	129	61.91812	30.27230	1874.40378
130	34.01245	35.29451	1200.45288	130	46.64866	32.61877	1521.62214	130	63.93046	30.28794	1936.32191
131	34.94780	35.32312	1234.46534	131	48.04812	32.63958	1568.27080	131	66.00820	30.30309	2000.25237
132	35.90886	35.35097	1269.41313	132	49.48957	32.65979	1616.31893	132	68.15347	30.31776	2066.26057
133	36.89635	35.37807	1305.32200	133	50.97425	32.67941	1665.80849	133	70.36846	30.33197	2134.41404
134	37.91100	35.40445	1342.21835	134	52.50348	32.69845	1716.78275	134	72.65543	30.34574	2204.78250
135	38.95356	35.43012	1380.12936	135	54.07859	32.71695	1769.28623	135	75.01673	30.35907	2277.43793
136	40.02478	35.45511	1419.08291	136	55.70094	32.73490	1823.36482	136	77.45478	30.37198	2352.45466
137	41.12546	35.47942	1459.10769	137	57.37197	32.75233	1879.06576	137	79.97206	30.38448	2429.90944
138	42.25641	35.50309	1500.23315	138	59.09313	32.76925	1936.43774	138	82.57115	30.39659	2509.88149
139	43.41846	35.52612	1542.48957	139	60.86593	32.78568	1995.53087	139	85.25471	30.40832	2592.45264
140	44.61247	35.54854	1585.90803	140	62.69190	32.80163	2056.39679	140	88.02549	30.41968	2677.70735
141	45.83931	35.57035	1630.52050	141	64.57266	32.81712	2119.08870	141	90.88632	30.43068	2765.73284
142	47.09989	35.59158	1676.35981	142	66.50984	32.83215	2183.66136	142	93.84012	30.44134	2856.61916
143	48.39514	35.61225	1723.45971	143	68.50514	32.84675	2250.17120	143	96.88993	30.45166	2950.45928
144	49.72601	35.63236	1771.85485	144	70.56029	32.86092	2318.67634	144	100.03885	30.46166	3047.34921
145	51.09347	35.65193	1821.58086	145	72.67710	32.87468	2389.23663	145	103.29011	30.47134	3147.38806
146	52.49854	35.67098	1872.67433	146	74.85741	32.88804	2461.91372	146	106.64704	30.48072	3250.67817
147	53.94225	35.68951	1925.17288	147	77.10313	32.90101	2536.77114	147	110.11307	30.48980	3357.32521
148	55.42567	35.70756	1979.11513	148	79.41623	32.91360	2613.87427	148	113.69174	30.49859	3467.43828
149	56.94987	35.72512	2034.54080	149	81.79871	32.92583	2693.29050	149	117.38673	30.50711	3581.13002
150	58.51599	35.74221	2091.49067	150	84.25268	32.93770	2775.08921	150	121.20179	30.51536	3698.51675
151	60.12518	35.75884	2150.00666	151	86.78026	32.94922	2859.34189	151	125.14085	30.52335	3819.71854
152	61.77863	35.77502	2210.13185	152	89.38366	32.96041	2946.12215	152	129.20793	30.53109	3944.85939
153	63.47754	35.79078	2271.91047	153	92.06517	32.97127	3035.50581	153	133.40719	30.53859	4074.06732
154	65.22317	35.80611	2335.38801	154	94.82713	32.98182	3127.57099	154	137.74292	30.54585	4207.47451
155	67.01681	35.82103	2400.61118	155	97.67194	32.99205	3222.39812	155	142.21957	30.55288	4345.21743
156	68.85977	35.83555	2467.62799	156	100.60210	33.00199	3320.07006	156	146.84170	30.55969	4487.43700
157	70.75341	35.84969	2536.48776	157	103.62016	33.01165	3420.67216	157	151.61406	30.56629	4634.27870
158	72.69913	35.86344	2607.24117	158	106.72877	33.02102	3524.29233	158	156.54151	30.57267	4785.89276
159	74.69836	35.87683	2679.94030	159	109.93063	33.03011	3631.02109	159	161.62911	30.57886	4942.43428

161	78.86326	35.90254	2831.39122	161	116.62541	33.04752	3854.18028	161	172.30573	30.59066	5270.94545
162	81.03200	35.91488	2910.25448	162	120.12417	33.05584	3970.80569	162	177.90566	30.59628	5443.25118
163	83.26038	35.92689	2991.28648	163	123.72790	33.06392	4090.92985	163	183.68760	30.60172	5621.15684
164	85.55004	35.93858	3074.54686	164	127.43973	33.07177	4214.65775	164	189.65744	30.60699	5804.84444
165	87.90266	35.94996	3160.09690	165	131.26292	33.07939	4342.09749	165	195.82131	30.61210	5994.50188
166	90.31999	35.96103	3247.99956	166	135.20081	33.08679	4473.36041	166	202.18550	30.61705	6190.32319
167	92.80379	35.97180	3338.31955	167	139.25684	33.09397	4608.56122	167	208.75653	30.62184	6392.50870
168	95.35589	35.98229	3431.12334	168	143.43454	33.10094	4747.81806	168	215.54112	30.62648	6601.26523
169	97.97818	35.99250	3526.47923	169	147.73758	33.10771	4891.25260	169	222.54621	30.63097	6816.80635
170	100.67258	36.00243	3624.45741	170	152.16971	33.11428	5038.99018	170	229.77896	30.63532	7039.35256
171	103.44107	36.01210	3725.12999	171	156.73480	33.12066	5191.15989	171	237.24677	30.63954	7269.13151
172	106.28570	36.02151	3828.57106	172	161.43684	33.12685	5347.89468	172	244.95729	30.64362	7506.37829
173	109.20856	36.03066	3934.85677	173	166.27995	33.13287	5509.33152	173	252.91841	30.64757	7751.33558
174	112.21180	36.03957	4044.06533	174	171.26834	33.13871	5675.61147	174	261.13825	30.65140	8004.25399
175	115.29762	36.04825	4156.27712	175	176.40639	33.14438	5846.87981	175	269.62525	30.65511	8265.39224
176	118.46831	36.05669	4271.57474	176	181.69859	33.14988	6023.28621	176	278.38807	30.65870	8535.01749
177	121.72618	36.06490	4390.04305	177	187.14954	33.15522	6204.98479	177	287.43568	30.66218	8813.40556
178	125.07365	36.07290	4511.76923	178	192.76403	33.16041	6392.13434	178	296.77734	30.66555	9100.84124
179	128.51318	36.08068	4636.84289	179	198.54695	33.16545	6584.89837	179	306.42260	30.66882	9397.61858
180	132.04729	36.08825	4765.35607	180	204.50336	33.17034	6783.44532	180	316.38134	30.67198	9704.04119
181	135.67859	36.09562	4897.40336	181	210.63846	33.17508	6987.94868	181	326.66373	30.67504	10020.42252
182	139.40975	36.10280	5033.08195	182	216.95761	33.17969	7198.58714	182	337.28030	30.67800	10347.08626
183	143.24352	36.10978	5172.49170	183	223.46634	33.18417	7415.54475	183	348.24191	30.68087	10684.36656
184	147.18272	36.11657	5315.73523	184	230.17033	33.18851	7639.01110	184	359.55978	30.68366	11032.60847
185	151.23024	36.12318	5462.91795	185	237.07544	33.19273	7869.18143	185	371.24547	30.68635	11392.16825
186	155.38908	36.12962	5614.14819	186	244.18771	33.19683	8106.25687	186	383.31095	30.68896	11763.41372
187	159.66227	36.13588	5769.53726	187	251.51334	33.20080	8350.44458	187	395.76855	30.69149	12146.72466
188	164.05299	36.14198	5929.19954	188	259.05874	33.20466	8601.95791	188	408.63103	30.69393	12542.49321
189	168.56444	36.14791	6093.25253	189	266.83050	33.20841	8861.01665	189	421.91154	30.69630	12951.12424
190	173.19997	36.15368	6261.81697	190	274.83541	33.21205	9127.84715	190	435.62366	30.69860	13373.03578
191	177.96297	36.15930	6435.01694	191	283.08048	33.21558	9402.68257	191	449.78143	30.70082	13808.65944
192	182.85695	36.16477	6612.97990	192	291.57289	33.21901	9685.76304	192	464.39933	30.70297	14258.44088
193	187.88551	36.17009	6795.83685	193	300.32008	33.22234	9977.33593	193	479.49231	30.70506	14722.84020
194	193.05236	36.17527	6983.72236	194	309.32968	33.22557	10277.65601	194	495.07581	30.70708	15202.33251
195	198.36131	36.18032	7176.77473	195	318.60957	33.22871	10586.98569	195	511.16577	30.70904	15697.40832
196	203.81624	36.18522	7375.13603	196	328.16786	33.23176	10905.59525	196	527.77866	30.71093	16208.57409
197	209.42119	36.19000	7578.95227	197	338.01289	33.23472	11233.75312	197	544.93146	30.71277	16736.35275
198	215.18027	36.19464	7788.37346	198	348.15328	33.23759	11571.77601	198	562.64174	30.71454	17281.28421
199	221.09773	36.19917	8003.55373	199	358.59788	33.24038	11919.92929	199	580.92759	30.71627	17843.92595
200	227.17792	36.20357	8224.65146	200	369.35582	33.24309	12278.52717	200	599.80774	30.71793	18424.85354

Table I. ANNUITIES (*Continued*)

M	C(14,M, 4)	A(14,M, 4)	S(14,M, 4)	M	C(15,M, 4)	A(15,M, 4)	S(15,M, 4)	M	C(16,M, 4)	A(16,M, 4)	S(16,M, 4)
1	1.03500	.96618	1.00000	1	1.03750	.96386	1.00000	1	1.04000	.96154	1.00000
2	1.07123	1.89969	2.03500	2	1.07641	1.89287	2.03750	2	1.08160	1.88609	2.04000
3	1.10872	2.80164	3.10622	3	1.11677	2.78831	3.11391	3	1.12486	2.77509	3.12160
4	1.14752	3.67308	4.21494	4	1.15865	3.65138	4.23068	4	1.16986	3.62990	4.24646
5	1.18769	4.51505	5.36247	5	1.20210	4.48326	5.38933	5	1.21665	4.45182	5.41632
6	1.22926	5.32855	6.55015	6	1.24718	5.28507	6.59143	6	1.26532	5.24214	6.63298
7	1.27228	6.11454	7.77941	7	1.29395	6.05790	7.83861	7	1.31593	6.00205	7.89829
8	1.31681	6.87396	9.05169	8	1.34247	6.80280	9.13255	8	1.36857	6.73274	9.21423
9	1.36290	7.60769	10.36850	9	1.39281	7.52077	10.47503	9	1.42331	7.43533	10.58280
10	1.41060	8.31661	11.73139	10	1.44504	8.21279	11.86784	10	1.48024	8.11090	12.00611
11	1.45997	9.00155	13.14199	11	1.49923	8.87979	13.31288	11	1.53945	8.76048	13.48635
12	1.51107	9.66333	14.60196	12	1.55545	9.52269	14.81212	12	1.60103	9.38507	15.02581
13	1.56396	10.30274	16.11303	13	1.61378	10.14236	16.36757	13	1.66507	9.98565	16.62684
14	1.61869	10.92052	17.67699	14	1.67430	10.73962	17.98135	14	1.73168	10.56312	18.29191
15	1.67535	11.51741	19.29568	15	1.73709	11.31530	19.65565	15	1.80094	11.11839	20.02359
16	1.73399	12.09412	20.97103	16	1.80223	11.87017	21.39274	16	1.87298	11.65230	21.82453
17	1.79468	12.65132	22.70502	17	1.86981	12.40498	23.19497	17	1.94790	12.16567	23.69751
18	1.85749	13.18968	24.49969	18	1.93993	12.92046	25.06478	18	2.02582	12.65930	25.64541
19	1.92250	13.70984	26.35718	19	2.01268	13.41731	27.00471	19	2.10685	13.13394	27.67123
20	1.98979	14.21240	28.27968	20	2.08815	13.89620	29.01739	20	2.19112	13.59033	29.77808
21	2.05943	14.69797	30.26947	21	2.16646	14.35779	31.10554	21	2.27877	14.02916	31.96920
22	2.13151	15.16712	32.32890	22	2.24770	14.80269	33.27200	22	2.36992	14.45112	34.24797
23	2.20611	15.62041	34.46041	23	2.33199	15.23151	35.51970	23	2.46472	14.85684	36.61789
24	2.28333	16.05837	36.66653	24	2.41944	15.64482	37.85168	24	2.56330	15.24696	39.08260
25	2.36324	16.48151	38.94986	25	2.51017	16.04320	40.27112	25	2.66584	15.62208	41.64591
26	2.44596	16.89035	41.31310	26	2.60430	16.42718	42.78129	26	2.77247	15.98277	44.31174
27	2.53157	17.28536	43.75906	27	2.70196	16.79729	45.38559	27	2.88337	16.32959	47.08421
28	2.62017	17.66702	46.29063	28	2.80328	17.15401	48.08755	28	2.99870	16.66306	49.96758
29	2.71188	18.03577	48.91080	29	2.90841	17.49784	50.89083	29	3.11865	16.98371	52.96629
30	2.80679	18.39205	51.62268	30	3.01747	17.82925	53.79924	30	3.24340	17.29203	56.08494
31	2.90503	18.73628	54.42947	31	3.13063	18.14867	56.81671	31	3.37313	17.58849	59.32834
32	3.00671	19.06887	57.33450	32	3.24803	18.45655	59.94734	32	3.50806	17.87355	62.70147
33	3.11194	19.39021	60.34121	33	3.36983	18.75330	63.19536	33	3.64838	18.14765	66.20953
34	3.22086	19.70068	63.45315	34	3.49619	19.03933	66.56519	34	3.79432	18.41120	69.85791
35	3.33359	20.00066	66.67401	35	3.62730	19.31501	70.06138	35	3.94609	18.66461	73.65222
36	3.45027	20.29049	70.00760	36	3.76333	19.58074	73.68868	36	4.10393	18.90828	77.59831
37	3.57103	20.57053	73.45787	37	3.90445	19.83685	77.45201	37	4.26809	19.14258	81.70225
38	3.69601	20.84109	77.02889	38	4.05087	20.08371	81.35646	38	4.43881	19.36786	85.97034
39	3.82537	21.10250	80.72491	39	4.20277	20.32165	85.40733	39	4.61637	19.58448	90.40915
40	3.95926	21.35507	84.55028	40	4.36038	20.55099	89.61010	40	4.80102	19.79277	95.02552
41	4.09783	21.59910	88.50954	41	4.52389	20.77204	93.97048	41	4.99306	19.99305	99.82654
42	4.24126	21.83488	92.60737	42	4.69354	20.98510	98.49437	42	5.19278	20.18563	104.81960
43	4.38970	22.06269	96.84863	43	4.86955	21.19046	103.18791	43	5.40050	20.37079	110.01238
44	4.54334	22.28279	101.23833	44	5.05215	21.38839	108.05746	44	5.61652	20.54884	115.41288
45	4.70236	22.49545	105.78167	45	5.24161	21.57917	113.10961	45	5.84118	20.72004	121.02939
46	4.86694	22.70092	110.48403	46	5.43817	21.76306	118.35122	46	6.07482	20.88465	126.87057
47	5.03728	22.89944	115.35097	47	5.64210	21.94030	123.78939	47	6.31782	21.04294	132.94539
48	5.21359	23.09124	120.38826	48	5.85368	22.11113	129.43150	48	6.57053	21.19513	139.26321
49	5.39606	23.27656	125.60185	49	6.07319	22.27579	135.28518	49	6.83335	21.34147	145.83373
50	5.58493	23.45562	130.99791	50	6.30094	22.43449	141.35837	50	7.10668	21.48218	152.66708
51	5.78040	23.62862	136.58284	51	6.53722	22.58746	147.65931	51	7.39095	21.61749	159.77377
52	5.98271	23.79576	142.36324	52	6.78237	22.73490	154.19653	52	7.68659	21.74758	167.16472
53	6.19211	23.95726	148.34595	53	7.03671	22.87702	160.97890	53	7.99405	21.87267	174.85131
54	6.40883	24.11330	154.53806	54	7.30059	23.01399	168.01561	54	8.31381	21.99296	182.84536
55	6.63314	24.26405	160.94689	55	7.57436	23.14602	175.31620	55	8.64637	22.10861	191.15917
56	6.86530	24.40971	167.58003	56	7.85840	23.27327	182.89055	56	8.99222	22.21982	199.80554

57	7.10559	24.55045	174.44533	57	8.15309	23.39592	190.74895	57	9.35191	22.32675	208.79776
58	7.35428	24.68642	181.55092	58	8.45883	23.51414	198.90204	58	9.72599	22.42957	218.14967
59	7.61168	24.81780	188.90520	59	8.77603	23.62809	207.36086	59	10.11503	22.52843	227.87566
60	7.87809	24.94473	196.51688	60	9.10513	23.73792	216.13690	60	10.51963	22.62349	237.99069
61	8.15382	25.06738	204.39497	61	9.44658	23.84377	225.24203	61	10.94041	22.71489	248.51031
62	8.43921	25.18587	212.54880	62	9.80082	23.94581	234.68861	62	11.37803	22.80278	259.45073
63	8.73458	25.30036	220.98801	63	10.16835	24.04415	244.48943	63	11.83315	22.88729	270.82875
64	9.04029	25.41097	229.72259	64	10.54967	24.13894	254.65778	64	12.30648	22.96855	282.66190
65	9.35670	25.51785	238.76288	65	10.94528	24.23030	265.20745	65	12.79874	23.04668	294.96838
66	9.68419	25.62111	248.11958	66	11.35573	24.31837	276.15273	66	13.31068	23.12181	307.76712
67	10.02313	25.72088	257.80376	67	11.78157	24.40324	287.50846	67	13.84311	23.19405	321.07780
68	10.37394	25.81727	267.82689	68	12.22338	24.48505	299.29002	68	14.39684	23.26351	334.92091
69	10.73703	25.91041	278.20084	69	12.68175	24.56391	311.51340	69	14.97271	23.33030	349.31775
70	11.11283	26.00040	288.93786	70	13.15732	24.63991	324.19515	70	15.57162	23.39451	364.29046
71	11.50177	26.08734	300.05069	71	13.65072	24.71317	337.35247	71	16.19448	23.45626	379.86208
72	11.90434	26.17134	311.55246	72	14.16262	24.78378	351.00319	72	16.84226	23.51564	396.05656
73	12.32099	26.25251	323.45680	73	14.69372	24.85183	365.16581	73	17.51595	23.57273	412.89882
74	12.75222	26.33092	335.77779	74	15.24473	24.91743	379.85952	74	18.21659	23.62762	430.41478
75	13.19855	26.40669	348.53001	75	15.81641	24.98065	395.10426	75	18.94525	23.68041	448.63137
76	13.66050	26.47989	361.72856	76	16.40952	25.04159	410.92067	76	19.70306	23.73116	467.57662
77	14.13862	26.55062	375.38906	77	17.02488	25.10033	427.33019	77	20.49119	23.77996	487.27969
78	14.63347	26.61896	389.52768	78	17.66332	25.15695	444.35507	78	21.31083	23.82689	507.77087
79	15.14564	26.68498	404.16115	79	18.32569	25.21151	462.01839	79	22.16327	23.87201	529.08171
80	15.67574	26.74878	419.30679	80	19.01290	25.26411	480.34408	80	23.04980	23.91539	551.24498
81	16.22439	26.81041	434.98252	81	19.72589	25.31481	499.35698	81	23.97179	23.95711	574.29478
82	16.79224	26.86996	451.20691	82	20.46561	25.36367	519.08287	82	24.93066	23.99722	598.26657
83	17.37997	26.92750	467.99915	83	21.23307	25.41076	539.54848	83	25.92789	24.03579	623.19723
84	17.98827	26.98309	485.37913	84	22.02931	25.45616	560.78154	84	26.96500	24.07287	649.12512
85	18.61786	27.03680	503.36739	85	22.85541	25.49991	582.81085	85	28.04360	24.10853	676.09012
86	19.26948	27.08870	521.98525	86	23.71248	25.54208	605.66626	86	29.16535	24.14282	704.13373
87	19.94392	27.13884	541.25474	87	24.60170	25.58273	629.37874	87	30.33196	24.17579	733.29908
88	20.64195	27.18728	561.19865	88	25.52427	25.62191	653.98045	88	31.54524	24.20749	763.63104
89	21.36442	27.23409	581.84061	89	26.48143	25.65967	679.50471	89	32.80705	24.23797	795.17628
90	22.11218	27.27932	603.20503	90	27.47448	25.69607	705.98614	90	34.11933	24.26728	827.98333
91	22.88610	27.32301	625.31720	91	28.50477	25.73115	733.46062	91	35.48411	24.29546	862.10267
92	23.68712	27.36523	648.20331	92	29.57370	25.76496	761.96539	92	36.90347	24.32256	897.58677
93	24.51616	27.40602	671.89042	93	30.68272	25.79756	791.53909	93	38.37961	24.34861	934.49024
94	25.37423	27.44543	696.40659	94	31.83332	25.82897	822.22181	94	39.91479	24.37367	972.86985
95	26.26233	27.48350	721.78082	95	33.02707	25.85925	854.05513	95	41.51139	24.39776	1012.78465
96	27.18151	27.52029	748.04314	96	34.26558	25.88843	887.08220	96	43.17184	24.42092	1054.29603
97	28.13286	27.55584	775.22465	97	35.55054	25.91656	921.34778	97	44.89872	24.44319	1097.46788
98	29.11751	27.59018	803.35752	98	36.88369	25.94367	956.89832	98	46.69466	24.46461	1142.36659
99	30.13663	27.62337	832.47503	99	38.26683	25.96981	993.78201	99	48.56245	24.48520	1189.06125
100	31.19141	27.65543	862.61166	100	39.70183	25.99499	1032.04883	100	50.50495	24.50500	1237.62370

Table I. ANNUITIES (*Continued*)

M	C(14,M, 4)	A(14,M, 4)	S(14,M, 4)	M	C(15,M, 4)	A(15,M, 4)	S(15,M, 4)	M	C(16,M, 4)	A(16,M, 4)	S(16,M, 4)
101	32.28311	27.68640	893.80306	101	41.19065	26.01927	1071.75066	101	52.52515	24.52404	1288.12865
102	33.41302	27.71633	926.08617	102	42.73530	26.04267	1112.94131	102	54.62615	24.54234	1340.65380
103	34.58247	27.74525	959.49919	103	44.33787	26.06522	1155.67661	103	56.81120	24.55995	1395.27995
104	35.79286	27.77318	994.08166	104	46.00054	26.08696	1200.01448	104	59.08365	24.57687	1452.09115
105	37.04561	27.80018	1029.87452	105	47.72556	26.10792	1246.01503	105	61.44699	24.59315	1511.17479
106	38.34220	27.82626	1066.92013	106	49.51527	26.12811	1293.74059	106	63.90487	24.60879	1572.62179
107	39.68418	27.85146	1105.26233	107	51.37209	26.14758	1343.25586	107	66.46107	24.62384	1636.52666
108	41.07313	27.87581	1144.94651	108	53.29855	26.16634	1394.62795	108	69.11951	24.63831	1702.98772
109	42.51069	27.89933	1186.01964	109	55.29724	26.18442	1447.92651	109	71.88429	24.65222	1772.10723
110	43.99856	27.92206	1228.53033	110	57.37089	26.20185	1503.22375	110	74.75966	24.66560	1843.99152
111	45.53851	27.94402	1272.52889	111	59.52230	26.21866	1560.59464	111	77.75005	24.67846	1918.75118
112	47.13236	27.96523	1318.06740	112	61.75439	26.23485	1620.11694	112	80.86005	24.69082	1996.50123
113	48.78199	27.98573	1365.19976	113	64.07017	26.25046	1681.87133	113	84.09445	24.70272	2077.36128
114	50.48936	28.00554	1413.98175	114	66.47281	26.26550	1745.94150	114	87.45823	24.71415	2161.45573
115	52.25649	28.02467	1464.47111	115	68.96554	26.28000	1812.41431	115	90.95656	24.72514	2248.91396
116	54.08547	28.04316	1516.72760	116	71.55174	26.29398	1881.37984	116	94.59482	24.73571	2339.87052
117	55.97846	28.06103	1570.81307	117	74.23493	26.30745	1952.93159	117	98.37861	24.74588	2434.46534
118	57.93770	28.07829	1626.79152	118	77.01874	26.32043	2027.16652	118	102.31376	24.75565	2532.84395
119	59.96552	28.09496	1684.72923	119	79.90695	26.33295	2104.18527	119	106.40631	24.76505	2635.15771
120	62.06432	28.11108	1744.69475	120	82.90345	26.34501	2184.09221	120	110.66256	24.77409	2741.56402
121	64.23657	28.12664	1806.75907	121	86.01234	26.35663	2266.99567	121	115.08906	24.78278	2852.22658
122	66.48485	28.14169	1870.99563	122	89.23780	26.36784	2353.00801	122	119.69263	24.79113	2967.31564
123	68.81182	28.15622	1937.48048	123	92.58422	26.37864	2442.24581	123	124.48033	24.79917	3087.00827
124	71.22023	28.17026	2006.29230	124	96.05613	26.38905	2534.83003	124	129.45954	24.80689	3211.48860
125	73.71294	28.18382	2077.51253	125	99.65823	26.39909	2630.88615	125	134.63793	24.81432	3340.94814
126	76.29289	28.19693	2151.22547	126	103.39541	26.40876	2730.54439	126	140.02344	24.82146	3475.58607
127	78.96314	28.20960	2227.51836	127	107.27274	26.41808	2833.93980	127	145.62438	24.82833	3615.60951
128	81.72685	28.22183	2306.48150	128	111.29547	26.42706	2941.21254	128	151.44936	24.83493	3761.23389
129	84.58729	28.23365	2388.20835	129	115.46905	26.43572	3052.50801	129	157.50733	24.84128	3912.68325
130	87.54785	28.24508	2472.79564	130	119.79914	26.44407	3167.97706	130	163.80762	24.84738	4070.19058
131	90.61202	28.25611	2560.34349	131	124.29161	26.45212	3287.77620	131	170.35993	24.85325	4233.99820
132	93.78344	28.26678	2650.95551	132	128.95254	26.45987	3412.06781	132	177.17433	24.85890	4404.35813
133	97.06586	28.27708	2744.73896	133	133.78826	26.46735	3541.02035	133	184.26130	24.86432	4581.53246
134	100.46317	28.28703	2841.80482	134	138.80532	26.47455	3674.80862	134	191.63175	24.86954	4765.79375
135	103.97938	28.29665	2942.26799	135	144.01052	26.48150	3813.61394	135	199.29702	24.87456	4957.42550
136	107.61866	28.30594	3046.24737	136	149.41092	26.48819	3957.62445	136	207.26890	24.87938	5156.72252
137	111.38531	28.31492	3153.86603	137	155.01383	26.49464	4107.03538	137	215.55966	24.88402	5363.99143
138	115.28380	28.32359	3265.25134	138	160.82685	26.50086	4262.04921	138	224.18204	24.88848	5579.55108
139	119.31873	28.33197	3380.53514	139	166.85785	26.50685	4422.87605	139	233.14933	24.89277	5803.73313
140	123.49489	28.34007	3499.85386	140	173.11502	26.51263	4589.73390	140	242.47530	24.89690	6036.88245
141	127.81721	28.34790	3623.34875	141	179.60683	26.51819	4762.84893	141	252.17431	24.90086	6279.35775
142	132.29081	28.35545	3751.16596	142	186.34209	26.52356	4942.45576	142	262.26128	24.90468	6531.53206
143	136.92099	28.36276	3883.45676	143	193.32992	26.52873	5128.79785	143	272.75173	24.90834	6793.79334
144	141.71322	28.36981	4020.37775	144	200.57979	26.53372	5322.12777	144	283.66180	24.91187	7066.54508
145	146.67318	28.37663	4162.09097	145	208.10153	26.53852	5522.70756	145	295.00828	24.91526	7350.20688
146	151.80675	28.38322	4308.76415	146	215.90534	26.54316	5730.80910	146	306.80861	24.91852	7645.21515
147	157.11998	28.38958	4460.57090	147	224.00179	26.54762	5946.71444	147	319.08095	24.92165	7952.02376
148	162.61918	28.39573	4617.69088	148	232.40186	26.55192	6170.71623	148	331.84419	24.92466	8271.10471
149	168.31085	28.40167	4780.31007	149	241.11693	26.55607	6403.11809	149	345.11796	24.92756	8602.94890
150	174.20173	28.40742	4948.62092	150	250.15881	26.56007	6644.23501	150	358.92267	24.93035	8948.06685
151	180.29879	28.41296	5122.82265	151	259.53977	26.56392	6894.39383	151	373.27958	24.93303	9306.98953
152	186.60925	28.41832	5303.12144	152	269.27251	26.56763	7153.93360	152	388.21076	24.93560	9680.26911
153	193.14057	28.42350	5489.73069	153	279.37023	26.57121	7423.20611	153	403.73919	24.93808	10068.47987
154	199.90049	28.42850	5682.87127	154	289.84661	26.57466	7702.57634	154	419.88876	24.94046	10472.21907
155	206.89701	28.43333	5882.77176	155	300.71586	26.57799	7992.42295	155	436.68431	24.94275	10892.10783
156	214.13841	28.43800	6089.66877	156	311.99271	26.58119	8293.13881	156	454.15169	24.94495	11328.79214
157	221.63325	28.44252	6303.80718	157	323.69243	26.58428	8605.13151	157	472.31775	24.94707	11782.94383
158	229.39042	28.44687	6525.44043	158	335.83090	26.58726	8928.82395	158	491.21046	24.94911	12255.26158
159	[illegible]	[illegible]	[illegible]	159	[illegible]	[illegible]	[illegible]	159	510.85888	24.95106	12746.47205

161	254.32925	28.45909	7237.97867	161	375.04637	26.59556	9974.56988	161	552.54497	24.95475	13788.62417
162	263.23078	28.46289	7492.30793	162	389.11061	26.59813	10349.61625	162	574.64677	24.95650	14341.16913
163	272.44385	28.46656	7755.53870	163	403.70226	26.60061	10738.72685	163	597.63264	24.95817	14915.81590
164	281.97939	28.47010	8027.98256	164	418.84109	26.60300	11142.42911	164	621.53794	24.95978	15513.44853
165	291.84867	28.47353	8309.96195	165	434.54763	26.60530	11561.27021	165	646.39946	24.96132	16134.98648
166	302.06337	28.47684	8601.81062	166	450.84317	26.60752	11995.81784	166	672.25544	24.96281	16781.38593
167	312.63559	28.48004	8903.87399	167	467.74979	26.60966	12446.66101	167	699.14565	24.96424	17453.64137
168	323.57784	28.48313	9216.50958	168	485.29040	26.61172	12914.41080	168	727.11148	24.96562	18152.78703
169	334.90306	28.48612	9540.08741	169	503.48880	26.61370	13399.70120	169	756.19594	24.96694	18879.89851
170	346.62467	28.48900	9874.99047	170	522.36962	26.61562	13903.19000	170	786.44378	24.96821	19636.09445
171	358.75653	28.49179	10221.61514	171	541.95849	26.61746	14425.55962	171	817.90153	24.96943	20422.53823
172	371.31301	28.49448	10580.37167	172	562.28193	26.61924	14967.51811	172	850.61759	24.97061	21240.43976
173	384.30896	28.49708	10951.68468	173	583.36750	26.62096	15529.80004	173	884.64229	24.97174	22091.05735
174	397.75978	28.49960	11335.99364	174	605.24378	26.62261	16113.16754	174	920.02799	24.97283	22975.69964
175	411.68137	28.50203	11733.75342	175	627.94042	26.62420	16718.41132	175	956.82910	24.97387	23895.72762
176	426.09022	28.50437	12145.43479	176	651.48819	26.62573	17346.35174	176	995.10227	24.97488	24852.55673
177	441.00338	28.50664	12571.52501	177	675.91900	26.62721	17997.83993	177	1034.90636	24.97584	25847.65900
178	456.43849	28.50883	13012.52838	178	701.26596	26.62864	18673.75893	178	1076.30261	24.97677	26882.56536
179	472.41384	28.51095	13468.96687	179	727.56343	26.63001	19375.02489	179	1119.35472	24.97767	27958.86797
180	488.94833	28.51299	13941.38072	180	754.84706	26.63134	20102.58832	180	1164.12891	24.97852	29078.22269
181	506.06152	28.51497	14430.32904	181	783.15383	26.63262	20857.43539	181	1210.69406	24.97935	30242.35160
182	523.77367	28.51688	14936.39056	182	812.52210	26.63385	21640.58921	182	1259.12183	24.98014	31453.04566
183	542.10575	28.51872	15460.16423	183	842.99167	26.63503	22453.11131	183	1309.48670	24.98091	32712.16749
184	561.07945	28.52051	16002.26997	184	874.60386	26.63618	23296.10298	184	1361.86617	24.98164	34021.65419
185	580.71723	28.52223	16563.34942	185	907.40151	26.63728	24170.70685	185	1416.34081	24.98235	35383.52036
186	601.04233	28.52389	17144.06665	186	941.42906	26.63834	25078.10835	186	1472.99445	24.98303	36799.86117
187	622.07881	28.52550	17745.10899	187	976.73265	26.63936	26019.53742	187	1531.91422	24.98368	38272.85562
188	643.85157	28.52705	18367.18780	188	1013.36013	26.64035	26996.27007	188	1593.19079	24.98431	39804.76984
189	666.38638	28.52855	19011.03937	189	1051.36113	26.64130	28009.63020	189	1656.91843	24.98491	41397.96064
190	689.70990	28.53000	19677.42575	190	1090.78717	26.64222	29060.99133	190	1723.19516	24.98549	43054.87906
191	713.84975	28.53140	20367.13565	191	1131.69169	26.64310	30151.77850	191	1792.12297	24.98605	44778.07423
192	738.83449	28.53276	21080.98540	192	1174.13013	26.64395	31283.47020	192	1863.80789	24.98659	46570.19719
193	764.69370	28.53407	21819.81989	193	1218.16001	26.64478	32457.60033	193	1938.36020	24.98710	48434.00508
194	791.45798	28.53533	22584.51359	194	1263.84101	26.64557	33675.76034	194	2015.89461	24.98760	50372.36529
195	819.15900	28.53655	23375.97156	195	1311.23505	26.64633	34939.60135	195	2096.53040	24.98808	52388.25990
196	847.82957	28.53773	24195.13057	196	1360.40637	26.64706	36250.83541	196	2180.39161	24.98853	54484.79029
197	877.50360	28.53887	25042.96014	197	1411.42160	26.64777	37611.24277	197	2267.60728	24.98898	56665.18190
198	908.21623	28.53997	25920.46374	198	1464.34991	26.64846	39022.66437	198	2358.31157	24.98940	58932.78918
199	940.00380	28.54103	26828.67997	199	1519.26304	26.64911	40487.01429	199	2452.64403	24.98981	61291.10075
200	972.90393	28.54206	27758.68377	200	1576.23540	26.64975	42006.27732	200	2550.74979	24.99020	63743.74478

Table I. ANNUITIES (*Continued*)

M	C(5,M,12)	A(5,M,12)	S(5,M,12)	M	C(6,M,12)	A(6,M,12)	S(6,M,12)	M	C(7,M,12)	A(7,M,12)	S(7,M,12)
1	1.00417	.99585	1.00000	1	1.00500	.99502	1.00000	1	1.00583	.99420	1.00000
2	1.00835	1.98757	2.00417	2	1.01003	1.98510	2.00500	2	1.01170	1.98264	2.00583
3	1.01255	2.97517	3.01252	3	1.01508	2.97025	3.01502	3	1.01760	2.96534	3.01753
4	1.01677	3.95868	4.02507	4	1.02015	3.95050	4.03010	4	1.02354	3.94234	4.03514
5	1.02101	4.93810	5.04184	5	1.02525	4.92587	5.05025	5	1.02951	4.91368	5.05867
6	1.02526	5.91346	6.06285	6	1.03038	5.89638	6.07550	6	1.03551	5.87938	6.08818
7	1.02953	6.88478	7.08811	7	1.03553	6.86207	7.10588	7	1.04155	6.83948	7.12370
8	1.03382	7.85206	8.11764	8	1.04071	7.82296	8.14141	8	1.04763	7.79402	8.16525
9	1.03813	8.81533	9.15147	9	1.04591	8.77906	9.18212	9	1.05374	8.74302	9.21288
10	1.04246	9.77460	10.18960	10	1.05114	9.73041	10.22803	10	1.05989	9.68651	10.26663
11	1.04680	10.72989	11.23206	11	1.05640	10.67703	11.27917	11	1.06607	10.62454	11.32651
12	1.05116	11.68122	12.27886	12	1.06168	11.61893	12.33556	12	1.07229	11.55712	12.39259
13	1.05554	12.62850	13.33002	13	1.06699	12.55615	13.39724	13	1.07855	12.48430	13.46488
14	1.05994	13.57205	14.38556	14	1.07232	13.48871	14.46423	14	1.08484	13.40609	14.54342
15	1.06436	14.51159	15.44550	15	1.07768	14.41652	15.53655	15	1.09116	14.32254	15.62826
16	1.06879	15.44722	16.50986	16	1.08307	15.33993	16.61423	16	1.09753	15.23368	16.71942
17	1.07324	16.37898	17.57865	17	1.08849	16.25863	17.69730	17	1.10393	16.13953	17.81695
18	1.07772	17.30687	18.65189	18	1.09393	17.17277	18.78579	18	1.11037	17.04013	18.92088
19	1.08221	18.23090	19.72961	19	1.09940	18.08236	19.87972	19	1.11685	17.93551	20.03126
20	1.08672	19.15111	20.81181	20	1.10490	18.98742	20.97912	20	1.12336	18.82569	21.14810
21	1.09124	20.06749	21.89853	21	1.11042	19.88798	22.08401	21	1.12992	19.71071	22.27147
22	1.09579	20.98008	22.98977	22	1.11597	20.78406	23.19443	22	1.13651	20.59060	23.40139
23	1.10036	21.88887	24.08556	23	1.12155	21.67568	24.31040	23	1.14314	21.46539	24.53789
24	1.10494	22.79390	25.18592	24	1.12716	22.56287	25.43196	24	1.14981	22.33510	25.68103
25	1.10955	23.69517	26.29086	25	1.13280	23.44564	26.55912	25	1.15651	23.19977	26.83084
26	1.11417	24.59270	27.40041	26	1.13846	24.32402	27.69191	26	1.16326	24.05942	27.98735
27	1.11881	25.48651	28.51458	27	1.14415	25.19803	28.83037	27	1.17005	24.91409	29.15061
28	1.12347	26.37660	29.63339	28	1.14987	26.06769	29.97452	28	1.17687	25.76380	30.32066
29	1.12815	27.26301	30.75686	29	1.15562	26.93302	31.12439	29	1.18374	26.60858	31.49753
30	1.13285	28.14573	31.88501	30	1.16140	27.79405	32.28002	30	1.19064	27.44847	32.68126
31	1.13757	29.02480	33.01787	31	1.16721	28.65080	33.44142	31	1.19759	28.28348	33.87190
32	1.14231	29.90021	34.15544	32	1.17304	29.50328	34.60862	32	1.20457	29.11365	35.06949
33	1.14707	30.77200	35.29776	33	1.17891	30.35153	35.78167	33	1.21160	29.93901	36.27406
34	1.15185	31.64016	36.44483	34	1.18480	31.19555	36.95058	34	1.21867	30.75958	37.48566
35	1.15665	32.50473	37.59668	35	1.19073	32.03537	38.14538	35	1.22578	31.57539	38.70433
36	1.16147	33.36570	38.75334	36	1.19668	32.87102	39.33610	36	1.23293	32.38646	39.93010
37	1.16631	34.22311	39.91481	37	1.20266	33.70250	40.53279	37	1.24012	33.19284	41.16303
38	1.17117	35.07695	41.08112	38	1.20868	34.52985	41.73545	38	1.24735	33.99454	42.40314
39	1.17605	35.92725	42.25229	39	1.21472	35.35309	42.94413	39	1.25463	34.79159	43.65050
40	1.18095	36.77403	43.42834	40	1.22079	36.17223	44.15885	40	1.26195	35.58401	44.90512
41	1.18587	37.61729	44.60929	41	1.22690	36.98729	45.37964	41	1.26931	36.37184	46.16707
42	1.19081	38.45705	45.79517	42	1.23303	37.79830	46.60654	42	1.27671	37.15511	47.43638
43	1.19577	39.29333	46.98598	43	1.23920	38.60527	47.83957	43	1.28416	37.93383	48.71309
44	1.20076	40.12614	48.18175	44	1.24539	39.40823	49.07877	44	1.29165	38.70803	49.99725
45	1.20576	40.95549	49.38251	45	1.25162	40.20720	50.32416	45	1.29919	39.47774	51.28890
46	1.21078	41.78140	50.58827	46	1.25788	41.00219	51.57578	46	1.30676	40.24299	52.58809
47	1.21583	42.60388	51.79906	47	1.26417	41.79322	52.83366	47	1.31439	41.00380	53.89485
48	1.22090	43.42296	53.01489	48	1.27049	42.58032	54.09783	48	1.32205	41.76020	55.20924
49	1.22598	44.23863	54.23578	49	1.27684	43.36350	55.36832	49	1.32977	42.51221	56.53129
50	1.23109	45.05092	55.46176	50	1.28323	44.14279	56.64516	50	1.33752	43.25986	57.86106
51	1.23622	45.85983	56.69285	51	1.28964	44.91820	57.92839	51	1.34533	44.00318	59.19858
52	1.24137	46.66539	57.92907	52	1.29609	45.68975	59.21803	52	1.35317	44.74218	60.54390
53	1.24654	47.46761	59.17045	53	1.30257	46.45746	60.51412	53	1.36107	45.47690	61.89708
54	1.25174	48.26650	60.41699	54	1.30908	47.22135	61.81669	54	1.36901	46.20736	63.25814
55	1.25695	49.06208	61.66873	55	1.31563	47.98145	63.12577	55	1.37699	46.93358	64.62715
56	1.26219	49.85435	62.92568	56	1.32221	48.73776	64.44140	56	1.38502	47.65559	66.00414
57	1.26745	50.64334	64.18787	57	1.32882	49.49031	65.76361	57	1.39310	48.37341	67.38916
58	1.27273	51.42905	65.45532	58	1.33546	50.23911	67.09243	58	1.40123	49.08707	68.78227

59	1.27803	52.21150	66.72805	59	1.34214	50.98419	68.42789	59	1.40940	49.79659	70.18350
60	1.28336	52.99071	68.00608	60	1.34885	51.72556	69.77003	60	1.41763	50.50199	71.59290
61	1.28871	53.76668	69.28944	61	1.35559	52.46324	71.11888	61	1.42589	51.20331	73.01053
62	1.29408	54.53943	70.57815	62	1.36237	53.19726	72.47448	62	1.43421	51.90055	74.43642
63	1.29947	55.30898	71.87222	63	1.36918	53.92762	73.83685	63	1.44258	52.59376	75.87063
64	1.30488	56.07533	73.17169	64	1.37603	54.65435	75.20603	64	1.45099	53.28294	77.31321
65	1.31032	56.83850	74.47657	65	1.38291	55.37746	76.58206	65	1.45946	53.96813	78.76421
66	1.31578	57.59851	75.78689	66	1.38982	56.09698	77.96497	66	1.46797	54.64934	80.22366
67	1.32126	58.35536	77.10267	67	1.39677	56.81291	79.35480	67	1.47653	55.32660	81.69164
68	1.32677	59.10907	78.42393	68	1.40376	57.52529	80.75157	68	1.48515	55.99993	83.16817
69	1.33229	59.85966	79.75070	69	1.41078	58.23411	82.15533	69	1.49381	56.66936	84.65332
70	1.33785	60.60713	81.08299	70	1.41783	58.93942	83.56611	70	1.50252	57.33491	86.14713
71	1.34342	61.35150	82.42084	71	1.42492	59.64121	84.98394	71	1.51129	57.99660	87.64965
72	1.34902	62.09278	83.76426	72	1.43204	60.33951	86.40886	72	1.52011	58.65444	89.16094
73	1.35464	62.83098	85.11328	73	1.43920	61.03434	87.84090	73	1.52897	59.30848	90.68105
74	1.36028	63.56612	86.46791	74	1.44640	61.72571	89.28010	74	1.53789	59.95872	92.21002
75	1.36595	64.29821	87.82820	75	1.45363	62.41365	90.72650	75	1.54686	60.60519	93.74791
76	1.37164	65.02727	89.19415	76	1.46090	63.09815	92.18014	76	1.55589	61.24791	95.29478
77	1.37736	65.75329	90.56579	77	1.46821	63.77926	93.64104	77	1.56496	61.88690	96.85066
78	1.38310	66.47631	91.94315	78	1.47555	64.45697	95.10924	78	1.57409	62.52219	98.41562
79	1.38886	67.19633	93.32624	79	1.48292	65.13132	96.58479	79	1.58327	63.15379	99.98972
80	1.39465	67.91335	94.71510	80	1.49034	65.80231	98.06771	80	1.59251	63.78173	101.57299
81	1.40046	68.62741	96.10975	81	1.49779	66.46996	99.55805	81	1.60180	64.40603	103.16550
82	1.40629	69.33850	97.51021	82	1.50528	67.13428	101.05584	82	1.61114	65.02671	104.76730
83	1.41215	70.04663	98.91650	83	1.51281	67.79531	102.56112	83	1.62054	65.64379	106.37844
84	1.41804	70.75183	100.32865	84	1.52037	68.45304	104.07393	84	1.62999	66.25729	107.99898
85	1.42394	71.45411	101.74669	85	1.52797	69.10750	105.59430	85	1.63950	66.86723	109.62897
86	1.42988	72.15347	103.17063	86	1.53561	69.75871	107.12227	86	1.64907	67.47363	111.26848
87	1.43584	72.84993	104.60051	87	1.54329	70.40668	108.65788	87	1.65869	68.07652	112.91754
88	1.44182	73.54350	106.03635	88	1.55101	71.05142	110.20117	88	1.66836	68.67591	114.57623
89	1.44783	74.23419	107.47816	89	1.55876	71.69296	111.75217	89	1.67809	69.27182	116.24459
90	1.45386	74.92201	108.92599	90	1.56655	72.33130	113.31094	90	1.68788	69.86428	117.92268
91	1.45992	75.60698	110.37985	91	1.57439	72.96647	114.87749	91	1.69773	70.45330	119.61057
92	1.46600	76.28911	111.83976	92	1.58226	73.59847	116.45188	92	1.70763	71.03891	121.30829
93	1.47211	76.96841	113.30576	93	1.59017	74.22734	118.03414	93	1.71759	71.62112	123.01593
94	1.47824	77.64489	114.77787	94	1.59812	74.85307	119.62431	94	1.72761	72.19995	124.73352
95	1.48440	78.31856	116.25611	95	1.60611	75.47569	121.22243	95	1.73769	72.77543	126.46113
96	1.49059	78.98944	117.74051	96	1.61414	76.09522	122.82854	96	1.74783	73.34757	128.19882
97	1.49680	79.65753	119.23110	97	1.62221	76.71166	124.44268	97	1.75802	73.91639	129.94665
98	1.50303	80.32286	120.72789	98	1.63032	77.32503	126.06490	98	1.76828	74.48191	131.70467
99	1.50930	80.98542	122.23093	99	1.63848	77.93536	127.69522	99	1.77859	75.04415	133.47295
100	1.51558	81.64523	123.74022	100	1.64667	78.54264	129.33370	100	1.78897	75.60314	135.25154

Table I. ANNUITIES (*Continued*)

M	C(5,M,12)	A(5,M,12)	S(5,M,12)	M	C(6,M,12)	A(6,M,12)	S(6,M,12)	M	C(7,M,12)	A(7,M,12)	S(7,M,12)
101	1.52190	82.30230	125.25581	101	1.65490	79.14691	130.98037	101	1.79940	76.15888	137.04051
102	1.52824	82.95665	126.77771	102	1.66318	79.74817	132.63527	102	1.80990	76.71139	138.83991
103	1.53461	83.60828	128.30595	103	1.67149	80.34644	134.29845	103	1.82046	77.26071	140.64981
104	1.54100	84.25721	129.84055	104	1.67985	80.94173	135.96994	104	1.83108	77.80683	142.47027
105	1.54742	84.90345	131.38156	105	1.68825	81.53406	137.64979	105	1.84176	78.34979	144.30134
106	1.55387	85.54700	132.92898	106	1.69669	82.12344	139.33804	106	1.85250	78.88960	146.14310
107	1.56035	86.18788	134.48285	107	1.70517	82.70989	141.03473	107	1.86331	79.42628	147.99560
108	1.56685	86.82611	136.04320	108	1.71370	83.29342	142.73990	108	1.87418	79.95985	149.85891
109	1.57338	87.46168	137.61004	109	1.72227	83.87405	144.45360	109	1.88511	80.49032	151.73309
110	1.57993	88.09462	139.18342	110	1.73088	84.45180	146.17587	110	1.89611	81.01772	153.61820
111	1.58651	88.72494	140.76335	111	1.73953	85.02666	147.90675	111	1.90717	81.54206	155.51430
112	1.59312	89.35263	142.34986	112	1.74823	85.59867	149.64628	112	1.91829	82.06335	157.42147
113	1.59976	89.97773	143.94299	113	1.75697	86.16783	151.39451	113	1.92948	82.58163	159.33976
114	1.60643	90.60023	145.54275	114	1.76576	86.73416	153.15148	114	1.94074	83.09690	161.26924
115	1.61312	91.22014	147.14918	115	1.77459	87.29767	154.91724	115	1.95206	83.60918	163.20998
116	1.61984	91.83748	148.76230	116	1.78346	87.85838	156.69183	116	1.96345	84.11849	165.16204
117	1.62659	92.45227	150.38214	117	1.79238	88.41630	158.47529	117	1.97490	84.62484	167.12548
118	1.63337	93.06450	152.00873	118	1.80134	88.97144	160.26766	118	1.98642	85.12826	169.10038
119	1.64018	93.67419	153.64210	119	1.81035	89.52382	162.06900	119	1.99801	85.62876	171.08680
120	1.64701	94.28135	155.28228	120	1.81940	90.07345	163.87935	120	2.00966	86.12635	173.08481
121	1.65387	94.88599	156.92929	121	1.82849	90.62035	165.69874	121	2.02138	86.62106	175.09447
122	1.66076	95.48812	158.58316	122	1.83764	91.16453	167.52724	122	2.03318	87.11291	177.11585
123	1.66768	96.08776	160.24392	123	1.84682	91.70600	169.35487	123	2.04504	87.60189	179.14903
124	1.67463	96.68491	161.91161	124	1.85606	92.24478	171.21170	124	2.05697	88.08805	181.19407
125	1.68161	97.27957	163.58624	125	1.86534	92.78087	173.06776	125	2.06896	88.57138	183.25103
126	1.68862	97.87177	165.26785	126	1.87467	93.31430	174.93310	126	2.08103	89.05191	185.31999
127	1.69565	98.46152	166.95646	127	1.88404	93.84507	176.80776	127	2.09317	89.52966	187.40103
128	1.70272	99.04882	168.65212	128	1.89346	94.37321	178.69180	128	2.10538	90.00463	189.49420
129	1.70981	99.63367	170.35483	129	1.90293	94.89871	180.58526	129	2.11766	90.47685	191.59958
130	1.71694	100.21611	172.06465	130	1.91244	95.42161	182.48818	130	2.13002	90.94633	193.71725
131	1.72409	100.79612	173.78158	131	1.92200	95.94190	184.40063	131	2.14244	91.41308	195.84727
132	1.73127	101.37373	175.50567	132	1.93161	96.45960	186.32263	132	2.15494	91.87713	197.98971
133	1.73849	101.94895	177.23694	133	1.94127	96.97473	188.25424	133	2.16751	92.33849	200.14465
134	1.74573	102.52177	178.97543	134	1.95098	97.48729	190.19551	134	2.18015	92.79718	202.31216
135	1.75300	103.09222	180.72116	135	1.96073	97.99730	192.14649	135	2.19287	93.25320	204.49231
136	1.76031	103.66030	182.47417	136	1.97054	98.50478	194.10722	136	2.20566	93.70658	206.68518
137	1.76764	104.22603	184.23448	137	1.98039	99.00973	196.07776	137	2.21853	94.15733	208.89085
138	1.77501	104.78941	186.00212	138	1.99029	99.51217	198.05815	138	2.23147	94.60546	211.10938
139	1.78240	105.35045	187.77713	139	2.00024	100.01211	200.04844	139	2.24449	95.05100	213.34085
140	1.78983	105.90916	189.55953	140	2.01024	100.50956	202.04868	140	2.25758	95.49395	215.58534
141	1.79729	106.46555	191.34937	141	2.02029	101.00454	204.05892	141	2.27075	95.93433	217.84292
142	1.80478	107.01964	193.14665	142	2.03040	101.49705	206.07922	142	2.28400	96.37216	220.11367
143	1.81230	107.57142	194.95143	143	2.04055	101.98712	208.10962	143	2.29732	96.80745	222.39766
144	1.81985	108.12092	196.76373	144	2.05075	102.47474	210.15016	144	2.31072	97.24022	224.69498
145	1.82743	108.66813	198.58358	145	2.06100	102.95994	212.20091	145	2.32420	97.67047	227.00571
146	1.83505	109.21308	200.41101	146	2.07131	103.44273	214.26192	146	2.33776	98.09823	229.32991
147	1.84269	109.75576	202.24606	147	2.08167	103.92311	216.33323	147	2.35139	98.52351	231.66766
148	1.85037	110.29620	204.08875	148	2.09207	104.40111	218.41489	148	2.36511	98.94632	234.01906
149	1.85808	110.83439	205.93912	149	2.10253	104.87673	220.50697	149	2.37891	99.36669	236.38417
150	1.86582	111.37034	207.79720	150	2.11305	105.34998	222.60950	150	2.39278	99.78461	238.76308
151	1.87360	111.90408	209.66302	151	2.12361	105.82087	224.72255	151	2.40674	100.20011	241.15586
152	1.88140	112.43559	211.53662	152	2.13423	106.28942	226.84616	152	2.42078	100.61320	243.56260
153	1.88924	112.96491	213.41802	153	2.14490	106.75565	228.98039	153	2.43490	101.02389	245.98339
154	1.89711	113.49202	215.30726	154	2.15563	107.21955	231.12530	154	2.44911	101.43220	248.41829
155	1.90502	114.01695	217.20437	155	2.16640	107.68114	233.28092	155	2.46339	101.83815	250.86740
156	1.91296	114.53970	219.10939	156	2.17724	108.14044	235.44733	156	2.47776	102.24174	253.33079
157	1.92093	115.06029	221.02235	157	2.18812	108.59745	237.62456	157	2.49222	102.64299	255.80855
158	[illegible]	[illegible]	[illegible]	158	[illegible]	[illegible]	[illegible]	158	[illegible]	[illegible]	[illegible]

161	1.95314	117.12110	228.75421	161	2.23221	110.40288	246.44292	161	2.55088	104.22485	265.86499
162	1.96128	117.63097	230.70735	162	2.24338	110.84864	248.67513	162	2.56576	104.61460	268.41586
163	1.96945	118.13873	232.66863	163	2.25459	111.29218	250.91851	163	2.58073	105.00208	270.98162
164	1.97766	118.64438	234.63809	164	2.26587	111.73351	253.17310	164	2.59578	105.38732	273.56235
165	1.98590	119.14793	236.61574	165	2.27719	112.17264	255.43897	165	2.61092	105.77033	276.15813
166	1.99417	119.64939	238.60164	166	2.28858	112.60960	257.71616	166	2.62615	106.15112	278.76905
167	2.00248	120.14877	240.59582	167	2.30002	113.04437	260.00474	167	2.64147	106.52969	281.39521
168	2.01083	120.64608	242.59830	168	2.31152	113.47699	262.30477	168	2.65688	106.90607	284.03668
169	2.01920	121.14132	244.60913	169	2.32308	113.90745	264.61629	169	2.67238	107.28027	286.69356
170	2.02762	121.63451	246.62833	170	2.33470	114.33577	266.93937	170	2.68797	107.65230	289.36594
171	2.03607	122.12565	248.65595	171	2.34637	114.76196	269.27407	171	2.70365	108.02217	292.05390
172	2.04455	122.61476	250.69201	172	2.35810	115.18603	271.62044	172	2.71942	108.38990	294.75755
173	2.05307	123.10184	252.73656	173	2.36989	115.60799	273.97854	173	2.73528	108.75549	297.47697
174	2.06162	123.58689	254.78963	174	2.38174	116.02785	276.34843	174	2.75124	109.11895	300.21225
175	2.07021	124.06993	256.85126	175	2.39365	116.44563	278.73018	175	2.76729	109.48033	302.96349
176	2.07884	124.55097	258.92147	176	2.40562	116.86132	281.12383	176	2.78343	109.83960	305.73078
177	2.08750	125.03001	261.00031	177	2.41765	117.27494	283.52945	177	2.79967	110.19678	308.51421
178	2.09620	125.50707	263.08781	178	2.42974	117.68651	285.94709	178	2.81600	110.55190	311.31387
179	2.10493	125.98214	265.18401	179	2.44188	118.09603	288.37683	179	2.83242	110.90495	314.12987
180	2.11370	126.45524	267.28894	180	2.45409	118.50351	290.81871	180	2.84895	111.25596	316.96230
181	2.12251	126.92638	269.40265	181	2.46636	118.90897	293.27281	181	2.86557	111.60493	319.81124
182	2.13135	127.39557	271.52516	182	2.47870	119.31241	295.73917	182	2.88228	111.95188	322.67681
183	2.14024	127.86281	273.65651	183	2.49109	119.71384	298.21787	183	2.89909	112.29681	325.55909
184	2.14915	128.32811	275.79675	184	2.50354	120.11327	300.70896	184	2.91601	112.63975	328.45819
185	2.15811	128.79147	277.94590	185	2.51606	120.51072	303.21250	185	2.93302	112.98069	331.37419
186	2.16710	129.25292	280.10401	186	2.52864	120.90619	305.72856	186	2.95013	113.31966	334.30721
187	2.17613	129.71245	282.27111	187	2.54129	121.29969	308.25721	187	2.96733	113.65666	337.25733
188	2.18520	130.17008	284.44724	188	2.55399	121.69123	310.79849	188	2.98464	113.99171	340.22467
189	2.19430	130.62580	286.63244	189	2.56676	122.08083	313.35248	189	3.00205	114.32482	343.20931
190	2.20344	131.07964	288.82674	190	2.57960	122.46849	315.91925	190	3.01957	114.65599	346.21137
191	2.21263	131.53159	291.03018	191	2.59249	122.85422	318.49884	191	3.03718	114.98524	349.23093
192	2.22185	131.98167	293.24281	192	2.60546	123.23803	321.09134	192	3.05490	115.31259	352.26811
193	2.23110	132.42987	295.46465	193	2.61848	123.61993	323.69679	193	3.07272	115.63803	355.32301
194	2.24040	132.87622	297.69576	194	2.63158	123.99993	326.31528	194	3.09064	115.96159	358.39573
195	2.24973	133.32072	299.93616	195	2.64473	124.37804	328.94685	195	3.10867	116.28327	361.48637
196	2.25911	133.76337	302.18589	196	2.65796	124.75426	331.59159	196	3.12680	116.60309	364.59504
197	2.26852	134.20419	304.44500	197	2.67125	125.12862	334.24955	197	3.14504	116.92105	367.72184
198	2.27797	134.64318	306.71352	198	2.68460	125.50112	336.92079	198	3.16339	117.23716	370.86689
199	2.28746	135.08034	308.99149	199	2.69803	125.87176	339.60540	199	3.18184	117.55145	374.03028
200	2.29700	135.51569	311.27896	200	2.71152	126.24055	342.30342	200	3.20040	117.86391	377.21212

Table I. ANNUITIES (*Continued*)

M	C(5,M,12)	A(5,M,12)	S(5,M,12)	M	C(6,M,12)	A(6,M,12)	S(6,M,12)	M	C(7,M,12)	A(7,M,12)	S(7,M,12)
201	2.30657	135.94924	313.57595	201	2.72507	126.60752	345.01494	201	3.21907	118.17455	380.41253
202	2.31618	136.38098	315.88252	202	2.73870	126.97265	347.74002	202	3.23785	118.48340	383.63160
203	2.32583	136.81094	318.19870	203	2.75239	127.33597	350.47872	203	3.25674	118.79046	386.86945
204	2.33552	137.23911	320.52452	204	2.76616	127.69749	353.23111	204	3.27574	119.09573	390.12619
205	2.34525	137.66550	322.86004	205	2.77999	128.05720	355.99727	205	3.29484	119.39924	393.40192
206	2.35502	138.09013	325.20529	206	2.79389	128.41512	358.77725	206	3.31406	119.70098	396.69677
207	2.36483	138.51299	327.56031	207	2.80786	128.77127	361.57114	207	3.33340	120.00097	400.01083
208	2.37469	138.93410	329.92515	208	2.82189	129.12564	364.37899	208	3.35284	120.29923	403.34423
209	2.38458	139.35346	332.29984	209	2.83600	129.47825	367.20089	209	3.37240	120.59575	406.69707
210	2.39452	139.77108	334.68442	210	2.85018	129.82910	370.03689	210	3.39207	120.89056	410.06947
211	2.40450	140.18697	337.07894	211	2.86444	130.17821	372.88708	211	3.41186	121.18365	413.46154
212	2.41451	140.60113	339.48343	212	2.87876	130.52558	375.75151	212	3.43176	121.47505	416.87340
213	2.42457	141.01357	341.89795	213	2.89315	130.87123	378.63027	213	3.45178	121.76475	420.30516
214	2.43468	141.42430	344.32252	214	2.90762	131.21515	381.52342	214	3.47192	122.05278	423.75694
215	2.44482	141.83333	346.75720	215	2.92216	131.55737	384.43104	215	3.49217	122.33914	427.22886
216	2.45501	142.24066	349.20202	216	2.93677	131.89788	387.35319	216	3.51254	122.62383	430.72103
217	2.46524	142.64630	351.65703	217	2.95145	132.23669	390.28996	217	3.53303	122.90687	434.23357
218	2.47551	143.05026	354.12227	218	2.96621	132.57382	393.24141	218	3.55364	123.18828	437.76660
219	2.48582	143.45254	356.59778	219	2.98104	132.90928	396.20762	219	3.57437	123.46805	441.32023
220	2.49618	143.85315	359.08360	220	2.99594	133.24306	399.18866	220	3.59522	123.74619	444.89460
221	2.50658	144.25210	361.57978	221	3.01092	133.57519	402.18460	221	3.61619	124.02273	448.48982
222	2.51703	144.64940	364.08637	222	3.02598	133.90566	405.19552	222	3.63729	124.29766	452.10601
223	2.52751	145.04504	366.60339	223	3.04111	134.23449	408.22150	223	3.65850	124.57099	455.74330
224	2.53805	145.43905	369.13091	224	3.05631	134.56168	411.26261	224	3.67984	124.84274	459.40180
225	2.54862	145.83141	371.66895	225	3.07159	134.88724	414.31892	225	3.70131	125.11292	463.08164
226	2.55924	146.22216	374.21757	226	3.08695	135.21118	417.39051	226	3.72290	125.38153	466.78295
227	2.56990	146.61128	376.77681	227	3.10239	135.53352	420.47747	227	3.74462	125.64858	470.50585
228	2.58061	146.99878	379.34672	228	3.11790	135.85425	423.57985	228	3.76646	125.91408	474.25047
229	2.59136	147.38468	381.92733	229	3.13349	136.17338	426.69775	229	3.78843	126.17804	478.01693
230	2.60216	147.76897	384.51869	230	3.14916	136.49092	429.83124	230	3.81053	126.44047	481.80536
231	2.61300	148.15167	387.12085	231	3.16490	136.80689	432.98040	231	3.83276	126.70138	485.61589
232	2.62389	148.53279	389.73386	232	3.18073	137.12128	436.14530	232	3.85512	126.96077	489.44865
233	2.63482	148.91232	392.35775	233	3.19663	137.43411	439.32603	233	3.87761	127.21866	493.30377
234	2.64580	149.29028	394.99257	234	3.21261	137.74539	442.52266	234	3.90022	127.47506	497.18138
235	2.65683	149.66667	397.63837	235	3.22868	138.05511	445.73527	235	3.92298	127.72997	501.08160
236	2.66790	150.04149	400.29520	236	3.24482	138.36329	448.96395	236	3.94586	127.98340	505.00458
237	2.67901	150.41477	402.96310	237	3.26104	138.66994	452.20877	237	3.96888	128.23536	508.95044
238	2.69018	150.78649	405.64211	238	3.27735	138.97507	455.46981	238	3.99203	128.48586	512.91931
239	2.70138	151.15667	408.33228	239	3.29374	139.27868	458.74716	239	4.01532	128.73490	516.91134
240	2.71264	151.52531	411.03367	240	3.31020	139.58077	462.04090	240	4.03874	128.98251	520.92666
241	2.72394	151.89243	413.74631	241	3.32676	139.88136	465.35110	241	4.06230	129.22867	524.96540
242	2.73529	152.25802	416.47025	242	3.34339	140.18046	468.67786	242	4.08599	129.47341	529.02770
243	2.74669	152.62209	419.20554	243	3.36011	140.47807	472.02124	243	4.10983	129.71673	533.11369
244	2.75813	152.98466	421.95223	244	3.37691	140.77420	475.38135	244	4.13380	129.95864	537.22352
245	2.76963	153.34572	424.71037	245	3.39379	141.06886	478.75826	245	4.15792	130.19914	541.35733
246	2.78117	153.70528	427.48000	246	3.41076	141.36205	482.15205	246	4.18217	130.43825	545.51524
247	2.79275	154.06335	430.26116	247	3.42781	141.65378	485.56281	247	4.20657	130.67598	549.69742
248	2.80439	154.41993	433.05392	248	3.44495	141.94406	488.99062	248	4.23111	130.91232	553.90398
249	2.81608	154.77504	435.85831	249	3.46218	142.23289	492.43558	249	4.25579	131.14730	558.13509
250	2.82781	155.12867	438.67438	250	3.47949	142.52029	495.89775	250	4.28061	131.38091	562.39088
251	2.83959	155.48083	441.50219	251	3.49689	142.80626	499.37724	251	4.30558	131.61316	566.67149
252	2.85142	155.83153	444.34179	252	3.51437	143.09081	502.87413	252	4.33070	131.84407	570.97708
253	2.86331	156.18078	447.19321	253	3.53194	143.37394	506.38850	253	4.35596	132.07364	575.30778
254	2.87524	156.52858	450.05652	254	3.54960	143.65566	509.92044	254	4.38137	132.30188	579.66374
255	2.88722	156.87493	452.93175	255	3.56735	143.93598	513.47004	255	4.40693	132.52880	584.04511
256	2.89925	157.21985	455.81897	256	3.58519	144.21490	517.03739	256	4.43264	132.75440	588.45204
257	2.91133	157.56333	458.71821	257	3.60311	144.49244	520.62258	257	4.45849	132.97869	592.88468
258	2.92346	157.90539	461.62954	258	3.62113	144.76860	524.22569	258	4.48450	133.20168	597.34317

261	2.96015	158.92308	470.43650	261	3.67572	145.58885	535.14349	261	4.56344	133.86292	610.87531
262	2.97249	159.25950	473.39665	262	3.69410	145.85956	538.81920	262	4.59006	134.08078	615.43875
263	2.98487	159.59453	476.36914	263	3.71257	146.12891	542.51330	263	4.61683	134.29738	620.02881
264	2.99731	159.92816	479.35401	264	3.73113	146.39693	546.22587	264	4.64377	134.51272	624.64564
265	3.00980	160.26041	482.35132	265	3.74978	146.66361	549.95700	265	4.67085	134.72682	629.28941
266	3.02234	160.59128	485.36112	266	3.76853	146.92896	553.70678	266	4.69810	134.93967	633.96026
267	3.03493	160.92077	488.38345	267	3.78738	147.19300	557.47532	267	4.72551	135.15129	638.65836
268	3.04758	161.24890	491.41839	268	3.80631	147.45572	561.26269	268	4.75307	135.36168	643.38387
269	3.06027	161.57567	494.46596	269	3.82535	147.71713	565.06901	269	4.78080	135.57085	648.13694
270	3.07303	161.90108	497.52624	270	3.84447	147.97725	568.89435	270	4.80869	135.77880	652.91774
271	3.08583	162.22515	500.59926	271	3.86369	148.23607	572.73882	271	4.83674	135.98555	657.72643
272	3.09869	162.54786	503.68509	272	3.88301	148.49360	576.60252	272	4.86495	136.19111	662.56317
273	3.11160	162.86924	506.78378	273	3.90243	148.74985	580.48553	273	4.89333	136.39547	667.42812
274	3.12456	163.18929	509.89538	274	3.92194	149.00483	584.38796	274	4.92188	136.59864	672.32145
275	3.13758	163.50800	513.01994	275	3.94155	149.25853	588.30990	275	4.95059	136.80064	677.24332
276	3.15066	163.82540	516.15753	276	3.96126	149.51098	592.25145	276	4.97946	137.00146	682.19391
277	3.16378	164.14147	519.30818	277	3.98106	149.76217	596.21270	277	5.00851	137.20112	687.17337
278	3.17697	164.45624	522.47197	278	4.00097	150.01211	600.19377	278	5.03773	137.39962	692.18188
279	3.19020	164.76970	525.64893	279	4.02097	150.26080	604.19474	279	5.06711	137.59697	697.21961
280	3.20350	165.08186	528.83914	280	4.04108	150.50826	608.21571	280	5.09667	137.79318	702.28673
281	3.21684	165.39272	532.04263	281	4.06128	150.75449	612.25679	281	5.12640	137.98825	707.38340
282	3.23025	165.70230	535.25948	282	4.08159	150.99949	616.31807	282	5.15631	138.18219	712.50980
283	3.24371	166.01058	538.48973	283	4.10200	151.24328	620.39966	283	5.18639	138.37500	717.66611
284	3.25722	166.31759	541.73343	284	4.12251	151.48585	624.50165	284	5.21664	138.56669	722.85250
285	3.27079	166.62333	544.99066	285	4.14312	151.72721	628.62417	285	5.24707	138.75728	728.06913
286	3.28442	166.92780	548.26145	286	4.16384	151.96737	632.76729	286	5.27768	138.94675	733.31620
287	3.29811	167.23100	551.54587	287	4.18466	152.20634	636.93113	287	5.30846	139.13513	738.59388
288	3.31185	167.53295	554.84398	288	4.20558	152.44412	641.11578	288	5.33943	139.32242	743.90235
289	3.32565	167.83364	558.15583	289	4.22661	152.68072	645.32136	289	5.37058	139.50862	749.24178
290	3.33951	168.13309	561.48148	290	4.24774	152.91614	649.54797	290	5.40191	139.69374	754.61235
291	3.35342	168.43129	564.82099	291	4.26898	153.15039	653.79571	291	5.43342	139.87778	760.01426
292	3.36739	168.72826	568.17441	292	4.29032	153.38347	658.06469	292	5.46511	140.06076	765.44768
293	3.38142	169.02399	571.54180	293	4.31178	153.61539	662.35501	293	5.49699	140.24268	770.91279
294	3.39551	169.31850	574.92323	294	4.33333	153.84616	666.66678	294	5.52906	140.42354	776.40978
295	3.40966	169.61178	578.31874	295	4.35500	154.07578	671.00012	295	5.56131	140.60336	781.93884
296	3.42387	169.90385	581.72840	296	4.37678	154.30426	675.35512	296	5.59375	140.78213	787.50015
297	3.43813	170.19470	585.15227	297	4.39866	154.53160	679.73189	297	5.62638	140.95986	793.09390
298	3.45246	170.48435	588.59040	298	4.42065	154.75781	684.13055	298	5.65920	141.13657	798.72028
299	3.46685	170.77280	592.04286	299	4.44276	154.98290	688.55121	299	5.69221	141.31224	804.37948
300	3.48129	171.06005	595.50971	300	4.46497	155.20686	692.99396	300	5.72542	141.48690	810.07169

Table I. ANNUITIES (*Continued*)

M	C(5,M,12)	A(5,M,12)	S(5,M,12)	M	C(6,M,12)	A(6,M,12)	S(6,M,12)	M	C(7,M,12)	A(7,M,12)	S(7,M,12)
301	3.49580	171.34610	598.99100	301	4.48729	155.42972	697.45893	301	5.75882	141.66055	815.79711
302	3.51036	171.63098	602.48679	302	4.50973	155.65146	701.94623	302	5.79241	141.83319	821.55593
303	3.52499	171.91466	605.99716	303	4.53228	155.87210	706.45596	303	5.82620	142.00483	827.34834
304	3.53968	172.19718	609.52214	304	4.55494	156.09164	710.98824	304	5.86018	142.17547	833.17454
305	3.55442	172.47852	613.06182	305	4.57772	156.31009	715.54318	305	5.89437	142.34512	839.03472
306	3.56923	172.75869	616.61624	306	4.60060	156.52745	720.12089	306	5.92875	142.51379	844.92909
307	3.58411	173.03770	620.18548	307	4.62361	156.74373	724.72150	307	5.96334	142.68149	850.85784
308	3.59904	173.31555	623.76958	308	4.64673	156.95894	729.34511	308	5.99812	142.84820	856.82118
309	3.61404	173.59225	627.36862	309	4.66996	157.17307	733.99183	309	6.03311	143.01396	862.81930
310	3.62909	173.86780	630.98266	310	4.69331	157.38614	738.66179	310	6.06831	143.17875	868.85242
311	3.64422	174.14221	634.61176	311	4.71678	157.59815	743.35510	311	6.10370	143.34258	874.92072
312	3.65940	174.41548	638.25597	312	4.74036	157.80911	748.07188	312	6.13931	143.50547	881.02443
313	3.67465	174.68761	641.91537	313	4.76406	158.01901	752.81224	313	6.17512	143.66741	887.16374
314	3.68996	174.95862	645.59002	314	4.78788	158.22787	757.57630	314	6.21114	143.82841	893.33886
315	3.70533	175.22850	649.27998	315	4.81182	158.43569	762.36418	315	6.24738	143.98848	899.55000
316	3.72077	175.49726	652.98531	316	4.83588	158.64248	767.17600	316	6.28382	144.14761	905.79738
317	3.73628	175.76491	656.70608	317	4.86006	158.84824	772.01188	317	6.32047	144.30583	912.08119
318	3.75184	176.03144	660.44236	318	4.88436	159.05297	776.87194	318	6.35734	144.46313	918.40167
319	3.76748	176.29687	664.19420	319	4.90878	159.25669	781.75630	319	6.39443	144.61951	924.75901
320	3.78317	176.56120	667.96168	320	4.93333	159.45939	786.66508	320	6.43173	144.77499	931.15344
321	3.79894	176.82443	671.74485	321	4.95799	159.66109	791.59840	321	6.46925	144.92957	937.58517
322	3.81477	177.08657	675.54379	322	4.98278	159.86178	796.55640	322	6.50698	145.08325	944.05441
323	3.83066	177.34762	679.35855	323	5.00770	160.06147	801.53918	323	6.54494	145.23604	950.56140
324	3.84662	177.60759	683.18921	324	5.03273	160.26017	806.54687	324	6.58312	145.38795	957.10634
325	3.86265	177.86648	687.03583	325	5.05790	160.45788	811.57961	325	6.62152	145.53897	963.68946
326	3.87874	178.12429	690.89848	326	5.08319	160.65461	816.63751	326	6.66015	145.68912	970.31098
327	3.89491	178.38104	694.77723	327	5.10860	160.85036	821.72069	327	6.69900	145.83839	976.97113
328	3.91113	178.63672	698.67213	328	5.13415	161.04513	826.82930	328	6.73808	145.98680	983.67013
329	3.92743	178.89134	702.58327	329	5.15982	161.23894	831.96344	329	6.77738	146.13435	990.40820
330	3.94379	179.14490	706.51070	330	5.18562	161.43178	837.12326	330	6.81692	146.28105	997.18558
331	3.96023	179.39741	710.45449	331	5.21154	161.62366	842.30888	331	6.85668	146.42689	1004.00250
332	3.97673	179.64888	714.41472	332	5.23760	161.81459	847.52042	332	6.89668	146.57189	1010.85918
333	3.99330	179.89930	718.39145	333	5.26379	162.00456	852.75802	333	6.93691	146.71604	1017.75586
334	4.00994	180.14868	722.38474	334	5.29011	162.19360	858.02181	334	6.97737	146.85936	1024.69277
335	4.02664	180.39702	726.39468	335	5.31656	162.38169	863.31192	335	7.01808	147.00185	1031.67014
336	4.04342	180.64434	730.42133	336	5.34314	162.56884	868.62848	336	7.05901	147.14351	1038.68822
337	4.06027	180.89063	734.46475	337	5.36986	162.75507	873.97163	337	7.10019	147.28436	1045.74723
338	4.07719	181.13589	738.52502	338	5.39671	162.94037	879.34149	338	7.14161	147.42438	1052.84743
339	4.09418	181.38014	742.60220	339	5.42369	163.12474	884.73819	339	7.18327	147.56359	1059.98904
340	4.11123	181.62338	746.69638	340	5.45081	163.30820	890.16188	340	7.22517	147.70200	1067.17230
341	4.12837	181.86561	750.80762	341	5.47806	163.49075	895.61269	341	7.26732	147.83960	1074.39748
342	4.14557	182.10683	754.93598	342	5.50545	163.67239	901.09076	342	7.30971	147.97640	1081.66480
343	4.16284	182.34705	759.08155	343	5.53298	163.85312	906.59621	343	7.35235	148.11242	1088.97451
344	4.18018	182.58627	763.24439	344	5.56065	164.03296	912.12919	344	7.39524	148.24764	1096.32686
345	4.19760	182.82450	767.42457	345	5.58845	164.21190	917.68984	345	7.43838	148.38208	1103.72210
346	4.21509	183.06175	771.62217	346	5.61639	164.38995	923.27829	346	7.48177	148.51573	1111.16048
347	4.23266	183.29800	775.83727	347	5.64447	164.56711	928.89468	347	7.52541	148.64862	1118.64225
348	4.25029	183.53328	780.06992	348	5.67270	164.74339	934.53915	348	7.56931	148.78073	1126.16766
349	4.26800	183.76758	784.32021	349	5.70106	164.91880	940.21185	349	7.61347	148.91208	1133.73697
350	4.28578	184.00091	788.58821	350	5.72956	165.09333	945.91291	350	7.65788	149.04266	1141.35044
351	4.30364	184.23328	792.87400	351	5.75821	165.26700	951.64247	351	7.70255	149.17249	1149.00831
352	4.32157	184.46467	797.17764	352	5.78700	165.43980	957.40068	352	7.74748	149.30156	1156.71086
353	4.33958	184.69511	801.49921	353	5.81594	165.61174	963.18769	353	7.79267	149.42989	1164.45834
354	4.35766	184.92459	805.83879	354	5.84502	165.78283	969.00362	354	7.83813	149.55747	1172.25102
355	4.37582	185.15312	810.19646	355	5.87424	165.95306	974.84864	355	7.88385	149.68431	1180.08915
356	4.39405	185.38070	814.57227	356	5.90361	166.12245	980.72289	356	7.92984	149.81042	1187.97300
357	4.41236	185.60734	818.96633	357	5.93313	166.29099	986.62650	357	7.97610	149.93579	1195.90284
358	4.43074	185.83303	823.37868	358	5.96280	166.45870	992.55963	358	8.02263	150.06044	1203.87894

361	4.48636	186.50451	836.72638	361	6.05269	166.95683	1010.53762	361	8.16384	150.43006	1228.08749
362	4.50505	186.72649	841.21274	362	6.08295	167.12122	1016.59031	362	8.21147	150.55184	1236.25134
363	4.52382	186.94754	845.71779	363	6.11337	167.28480	1022.67326	363	8.25937	150.67291	1244.46280
364	4.54267	187.16767	850.24162	364	6.14393	167.44756	1028.78662	364	8.30755	150.79329	1252.72217
365	4.56160	187.38690	854.78429	365	6.17465	167.60951	1034.93056	365	8.35601	150.91296	1261.02972
366	4.58061	187.60521	859.34589	366	6.20553	167.77066	1041.10521	366	8.40475	151.03194	1269.38572
367	4.59969	187.82261	863.92650	367	6.23655	167.93101	1047.31074	367	8.45378	151.15023	1277.79047
368	4.61886	188.03912	868.52619	368	6.26774	168.09055	1053.54729	368	8.50309	151.26784	1286.24425
369	4.63810	188.25472	873.14505	369	6.29908	168.24931	1059.81503	369	8.55269	151.38476	1294.74734
370	4.65743	188.46943	877.78316	370	6.33057	168.40727	1066.11410	370	8.60258	151.50100	1303.30003
371	4.67684	188.68325	882.44059	371	6.36222	168.56445	1072.44467	371	8.65277	151.61657	1311.90262
372	4.69632	188.89619	887.11742	372	6.39403	168.72084	1078.80689	372	8.70324	151.73147	1320.55538
373	4.71589	189.10823	891.81374	373	6.42600	168.87646	1085.20093	373	8.75401	151.84571	1329.25862
374	4.73554	189.31940	896.52964	374	6.45813	169.03131	1091.62693	374	8.80507	151.95928	1338.01263
375	4.75527	189.52970	901.26518	375	6.49043	169.18538	1098.08507	375	8.85644	152.07219	1346.81771
376	4.77509	189.73912	906.02045	376	6.52288	169.33869	1104.57549	376	8.90810	152.18445	1355.67414
377	4.79498	189.94767	910.79553	377	6.55549	169.49123	1111.09837	377	8.96006	152.29605	1364.58224
378	4.81496	190.15535	915.59051	378	6.58827	169.64301	1117.65386	378	9.01233	152.40701	1373.54230
379	4.83502	190.36218	920.40547	379	6.62121	169.79404	1124.24213	379	9.06490	152.51733	1382.55463
380	4.85517	190.56814	925.24050	380	6.65432	169.94432	1130.86334	380	9.11778	152.62700	1391.61954
381	4.87540	190.77326	930.09567	381	6.68759	170.09385	1137.51766	381	9.17097	152.73604	1400.73732
382	4.89571	190.97752	934.97106	382	6.72103	170.24264	1144.20525	382	9.22446	152.84445	1409.90828
383	4.91611	191.18093	939.86678	383	6.75463	170.39069	1150.92627	383	9.27827	152.95223	1419.13275
384	4.93660	191.38350	944.78289	384	6.78840	170.53800	1157.68091	384	9.33240	153.05938	1428.41102
385	4.95716	191.58523	949.71948	385	6.82235	170.68457	1164.46931	385	9.38684	153.16592	1437.74342
386	4.97782	191.78612	954.67665	386	6.85646	170.83042	1171.29166	386	9.44159	153.27183	1447.13026
387	4.99856	191.98617	959.65447	387	6.89074	170.97554	1178.14812	387	9.49667	153.37713	1456.57185
388	5.01939	192.18540	964.65303	388	6.92519	171.11994	1185.03885	388	9.55207	153.48182	1466.06852
389	5.04030	192.38380	969.67242	389	6.95982	171.26363	1191.96405	389	9.60779	153.58590	1475.62059
390	5.06130	192.58138	974.71272	390	6.99462	171.40659	1198.92387	390	9.66383	153.68938	1485.22837
391	5.08239	192.77814	979.77402	391	7.02959	171.54885	1205.91849	391	9.72020	153.79226	1494.89221
392	5.10357	192.97408	984.85641	392	7.06474	171.69040	1212.94808	392	9.77691	153.89454	1504.61241
393	5.12483	193.16921	989.95998	393	7.10006	171.83124	1220.01282	393	9.83394	153.99623	1514.38932
394	5.14619	193.36353	995.08481	394	7.13556	171.97138	1227.11289	394	9.89130	154.09733	1524.22325
395	5.16763	193.55704	1000.23100	395	7.17124	172.11083	1234.24845	395	9.94900	154.19784	1534.11456
396	5.18916	193.74975	1005.39863	396	7.20710	172.24958	1241.41969	396	10.00704	154.29777	1544.06356
397	5.21078	193.94166	1010.58779	397	7.24313	172.38764	1248.62679	397	10.06541	154.39712	1554.07059
398	5.23249	194.13277	1015.79857	398	7.27935	172.52502	1255.86993	398	10.12413	154.49589	1564.13601
399	5.25430	194.32309	1021.03107	399	7.31575	172.66171	1263.14928	399	10.18318	154.59410	1574.26013
400	5.27619	194.51262	1026.28536	400	7.35233	172.79772	1270.46502	400	10.24259	154.69173	1584.44332

Table I. ANNUITIES (*Continued*)

M	C(5,M,12)	A(5,M,12)	S(5,M,12)	M	C(6,M,12)	A(6,M,12)	S(6,M,12)	M	C(7,M,12)	A(7,M,12)	S(7,M,12)
401	5.29817	194.70137	1031.56155	401	7.38909	172.93306	1277.81735	401	10.30233	154.78879	1594.68590
402	5.32025	194.88933	1036.85973	402	7.42603	173.06772	1285.20643	402	10.36243	154.88529	1604.98824
403	5.34242	195.07651	1042.17997	403	7.46316	173.20171	1292.63247	403	10.42288	154.98124	1615.35067
404	5.36468	195.26291	1047.52239	404	7.50048	173.33503	1300.09563	404	10.48368	155.07662	1625.77355
405	5.38703	195.44855	1052.88707	405	7.53798	173.46769	1307.59611	405	10.54483	155.17146	1636.25723
406	5.40948	195.63341	1058.27410	406	7.57567	173.59970	1315.13409	406	10.60635	155.26574	1646.80206
407	5.43201	195.81750	1063.68357	407	7.61355	173.73104	1322.70976	407	10.66822	155.35948	1657.40841
408	5.45465	196.00083	1069.11559	408	7.65162	173.86173	1330.32331	408	10.73045	155.45267	1668.07662
409	5.47738	196.18340	1074.57024	409	7.68987	173.99177	1337.97492	409	10.79304	155.54532	1678.80707
410	5.50020	196.36521	1080.04761	410	7.72832	174.12117	1345.66480	410	10.85600	155.63744	1689.60011
411	5.52312	196.54627	1085.54781	411	7.76697	174.24992	1353.39312	411	10.91933	155.72902	1700.45611
412	5.54613	196.72657	1091.07093	412	7.80580	174.37803	1361.16009	412	10.98302	155.82007	1711.37544
413	5.56924	196.90613	1096.61705	413	7.84483	174.50550	1368.96589	413	11.04709	155.91059	1722.35846
414	5.59244	197.08494	1102.18629	414	7.88405	174.63234	1376.81072	414	11.11153	156.00058	1733.40555
415	5.61574	197.26301	1107.77874	415	7.92347	174.75855	1384.69477	415	11.17635	156.09006	1744.51709
416	5.63914	197.44035	1113.39448	416	7.96309	174.88413	1392.61824	416	11.24155	156.17902	1755.69343
417	5.66264	197.61694	1119.03362	417	8.00291	175.00908	1400.58134	417	11.30712	156.26746	1766.93498
418	5.68623	197.79281	1124.69626	418	8.04292	175.13341	1408.58424	418	11.37308	156.35538	1778.24210
419	5.70993	197.96794	1130.38250	419	8.08314	175.25713	1416.62716	419	11.43942	156.44280	1789.61518
420	5.73372	198.14235	1136.09243	420	8.12355	175.38023	1424.71030	420	11.50615	156.52971	1801.05460
421	5.75761	198.31603	1141.82614	421	8.16417	175.50271	1432.83385	421	11.57327	156.61612	1812.56075
422	5.78160	198.48899	1147.58375	422	8.20499	175.62459	1440.99802	422	11.64078	156.70202	1824.13402
423	5.80569	198.66124	1153.36535	423	8.24602	175.74586	1449.20301	423	11.70869	156.78743	1835.77481
424	5.82988	198.83277	1159.17104	424	8.28725	175.86653	1457.44902	424	11.77699	156.87234	1847.48349
425	5.85417	199.00359	1165.00092	425	8.32868	175.98659	1465.73627	425	11.84569	156.95676	1859.26048
426	5.87856	199.17370	1170.85509	426	8.37032	176.10606	1474.06495	426	11.91479	157.04069	1871.10617
427	5.90306	199.34310	1176.73365	427	8.41218	176.22494	1482.43528	427	11.98429	157.12413	1883.02095
428	5.92765	199.51180	1182.63671	428	8.45424	176.34322	1490.84745	428	12.05420	157.20709	1895.00524
429	5.95235	199.67980	1188.56436	429	8.49651	176.46092	1499.30169	429	12.12451	157.28957	1907.05944
430	5.97715	199.84710	1194.51671	430	8.53899	176.57803	1507.79820	430	12.19524	157.37156	1919.18395
431	6.00206	200.01371	1200.49387	431	8.58169	176.69456	1516.33719	431	12.26638	157.45309	1931.37919
432	6.02707	200.17963	1206.49593	432	8.62459	176.81050	1524.91887	432	12.33793	157.53414	1943.64557
433	6.05218	200.34486	1212.52299	433	8.66772	176.92587	1533.54347	433	12.40990	157.61472	1955.98350
434	6.07740	200.50941	1218.57517	434	8.71106	177.04067	1542.21119	434	12.48229	157.69483	1968.39341
435	6.10272	200.67327	1224.65257	435	8.75461	177.15490	1550.92224	435	12.55511	157.77448	1980.87570
436	6.12815	200.83645	1230.75529	436	8.79838	177.26855	1559.67685	436	12.62835	157.85367	1993.43081
437	6.15368	200.99895	1236.88343	437	8.84238	177.38165	1568.47524	437	12.70201	157.93240	2006.05916
438	6.17932	201.16078	1243.03711	438	8.88659	177.49417	1577.31761	438	12.77611	158.01067	2018.76117
439	6.20507	201.32194	1249.21644	439	8.93102	177.60614	1586.20420	439	12.85063	158.08848	2031.53727
440	6.23092	201.48243	1255.42150	440	8.97568	177.71756	1595.13522	440	12.92560	158.16585	2044.38791
441	6.25689	201.64226	1261.65243	441	9.02055	177.82841	1604.11090	441	13.00100	158.24277	2057.31350
442	6.28296	201.80142	1267.90931	442	9.06566	177.93872	1613.13145	442	13.07683	158.31924	2070.31450
443	6.30913	201.95992	1274.19227	443	9.11099	178.04848	1622.19711	443	13.15312	158.39527	2083.39133
444	6.33542	202.11776	1280.50140	444	9.15654	178.15769	1631.30810	444	13.22984	158.47085	2096.54445
445	6.36182	202.27495	1286.83682	445	9.20232	178.26636	1640.46464	445	13.30702	158.54600	2109.77429
446	6.38833	202.43148	1293.19864	446	9.24833	178.37449	1649.66696	446	13.38464	158.62071	2123.08131
447	6.41495	202.58737	1299.58697	447	9.29458	178.48207	1658.91530	447	13.46272	158.69499	2136.46595
448	6.44167	202.74261	1306.00192	448	9.34105	178.58913	1668.20987	448	13.54125	158.76884	2149.92867
449	6.46851	202.89720	1312.44359	449	9.38775	178.69565	1677.55092	449	13.62024	158.84226	2163.46992
450	6.49547	203.05116	1318.91211	450	9.43469	178.80164	1686.93868	450	13.69969	158.91526	2177.09016
451	6.52253	203.20447	1325.40758	451	9.48187	178.90711	1696.37337	451	13.77961	158.98783	2190.78985
452	6.54971	203.35715	1331.93011	452	9.52928	179.01205	1705.85524	452	13.85999	159.05998	2204.56946
453	6.57700	203.50919	1338.47982	453	9.57692	179.11646	1715.38451	453	13.94084	159.13171	2218.42945
454	6.60440	203.66061	1345.05681	454	9.62481	179.22036	1724.96143	454	14.02216	159.20302	2232.37029
455	6.63192	203.81139	1351.66122	455	9.67293	179.32374	1734.58624	455	14.10396	159.27393	2246.39245
456	6.65955	203.96155	1358.29314	456	9.72130	179.42661	1744.25917	456	14.18623	159.34442	2260.49640
457	6.68730	204.11109	1364.95269	457	9.76990	179.52897	1753.98047	457	14.26898	159.41450	2274.68263
458	6.71517	204.26001	1371.64000	458	9.81875	179.63081	1763.75037	458	14.35222	159.48418	2288.95161

461	6.79946	204.70306	1391.86955	461	9.96677	179.93332	1793.35415	461	14.60485	159.69079	2332.25992
462	6.82779	204.84952	1398.66901	462	10.01660	180.03315	1803.32092	462	14.69004	159.75886	2346.86477
463	6.85624	204.99537	1405.49680	463	10.06669	180.13249	1813.33753	463	14.77574	159.82654	2361.55481
464	6.88480	205.14062	1412.35303	464	10.11702	180.23134	1823.40422	464	14.86193	159.89383	2376.33055
465	6.91349	205.28527	1419.23784	465	10.16761	180.32969	1833.52124	465	14.94862	159.96072	2391.19248
466	6.94230	205.42931	1426.15133	466	10.21844	180.42755	1843.68884	466	15.03582	160.02723	2406.14110
467	6.97122	205.57276	1433.09363	467	10.26954	180.52492	1853.90729	467	15.12353	160.09335	2421.17692
468	7.00027	205.71561	1440.06485	468	10.32088	180.62182	1864.17682	468	15.21175	160.15909	2436.30046
469	7.02944	205.85787	1447.06512	469	10.37249	180.71822	1874.49771	469	15.30049	160.22445	2451.51221
470	7.05873	205.99954	1454.09456	470	10.42435	180.81415	1884.87020	470	15.38974	160.28943	2466.81270
471	7.08814	206.14062	1461.15329	471	10.47647	180.90961	1895.29455	471	15.47951	160.35403	2482.20244
472	7.11767	206.28111	1468.24142	472	10.52886	181.00458	1905.77102	472	15.56981	160.41825	2497.68195
473	7.14733	206.42103	1475.35910	473	10.58150	181.09909	1916.29988	473	15.66064	160.48211	2513.25176
474	7.17711	206.56036	1482.50643	474	10.63441	181.19312	1926.88138	474	15.75199	160.54559	2528.91240
475	7.20701	206.69911	1489.68354	475	10.68758	181.28669	1937.51578	475	15.84388	160.60871	2544.66439
476	7.23704	206.83729	1496.89055	476	10.74102	181.37979	1948.20336	476	15.93630	160.67146	2560.50826
477	7.26720	206.97489	1504.12760	477	10.79472	181.47243	1958.94438	477	16.02926	160.73384	2576.44456
478	7.29748	207.11193	1511.39479	478	10.84870	181.56460	1969.73910	478	16.12276	160.79587	2592.47382
479	7.32788	207.24839	1518.69227	479	10.90294	181.65632	1980.58780	479	16.21681	160.85753	2608.59658
480	7.35842	207.38429	1526.02016	480	10.95745	181.74758	1991.49073	480	16.31141	160.91884	2624.81340
481	7.38908	207.51963	1533.37857	481	11.01224	181.83839	2002.44819	481	16.40656	160.97979	2641.12481
482	7.41987	207.65440	1540.76765	482	11.06730	181.92875	2013.46043	482	16.50227	161.04039	2657.53137
483	7.45078	207.78861	1548.18752	483	11.12264	182.01866	2024.52773	483	16.59853	161.10063	2674.03364
484	7.48183	207.92227	1555.63830	484	11.17825	182.10811	2035.65037	484	16.69535	161.16053	2690.63217
485	7.51300	208.05537	1563.12012	485	11.23414	182.19713	2046.82862	485	16.79274	161.22008	2707.32752
486	7.54430	208.18792	1570.63312	486	11.29031	182.28570	2058.06276	486	16.89070	161.27928	2724.12027
487	7.57574	208.31992	1578.17743	487	11.34677	182.37383	2069.35308	487	16.98923	161.33815	2741.01097
488	7.60730	208.45138	1585.75317	488	11.40350	182.46152	2080.69984	488	17.08833	161.39667	2758.00020
489	7.63900	208.58228	1593.36047	489	11.46052	182.54878	2092.10334	489	17.18802	161.45485	2775.08853
490	7.67083	208.71265	1600.99948	490	11.51782	182.63560	2103.56386	490	17.28828	161.51269	2792.27655
491	7.70279	208.84247	1608.67031	491	11.57541	182.72199	2115.08168	491	17.38913	161.57019	2809.56483
492	7.73489	208.97175	1616.37310	492	11.63329	182.80795	2126.65709	492	17.49056	161.62737	2826.95396
493	7.76712	209.10050	1624.10799	493	11.69145	182.89348	2138.29037	493	17.59259	161.68421	2844.44452
494	7.79948	209.22872	1631.87510	494	11.74991	182.97859	2149.98182	494	17.69522	161.74072	2862.03711
495	7.83198	209.35640	1639.67458	495	11.80866	183.06328	2161.73173	495	17.79844	161.79691	2879.73233
496	7.86461	209.48355	1647.50656	496	11.86770	183.14754	2173.54039	496	17.90226	161.85277	2897.53077
497	7.89738	209.61017	1655.37117	497	11.92704	183.23138	2185.40809	497	18.00669	161.90830	2915.43303
498	7.93029	209.73627	1663.26855	498	11.98668	183.31481	2197.33514	498	18.11173	161.96351	2933.43972
499	7.96333	209.86185	1671.19884	499	12.04661	183.39782	2209.32181	499	18.21738	162.01841	2951.55146
500	7.99651	209.98690	1679.16217	500	12.10684	183.48042	2221.36842	500	18.32365	162.07298	2969.76884

Table I. ANNUITIES (*Continued*)

M	C(8,M,12)	A(8,M,12)	S(8,M,12)	M	C(9,M,12)	A(9,M,12)	S(9,M,12)	M	C(10,M,12)	A(10,M,12)	S(10,M,12)
1	1.00667	.99338	1.00000	1	1.00750	.99256	1.00000	1	1.00833	.99174	1.00000
2	1.01338	1.98018	2.00667	2	1.01506	1.97772	2.00750	2	1.01674	1.97527	2.00833
3	1.02013	2.96044	3.02004	3	1.02267	2.95556	3.02256	3	1.02521	2.95069	3.02507
4	1.02693	3.93421	4.04018	4	1.03034	3.92611	4.04523	4	1.03375	3.91804	4.05028
5	1.03378	4.90154	5.06711	5	1.03807	4.88944	5.07556	5	1.04237	4.87739	5.08403
6	1.04067	5.86245	6.10089	6	1.04585	5.84560	6.11363	6	1.05105	5.82882	6.12640
7	1.04761	6.81701	7.14157	7	1.05370	6.79464	7.15948	7	1.05981	6.77238	7.17745
8	1.05459	7.76524	8.18918	8	1.06160	7.73661	8.21318	8	1.06864	7.70815	8.23726
9	1.06163	8.70719	9.24377	9	1.06956	8.67158	9.27478	9	1.07755	8.63618	9.30591
10	1.06870	9.64290	10.30540	10	1.07758	9.59958	10.34434	10	1.08653	9.55654	10.38346
11	1.07583	10.57242	11.37410	11	1.08566	10.52067	11.42192	11	1.09558	10.46930	11.46998
12	1.08300	11.49578	12.44993	12	1.09381	11.43491	12.50759	12	1.10471	11.37451	12.56557
13	1.09022	12.41303	13.53293	13	1.10201	12.34235	13.60139	13	1.11392	12.27224	13.67028
14	1.09749	13.32420	14.62315	14	1.11028	13.24302	14.70340	14	1.12320	13.16255	14.78420
15	1.10480	14.22934	15.72063	15	1.11860	14.13699	15.81368	15	1.13256	14.04551	15.90740
16	1.11217	15.12848	16.82544	16	1.12699	15.02431	16.93228	16	1.14200	14.92116	17.03996
17	1.11958	16.02167	17.93761	17	1.13544	15.90502	18.05927	17	1.15152	15.78958	18.18196
18	1.12705	16.90894	19.05719	18	1.14396	16.77918	19.19472	18	1.16111	16.65083	19.33348
19	1.13456	17.79034	20.18424	19	1.15254	17.64683	20.33868	19	1.17079	17.50495	20.49459
20	1.14213	18.66590	21.31880	20	1.16118	18.50802	21.49122	20	1.18054	18.35202	21.66538
21	1.14974	19.53566	22.46093	21	1.16989	19.36280	22.65240	21	1.19038	19.19208	22.84593
22	1.15740	20.39967	23.61066	22	1.17867	20.21121	23.82230	22	1.20030	20.02521	24.03631
23	1.16512	21.25795	24.76807	23	1.18751	21.05331	25.00096	23	1.21031	20.85145	25.23661
24	1.17289	22.11054	25.93319	24	1.19641	21.88915	26.18847	24	1.22039	21.67085	26.44692
25	1.18071	22.95749	27.10608	25	1.20539	22.71876	27.38488	25	1.23056	22.48349	27.66731
26	1.18858	23.79883	28.28678	26	1.21443	23.54219	28.59027	26	1.24082	23.28941	28.89787
27	1.19650	24.63460	29.47536	27	1.22354	24.35949	29.80470	27	1.25116	24.08867	30.13868
28	1.20448	25.46484	30.67187	28	1.23271	25.17071	31.02823	28	1.26158	24.88133	31.38984
29	1.21251	26.28957	31.87634	29	1.24196	25.97589	32.26094	29	1.27210	25.66744	32.65142
30	1.22059	27.10885	33.08885	30	1.25127	26.77508	33.50290	30	1.28270	26.44704	33.92352
31	1.22873	27.92270	34.30945	31	1.26066	27.56832	34.75417	31	1.29339	27.22021	35.20621
32	1.23692	28.73116	35.53818	32	1.27011	28.35565	36.01483	32	1.30416	27.98698	36.49960
33	1.24517	29.53426	36.77510	33	1.27964	29.13712	37.28494	33	1.31503	28.74742	37.80376
34	1.25347	30.33205	38.02026	34	1.28923	29.91278	38.56458	34	1.32599	29.50158	39.11879
35	1.26182	31.12455	39.27373	35	1.29890	30.68266	39.85381	35	1.33704	30.24950	40.44478
36	1.27024	31.91181	40.53556	36	1.30865	31.44681	41.15272	36	1.34818	30.99124	41.78182
37	1.27871	32.69385	41.80579	37	1.31846	32.20527	42.46136	37	1.35942	31.72685	43.13000
38	1.28723	33.47071	43.08450	38	1.32835	32.95808	43.77982	38	1.37075	32.45638	44.48942
39	1.29581	34.24243	44.37173	39	1.33831	33.70529	45.10817	39	1.38217	33.17988	45.86016
40	1.30445	35.00903	45.66754	40	1.34835	34.44694	46.44648	40	1.39369	33.89740	47.24233
41	1.31315	35.77056	46.97199	41	1.35846	35.18307	47.79483	41	1.40530	34.60899	48.63602
42	1.32190	36.52705	48.28514	42	1.36865	35.91371	49.15329	42	1.41701	35.31470	50.04132
43	1.33071	37.27852	49.60704	43	1.37891	36.63892	50.52194	43	1.42882	36.01458	51.45833
44	1.33959	38.02502	50.93775	44	1.38926	37.35873	51.90086	44	1.44073	36.70867	52.88715
45	1.34852	38.76658	52.27734	45	1.39968	38.07318	53.29011	45	1.45273	37.39703	54.32788
46	1.35751	39.50323	53.62585	46	1.41017	38.78231	54.68979	46	1.46484	38.07970	55.78061
47	1.36656	40.23499	54.98336	47	1.42075	39.48617	56.09996	47	1.47705	38.75673	57.24545
48	1.37567	40.96191	56.34992	48	1.43141	40.18478	57.52071	48	1.48935	39.42816	58.72249
49	1.38484	41.68402	57.72558	49	1.44214	40.87820	58.95212	49	1.50177	40.09404	60.21185
50	1.39407	42.40134	59.11042	50	1.45296	41.56645	60.39426	50	1.51428	40.75442	61.71361
51	1.40336	43.11392	60.50449	51	1.46385	42.24958	61.84721	51	1.52690	41.40935	63.22789
52	1.41272	43.82177	61.90785	52	1.47483	42.92762	63.31107	52	1.53962	42.05885	64.75479
53	1.42214	44.52494	63.32057	53	1.48589	43.60061	64.78590	53	1.55245	42.70300	66.29441
54	1.43162	45.22345	64.74271	54	1.49704	44.26860	66.27180	54	1.56539	43.34181	67.84687
55	1.44116	45.91733	66.17433	55	1.50827	44.93161	67.76883	55	1.57844	43.97535	69.41226
56	1.45077	46.60662	67.61549	56	1.51958	45.58969	69.27710	56	1.59159	44.60366	70.99069
57	1.46044	47.29135	69.06626	57	1.53098	46.24287	70.79668	57	1.60485	45.22677	72.58228
[illegible]	[illegible]	[illegible]	[illegible]	58	[illegible]	[illegible]	[illegible]	58	1.61823	45.84473	74.18713

59	1.47998	48.64722	71.99688	59	1.55403	47.53467	73.87011	59	1.63171	46.45758	75.80536
60	1.48985	49.31843	73.47686	60	1.56568	48.17337	75.42414	60	1.64531	47.06537	77.43707
61	1.49978	49.98520	74.96670	61	1.57742	48.80732	76.98982	61	1.65902	47.66813	79.08238
62	1.50978	50.64755	76.46648	62	1.58925	49.43654	78.56724	62	1.67285	48.26592	80.74140
63	1.51984	51.30551	77.97626	63	1.60117	50.06109	80.15650	63	1.68679	48.85876	82.41425
64	1.52997	51.95912	79.49610	64	1.61318	50.68098	81.75767	64	1.70084	49.44671	84.10103
65	1.54017	52.60839	81.02607	65	1.62528	51.29626	83.37085	65	1.71502	50.02979	85.80187
66	1.55044	53.25337	82.56625	66	1.63747	51.90695	84.99613	66	1.72931	50.60806	87.51689
67	1.56078	53.89408	84.11669	67	1.64975	52.51311	86.63360	67	1.74372	51.18154	89.24620
68	1.57118	54.53054	85.67747	68	1.66213	53.11475	88.28336	68	1.75825	51.75029	90.98991
69	1.58166	55.16279	87.24865	69	1.67459	53.71191	89.94548	69	1.77290	52.31434	92.74816
70	1.59220	55.79085	88.83031	70	1.68715	54.30462	91.62007	70	1.78768	52.87373	94.52107
71	1.60282	56.41475	90.42251	71	1.69980	54.89293	93.30722	71	1.80257	53.42849	96.30874
72	1.61350	57.03452	92.02533	72	1.71255	55.47685	95.00703	72	1.81759	53.97867	98.11131
73	1.62426	57.65019	93.63883	73	1.72540	56.05643	96.71958	73	1.83274	54.52430	99.92891
74	1.63509	58.26178	95.26309	74	1.73834	56.63169	98.44498	74	1.84801	55.06542	101.76165
75	1.64599	58.86931	96.89817	75	1.75137	57.20267	100.18331	75	1.86341	55.60207	103.60966
76	1.65696	59.47283	98.54416	76	1.76451	57.76940	101.93469	76	1.87894	56.13428	105.47308
77	1.66801	60.07235	100.20112	77	1.77774	58.33191	103.69920	77	1.89460	56.66210	107.35202
78	1.67913	60.66789	101.86913	78	1.79108	58.89023	105.47694	78	1.91039	57.18555	109.24662
79	1.69032	61.25950	103.54826	79	1.80451	59.44440	107.26802	79	1.92631	57.70468	111.15701
80	1.70159	61.84718	105.23858	80	1.81804	59.99444	109.07253	80	1.94236	58.21952	113.08332
81	1.71293	62.43098	106.94017	81	1.83168	60.54039	110.89057	81	1.95855	58.73010	115.02568
82	1.72435	63.01090	108.65310	82	1.84542	61.08227	112.72225	82	1.97487	59.23646	116.98422
83	1.73585	63.58699	110.37746	83	1.85926	61.62012	114.56767	83	1.99133	59.73864	118.95909
84	1.74742	64.15926	112.11331	84	1.87320	62.15396	116.42693	84	2.00792	60.23667	120.95042
85	1.75907	64.72774	113.86073	85	1.88725	62.68384	118.30013	85	2.02465	60.73058	122.95834
86	1.77080	65.29246	115.61980	86	1.90141	63.20976	120.18738	86	2.04152	61.22041	124.98299
87	1.78260	65.85344	117.39060	87	1.91567	63.73177	122.08879	87	2.05854	61.70619	127.02452
88	1.79449	66.41070	119.17320	88	1.93003	64.24990	124.00445	88	2.07569	62.18796	129.08305
89	1.80645	66.96427	120.96769	89	1.94451	64.76417	125.93449	89	2.09299	62.66574	131.15875
90	1.81849	67.51418	122.77414	90	1.95909	65.27461	127.87899	90	2.11043	63.13958	133.25174
91	1.83062	68.06044	124.59264	91	1.97379	65.78125	129.83809	91	2.12802	63.60950	135.36217
92	1.84282	68.60309	126.42326	92	1.98859	66.28412	131.81187	92	2.14575	64.07554	137.49018
93	1.85511	69.14214	128.26608	93	2.00350	66.78324	133.80046	93	2.16363	64.53772	139.63594
94	1.86747	69.67762	130.12118	94	2.01853	67.27865	135.80397	94	2.18166	64.99609	141.79957
95	1.87992	70.20956	131.98866	95	2.03367	67.77038	137.82250	95	2.19984	65.45067	143.98123
96	1.89246	70.73797	133.86858	96	2.04892	68.25844	139.85616	96	2.21818	65.90149	146.18108
97	1.90507	71.26288	135.76104	97	2.06429	68.74287	141.90508	97	2.23666	66.34858	148.39925
98	1.91777	71.78432	137.66611	98	2.07977	69.22369	143.96937	98	2.25530	66.79198	150.63591
99	1.[illegible]3056	72.30231	139.58389	99	2.09537	69.70093	146.04914	99	2.27409	67.23172	152.89121
100	1.94343	72.81686	141.51445	100	2.11108	70.17462	148.14451	100	2.29304	67.66782	155.16530

Table I. ANNUITIES (*Continued*)

M	C(8,M,12)	A(8,M,12)	S(8,M,12)	M	C(9,M,12)	A(9,M,12)	S(9,M,12)	M	C(10,M,12)	A(10,M,12)	S(10,M,12)
101	1.95639	73.32801	143.45788	101	2.12692	70.64479	150.25560	101	2.31215	68.10032	157.45835
102	1.96943	73.83577	145.41426	102	2.14287	71.11145	152.38251	102	2.33142	68.52924	159.77050
103	1.98256	74.34017	147.38369	103	2.15894	71.57464	154.52538	103	2.35085	68.95462	162.10192
104	1.99577	74.84123	149.36625	104	2.17513	72.03438	156.68432	104	2.37044	69.37648	164.45277
105	2.00908	75.33897	151.36202	105	2.19145	72.49070	158.85945	105	2.39019	69.79486	166.82321
106	2.02247	75.83341	153.37110	106	2.20788	72.94363	161.05090	106	2.41011	70.20978	169.21340
107	2.03596	76.32458	155.39358	107	2.22444	73.39318	163.25878	107	2.43020	70.62127	171.62352
108	2.04953	76.81250	157.42954	108	2.24112	73.83938	165.48322	108	2.45045	71.02935	174.05371
109	2.06319	77.29718	159.47907	109	2.25793	74.28226	167.72435	109	2.47087	71.43407	176.50416
110	2.07695	77.77866	161.54226	110	2.27487	74.72185	169.98228	110	2.49146	71.83544	178.97503
111	2.09079	78.25695	163.61921	111	2.29193	75.15816	172.25715	111	2.51222	72.23350	181.46649
112	2.10473	78.73206	165.71000	112	2.30912	75.59123	174.54908	112	2.53316	72.62826	183.97871
113	2.11876	79.20404	167.81474	113	2.32644	76.02107	176.85819	113	2.55427	73.01976	186.51186
114	2.13289	79.67289	169.93350	114	2.34388	76.44771	179.18463	114	2.57555	73.40803	189.06613
115	2.14711	80.13863	172.06639	115	2.36146	76.87118	181.52851	115	2.59701	73.79309	191.64168
116	2.16142	80.60129	174.21350	116	2.37917	77.29149	183.88998	116	2.61866	74.17496	194.23869
117	2.17583	81.06088	176.37492	117	2.39702	77.70868	186.26915	117	2.64048	74.55368	196.85735
118	2.19034	81.51743	178.55076	118	2.41500	78.12276	188.66617	118	2.66248	74.92927	199.49783
119	2.20494	81.97096	180.74109	119	2.43311	78.53376	191.08117	119	2.68467	75.30176	202.16031
120	2.21964	82.42148	182.94604	120	2.45136	78.94169	193.51428	120	2.70704	75.67115	204.84498
121	2.23444	82.86902	185.16568	121	2.46974	79.34659	195.96563	121	2.72960	76.03752	207.55202
122	2.24933	83.31360	187.40011	122	2.48827	79.74848	198.43538	122	2.75235	76.40084	210.28162
123	2.26433	83.75523	189.64945	123	2.50693	80.14737	200.92364	123	2.77528	76.76117	213.03397
124	2.27943	84.19394	191.91378	124	2.52573	80.54330	203.43057	124	2.79841	77.11851	215.80925
125	2.29462	84.62974	194.19320	125	2.54467	80.93628	205.95630	125	2.82173	77.47291	218.60766
126	2.30992	85.06265	196.48782	126	2.56376	81.32633	208.50097	126	2.84524	77.82437	221.42939
127	2.32532	85.49270	198.79774	127	2.58299	81.71348	211.06473	127	2.86896	78.17293	224.27464
128	2.34082	85.91990	201.12306	128	2.60236	82.09775	213.64771	128	2.89286	78.51861	227.14359
129	2.35643	86.34427	203.46388	129	2.62188	82.47915	216.25007	129	2.91697	78.86143	230.03645
130	2.37214	86.76583	205.82031	130	2.64154	82.85772	218.87195	130	2.94128	79.20142	232.95343
131	2.38795	87.18460	208.19244	131	2.66135	83.23347	221.51349	131	2.96579	79.53859	235.89470
132	2.40387	87.60060	210.58039	132	2.68131	83.60642	224.17484	132	2.99050	79.87299	238.86049
133	2.41990	88.01384	212.98426	133	2.70142	83.97660	226.85615	133	3.01542	80.20461	241.85100
134	2.43603	88.42435	215.40416	134	2.72168	84.34402	229.55757	134	3.04055	80.53350	244.86642
135	2.45227	88.83213	217.84018	135	2.74209	84.70870	232.27925	135	3.06589	80.85967	247.90698
136	2.46862	89.23722	220.29245	136	2.76266	85.07067	235.02135	136	3.09144	81.18314	250.97287
137	2.48507	89.63962	222.76107	137	2.78338	85.42995	237.78401	137	3.11720	81.50395	254.06431
138	2.50164	90.03936	225.24614	138	2.80426	85.78655	240.56739	138	3.14318	81.82209	257.18151
139	2.51832	90.43645	227.74778	139	2.82529	86.14049	243.37164	139	3.16937	82.13761	260.32469
140	2.53511	90.83091	230.26610	140	2.84648	86.49180	246.19693	140	3.19578	82.45053	263.49406
141	2.55201	91.22276	232.80121	141	2.86783	86.84050	249.04341	141	3.22242	82.76085	266.68985
142	2.56902	91.61201	235.35322	142	2.88933	87.18660	251.91123	142	3.24927	83.06861	269.91226
143	2.58615	91.99868	237.92224	143	2.91100	87.53013	254.80057	143	3.27635	83.37383	273.16153
144	2.60339	92.38280	240.50839	144	2.93284	87.87109	257.71157	144	3.30365	83.67653	276.43788
145	2.62075	92.76437	243.11178	145	2.95483	88.20952	260.64441	145	3.33118	83.97672	279.74153
146	2.63822	93.14341	245.73252	146	2.97699	88.54543	263.59924	146	3.35894	84.27444	283.07270
147	2.65580	93.51995	248.37074	147	2.99932	88.87884	266.57623	147	3.38693	84.56969	286.43164
148	2.67351	93.89399	251.02654	148	3.02182	89.20977	269.57556	148	3.41515	84.86250	289.81857
149	2.69133	94.26555	253.70005	149	3.04448	89.53823	272.59737	149	3.44361	85.15289	293.23373
150	2.70928	94.63465	256.39139	150	3.06731	89.86425	275.64185	150	3.47231	85.44089	296.67734
151	2.72734	95.00131	259.10066	151	3.09032	90.18784	278.70917	151	3.50125	85.72650	300.14965
152	2.74552	95.36554	261.82800	152	3.11350	90.50902	281.79949	152	3.53042	86.00975	303.65090
153	2.76382	95.72736	264.57352	153	3.13685	90.82781	284.91298	153	3.55984	86.29066	307.18133
154	2.78225	96.08678	267.33734	154	3.16037	91.14423	288.04983	154	3.58951	86.56925	310.74117
155	2.80080	96.44382	270.11959	155	3.18408	91.45829	291.21020	155	3.61942	86.84554	314.33068
156	2.81947	96.79850	272.92039	156	3.20796	91.77002	294.39428	156	3.64958	87.11954	317.95010
157	2.83827	97.15083	275.73986	157	3.23202	92.07942	297.60224	157	3.68000	87.39128	321.59969

161	2.91471	98.53696	287.20696	161	3.33007	93.29418	310.67647	161	3.80421	88.45597	336.50470
162	2.93414	98.87777	290.12167	162	3.35505	93.59224	314.00655	162	3.83591	88.71666	340.30891
163	2.95371	99.21633	293.05582	163	3.38021	93.88808	317.36160	163	3.86787	88.97520	344.14481
164	2.97340	99.55265	296.00952	164	3.40556	94.18171	320.74181	164	3.90011	89.23160	348.01269
165	2.99322	99.88673	298.98292	165	3.43111	94.47316	324.14737	165	3.93261	89.48589	351.91279
166	3.01317	100.21861	301.97614	166	3.45684	94.76245	327.57848	166	3.96538	89.73807	355.84540
167	3.03326	100.54829	304.98931	167	3.48276	95.04957	331.03531	167	3.99842	89.98817	359.81078
168	3.05348	100.87578	308.02257	168	3.50889	95.33456	334.51808	168	4.03174	90.23620	363.80920
169	3.07384	101.20111	311.07606	169	3.53520	95.61743	338.02696	169	4.06534	90.48218	367.84094
170	3.09433	101.52428	314.14990	170	3.56172	95.89820	341.56217	170	4.09922	90.72613	371.90629
171	3.11496	101.84531	317.24423	171	3.58843	96.17687	345.12388	171	4.13338	90.96806	376.00550
172	3.13573	102.16422	320.35919	172	3.61534	96.45347	348.71231	172	4.16782	91.20800	380.13888
173	3.15663	102.48101	323.49492	173	3.64246	96.72801	352.32765	173	4.20256	91.44595	384.30671
174	3.17768	102.79571	326.65155	174	3.66978	97.00051	355.97011	174	4.23758	91.68193	388.50926
175	3.19886	103.10832	329.82923	175	3.69730	97.27097	359.63989	175	4.27289	91.91597	392.74684
176	3.22019	103.41886	333.02809	176	3.72503	97.53943	363.33719	176	4.30850	92.14806	397.01973
177	3.24166	103.72734	336.24828	177	3.75297	97.80588	367.06222	177	4.34440	92.37825	401.32823
178	3.26327	104.03378	339.48993	178	3.78111	98.07036	370.81518	178	4.38061	92.60653	405.67263
179	3.28502	104.33820	342.75320	179	3.80947	98.33286	374.59630	179	4.41711	92.83292	410.05324
180	3.30692	104.64059	346.03822	180	3.83804	98.59341	378.40577	180	4.45392	93.05744	414.47035
181	3.32897	104.94099	349.34514	181	3.86683	98.85202	382.24381	181	4.49104	93.28010	418.92427
182	3.35116	105.23939	352.67411	182	3.89583	99.10870	386.11064	182	4.52846	93.50093	423.41530
183	3.37350	105.53582	356.02527	183	3.92505	99.36348	390.00647	183	4.56620	93.71993	427.94376
184	3.39599	105.83028	359.39877	184	3.95449	99.61635	393.93152	184	4.60425	93.93712	432.50996
185	3.41863	106.12280	362.79477	185	3.98415	99.86735	397.88601	185	4.64262	94.15252	437.11421
186	3.44142	106.41337	366.21340	186	4.01403	100.11648	401.87015	186	4.68131	94.36613	441.75683
187	3.46437	106.70203	369.65482	187	4.04413	100.36375	405.88418	187	4.72032	94.57798	446.43814
188	3.48746	106.98877	373.11918	188	4.07446	100.60918	409.92831	188	4.75965	94.78808	451.15845
189	3.51071	107.27361	376.60665	189	4.10502	100.85278	414.00277	189	4.79932	94.99645	455.91811
190	3.53412	107.55657	380.11736	190	4.13581	101.09457	418.10779	190	4.83931	95.20309	460.71742
191	3.55768	107.83765	383.65147	191	4.16683	101.33456	422.24360	191	4.87964	95.40802	465.55674
192	3.58139	108.11687	387.20915	192	4.19808	101.57277	426.41043	192	4.92030	95.61126	470.43638
193	3.60527	108.39424	390.79054	193	4.22956	101.80920	430.60850	193	4.96131	95.81282	475.35668
194	3.62931	108.66978	394.39581	194	4.26129	102.04387	434.83807	194	5.00265	96.01271	480.31798
195	3.65350	108.94349	398.02512	195	4.29325	102.27679	439.09935	195	5.04434	96.21095	485.32063
196	3.67786	109.21539	401.67862	196	4.32544	102.50798	443.39260	196	5.08637	96.40756	490.36497
197	3.70238	109.48548	405.35648	197	4.35789	102.73745	447.71804	197	5.12876	96.60254	495.45135
198	3.72706	109.75379	409.05885	198	4.39057	102.96521	452.07593	198	5.17150	96.79590	500.58011
199	3.75191	110.02032	412.78591	199	4.42350	103.19128	456.46650	199	5.21460	96.98767	505.75161
200	3.77692	110.28509	416.53782	200	4.45667	103.41566	460.89000	200	5.25805	97.17786	510.96621

Table I. ANNUITIES (*Continued*)

M	C(8,M,12)	A(8,M,12)	S(8,M,12)	M	C(9,M,12)	A(9,M,12)	S(9,M,12)	M	C(10,M,12)	A(10,M,12)	S(10,M,12)
201	3.80210	110.54810	420.31474	201	4.49010	103.63838	465.34667	201	5.30187	97.35647	516.22426
202	3.82745	110.80937	424.11584	202	4.52378	103.85943	469.83677	202	5.34605	97.55353	521.52613
203	3.85296	111.06891	427.94428	203	4.55770	104.07884	474.36055	203	5.39060	97.73903	526.87218
204	3.87865	111.32673	431.79724	204	4.59189	104.29661	478.91825	204	5.43552	97.92301	532.26278
205	3.90451	111.58285	435.67589	205	4.62633	104.51277	483.51014	205	5.48082	98.10546	537.69830
206	3.93054	111.83727	439.58040	206	4.66102	104.72731	488.13647	206	5.52649	98.28641	543.17912
207	3.95674	112.09000	443.51093	207	4.69598	104.94026	492.79749	207	5.57255	98.46586	548.70561
208	3.98312	112.34106	447.46767	208	4.73120	105.15162	497.49347	208	5.61898	98.64383	554.27816
209	4.00967	112.59046	451.45079	209	4.76669	105.36141	502.22467	209	5.66581	98.82033	559.89715
210	4.03640	112.83820	455.46046	210	4.80244	105.56964	506.99135	210	5.71302	98.99536	565.56296
211	4.06331	113.08431	459.49687	211	4.83845	105.77632	511.79379	211	5.76063	99.16896	571.27598
212	4.09040	113.32878	463.56018	212	4.87474	105.98146	516.63224	212	5.80864	99.34111	577.03661
213	4.11767	113.57164	467.65058	213	4.91130	106.18507	521.50699	213	5.85704	99.51185	582.84525
214	4.14512	113.81288	471.76825	214	4.94814	106.38717	526.41829	214	5.90585	99.68117	588.70230
215	4.17276	114.05253	475.91337	215	4.98525	106.58776	531.36643	215	5.95507	99.84910	594.60815
216	4.20057	114.29060	480.08613	216	5.02264	106.78686	536.35167	216	6.00469	100.01563	600.56322
217	4.22858	114.52708	484.28670	217	5.06031	106.98447	541.37431	217	6.05473	100.18079	606.56791
218	4.25677	114.76200	488.51528	218	5.09826	107.18062	546.43462	218	6.10519	100.34459	612.62264
219	4.28515	114.99537	492.77205	219	5.13650	107.37530	551.53288	219	6.15607	100.50703	618.72783
220	4.31371	115.22719	497.05720	220	5.17502	107.56854	556.66938	220	6.20737	100.66813	624.88390
221	4.34247	115.45747	501.37091	221	5.21383	107.76034	561.84440	221	6.25909	100.82790	631.09126
222	4.37142	115.68623	505.71338	222	5.25294	107.95071	567.05823	222	6.31125	100.98634	637.35036
223	4.40057	115.91347	510.08481	223	5.29233	108.13966	572.31117	223	6.36385	101.14348	643.66161
224	4.42990	116.13921	514.48537	224	5.33203	108.32720	577.60350	224	6.41688	101.29932	650.02546
225	4.45944	116.36345	518.91527	225	5.37202	108.51335	582.93553	225	6.47035	101.45387	656.44233
226	4.48916	116.58621	523.37471	226	5.41231	108.69812	588.30754	226	6.52427	101.60714	662.91269
227	4.51909	116.80750	527.86387	227	5.45290	108.88151	593.71985	227	6.57864	101.75915	669.43696
228	4.54922	117.02731	532.38297	228	5.49380	109.06353	599.17275	228	6.63346	101.90990	676.01560
229	4.57955	117.24568	536.93219	229	5.53500	109.24420	604.66654	229	6.68874	102.05941	682.64906
230	4.61008	117.46259	541.51173	230	5.57651	109.42352	610.20154	230	6.74448	102.20768	689.33781
231	4.64081	117.67807	546.12181	231	5.61834	109.60151	615.77805	231	6.80069	102.35472	696.08229
232	4.67175	117.89212	550.76262	232	5.66047	109.77818	621.39639	232	6.85736	102.50055	702.88297
233	4.70290	118.10476	555.43437	233	5.70293	109.95352	627.05686	233	6.91450	102.64517	709.74033
234	4.73425	118.31598	560.13727	234	5.74570	110.12757	632.75979	234	6.97212	102.78860	716.65483
235	4.76581	118.52581	564.87152	235	5.78879	110.30031	638.50549	235	7.03022	102.93084	723.62696
236	4.79758	118.73425	569.63733	236	5.83221	110.47178	644.29428	236	7.08881	103.07191	730.65718
237	4.82957	118.94131	574.43491	237	5.87595	110.64196	650.12648	237	7.14788	103.21181	737.74599
238	4.86176	119.14700	579.26448	238	5.92002	110.81088	656.00243	238	7.20745	103.35056	744.89388
239	4.89417	119.35132	584.12624	239	5.96442	110.97854	661.92245	239	7.26751	103.48816	752.10132
240	4.92680	119.55429	589.02042	240	6.00915	111.14495	667.88687	240	7.32807	103.62462	759.36884
241	4.95965	119.75592	593.94722	241	6.05422	111.31013	673.89602	241	7.38914	103.75995	766.69691
242	4.99271	119.95621	598.90687	242	6.09963	111.47407	679.95024	242	7.45072	103.89417	774.08605
243	5.02600	120.15518	603.89958	243	6.14537	111.63680	686.04987	243	7.51281	104.02727	781.53677
244	5.05950	120.35282	608.92558	244	6.19146	111.79831	692.19524	244	7.57541	104.15928	789.04957
245	5.09323	120.54916	613.98508	245	6.23790	111.95862	698.38671	245	7.63854	104.29019	796.62499
246	5.12719	120.74420	619.07831	246	6.28468	112.11774	704.62461	246	7.70220	104.42003	804.26353
247	5.16137	120.93795	624.20550	247	6.33182	112.27567	710.90929	247	7.76638	104.54879	811.96572
248	5.19578	121.13041	629.36687	248	6.37931	112.43243	717.24111	248	7.83110	104.67648	819.73211
249	5.23042	121.32160	634.56265	249	6.42715	112.58802	723.62042	249	7.89636	104.80312	827.56321
250	5.26529	121.51153	639.79307	250	6.47536	112.74245	730.04757	250	7.96216	104.92872	835.45957
251	5.30039	121.70019	645.05836	251	6.52392	112.89573	736.52293	251	8.02851	105.05327	843.42173
252	5.33572	121.88761	650.35875	252	6.57285	113.04787	743.04685	252	8.09542	105.17680	851.45024
253	5.37130	122.07378	655.69447	253	6.62215	113.19888	749.61970	253	8.16288	105.29931	859.54566
254	5.40711	122.25872	661.06577	254	6.67181	113.34876	756.24185	254	8.23090	105.42080	867.70854
255	5.44315	122.44244	666.47287	255	6.72185	113.49753	762.91366	255	8.29950	105.54129	875.93945
256	5.47944	122.62494	671.91602	256	6.77227	113.64519	769.63552	256	8.36866	105.66078	884.23894
257	5.51597	122.80623	677.39546	257	6.82306	113.79175	776.40778	257	8.43840	105.77929	892.60760
[illegible]	[illegible]	[illegible]	[illegible]	[illegible]	[illegible]	[illegible]	[illegible]	258	8.50872	105.89682	901.04600

261	5.66454	123.51947	699.68096	261	7.03006	114.36717	804.00859	261	8.72321	106.24360	926.78546
262	5.70230	123.69484	705.34550	262	7.08279	114.50836	811.03866	262	8.79591	106.35729	935.50867
263	5.74032	123.86905	711.04781	263	7.13591	114.64850	818.12145	263	8.86920	106.47004	944.30457
264	5.77859	124.04210	716.78813	264	7.18943	114.78759	825.25736	264	8.94311	106.58186	953.17378
265	5.81711	124.21401	722.56671	265	7.24335	114.92565	832.44679	265	9.01764	106.69275	962.11689
266	5.85589	124.38477	728.38383	266	7.29768	115.06268	839.69014	266	9.09279	106.80273	971.13453
267	5.89493	124.55441	734.23972	267	7.35241	115.19869	846.98782	267	9.16856	106.91180	980.22732
268	5.93423	124.72293	740.13465	268	7.40755	115.33368	854.34022	268	9.24497	107.01996	989.39588
269	5.97379	124.89032	746.06888	269	7.46311	115.46768	861.74778	269	9.32201	107.12724	998.64085
270	6.01362	125.05661	752.04267	270	7.51908	115.60067	869.21088	270	9.39969	107.23362	1007.96286
271	6.05371	125.22180	758.05629	271	7.57547	115.73268	876.72997	271	9.47802	107.33913	1017.36255
272	6.09407	125.38589	764.11000	272	7.63229	115.86370	884.30544	272	9.55700	107.44376	1026.84057
273	6.13469	125.54890	770.20407	273	7.68953	115.99375	891.93773	273	9.63665	107.54754	1036.39757
274	6.17559	125.71083	776.33876	274	7.74720	116.12282	899.62726	274	9.71695	107.65045	1046.03422
275	6.21676	125.87169	782.51435	275	7.80531	116.25094	907.37447	275	9.79793	107.75251	1055.75117
276	6.25821	126.03148	788.73111	276	7.86385	116.37811	915.17978	276	9.87958	107.85373	1065.54910
277	6.29993	126.19021	794.98932	277	7.92283	116.50432	923.04363	277	9.96191	107.95411	1075.42867
278	6.34193	126.34789	801.28925	278	7.98225	116.62960	930.96645	278	10.04492	108.05366	1085.39058
279	6.38421	126.50452	807.63118	279	8.04212	116.75395	938.94870	279	10.12863	108.15239	1095.43550
280	6.42677	126.66012	814.01539	280	8.10243	116.87737	946.99082	280	10.21303	108.25031	1105.56413
281	6.46961	126.81469	820.44216	281	8.16320	116.99987	955.09325	281	10.29814	108.34741	1115.77716
282	6.51275	126.96824	826.91177	282	8.22442	117.12146	963.25645	282	10.38396	108.44372	1126.07531
283	6.55616	127.12077	833.42451	283	8.28611	117.24214	971.48087	283	10.47049	108.53922	1136.45927
284	6.59987	127.27228	839.98068	284	8.34825	117.36193	979.76698	284	10.55775	108.63394	1146.92976
285	6.64387	127.42280	846.58055	285	8.41086	117.48082	988.11523	285	10.64573	108.72787	1157.48751
286	6.68816	127.57232	853.22442	286	8.47395	117.59883	996.52609	286	10.73444	108.82103	1168.13324
287	6.73275	127.72084	859.91258	287	8.53750	117.71596	1005.00004	287	10.82390	108.91342	1178.86768
288	6.77764	127.86839	866.64533	288	8.60153	117.83222	1013.53754	288	10.91410	109.00504	1189.69158
289	6.82282	128.01496	873.42297	289	8.66604	117.94761	1022.13907	289	11.00505	109.09591	1200.60568
290	6.86831	128.16055	880.24579	290	8.73104	118.06214	1030.80511	290	11.09676	109.18603	1211.61072
291	6.91409	128.30518	887.11409	291	8.79652	118.17583	1039.53615	291	11.18923	109.27540	1222.70748
292	6.96019	128.44886	894.02819	292	8.86250	118.28866	1048.33267	292	11.28247	109.36403	1233.89671
293	7.00659	128.59158	900.98838	293	8.92896	118.40066	1057.19517	293	11.37649	109.45193	1245.17918
294	7.05330	128.73336	907.99496	294	8.99593	118.51182	1066.12413	294	11.47130	109.53911	1256.55567
295	7.10032	128.87420	915.04826	295	9.06340	118.62215	1075.12006	295	11.56689	109.62556	1268.02697
296	7.14766	129.01410	922.14859	296	9.13138	118.73166	1084.18346	296	11.66328	109.71130	1279.59386
297	7.19531	129.15308	929.29624	297	9.19986	118.84036	1093.31484	297	11.76048	109.79633	1291.25715
298	7.24328	129.29114	936.49155	298	9.26886	118.94825	1102.51470	298	11.85848	109.88066	1303.01762
299	7.29157	129.42829	943.73483	299	9.33838	119.05533	1111.78356	299	11.95730	109.96429	1314.87610
300	7.34018	129.56452	951.02639	300	9.40841	119.16162	1121.12194	300	12.05695	110.04723	1326.83340

Table I. ANNUITIES (*Continued*)

M	C(8,M,12)	A(8,M,12)	S(8,M,12)	M	C(9,M,12)	A(9,M,12)	S(9,M,12)	M	C(10,M,12)	A(10,M,12)	S(10,M,12)
301	7.38911	129.69986	958.36657	301	9.47898	119.26712	1130.53035	301	12.15742	110.12948	1338.89035
302	7.43837	129.83429	965.75568	302	9.55007	119.37183	1140.00933	302	12.25873	110.21106	1351.04777
303	7.48796	129.96784	973.19405	303	9.62170	119.47576	1149.55940	303	12.36089	110.29196	1363.30650
304	7.53788	130.10051	980.68201	304	9.69386	119.57892	1159.18109	304	12.46389	110.37219	1375.66739
305	7.58813	130.23229	988.21989	305	9.76655	119.68131	1168.87495	305	12.56776	110.45176	1388.13128
306	7.63872	130.36320	995.80803	306	9.83981	119.78294	1178.64152	306	12.67249	110.53067	1400.69904
307	7.68964	130.49325	1003.44675	307	9.91361	119.88381	1188.48133	307	12.77810	110.60893	1413.37153
308	7.74091	130.62243	1011.13639	308	9.98796	119.98393	1198.39494	308	12.88458	110.68654	1426.14963
309	7.79252	130.75076	1018.87730	309	10.06287	120.08331	1208.38290	309	12.99195	110.76351	1439.03421
310	7.84447	130.87824	1026.66981	310	10.13834	120.18194	1218.44577	310	13.10022	110.83985	1452.02616
311	7.89676	131.00487	1034.51428	311	10.21438	120.27984	1228.58411	311	13.20939	110.91555	1465.12638
312	7.94941	131.13067	1042.41104	312	10.29099	120.37701	1238.79849	312	13.31946	110.99063	1478.33577
313	8.00240	131.25563	1050.36045	313	10.36817	120.47346	1249.08948	313	13.43046	111.06509	1491.65523
314	8.05575	131.37977	1058.36285	314	10.44593	120.56919	1259.45765	314	13.54238	111.13893	1505.08569
315	8.10946	131.50308	1066.41860	315	10.52428	120.66421	1269.90359	315	13.65523	111.21216	1518.62807
316	8.16352	131.62557	1074.52806	316	10.60321	120.75852	1280.42786	316	13.76903	111.28479	1532.28331
317	8.21794	131.74726	1082.69158	317	10.68273	120.85213	1291.03107	317	13.88377	111.35681	1546.05233
318	8.27273	131.86814	1090.90953	318	10.76285	120.94504	1301.71381	318	13.99947	111.42825	1559.93610
319	8.32788	131.98822	1099.18226	319	10.84357	121.03727	1312.47666	319	14.11613	111.49909	1573.93557
320	8.38340	132.10750	1107.51014	320	10.92490	121.12880	1323.32023	320	14.23376	111.56934	1588.05170
321	8.43929	132.22599	1115.89354	321	11.00684	121.21965	1334.24514	321	14.35238	111.63902	1602.28546
322	8.49555	132.34370	1124.33283	322	11.08939	121.30983	1345.25197	322	14.47198	111.70812	1616.63784
323	8.55219	132.46063	1132.82838	323	11.17256	121.39933	1356.34136	323	14.59258	111.77664	1631.10983
324	8.60920	132.57679	1141.38057	324	11.25635	121.48817	1367.51392	324	14.71419	111.84461	1645.70241
325	8.66660	132.69217	1149.98977	325	11.34078	121.57635	1378.77028	325	14.83680	111.91201	1660.41659
326	8.72438	132.80679	1158.65637	326	11.42583	121.66387	1390.11105	326	14.96044	111.97885	1675.25340
327	8.78254	132.92066	1167.38075	327	11.51153	121.75074	1401.53689	327	15.08512	112.04514	1690.21384
328	8.84109	133.03376	1176.16329	328	11.59786	121.83696	1413.04842	328	15.21082	112.11088	1705.29896
329	8.90003	133.14612	1185.00438	329	11.68485	121.92254	1424.64628	329	15.33758	112.17608	1720.50978
330	8.95936	133.25774	1193.90440	330	11.77248	122.00749	1436.33113	330	15.46539	112.24074	1735.84737
331	9.01909	133.36861	1202.86377	331	11.86078	122.09180	1448.10361	331	15.59427	112.30487	1751.31276
332	9.07922	133.47876	1211.88286	332	11.94973	122.17548	1459.95439	332	15.72423	112.36846	1766.90703
333	9.13975	133.58817	1220.96208	333	12.03936	122.25854	1471.91412	333	15.85526	112.43153	1782.63126
334	9.20068	133.69686	1230.10183	334	12.12965	122.34099	1483.95348	334	15.98739	112.49408	1798.48652
335	9.26202	133.80482	1239.30250	335	12.22062	122.42282	1496.08313	335	16.12062	112.55612	1814.47391
336	9.32376	133.91208	1248.56452	336	12.31228	122.50403	1508.30375	336	16.25495	112.61764	1830.59452
337	9.38592	134.01862	1257.88828	337	12.40462	122.58465	1520.61603	337	16.39041	112.67865	1846.84948
338	9.44849	134.12446	1267.27421	338	12.49765	122.66467	1533.02065	338	16.52700	112.73915	1863.23989
339	9.51148	134.22959	1276.72270	339	12.59139	122.74408	1545.51830	339	16.66472	112.79916	1879.76689
340	9.57489	134.33403	1286.23419	340	12.68582	122.82291	1558.10969	340	16.80360	112.85867	1896.43161
341	9.63873	134.43778	1295.80908	341	12.78097	122.90115	1570.79551	341	16.94363	112.91769	1913.23521
342	9.70299	134.54084	1305.44781	342	12.87682	122.97881	1583.57648	342	17.08482	112.97622	1930.17884
343	9.76767	134.64322	1315.15079	343	12.97340	123.05589	1596.45330	343	17.22720	113.03427	1947.26366
344	9.83279	134.74492	1324.91847	344	13.07070	123.13240	1609.42670	344	17.37076	113.09184	1964.49086
345	9.89834	134.84595	1334.75125	345	13.16873	123.20834	1622.49740	345	17.51551	113.14893	1981.86161
346	9.96433	134.94630	1344.64960	346	13.26750	123.28371	1635.66613	346	17.66148	113.20555	1999.37713
347	10.03076	135.04600	1354.61393	347	13.36700	123.35852	1648.93363	347	17.80866	113.26170	2017.03860
348	10.09763	135.14503	1364.64469	348	13.46725	123.43278	1662.30063	348	17.95706	113.31739	2034.84726
349	10.16495	135.24341	1374.74232	349	13.56826	123.50648	1675.76789	349	18.10670	113.37262	2052.80432
350	10.23272	135.34113	1384.90727	350	13.67002	123.57963	1689.33615	350	18.25759	113.42739	2070.91102
351	10.30093	135.43821	1395.13998	351	13.77255	123.65224	1703.00617	351	18.40974	113.48171	2089.16861
352	10.36961	135.53465	1405.44092	352	13.87584	123.72431	1716.77871	352	18.56315	113.53558	2107.57835
353	10.43874	135.63045	1415.81052	353	13.97991	123.79584	1730.65455	353	18.71785	113.58901	2126.14150
354	10.50833	135.72561	1426.24926	354	14.08476	123.86684	1744.63446	354	18.87383	113.64199	2144.85935
355	10.57838	135.82014	1436.75759	355	14.19039	123.93731	1758.71922	355	19.03111	113.69453	2163.73318
356	10.64891	135.91405	1447.33597	356	14.29682	124.00725	1772.90961	356	19.18970	113.74665	2182.76429
357	10.71990	136.00733	1457.98488	357	14.40405	124.07668	1787.20644	357	19.34962	113.79833	2201.95399
358	10.79137	136.10000	1468.70478	358	14.51208	124.14558	1801.61049	356	19.51086	113.84958	2221.30361

361	11.00863	136.37433	1501.29518	361	14.84106	124.34925	1845.47406	361	20.00271	114.00081	2280.32532
362	11.08203	136.46457	1512.30381	362	14.95236	124.41613	1860.31511	362	20.16940	114.05039	2300.32804
363	11.15591	136.55421	1523.38584	363	15.06451	124.48251	1875.26748	363	20.33748	114.09956	2320.49744
364	11.23028	136.64325	1534.54174	364	15.17749	124.54839	1890.33193	364	20.50696	114.14833	2340.83491
365	11.30515	136.73171	1545.77202	365	15.29132	124.61379	1905.50947	365	20.67785	114.19669	2361.34187
366	11.38051	136.81958	1557.07717	366	15.40601	124.67870	1920.80080	366	20.85016	114.24465	2382.01972
367	11.45638	136.90686	1568.45768	367	15.52155	124.74313	1936.20680	367	21.02392	114.29221	2402.86989
368	11.53276	136.99357	1579.91407	368	15.63796	124.80707	1951.72835	368	21.19912	114.33939	2423.89380
369	11.60965	137.07971	1591.44683	369	15.75525	124.87054	1967.36631	369	21.37577	114.38617	2445.09292
370	11.68704	137.16527	1603.05647	370	15.87341	124.93354	1983.12156	370	21.55391	114.43256	2466.46869
371	11.76496	137.25027	1614.74352	371	15.99246	124.99607	1998.99497	371	21.73352	114.47858	2488.02260
372	11.84339	137.33471	1626.50847	372	16.11241	125.05814	2014.98744	372	21.91463	114.52421	2509.75612
373	11.92235	137.41858	1638.35186	373	16.23325	125.11974	2031.09984	373	22.09726	114.56946	2531.67075
374	12.00183	137.50190	1650.27421	374	16.35500	125.18088	2047.33309	374	22.28140	114.61434	2553.76801
375	12.08184	137.58467	1662.27604	375	16.47766	125.24157	2063.68809	375	22.46708	114.65885	2576.04941
376	12.16239	137.66689	1674.35788	376	16.60124	125.30181	2080.16575	376	22.65430	114.70299	2598.51649
377	12.24347	137.74857	1686.52026	377	16.72575	125.36159	2096.76699	377	22.84309	114.74677	2621.17079
378	12.32509	137.82971	1698.76373	378	16.85120	125.42094	2113.49274	378	23.03345	114.79019	2644.01388
379	12.40726	137.91030	1711.08882	379	16.97758	125.47984	2130.34394	379	23.22539	114.83324	2667.04733
380	12.48997	137.99037	1723.49608	380	17.10491	125.53830	2147.32152	380	23.41894	114.87594	2690.27272
381	12.57324	138.06990	1735.98606	381	17.23320	125.59633	2164.42643	381	23.61410	114.91829	2713.69166
382	12.65706	138.14891	1748.55930	382	17.36245	125.65392	2181.65963	382	23.81088	114.96029	2737.30576
383	12.74144	138.22739	1761.21636	383	17.49267	125.71109	2199.02208	383	24.00931	115.00194	2761.11664
384	12.82639	138.30536	1773.95780	384	17.62386	125.76783	2216.51474	384	24.20938	115.04324	2785.12595
385	12.91189	138.38280	1786.78419	385	17.75604	125.82415	2234.13860	385	24.41113	115.08421	2809.33533
386	12.99797	138.45974	1799.69608	386	17.88921	125.88005	2251.89464	386	24.61455	115.12484	2833.74646
387	13.08463	138.53617	1812.69405	387	18.02338	125.93553	2269.78385	387	24.81968	115.16513	2858.36101
388	13.17186	138.61208	1825.77868	388	18.15855	125.99060	2287.80723	388	25.02651	115.20508	2883.18069
389	13.25967	138.68750	1838.95054	389	18.29474	126.04527	2305.96579	389	25.23506	115.24471	2908.20719
390	13.34807	138.76242	1852.21021	390	18.43195	126.09952	2324.26053	390	25.44535	115.28401	2933.44225
391	13.43706	138.83684	1865.55828	391	18.57019	126.15337	2342.69248	391	25.65740	115.32299	2958.88760
392	13.52664	138.91077	1878.99533	392	18.70947	126.20682	2361.26268	392	25.87121	115.36164	2984.54500
393	13.61681	138.98421	1892.52197	393	18.84979	126.25987	2379.97215	393	26.08680	115.39997	3010.41621
394	13.70759	139.05716	1906.13878	394	18.99116	126.31252	2398.82194	394	26.30419	115.43799	3036.50301
395	13.79898	139.12963	1919.84637	395	19.13360	126.36479	2417.81310	395	26.52339	115.47569	3062.80720
396	13.89097	139.20162	1933.64535	396	19.27710	126.41666	2436.94670	396	26.74442	115.51308	3089.33060
397	13.98358	139.27313	1947.53632	397	19.42168	126.46815	2456.22380	397	26.96729	115.55016	3116.07502
398	14.07680	139.34417	1961.51989	398	19.56734	126.51926	2475.64548	398	27.19202	115.58694	3143.04231
399	14.17064	139.41474	1975.59669	399	19.71410	126.56998	2495.21282	399	27.41862	115.62341	3170.23433
400	14.26512	139.48484	1989.76734	400	19.86195	126.62033	2514.92692	400	27.64711	115.65958	3197.65295

Table I. ANNUITIES (*Continued*)

M	C(8,M,12)	A(8,M,12)	S(8,M,12)	M	C(9,M,12)	A(9,M,12)	S(9,M,12)	M	C(10,M,12)	A(10,M,12)	S(10,M,12)
401	14.36022	139.55447	2004.03245	401	20.01092	126.67030	2534.78887	401	27.87750	115.69545	3225.30006
402	14.45595	139.62365	2018.39267	402	20.16100	126.71990	2554.79978	402	28.10981	115.73103	3253.17756
403	14.55232	139.69237	2032.84862	403	20.31221	126.76914	2574.96078	403	28.34406	115.76631	3281.28737
404	14.64934	139.76063	2047.40095	404	20.46455	126.81800	2595.27299	404	28.58026	115.80130	3309.63143
405	14.74700	139.82844	2062.05028	405	20.61803	126.86650	2615.73754	405	28.81843	115.83600	3338.21169
406	14.84532	139.89580	2076.79729	406	20.77267	126.91464	2636.35557	406	29.05858	115.87041	3367.03012
407	14.94428	139.96272	2091.64260	407	20.92846	126.96242	2657.12823	407	29.30074	115.90454	3396.08871
408	15.04391	140.02919	2106.58689	408	21.08543	127.00985	2678.05670	408	29.54491	115.93839	3425.38945
409	15.14421	140.09522	2121.63080	409	21.24357	127.05692	2699.14212	409	29.79112	115.97195	3454.93436
410	15.24517	140.16082	2136.77500	410	21.40289	127.10365	2720.38569	410	30.03938	116.00524	3484.72548
411	15.34680	140.22598	2152.02017	411	21.56341	127.15002	2741.78858	411	30.28971	116.03826	3514.76486
412	15.44911	140.29070	2167.36697	412	21.72514	127.19605	2763.35199	412	30.54212	116.07100	3545.05457
413	15.55211	140.35500	2182.81608	413	21.88808	127.24174	2785.07713	413	30.79664	116.10347	3575.59669
414	15.65579	140.41888	2198.36819	414	22.05224	127.28708	2806.96521	414	31.05328	116.13567	3606.39333
415	15.76016	140.48233	2214.02398	415	22.21763	127.33209	2829.01745	415	31.31206	116.16761	3637.44660
416	15.86523	140.54536	2229.78414	416	22.38426	127.37677	2851.23508	416	31.57299	116.19928	3668.75866
417	15.97100	140.60797	2245.64937	417	22.55215	127.42111	2873.61935	417	31.83610	116.23069	3700.33165
418	16.07747	140.67017	2261.62036	418	22.72129	127.46512	2896.17149	418	32.10140	116.26185	3732.16774
419	16.18465	140.73196	2277.69783	419	22.89170	127.50880	2918.89278	419	32.36891	116.29274	3764.26914
420	16.29255	140.79334	2293.88248	420	23.06338	127.55216	2941.78447	420	32.63865	116.32338	3796.63805
421	16.40117	140.85431	2310.17503	421	23.23636	127.59520	2964.84786	421	32.91064	116.35376	3829.27670
422	16.51051	140.91488	2326.57620	422	23.41063	127.63792	2988.08422	422	33.18489	116.38390	3862.18734
423	16.62058	140.97504	2343.08671	423	23.58621	127.68031	3011.49485	423	33.46144	116.41378	3895.37224
424	16.73138	141.03481	2359.70729	424	23.76311	127.72239	3035.08106	424	33.74028	116.44342	3928.83367
425	16.84292	141.09418	2376.43867	425	23.94133	127.76416	3058.84417	425	34.02145	116.47281	3962.57395
426	16.95521	141.15316	2393.28159	426	24.12089	127.80562	3082.78550	426	34.30496	116.50196	3996.59540
427	17.06825	141.21175	2410.23680	427	24.30180	127.84677	3106.90639	427	34.59084	116.53087	4030.90036
428	17.18203	141.26995	2427.30505	428	24.48406	127.88761	3131.20819	428	34.87909	116.55954	4065.49120
429	17.29658	141.32777	2444.48708	429	24.66769	127.92815	3155.69225	429	35.16975	116.58798	4100.37029
430	17.41189	141.38520	2461.78366	430	24.85270	127.96839	3180.35994	430	35.46283	116.61618	4135.54005
431	17.52797	141.44225	2479.19556	431	25.03909	128.00833	3205.21264	431	35.75836	116.64414	4171.00288
432	17.64482	141.49892	2496.72353	432	25.22689	128.04797	3230.25173	432	36.05634	116.67188	4206.76124
433	17.76246	141.55522	2514.36835	433	25.41609	128.08731	3255.47862	433	36.35681	116.69938	4242.81758
434	17.88087	141.61115	2532.13080	434	25.60671	128.12636	3280.89471	434	36.65979	116.72666	4279.17439
435	18.00008	141.66670	2550.01168	435	25.79876	128.16513	3306.50142	435	36.96528	116.75371	4315.83418
436	18.12008	141.72189	2568.01175	436	25.99225	128.20360	3332.30018	436	37.27333	116.78054	4352.79946
437	18.24088	141.77671	2586.13183	437	26.18719	128.24179	3358.29244	437	37.58394	116.80715	4390.07279
438	18.36248	141.83117	2604.37271	438	26.38360	128.27969	3384.47963	438	37.89714	116.83353	4427.65673
439	18.48490	141.88527	2622.73520	439	26.58147	128.31731	3410.86323	439	38.21295	116.85970	4465.55387
440	18.60813	141.93901	2641.22010	440	26.78084	128.35465	3437.44470	440	38.53139	116.88566	4503.76682
441	18.73219	141.99239	2659.82823	441	26.98169	128.39171	3464.22553	441	38.85249	116.91139	4542.29821
442	18.85707	142.04542	2678.56042	442	27.18405	128.42850	3491.20723	442	39.17626	116.93692	4581.15070
443	18.98278	142.09810	2697.41749	443	27.38793	128.46501	3518.39128	443	39.50272	116.96223	4620.32695
444	19.10934	142.15043	2716.40027	444	27.59334	128.50125	3545.77922	444	39.83191	116.98734	4659.82968
445	19.23673	142.20242	2735.50961	445	27.80029	128.53722	3573.37256	445	40.16385	117.01224	4699.66159
446	19.36498	142.25406	2754.74634	446	28.00880	128.57292	3601.17285	446	40.49855	117.03693	4739.82544
447	19.49408	142.30535	2774.11131	447	28.21886	128.60836	3629.18165	447	40.83603	117.06142	4780.32398
448	19.62404	142.35631	2793.60539	448	28.43050	128.64353	3657.40051	448	41.17633	117.08570	4821.16002
449	19.75486	142.40693	2813.22943	449	28.64373	128.67845	3685.83102	449	41.51947	117.10979	4862.33635
450	19.88656	142.45722	2832.98429	450	28.85856	128.71310	3714.47475	450	41.86547	117.13368	4903.85582
451	20.01914	142.50717	2852.87085	451	29.07500	128.74749	3743.33331	451	42.21434	117.15736	4945.72128
452	20.15260	142.55679	2872.88999	452	29.29306	128.78163	3772.40831	452	42.56613	117.18086	4987.93563
453	20.28695	142.60608	2893.04259	453	29.51276	128.81551	3801.70137	453	42.92085	117.20416	5030.50176
454	20.42220	142.65505	2913.32954	454	29.73411	128.84914	3831.21413	454	43.27852	117.22726	5073.42261
455	20.55834	142.70369	2933.75174	455	29.95711	128.88253	3860.94824	455	43.63918	117.25018	5116.70113
456	20.69540	142.75201	2954.31008	456	30.18179	128.91566	3890.90535	456	44.00284	117.27290	5160.34030
457	20.83337	142.80001	2975.00548	457	30.40815	128.94854	3921.08714	457	44.36953	117.29544	5204.34314
458	[illegible]	[illegible]	[illegible]	458	[illegible]	[illegible]	[illegible]	458	44.73927	117.31779	5248.71267

461	21.39451	142.98885	3059.17601	461	31.33071	129.07766	4044.09498	461	45.86710	117.38375	5384.05207
462	21.53714	143.03529	3080.57051	462	31.56569	129.10934	4075.42569	462	46.24933	117.40537	5429.91917
463	21.68072	143.08141	3102.10765	463	31.80244	129.14078	4106.99138	463	46.63474	117.42681	5476.16850
464	21.82526	143.12723	3123.79837	464	32.04095	129.17199	4138.79382	464	47.02336	117.44808	5522.80324
465	21.97076	143.17274	3145.61362	465	32.28126	129.20297	4170.83477	465	47.41522	117.46917	5569.82660
466	22.11723	143.21796	3167.58438	466	32.52337	129.23372	4203.11603	466	47.81035	117.49008	5617.24182
467	22.26468	143.26287	3189.70161	467	32.76730	129.26424	4235.63940	467	48.20877	117.51083	5665.05217
468	22.41311	143.30749	3211.96629	468	33.01305	129.29453	4268.40670	468	48.61051	117.53140	5713.26094
469	22.56253	143.35181	3234.37940	469	33.26065	129.32459	4301.41975	469	49.01560	117.55180	5761.87144
470	22.71295	143.39584	3256.94193	470	33.51010	129.35443	4334.68039	470	49.42406	117.57203	5810.88704
471	22.86437	143.43957	3279.65487	471	33.76143	129.38405	4368.19050	471	49.83593	117.59210	5860.31110
472	23.01679	143.48302	3302.51924	472	34.01464	129.41345	4401.95193	472	50.25123	117.61200	5910.14702
473	23.17024	143.52618	3325.53603	473	34.26975	129.44263	4435.96657	473	50.66999	117.63173	5960.39825
474	23.32471	143.56905	3348.70627	474	34.52677	129.47160	4470.23631	474	51.09224	117.65131	6011.06823
475	23.48021	143.61164	3372.03098	475	34.78572	129.50034	4504.76309	475	51.51800	117.67072	6062.16047
476	23.63674	143.65395	3395.51119	476	35.04662	129.52888	4539.54881	476	51.94732	117.68997	6113.67847
477	23.79432	143.69597	3419.14793	477	35.30947	129.55720	4574.59543	477	52.38021	117.70906	6165.62579
478	23.95295	143.73772	3442.94225	478	35.57429	129.58531	4609.90489	478	52.81672	117.72799	6218.00601
479	24.11263	143.77919	3466.89520	479	35.84109	129.61321	4645.47918	479	53.25686	117.74677	6270.82272
480	24.27339	143.82039	3491.00783	480	36.10990	129.64090	4681.32027	480	53.70066	117.76539	6324.07958
481	24.43521	143.86132	3515.28122	481	36.38073	129.66839	4717.43017	481	54.14817	117.78386	6377.78024
482	24.59811	143.90197	3539.71643	482	36.65358	129.69567	4753.81090	482	54.59940	117.80217	6431.92841
483	24.76210	143.94235	3564.31453	483	36.92848	129.72275	4790.46449	483	55.05440	117.82034	6486.52782
484	24.92718	143.98247	3589.07663	484	37.20545	129.74963	4827.39297	484	55.51319	117.83835	6541.58221
485	25.09336	144.02232	3614.00381	485	37.48449	129.77631	4864.59841	485	55.97579	117.85622	6597.09540
486	25.26065	144.06191	3639.09717	486	37.76562	129.80279	4902.08290	486	56.44226	117.87393	6653.07119
487	25.42905	144.10124	3664.35782	487	38.04886	129.82907	4939.84852	487	56.91261	117.89150	6709.51345
488	25.59858	144.14030	3689.78687	488	38.33423	129.85515	4977.89739	488	57.38688	117.90893	6766.42607
489	25.76924	144.17911	3715.38545	489	38.62174	129.88105	5016.23162	489	57.86511	117.92621	6823.81295
490	25.94103	144.21765	3741.15468	490	38.91140	129.90675	5054.85335	490	58.34732	117.94335	6881.67806
491	26.11397	144.25595	3767.09571	491	39.20324	129.93225	5093.76475	491	58.83354	117.96035	6940.02538
492	26.28806	144.29399	3793.20969	492	39.49726	129.95757	5132.95799	492	59.32382	117.97720	6998.85892
493	26.46332	144.33178	3819.49775	493	39.79349	129.98270	5172.45525	493	59.81819	117.99392	7058.18275
494	26.63974	144.36931	3845.96107	494	40.09194	130.00764	5212.25874	494	60.31667	118.01050	7118.00093
495	26.81734	144.40660	3872.60081	495	40.39263	130.03240	5252.35068	495	60.81931	118.02694	7178.31761
496	26.99612	144.44365	3899.41815	496	40.69557	130.05697	5292.74331	496	61.32614	118.04325	7239.13692
497	27.17610	144.48044	3926.41427	497	41.00079	130.08136	5333.43889	497	61.83719	118.05942	7300.46306
498	27.35727	144.51700	3953.59036	498	41.30830	130.10557	5374.43968	498	62.35250	118.07546	7362.30026
499	27.53965	144.55331	3980.94763	499	41.61811	130.12960	5415.74797	499	62.87211	118.09136	7424.65276
500	27.72325	144.58938	4008.48728	500	41.93025	130.15345	5457.35608	500	63.39604	118.10714	7487.52486

Table I. ANNUITIES (*Continued*)

M	C(11,M,12)	A(11,M,12)	S(11,M,12)	M	C(12,M,12)	A(12,M,12)	S(12,M,12)	M	C(13,M,12)	A(13,M,12)	S(13,M,12)
1	1.00917	.99092	1.00000	1	1.01000	.99010	1.00000	1	1.01083	.98928	1.00000
2	1.01842	1.97283	2.00917	2	1.02010	1.97040	2.01000	2	1.02178	1.96796	2.01083
3	1.02775	2.94583	3.02758	3	1.03030	2.94099	3.03010	3	1.03285	2.93515	3.03262
4	1.03717	3.90999	4.05534	4	1.04060	3.90197	4.06040	4	1.04404	3.89397	4.06547
5	1.04668	4.86539	5.09251	5	1.05101	4.85343	5.10101	5	1.05535	4.84152	5.10951
6	1.05628	5.81211	6.13919	6	1.06152	5.79548	6.15202	6	1.06679	5.77892	6.16487
7	1.06596	6.75023	7.19547	7	1.07214	6.72819	7.21354	7	1.07834	6.70526	7.23165
8	1.07573	7.67983	8.26143	8	1.08286	7.65168	8.28567	8	1.09002	7.62367	8.31000
9	1.08559	8.60099	9.33716	9	1.09369	8.56602	9.36853	9	1.10183	8.53125	9.40002
10	1.09554	9.51378	10.42275	10	1.10462	9.47130	10.46221	10	1.11377	9.42910	10.50185
11	1.10558	10.41828	11.51829	11	1.11567	10.36763	11.56683	11	1.12584	10.31733	11.61562
12	1.11572	11.31456	12.62387	12	1.12683	11.25508	12.68250	12	1.13803	11.19604	12.74146
13	1.12595	12.20271	13.73959	13	1.13809	12.13374	13.80933	13	1.15036	12.06533	13.87949
14	1.13627	13.08278	14.86554	14	1.14947	13.00370	14.94742	14	1.16282	12.92531	15.02985
15	1.14668	13.95486	16.00181	15	1.16097	13.86505	16.09690	15	1.17542	13.77607	16.19268
16	1.15719	14.81902	17.14849	16	1.17258	14.71787	17.25786	16	1.18815	14.61771	17.36810
17	1.16780	15.67533	18.30568	17	1.18430	15.56225	18.43044	17	1.20103	15.45033	18.55625
18	1.17851	16.52386	19.47349	18	1.19615	16.39827	19.61475	18	1.21404	16.27403	19.75728
19	1.18931	17.36469	20.65199	19	1.20811	17.22601	20.81090	19	1.22719	17.08890	20.97132
20	1.20021	18.19787	21.84130	20	1.22019	18.04555	22.01900	20	1.24048	17.89504	22.19850
21	1.21121	19.02349	23.04151	21	1.23239	18.85698	23.23919	21	1.25392	18.69254	23.43899
22	1.22232	19.84161	24.25273	22	1.24472	19.66038	24.47159	22	1.26751	19.48149	24.69291
23	1.23352	20.65230	25.47504	23	1.25716	20.45582	25.71630	23	1.28124	20.26198	25.96042
24	1.24483	21.45562	26.70857	24	1.26973	21.24339	26.97346	24	1.29512	21.03411	27.24166
25	1.25624	22.25165	27.95339	25	1.28243	22.02316	28.24320	25	1.30915	21.79797	28.53677
26	1.26775	23.04044	29.20963	26	1.29526	22.79520	29.52563	26	1.32333	22.55364	29.84592
27	1.27938	23.82207	30.47739	27	1.30821	23.55961	30.82089	27	1.33767	23.30121	31.16925
28	1.29110	24.59660	31.75676	28	1.32129	24.31644	32.12910	28	1.35216	24.04076	32.50692
29	1.30294	25.36410	33.04787	29	1.33450	25.06579	33.45039	29	1.36681	24.77240	33.85908
30	1.31488	26.12462	34.35081	30	1.34785	25.80771	34.78489	30	1.38161	25.49619	35.22588
31	1.32694	26.87824	35.66569	31	1.36133	26.54229	36.13274	31	1.39658	26.21222	36.60750
32	1.33910	27.62501	36.99263	32	1.37494	27.26959	37.49407	32	1.41171	26.92058	38.00408
33	1.35137	28.36500	38.33172	33	1.38869	27.98969	38.86901	33	1.42700	27.62135	39.41579
34	1.36376	29.09826	39.68310	34	1.40258	28.70267	40.25770	34	1.44246	28.31461	40.84279
35	1.37626	29.82487	41.04686	35	1.41660	29.40858	41.66028	35	1.45809	29.00044	42.28526
36	1.38888	30.54487	42.42312	36	1.43077	30.10751	43.07688	36	1.47389	29.67892	43.74335
37	1.40161	31.25834	43.81200	37	1.44508	30.79951	44.50765	37	1.48985	30.35012	45.21723
38	1.41446	31.96532	45.21361	38	1.45953	31.48466	45.95272	38	1.50599	31.01414	46.70709
39	1.42742	32.66589	46.62807	39	1.47412	32.16303	47.41225	39	1.52231	31.67103	48.21308
40	1.44051	33.36009	48.05549	40	1.48886	32.83469	48.88637	40	1.53880	32.32089	49.73539
41	1.45371	34.04798	49.49600	41	1.50375	33.49969	50.37524	41	1.55547	32.96378	51.27419
42	1.46704	34.72962	50.94972	42	1.51879	34.15811	51.87899	42	1.57232	33.59979	52.82966
43	1.48049	35.40508	52.41676	43	1.53398	34.81001	53.39778	43	1.58935	34.22897	54.40198
44	1.49406	36.07440	53.89724	44	1.54932	35.45545	54.93176	44	1.60657	34.85142	55.99134
45	1.50775	36.73763	55.39130	45	1.56481	36.09451	56.48107	45	1.62398	35.46719	57.59791
46	1.52157	37.39485	56.89905	46	1.58046	36.72724	58.04589	46	1.64157	36.07636	59.22189
47	1.53552	38.04609	58.42063	47	1.59626	37.35370	59.62634	47	1.65935	36.67900	60.86346
48	1.54960	38.69142	59.95615	48	1.61223	37.97396	61.22261	48	1.67733	37.27519	62.52281
49	1.56380	39.33089	61.50575	49	1.62835	38.58808	62.83483	49	1.69550	37.86499	64.20014
50	1.57814	39.96455	63.06955	50	1.64463	39.19612	64.46318	50	1.71387	38.44846	65.89564
51	1.59260	40.59245	64.64769	51	1.66108	39.79814	66.10781	51	1.73244	39.02568	67.60951
52	1.60720	41.21465	66.24029	52	1.67769	40.39419	67.75889	52	1.75120	39.59672	69.34195
53	1.62194	41.83120	67.84750	53	1.69447	40.98435	69.44658	53	1.77018	40.16163	71.09315
54	1.63680	42.44214	69.46943	54	1.71141	41.56866	71.14105	54	1.78935	40.72050	72.86333
55	1.65181	43.04754	71.10623	55	1.72852	42.14719	72.85246	55	1.80874	41.27337	74.65268
56	1.66695	43.64744	72.75804	56	1.74581	42.71999	74.58098	56	1.82833	41.82031	76.46142

57	1.68223	44.24189	74.42499	57	1.76327	43.28712	76.32679	57	1.84814	42.36140	78.28975
58	1.69765	44.83094	76.10722	58	1.78090	43.84863	78.09006	58	1.86816	42.89668	80.13789
59	1.71321	45.41464	77.80487	59	1.79871	44.40459	79.87096	59	1.88840	43.42623	82.00605
60	1.72892	45.99303	79.51808	60	1.81670	44.95504	81.66967	60	1.90886	43.95011	83.89445
61	1.74476	46.56618	81.24700	61	1.83486	45.50004	83.48637	61	1.92954	44.46837	85.80331
62	1.76076	47.13411	82.99176	62	1.85321	46.03964	85.32123	62	1.95044	44.98107	87.73284
63	1.77690	47.69689	84.75252	63	1.87174	46.57390	87.17444	63	1.97157	45.48828	89.68328
64	1.79319	48.25456	86.52942	64	1.89046	47.10287	89.04619	64	1.99293	45.99006	91.65485
65	1.80962	48.80716	88.32260	65	1.90937	47.62661	90.93665	65	2.01452	46.48645	93.64778
66	1.82621	49.35474	90.13223	66	1.92846	48.14516	92.84602	66	2.03634	46.97753	95.66229
67	1.84295	49.89735	91.95844	67	1.94774	48.65857	94.77448	67	2.05840	47.46334	97.69864
68	1.85985	50.43503	93.80139	68	1.96722	49.16690	96.72222	68	2.08070	47.94395	99.75704
69	1.87689	50.96782	95.66124	69	1.98689	49.67020	98.68944	69	2.10324	48.41941	101.83774
70	1.89410	51.49578	97.53813	70	2.00676	50.16851	100.67634	70	2.12603	48.88977	103.94098
71	1.91146	52.01894	99.43223	71	2.02683	50.66190	102.68310	71	2.14906	49.35509	106.06701
72	1.92898	52.53735	101.34369	72	2.04710	51.15039	104.70993	72	2.17234	49.81542	108.21607
73	1.94667	53.05105	103.27268	73	2.06757	51.63405	106.75703	73	2.19587	50.27082	110.38841
74	1.96451	53.56008	105.21934	74	2.08825	52.11292	108.82460	74	2.21966	50.72134	112.58428
75	1.98252	54.06449	107.18385	75	2.10913	52.58705	110.91285	75	2.24371	51.16703	114.80395
76	2.00069	54.56431	109.16637	76	2.13022	53.05649	113.02198	76	2.26802	51.60794	117.04766
77	2.01903	55.05960	111.16706	77	2.15152	53.52127	115.15220	77	2.29259	52.04413	119.31567
78	2.03754	55.55039	113.18609	78	2.17304	53.98146	117.30372	78	2.31742	52.47565	121.60826
79	2.05622	56.03672	115.22363	79	2.19477	54.43709	119.47675	79	2.34253	52.90254	123.92568
80	2.07507	56.51863	117.27985	80	2.21672	54.88821	121.67152	80	2.36791	53.32485	126.26821
81	2.09409	56.99617	119.35492	81	2.23888	55.33486	123.88824	81	2.39356	53.74264	128.63612
82	2.11328	57.46936	121.44900	82	2.26127	55.77709	126.12712	82	2.41949	54.15595	131.02967
83	2.13265	57.93826	123.56229	83	2.28388	56.21494	128.38839	83	2.44570	54.56483	133.44916
84	2.15220	58.40290	125.69494	84	2.30672	56.64845	130.67227	84	2.47219	54.96933	135.89486
85	2.17193	58.86332	127.84714	85	2.32979	57.07768	132.97900	85	2.49898	55.36949	138.36705
86	2.19184	59.31956	130.01908	86	2.35309	57.50265	135.30879	86	2.52605	55.76537	140.86603
87	2.21193	59.77165	132.21092	87	2.37662	57.92342	137.66187	87	2.55341	56.15700	143.39208
88	2.23221	60.21964	134.42285	88	2.40038	58.34002	140.03849	88	2.58108	56.54443	145.94549
89	2.25267	60.66356	136.65506	89	2.42439	58.75249	142.43888	89	2.60904	56.92772	148.52657
90	2.27332	61.10344	138.90773	90	2.44863	59.16088	144.86327	90	2.63730	57.30689	151.13561
91	2.29416	61.53933	141.18105	91	2.47312	59.56523	147.31190	91	2.66587	57.68200	153.77291
92	2.31519	61.97126	143.47521	92	2.49785	59.96557	149.78502	92	2.69475	58.05310	156.43878
93	2.33641	62.39927	145.79040	93	2.52283	60.36195	152.28287	93	2.72395	58.42021	159.13354
94	2.35783	62.82339	148.12681	94	2.54806	60.75441	154.80570	94	2.75346	58.78339	161.85748
95	2.37944	63.24365	150.48464	95	2.57354	61.14298	157.35375	95	2.78329	59.14268	164.61094
96	2.40125	63.66010	152.86408	96	2.59927	61.52770	159.92729	96	2.81344	59.49812	167.39423
97	2.42327	64.07277	155.26534	97	2.62527	61.90862	162.52657	97	2.84392	59.84974	170.20766
98	2.44548	64.48169	157.68860	98	2.65152	62.28576	165.15183	98	2.87473	60.19760	173.05158
99	2.46790	64.88689	160.13408	99	2.67803	62.65917	167.80335	99	2.90587	60.54173	175.92630
100	2.49052	65.28841	162.60198	100	2.70481	63.02888	170.48138	100	2.93735	60.88218	178.83217

Table I. ANNUITIES (*Continued*)

M	C(11,M,12)	A(11,M,12)	S(11,M,12)	M	C(12,M,12)	A(12,M,12)	S(12,M,12)	M	C(13,M,12)	A(13,M,12)	S(13,M,12)
101	2.51335	65.68629	165.09250	101	2.73186	63.39493	173.18620	101	2.96917	61.21897	181.76952
102	2.53639	66.08055	167.60585	102	2.75918	63.75736	175.91806	102	3.00134	61.55216	184.73869
103	2.55964	66.47123	170.14223	103	2.78677	64.11619	178.67724	103	3.03385	61.88177	187.74003
104	2.58310	66.85836	172.70187	104	2.81464	64.47148	181.46401	104	3.06672	62.20785	190.77388
105	2.60678	67.24198	175.28497	105	2.84279	64.82325	184.27865	105	3.09994	62.53044	193.84059
106	2.63067	67.62211	177.89175	106	2.87121	65.17153	187.12144	106	3.13352	62.84957	196.94053
107	2.65479	67.99879	180.52242	107	2.89993	65.51637	189.99265	107	3.16747	63.16528	200.07406
108	2.67912	68.37204	183.17721	108	2.92893	65.85779	192.89258	108	3.20178	63.47760	203.24153
109	2.70368	68.74191	185.85634	109	2.95822	66.19583	195.82151	109	3.23647	63.78658	206.44331
110	2.72847	69.10842	188.56002	110	2.98780	66.53053	198.77972	110	3.27153	64.09225	209.67978
111	2.75348	69.47159	191.28849	111	3.01768	66.86191	201.75752	111	3.30697	64.39464	212.95131
112	2.77872	69.83147	194.04196	112	3.04785	67.19001	204.78519	112	3.34280	64.69379	216.25828
113	2.80419	70.18808	196.82068	113	3.07833	67.51486	207.83304	113	3.37901	64.98974	219.60108
114	2.82989	70.54145	199.62487	114	3.10911	67.83649	210.91137	114	3.41562	65.28251	222.98009
115	2.85584	70.89161	202.45477	115	3.14020	68.15494	214.02049	115	3.45262	65.57214	226.39571
116	2.88201	71.23859	205.31060	116	3.17161	68.47024	217.16069	116	3.49002	65.85868	229.84833
117	2.90843	71.58242	208.19262	117	3.20332	68.78242	220.33230	117	3.52783	66.14214	233.33835
118	2.93509	71.92312	211.10105	118	3.23536	69.09150	223.53562	118	3.56605	66.42256	236.86618
119	2.96200	72.26073	214.03614	119	3.26771	69.39753	226.77098	119	3.60468	66.69997	240.43223
120	2.98915	72.59528	216.99814	120	3.30039	69.70052	230.03869	120	3.64373	66.97442	244.03692
121	3.01655	72.92678	219.98729	121	3.33339	70.00052	233.33908	121	3.68321	67.24592	247.68065
122	3.04420	73.25527	223.00384	122	3.36672	70.29754	236.67247	122	3.72311	67.51451	251.36386
123	3.07211	73.58078	226.04804	123	3.40039	70.59163	240.03919	123	3.76344	67.78023	255.08697
124	3.10027	73.90334	229.12015	124	3.43440	70.88280	243.43958	124	3.80421	68.04309	258.85041
125	3.12869	74.22296	232.22042	125	3.46874	71.17109	246.87398	125	3.84543	68.30314	262.65462
126	3.15737	74.53968	235.34910	126	3.50343	71.45652	250.34272	126	3.88708	68.56041	266.50005
127	3.18631	74.85352	238.50647	127	3.53846	71.73913	253.84615	127	3.92919	68.81491	270.38713
128	3.21552	75.16451	241.69278	128	3.57385	72.01894	257.38461	128	3.97176	69.06669	274.31632
129	3.24499	75.47268	244.90830	129	3.60958	72.29598	260.95845	129	4.01479	69.31577	278.28808
130	3.27474	75.77805	248.15329	130	3.64568	72.57028	264.56804	130	4.05828	69.56218	282.30287
131	3.30476	76.08064	251.42803	131	3.68214	72.84186	268.21372	131	4.10225	69.80595	286.36115
132	3.33505	76.38049	254.73278	132	3.71896	73.11075	271.89586	132	4.14669	70.04710	290.46340
133	3.36562	76.67761	258.06783	133	3.75615	73.37698	275.61481	133	4.19161	70.28567	294.61009
134	3.39647	76.97203	261.43346	134	3.79371	73.64058	279.37096	134	4.23702	70.52169	298.80169
135	3.42761	77.26378	264.82993	135	3.83165	73.90156	283.16467	135	4.28292	70.75518	303.03871
136	3.45903	77.55288	268.25754	136	3.86996	74.15996	286.99632	136	4.32932	70.98616	307.32163
137	3.49074	77.83935	271.71656	137	3.90866	74.41580	290.86628	137	4.37622	71.21467	311.65095
138	3.52273	78.12322	275.20730	138	3.94775	74.66911	294.77495	138	4.42363	71.44073	316.02717
139	3.55503	78.40451	278.73003	139	3.98723	74.91991	298.72269	139	4.47155	71.66436	320.45080
140	3.58761	78.68325	282.28506	140	4.02710	75.16823	302.70992	140	4.51999	71.88560	324.92235
141	3.62050	78.95946	285.87267	141	4.06737	75.41409	306.73702	141	4.56896	72.10447	329.44234
142	3.65369	79.23315	289.49317	142	4.10804	75.65751	310.80439	142	4.61846	72.32099	334.01130
143	3.68718	79.50436	293.14686	143	4.14912	75.89853	314.91244	143	4.66849	72.53519	338.62975
144	3.72098	79.77311	296.83404	144	4.19062	76.13716	319.06156	144	4.71906	72.74710	343.29824
145	3.75509	80.03941	300.55502	145	4.23252	76.37342	323.25217	145	4.77019	72.95674	348.01731
146	3.78951	80.30330	304.31010	146	4.27485	76.60735	327.48470	146	4.82186	73.16412	352.78749
147	3.82425	80.56479	308.09961	147	4.31760	76.83896	331.75954	147	4.87410	73.36929	357.60936
148	3.85930	80.82390	311.92386	148	4.36077	77.06828	336.07714	148	4.92690	73.57226	362.48346
149	3.89468	81.08066	315.78316	149	4.40438	77.29532	340.43791	149	4.98028	73.77305	367.41036
150	3.93038	81.33509	319.67784	150	4.44842	77.52012	344.84229	150	5.03423	73.97169	372.39064
151	3.96641	81.58721	323.60822	151	4.49291	77.74270	349.29071	151	5.08877	74.16820	377.42487
152	4.00277	81.83704	327.57463	152	4.53784	77.96307	353.78362	152	5.14390	74.36261	382.51364
153	4.03946	82.08460	331.57740	153	4.58321	78.18125	358.32146	153	5.19962	74.55493	387.65754
154	4.07649	82.32990	335.61686	154	4.62905	78.39728	362.90467	154	5.25595	74.74519	392.85717
155	4.11386	82.57299	339.69334	155	4.67534	78.61117	367.53372	155	5.31289	74.93341	398.11312
156	4.15157	82.81386	343.80720	156	4.72209	78.82294	372.20905	156	5.37045	75.11961	403.42601
157	4.18962	83.05254	347.95877	157	4.76931	79.03261	376.93114	157	5.42863	75.30382	408.79646

161	4.34537	83.98580	364.94910	161	4.96296	79.85075	396.29646	161	5.66772	76.02112	430.86639
162	4.38520	84.21384	369.29446	162	5.01259	80.05025	401.25943	162	5.72912	76.19567	436.53411
163	4.42540	84.43981	373.67966	163	5.06272	80.24777	406.27202	163	5.79118	76.36835	442.26323
164	4.46596	84.66372	378.10506	164	5.11335	80.44334	411.33474	164	5.85392	76.53917	448.05441
165	4.50690	84.88561	382.57102	165	5.16448	80.63697	416.44809	165	5.91734	76.70817	453.90833
166	4.54821	85.10547	387.07792	166	5.21613	80.82868	421.61257	166	5.98144	76.87535	459.82567
167	4.58991	85.32334	391.62614	167	5.26829	81.01850	426.82859	167	6.04624	77.04074	465.80712
168	4.63198	85.53923	396.21604	168	5.32097	81.20643	432.09698	168	6.11174	77.20436	471.85336
169	4.67444	85.75316	400.84802	169	5.37418	81.39251	437.41795	169	6.17796	77.36623	477.96511
170	4.71729	85.96515	405.52246	170	5.42792	81.57674	442.79213	170	6.24488	77.52636	484.14306
171	4.76053	86.17521	410.23975	171	5.48220	81.75915	448.22005	171	6.31254	77.68478	490.38795
172	4.80417	86.38336	415.00028	172	5.53702	81.93975	453.70225	172	6.38092	77.84149	496.70048
173	4.84821	86.58962	419.80445	173	5.59239	82.11857	459.23928	173	6.45005	77.99653	503.08140
174	4.89265	86.79401	424.65266	174	5.64832	82.29561	464.83167	174	6.51992	78.14991	509.53145
175	4.93750	86.99654	429.54531	175	5.70480	82.47090	470.47998	175	6.59056	78.30164	516.05138
176	4.98276	87.19723	434.48281	176	5.76185	82.64446	476.18478	176	6.66195	78.45174	522.64193
177	5.02843	87.39610	439.46557	177	5.81947	82.81629	481.94663	177	6.73413	78.60024	529.30389
178	5.07453	87.59317	444.49400	178	5.87766	82.98643	487.76610	178	6.80708	78.74715	536.03801
179	5.12104	87.78844	449.56853	179	5.93644	83.15488	493.64376	179	6.88082	78.89248	542.84509
180	5.16799	87.98194	454.68957	180	5.99580	83.32166	499.58020	180	6.95536	79.03625	549.72591
181	5.21536	88.17368	459.85756	181	6.05576	83.48680	505.57600	181	7.03071	79.17849	556.68128
182	5.26317	88.36368	465.07292	182	6.11632	83.65029	511.63176	182	7.10688	79.31919	563.71199
183	5.31141	88.55195	470.33609	183	6.17748	83.81217	517.74808	183	7.18387	79.45840	570.81887
184	5.36010	88.73852	475.64751	184	6.23926	83.97245	523.92556	184	7.26170	79.59610	578.00274
185	5.40924	88.92338	481.00761	185	6.30165	84.13114	530.16481	185	7.34036	79.73234	585.26444
186	5.45882	89.10657	486.41684	186	6.36466	84.28825	536.46646	186	7.41989	79.86711	592.60480
187	5.50886	89.28810	491.87567	187	6.42831	84.44381	542.83113	187	7.50027	80.00044	600.02469
188	5.55936	89.46798	497.38453	188	6.49259	84.59784	549.25944	188	7.58152	80.13234	607.52496
189	5.61032	89.64622	502.94388	189	6.55752	84.75033	555.75203	189	7.66365	80.26282	615.10648
190	5.66175	89.82284	508.55420	190	6.62310	84.90132	562.30955	190	7.74668	80.39191	622.77013
191	5.71365	89.99786	514.21595	191	6.68933	85.05081	568.93265	191	7.83060	80.51962	630.51681
192	5.76602	90.17129	519.92960	192	6.75622	85.19882	575.62197	192	7.91543	80.64595	638.34741
193	5.81888	90.34315	525.69562	193	6.82378	85.34537	582.37819	193	8.00118	80.77093	646.26284
194	5.87222	90.51344	531.51449	194	6.89202	85.49047	589.20198	194	8.08786	80.89458	654.26402
195	5.92604	90.68219	537.38671	195	6.96094	85.63412	596.09400	195	8.17548	81.01689	662.35188
196	5.98037	90.84940	543.31276	196	7.03055	85.77636	603.05494	196	8.26405	81.13790	670.52736
197	6.03519	91.01510	549.29312	197	7.10085	85.91719	610.08548	197	8.35357	81.25761	678.79140
198	6.09051	91.17929	555.32831	198	7.17186	86.05662	617.18634	198	8.44407	81.37603	687.14498
199	6.14634	91.34198	561.41882	199	7.24358	86.19468	624.35820	199	8.53555	81.49319	695.58905
200	6.20268	91.50321	567.56516	200	7.31602	86.33136	631.60179	200	8.62802	81.60909	704.12459

Table I. ANNUITIES (*Continued*)

M	C(11,M,12)	A(11,M,12)	S(11,M,12)	M	C(12,M,12)	A(12,M,12)	S(12,M,12)	M	C(13,M,12)	A(13,M,12)	S(13,M,12)
201	6.25954	91.66296	573.76784	201	7.38918	86.46669	638.91780	201	8.72149	81.72375	712.75261
202	6.31692	91.82127	580.02738	202	7.46307	86.60069	646.30698	202	8.81597	81.83718	721.47410
203	6.37482	91.97813	586.34429	203	7.53770	86.73335	653.77005	203	8.91148	81.94940	730.29007
204	6.43326	92.13358	592.71912	204	7.61308	86.86471	661.30775	204	9.00802	82.06041	739.20154
205	6.49223	92.28761	599.15238	205	7.68921	86.99476	668.92083	205	9.10560	82.17023	748.20956
206	6.55174	92.44024	605.64461	206	7.76610	87.12352	676.61004	206	9.20425	82.27888	757.31516
207	6.61180	92.59148	612.19635	207	7.84376	87.25101	684.37614	207	9.30396	82.38636	766.51941
208	6.67241	92.74135	618.80815	208	7.92220	87.37724	692.21990	208	9.40475	82.49269	775.82337
209	6.73357	92.88986	625.48056	209	8.00142	87.50222	700.14210	209	9.50664	82.59788	785.22812
210	6.79530	93.03702	632.21413	210	8.08144	87.62596	708.14352	210	9.60963	82.70194	794.73476
211	6.85759	93.18285	639.00942	211	8.16225	87.74848	716.22495	211	9.71373	82.80489	804.34439
212	6.92045	93.32735	645.86701	212	8.24387	87.86978	724.38720	212	9.81896	82.90673	814.05812
213	6.98389	93.47053	652.78746	213	8.32631	87.98988	732.63108	213	9.92534	83.00748	823.87708
214	7.04790	93.61242	659.77134	214	8.40957	88.10879	740.95739	214	10.03286	83.10716	833.80242
215	7.11251	93.75302	666.81925	215	8.49367	88.22653	749.36696	215	10.14155	83.20576	843.83528
216	7.17771	93.89234	673.93176	216	8.57861	88.34309	757.86063	216	10.25142	83.30331	853.97683
217	7.24350	94.03039	681.10946	217	8.66439	88.45851	766.43924	217	10.36247	83.39981	864.22824
218	7.30990	94.16719	688.35297	218	8.75104	88.57278	775.10363	218	10.47473	83.49528	874.59071
219	7.37691	94.30275	695.66287	219	8.83855	88.68592	783.85466	219	10.58821	83.58972	885.06545
220	7.44453	94.43708	703.03978	220	8.92693	88.79794	792.69321	220	10.70291	83.68315	895.65366
221	7.51277	94.57018	710.48431	221	9.01620	88.90885	801.62014	221	10.81886	83.77559	906.35657
222	7.58164	94.70208	717.99708	222	9.10636	89.01867	810.63635	222	10.93607	83.86703	917.17543
223	7.65114	94.83278	725.57872	223	9.19743	89.12739	819.74271	223	11.05454	83.95749	928.11150
224	7.72127	94.96229	733.22986	224	9.28940	89.23504	828.94014	224	11.17430	84.04698	939.16604
225	7.79205	95.09063	740.95114	225	9.38230	89.34163	838.22954	225	11.29535	84.13551	950.34034
226	7.86348	95.21780	748.74319	226	9.47612	89.44716	847.61183	226	11.41772	84.22309	961.63569
227	7.93556	95.34381	756.60667	227	9.57088	89.55164	857.08795	227	11.54141	84.30974	973.05341
228	8.00830	95.46868	764.54223	228	9.66659	89.65509	866.65883	228	11.66644	84.39545	984.59483
229	8.08171	95.59242	772.55053	229	9.76325	89.75751	876.32542	229	11.79283	84.48025	996.26127
230	8.15580	95.71503	780.63225	230	9.86089	89.85892	886.08867	230	11.92059	84.56414	1008.05410
231	8.23056	95.83653	788.78804	231	9.95950	89.95933	895.94956	231	12.04973	84.64713	1019.97469
232	8.30600	95.95693	797.01860	232	10.05909	90.05874	905.90905	232	12.18026	84.72923	1032.02441
233	8.38214	96.07623	805.32460	233	10.15968	90.15717	915.96815	233	12.31222	84.81045	1044.20468
234	8.45898	96.19445	813.70674	234	10.26128	90.25463	926.12783	234	12.44560	84.89080	1056.51689
235	8.53652	96.31159	822.16572	235	10.36389	90.35111	936.38911	235	12.58043	84.97029	1068.96249
236	8.61477	96.42767	830.70224	236	10.46753	90.44665	946.75300	236	12.71671	85.04892	1081.54292
237	8.69374	96.54269	839.31701	237	10.57221	90.54124	957.22053	237	12.85448	85.12672	1094.25964
238	8.77343	96.65667	848.01075	238	10.67793	90.63489	967.79273	238	12.99374	85.20368	1107.11411
239	8.85386	96.76962	856.78418	239	10.78471	90.72761	978.47066	239	13.13450	85.27981	1120.10785
240	8.93502	96.88154	865.63804	240	10.89255	90.81942	989.25537	240	13.27679	85.35513	1133.24235
241	9.01692	96.99244	874.57305	241	11.00148	90.91031	1000.14792	241	13.42062	85.42964	1146.51914
242	9.09957	97.10234	883.58997	242	11.11149	91.00031	1011.14940	242	13.56601	85.50336	1159.93977
243	9.18299	97.21123	892.68955	243	11.22261	91.08942	1022.26089	243	13.71298	85.57628	1173.50578
244	9.26716	97.31914	901.87254	244	11.33484	91.17764	1033.48350	244	13.86154	85.64842	1187.21876
245	9.35211	97.42607	911.13970	245	11.44818	91.26499	1044.81834	245	14.01170	85.71979	1201.08030
246	9.43784	97.53203	920.49181	246	11.56267	91.35147	1056.26652	246	14.16350	85.79040	1215.09200
247	9.52436	97.63702	929.92966	247	11.67829	91.43710	1067.82918	247	14.31693	85.86024	1229.25550
248	9.61166	97.74106	939.45401	248	11.79507	91.52189	1079.50748	248	14.47203	85.92934	1243.57243
249	9.69977	97.84416	949.06567	249	11.91303	91.60583	1091.30255	249	14.62882	85.99770	1258.04447
250	9.78868	97.94631	958.76544	250	12.03216	91.68894	1103.21558	250	14.78729	86.06533	1272.67328
251	9.87841	98.04755	968.55412	251	12.15248	91.77123	1115.24773	251	14.94749	86.13223	1287.46058
252	9.96896	98.14786	978.43254	252	12.27400	91.85270	1127.40021	252	15.10942	86.19841	1302.40807
253	10.06035	98.24726	988.40150	253	12.39674	91.93336	1139.67421	253	15.27311	86.26389	1317.51749
254	10.15257	98.34575	998.46185	254	12.52071	92.01323	1152.07095	254	15.43856	86.32866	1332.79059
255	10.24563	98.44336	1008.61442	255	12.64592	92.09231	1164.59166	255	15.60582	86.39274	1348.22916
256	10.33955	98.54007	1018.86005	256	12.77238	92.17060	1177.23758	256	15.77488	86.45613	1363.83497
257	10.43433	98.63591	1029.19960	257	12.90010	92.24812	1190.00996	257	15.94577	86.51884	1379.60985
258	10.52998	98.73088	1039.63393	258	13.02910	92.32487	1202.91006	258	16.11852	86.58088	1395.55563

261	10.82221	99.01063	1071.51432	261	13.42390	92.55060	1242.38953	261	16.64807	86.76304	1444.43693
262	10.92142	99.10220	1082.33654	262	13.55813	92.62435	1255.81343	262	16.82842	86.82247	1461.08499
263	11.02153	99.19293	1093.25795	263	13.69372	92.69738	1269.37156	263	17.01073	86.88125	1477.91342
264	11.12256	99.28284	1104.27949	264	13.83065	92.76968	1283.06528	264	17.19501	86.93941	1494.92414
265	11.22452	99.37193	1115.40205	265	13.96896	92.84127	1296.89593	265	17.38129	86.99694	1512.11916
266	11.32741	99.46021	1126.62657	266	14.10865	92.91215	1310.85489	266	17.56959	87.05386	1529.50045
267	11.43124	99.54769	1137.95398	267	14.24974	92.98233	1324.97354	267	17.75993	87.11017	1547.07003
268	11.53603	99.63437	1149.38522	268	14.39223	93.05181	1339.22327	268	17.95232	87.16587	1564.82996
269	11.64178	99.72027	1160.92125	269	14.53616	93.12060	1353.61551	269	18.14681	87.22097	1582.78228
270	11.74849	99.80539	1172.56303	270	14.68152	93.18871	1368.15166	270	18.34340	87.27549	1600.92909
271	11.85619	99.88973	1184.31152	271	14.82833	93.25615	1382.83318	271	18.54212	87.32942	1619.27249
272	11.96487	99.97331	1196.16771	272	14.97662	93.32292	1397.66151	272	18.74299	87.38277	1637.81461
273	12.07455	100.05613	1208.13258	273	15.12638	93.38903	1412.63813	273	18.94604	87.43556	1656.55760
274	12.18523	100.13819	1220.20713	274	15.27765	93.45449	1427.76451	274	19.15129	87.48777	1675.50364
275	12.29693	100.21952	1232.39236	275	15.43042	93.51930	1443.04215	275	19.35876	87.53943	1694.65493
276	12.40965	100.30010	1244.68929	276	15.58473	93.58346	1458.47257	276	19.56848	87.59053	1714.01369
277	12.52341	100.37995	1257.09895	277	15.74057	93.64699	1474.05730	277	19.78047	87.64109	1733.58218
278	12.63820	100.45907	1269.62235	278	15.89798	93.70989	1489.79787	278	19.99476	87.69110	1753.36265
279	12.75406	100.53748	1282.26056	279	16.05696	93.77217	1505.69585	279	20.21137	87.74058	1773.35741
280	12.87097	100.61517	1295.01461	280	16.21753	93.83383	1521.75281	280	20.43033	87.78952	1793.56878
281	12.98895	100.69216	1307.88558	281	16.37970	93.89488	1537.97034	281	20.65166	87.83794	1813.99911
282	13.10802	100.76845	1320.87453	282	16.54350	93.95533	1554.35004	282	20.87538	87.88585	1834.65077
283	13.22817	100.84405	1333.98255	283	16.70894	94.01518	1570.89354	283	21.10153	87.93324	1855.52615
284	13.34943	100.91896	1347.21072	284	16.87602	94.07443	1587.60248	284	21.33013	87.98012	1876.62768
285	13.47180	100.99319	1360.56015	285	17.04479	94.13310	1604.47850	285	21.56121	88.02650	1897.95782
286	13.59529	101.06674	1374.03196	286	17.21523	94.19119	1621.52329	286	21.79479	88.07238	1919.51903
287	13.71992	101.13963	1387.62725	287	17.38739	94.24870	1638.73852	287	22.03090	88.11777	1941.31382
288	13.84568	101.21185	1401.34716	288	17.56126	94.30565	1656.12591	288	22.26957	88.16268	1963.34472
289	13.97260	101.28342	1415.19285	289	17.73687	94.36203	1673.68716	289	22.51082	88.20710	1985.61428
290	14.10068	101.35434	1429.16545	290	17.91424	94.41785	1691.42404	290	22.75469	88.25105	2008.12511
291	14.22994	101.42461	1443.26613	291	18.09338	94.47312	1709.33828	291	23.00120	88.29452	2030.87979
292	14.36038	101.49425	1457.49607	292	18.27432	94.52784	1727.43166	292	23.25038	88.33753	2053.88099
293	14.49202	101.56325	1471.85645	293	18.45706	94.58202	1745.70598	293	23.50226	88.38008	2077.13137
294	14.62486	101.63163	1486.34847	294	18.64163	94.63566	1764.16304	294	23.75686	88.42218	2100.63363
295	14.75892	101.69939	1500.97333	295	18.82805	94.68877	1782.80467	295	24.01423	88.46382	2124.39049
296	14.89421	101.76653	1515.73225	296	19.01633	94.74136	1801.63271	296	24.27438	88.50501	2148.40472
297	15.03074	101.83306	1530.62646	297	19.20649	94.79343	1820.64904	297	24.53736	88.54577	2172.67911
298	15.16852	101.89898	1545.65721	298	19.39856	94.84498	1839.85553	298	24.80318	88.58608	2197.21646
299	15.30757	101.96431	1560.82573	299	19.59254	94.89602	1859.25409	299	25.07188	88.62597	2222.01964
300	15.44789	102.02904	1576.13330	300	19.78847	94.94655	1878.84663	300	25.34349	88.66543	2247.09152

Table I. ANNUITIES (*Continued*)

M	C(11,M,12)	A(11,M,12)	S(11,M,12)
301	15.58949	102.09319	1591.58119
302	15.73240	102.15675	1607.17068
303	15.87661	102.21974	1622.90308
304	16.02215	102.28215	1638.77969
305	16.16902	102.34400	1654.80184
306	16.31723	102.40528	1670.97086
307	16.46681	102.46601	1687.28809
308	16.61775	102.52619	1703.75490
309	16.77008	102.58582	1720.37265
310	16.92381	102.64491	1737.14273
311	17.07894	102.70346	1754.06654
312	17.23550	102.76148	1771.14548
313	17.39349	102.81897	1788.38099
314	17.55293	102.87594	1805.77448
315	17.71383	102.93239	1823.32741
316	17.87621	102.98833	1841.04124
317	18.04008	103.04377	1858.91746
318	18.20544	103.09870	1876.95753
319	18.37233	103.15313	1895.16298
320	18.54074	103.20706	1913.53530
321	18.71070	103.26051	1932.07604
322	18.88221	103.31347	1950.78674
323	19.05530	103.36594	1969.66895
324	19.22997	103.41795	1988.72425
325	19.40625	103.46948	2007.95422
326	19.58414	103.52054	2027.36047
327	19.76366	103.57114	2046.94461
328	19.94483	103.62127	2066.70827
329	20.12765	103.67096	2086.65309
330	20.31216	103.72019	2106.78075
331	20.49835	103.76897	2127.09290
332	20.68625	103.81731	2147.59126
333	20.87588	103.86522	2168.27751
334	21.06724	103.91268	2189.15339
335	21.26036	103.95972	2210.22063
336	21.45524	104.00633	2231.48098
337	21.65192	104.05251	2252.93622
338	21.85039	104.09828	2274.58814
339	22.05069	104.14363	2296.43853
340	22.25282	104.18857	2318.48922
341	22.45680	104.23310	2340.74203
342	22.66266	104.27722	2363.19884
343	22.87040	104.32095	2385.86149
344	23.08004	104.36428	2408.73189
345	23.29161	104.40721	2431.81193
346	23.50512	104.44975	2455.10354
347	23.72058	104.49191	2478.60866
348	23.93802	104.53369	2502.32924
349	24.15745	104.57508	2526.26725
350	24.37889	104.61610	2550.42470
351	24.60237	104.65675	2574.80360
352	24.82789	104.69702	2599.40596
353	25.05548	104.73693	2624.23385
354	25.28515	104.77648	2649.28933
355	25.51693	104.81567	2674.57448
356	25.75084	104.85451	2700.09141
357	25.98689	104.89299	2725.84225
358	26.22510	104.93112	2751.82914

M	C(12,M,12)	A(12,M,12)	S(12,M,12)
301	19.98635	94.99659	1898.63509
302	20.18621	95.04612	1918.62144
303	20.38808	95.09517	1938.80766
304	20.59196	95.14374	1959.19573
305	20.79788	95.19182	1979.78769
306	21.00586	95.23942	2000.58557
307	21.21591	95.28656	2021.59142
308	21.42807	95.33322	2042.80734
309	21.64235	95.37943	2064.23541
310	21.85878	95.42518	2085.87777
311	22.07737	95.47047	2107.73654
312	22.29814	95.51532	2129.81391
313	22.52112	95.55972	2152.11205
314	22.74633	95.60369	2174.63317
315	22.97380	95.64721	2197.37950
316	23.20353	95.69031	2220.35330
317	23.43557	95.73298	2243.55683
318	23.66992	95.77523	2266.99240
319	23.90662	95.81706	2290.66232
320	24.14569	95.85847	2314.56894
321	24.38715	95.89948	2338.71463
322	24.63102	95.94008	2363.10178
323	24.87733	95.98028	2387.73280
324	25.12610	96.02007	2412.61013
325	25.37736	96.05948	2437.73623
326	25.63114	96.09850	2463.11359
327	25.88745	96.13712	2488.74472
328	26.14632	96.17537	2514.63217
329	26.40778	96.21324	2540.77849
330	26.67186	96.25073	2567.18628
331	26.93858	96.28785	2593.85814
332	27.20797	96.32461	2620.79672
333	27.48005	96.36100	2648.00469
334	27.75485	96.39703	2675.48474
335	28.03240	96.43270	2703.23958
336	28.31272	96.46802	2731.27198
337	28.59585	96.50299	2759.58470
338	28.88181	96.53761	2788.18055
339	29.17062	96.57189	2817.06235
340	29.46233	96.60584	2846.23298
341	29.75695	96.63944	2875.69531
342	30.05452	96.67271	2905.45226
343	30.35507	96.70566	2935.50678
344	30.65862	96.73827	2965.86185
345	30.96520	96.77057	2996.52047
346	31.27486	96.80254	3027.48567
347	31.58761	96.83420	3058.76053
348	31.90348	96.86555	3090.34813
349	32.22252	96.89658	3122.25162
350	32.54474	96.92731	3154.47413
351	32.87019	96.95773	3187.01887
352	33.19889	96.98785	3219.88906
353	33.53088	97.01767	3253.08795
354	33.86619	97.04720	3286.61883
355	34.20485	97.07644	3320.48502
356	34.54690	97.10538	3354.68987
357	34.89237	97.13404	3389.23677
358	35.24129	97.16242	3424.12914

M	C(13,M,12)	A(13,M,12)	S(13,M,12)
301	25.61805	88.70446	2272.43501
302	25.89557	88.74308	2298.05306
303	26.17611	88.78128	2323.94863
304	26.45968	88.81908	2350.12474
305	26.74633	88.85646	2376.58443
306	27.03608	88.89345	2403.33076
307	27.32897	88.93004	2430.36684
308	27.62504	88.96624	2457.69582
309	27.92431	89.00205	2485.32085
310	28.22682	89.03748	2513.24516
311	28.53261	89.07253	2541.47199
312	28.84172	89.10720	2570.00460
313	29.15417	89.14150	2598.84632
314	29.47001	89.17543	2628.00048
315	29.78926	89.20900	2657.47049
316	30.11198	89.24221	2687.25975
317	30.43819	89.27507	2717.37173
318	30.76794	89.30757	2747.80993
319	31.10126	89.33972	2778.57787
320	31.43819	89.37153	2809.67913
321	31.77877	89.40300	2841.11732
322	32.12304	89.43413	2872.89609
323	32.47104	89.46492	2905.01913
324	32.82281	89.49539	2937.49017
325	33.17839	89.52553	2970.31298
326	33.53782	89.55535	3003.49137
327	33.90115	89.58484	3037.02920
328	34.26841	89.61403	3070.93035
329	34.63965	89.64289	3105.19876
330	35.01492	89.67145	3139.83841
331	35.39424	89.69971	3174.85333
332	35.77768	89.72766	3210.24757
333	36.16527	89.75531	3246.02525
334	36.55706	89.78266	3282.19053
335	36.95310	89.80972	3318.74759
336	37.35342	89.83649	3355.70069
337	37.75809	89.86298	3393.05411
338	38.16713	89.88918	3430.81220
339	38.58061	89.91510	3468.97933
340	38.99857	89.94074	3507.55994
341	39.42105	89.96611	3546.55851
342	39.84811	89.99120	3585.97956
343	40.27980	90.01603	3625.82767
344	40.71616	90.04059	3666.10747
345	41.15726	90.06489	3706.82363
346	41.60313	90.08892	3747.98089
347	42.05383	90.11270	3789.58402
348	42.50941	90.13623	3831.63784
349	42.96993	90.15950	3874.14725
350	43.43544	90.18252	3917.11718
351	43.90599	90.20530	3960.55262
352	44.38163	90.22783	4004.45860
353	44.86244	90.25012	4048.84024
354	45.34845	90.27217	4093.70268
355	45.83972	90.29399	4139.05112
356	46.33632	90.31557	4184.89084
357	46.83829	90.33692	4231.22716
358	47.34571	90.35804	4278.06545

361	26.95292	105.04345	2831.22783	361	36.30914	97.24587	3530.91377	361	48.90117	90.42005	4421.64687
362	27.19999	105.08021	2858.18076	362	36.67223	97.27314	3567.22291	362	49.43094	90.44029	4470.54805
363	27.44932	105.11664	2885.38075	363	37.03895	97.30014	3603.89514	363	49.96644	90.46030	4519.97898
364	27.70094	105.15274	2912.83007	364	37.40934	97.32687	3640.93409	364	50.50774	90.48010	4569.94542
365	27.95487	105.18852	2940.53101	365	37.78343	97.35334	3678.34343	365	51.05491	90.49968	4620.45317
366	28.21112	105.22396	2968.48588	366	38.16127	97.37954	3716.12687	366	51.60800	90.51906	4671.50807
367	28.46972	105.25909	2996.69700	367	38.54288	97.40549	3754.28814	367	52.16709	90.53823	4723.11608
368	28.73069	105.29389	3025.16672	368	38.92831	97.43118	3792.83102	368	52.73223	90.55719	4775.28317
369	28.99406	105.32838	3053.89742	369	39.31759	97.45661	3831.75933	369	53.30350	90.57595	4828.01540
370	29.25984	105.36256	3082.89148	370	39.71077	97.48179	3871.07692	370	53.88095	90.59451	4881.31890
371	29.52805	105.39643	3112.15132	371	40.10788	97.50672	3910.78769	371	54.46467	90.61287	4935.19986
372	29.79873	105.42998	3141.67937	372	40.50896	97.53141	3950.89557	372	55.05470	90.63104	4989.66452
373	30.07188	105.46324	3171.47810	373	40.91405	97.55585	3991.40452	373	55.65112	90.64901	5044.71922
374	30.34754	105.49619	3201.54998	374	41.32319	97.58005	4032.31857	374	56.25401	90.66678	5100.37035
375	30.62573	105.52884	3231.89752	375	41.73642	97.60401	4073.64175	375	56.86343	90.68437	5156.62436
376	30.90646	105.56120	3262.52325	376	42.15378	97.62773	4115.37817	376	57.47945	90.70177	5213.48779
377	31.18977	105.59326	3293.42971	377	42.57532	97.65122	4157.53195	377	58.10215	90.71898	5270.96724
378	31.47568	105.62503	3324.61948	378	43.00107	97.67448	4200.10727	378	58.73159	90.73600	5329.06939
379	31.76421	105.65651	3356.09516	379	43.43108	97.69750	4243.10835	379	59.36784	90.75285	5387.80097
380	32.05538	105.68771	3387.85937	380	43.86539	97.72030	4286.53943	380	60.01100	90.76951	5447.16882
381	32.34922	105.71862	3419.91475	381	44.30405	97.74287	4330.40482	381	60.66111	90.78600	5507.17981
382	32.64575	105.74925	3452.26396	382	44.74709	97.76522	4374.70887	382	61.31828	90.80231	5567.84093
383	32.94501	105.77961	3484.90972	383	45.19456	97.78734	4419.45596	383	61.98256	90.81844	5629.15920
384	33.24700	105.80968	3517.85472	384	45.64651	97.80925	4464.55052	384	62.65404	90.83440	5691.14176
385	33.55177	105.83949	3551.10172	385	46.10297	97.83094	4510.29702	385	63.33279	90.85019	5753.79580
386	33.85932	105.86902	3584.65349	386	46.56400	97.85242	4556.40000	386	64.01889	90.86581	5817.12858
387	34.16970	105.89829	3618.51281	387	47.02964	97.87368	4602.96399	387	64.71243	90.88126	5881.14748
388	34.48292	105.92729	3652.68251	388	47.49994	97.89473	4649.99363	388	65.41348	90.89655	5945.85991
389	34.79902	105.95602	3687.16544	389	47.97494	97.91558	4697.49357	389	66.12213	90.91167	6011.27339
390	35.11801	105.98450	3721.96445	390	48.45469	97.93622	4745.46851	390	66.83845	90.92664	6077.39552
391	35.43992	106.01272	3757.08246	391	48.93923	97.95665	4793.92319	391	67.56253	90.94144	6144.23397
392	35.76479	106.04068	3792.52238	392	49.42862	97.97688	4842.86242	392	68.29446	90.95608	6211.79650
393	36.09263	106.06838	3828.28717	393	49.92291	97.99691	4892.29105	393	69.03432	90.97056	6280.09097
394	36.42348	106.09584	3864.37981	394	50.42214	98.01674	4942.21396	394	69.78219	90.98490	6349.12529
395	36.75736	106.12304	3900.80329	395	50.92636	98.03638	4992.63610	395	70.53816	90.99907	6418.90748
396	37.09431	106.15000	3937.56065	396	51.43562	98.05582	5043.56246	396	71.30233	91.01310	6489.44564
397	37.43434	106.17672	3974.65496	397	51.94998	98.07507	5094.99808	397	72.07477	91.02697	6560.74797
398	37.77749	106.20319	4012.08929	398	52.46948	98.09413	5146.94806	398	72.85558	91.04070	6632.82274
399	38.12378	106.22942	4049.86678	399	52.99418	98.11300	5199.41755	399	73.64485	91.05428	6705.67832
400	38.47325	106.25541	4087.99056	400	53.52412	98.13168	5252.41172	400	74.44267	91.06771	6779.32317

Table I. ANNUITIES (*Continued*)

M	C(11,M,12)	A(11,M,12)	S(11,M,12)	M	C(12,M,12)	A(12,M,12)	S(12,M,12)	M	C(13,M,12)	A(13,M,12)	S(13,M,12)
401	38.82592	106.28116	4126.46380	401	54.05936	98.15018	5305.93584	401	75.24913	91.08100	6853.76583
402	39.18182	106.30669	4165.28972	402	54.59995	98.16850	5359.99520	402	76.06433	91.09414	6929.01496
403	39.54099	106.33198	4204.47154	403	55.14595	98.18663	5414.59515	403	76.88836	91.10715	7005.07929
404	39.90345	106.35704	4244.01253	404	55.69741	98.20458	5469.74110	404	77.72132	91.12002	7081.96765
405	40.26923	106.38187	4283.91598	405	56.25439	98.22236	5525.43851	405	78.56330	91.13275	7159.68897
406	40.63836	106.40648	4324.18521	406	56.81693	98.23996	5581.69290	406	79.41440	91.14534	7238.25227
407	41.01088	106.43086	4364.82358	407	57.38510	98.25739	5638.50982	407	80.27472	91.15779	7317.66656
408	41.38682	106.45502	4405.83446	408	57.95895	98.27464	5695.89492	408	81.14437	91.17012	7397.94139
409	41.76620	106.47897	4447.22128	409	58.53854	98.29172	5753.85387	409	82.02343	91.18231	7479.08575
410	42.14905	106.50269	4488.98747	410	59.12392	98.30864	5812.39241	410	82.91202	91.19437	7561.10918
411	42.53542	106.52620	4531.13652	411	59.71516	98.32538	5871.51634	411	83.81023	91.20630	7644.02120
412	42.92533	106.54950	4573.67194	412	60.31231	98.34196	5931.23150	412	84.71817	91.21811	7727.83143
413	43.31881	106.57258	4616.59727	413	60.91544	98.35838	5991.54381	413	85.63595	91.22978	7812.54960
414	43.71590	106.59546	4659.91607	414	61.52459	98.37463	6052.45925	414	86.56368	91.24134	7898.18555
415	44.11663	106.61812	4703.63197	415	62.13984	98.39073	6113.98384	415	87.50145	91.25276	7984.74923
416	44.52103	106.64059	4747.74860	416	62.76124	98.40666	6176.12368	416	88.44938	91.26407	8072.25068
417	44.92914	106.66284	4792.26963	417	63.38885	98.42244	6238.88492	417	89.40758	91.27526	8160.70006
418	45.34099	106.68490	4837.19877	418	64.02274	98.43805	6302.27377	418	90.37617	91.28632	8250.10765
419	45.75661	106.70675	4882.53975	419	64.66297	98.45352	6366.29651	419	91.35524	91.29727	8340.48381
420	46.17605	106.72841	4928.29637	420	65.30959	98.46883	6430.95947	420	92.34492	91.30810	8431.83906
421	46.59933	106.74987	4974.47242	421	65.96269	98.48399	6496.26907	421	93.34533	91.31881	8524.18398
422	47.02649	106.77113	5021.07175	422	66.62232	98.49900	6562.23176	422	94.35657	91.32941	8617.52930
423	47.45757	106.79220	5068.09824	423	67.28854	98.51386	6628.85407	423	95.37876	91.33989	8711.88587
424	47.89259	106.81308	5115.55581	424	67.96143	98.52858	6696.14262	424	96.41203	91.35026	8807.26464
425	48.33161	106.83378	5163.44840	425	68.64104	98.54315	6764.10404	425	97.45650	91.36052	8903.67667
426	48.77465	106.85428	5211.78001	426	69.32745	98.55757	6832.74508	426	98.51228	91.37068	9001.13317
427	49.22175	106.87459	5260.55466	427	70.02073	98.57185	6902.07253	427	99.57949	91.38072	9099.64544
428	49.67295	106.89473	5309.77641	428	70.72093	98.58599	6972.09326	428	100.65827	91.39065	9199.22493
429	50.12829	106.91467	5359.44936	429	71.42814	98.59999	7042.81419	429	101.74873	91.40048	9299.88320
430	50.58780	106.93444	5409.57765	430	72.14242	98.61385	7114.24233	430	102.85101	91.41020	9401.63194
431	51.05152	106.95403	5460.16544	431	72.86385	98.62758	7186.38476	431	103.96523	91.41982	9504.48295
432	51.51949	106.97344	5511.21696	432	73.59249	98.64117	7259.24860	432	105.09152	91.42934	9608.44818
433	51.99175	106.99267	5562.73645	433	74.32841	98.65462	7332.84109	433	106.23001	91.43875	9713.53971
434	52.46834	107.01173	5614.72820	434	75.07170	98.66794	7407.16950	434	107.38084	91.44806	9819.76972
435	52.94930	107.03062	5667.19654	435	75.82241	98.68113	7482.24120	435	108.54413	91.45728	9927.15056
436	53.43467	107.04933	5720.14584	436	76.58064	98.69419	7558.06361	436	109.72003	91.46639	10035.69469
437	53.92449	107.06788	5773.58051	437	77.34644	98.70712	7634.64424	437	110.90866	91.47541	10145.41472
438	54.41880	107.08625	5827.50500	438	78.11991	98.71992	7711.99069	438	112.11017	91.48433	10256.32337
439	54.91763	107.10446	5881.92380	439	78.90111	98.73259	7790.11059	439	113.32470	91.49315	10368.43354
440	55.42105	107.12251	5936.84143	440	79.69012	98.74514	7869.01170	440	114.55238	91.50188	10481.75824
441	55.92907	107.14039	5992.26248	441	80.48702	98.75756	7948.70182	441	115.79337	91.51052	10596.31062
442	56.44176	107.15810	6048.19155	442	81.29189	98.76986	8029.18883	442	117.04779	91.51906	10712.10399
443	56.95914	107.17566	6104.63331	443	82.10481	98.78204	8110.48072	443	118.31581	91.52751	10829.15178
444	57.48126	107.19306	6161.59245	444	82.92586	98.79410	8192.58553	444	119.59757	91.53587	10947.46759
445	58.00818	107.21030	6219.07371	445	83.75511	98.80604	8275.51138	445	120.89321	91.54414	11067.06516
446	58.53992	107.22738	6277.08189	446	84.59266	98.81786	8359.26650	446	122.20288	91.55233	11187.95836
447	59.07653	107.24431	6335.62180	447	85.43859	98.82957	8443.85916	447	123.52675	91.56042	11310.16125
448	59.61807	107.26108	6394.69834	448	86.29298	98.84116	8529.29775	448	124.86495	91.56843	11433.68799
449	60.16457	107.27770	6454.31641	449	87.15591	98.85263	8615.59073	449	126.21766	91.57635	11558.55295
450	60.71608	107.29417	6514.48097	450	88.02747	98.86399	8702.74664	450	127.58501	91.58419	11684.77060
451	61.27264	107.31049	6575.19705	451	88.90774	98.87524	8790.77411	451	128.96719	91.59195	11812.35562
452	61.83431	107.32666	6636.46969	452	89.79682	98.88637	8879.68185	452	130.36433	91.59962	11941.32280
453	62.40112	107.34269	6698.30399	453	90.69479	98.89740	8969.47867	453	131.77661	91.60721	12071.68713
454	62.97313	107.35857	6760.70511	454	91.60173	98.90832	9060.17345	454	133.20419	91.61471	12203.46374
455	63.55038	107.37430	6823.67824	455	92.51775	98.91913	9151.77519	455	134.64724	91.62214	12336.66793
456	64.13293	107.38990	6887.22863	456	93.44293	98.92983	9244.29294	456	136.10591	91.62949	12471.31517
457	64.72081	107.40535	6951.36156	457	94.37736	98.94042	9337.73587	457	137.58040	91.63676	12607.42108
458	65.31409	107.42066	7016.08237	458	95.32113	98.95091	9432.11323	458	139.07085	91.64395	12745.00148
[illegible]	[illegible]	[illegible]	[illegible]	459	96.27434	98.96130	9527.43436	459	140.57745	91.65106	12884.07233

461	67.12674	107.46576	7213.82626
462	67.74207	107.48052	7280.95300
463	68.36304	107.49515	7348.69507
464	68.98970	107.50965	7417.05811
465	69.62210	107.52401	7486.04781
466	70.26031	107.53824	7555.66991
467	70.90436	107.55234	7625.93022
468	71.55432	107.56632	7696.83458
469	72.21023	107.58017	7768.38890
470	72.87216	107.59389	7840.59913
471	73.54015	107.60749	7913.47129
472	74.21427	107.62096	7987.01144
473	74.89457	107.63432	8061.22571
474	75.58110	107.64755	8136.12028
475	76.27393	107.66066	8211.70139
476	76.97311	107.67365	8287.97532
477	77.67869	107.68652	8364.94842
478	78.39075	107.69928	8442.62712
479	79.10933	107.71192	8521.01786
480	79.83450	107.72445	8600.12720
481	80.56632	107.73686	8679.96169
482	81.30484	107.74916	8760.52801
483	82.05013	107.76135	8841.83285
484	82.80226	107.77342	8923.88298
485	83.56128	107.78539	9006.68525
486	84.32726	107.79725	9090.24653
487	85.10026	107.80900	9174.57379
488	85.88035	107.82064	9259.67405
489	86.66758	107.83218	9345.55439
490	87.46203	107.84361	9432.22197
491	88.26377	107.85494	9519.68401
492	89.07285	107.86617	9607.94778
493	89.88936	107.87730	9697.02063
494	90.71334	107.88832	9786.90999
495	91.54488	107.89924	9877.62333
496	92.38404	107.91007	9969.16821
497	93.23090	107.92079	10061.55225
498	94.08551	107.93142	10154.78315
499	94.94796	107.94195	10248.86866
500	95.81832	107.95239	10343.81662

461	98.20946	98.98177	9720.94579
462	99.19155	98.99185	9819.15525
463	100.18347	99.00183	9918.34680
464	101.18530	99.01171	10018.53027
465	102.19716	99.02150	10119.71557
466	103.21913	99.03119	10221.91273
467	104.25132	99.04078	10325.13185
468	105.29383	99.05028	10429.38317
469	106.34677	99.05968	10534.67700
470	107.41024	99.06899	10641.02377
471	108.48434	99.07821	10748.43401
472	109.56918	99.08733	10856.91835
473	110.66488	99.09637	10966.48754
474	111.77152	99.10532	11077.15241
475	112.88924	99.11418	11188.92393
476	114.01813	99.12295	11301.81317
477	115.15831	99.13163	11415.83131
478	116.30990	99.14023	11530.98962
479	117.47300	99.14874	11647.29952
480	118.64773	99.15717	11764.77251
481	119.83420	99.16551	11883.42024
482	121.03254	99.17378	12003.25444
483	122.24287	99.18196	12124.28698
484	123.46530	99.19006	12246.52985
485	124.69995	99.19808	12369.99515
486	125.94695	99.20601	12494.69510
487	127.20642	99.21388	12620.64205
488	128.47848	99.22166	12747.84847
489	129.76327	99.22937	12876.32696
490	131.06090	99.23700	13006.09023
491	132.37151	99.24455	13137.15113
492	133.69523	99.25203	13269.52264
493	135.03218	99.25944	13403.21787
494	136.38250	99.26677	13538.25005
495	137.74633	99.27403	13674.63255
496	139.12379	99.28122	13812.37887
497	140.51503	99.28833	13951.50266
498	141.92018	99.29538	14092.01769
499	143.33938	99.30236	14233.93786
500	144.77277	99.30926	14377.27724

461	143.63979	91.66506	13166.75015
462	145.19589	91.67195	13310.38995
463	146.76885	91.67876	13455.58584
464	148.35884	91.68550	13602.35468
465	149.96606	91.69217	13750.71353
466	151.59070	91.69877	13900.67959
467	153.23293	91.70529	14052.27028
468	154.89295	91.71175	14205.50321
469	156.57096	91.71813	14360.39616
470	158.26714	91.72445	14516.96712
471	159.98170	91.73070	14675.23427
472	161.71484	91.73689	14835.21597
473	163.46675	91.74300	14996.93081
474	165.23764	91.74906	15160.39756
475	167.02771	91.75504	15325.63520
476	168.83718	91.76097	15492.66292
477	170.66625	91.76683	15661.50010
478	172.51514	91.77262	15832.16635
479	174.38405	91.77836	16004.68148
480	176.27321	91.78403	16179.06553
481	178.18284	91.78964	16355.33874
482	180.11315	91.79519	16533.52158
483	182.06438	91.80069	16713.63473
484	184.03674	91.80612	16895.69911
485	186.03047	91.81150	17079.73585
486	188.04580	91.81681	17265.76632
487	190.08296	91.82207	17453.81212
488	192.14220	91.82728	17643.89508
489	194.22374	91.83243	17836.03728
490	196.32783	91.83752	18030.26102
491	198.45471	91.84256	18226.58885
492	200.60464	91.84754	18425.04356
493	202.77786	91.85248	18625.64820
494	204.97462	91.85736	18828.42605
495	207.19517	91.86218	19033.40067
496	209.43979	91.86696	19240.59584
497	211.70872	91.87168	19450.03563
498	214.00223	91.87635	19661.74435
499	216.32059	91.88098	19875.74658
500	218.66406	91.88555	20092.06717

Table I. ANNUITIES (*Continued*)

M	C(14,M,12)	A(14,M,12)	S(14,M,12)	M	C(15,M,12)	A(15,M,12)	S(15,M,12)	M	C(16,M,12)	A(16,M,12)	S(16,M,12)
1	1.01167	.98847	1.00000	1	1.01250	.98765	1.00000	1	1.01333	.98684	1.00000
2	1.02347	1.96554	2.01167	2	1.02516	1.96312	2.01250	2	1.02684	1.96070	2.01333
3	1.03541	2.93134	3.03514	3	1.03797	2.92653	3.03766	3	1.04054	2.92174	3.04018
4	1.04749	3.88600	4.07055	4	1.05095	3.87806	4.07563	4	1.05441	3.87014	4.08071
5	1.05971	4.82966	5.11804	5	1.06408	4.81784	5.12657	5	1.06847	4.80606	5.13512
6	1.07207	5.76243	6.17775	6	1.07738	5.74601	6.19065	6	1.08271	5.72966	6.20359
7	1.08458	6.68444	7.24982	7	1.09085	6.66273	7.26804	7	1.09715	6.64112	7.28631
8	1.09723	7.59582	8.33440	8	1.10449	7.56812	8.35889	8	1.11178	7.54058	8.38346
9	1.11004	8.49670	9.43164	9	1.11829	8.46234	9.46337	9	1.12660	8.42820	9.49524
10	1.12299	9.38718	10.54167	10	1.13227	9.34553	10.58167	10	1.14162	9.30414	10.62184
11	1.13609	10.26739	11.66466	11	1.14642	10.21780	11.71394	11	1.15685	10.16856	11.76346
12	1.14934	11.13746	12.80075	12	1.16075	11.07931	12.86036	12	1.17227	11.02161	12.92031
13	1.16275	11.99748	13.95009	13	1.17526	11.93018	14.02112	13	1.18790	11.86343	14.09258
14	1.17632	12.84760	15.11284	14	1.18995	12.77055	15.19638	14	1.20374	12.69417	15.28048
15	1.19004	13.68790	16.28915	15	1.20483	13.60055	16.38633	15	1.21979	13.51399	16.48422
16	1.20392	14.51852	17.47919	16	1.21989	14.42029	17.59116	16	1.23605	14.32301	17.70401
17	1.21797	15.33956	18.68312	17	1.23514	15.22992	18.81105	17	1.25253	15.12140	18.94006
18	1.23218	16.15113	19.90109	18	1.25058	16.02955	20.04619	18	1.26923	15.90927	20.19260
19	1.24655	16.95334	21.13327	19	1.26621	16.81931	21.29677	19	1.28616	16.68678	21.46183
20	1.26110	17.74630	22.37982	20	1.28204	17.59932	22.55298	20	1.30331	17.45406	22.74799
21	1.27581	18.53012	23.64092	21	1.29806	18.36969	23.84502	21	1.32068	18.21124	24.05130
22	1.29070	19.30489	24.91673	22	1.31429	19.13056	25.14308	22	1.33829	18.95846	25.37198
23	1.30575	20.07073	26.20743	23	1.33072	19.88204	26.45737	23	1.35614	19.69585	26.71027
24	1.32099	20.82774	27.51318	24	1.34735	20.62423	27.78808	24	1.37422	20.42354	28.06641
25	1.33640	21.57602	28.83417	25	1.36419	21.35727	29.13544	25	1.39254	21.14165	29.44063
26	1.35199	22.31567	30.17057	26	1.38125	22.08125	30.49963	26	1.41111	21.85031	30.83317
27	1.36776	23.04679	31.52256	27	1.39851	22.79630	31.88087	27	1.42992	22.54965	32.24428
28	1.38372	23.76948	32.89032	28	1.41599	23.50252	33.27938	28	1.44899	23.23979	33.67421
29	1.39986	24.48384	34.27404	29	1.43369	24.20002	34.69538	29	1.46831	23.92084	35.12319
30	1.41620	25.18996	35.67390	30	1.45161	24.88891	36.12907	30	1.48789	24.59294	36.59150
31	1.43272	25.88793	37.09010	31	1.46976	25.56929	37.58068	31	1.50773	25.25619	38.07939
32	1.44943	26.57786	38.52282	32	1.48813	26.24127	39.05044	32	1.52783	25.91071	39.58712
33	1.46634	27.25982	39.97225	33	1.50673	26.90496	40.53857	33	1.54820	26.55662	41.11494
34	1.48345	27.93393	41.43859	34	1.52557	27.56046	42.04530	34	1.56884	27.19404	42.66314
35	1.50076	28.60026	42.92204	35	1.54464	28.20786	43.57087	35	1.58976	27.82306	44.23199
36	1.51827	29.25890	44.42280	36	1.56394	28.84727	45.11551	36	1.61096	28.44381	45.82174
37	1.53598	29.90995	45.94107	37	1.58349	29.47878	46.67945	37	1.63244	29.05639	47.43270
38	1.55390	30.55350	47.47704	38	1.60329	30.10250	48.26294	38	1.65420	29.66091	49.06514
39	1.57203	31.18962	49.03094	39	1.62333	30.71852	49.86623	39	1.67626	30.25748	50.71934
40	1.59037	31.81840	50.60297	40	1.64362	31.32693	51.48956	40	1.69861	30.84620	52.39560
41	1.60892	32.43994	52.19334	41	1.66416	31.92784	53.13318	41	1.72126	31.42717	54.09421
42	1.62769	33.05430	53.80226	42	1.68497	32.52132	54.79734	42	1.74421	32.00050	55.81546
43	1.64668	33.66159	55.42995	43	1.70603	33.10748	56.48231	43	1.76746	32.56628	57.55967
44	1.66589	34.26186	57.07664	44	1.72735	33.68640	58.18834	44	1.79103	33.12462	59.32713
45	1.68533	34.85522	58.74253	45	1.74895	34.25817	59.91569	45	1.81491	33.67561	61.11816
46	1.70499	35.44173	60.42786	46	1.77081	34.82288	61.66464	46	1.83911	34.21935	62.93307
47	1.72488	36.02148	62.13285	47	1.79294	35.38062	63.43545	47	1.86363	34.75594	64.77217
48	1.74501	36.59455	63.85774	48	1.81535	35.93148	65.22839	48	1.88848	35.28547	66.63580
49	1.76537	37.16100	65.60274	49	1.83805	36.47554	67.04374	49	1.91366	35.80803	68.52428
50	1.78596	37.72092	67.36811	50	1.86102	37.01288	68.88179	50	1.93917	36.32371	70.43794
51	1.80680	38.27439	69.15407	51	1.88429	37.54358	70.74281	51	1.96503	36.83261	72.37711
52	1.82788	38.82147	70.96087	52	1.90784	38.06773	72.62710	52	1.99123	37.33481	74.34214
53	1.84920	39.36225	72.78874	53	1.93169	38.58542	74.53494	53	2.01778	37.83040	76.33337
54	1.87078	39.89678	74.63795	54	1.95583	39.09671	76.46662	54	2.04468	38.31948	78.35115
55	1.89260	40.42516	76.50872	55	1.98028	39.60169	78.42246	55	2.07194	38.80212	80.39583
56	1.91468	40.94744	78.40132	56	2.00503	40.10043	80.40274	56	2.09957	39.27840	82.46777

57	1.93702	41.46369	80.31601	57	2.03010	40.59302	82.40777	57	2.12756	39.74843	84.56734
58	1.95962	41.97400	82.25303	58	2.05547	41.07952	84.43787	58	2.15593	40.21226	86.69491
59	1.98248	42.47841	84.21264	59	2.08117	41.56002	86.49334	59	2.18468	40.67000	88.85084
60	2.00561	42.97702	86.19513	60	2.10718	42.03459	88.57451	60	2.21381	41.12171	91.03552
61	2.02901	43.46987	88.20073	61	2.13352	42.50330	90.68169	61	2.24332	41.56747	93.24932
62	2.05268	43.95704	90.22974	62	2.16019	42.96622	92.81521	62	2.27324	42.00737	95.49265
63	2.07663	44.43859	92.28242	63	2.18719	43.42343	94.97540	63	2.30355	42.44149	97.76588
64	2.10086	44.91458	94.35905	64	2.21453	43.87499	97.16259	64	2.33426	42.86989	100.06943
65	2.12537	45.38509	96.45991	65	2.24221	44.32098	99.37713	65	2.36538	43.29265	102.40369
66	2.15016	45.85017	98.58527	66	2.27024	44.76146	101.61934	66	2.39692	43.70986	104.76907
67	2.17525	46.30989	100.73543	67	2.29862	45.19651	103.88958	67	2.42888	44.12157	107.16599
68	2.20062	46.76431	102.91068	68	2.32735	45.62618	106.18820	68	2.46126	44.52786	109.59487
69	2.22630	47.21348	105.11131	69	2.35644	46.05055	108.51555	69	2.49408	44.92881	112.05614
70	2.25227	47.65748	107.33760	70	2.38590	46.46968	110.87200	70	2.52734	45.32449	114.55022
71	2.27855	48.09635	109.58988	71	2.41572	46.88363	113.25790	71	2.56103	45.71495	117.07755
72	2.30513	48.53017	111.86843	72	2.44592	47.29247	115.67362	72	2.59518	46.10028	119.63859
73	2.33202	48.95898	114.17356	73	2.47649	47.69627	118.11954	73	2.62978	46.48054	122.23377
74	2.35923	49.38285	116.50558	74	2.50745	48.09508	120.59604	74	2.66485	46.85580	124.86355
75	2.38676	49.80183	118.86481	75	2.53879	48.48897	123.10349	75	2.70038	47.22612	127.52840
76	2.41460	50.21597	121.25157	76	2.57053	48.87800	125.64228	76	2.73638	47.59156	130.22878
77	2.44277	50.62534	123.66617	77	2.60266	49.26222	128.21281	77	2.77287	47.95220	132.96516
78	2.47127	51.02999	126.10894	78	2.63519	49.64170	130.81547	78	2.80984	48.30809	135.73803
79	2.50010	51.42998	128.58021	79	2.66813	50.01649	133.45066	79	2.84730	48.65930	138.54787
80	2.52927	51.82535	131.08032	80	2.70148	50.38666	136.11880	80	2.88527	49.00589	141.39518
81	2.55878	52.21616	133.60959	81	2.73525	50.75225	138.82028	81	2.92374	49.34792	144.28044
82	2.58863	52.60246	136.16837	82	2.76944	51.11334	141.55553	82	2.96272	49.68545	147.20418
83	2.61883	52.98431	138.75700	83	2.80406	51.46996	144.32498	83	3.00223	50.01853	150.16691
84	2.64938	53.36176	141.37583	84	2.83911	51.82219	147.12904	84	3.04226	50.34723	153.16913
85	2.68029	53.73485	144.02521	85	2.87460	52.17006	149.96815	85	3.08282	50.67161	156.21139
86	2.71156	54.10364	146.70551	86	2.91053	52.51364	152.84275	86	3.12392	50.99172	159.29421
87	2.74320	54.46818	149.41707	87	2.94692	52.85298	155.75329	87	3.16558	51.30762	162.41813
88	2.77520	54.82852	152.16027	88	2.98375	53.18813	158.70021	88	3.20778	51.61936	165.58370
89	2.80758	55.18469	154.93547	89	3.02105	53.51914	161.68395	89	3.25055	51.92700	168.79149
90	2.84034	55.53677	157.74305	90	3.05881	53.84606	164.70501	90	3.29389	52.23060	172.04204
91	2.87347	55.88478	160.58339	91	3.09705	54.16895	167.76382	91	3.33781	52.53019	175.33593
92	2.90700	56.22877	163.45686	92	3.13576	54.48785	170.86087	92	3.38232	52.82585	178.67375
93	2.94091	56.56880	166.36386	93	3.17496	54.80282	173.99663	93	3.42741	53.11761	182.05606
94	2.97522	56.90491	169.30477	94	3.21464	55.11389	177.17159	94	3.47311	53.40554	185.48348
95	3.00993	57.23715	172.27999	95	3.25483	55.42113	180.38623	95	3.51942	53.68968	188.95659
96	3.04505	57.56555	175.28993	96	3.29551	55.72457	183.64106	96	3.56635	53.97008	192.47601
97	3.08057	57.89016	178.33498	97	3.33671	56.02427	186.93657	97	3.61390	54.24679	196.04236
98	3.11651	58.21104	181.41555	98	3.37842	56.32026	190.27328	98	3.66208	54.51985	199.65626
99	3.15287	58.52821	184.53207	99	3.42065	56.61261	193.65170	99	3.71091	54.78933	203.31834
100	3.18966	58.84172	187.68494	100	3.46340	56.90134	197.07234	100	3.76039	55.05526	207.02925

Table I. ANNUITIES (*Continued*)

M	C(14,M,12)	A(14,M,12)	S(14,M,12)	M	C(15,M,12)	A(15,M,12)	S(15,M,12)	M	C(16,M,12)	A(16,M,12)	S(16,M,12)
101	3.22687	59.15162	190.87460	101	3.50670	57.18651	200.53575	101	3.81053	55.31769	210.78964
102	3.26452	59.45794	194.10147	102	3.55053	57.46816	204.04244	102	3.86134	55.57667	214.60017
103	3.30260	59.76073	197.36598	103	3.59491	57.74633	207.59297	103	3.91282	55.83224	218.46150
104	3.34113	60.06003	200.66859	104	3.63985	58.02106	211.18789	104	3.96499	56.08445	222.37432
105	3.38011	60.35588	204.00972	105	3.68535	58.29241	214.82773	105	4.01786	56.33334	226.33932
106	3.41955	60.64832	207.38983	106	3.73141	58.56040	218.51308	106	4.07143	56.57895	230.35717
107	3.45944	60.93738	210.80938	107	3.77806	58.82509	222.24449	107	4.12571	56.82133	234.42860
108	3.49980	61.22311	214.26883	108	3.82528	59.08651	226.02255	108	4.18072	57.06052	238.55432
109	3.54063	61.50555	217.76863	109	3.87310	59.34470	229.84783	109	4.23647	57.29657	242.73504
110	3.58194	61.78472	221.30926	110	3.92151	59.59970	233.72093	110	4.29295	57.52951	246.97151
111	3.62373	62.06068	224.89120	111	3.97053	59.85156	237.64244	111	4.35019	57.75938	251.26446
112	3.66601	62.33346	228.51493	112	4.02016	60.10031	241.61297	112	4.40820	57.98624	255.61465
113	3.70878	62.60309	232.18094	113	4.07041	60.34598	245.63313	113	4.46697	58.21010	260.02285
114	3.75205	62.86961	235.88972	114	4.12129	60.58862	249.70355	114	4.52653	58.43102	264.48982
115	3.79582	63.13306	239.64177	115	4.17281	60.82827	253.82484	115	4.58688	58.64903	269.01635
116	3.84011	63.39347	243.43759	116	4.22497	61.06496	257.99765	116	4.64804	58.86418	273.60324
117	3.88491	63.65088	247.27769	117	4.27778	61.29872	262.22262	117	4.71002	59.07649	278.25128
118	3.93023	63.90531	251.16260	118	4.33126	61.52960	266.50041	118	4.77282	59.28601	282.96130
119	3.97608	64.15682	255.09283	119	4.38540	61.75763	270.83166	119	4.83645	59.49277	287.73411
120	4.02247	64.40542	259.06891	120	4.44021	61.98285	275.21706	120	4.90094	59.69682	292.57057
121	4.06940	64.65116	263.09138	121	4.49572	62.20528	279.65727	121	4.96629	59.89817	297.47151
122	4.11688	64.89406	267.16078	122	4.55191	62.42497	284.15299	122	5.03250	60.09688	302.43780
123	4.16491	65.13416	271.27766	123	4.60881	62.64194	288.70490	123	5.09960	60.29298	307.47030
124	4.21350	65.37149	275.44256	124	4.66642	62.85624	293.31371	124	5.16760	60.48649	312.56990
125	4.26265	65.60609	279.65606	125	4.72475	63.06789	297.98013	125	5.23650	60.67746	317.73750
126	4.31239	65.83798	283.91871	126	4.78381	63.27693	302.70488	126	5.30632	60.86591	322.97400
127	4.36270	66.06720	288.23110	127	4.84361	63.48339	307.48870	127	5.37707	61.05189	328.28032
128	4.41359	66.29377	292.59380	128	4.90415	63.68730	312.33230	128	5.44877	61.23541	333.65739
129	4.46509	66.51773	297.00739	129	4.96546	63.88869	317.23646	129	5.52142	61.41653	339.10616
130	4.51718	66.73911	301.47248	130	5.02752	64.08759	322.20191	130	5.59503	61.59526	344.62757
131	4.56988	66.95793	305.98966	131	5.09037	64.28404	327.22944	131	5.66963	61.77163	350.22261
132	4.62319	67.17423	310.55953	132	5.15400	64.47807	332.31981	132	5.74523	61.94569	355.89224
133	4.67713	67.38804	315.18273	133	5.21842	64.66970	337.47380	133	5.82183	62.11746	361.63747
134	4.73170	67.59938	319.85986	134	5.28365	64.85896	342.69223	134	5.89946	62.28697	367.45931
135	4.78690	67.80828	324.59156	135	5.34970	65.04589	347.97588	135	5.97812	62.45424	373.35876
136	4.84275	68.01477	329.37846	136	5.41657	65.23050	353.32558	136	6.05783	62.61932	379.33688
137	4.89925	68.21889	334.22121	137	5.48428	65.41284	358.74215	137	6.13860	62.78222	385.39471
138	4.95641	68.42065	339.12046	138	5.55283	65.59293	364.22642	138	6.22044	62.94298	391.53330
139	5.01423	68.62008	344.07686	139	5.62224	65.77080	369.77925	139	6.30338	63.10163	397.75375
140	5.07273	68.81721	349.09109	140	5.69252	65.94647	375.40149	140	6.38743	63.25819	404.05713
141	5.13191	69.01207	354.16382	141	5.76368	66.11997	381.09401	141	6.47259	63.41268	410.44456
142	5.19178	69.20468	359.29573	142	5.83572	66.29133	386.85769	142	6.55890	63.56515	416.91715
143	5.25235	69.39507	364.48752	143	5.90867	66.46057	392.69341	143	6.64635	63.71561	423.47605
144	5.31363	69.58327	369.73987	144	5.98253	66.62772	398.60208	144	6.73497	63.86409	430.12239
145	5.37562	69.76929	375.05350	145	6.05731	66.79281	404.58460	145	6.82476	64.01061	436.85736
146	5.43834	69.95317	380.42913	146	6.13302	66.95586	410.64191	146	6.91576	64.15521	443.68212
147	5.50179	70.13493	385.86747	147	6.20969	67.11690	416.77493	147	7.00797	64.29790	450.59789
148	5.56597	70.31460	391.36925	148	6.28731	67.27595	422.98462	148	7.10141	64.43872	457.60586
149	5.63091	70.49219	396.93523	149	6.36590	67.43304	429.27193	149	7.19610	64.57768	464.70727
150	5.69660	70.66773	402.56614	150	6.44547	67.58819	435.63783	150	7.29204	64.71482	471.90337
151	5.76307	70.84125	408.26274	151	6.52604	67.74142	442.08330	151	7.38927	64.85015	479.19541
152	5.83030	71.01277	414.02581	152	6.60762	67.89276	448.60934	152	7.48780	64.98370	486.58468
153	5.89832	71.18231	419.85611	153	6.69021	68.04223	455.21696	153	7.58763	65.11549	494.07248
154	5.96714	71.34989	425.75443	154	6.77384	68.18986	461.90717	154	7.68880	65.24555	501.66011
155	6.03675	71.51554	431.72157	155	6.85851	68.33566	468.68101	155	7.79132	65.37390	509.34891
156	6.10718	71.67928	437.75832	156	6.94424	68.47967	475.53952	156	7.89520	65.50056	517.14023
157	6.17843	71.84114	443.86550	157	7.03105	68.62189	482.48377	157	8.00047	65.62555	525.03544
158	6.25051	72.00112	450.04393	158	7.11894	68.76236	489.51481	158	8.10715	65.74890	533.03591

161	6.47184	72.47010	469.01509	161	7.38925	69.17346	511.13969	161	8.43577	66.10929	557.68307
162	6.54735	72.62283	475.48693	162	7.48161	69.30712	518.52894	162	8.54825	66.22628	566.11885
163	6.62373	72.77381	482.03428	163	7.57513	69.43913	526.01055	163	8.66223	66.34172	574.66710
164	6.70101	72.92304	488.65801	164	7.66982	69.56951	533.58568	164	8.77772	66.45564	583.32933
165	6.77919	73.07055	495.35902	165	7.76569	69.69828	541.25550	165	8.89476	66.56807	592.10705
166	6.85828	73.21636	502.13821	166	7.86276	69.82546	549.02120	166	9.01336	66.67902	601.00181
167	6.93829	73.36048	508.99649	167	7.96105	69.95107	556.88396	167	9.13354	66.78850	610.01517
168	7.01924	73.50295	515.93478	168	8.06056	70.07513	564.84501	168	9.25532	66.89655	619.14870
169	7.10113	73.64377	522.95402	169	8.16132	70.19766	572.90557	169	9.37872	67.00317	628.40402
170	7.18398	73.78297	530.05515	170	8.26334	70.31868	581.06589	170	9.50377	67.10839	637.78274
171	7.26779	73.92056	537.23913	171	8.36663	70.43820	589.33023	171	9.63049	67.21223	647.28651
172	7.35258	74.05657	544.50692	172	8.47121	70.55625	597.69686	172	9.75889	67.31470	656.91700
173	7.43836	74.19101	551.85950	173	8.57710	70.67284	606.16807	173	9.88901	67.41582	666.67589
174	7.52514	74.32390	559.29786	174	8.68431	70.78799	614.74517	174	10.02087	67.51562	676.56490
175	7.61293	74.45525	566.82300	175	8.79287	70.90172	623.42948	175	10.15448	67.61410	686.58577
176	7.70175	74.58509	574.43593	176	8.90278	71.01404	632.22235	176	10.28987	67.71128	696.74024
177	7.79161	74.71344	582.13769	177	9.01406	71.12498	641.12513	177	10.42707	67.80718	707.03011
178	7.88251	74.84030	589.92929	178	9.12674	71.23455	650.13920	178	10.56610	67.90182	717.45718
179	7.97447	74.96570	597.81180	179	9.24082	71.34276	659.26594	179	10.70698	67.99522	728.02328
180	8.06751	75.08965	605.78627	180	9.35633	71.44964	668.50675	180	10.84974	68.08739	738.73025
181	8.16163	75.21218	613.85378	181	9.47329	71.55520	677.86309	181	10.99440	68.17835	749.57999
182	8.25685	75.33329	622.01541	182	9.59170	71.65946	687.33638	182	11.14099	68.26810	760.57439
183	8.35318	75.45301	630.27225	183	9.71160	71.76243	696.92809	183	11.28954	68.35668	771.71538
184	8.45063	75.57134	638.62543	184	9.83300	71.86413	706.63969	184	11.44007	68.44409	783.00492
185	8.54922	75.68831	647.07606	185	9.95591	71.96457	716.47268	185	11.59260	68.53036	794.44499
186	8.64896	75.80393	655.62528	186	10.08036	72.06377	726.42859	186	11.74717	68.61548	806.03759
187	8.74987	75.91822	664.27424	187	10.20636	72.16175	736.50895	187	11.90380	68.69949	817.78475
188	8.85195	76.03119	673.02411	188	10.33394	72.25852	746.71531	188	12.06251	68.78239	829.68855
189	8.95522	76.14285	681.87606	189	10.46312	72.35409	757.04925	189	12.22335	68.86420	841.75107
190	9.05970	76.25323	690.83128	190	10.59390	72.44849	767.51237	190	12.38633	68.94494	853.97441
191	9.16539	76.36234	699.89097	191	10.72633	72.54172	778.10627	191	12.55148	69.02461	866.36074
192	9.27232	76.47019	709.05637	192	10.86041	72.63379	788.83260	192	12.71883	69.10323	878.91222
193	9.38050	76.57679	718.32869	193	10.99616	72.72473	799.69301	193	12.88841	69.18082	891.63104
194	9.48994	76.68217	727.70919	194	11.13361	72.81455	810.68917	194	13.06026	69.25739	904.51946
195	9.60066	76.78632	737.19914	195	11.27278	72.90326	821.82279	195	13.23440	69.33295	917.57972
196	9.71266	76.88928	746.79979	196	11.41369	72.99088	833.09557	196	13.41085	69.40752	930.81411
197	9.82598	76.99105	756.51246	197	11.55637	73.07741	844.50927	197	13.58967	69.48110	944.22497
198	9.94062	77.09165	766.33843	198	11.70082	73.16287	856.06563	198	13.77086	69.55372	957.81464
199	10.05659	77.19109	776.27905	199	11.84708	73.24728	867.76645	199	13.95447	69.62538	971.58550
200	10.17392	77.28938	786.33564	200	11.99517	73.33065	879.61353	200	14.14053	69.69610	985.53997

Table I. ANNUITIES (*Continued*)

M	C(14,M,12)	A(14,M,12)	S(14,M,12)
201	10.29261	77.38654	796.50955
202	10.41269	77.48257	806.80217
203	10.53417	77.57750	817.21486
204	10.65707	77.67134	827.74903
205	10.78140	77.76409	838.40610
206	10.90719	77.85577	849.18751
207	11.03444	77.94640	860.09470
208	11.16317	78.03598	871.12913
209	11.29341	78.12452	882.29231
210	11.42517	78.21205	893.58572
211	11.55846	78.29857	905.01088
212	11.69331	78.38409	916.56934
213	11.82973	78.46862	928.26265
214	11.96774	78.55218	940.09238
215	12.10737	78.63477	952.06013
216	12.24862	78.71641	964.16750
217	12.39152	78.79711	976.41612
218	12.53609	78.87688	988.80764
219	12.68234	78.95573	1001.34373
220	12.83030	79.03367	1014.02607
221	12.97999	79.11072	1026.85638
222	13.13142	79.18687	1039.83637
223	13.28462	79.26214	1052.96779
224	13.43961	79.33655	1066.25241
225	13.59641	79.41010	1079.69203
226	13.75503	79.48280	1093.28843
227	13.91551	79.55466	1107.04347
228	14.07785	79.62570	1120.95897
229	14.24210	79.69591	1135.03683
230	14.40825	79.76531	1149.27892
231	14.57635	79.83392	1163.68718
232	14.74641	79.90173	1178.26353
233	14.91845	79.96876	1193.00994
234	15.09250	80.03502	1207.92838
235	15.26858	80.10052	1223.02088
236	15.44671	80.16525	1238.28946
237	15.62692	80.22925	1253.73617
238	15.80924	80.29250	1269.36309
239	15.99368	80.35502	1285.17233
240	16.18027	80.41683	1301.16601
241	16.36904	80.47792	1317.34628
242	16.56001	80.53831	1333.71531
243	16.75321	80.59800	1350.27533
244	16.94867	80.65700	1367.02854
245	17.14640	80.71532	1383.97721
246	17.34644	80.77297	1401.12361
247	17.54882	80.82995	1418.47005
248	17.75355	80.88628	1436.01887
249	17.96068	80.94196	1453.77242
250	18.17022	80.99699	1471.73310
251	18.38221	81.05139	1489.90332
252	18.59666	81.10516	1508.28552
253	18.81363	81.15832	1526.88219
254	19.03312	81.21086	1545.69581
255	19.25517	81.26279	1564.72893
256	19.47981	81.31413	1583.98410
257	19.70708	81.36487	1603.46392

M	C(15,M,12)	A(15,M,12)	S(15,M,12)
201	12.14511	73.41299	891.60870
202	12.29692	73.49431	903.75381
203	12.45063	73.57462	916.05073
204	12.60627	73.65395	928.50137
205	12.76385	73.73230	941.10764
206	12.92339	73.80968	953.87148
207	13.08494	73.88610	966.79487
208	13.24850	73.96158	979.87981
209	13.41410	74.03613	993.12831
210	13.58178	74.10976	1006.54241
211	13.75155	74.18247	1020.12419
212	13.92345	74.25430	1033.87574
213	14.09749	74.32523	1047.79919
214	14.27371	74.39529	1061.89668
215	14.45213	74.46448	1076.17039
216	14.63278	74.53282	1090.62252
217	14.81569	74.60032	1105.25530
218	15.00089	74.66698	1120.07099
219	15.18840	74.73282	1135.07188
220	15.37825	74.79785	1150.26028
221	15.57048	74.86207	1165.63853
222	15.76511	74.92550	1181.20901
223	15.96218	74.98815	1196.97413
224	16.16170	75.05003	1212.93630
225	16.36373	75.11114	1229.09801
226	16.56827	75.17149	1245.46173
227	16.77538	75.23111	1262.03000
228	16.98507	75.28998	1278.80538
229	17.19738	75.34813	1295.79045
230	17.41235	75.40556	1312.98783
231	17.63000	75.46228	1330.40017
232	17.85038	75.51830	1348.03018
233	18.07351	75.57363	1365.88055
234	18.29943	75.62828	1383.95406
235	18.52817	75.68225	1402.25349
236	18.75977	75.73556	1420.78165
237	18.99427	75.78820	1439.54143
238	19.23170	75.84020	1458.53569
239	19.47209	75.89156	1477.76739
240	19.71549	75.94228	1497.23948
241	19.96194	75.99237	1516.95497
242	20.21146	76.04185	1536.91691
243	20.46410	76.09072	1557.12837
244	20.71991	76.13898	1577.59248
245	20.97890	76.18665	1598.31238
246	21.24114	76.23372	1619.29129
247	21.50666	76.28022	1640.53243
248	21.77549	76.32614	1662.03909
249	22.04768	76.37150	1683.81457
250	22.32328	76.41630	1705.86225
251	22.60232	76.46054	1728.18553
252	22.88485	76.50424	1750.78785
253	23.17091	76.54739	1773.67270
254	23.46055	76.59002	1796.84361
255	23.75380	76.63212	1820.30416
256	24.05072	76.67370	1844.05796
257	24.35136	76.71476	1868.10868

M	C(16,M,12)	A(16,M,12)	S(16,M,12)
201	14.32907	69.76589	999.68050
202	14.52013	69.83475	1014.00958
203	14.71373	69.90272	1028.52970
204	14.90991	69.96979	1043.24343
205	15.10871	70.03598	1058.15335
206	15.31016	70.10129	1073.26206
207	15.51430	70.16575	1088.57222
208	15.72115	70.22936	1104.08651
209	15.93077	70.29213	1119.80767
210	16.14318	70.35407	1135.73844
211	16.35842	70.41521	1151.88162
212	16.57653	70.47553	1168.24004
213	16.79755	70.53506	1184.81657
214	17.02152	70.59381	1201.61413
215	17.24848	70.65179	1218.63565
216	17.47845	70.70900	1235.88412
217	17.71150	70.76546	1253.36258
218	17.94765	70.82118	1271.07408
219	18.18696	70.87617	1289.02173
220	18.42945	70.93043	1307.20869
221	18.67518	70.98397	1325.63814
222	18.92418	71.03682	1344.31331
223	19.17650	71.08896	1363.23749
224	19.43219	71.14042	1382.41399
225	19.69128	71.19121	1401.84618
226	19.95383	71.24132	1421.53746
227	20.21988	71.29078	1441.49129
228	20.48948	71.33959	1461.71118
229	20.76268	71.38775	1482.20066
230	21.03951	71.43528	1502.96334
231	21.32004	71.48218	1524.00285
232	21.60431	71.52847	1545.32288
233	21.89236	71.57415	1566.92719
234	22.18426	71.61922	1588.81955
235	22.48005	71.66371	1611.00381
236	22.77978	71.70761	1633.48386
237	23.08352	71.75093	1656.26365
238	23.39130	71.79368	1679.34716
239	23.70318	71.83587	1702.73846
240	24.01922	71.87750	1726.44164
241	24.33948	71.91859	1750.46086
242	24.66400	71.95913	1774.80034
243	24.99286	71.99914	1799.46434
244	25.32610	72.03863	1824.45720
245	25.66378	72.07759	1849.78330
246	26.00596	72.11605	1875.44707
247	26.35271	72.15399	1901.45304
248	26.70408	72.19144	1927.80574
249	27.06013	72.22839	1954.50982
250	27.42093	72.26486	1981.56995
251	27.78655	72.30085	2008.99088
252	28.15703	72.33637	2036.77743
253	28.53246	72.37141	2064.93446
254	28.91289	72.40600	2093.46692
255	29.29840	72.44013	2122.37981
256	29.68904	72.47382	2151.67821
257	30.08490	72.50705	2181.36725
258	30.48603	72.53986	2211.45215

261	20.64296	81.56206	1683.68249	261	25.59195	76.87402	1967.35574	261	31.72180	72.63570	2304.13510
262	20.88380	81.60994	1704.32545	262	25.91185	76.91261	1992.94768	262	32.14476	72.66680	2335.85690
263	21.12744	81.65727	1725.20925	263	26.23574	76.95072	2018.85953	263	32.57336	72.69750	2368.00166
264	21.37393	81.70406	1746.33669	264	26.56369	76.98837	2045.09527	264	33.00767	72.72780	2400.57501
265	21.62329	81.75031	1767.71062	265	26.89574	77.02555	2071.65896	265	33.44777	72.75770	2433.58268
266	21.87556	81.79602	1789.33391	266	27.23193	77.06227	2098.55470	266	33.89374	72.78720	2467.03045
267	22.13078	81.84121	1811.20947	267	27.57233	77.09854	2125.78663	267	34.34566	72.81632	2500.92419
268	22.38897	81.88587	1833.34025	268	27.91699	77.13436	2153.35897	268	34.80360	72.84505	2535.26984
269	22.65017	81.93002	1855.72922	269	28.26595	77.16974	2181.27595	269	35.26765	72.87340	2570.07344
270	22.91443	81.97366	1878.37939	270	28.61927	77.20468	2209.54190	270	35.73788	72.90139	2605.34109
271	23.18176	82.01680	1901.29382	271	28.97701	77.23919	2238.16118	271	36.21439	72.92900	2641.07897
272	23.45222	82.05944	1924.47558	272	29.33923	77.27328	2267.13819	272	36.69724	72.95625	2677.29335
273	23.72582	82.10159	1947.92779	273	29.70597	77.30694	2296.47742	273	37.18654	72.98314	2713.99060
274	24.00263	82.14325	1971.65362	274	30.07729	77.34019	2326.18339	274	37.68236	73.00968	2751.17714
275	24.28266	82.18443	1995.65624	275	30.45326	77.37302	2356.26068	275	38.18479	73.03587	2788.85950
276	24.56595	82.22514	2019.93890	276	30.83392	77.40546	2386.71394	276	38.69392	73.06171	2827.04429
277	24.85256	82.26537	2044.50485	277	31.21935	77.43749	2417.54786	277	39.20984	73.08721	2865.73822
278	25.14250	82.30515	2069.35741	278	31.60959	77.46912	2448.76721	278	39.73264	73.11238	2904.94806
279	25.43583	82.34446	2094.49991	279	32.00471	77.50037	2480.37680	279	40.26241	73.13722	2944.68070
280	25.73258	82.38332	2119.93574	280	32.40477	77.53123	2512.38151	280	40.79924	73.16173	2984.94311
281	26.03280	82.42174	2145.66833	281	32.80983	77.56171	2544.78628	281	41.34323	73.18592	3025.74235
282	26.33651	82.45971	2171.70112	282	33.21995	77.59181	2577.59611	282	41.89447	73.20979	3067.08558
283	26.64377	82.49724	2198.03764	283	33.63520	77.62154	2610.81606	283	42.45307	73.23334	3108.98006
284	26.95462	82.53434	2224.68141	284	34.05564	77.65090	2644.45126	284	43.01911	73.25659	3151.43313
285	27.26909	82.57101	2251.63603	285	34.48134	77.67990	2678.50690	285	43.59270	73.27953	3194.45223
286	27.58723	82.60726	2278.90511	286	34.91235	77.70855	2712.98824	286	44.17393	73.30217	3238.04493
287	27.90908	82.64309	2306.49234	287	35.34876	77.73684	2747.90059	287	44.76292	73.32451	3282.21886
288	28.23468	82.67851	2334.40142	288	35.79062	77.76478	2783.24935	288	45.35976	73.34655	3326.98178
289	28.56409	82.71351	2362.63610	289	36.23800	77.79237	2819.03996	289	45.96455	73.36831	3372.34154
290	28.89734	82.74812	2391.20019	290	36.69097	77.81963	2855.27796	290	46.57741	73.38978	3418.30609
291	29.23447	82.78233	2420.09752	291	37.14961	77.84655	2891.96894	291	47.19845	73.41096	3464.88351
292	29.57554	82.81614	2449.33199	292	37.61398	77.87313	2929.11855	292	47.82776	73.43187	3512.08195
293	29.92059	82.84956	2478.90753	293	38.08416	77.89939	2966.73253	293	48.46546	73.45251	3559.90971
294	30.26966	82.88260	2508.82812	294	38.56021	77.92532	3004.81669	294	49.11167	73.47287	3608.37518
295	30.62281	82.91525	2539.09778	295	39.04221	77.95094	3043.37690	295	49.76649	73.49296	3657.48684
296	30.98007	82.94753	2569.72059	296	39.53024	77.97623	3082.41911	296	50.43004	73.51279	3707.25334
297	31.34151	82.97944	2600.70066	297	40.02437	78.00122	3121.94935	297	51.10245	73.53236	3757.68338
298	31.70716	83.01098	2632.04217	298	40.52467	78.02589	3161.97371	298	51.78381	73.55167	3808.78583
299	32.07708	83.04215	2663.74933	299	41.03123	78.05027	3202.49839	299	52.47426	73.57073	3860.56964
300	32.45131	83.07297	2695.82641	300	41.54412	78.07434	3243.52962	300	53.17392	73.58953	3913.04390

Table I. ANNUITIES (*Continued*)

M	C(14,M,12)	A(14,M,12)	S(14,M,12)
301	32.82991	83.10343	2728.27772
302	33.21292	83.13353	2761.10762
303	33.60041	83.16330	2794.32054
304	33.99241	83.19271	2827.92095
305	34.38899	83.22179	2861.91336
306	34.79019	83.25054	2896.30235
307	35.19608	83.27895	2931.09254
308	35.60670	83.30703	2966.28862
309	36.02211	83.33479	3001.89533
310	36.44237	83.36224	3037.91744
311	36.86753	83.38936	3074.35981
312	37.29765	83.41617	3111.22734
313	37.73279	83.44267	3148.52499
314	38.17301	83.46887	3186.25778
315	38.61836	83.49476	3224.43079
316	39.06891	83.52036	3263.04915
317	39.52471	83.54566	3302.11806
318	39.98583	83.57067	3341.64277
319	40.45233	83.59539	3381.62860
320	40.92428	83.61983	3422.08093
321	41.40173	83.64398	3463.00521
322	41.88475	83.66785	3504.40694
323	42.37340	83.69145	3546.29168
324	42.86776	83.71478	3588.66509
325	43.36788	83.73784	3631.53285
326	43.87384	83.76063	3674.90073
327	44.38570	83.78316	3718.77457
328	44.90354	83.80543	3763.16028
329	45.42741	83.82745	3808.06381
330	45.95740	83.84920	3853.49122
331	46.49357	83.87071	3899.44862
332	47.03599	83.89197	3945.94219
333	47.58475	83.91299	3992.97818
334	48.13990	83.93376	4040.56293
335	48.70153	83.95429	4088.70283
336	49.26972	83.97459	4137.40436
337	49.84453	83.99465	4186.67408
338	50.42605	84.01448	4236.51861
339	51.01435	84.03409	4286.94466
340	51.60952	84.05346	4337.95901
341	52.21163	84.07262	4389.56853
342	52.82077	84.09155	4441.78017
343	53.43701	84.11026	4494.60094
344	54.06044	84.12876	4548.03795
345	54.69115	84.14704	4602.09839
346	55.32921	84.16512	4656.78954
347	55.97472	84.18298	4712.11875
348	56.62776	84.20064	4768.09347
349	57.28841	84.21810	4824.72122
350	57.95678	84.23535	4882.00964
351	58.63294	84.25241	4939.96642
352	59.31699	84.26926	4998.59936
353	60.00902	84.28593	5057.91635
354	60.70913	84.30240	5117.92538
355	61.41740	84.31868	5178.63451
356	62.13394	84.33478	5240.05191
357	62.85883	84.35069	5302.18585
358	63.59219	84.36641	5365.04468

M	C(15,M,12)	A(15,M,12)	S(15,M,12)
301	42.06342	78.09811	3285.07374
302	42.58921	78.12159	3327.13716
303	43.12158	78.14478	3369.72637
304	43.66060	78.16768	3412.84795
305	44.20636	78.19031	3456.50855
306	44.75894	78.21265	3500.71491
307	45.31842	78.23471	3545.47384
308	45.88490	78.25651	3590.79227
309	46.45846	78.27803	3636.67717
310	47.03920	78.29929	3683.13563
311	47.62719	78.32029	3730.17483
312	48.22253	78.34102	3777.80202
313	48.82531	78.36151	3826.02454
314	49.43562	78.38173	3874.84985
315	50.05357	78.40171	3924.28547
316	50.67924	78.42144	3974.33904
317	51.31273	78.44093	4025.01828
318	51.95414	78.46018	4076.33101
319	52.60356	78.47919	4128.28514
320	53.26111	78.49797	4180.88871
321	53.92687	78.51651	4234.14982
322	54.60096	78.53482	4288.07669
323	55.28347	78.55291	4342.67765
324	55.97451	78.57078	4397.95112
325	56.67420	78.58842	4453.93563
326	57.38262	78.60585	4510.60983
327	58.09991	78.62306	4567.99245
328	58.82615	78.64006	4626.09236
329	59.56148	78.65685	4684.91851
330	60.30600	78.67343	4744.47999
331	61.05982	78.68981	4804.78599
332	61.82307	78.70598	4865.84582
333	62.59586	78.72196	4927.66889
334	63.37831	78.73774	4990.26475
335	64.17054	78.75332	5053.64306
336	64.97267	78.76871	5117.81360
337	65.78483	78.78391	5182.78627
338	66.60714	78.79893	5248.57110
339	67.43973	78.81376	5315.17823
340	68.28272	78.82840	5382.61796
341	69.13626	78.84286	5450.90069
342	70.00046	78.85715	5520.03695
343	70.87547	78.87126	5590.03741
344	71.76141	78.88519	5660.91288
345	72.65843	78.89896	5732.67429
346	73.56666	78.91255	5805.33271
347	74.48624	78.92598	5878.89937
348	75.41732	78.93924	5953.38562
349	76.36004	78.95233	6028.80294
350	77.31454	78.96527	6105.16297
351	78.28097	78.97804	6182.47751
352	79.25948	78.99066	6260.75848
353	80.25022	79.00312	6340.01796
354	81.25335	79.01543	6420.26818
355	82.26902	79.02758	6501.52154
356	83.29738	79.03959	6583.79056
357	84.33860	79.05144	6667.08794
358	85.39283	79.06315	6751.42654

M	C(16,M,12)	A(16,M,12)	S(16,M,12)
301	53.89290	73.60809	3966.21782
302	54.60134	73.62641	4020.10072
303	55.32936	73.64448	4074.70206
304	56.06709	73.66232	4130.03142
305	56.81465	73.67992	4186.09851
306	57.57218	73.69729	4242.91316
307	58.33980	73.71443	4300.48533
308	59.11767	73.73134	4358.82514
309	59.90590	73.74804	4417.94281
310	60.70465	73.76451	4477.84871
311	61.51404	73.78077	4538.55336
312	62.33423	73.79681	4600.06740
313	63.16536	73.81264	4662.40164
314	64.00756	73.82826	4725.56699
315	64.86099	73.84368	4789.57455
316	65.72581	73.85890	4854.43554
317	66.60215	73.87391	4920.16135
318	67.49018	73.88873	4986.76350
319	68.39005	73.90335	5054.25368
320	69.30192	73.91778	5122.64373
321	70.22594	73.93202	5191.94565
322	71.16229	73.94607	5262.17159
323	72.11112	73.95994	5333.33388
324	73.07260	73.97362	5405.44500
325	74.04690	73.98713	5478.51760
326	75.03419	74.00046	5552.56450
327	76.03465	74.01361	5627.59869
328	77.04844	74.02659	5703.63334
329	78.07576	74.03939	5780.68179
330	79.11677	74.05203	5858.75754
331	80.17166	74.06451	5937.87431
332	81.24061	74.07682	6018.04597
333	82.32382	74.08896	6099.28658
334	83.42147	74.10095	6181.61040
335	84.53376	74.11278	6265.03187
336	85.66088	74.12445	6349.56563
337	86.80302	74.13597	6435.22651
338	87.96039	74.14734	6522.02953
339	89.13320	74.15856	6609.98992
340	90.32164	74.16963	6699.12312
341	91.52593	74.18056	6789.44476
342	92.74628	74.19134	6880.97069
343	93.98289	74.20198	6973.71697
344	95.23600	74.21248	7067.69986
345	96.50581	74.22284	7162.93586
346	97.79256	74.23307	7259.44167
347	99.09646	74.24316	7357.23423
348	100.41774	74.25312	7456.33068
349	101.75665	74.26295	7556.74842
350	103.11340	74.27265	7658.50507
351	104.48825	74.28222	7761.61847
352	105.88142	74.29166	7866.10672
353	107.29318	74.30098	7971.98814
354	108.72375	74.31018	8079.28132
355	110.17340	74.31925	8188.00507
356	111.64238	74.32821	8298.17847
357	113.13094	74.33705	8409.82085
358	114.63936	74.34577	8522.95179

361	65.84398	84.41251	5558.05563	361	88.63526	79.09742	7010.82061	361	119.28634	74.37126	8871.47582
362	66.61216	84.42752	5623.89961	362	89.74320	79.10857	7099.45586	362	120.87683	74.37953	8990.76216
363	67.38930	84.44236	5690.51177	363	90.86499	79.11957	7189.19906	363	122.48852	74.38770	9111.63899
364	68.17551	84.45703	5757.90108	364	92.00080	79.13044	7280.06405	364	124.12170	74.39575	9234.12751
365	68.97089	84.47153	5826.07659	365	93.15081	79.14118	7372.06485	365	125.77666	74.40370	9358.24921
366	69.77555	84.48586	5895.04748	366	94.31520	79.15178	7465.21555	366	127.45368	74.41155	9484.02587
367	70.58960	84.50002	5964.82304	367	95.49414	79.16225	7559.53086	367	129.15306	74.41929	9611.47954
368	71.41315	84.51403	6035.41264	368	96.68781	79.17259	7655.02499	368	130.87510	74.42693	9740.63261
369	72.24630	84.52787	6106.82579	369	97.89641	79.18281	7751.71281	369	132.62010	74.43447	9871.50771
370	73.08917	84.54155	6179.07209	370	99.12012	79.19290	7849.60922	370	134.38837	74.44192	10004.12781
371	73.94188	84.55507	6252.16126	371	100.35912	79.20286	7948.72933	371	136.18022	74.44926	10138.51618
372	74.80454	84.56844	6326.10314	372	101.61361	79.21270	8049.08845	372	137.99595	74.45651	10274.69640
373	75.67726	84.58166	6400.90768	373	102.88378	79.22242	8150.70205	373	139.83590	74.46366	10412.69235
374	76.56016	84.59472	6476.58494	374	104.16982	79.23202	8253.58583	374	141.70038	74.47071	10552.52825
375	77.45336	84.60763	6553.14509	375	105.47195	79.24150	8357.75555	375	143.58971	74.47768	10694.22862
376	78.35698	84.62039	6630.59845	376	106.79034	79.25087	8463.22760	376	145.50424	74.48455	10837.81834
377	79.27115	84.63301	6708.95543	377	108.12522	79.26012	8570.01794	377	147.44430	74.49133	10983.32258
378	80.19598	84.64548	6788.22658	378	109.47679	79.26925	8678.14317	378	149.41023	74.49803	11130.76688
379	81.13160	84.65780	6868.42256	379	110.84525	79.27827	8787.51996	379	151.40236	74.50463	11280.17711
380	82.07813	84.66998	6949.55415	380	112.23082	79.28718	8898.46521	380	153.42106	74.51115	11431.57947
381	83.03571	84.68203	7031.63229	381	113.63370	79.29598	9010.69602	381	155.46667	74.51758	11585.00053
382	84.00446	84.69393	7114.66800	382	115.05412	79.30468	9124.32972	382	157.53956	74.52393	11740.46720
383	84.98451	84.70570	7198.67246	383	116.49230	79.31326	9239.38384	383	159.64009	74.53019	11898.00677
384	85.97600	84.71733	7283.65697	384	117.94845	79.32174	9355.87614	384	161.76862	74.53637	12057.64686
385	86.97905	84.72883	7369.63297	385	119.42281	79.33011	9473.82459	385	163.92554	74.54248	12219.41548
386	87.99381	84.74019	7455.61202	386	120.91559	79.33838	9593.24740	386	166.11121	74.54850	12383.34102
387	89.02040	84.75142	7544.60582	387	122.42704	79.34655	9714.16299	387	168.32603	74.55444	12549.45223
388	90.05897	84.76253	7633.62623	388	123.95738	79.35462	9836.59003	388	170.57038	74.56030	12717.77826
389	91.10966	84.77350	7723.68520	389	125.50684	79.36258	9960.54740	389	172.84465	74.56608	12888.34864
390	92.17261	84.78435	7814.79486	390	127.07568	79.37045	10086.05425	390	175.14924	74.57179	13061.19329
391	93.24795	84.79508	7906.96747	391	128.66412	79.37823	10213.12993	391	177.48457	74.57743	13236.34253
392	94.33585	84.80568	8000.21542	392	130.27243	79.38590	10341.79405	392	179.85103	74.58299	13413.82710
393	95.43643	84.81616	8094.55127	393	131.90083	79.39348	10472.06647	393	182.24904	74.58848	13593.67813
394	96.54986	84.82651	8189.98770	394	133.54959	79.40097	10603.96731	394	184.67903	74.59389	13775.92717
395	97.67627	84.83675	8286.53755	395	135.21896	79.40837	10737.51690	395	187.14142	74.59923	13960.60620
396	98.81583	84.84687	8384.21383	396	136.90920	79.41567	10872.73586	396	189.63663	74.60451	14147.74761
397	99.96868	84.85687	8483.02965	397	138.62056	79.42289	11009.64506	397	192.16512	74.60971	14337.38425
398	101.13498	84.86676	8582.99833	398	140.35332	79.43001	11148.26562	398	194.72732	74.61485	14529.54937
399	102.31489	84.87654	8684.13331	399	142.10774	79.43705	11288.51894	399	197.32369	74.61991	14724.27670
400	103.50856	84.88620	8786.44820	400	143.88408	79.44400	11430.72668	400	199.95467	74.62491	14921.60039

Table I. ANNUITIES (*Continued*)

M	C(14,M,12)	A(14,M,12)	S(14,M,12)
401	104.71616	84.89575	8889.95676
402	105.93785	84.90519	8994.67293
403	107.17379	84.91452	9100.61078
404	108.42415	84.92374	9207.78457
405	109.68910	84.93286	9316.20872
406	110.96881	84.94187	9425.89782
407	112.26344	84.95078	9536.86663
408	113.57318	84.95958	9649.13008
409	114.89820	84.96828	9762.70326
410	116.23868	84.97689	9877.60147
411	117.59480	84.98539	9993.84015
412	118.96674	84.99380	10111.43495
413	120.35469	85.00211	10230.40169
414	121.75882	85.01032	10350.75638
415	123.17934	85.01844	10472.51520
416	124.61644	85.02646	10595.69455
417	126.07029	85.03439	10720.31098
418	127.54111	85.04223	10846.38128
419	129.02909	85.04998	10973.92239
420	130.53443	85.05764	11102.95149
421	132.05734	85.06522	11233.48592
422	133.59800	85.07270	11365.54326
423	135.15665	85.08010	11499.14126
424	136.73348	85.08741	11634.29791
425	138.32870	85.09464	11771.03139
426	139.94253	85.10179	11909.36009
427	141.57520	85.10885	12049.30262
428	143.22691	85.11583	12190.87782
429	144.89789	85.12274	12334.10472
430	146.58836	85.12956	12479.00261
431	148.29856	85.13630	12625.59098
432	150.02871	85.14297	12773.88954
433	151.77905	85.14956	12923.91825
434	153.54980	85.15607	13075.69730
435	155.34122	85.16251	13229.24710
436	157.15353	85.16887	13384.58831
437	158.98699	85.17516	13541.74184
438	160.84184	85.18138	13700.72883
439	162.71832	85.18752	13861.57067
440	164.61670	85.19360	14024.28899
441	166.53723	85.19960	14188.90570
442	168.48017	85.20554	14355.44293
443	170.44577	85.21140	14523.92310
444	172.43430	85.21720	14694.36887
445	174.44604	85.22293	14866.80317
446	176.48124	85.22860	15041.24921
447	178.54019	85.23420	15217.73045
448	180.62316	85.23974	15396.27064
449	182.73043	85.24521	15576.89380
450	184.86228	85.25062	15759.62422
451	187.01901	85.25597	15944.48651
452	189.20090	85.26125	16131.50552
453	191.40824	85.26648	16320.70641
454	193.64134	85.27164	16512.11465
455	195.90049	85.27675	16705.75599
456	198.18599	85.28179	16901.65648
457	200.49816	85.28678	17099.84247
458	202.83731	85.29171	17300.34063

M	C(15,M,12)	A(15,M,12)	S(15,M,12)
401	145.68263	79.45086	11574.61076
402	147.50367	79.45764	11720.29339
403	149.34746	79.46434	11867.79706
404	151.21431	79.47095	12017.14453
405	153.10449	79.47748	12168.35883
406	155.01829	79.48393	12321.46332
407	156.95602	79.49030	12476.48161
408	158.91797	79.49660	12633.43763
409	160.90444	79.50281	12792.35560
410	162.91575	79.50895	12953.26004
411	164.95220	79.51501	13116.17579
412	167.01410	79.52100	13281.12799
413	169.10178	79.52691	13448.14209
414	171.21555	79.53275	13617.24387
415	173.35574	79.53852	13788.45942
416	175.52269	79.54422	13961.81516
417	177.71672	79.54985	14137.33785
418	179.93818	79.55540	14315.05457
419	182.18741	79.56089	14494.99275
420	184.46475	79.56631	14677.18015
421	186.77056	79.57167	14861.64492
422	189.10519	79.57696	15048.41548
423	191.46901	79.58218	15237.52067
424	193.86237	79.58734	15428.98968
425	196.28565	79.59243	15622.85205
426	198.73922	79.59746	15819.13770
427	201.22346	79.60243	16017.87692
428	203.73875	79.60734	16219.10038
429	206.28549	79.61219	16422.83914
430	208.86406	79.61698	16629.12463
431	211.47486	79.62170	16837.98869
432	214.11829	79.62637	17049.46354
433	216.79477	79.63099	17263.58184
434	219.50471	79.63554	17480.37661
435	222.24852	79.64004	17699.88132
436	225.02662	79.64449	17922.12983
437	227.83946	79.64888	18147.15646
438	230.68745	79.65321	18374.99591
439	233.57104	79.65749	18605.68336
440	236.49068	79.66172	18839.25440
441	239.44681	79.66590	19075.74508
442	242.43990	79.67002	19315.19190
443	245.47040	79.67410	19557.63180
444	248.53878	79.67812	19803.10219
445	251.64551	79.68209	20051.64097
446	254.79108	79.68602	20303.28648
447	257.97597	79.68989	20558.07757
448	261.20067	79.69372	20816.05353
449	264.46568	79.69750	21077.25420
450	267.77150	79.70124	21341.71988
451	271.11864	79.70493	21609.49138
452	274.50763	79.70857	21880.61002
453	277.93897	79.71217	22155.11765
454	281.41321	79.71572	22433.05662
455	284.93087	79.71923	22714.46983
456	288.49251	79.72270	22999.40070
457	292.09867	79.72612	23287.89321
458	295.74990	79.72950	23579.99187
[illegible]	[illegible]	79.73284	23875.74177

M	C(16,M,12)	A(16,M,12)	S(16,M,12)
401	202.62073	74.62985	15121.55506
402	205.32234	74.63472	15324.17579
403	208.05998	74.63953	15529.49814
404	210.83411	74.64427	15737.55811
405	213.64523	74.64895	15948.39222
406	216.49383	74.65357	16162.03745
407	219.38042	74.65813	16378.53128
408	222.30549	74.66263	16597.91170
409	225.26955	74.66707	16820.21719
410	228.27316	74.67145	17045.48675
411	231.31680	74.67577	17273.75991
412	234.40102	74.68004	17505.07671
413	237.52637	74.68425	17739.47773
414	240.69339	74.68840	17977.00410
415	243.90263	74.69250	18217.69749
416	247.15467	74.69655	18461.60012
417	250.45006	74.70054	18708.75479
418	253.78940	74.70448	18959.20485
419	257.17326	74.70837	19212.99425
420	260.60223	74.71221	19470.16751
421	264.07693	74.71599	19730.76974
422	267.59796	74.71973	19994.84667
423	271.16593	74.72342	20262.44463
424	274.78147	74.72706	20533.61055
425	278.44523	74.73065	20808.39203
426	282.15783	74.73419	21086.83726
427	285.91993	74.73769	21368.99509
428	289.73220	74.74114	21654.91502
429	293.59530	74.74455	21944.64722
430	297.50990	74.74791	22238.24252
431	301.47670	74.75122	22535.75242
432	305.49639	74.75450	22837.22912
433	309.56967	74.75773	23142.72550
434	313.69727	74.76092	23452.29518
435	317.87990	74.76406	23765.99245
436	322.11830	74.76717	24083.87235
437	326.41321	74.77023	24405.99064
438	330.76538	74.77325	24732.40385
439	335.17559	74.77624	25063.16924
440	339.64460	74.77918	25398.34483
441	344.17319	74.78209	25737.98942
442	348.76217	74.78495	26082.16262
443	353.41233	74.78778	26430.92479
444	358.12449	74.79058	26784.33712
445	362.89949	74.79333	27142.46161
446	367.73815	74.79605	27505.36110
447	372.64132	74.79873	27873.09925
448	377.60987	74.80138	28245.74057
449	382.64467	74.80400	28623.35044
450	387.74660	74.80657	29005.99512
451	392.91656	74.80912	29393.74172
452	398.15544	74.81163	29786.65827
453	403.46418	74.81411	30184.81372
454	408.84371	74.81656	30588.27790
455	414.29495	74.81897	30997.12161
456	419.81889	74.82135	31411.41656
457	425.41647	74.82370	31831.23545
458	431.08869	74.82602	32256.65192
459	436.83654	74.82831	32687.74061

461	210.01976	85.30616	17915.97947	461	306.97973	79.73940	24478.37840	461	448.56318	74.83280	33567.23818
462	212.46999	85.31087	18125.99923	462	310.81698	79.74261	24785.35813	462	454.54402	74.83500	34015.80136
463	214.94881	85.31552	18338.46922	463	314.70219	79.74579	25096.17511	463	460.60461	74.83717	34470.34538
464	217.45654	85.32012	18553.41803	464	318.63597	79.74893	25410.87730	464	466.74600	74.83931	34930.94998
465	219.99354	85.32466	18770.87457	465	322.61892	79.75203	25729.51326	465	472.96928	74.84143	35397.69598
466	222.56013	85.32916	18990.86811	466	326.65165	79.75509	26052.13218	466	479.27554	74.84351	35870.66526
467	225.15666	85.33360	19213.42824	467	330.73480	79.75811	26378.78383	467	485.66588	74.84557	36349.94080
468	227.78349	85.33799	19438.58490	468	334.86898	79.76110	26709.51863	468	492.14142	74.84760	36835.60668
469	230.44096	85.34233	19666.36839	469	339.05485	79.76405	27044.38761	469	498.70331	74.84961	37327.74810
470	233.12944	85.34662	19896.80935	470	343.29303	79.76696	27383.44246	470	505.35269	74.85159	37826.45141
471	235.84929	85.35086	20129.93880	471	347.58419	79.76984	27726.73549	471	512.09072	74.85354	38331.80409
472	238.60086	85.35505	20365.78808	472	351.92900	79.77268	28074.31968	472	518.91860	74.85547	38843.89481
473	241.38454	85.35919	20604.38894	473	356.32811	79.77549	28426.24868	473	525.83751	74.85737	39362.81341
474	244.20069	85.36329	20845.77348	474	360.78221	79.77826	28782.57678	474	532.84868	74.85925	39888.65092
475	247.04970	85.36733	21089.97417	475	365.29199	79.78100	29143.35899	475	539.95333	74.86110	40421.49960
476	249.93195	85.37134	21337.02387	476	369.85814	79.78370	29508.65098	476	547.15271	74.86293	40961.45293
477	252.84782	85.37529	21586.95582	477	374.48136	79.78637	29878.50912	477	554.44808	74.86473	41508.60564
478	255.79771	85.37920	21839.80363	478	379.16238	79.78901	30252.99048	478	561.84072	74.86651	42063.05371
479	258.78202	85.38306	22095.60134	479	383.90191	79.79161	30632.15285	479	569.33193	74.86827	42624.89443
480	261.80114	85.38688	22354.38336	480	388.70068	79.79419	31016.05477	480	576.92302	74.87000	43194.22635
481	264.85549	85.39066	22616.18450	481	393.55944	79.79673	31404.75546	481	584.61532	74.87171	43771.14937
482	267.94547	85.39439	22881.03998	482	398.47894	79.79924	31798.31490	482	592.41020	74.87340	44355.76470
483	271.07150	85.39808	23148.98545	483	403.45992	79.80172	32196.79384	483	600.30900	74.87506	44948.17489
484	274.23400	85.40173	23420.05695	484	408.50317	79.80416	32600.25376	484	608.31312	74.87671	45548.48389
485	277.43339	85.40533	23694.29094	485	413.60946	79.80658	33008.75693	485	616.42396	74.87833	46156.79701
486	280.67012	85.40889	23971.72434	486	418.77958	79.80897	33422.36639	486	624.64295	74.87993	46773.22097
487	283.94460	85.41242	24252.39446	487	424.01432	79.81133	33841.14597	487	632.97152	74.88151	47397.86392
488	287.25729	85.41590	24536.33906	488	429.31450	79.81366	34265.16030	488	641.41114	74.88307	48030.83543
489	290.60862	85.41934	24823.59635	489	434.68094	79.81596	34694.47480	489	649.96329	74.88461	48672.24657
490	293.99906	85.42274	25114.20497	490	440.11445	79.81823	35129.15574	490	658.62946	74.88613	49322.20986
491	297.42905	85.42610	25408.20403	491	445.61588	79.82047	35569.27019	491	667.41119	74.88763	49980.83933
492	300.89905	85.42943	25705.63308	492	451.18608	79.82269	36014.88606	492	676.31001	74.88910	50648.25052
493	304.40954	85.43271	26006.53213	493	456.82590	79.82488	36466.07214	493	685.32747	74.89056	51324.56052
494	307.96099	85.43596	26310.94167	494	462.53623	79.82704	36922.89804	494	694.46517	74.89200	52009.88800
495	311.55386	85.43917	26618.90266	495	468.31793	79.82918	37385.43427	495	703.72471	74.89342	52704.35317
496	315.18866	85.44234	26930.45652	496	474.17190	79.83128	37853.75219	496	713.10771	74.89483	53408.07788
497	318.86586	85.44548	27245.64518	497	480.09905	79.83337	38327.92410	497	722.61581	74.89621	54121.18559
498	322.58596	85.44858	27564.51104	498	486.10029	79.83542	38808.02315	498	732.25069	74.89758	54843.80139
499	326.34947	85.45164	27887.09700	499	492.17654	79.83746	39294.12344	499	742.01403	74.89892	55576.05208
500	330.15688	85.45467	28213.44647	500	498.32875	79.83946	39785.29998	500	751.90755	74.90025	56318.06611

TABLE II
Day Numbers

The number of each day of the year is used for allocating costs between parties, usually between a buyer and a seller.

Number of Each Day of the Year*
(Counting from January 1)

Day of Mo.	Jan.	Feb.	Mar.	Apr.	May	June	July	Aug.	Sept.	Oct.	Nov.	Dec.
1	1	32	60	91	121	152	182	213	244	274	305	335
2	2	33	61	92	122	153	183	214	245	275	306	336
3	3	34	62	93	123	154	184	215	246	276	307	337
4	4	35	63	94	124	155	185	216	247	277	308	338
5	5	36	64	95	125	156	186	217	248	278	309	339
6	6	37	65	96	126	157	187	218	249	279	310	340
7	7	38	66	97	127	158	188	219	250	280	311	341
8	8	39	67	98	128	159	189	220	251	281	312	342
9	9	40	68	99	129	160	190	221	252	282	313	343
10	10	41	69	100	130	161	191	222	253	283	314	344
11	11	42	70	101	131	162	192	223	254	284	315	345
12	12	43	71	102	132	163	193	224	255	285	316	346
13	13	44	72	103	133	164	194	225	256	286	317	347
14	14	45	73	104	134	165	195	226	257	287	318	348
15	15	46	74	105	135	166	196	227	258	288	319	349
16	16	47	75	106	136	167	197	228	259	289	320	350
17	17	48	76	107	137	168	198	229	260	290	321	351
18	18	49	77	108	138	169	199	230	261	291	322	352
19	19	50	78	109	139	170	200	231	262	292	323	353
20	20	51	79	110	140	171	201	232	263	293	324	354
21	21	52	80	111	141	172	202	233	264	294	325	355
22	22	53	81	112	142	173	203	234	265	295	326	356
23	23	54	82	113	143	174	204	235	266	296	327	357
24	24	55	83	114	144	175	205	236	267	297	328	358
25	25	56	84	115	145	176	206	237	268	298	329	359

Table II. DAY NUMBERS (*Continued*)

Day of Mo.	Jan.	Feb.	Mar.	Apr.	May	June	July	Aug.	Sept.	Oct.	Nov.	Dec.
26	26	57	85	116	146	177	207	238	269	299	330	360
27	27	58	86	117	147	178	208	239	270	300	331	361
28	28	59	87	118	148	179	209	240	271	301	332	362
29	29	...	88	119	149	180	210	241	272	302	333	363
30	30	...	89	120	150	181	211	242	273	303	334	364
31	31	...	90	....	151	....	212	243	....	304	....	365

* For leap years, add one to each number after 59; i.e., after February 28.

Index

O

P

R